The
DYNAMICS
of
FASHION

Fairchild Books, Inc.
NEW YORK

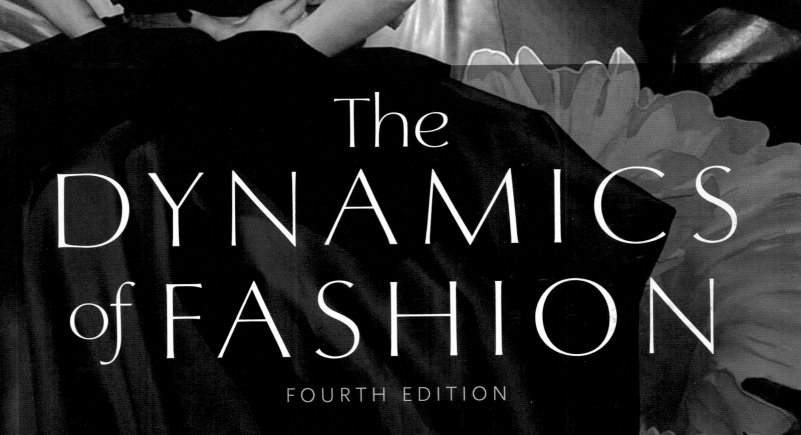

The
DYNAMICS
of FASHION

FOURTH EDITION

Elaine Stone, *Professor Emerita*

FASHION INSTITUTE OF TECHNOLOGY, NEW YORK

Fairchild Books

An imprint of Bloomsbury Publishing Inc.

1385 Broadway	50 Bedford Square
New York	London
NY 10018	WC1B 3DP
USA	UK

www.fairchildbooks.com

First edition published 1999
Second edition published 2003
Third edition published 2008
This edition first published 2013

© Bloomsbury Publishing Inc., 2013

All rights reserved. No part of this publication may be reproduced or transmitted in any form or by any means, electronic or mechanical, including photocopying, recording, or any information storage or retrieval system, without prior permission in writing from the publishers.

No responsibility for loss caused to any individual or organization acting on or refraining from action as a result of the material in this publication can be accepted by Bloomsbury Publishing Inc or the author.

Library of Congress Cataloging-in-Publication Data
A catalog record for this book is available from the Library of Congress.

ISBN: 978-1-60901-500-8

Typeset by Barbara Barg Medley
Features design by Carly Grafstein
Cover design by Sarah Silberg
Cover Art: Jamie Beck & Kevin Burg
Printed and bound in Canada

CONTENTS

v

Extended CONTENTS

PREFACE

Fashion is fast and forward, challenging and changing, and constantly in motion. This new edition of *The Dynamics of Fashion* is presented to students and instructors so that they can be on the cutting edge of what is happening in the business known as *fashion*. This updated text will prepare students to learn and understand the innovation and challenge of careers in the global world of today's fashion business.

The fourth edition of *The Dynamics of Fashion* brings new perspectives of the fashion business to students' attention. All chapters have been substantially updated with current theories added. The text covers the broad scope of fashion and adds the newest and most up-to-date facts and figures used by professionals, to keep the industry a vital and challenging career path.

New to This Edition

- More than 150 new full-color photographs highlighting the people, principles, practices, and techniques of the fashion business
- Updated coverage throughout the text includes the latest industry trends, such as developments in sustainability (Chapters 2, 6, 7, and 15), e-commerce (Chapters 3, 4, 5, 18, and 19), globalization (Chapters 4, 5, 6, 8, 16, and 17), technology (Chapters 6, 8, 18, 19, and 20), and the use of social media (Chapters 3, 4, 19, and 20) for fashion marketing
- Revised and new Review questions spark discussion about the most recent developments in the industry
- Up-to-date data in charts and illustrations
- New terms in Trade Talk and updated glossary

Brand-new content and illustrative features in every chapter:
- Fashion Focus features highlight the interesting people and events that are influencing fashion right now.
- Then and Now features show the cyclical nature of fashion as seen through yesterday's classics and today's emerging trends.

Organization of the Text

This edition of *The Dynamics of Fashion* uses the successful classroom-tested organization of the previous editions. It is structured in the following sequential learning order:

Unit One: The Changing World of Fashion

This unit examines how and why fashion evolves and changes. Chapter 1 teaches the student about fashion history, focusing on the development of fashion design and how it has grown into a major force for the future. A special project at the end of this chapter helps students learn how key designers relate to fashion throughout the decades. Chapter 2 explains the cyclical nature of fashion, including the core principles of the business. Chapter 3 examines the basic psychological and environmental factors that affect fashion. Chapter 4 discusses the movement of fashion, forecasting, and theories of fashion adoption. Moreover, the text shows how fashion leaders can be influential and spark trends. Chapter 5 covers the business scope of the industry, including licensing and franchising.

Fashion operates in a far different way today than it did years ago. It moves faster and reaches more people. Perhaps most important, it is more businesslike. To understand the changes that have occurred and will occur in the future of the fashion industry, you must first understand the foundation of the fashion business.

Unit Two: The Primary Level: The Materials of Fashion

The growers and producers of the raw material of fashion—fibers, fabrics, trimming, leather, and fur—are covered in this unit. New and fast-moving advances in these industries coupled with an increasing variety of fashion goods using these materials are explained. The difference between natural and manufactured fibers is explained, along with the sustainability of products made from "green" fibers, and the production process of most fabrics (Chapter 6). Leather and fur are also covered in detail. Different categories of leather, special finishes, real and faux fur, the development of these industries, and the steps in producing and marketing are examined (Chapter 7).

Unit Three: The Secondary Level: The Producers of Apparel

The third unit begins with a chapter on product development. Students will learn about the six-stage process of developing and producing a line, supply chain management, licensing, private labels, brand extension, specification buying, offshore production, and trade agreements (Chapter 8). Industry trends in apparel are then broken down into separate chapters focusing on women's (Chapter 9), men's (Chapter 10), and children's apparel (Chapter 11).

Chapter 9 describes the history of the women's apparel industry, along with the categories, size ranges, price zones, and brand and designer names used in marketing. Chapter 10 compares and contrasts all the factors that are common to both men's and women's apparel and explains the differences that exist in producing and marketing menswear. Chapter 11 discusses children's apparel, including the impact of demographics, the influence of fashion on children's wear, licensing, industry trends, and responses to social issues.

Unit Four: The Secondary Level: The Other Producers

The producers of innerwear, accessories, beauty, and home fashions no longer exist just to coordinate with apparel. These industries have become innovators and fashion trendsetters. This unit explains how each industry functions and covers current and future practices and trends.

There is a discussion of the history of innerwear, bodywear, and legwear, as well as the latest merchandising and marketing trends (Chapter 12). The ever-expanding accessories industries are explored from their past to the present (Chapter 13). Chapter 14 discusses the beauty industry (formerly referred to as "cosmetics and fragrances"), and the text illustrates the different growing market segments in this sector of the fashion business. Chapter 15 examines the rapidly growing area of home fashions. This chapter also explores the influence of top and young designers who are increasingly expanding their range of products, from apparel to home.

Unit Five: The Retail Level: The Markets for Fashion

This unit focuses on the elements of fashion marketing and reveals how markets operate to help manufacturers sell their products and how retailers satisfy the needs of their target customers. Different types of retailers and strategies are also explained in this unit.

Chapter 16 is devoted to global fashion markets and their unique offerings and personalities. Chapter 17 explores global sourcing and merchandising—both the advantages and disadvantages as American industries continue to expand into foreign markets. There is also a discussion about importing, exporting, quotas, and the trade deficit. Chapter 18 discusses the history and development of fashion retailing in the United States, including the different types of retailers and changing retail patterns. For example, the growth of e-commerce, international brands in America, and discount stores. Chapter 19 focuses on current policies and major strategies in fashion retailing, including e-tailing and how businesses use social media and online promotion to reach out to customers. Additionally, Chapter 19 discusses the methods of merchandising, such as fashion cycle emphasis, quality, price ranges, merchandise assortments, brand policies, and exclusivity. There is an evaluation of operational policies as well, including customer services, promotional activities, and selling services.

Unit Six: The Auxiliary Level: Supporting Services

The final unit in this book covers a myriad of fashion services and explains their interconnecting roles in the fashion business, from design to consumer (Chapter 20). Advertising, print, and online media such as fashion magazines and newspapers are discussed, along with television, broadcast, and social media. Additionally, Chapter 20 explores the role of advertising agencies, fashion consultants, and public relations firms. Visual merchandising and store design are also covered as important aspects of promotion. Finally, this chapter looks at the industry publications and organizations that work to provide information and other services.

Text Features

The Dynamics of Fashion provides a wide range of examples, color illustrations, tables, and many exciting special features that make the people, principles, practices, and techniques of the fashion business come alive. All these features are appropriate for class discussion, library research projects, and group projects.

Fashion Focus

"Fashion Focus" is a popular feature that highlights interesting people, places, and products in the fashion business. This feature makes the chapter material more relevant to the reader. For example, key people discussed include Ralph Rucci (Chapter 1), Michael Kors (Chapter 2), Sarah Burton (Chapter 5), Billy Reid (Chapter 10), and Bobbie Brown (Chapter 14).

Then and Now

"Then and Now" is a feature that encourages the student to look to the past, present, and future of subjects that have a lasting imprint on fashion. It also teaches how fashion is cyclical, with comparisons of trends from different points in time. For example, topics include denim through the decades (Chapter 6), vanity sizing (Chapter 8), counterfeiting (Chapter 17), discounters and retailing strategies (Chapter 19), and CFDA (Chapter 20).

Glossary

The glossary has been updated to reflect revised content from the text. A knowledge and understanding of the language of fashion gives students a firm footing upon which they can step out into the industry and know they are speaking the right language.

Summary and Review

The chapters conclude with student-oriented activities designed to enrich and reinforce the instructional material. A summary gives a quick reminder of key concepts.

The "Trade Talk" section explains fashion and merchandising terms introduced for the first time in that chapter. The student will recognize these terms when they appear in subsequent chapters. Terms have been added throughout the text based on revised content in the fourth edition.

"For Review" asks questions about the key concepts of each chapter. These questions provoke thought, encourage classroom discussion, and recall the material presented in the text. Questions have been added and revised for the fourth edition.

"For Discussion" asks the student to explain the significance of a major concept and to support the explanation with specific illustrations. This activity affords the student an opportunity to apply theory to actual situations and to draw on his or her own background and experiences.

Instructor's Resources

Fairchild Books is pleased to offer a robust ancillary package to instructors for the fourth edition of *The Dynamics of Fashion*. The Instructor's Guide features answers to end-of-chapter activities; supplemental student activities and assignments; a comprehensive test bank of multiple choice, identification, true or false, and essay questions for each chapter *and* unit; and a guide to exploring careers with an expanded focus on using social media, social and environmental responsibility, and key functionalities and skill sets for the millennial generation. The PowerPoint presentation reproduces the text's expanded full-color art program, featuring more than 150 images. The PowerPoint also offers a concise, bulleted basis for classroom lectures and discussions for each chapter. Finally, a curated digital library of special supplemental resources for all of the text's features is available for instructors. This collection includes categorical links to articles, image galleries, and videos from respected trade, fashion, and news websites.

ACKNOWLEDGMENTS

I am grateful to the many educators and business people who have given me encouragement, information, and helpful suggestions. Among these are my teaching colleagues at the Fashion Institute of Technology, who have supported the writing of *The Dynamics of Fashion*, and the very helpful staff of professionals in the FIT library.

I am also indebted to the industry experts and professionals, both domestic and foreign, who gave of their time and expertise to ensure the timeliness and accuracy of the information in this book. Thank you to the reviewers selected by the publisher: Karol Blaylock, Tarleton State University; Melissa Carr, Dominican University; Carol Salusso, Washington State University; Leslie Bush, Phoenix College; Pamela Stoessell, Mary Mount University; Elizabeth Heuisler, Art Institute of Tucson; Jan Salcido, Art Institute of California—Orange County; Sharon Scalise, College of DuPage; and Andrea Kolasinski Marcinkus, The Illinois Institute of Art—Schaumburg. Special thanks to Michael Londrigan, LIM College, for his revisions to the text and Instructor's Guide. Additional thanks to Maritza Buritica for her diligent work on the supplemental digital library and Pam Zuckerman, Fashion Institute of Technology, for her contributions to the instructor's resources.

My heartfelt gratitude and sincere appreciation goes to the staff at Fairchild Books. I particularly want to mention Elizabeth Marotta, the senior production editor at Fairchild and the person who really made this edition possible by her complete attention to every detail, and most of all for being a friend in need, who helped me on all phases of producing this book. To the art department, Sara Silberg, Barbara Barg Medley, and Carly Grafstein, who made this edition of *The Dynamics of Fashion* truly dynamic. To Anne Sanow for her contributions to Chapter 1. Thanks to Amy Butler for her wonderful work on the PowerPoint presentation and Instructor's Guide. Finally, to the former executive editor, Olga Kontzias, I say a heartfelt thank you for all the years we have worked together.

I regret that space does not permit me to personally list and thank my friends in all segments of the fashion business who supplied, throughout the development of this edition, their encouragement as well as significant amounts of current and trend trade information. As always, I welcome instructors' and students' comments. They can be sent to me through Fairchild Books or to my e-mail address: elaine_stone@fitnyc.edu.

This book is dedicated to Minnie M. Stone, who served as a mentor, friend, and critic throughout my career. Best of all, she was a terrific mother.

—Elaine Stone

The
DYNAMICS
of
FASHION

Unit One THE CHANGING WORLD OF FASHION

FASHION—the very word conjures up excitement and interest in all of us. Fashion is the ultimate F word! It is faddish, familiar, fantasy, form, fatal, feasible, festive, finite, fit, fresh, and fun. Fashion is the most dynamic of American businesses. It thrives on change, and change is the engine that fuels it.

In Unit 1 you will learn how and why fashion evolves and changes. You will begin to develop a basic vocabulary and a working knowledge of the following:

- Chapter 1: The history and foundation of fashion from the 19th century through today.
- Chapter 2: The principles around which the fashion world revolves.
- Chapter 3: The environmental forces—the role that economic, demographic, sociological, and psychological elements play in the fashion business.

- Chapter 4: The cyclical forces—how fashions change and how an understanding of this constant cycle of change can be used to predict and analyze current and future fashion trends.
- Chapter 5: The business forces—the scope of the industry, its recent growth and expansion, and various new forms of ownership, along with the design forces, and the roles played by designers, manufacturers, and retailers in creating fashion.

The fashion world operates in a far different way today than in the past. It moves faster and reaches more people. To understand the changes that have occurred and will occur in the future, you must first understand the dynamics that underlie the fashion business.

KEY CONCEPTS

- The social and cultural conditions that affect fashion
- Major developments and trends, decade by decade
- The designers and other innovators who influence fashion

Turn on your television today, or log on to the Internet, and you're constantly being told what people are wearing. On the red carpet at the Oscars, every actress will be asked who designed her gown; less than a week later, she'll show up in *Star* or *People* magazine on either the best-dressed or worst-dressed list, and a stylist will have written a sidebar telling you where you can buy an inexpensive replica of the dress—along with the shoes, jewelry, handbag, and cosmetics. When Katie Couric became the first woman to head up the CBS evening news broadcast in 2006, critics discussed her choice in suits as much as they did her reporting style. Suiting styles for men are worn with cool élan by actor George Clooney, rapper Jay-Z, and soccer star David Beckham. Socialites design clothing or handbag lines. Everyone is in on the act, it seems, from the reality show participants of *Project Runway* to those who want to laugh at it all by reading what the Fug Girls have to say online. The newest looks are seen and talked about and copied more quickly than ever—never before have we had so much information at our fingertips and so many options from which to choose.

But how did we get here? It's true that we can see the latest from music videos, award shows, and the fashion runway almost immediately. Almost a hundred years ago, however, American women went wild for anything worn by the actress Mary Pickford, and newspapers and magazines hastened to provide photographs and drawings of her ingenue style as soon as they could roll them off the press. Factory and "office girls" from the turn of the twentieth century had a role in shaping the apparel industry with their demands for functional, streamlined clothing, and the famous Rosie the Riveter poster from World War II boldly depicted fashion on duty: coveralls, along with a feminine swoosh of bright-red patriotic lipstick. Today's In and Out lists have their precedent in that wartime era, too, with the inauguration of the U.S.-based Best-Dressed List in 1940, formerly the domain of Paris. And one of the Best-Dressed's notable men was the suave Cary Grant—emulated by none other than Mr. Clooney today.

The point is that fashion has *always* been changing and evolving—and at any time in the past, though it may be history to us now, that change was usually dramatic. The evolution of fashion is an exciting one, full of innovations and imitations. Fashion history tells us where we've been and suggests where fashion might be going. In this chapter, our focus is the last hundred years or so, from the turn of the twentieth century to the present day. There are different ways to determine when one decade begins and the former one ends—sometimes it's a momentous event, such as the stock market crash of 1929 or the end of World War II, in 1945. Whatever the event may be, it's important to remember that there are many changes that occur over any ten-year period. In the following sections, we give an overview of the events of each decade—social, cultural, and economic; these events are related to major fashion trends and developments of the period, and the designers and other individuals who had a strong influence at the time are noted.

Social and Cultural Conditions

You may have heard the old adage about hemlines going up when the stock market is on the rise—and falling when times get tough. Interestingly, this is often true: think of the miniskirts worn during the stock market boom of the 1980s, contrasted with the longer, more sedate skirts that were popular during the recession in the early 1990s. It isn't quite that simple, however, and examining other events in each decade provides more clues to what people were wearing and why. Significant issues are wars and revolutions; peacetime and prosperity; civil rights; travel; transportation; communication; literacy and education; developments in science, technology, and medicine; sports and recreation; and of course the entertainment industry, from vaudeville and theater to film and the Internet.

Fashion Trends and Developments

It's said that for every action there's an equal and opposite reaction, and we'll see how this holds true for fashion. Sometimes the reactions are a response to horrific events: both the attack on Pearl Harbor in 1941 and the terrorist bombings on September 11, 2001, resulted in a trend for red, white, and blue clothing and accessories. Other times, fashion takes advantage of new technology and scientific breakthroughs, such as the invention of nylon. Along with apparel, trends include changes in accessories, hairstyles, and cosmetics. For every major trend that seems particular to its time—think flapper dresses from the 1920s, Jackie Kennedy's ladylike suits, and bell-bottom pants from the 1970s—there is often a reinterpretation later on (contemporary Marc Jacobs or Michael Kors, the resurgence and refinement of low-slung pants). From the Gibson Girl's blouse to Twiggy's microminis, from the Man in the Gray Flannel Suit to Calvin Klein's underwear on display, the past hundred years have produced some memorable fashion

FIGURE 1.1 Audrey Hepburn and Grace Kelly waiting backstage at the Academy Awards in 1958 (top) and Anne Hathaway on the red carpet at the Academy Awards in 2013 (bottom).

moments. Some of them were a flash in the pan, but others influence us today—and will continue to do so in the future.

Designers and Other Influences

Someone has to be the creative force behind all of this change, and this is where fashion designers take center stage. Twentieth-century modernization saw the rise of mass apparel production and the rise of the designer as fashion arbiter—and fashion star. Many fashion staples in our closets today, such as the little black dress, can be accredited to a particular designer (in this case, Chanel). Innovators, artists, and often followers, too, designers have put their stamp on major fashion trends throughout the years. We will also see how other elements, such as urban or street culture, influence design.

PRELUDE TO THE TWENTIETH CENTURY

Before we learn how fashion developed and evolved over the past century, we need to look at the state of things before that time—when the United States was a very young country, forging its own identity while still retaining close ties to Europe. In the mid-nineteenth century, New York City's population was still under one million, and other prominent East Coast cities, such as Boston and Philadelphia, boasted only 137,000 and 121,000 respectively. The western cities were much smaller outposts; Saint Louis, famed as the Gateway to the West, was the largest with nearly 80,000, and San Francisco had just 35,000 pioneering inhabitants. Contrast this with the 1.5 million citizens of Paris at the time, or London's 2.3 million—these were long-established urban centers of culture and industry that Americans hoped to emulate. The years leading up to 1900 brought enormous expansion and change to the United States, and with that, a new national identity.

Social and Cultural Conditions

As the United States expanded, it experienced severe growing pains. The Civil War of 1861–1865 threatened the country's very survival, and the aftermath saw social upheavals in race and class. Industrialization brought improved modes of transportation such as safer railroads and electric trolleys; people could receive news faster because of the telegraph and telephone; and the cycle of the day (and therefore the workday) was altered forever with the widespread use of electric lights.

By the turn of the twentieth century, there were nearly 3.5 million people living in New York City alone, and other urban centers were rapidly expanding as well. The western part of the country gave way from frontier settlement to modernization, which was altogether different from the European-influenced East.

Fashion Trends and Developments

During much of the nineteenth century, particularly the conservative Victorian era, clothing was strait-laced and bodies were covered up. While the wealthier population had always looked to Europe for aristocratic fashion design, the desire for gentility and refinement became a broader concern as Americans on the whole became more settled and established. Women's dress was carefully chosen to show their respectability. Restricted by corsets and hoop skirts, with layer upon layer of undergarments, inner and outer skirts, and flounces, the decorative aspect of dressing conveyed femininity.

The voluminous skirts of the mid-1800s were reduced to the slimmer bustle silhouette. The fashion cycle ebbed and flowed, with a continual struggle between gentility and practicality. A "respectable" wife from the East Coast accustomed to wearing corsets and heavy skirts might get rid of some layers should she migrate westward overland, where such restrictions would be impractical for cooking over fires outdoors. Once settled in her new home, however, she'd be likely to resurrect her finery to show that she was a woman knowledgeable about fashion and culture.

The change from homemade to ready-made apparel was another significant fashion trend. Mass production of garments such as corsets and men's shirts began in the mid-1800s; by the mid-1890s, as more men—and also women—began working in factories and offices, the apparel industry responded to the demand for practical clothing by adapting the men's shirt for women in a blouselike form. The shirtwaist would keep manufacturers rushing to meet demand into the new century. Ready-made apparel became widespread, available from mail-order catalogs such as Sears, Roebuck and Co. and Montgomery Ward (popularized with the expansion of mail delivery) and the advent of department stores in major urban centers.

Designers and Other Influences

Fashion before 1870 meant that every woman was essentially a dressmaker. For inspiration she would look to her friends and neighbors, most of whom would

FIGURE 1.2 Cover of *Vogue* from 1894.

be concerned with some degree of respectability, just as she was. Influence from Europe found its way to the United States through publications such as *Godey's Lady's Book*, where the latest styles were illustrated.

Respectability meant looking to one's social betters—which meant, for all practical purposes, being somehow influenced by the designer Charles Frederick Worth. An Englishman who established the House of Worth in Paris in 1857, he dressed society women in Europe and the United States, along with royalty and others seeking social status. Along with Worth (who is often considered to be the father of haute couture), other designers based in Paris included Jeanne Paquin, a competitor, and Jacques Doucet of the House of Doucet, established in the mid-1800s as a producer of lingerie and men's clothing and accessories.

In addition to more widely available information about fashion (including *Vogue* magazine, which began its publication in 1892), photography was a significant factor in fashion's development in the nineteenth century. First in use in the 1840s, its technology continued to improve, and many Americans, particularly after the Civil War, had more opportunities to see what they—and other people—looked like. Comparison being a surefire way to encourage criticism or envy, no doubt more than one woman saw a photograph and thought, I want to wear *that*.

When Queen Victoria died in 1901, the new century had just turned and progress was evident. The so-called Edwardian Age, during the reign of King Edward VII, clung to the classical and opulent in dress and manner. Changes certainly occurred, and what was known as La Belle Epoque ("The Beautiful Age") would vanish in the upheaval of World War I.

Social and Cultural Conditions

The U.S. population had reached 75.9 million by 1900—and it continued to grow, with immigrants pouring in through Ellis Island and other ports. In contrast to the opulence enjoyed by the wealthy, many of these new immigrants, mostly city dwellers, lived in extreme poverty and hardship. As the divide between rich and poor became more pronounced, charities and other social institutions struggled to improve conditions while these new workers entered the U.S. economy. Women continued working, with 20 percent earning wages outside the home in 1902; by 1910, nearly 25 percent did so.

Mobility was increasing everywhere. Bicycling became a popular recreational pastime. Automobiles, a novelty in the late 1800s, were produced by the thousands by 1907, and Americans who could afford them were eager to get in the driver's seat. Wilbur and Orville Wright introduced the country to the possibility of air travel in 1903. Telephones became widespread, facilitating communication.

Aside from a brief economic downturn in 1907, most of the country was prospering during this decade—which means that more people had money to spend on entertainment. Theater, opera, and vaudeville were all enormously popular, and "moving pictures," which had sprouted up in the late 1890s, became a hit when *The Great Train Robbery*, the first movie with a real storyline, was shown in 1903. And while the devastation of the San Francisco earthquake in 1906 may have shocked the nation, the photographs and film reels of the city also served to unite the United States.

Fashion Trends and Developments

The turn of the century featured a preference for a mature female silhouette compatible with the Edwardian fashions of the day. This Pouter pigeon figure, accentuating a small waist with rounded curves above and below, required the S-bend corset (also known as the straight or erect form). Bodices were also boned,

FIGURE 1.3 Bicycling increased mobility everywhere and fashioned the "new woman."

and bloused out above; sleeves were long, and skirts were worn close to the hip and featured gores that flared into a trumpet shape. Sleeves became shorter and fuller—including the famously exaggerated leg o' mutton look—but the basic components did not change drastically until the middle of the decade, when the princess shape slimmed the look down considerably. Still voluminous were hair and hats, the former piled and poufed, the latter wide, round, and elaborately decked out with ribbon, feathers, and bows.

Men's fashion tended toward a blockier shape, with three-piece suits and the sack coat with no waistline seams. Shirt tailoring was stiff and formal, with starched fronts; these later gave way to more relaxed styles, and men eventually began to omit vests and even jackets.

Recreation had an impact on fashion in this period, too, most notably with the full, knee-length pants known as bloomers (for women) and knickers (for men) adopted for cycling. Modesty nevertheless prevailed in swimwear, with women's costumes featuring over-the-knee skirts and dark stockings. Though sportswear was in its infancy, the concept of practical clothing took hold.

Designers and Other Influences

The overall formality of the decade kept the Paris designers in business, with Doucet responding to the Art Nouveau influences with decorative designs, and the house of Callot Soeurs specializing in lace. Paquin and the House of Worth remained prominent, with Jean-Philippe Worth taking over the business from his father.

Perhaps the most indelible fashion image of the early 1900s is the Gibson Girl, created by illustrator Charles Dana Gibson. Though she featured the popular curved figure of the day, the twist was that she was also a "new woman" who was independent and active in addition to being beautiful. Her counterpart was the Arrow Collar Man, fashioned as a clean-cut and sporty version of masculinity.

This was also a decade when fashion began to get into the streets. As more working-class men and women went to amusement parks, dance halls, and movie theaters, they had more opportunity to see what "the swells" were wearing and could attempt to imitate a frill on a blouse or the flip on the brim of a hat. The pace of fashion news picked up and spread from cities to towns and the country, paving the way for even more radical change with the advent of a war that would redraw the boundaries of the world.

THE 1910s: NEW FASHIONS TAKE HOLD

The twentieth century can be said to have really gotten under way after 1910, and the decade saw the full changeover to mass production of everything from clothing to foodstuffs to Model T Fords. Manufacturing continued to step up with the production of armaments and other supplies to assist the Allied European countries when World War I broke out in 1914. Long before the United States officially entered the war in 1917, the mood was one of preparation. The first income tax was introduced in 1913 as one way to cover war expenditures. Women took over jobs in heavy industry when men were drafted into the armed forces.

Social and Cultural Conditions

Entertainment thrived in the United States, with a flourishing of popular songs and the public's newfound fascination with movies and movie stars. The film industry established itself in Hollywood, and the studio "star system" was born—along with movie fan magazines, which made household names of the players. Old-fashioned dances like the waltz and minuet were superseded by the new fox-trot and Castle Walk, made popular by the performing duo Irene and Vernon Castle.

Fashion Trends and Developments

Even before the United States officially entered World War I, the operating principle was about cutting back—and fashion followed suit. Manufacturers used lighter materials and construction, and the fussy silhouettes of the previous decade disappeared. Narrower lines and brighter colors prevailed. Styles gave a nod to modernism and other avant-garde influences, such as the theatrical costumes worn by the Ballets Russes troupe of dancers, who performed to great acclaim in Paris. This resulted in some new and startling designs, such as harem trousers, turbans, the hobble skirt, and the lampshade dress. These bohemian styles weren't for everyone, but the slimmed-down and sloping shapes carried over into more day-to-day styles as well.

Men's fashion followed a similar trend, with boxy suits replaced by a less full line and lighter fabrics. The war introduced the streamlined trench coat, which was then adopted by the general public and remains a fashion classic today. War shortages included color dyes, and for the years 1914–1918 basic black, white, tan, and blue were popular. Hemlines crept up to conserve fabric. As utilitarian styles took hold, accessorizing became popular: exposed ankles showed off embroidered stockings, and eyes and lips were darkened with newly available cosmetics that complemented the new short bobbed or permed hairstyles under smaller hats. Concurrent to Keds in 1917, Marquis M. Converse of the Converse Rubber Shoe Company created what would come to define the rubberized shoe, the Converse All-Star.

Designers and Other Influences

Paris was the epicenter for innovation, and many designers started their businesses during this period, including Jean Patou, Coco Chanel, and Madeleine Vionnet. Forced to close up shop briefly during the war, they would rise to prominence in the 1920s. Fashion leaders of the 1910s were Paul Poiret, whose style was dramatic and introduced the most cutting-edge styles; Jeanne Sacerdote, known as Madame Jenny, worked in a style that was simpler than Poiret's and was widely copied; Mariano Fortuny was known for

FIGURE 1.4 The Ballets Russes, 1916.

his reinterpretation of classic Grecian draping and pleating used in gowns and robes. As the war brought more Americans overseas for the first time, interest in French designers increased, and American ready-to-wear manufacturers rushed to copy them.

The new American stars of stage and screen were also a significant influence during this time. Women were enthralled with the frilly ingenue dresses worn by Mary Pickford and the vampish look of Theda Bara, and men copied Charlie Chaplin or Rudolph Valentino.

FIGURE 1.5 Design by Madeleine Vionnet.

THE 1920s: FASHION GETS MODERN

Americans were ready to move on when the war ended, and move they did. The 1920s were a time when nostalgia for the past was pushed aside for the fast and fun pursuits of a younger generation—who delighted in shocking their elders. Jazz music and new dances became all the rage, and when Prohibition was passed in 1919, it provided another excuse to break the rules. Women responded to the ratification of suffrage in 1920 by taking liberties they felt were due to them, from smoking and cursing in public to wearing heavy makeup and baring their arms. These flappers and their loose, daring styles were imitated by anyone who wanted to appear young.

Social and Cultural Conditions

The cinema—now a full-fledged industry—provided new idols to aspire to, such as It girl Clara Bow, Myrna Loy, and Claudette Colbert, and for the men, the dashing, masculine ideal of Douglas Fairbanks. Ever fickle, the young population abandoned silent film stars who couldn't measure up when films with sound, dubbed *talkies*, were introduced in 1927 (the same year the first Academy Awards were presented), and Americans became enamored of a talking mouse when Walt Disney introduced Mickey in 1928. Mass media continued its expansion with the first commercial radio station in 1920, and by the end of the decade, many, if not most, Americans owned or had access to radios of their own. Prosperity ended with the stock market crash of 1929, and the next ten years would carry a more somber tone.

Fashion Trends and Developments

As conventions fell away, so did restricting waistlines and skirts. To dance the Charleston, the tango, or the Black Bottom, spirited flappers wanted clothing that was loose, free, and above all, fun. The straight-cut chemise dress (often sleeveless) flattened the line of the body, and as hemlines rose to knee length, the dresses were augmented with fringe and beads that swung as one moved. The boyish silhouette was complemented by costume finery such as long necklaces and T-strap shoes for dancing, often with highly decorative heels. Hair became even shorter with the shingle bob, and hats were close-fitting cloches; makeup, now widely available, was worn dark around the eyes and emphasized a bow-pointed lip. The extremely short and bare styles changed again toward the end of the decade, as flappers grew up. By 1928, hemlines were longer again and pointed in back, and dresses at least skimmed the waistline again.

Men's fashions were still more conventional, with suits being the norm. There was a rise in sportswear for both men and women, and the layers of times past were streamlined to fit modern life. Clothing for tennis and golf popularized short-sleeved shirts, argyle sweaters, and saddle oxfords. Women's swimwear used knits, became shorter, and revealed bare arms and legs, the better for achieving the now-desirable suntan—resulting in the arrest of young women at public beaches who sported the more daring styles.

TOUJOURS COUTURE

OVER THE YEARS haute couture has been declared dead many times. *The New York Times* stated in 1965, "Every ten years, the doctors assemble at the bedside of French haute couture and announce that death is imminent." But perhaps the reports of haute couture's death have been greatly exaggerated. Haute couture has survived world wars, the cultural revolution, and economic meltdowns—and it has always reshaped to fit the times.

What is this phenomenon called haute couture, which cyclically dies only to be reborn? According to the bylaws of the Chambre Syndicate de la Haute Couture, "an haute couturier is a designer who presides over the creation of hand-finished made-to-order clothing in a 'laboratory' that employs at least twenty workers in Paris." From a peak of 200 before World War II, only eleven authentic haute couturiers remain, and there are four correspondent members. Just two Americans have ever been classified as haute couturiers: Mainbocher (who retired in 1971) and Ralph Rucci.

The founding father of haute couture was an Englishman, Charles Frederick Worth, who opened his shop in Paris on the Rue de la Paix in 1858. The house of Worth lasted one hundred years, during which a former Worth employee—Paul Poiret—brought the clothing up-to-date with an avant-garde primitivism of the World War I era.

Haute couture is a mesmerizing showcase of ultrafashion indulgences that bring entertainment to the forefront on the world's fashion runways. Each couture garment is a one-of-a-kind, made-to-measure piece that has been stitched inch-by-inch by the couture house's atelier seamstresses. Although the designers get full credit for the design, these time-honored seamstresses are the ones who labor for hours, days, and sometimes months behind the scenes, using the best of their craft to create a garment of exquisite beauty—that sells for an exorbitant price.

But do not be discouraged if you can't afford the over-the-top couture prices, which tend to run into the tens of thousands of dollars. More accessibly priced products are available through couture houses' accessories collections: scarfs, handbags, wallets, costume jewelry, shoes, and millinery. Many couture designers are selling their brands to the mass market as less-expensive, but no-less-chic versions of their couture creations. This is giving couture a new lease on life through marketing and publicity. At the same time, marketers are hoping that women will eventually graduate to high-end fashion. Couture is something to be coveted. As Polly Guerin, the fashion historian, says, "Viva Haute Couture!! It's in the fashion world, a compelling lure for ladies who lunch and rich fashionistas worldwide. Couture titillates the imagination, it serves as inspiration, and in its finest hour it is the greatest show in the fashion galaxy."

Jean Paul Gaultier Fall 2011

Chanel Spring 2013

Jean Paul Gaultier Spring 2013

Designers and Other Influences

Parisian designers flourished in the postwar period. This was the heyday of Coco Chanel, who introduced the little black dress coveted by modern women everywhere and pioneered the use of casual fabrics and chic sportswear separates. Also emphasizing new sportswear designs was Jean Patou, whose pleated skirts and pullover tops were a hit with sports stars and café society alike. Madeleine Vionnet created inventive styles with handkerchief and asymmetrical hems, geometric shapes, and cowl and halter necklines. More romantic interpretations from the period include those of Jeanne Lanvin, whose dresses were longer and fuller; her wide-ranging talent also led her to produce tubular dresses and coordinated separates. Also important among the Paris ateliers was Edward Molyneux, whose British heritage influenced his designs for modern, streamlined suits.

French designers also began to turn an eye to what American consumers were buying. As ready-to-wear apparel became more fashionable and desirable, U.S. manufacturers produced copies, or knockoffs, of popular Parisian looks.

THE 1930s: MAKING DO

If the previous ten years had been freewheeling, the worldwide economic downturn that ushered in the 1930s brought a new frugality. The Depression was a time when people were encouraged to make do with what they had—and many had little, with unemployment at an all-time high. In the United States, Franklin Delano Roosevelt was elected president in 1932 and instituted a wide-ranging program of social relief, from the Works Progress Administration and National Industrial Recovery Administration to the very practical repeal of Prohibition.

Social and Cultural Conditions

As a relief from what seemed like constant bad news, Americans turned in droves to Hollywood, which provided the glamour of musicals, sharp-tongued comedies, and gangster films. The exploits of British royalty also provided a distraction, and when King Edward VIII gave up his throne for the love of divorcée Wallis Simpson, the media crowned them fashion icons. It was also a decade in which many literary classics were penned, including John Steinbeck's *The Grapes of Wrath* and Margaret Mitchell's *Gone with the Wind*. With Germany's invasion of Poland in 1939, the economic woes of the decade lessened as industries in the United States and abroad began gearing up for war.

Fashion Trends and Developments

Hemlines fell along with the stock market and stayed long throughout the decade. The overall look was softer and more feminine, with clothing fitting closer to the body. A slender silhouette still dominated, and the waistline returned, accentuated with belts. Both day and evening dresses were long and narrow, often offset by broader shoulders or draped necklines, emulating slinky Hollywood glamour with bias cuts and light fabrics. Skirts were featured with yokes and gathers. The new rubberized Lastex fabric revolutionized the undergarment industry by introducing two-way stretch, and girdles and bras offered better shaping under clingy fabrics. Nylon stockings were introduced in 1938 and were an overnight sensation (though they would be rationed just short years later). Gloves and hats remained important accessories, and women favored the Marcel wave for hair and the platinum color of actress Jean Harlow. Men's clothing in the 1930s followed trends similar to those of women's apparel, streamlining throughout the decade and gradually acquiring broader, padded shoulders.

Casual styles continued to gain popularity for both men and women as more people participated in sports.

FIGURE 1.6 Elsa Schiaparelli, 1932.

Here, too, Hollywood exerted an influence: as more starlets were wearing one-piece swimsuits or the snug dancing costumes of lavish musical productions, body consciousness became widely accepted. Sportswear styles such as the cardigan coat or sweater were adopted for leisure time, and the 1932 Winter Olympics in Lake Placid, New York, encouraged sleeker trousers with stretch cuffs for many sports.

Designers and Other Influences

Fewer American department store buyers made the trip to Paris during the 1930s, and American designers in New York and on the West Coast began to achieve prominence. Designers such as Elizabeth Hawes and Clare Potter addressed the growing demand for clothes to suit an active lifestyle, producing sportswear and softer, casual designs. Dressmakers such as Hattie Carnegie and Nettie Rosenstein ran highly successful businesses, and others, such as Muriel King, began their careers in art and illustration and designed costumes for films. Hollywood-influenced designs were epitomized by the flowing, ruffle-sleeved dress worn by Joan Crawford in *Letty Lynton* (designed by Adrian)— and a new kind of California glamour turned up in the form of the tailored men's trousers worn by Marlene Dietrich and Katharine Hepburn.

One American designer who successfully established himself in Paris was Mainbocher, whose elegant evening designs were favored by the Duchess of Windsor. There he joined a strong fashion group dominated at the time by Chanel and Elsa Schiaparelli, who experimented with the surrealist art of Salvador Dalí and Jean Cocteau to design wearable fashion. Molyneux remained a force, with his slim-lined suiting, and Vionnet's bias cut was a signature look of the decade. Madame Grès was known for her intricate draped, wrapped, and pleated gowns.

THE 1940s: WAR AND DUTY

For the second time in the twentieth century, the world was engaged in large-scale war. From the years 1939–1945, war was the dominating factor of life, most devastatingly in Continental Europe but also in Asia and the Pacific. While the United States avoided attacks on its mainland, Japan's surprise attack on the Hawaiian base of Pearl Harbor in December 1941 pushed the country into a grueling four years. Wartime rationing affected food, transportation, and the apparel industry, with governmental controls over the amount of fabric that could be used for clothing. As men went off to battle, women—as they had during World War I—assumed industrial and other jobs formerly occupied by men.

Social and Cultural Conditions

As the roles of men and women shifted, society moved toward a loosening of formality and convention—a trend that has continued to this day. Another westward migration (no less significant than the one that had occurred in the 1800s) took place, with thousands of men and women relocating across the country to munitions plants and military bases. California's population grew by more than 70 percent during this time. The film industry still provided an escape from the wartime headlines, but Hollywood was pressed into patriotic duty, with many stars spending time entertaining the troops or selling war bonds.

A return to traditional family values began to take hold after 1946, when returning soldiers completed college on the GI Bill and started families. Americans would experience a new prosperity and shift in values.

Fashion Trends and Developments

Fashion for more than half of the decade was "on duty": subject to restrictions to conserve fabric and therefore shorter, sharper, and with a distinct military influence. Women's suits were tailored and mannish looking, with padded shoulders and peplum jackets nipped in at the waist. Shoes were rationed and became more practical for walking (with gasoline rationed as well). To offset the sharp lines of clothing, accessories, hair, and makeup imitated the carefree glamour of stars like pinup girl Betty Grable. Hair was longer and rolled, lipstick a patriotic red, and hats, though small, were jauntily perched and often whimsically decorated. With more severe shortages in Europe, fashionable women in both Europe and the United States adopted the turban or scarf as a head covering.

Hawaiian shirts and other Pacific-inspired designs like the sarong enjoyed popularity. The growing teenage population in the United States adopted the bobby-soxer look, including slacks for girls.

When wartime restrictions were lifted, clothing began to become fuller and more formal again. French designer Christian Dior made a splash with the introduction of his full, feminine New Look in 1947. With this success, he was credited with rescuing French haute couture from obsolescence—though Parisian designers would now have to share fashion's stage with the Americans, who had risen in prominence during the years of the war.

FIGURE 1.7 The head covering was a popular trend in the 1940s.

Designers and Other Influences

Perhaps the biggest shift that occurred during the 1940s was that the designers in occupied Paris were effectively shut down. With a lack of European influence, American designers earned their due. Claire McCardell worked within rationing guidelines to produce dresses and playclothes that were simple in shape, including practical wardrobe staples like the dirndl skirt and pop-over dress. Other designers who successfully created clothes that were both stylish and practical were Tina Leser, Norman Norell, and Mildred Orrick, and Hattie Carnegie's ready-to-wear business thrived. Essential in shifting the focus from French to American designers was the appropriation of the Best-Dressed List from Paris, where it had originated as a publicity stunt for the venerable Mainbocher. As reinterpreted by publicist Eleanor Lambert, the annual list highlighted American women and an American sensibility of style.

In the later 1940s, Paris regained its foothold as a design center. Along with Dior were Pierre Balmain (who claimed credit for the New Look that Dior became celebrated for), Jacques Fath, and Nina Ricci, all of whom would make significant contributions to the feminine, more formal styles of the 1950s.

Postwar was a boom period for Americans, who experienced an explosion in both the birth rate and the economy. All that wartime industry matured into the production of new consumer goods to fill the home: electric stoves and vacuum cleaners, toys, games, and gadgets. Televisions became the latest form of family entertainment, and shows such as *I Love Lucy* and *The Honeymooners* gave films stiff competition. With an overriding mood of conservatism, men and women reassumed more traditional masculine and feminine roles; many women who had worked outside of the home in the previous decade returned to homemaking, and the nuclear family was held up as the ideal.

Social and Cultural Conditions

Bolstering the mood were film and television icons who seemed almost a throwback to the more independent icons of the wartime years: curvy sexpots like Marilyn Monroe and girl-next-door Doris Day, along with well-dressed housewife models such as Donna Reed.

The West Coast lured Beat writers Allen Ginsberg and Jack Kerouac; Kerouac's road novel *On the Road* became a classic for the disaffected. Civil rights issues were brewing, and Rosa Parks's arrest in 1955 for refusing to relinquish her bus seat to a white passenger resulted in widespread protests. When the Civil Rights Act was passed in 1957, the struggle gained momentum. And though the majority of America's teenagers during the 1950s seemed happily and selfishly absorbed with their rock and roll (including parental shocker Elvis Presley), they were also drawn to films like *Rebel Without a Cause*. They would indeed rebel in earnest once they got a little older.

Fashion Trends and Developments

The return to more traditional roles meant softer and fuller styles for women. Fashion also tended toward more conformity, with fashion editors in *Vogue* and *Harper's Bazaar* issuing decrees about the appropriate length and width for skirts. Full-skirted dresses as well as the narrower shirtwaist dress were available for daytime wear, but dressing for cocktails and other evening social events became more constructed for women again, with dresses featuring crinolines under wide skirts, boned bodices, and structured undergarments. When the stiletto heel was introduced in 1951, the thicker heels from the wartime era all but disappeared. Many of these feminine styles were worn by

Spring 2013

Fall 2013

Spring 2013

RUCCI'S RULES:
CUTTING HIS OWN WAY

IN 1994, THE Chado Ralph Rucci line was born and a new standard was set for luxurious dressing with an artistic twist. Because of his sculptural silhouettes, impeccable craftsmanship, and use of the most fabulous materials, Ralph Rucci became a favorite with society mavens and mature fashionistas. In 2002, Rucci was the first American designer since Mainbocher in the 1930s to be invited to present his line at the Paris Haute Couture show under his own name. He designs all of his own prints and works with mills to create new fabrics and revive historically important textiles.

Born and raised in Philadelphia, Rucci graduated from Temple University with a degree in philosophy. At the age of twenty-one, he moved to New York City to study at the Fashion Institute of Technology and then trained at Halston and Balenciaga.

In an interview in *WWD*, Rucci said that during the thirty years he has been in business, the common thread has been "cut, cut, cut, and finding new ways to make clothes so a woman becomes empowered and not decorated. I detest decoration." Rucci has also found the ongoing and still-growing trend of celebrity designers alarming. He said, "You see, when I entered the profession, collections were made by professionals making clothes. Today, lending the name just for magazine readers is the norm, and I hope it passes us quickly."

Rucci continues to expand his horizons and explore potential licenses. He is launching a home collection with Holly Hunt and is planning an accessory line of shoes, handbags, and leather goods. These moves are marking the next chapter in the designer's career.

Among the many honors Rucci has received throughout his career include the Cooper-Hewitt National Design Award (2008); the Couture Council of the Museum at FIT (2006); Pratt Institute Icon Award (2009); the Philadelphia International Festival of the Arts Visionary Award for Fashion (2011); and induction into the Fashion Walk of Fame (2011).

Ralph Rucci

teenage girls, too—though often given a more playful feel, with full poodle skirts and ballerina shoes. The twin set (cardigan and shell) was worn by women and teens alike, and matching mother–daughter dresses were popular as well.

For men, the 1950s was the time of the gray flannel suit, often accompanied by a fedora hat. While formality in the workplace was the accepted standard, leisure-time separates such as sports jackets and short-sleeved shirts were also worn. Casual clothes for all members of the family were given a boost with the invention of wash-and-wear fabrics such as acrylic and Orlon. Dungarees or jeans were another popular youth style, cuffed for after-school dress or, for truly rebellious types, worn with a white T-shirt and leather jacket like Marlon Brando.

Designers and Other Influences

The trend toward formality brought French designers back into the spotlight, with Dior and Balmain leading the way. Jacques Fath introduced a slightly leaner silhouette and was known for his pointed collars; he also made inroads into the American ready-to-wear market before his death in 1954. Chanel reopened her atelier in that same year, and her collarless wool tweed suits, while not popular in France, achieved near-cult status in the United States. Italian designers arranged their first collective couture show in 1951 and started to become noticed; the House of Gucci, in particular, had a good deal of success with leather accessories. Other European influences included Queen Elizabeth II of England, who wore a dress by British designer Norman Hartnell at her 1953 coronation, and polished, ladylike film star Grace Kelly, who retired from film in 1956 when she married Prince Rainier of Monaco.

American designers like Claire McCardell continued to gain recognition—even earning coverage in the French fashion press. The generally less-structured styles being produced in New York and California were more appropriate for the ready-to-wear market. Norman Norell showed collections featuring a range of suits, day dresses, and formal wear. Charles James and Arnold Scaasi were known for their structured and dramatic clothing, while on the other end of the spectrum, Californian Bonnie Cashin, who had worked as a costume designer in Hollywood, specialized in layered, comfortable clothing for active women. Perhaps heralding the end of designer-dictated fashion, an unlikely fashion icon was introduced in 1959 in the form of Barbie, the doll who would come to incur both admiration and wrath for her idealized figure and fashion-forwardness.

FIGURE 1.8 The gray flannel suit and fedora hat, as popularized by Gregory Peck, 1956.

THE 1960s: TIMES ARE A-CHANGING

The so-called baby boom generation came of age during the 1960s and set off a fast-forward "youthquake" surpassing even that of the 1920s. In a period of protests, antiwar demonstrations, and generational conflicts, the world seemed to be in constant chaos. The decade began on a note of progressiveness and optimism with the election of President John F. Kennedy but soured dramatically when he was assassinated in 1963. The conflict in Vietnam escalated and race riots dominated the evening news; 1968 was one of the most violent on record, with student revolts in France, Germany, Eastern Europe, and Mexico and, in the United States, the assassinations of civil rights leader Martin Luther King Jr. and favored Democratic presidential candidate Bobby Kennedy within two months of each other.

Social and Cultural Conditions

Turmoil proved conducive to arts and music, however, and a cross-fertilization of styles emerged from the "British Invasion" of the Beatles and Rolling Stones to American homegrown talents such as Janis Joplin, Bob Dylan, and the Beach Boys. The San Francisco neighborhood of Haight-Ashbury became synonymous with flower power and hippies during the 1967 Summer of Love, and the Woodstock music festival in 1969 was a defining moment for youth culture. And it is important not to forget that the 1960s were a time when advances in science and technology outpaced anything seen before, with the introduction of the birth-control pill igniting a sexual revolution and astronaut Neil Armstrong stepping out onto the moon in 1969.

Fashion Trends and Developments

In the first years of the decade, conservatism was in evidence to a degree: women still wore full or longer skirts and fitted suits, although the teen crowd had already experimented with slightly higher hemlines. Men wore pressed slacks and sports jackets and were short-haired and clean-cut in the manner of "safe" pop and folk singers such as Pat Boone and the Kingston Trio. Women raced to copy First Lady Jackie Kennedy's suits with boxy little jackets and her signature pillbox hat. The Best-Dressed List continued to identify prominent socialites and actresses, such as Audrey Hepburn, as arbiters of American chic, although the concept of "dressing well" would change in interesting ways as the decade progressed.

The most visible fashions of the times were the most radical. Shift dresses climbed over the knee and then higher still, with the miniskirt making its debut in 1966 (and the even shorter micromini a few years later). Eastern influences showed up in caftans and Nehru jackets. Wild colors, op-art designs, and swirling Pucci prints became popular. Complementing these shorter styles was the white midcalf boot known as the go-go boot, and brightly colored and patterned tights completed the look. Other new shapes included the baby-doll dress and bell-bottom pants and jeans. Beach and surf culture made the bikini a swimwear staple, though designer Rudi Gernreich's topless monokini was too wild for most.

More than in any other decade, the 1960s produced styles that demanded niche marketing to specific customers. More mature adults gravitated toward more tailored looks, while the fashionable youth crowd browsed trendy boutiques. And once the counterculture really got under way, young people ransacked Army-Navy stores, their grandmother's closet, and anywhere else to pull together their flower-child costumes—elements of which were then appropriated by haute couture at a much higher price.

This was also the decade for hair as fashion. From bouffants and falls to wigs, ironing, pixie cuts, or simply long and untamed styles, hair became an expression of individuality for women. The same applied to men as well. The Beatles' mop top, which had been considered too long in 1963, was by the end of the 1960s practically uptight. In 1968, the rock musical *Hair* gloried in long locks, the Age of Aquarius, and love beads.

Designers and Other Influences

The big fashion story of the decade was swinging London, where Mary Quant introduced the miniskirt (cut shorter than in New York) and the Biba boutique sold a "total look" that coordinated dresses with tights and shoes. The rock group the Rolling Stones introduced the Carnaby Street "peacock" look for men to the United States. With styles that were easier to copy—and with rapid knockoffs being an increasing trend—French designers accustomed to the world of the atelier

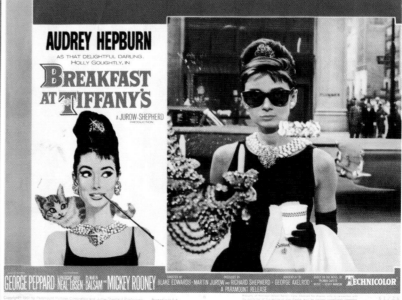

FIGURE 1.9 Gernreich design, 1967 (left) and Audrey Hepburn stars in *Breakfast at Tiffany's*, 1961 (right).

struggled to keep pace. Those influenced by futuristic design were Andre Courrèges, Paco Rabanne, Pierre Cardin, and Emanuel Ungaro. On the more conservative side of things, Hubert de Givenchy, known for dressing Jackie Kennedy and Audrey Hepburn, was successful with an older clientele. In the United States, designers such as Bill Blass and Oscar de la Renta succeeded in providing styles that were updated but still ladylike, while up-and-comer Betsey Johnson catered to the youth market. Bonnie Cashin, working in California, continued her line of sportswear separates (including shorts, ponchos, and culottes), while another California designer, James Galanos, became known for the floaty chiffon evening look, a more formal turn.

THE 1970s: FASHION AND THE ME DECADE

Social unrest remained a hallmark of the 1970s. Americans were divided by the war in Vietnam and the struggle of women and minorities to achieve equal rights. By the mid-1970s, the economy was at its lowest point since the Great Depression. Baby boomers, partly as a reaction to the chaos of the 1960s (and also simply because they were getting older), set out to "find themselves" by whatever means possible.

Social and Cultural Conditions

Television was quick to adapt, featuring shows depicting single working women who ran the gamut from *The Mary Tyler Moore Show* to *Charlie's Angels* and families who gave a nod to unconventionality, like the *Brady Bunch*. Magazines also saw change during this time. American *Vogue* featured a black model on the front cover for the first time in August 1974.

Fashion Trends and Developments

Fashionwise, "anything goes" was the mantra of the 1970s. The hippie style of the counterculture continued to be popular with the younger generation (particularly those who had missed out on Woodstock), and also persisting throughout the decade were short skirts and long hair. Nobody could seem to make up their minds about skirt lengths, and along with minis there were midi and maxi lengths. (Many women, faced with confusing choices, gave up and simply wore pants instead; a more extreme choice was hot pants, or short shorts.) For men, the polyester leisure suit, with pointed collars and open shirts, was the stylish outfit of choice.

FIGURE 1.10 Beverly Johnson was the first black model to be featured on the front cover of American *Vogue* in 1974.

Denim (especially designer jeans) soared in popularity for everyone, becoming acceptable for dress as well as casual wear. Platform shoes reached new heights and were worn by both sexes, and the 1970s might also be called the decade of the boot, which was produced in all kinds of leather, suede, vinyl, and patchwork prints.

Although there were many options, with influences ranging from ethnic designs and disco to glam rock and punk, the entrance of significant numbers of women into the professional workforce created a demand for appropriate office attire. With the publication of *Dress for Success* in 1975 and *The Woman's Dress for Success Book* in 1977, men's suits were feminized for women in slim, no-nonsense shapes.

Designers and Other Influences

Designers responded to the times by introducing a variety of styles, but even fashion editors admitted that there were no longer "rules" to dictate one's choices. As a result, the business of French haute couture suffered. An exception was Yves Saint Laurent, whose often romantic designs and haute-bohemian looks were deemed easy enough to emulate with knockoffs. The Italian design team Missoni emerged with elegant, patterned knitwear. In London, British designer Vivienne Westwood brought the deconstructed, anarchist elements of punk style to the fore, while her compatriot Zandra Rhodes worked the aesthetic in a more glamorous mode.

With casual wear as the dominant mode, however, the 1970s were really a time for American designers to shine. In 1973, Eleanor Lambert produced a benefit fashion show at the palace of Versailles, which featured both French and American designers. The show was a hit, and this eventually led to the spread of American fashion around the world. Ralph Lauren and Calvin Klein made their debuts, both producing wearable wardrobe separates with a nod to menswear. Klein became known for his neutral colors and minimalist approach to design, while Lauren traded in classic nostalgia (he designed the costumes for two popular films of the era, *Annie Hall* and *The Great Gatsby*). Diane von Furstenberg introduced her one-piece wrap dress in 1973, and its immediate success landed her on the cover of *Time* magazine. Anne Klein was another well-known designer of high-quality sportswear until her death in 1974; one of the design successors of her company was the young Donna Karan, who would make her mark in the 1980s. And no discussion of the 1970s would be complete without mention of Halston, whose simple, clinging dresses—a staple of the Studio 54 nightlife clique—became instant classics.

Fashion was influenced by popular culture more than ever. From John Travolta's white suit in *Saturday Night Fever* to Farrah Fawcett's feathered hair, trends in the 1970s came and went as fast as new media idols appeared. It's almost no wonder that nostalgia for this decade of self-expression didn't take long to come back around.

THE 1980s: POP CULTURE AND EXCESS

No other decade exemplifies excess quite like the 1980s. Although the decade began on a low note, with continued inflation and the ongoing hostage crisis in Iran, the social landscape changed when Ronald Reagan came into office as president. He and his wife, Nancy, set a more glamorous stamp on the White House. Americans, eager for new wealth themselves, played along. This was the era of the yuppie, or young urban professional, who engaged in conspicuous consumption—and many were women, primarily baby boomers who had worked their way up to executive-level positions and wanted to enjoy their newfound financial security. Food and fashion were status symbols, and it seemed that these yuppies couldn't get enough of sushi or arugula or the latest Gucci bag. The stock market was suddenly sexy—even middle-class investors joined the game. "Greed is good" went the tagline from the

hit movie *Wall Street*—and most seemed to agree. The mood lasted until the stock market crashed in 1987.

Social and Cultural Conditions

The corresponding advancements in technology had a profound effect on the way Americans spent their leisure time. Apple introduced the Macintosh in 1984, and by the end of the decade, computers were used in offices, homes, and schools. Videocassette players (VCRs) and cable television brought movies into the home, and with the Sony Walkman, users could take music cassette tapes (and later, CDs) along on their commute or to the gym. Exercising became an industry in itself, with shiny new gyms boasting the latest in Nautilus fitness machines. But perhaps nothing revolutionized pop culture (and the emerging generation X, born after the baby boomers) like the advent of MTV in 1981. The art of the music video was born, and it made international stars of those performers who could best exploit the medium: Madonna, Michael Jackson, and many more.

Fashion Trends and Developments

There were a variety of fashion influences in the 1980s, but whatever the source of inspiration, the general idea was that bigger was better. Whether it was the shoulders on one of Nancy Reagan's red suits, the romantic style and signature hats of Princess Di, or the bleached, permed, ratted, and tied-up hair flaunted by pop star Madonna, this principle held true. More disposable income meant that conspicuous consumption was acceptable, and dressing for success took on a new meaning. Suits were slick and sharp, and the padded shoulder, for both women and men, was everywhere. "Power dressing" was the name of the game, and women embraced it in executive-style outfits featuring big shoulders, close-fitting skirts, and blouses with dolman or batwing sleeves. The sharp wedge cut (an inverted triangle) was popular for dresses. This was a style to aspire to, even if you hadn't yet worked your way up the executive ladder, and it gave birth to another trend (still sometimes visible today): white high-top Reebok athletic shoes (a 1980s staple) worn with the suits, over pantyhose, for the commute to the office, with pumps tucked safely in the briefcase. For nighttime, no amount of pouf or glitz was too much. As exemplified by actresses Joan Collins and Linda Evans in the nighttime television drama *Dynasty* (with costumes designed by Nolan Miller), fabrics were printed, shiny, threaded with gold, and often period-inspired.

FIGURE 1.11 Rosanna Arquette and Madonna in *Desperately Seeking Susan*, 1985.

Men had options as well—and there was more on the market for them to choose from. The emphasis on the yuppie lifestyle meant that owning at least one good suit was key, and those by Giorgio Armani were a favored choice. Wall Streeters (or those who wanted to look like them) also imitated the suspender look worn by actor Michael Douglas. As a casual alternative, the unstructured jackets worn over T-shirts and shoes worn without socks, popularized by Don Johnson and Philip Michael Thomas in the television show *Miami Vice*, were the dominant look.

The pop music scene played an enormous part in 1980s fashion, due to the visibility of MTV. This was true especially for teenagers and those in their early twenties, who rushed out to shopping malls to imitate the short skirts, lace stockings, leggings, and see-through shirts worn by Madonna in her earliest incarnation. Later, when she changed her look to the more polished costumes of her Material Girl persona, accessorizing changed again. Other pop and synth-pop group members provided inspiration with deconstructed looks and big or wedge-cut hair. And perhaps no movie had such a fashion impact as *Flashdance*, which caused thousands of young women to don dancers' leg warmers and off-the-shoulder tops.

Designers and Other Influences

The desire for luxury in the 1980s allowed French couture designers to make their mark with extravagant designs. Christian Lacroix's pouf skirt was one of the most widely copied designs. Jean Paul Gaultier designed Madonna's famous conical bra and other gender-bending ensembles featuring tailored suits and corsetry. Thierry Mugler put his stamp on the power suit with broad-shouldered, nipped-waist versions that combined both historic and futuristic elements. Azzedine Alaïa redefined the little black dress as short, tight, and sexy, and Karl Lagerfeld reinvigorated the house of Chanel when he assumed the role of head designer in 1982 by updating the classic boxy suit in a modern mode—along with heaps of accessories.

The fashion world also began to take note of Japanese designers, such as Rei Kawakubo and Yohji Yamamoto—both of whom worked in avant-garde and often deconstructed styles. Kenzo Takada introduced colorful designs for both men and women. Issey Miyake, an innovator of experimental twists and pleats, created clothing that was always challenging, often more art than apparel.

Other significant designers, in addition to Armani (best known for his suiting looks), were fellow Italians Gianni Versace and Franco Moschino. London designer Vivienne Westwood shifted her focus from punk to pirate. Designers in the United States produced ready-to-wear collections that were less extravagant than those of their European counterparts: Calvin Klein and Ralph Lauren expanded their range of sportswear and suiting, Donna Karan introduced a more feminine (yet practical) look for working women, and Liz Claiborne produced affordable women's separates.

THE 1990s: FASHION IN THE INFORMATION AGE

Faced with a new recession, Americans retrenched after the 1987 stock market crash. The country saw the Persian Gulf War in 1991, which polarized Americans, and President George H.W. Bush was defeated by Democrat Bill Clinton in 1992. There was a rapid rise of new technologies, computer culture expanded to include e-mail and the Internet, and cell phones became commonplace items (earlier in Europe and Asia, later in the United States).

Social and Cultural Conditions

Generation X was now a significant part of the workforce, and they tried to define themselves against the previous decade's excesses. More technologically savvy than the baby boomers but less sure of pursuing high-pressure careers, this group—some of whom ironically tagged themselves with the moniker *slacker*—made their presence known in music and other areas of entertainment.

Digital know-how gave rise to a do-it-yourself style of filming and showed up too in the growing prominence of electronic and hip-hop music. But perhaps the loudest influence was from the "alternative" scene, when garage rock bands (many from the Seattle area) burst onto the music scene in the early 1990s. Bands such as Nirvana, Soundgarden, and Pearl Jam popularized the grunge aesthetic and shifted the terrain from pop to harder rock. As the economy rebounded in the late 1990s, brighter sounds in music came again, with manufactured pop stars such as the teenaged Britney Spears making their mark.

Fashion Trends and Developments

The somber mood of the early 1990s reflected the way people dressed, with laid-back minimalism and informality. Office attire became more casual, as gen Xers in their twenties showed up to work in casual separates at new high-tech companies, and "casual Fridays" relaxed the dress code for men and women at all but the stuffiest of firms. The classic chino pant was a beneficiary of these relaxed office environments and was offered in many variations for both men and women by newly prominent ready-to-wear companies such as the Gap, J. Crew, and Banana Republic. Fashion took its inspiration from many places, and individualism, rather than fashion rules, became the norm.

Layering was a popular look, with women often in longer skirts, jackets, and vests; more stretch fabrics were introduced, and styles were generally looser and flowing. The slip dress enjoyed a fairly long run of popularity—either worn over a T-shirt for a casual look, in sinuous silk for evening, and, for the grunge crowd, often worn with clunky combat-style boots such as Doc Martens. The grunge look also instigated a run on old plaid flannel shirts and ratty lingerie slips, worn as outerwear—though an attempt by young designer Marc Jacobs to bring this look to the runway was a failure. Clothing for active sports became more specialized, with some pieces, like stretchy yoga pants, becoming acceptable for daywear. As the economy enjoyed an upswing in the late 1990s, more polished and playful clothing was desirable.

Designers and Other Influences

Minimalist Calvin Klein's streamlined suits and slim, bias-cut slip dresses were a distinctive and widely copied look in the early 1990s. For those interested in a more deconstructed or avant-garde take on minimalism, Belgian designers Ann Demeulemeester and Dries Van Noten, along with German Jil Sander, filled the requirement. Classic styles in a new mix of neutrals and patterns were offered by Miuccia Prada, and the black nylon Prada backpack became a much-copied status item. France experienced a changing of the guard when British designers John Galliano and Alexander McQueen were chosen to head up the venerable houses of Dior and Givenchy respectively. This started a trend toward internationalism, as increasingly design houses merged into large corporate groups and brought in talent from other countries to reinvigorate their products and image. American Tom Ford was hired as creative director of the Gucci group and made a splash with his high-cut, revealing long dresses. Michael Kors, another American, worked during the 1990s at Céline, and Marc Jacobs was hired by Louis Vuitton.

Branding, rather than the signature style of any one design house or designer, became the norm during this time, and "lifestyle" dressing was the operative term. This allowed designers to assume more than one identity. In the United States, Tommy Hilfiger initially made his mark with rap-inspired styles, later turning to a more casual American preppy look and jeans. Anna Sui caught the pulse of the retro trend and incorporated touches from the 1940s and 1960s—as well as street looks—into her designs. Isaac Mizrahi worked in the classic chic mode of Geoffrey Beene. And rap star Sean Combs became one of the first celebrities to launch a fashion line with his Sean John line, which took the hip-hop look high-class.

FIGURE 1.12 The grunge look of the 1990s.

THE TWENTY-FIRST CENTURY: FASHION AND TECHNOLOGY

The effects of the economic downturn were still in evidence following the high-tech industry's peak and fall. The first year of the new millennium brought the election of George W. Bush in a hotly contested election that was decided only by the Supreme Court—setting off the age of voting recounts (which would be revisited in the 2004 election as well) and further polarizing the country into a bitter, two-party deadlock. But the most devastating event of the early decade was the terrorist attacks in the United States on September 11, 2001, which shattered Americans' perception of security and invulnerability. After an outpouring of sympathy worldwide, the global tide took a different turn following the U.S. invasions of Afghanistan in 2002 and, especially, the invasion of Iraq in 2003. Terrorist attacks also persisted in various parts of the world, from London to Madrid. At the same time, technology and industry continued to extend itself with the outsourcing of jobs to Asian countries such as China and India—both of which have become international economic contenders. Combined with the emergence of the euro and the subsequent fall of the dollar's power, Americans today find that globalization has both significant benefits and challenges.

Social and Cultural Conditions

The new century has also seen the continued rise in technology, with cell phones now used by almost everyone and the Internet often the first stop for purchasing merchandise ranging from clothing to cosmetics to food. These days it's unthinkable for a retailer to be without a website or social media site to display the company's image. The remarkable success of eBay paved the way for almost anyone to set up a website and become a merchant. Apple's introduction of the portable iPad again revolutionized the entertainment industry by offering yet another way for users to personalize their choices and connect with the world. More and more people worldwide participate in social media sites such as Facebook, Twitter, Pinterest, Instagram, and YouTube. The ability to expose oneself to the masses is also reflected in reality television and a watered-down celebrity culture, where trivia is news and news is often trivial. And taking stock of what the last century of progress has brought us—and what it will cost us—concern for the very earth itself has reached a critical point, with global warming providing a new impetus for technology to find solutions.

It remains to be seen how these many choices will play out, but one thing is for certain: consumers are now accustomed to having more of a say in what they buy and from whom. This new level of individualism will lead to more challenges and opportunities.

Fashion Trends and Developments

More than ever, celebrity culture provides the inspiration for how people want to dress. And the very idea of *celebrity* itself has become more attainable: socialites such as Paris Hilton are essentially famous for being famous, and reality television stars are watched for their style choices as well. The act of participating in fashion by attending runway shows is seen as a legitimizing factor, with many a young starlet fighting for prominent front-row seats. A hierarchy still exists, of course, with serious actresses such as Nicole Kidman, Cate Blanchett, and Gwyneth Paltrow embodying a more classic and glamorous approach to style. Glamour may have been put away abruptly after the 9/11 attacks, when the uniform of choice at the 2002 Academy Awards was a sober black suit for both men and women, accented with tasteful jewels in patriotic red, white, and blue, but it has enjoyed a resurgence since then. For example, the television show *Sex and the City* set off the popularity of feminine, ladylike styles for high-powered women. This look has coexisted with more casual, mix-and-match styles with a variety of textures and patterns.

The most notable change in proportion has been short over long, and boxy swing coats and trapeze jackets that are worn over blouses or long T-shirts, often with skinny jeans. The baby-doll dress has resurfaced, as have minidresses and short tunics. The idea of organic or sustainable fashion also took hold in the twenty-first century (as a more knowledgeable, modern version of the 1970s back-to-nature theme). Retro and vintage looks are an inspiration, too, with many twists on old designs given a fresh hand by young and often local designers. In addition to New York, the cities of Los Angeles and Austin, Texas, are fertile ground. In Europe, the 2000s saw the emergence of Berlin as the choice city of cool for fashion and other art. One surefire way of taking a local design shop national (or international) is to offer up a variation on the T-shirt, which emerged in this decade as a true fashion item with many interpretations and price levels: companies such as American Apparel, C&C California, Urban Outfitters, and James Perse are well known.

Designers and Other Influences

Celebrity culture has given us more celebrities as designers, such as Victoria Beckham, Jessica Simpson, Kanye West, Mary-Kate and Ashley Olsen, Jennifer Lopez,

FIGURE 1.13 Designs from Victoria Beckham in 2012 (left) and Jason Wu in 2013 (right).

Gwen Stefani, Jay-Z, Nicole Richie, Justin Timberlake, Beyoncé, Rihanna, Sofía Vergara, among others. And designers have become celebrities themselves—no longer secluded in a rarefied atmosphere, they are household names. This democratization of fashion has led established designers to embrace the concept of "design for all" by associating themselves with retail chain stores looking for an image boost. For example, the trendy Scandinavia-based chain H&M introduced the idea of limited-edition lines of clothing from designers such as Karl Lagerfeld, Roberto Cavalli, and Stella McCartney. Target and Kohl's also sell lower-priced lines from well-known designers. Major fashion houses have continued to come under the corporate umbrella of large luxury-brand conglomerates such as the French-owned LMVH and the Gucci Group, and designers come and go. In Britain, Christopher Bailey modernized the Burberry line. Donatella Versace, who assumed design control of the line after her brother Gianni's shocking murder in 1997, has not only kept the house alive but brought it up-to-date with a ready-to-wear line.

Ready-to-wear is indeed the predominant aspect of design today; couture is more widely understood to be something a designer does to create hype, but successful styles will be modified in a more casual vein. In the United States, both Michael Kors and Marc Jacobs have grasped this principle well by running both high-end and more affordable bridge lines. Among younger designers, those who have made their mark are Zac Posen, Jason Wu, Alexander Wang, Behnaz Sarafpour, and the design teams Rodarte, Proenza Schouler, and Viktor & Rolf.

Summary and Review

It is said that for every action there's an equal and opposite reaction—and this is very true for fashion. In the 1900s fashion began to be seen in the streets, as the public went to amusement parks, dance halls, and movie theaters. The indelible fashion image of the early 1900s was the Gibson Girl. Featured with a popular curved figure, she was considered a "new woman" who was independent, active, and beautiful. Jeanne Paquin and the House of Worth were leading designers and Charles Frederick Worth gained recognition as the father of haute couture.

During the 1910s, the operating principle was about cutting back—and fashion followed suit. Manufacturers used lighter materials and construction, and fussy silhouettes disappeared. Entertainment thrived in the United States, and the public had a newfound fascination with movies and Hollywood stars. Jean Patou, Coco Chanel, Madeleine Vionnet, and Paul Poiret were the fashion leaders, with Mariano Fortuny introducing classic draping and pleating.

The 1920s brought jazz music and flappers, who wore loose and daring styles. Coco Chanel became famous for her little black dress; Jean Patou emphasized new sportswear designs; Jeanne Lanvin produced tubular dresses and coordinated separates; and Madeleine Vionnet created inventive styles with handkerchief and asymmetrical hems.

The 1930s and early 1940s were the Depression era, and in the early '40s World War II encompassed Europe, Asia, and America. These years proved to be a boon to American design and creativity. Elizabeth Havens, Clare Potter, Hattie Carnegie, Nettie Rosenstein, and Claire McCardell were all successful designer entrepreneurs of the time. In Hollywood, Adrian, the famous designer for successful films, came into the public eye. After the war's end, Christian Dior introduced the New Look in 1947. Along with Dior, Pierre Balmain and Nina Ricci helped Paris regain its foothold as a design center.

The 1950s and 1960s brought American design to the forefront of the fashion industry. The baby-boom generation came of age during the 1950s and 1960s, wearing Pucci prints, baby-doll dresses, and bell-bottom pants and jeans. Mary Quant, Paco Rabanne, Pierre Cardin, Emanuel Ungaro, and Hubert de Givenchy were popular French and English designers, while Bill Blass, Oscar de la Renta, and James Galanos were American stars.

The 1970s was the "anything goes" decade. Skirt lengths ranged from microminis and minis to midis and maxi lengths. Fashion influences ranged from ethnic design and disco to glam rock and punk. This was the time of Yves Saint Laurent, Missoni suits, Vivienne Westwood, and Zandra Rhodes, from Britain. Ralph Lauren and Calvin Klein made their debut; Diane von Furstenberg introduced her one-piece wrap dress in 1973, and Halston's simple, clinging dresses became instant classics.

Excess exemplifies the decade of the 1980s. There were a variety of fashion influences, but the general idea was that bigger is better. For women, power dressing was the name of the game. The 1980s were a boon to French couture designers Christian Lacroix, Jean-Paul Gaultier, Thierry Mugler, Azzedine Alaïa, and Karl Lagerfeld, who designed new and exciting silhouettes. The fashion world began to take note of Japanese designers Rei Kawakubo, Yohji Yamamoto, Kenzo Takada, and Issey Miyake, who worked in avant-garde and deconstructed styles. Prominent Italian designers included Gianni Versace and Franco Moschino.

The somber mood of the 1990s reflected the way people dressed, with minimalism and informality prevalent. Casual Friday dress codes emerged; layering was a popular look, as was grunge. Belgian designers Ann Demeulemeester and Dries Van Noten and German Jil Sander made their mark, as did Italian Miuccia Prada, whose black nylon Prada backpack became a much-copied status item.

The entry into the twenty-first century brought about technological advances, with the explosion of social media sites and online shopping. The 2000s became the decade of celebrities, socialites, and reality-TV stars. Celebrity culture has given us more "designers," while the fashion designers have become celebrities themselves.

We now look to the future, and at the same time, the past. Where and how fashion will evolve will still be based upon hundreds of years of history—but it all depends on you!

For Discussion

There seem to be definite correlations between fashion and the times. As times change, so do fashions, and when a fashion changes, the total look changes. Accessories, makeup, and hairstyles are all part of this total fashion look. When styles are revised, they are revived in new forms, adapted for new lifestyles and occasions.

Study Table 1.1 on the following pages and answer the questions below.

1. Find examples in magazines or draw, sketch, or photograph examples of one or more fashion items listed in the table.

2. What similarities in fashion and their causes can you find in the decades listed?

3. What environmental changes do you feel will have lasting effects over the next ten to twenty years?

4. What examples from the decades listed can you find to support the theory that fashion is evolutionary?

5. During what time period was fashion closest to being revolutionary?

6. What additions can you make to the information on past decades listed?

7. From your interpretation of the information on past decades, what conclusions can you draw about the evolution of fashions and their relationship to current events?

Era	Events Taking Place	Public Reactions	Interpretation in Apparel and Dress	Designers of the Decades

1920s	Post–World War I, Paris influence
	Voting rights for women
	Prohibition
	Talking movies
	Increasing prosperity
	Modern art, music, literature
	Birth of sportswear
		Daring looks and behavior
		Freedom for the body
		Short hairstyles
		Women begin to smoke
		Dancing (Charleston)
			Chemise dresses
			Short skirts
			T-strap shoes
			Cloche hats
			Luxurious fabrics:
			   silks,
			   satins,
			   crepes
			Costume looks
			Long strands of beads
				Madeleine Vionnet
				Jean Patou
				Edward Molyneux
				Coco Chanel
				Norman Hartnell
				Jeanne Lanvin

1930s	Depression era Unemployment, little money Hollywood influence: stars and designers Rayon and acetate fabrics Big bands, swing music	Frugality, conservatism "The little woman" "Make do" attitude	Soft looks: loose, light fabrics Long hemlines, bias cuts Big hats, big brims The housedress Fox fur-collared coats Wraps Platform shoes Broad-shouldered jackets	Jean Desses Madame Grès Elsa Schiaparelli Vera Maxwell Mainbocher

1940s	World War II:
	   government restrictions
	Exit France as fashion source
	Shortage of materials
	Emergence of American designers
	Radio, records
	Crooners: Crosby, Sinatra
	Dior—1947 "New Look"
		Women take men's jobs
		Glamour, pinup girls
		Strong nationalism
		Common cause philosophy
			Tailored, mannish suits,
			   peplum jackets
			Padded shoulders
			Knee-length straight skirts
			Soft, shoulder-length hair
			   (pageboy)
			¾–length coats
			Debut of bikini
				Bonnie Cashin
				Claire McCardell
				Adrian
				Norman Norell
				Pauline Trigère
				Christian Dior
				Cristóbal Balenciaga
				Hattie Carnegie
				Adele Simpson
				Charles James
				Nina Ricci

1950s	Population increasing; baby boom
	Korean War
	Films expand, go public, diversify
	Move to suburbs
	Incomes rising
	More imports
	Improved transportation
	Improved communications: TV
	Development of more
	   synthetics, finishes
	Birth of rock 'n' roll
		Buy new homes,
		   appliances,
		   furnishings
		Conformity
		Improve quality
		   of family life
		Use of increased
		   leisure time
		   for sports and
		   recreation
		The station wagon
			Classics: shirtwaist dress
			At-home clothes
			Mink coats
			Sack dress (too quickly copied)
			Sportswear
			Ivy League look:
			   gray flannel suit,
			   skinny ties,
			   button-down shirts
			Car coats
			Wash 'n' wear fabrics
			Sweater sets
			Unisex looks
				Hubert de Givenchy
				Mary Quant
				Yves Saint Laurent
				James Galanos
				Ceil Chapman
				Donald Brooks
				Gucci
				Anne Fogarty
				Missoni

1960s	Rise of shopping centers:
	   boutiques
	New technology: stretch fabrics,
	   new knitting methods
	Big business expansion; prosperity
	Designer names
	Civil rights movement
	Woodstock
	Vietnam War:
	   youth rebellion,
	   antiwar movement
	London influence: The Beatles,
	   Twiggy, Mod, Mary Quant,
	   Carnaby Street
	Peacock revolution, rock music,
	   youth cult
		New sexual freedom
		Experimental in fashion
		Anti-establishment
		   attitudes
		Generation gap
		Identity seeking,
		   new values
		Divorce, singles
		Drug experimentation
			Street fashions: jeans
			Vinyl, synthetics, wetlook
			Miniskirts
			Wild use of color patterns
			Knits, polyester
			Ethnic clothing and crafts
			Fun furs
			Long hair, wigs
			Men: turtlenecks,
			   wide ties,
			   Nehru jackets,
			   golf coordinates,
			   nylon printed shirts
				André Courrèges
				Pierre Cardin
				Anne Klein
				Geoffrey Beene
				Halston
				Rudi Gernreich
				Emilio Pucci
				Emanuel Ungaro
				Valentino
				Mila Schön
				Jean Muir

Era	Events Taking Place	Public Reactions	Interpretation in Apparel and Dress	Designers of the Decades
1970s	Equal rights, women's liberation movement Women working outside the home Watergate, disenchantment with politics Recessions Ecology, conservation; energy crisis Stabilizing economy End of Vietnam War Disco dancing, clubs Consumerism Hostage crisis in Iran	Individualism Return-to-sanity reaction to 1960s chaos Back to nature, health foods, natural fibers New conservatism Urban renewal, interest in cities & their problems Equal Rights Amendment Minority organizations Overseas manufacturing	Pantsuits (women), leisure suits (men) Maxi and longuette (1970s disaster) Jeans: bell-bottoms, straight leg, tapered legs, peg leg; denim acceptable for dress and casual wear T-shirts, tank tops, boots Eclecticism Classic look: blazers, shirts, investment clothing Separates, not coordinates Hot pants Romantic look: soft, feminine	Bill Blass Ralph Lauren Zandra Rhodes Diane von Furstenberg Giorgio Armani Gianfranco Ferré Vivienne Westwood Calvin Klein Kenzo Betsey Johnson Adolfo Norma Kamali Mary McFadden Oscar de la Renta Sonia Rykiel Stephen Burrows Bob Mackie Paco Rabanne
1980s	Computer explosion Music videos Nuclear weapons buildup in Europe Yuppie (Young Urban Professional) Recessions and unemployment Wars in Central America, Middle East Movies: *Fame, E.T., Flashdance* First black presidential and first woman vice-presidential candidates Japanese fashion explosion Executive-level women; two-income families New baby boom Licensing "arrangements" Birth of MTV	Buy home computers Michael Jackson, youth hero Nuclear freeze movement Entrepreneurship Immigration legislation Day-care centers Graffiti art London influence: punk, Boy George, and Culture Club Patriotism flourishes Convertibles return Proliferation of malls	Return of chemise Punk hairdos Androgynous dressing Tailored suits and classic dressing for men and women Torn-clothes fad Return to pants in mid-decade Hats return for everyone Furs Backpacks as fashion Sneakers for everyday wear	Donna Karan Perry Ellis Rei Kawakubo Christian Lacroix Gianni Versace Claude Montana Adrienne Vittadini Tommy Hilfiger Stephen Sprouse Issey Miyake Yohji Yamamoto Michael Kors Thierry Mugler Carolina Herrera Franco Moschino Karl Lagerfeld Jean-Paul Gaultier Liz Claiborne
1990s	Creation of the European Monetary Union Gulf War Economic recession High-tech industry growth NAFTA GATT Rise of terrorism Cellular phones proliferate Sports participation increases *Sex and the City*	Expansion of companies overseas Business failures, consolidations and takeovers Casual Fridays Proliferation of foreign manufacturing	Patriotic designs Grunge Retro Chunky shoes Rise of vintage Layering Innerwear as outerwear The decade of the supermodel and fashion photographer Sports gear becomes fashionable as each sport develops its own style Image and branding becomes more important than seasonal style changes Slip dresses Chinos	Anna Sui Josie Natori Isaac Mizrahi Todd Oldham Tracy Reese Nicole Miller John Galliano Vera Wang Prada Marc Jacobs Donatella Versace Martin Margiela Ann Demeulemeester Tom Ford Jil Sander Helmut Lang Narcisco Rodriguez Alber Elbaz Alexander McQueen Patrick Kelly Dries Van Noten Dominico Dolce & Stefano Gabbana
2000s	Expansion of communication technology September 11th terrorist attacks Emergence of the euro	Online shopping Social media Merchant/vendor data sharing	Mixing color, texture, and pattern Short layers over long End of haute couture influence	Zac Posen Peter Som Phillip Lim Rodarte Nicolas Ghesquière Hussein Chalayan Stella McCartney Proenza Schouler Ralph Rucci Roberto Cavalli Behnaz Sarafpour Viktor & Rolf Jason Wu Prabal Gurung

Chapter Two
THE NATURE OF FASHION

KEY CONCEPTS

- Marketing and merchandising in the fashion business
- The stages of the fashion cycle
- The intangibles of fashion

In his 1850 book *Fashion: The Power That Influences the World*, George P. Fox said, "Fashion is and has been and will be, through all ages, the outward form through which the mind speaks to the universe. Fashion in all languages designs to make, shape, model, adapt, embellish, and adorn."[1]

More recently, the famous designer Miuccia Prada said, "What you wear is how you present yourself to the world, especially today, when human contacts are so quick. Fashion is instant language."[2]

Fashion involves our outward, visible lives. It involves the clothes we wear, the dances we dance, the cars we drive, and the way we cut our hair. Fashion also influences architecture, forms of worship, and lifestyles. It has an impact on every stage of life from the womb to the tomb.

People started covering their bodies with clothes to keep warm and to be modest, but adornment—decoration—was already an important part of dressing. Pressure from peer groups and changes in lifestyle influence the type of adornment considered acceptable in a particular time or for a particular group. Basically, the reasons people have for wearing clothes have not changed. Today, we still wear clothes to keep warm or cool and for the sake of modesty, but what we select for those purposes are very much influenced by a desire to adorn ourselves.

Because people are social animals, clothing is very much a social statement. By looking at the way a person dresses, you can often make good guesses about his or her social and business standing, sex-role identification, political orientation, ethnicity, lifestyle, and aesthetic priorities. Clothing is a forceful and highly visible medium of communication that carries with it information about who a person is, who a person is not, and who a person would like to be.

The Importance of Fashion

Webster's Dictionary defines fashion as "prevailing custom, usage, or style,"[3] and in this sense it covers a wide range of human activity. The term is used in this book in a narrower sense: **fashion** here means the style or styles of clothing and accessories worn at a particular time by a particular group of people. Fashion in cosmetics and fragrances and in home furnishings is also covered.

General interest in fashion has increased enormously over the years. Fashion is one of the greatest economic forces in present-day life. To a great extent, it determines what people buy. Change in fashion is often the motivating factor for replacing clothes, cosmetics, furniture, housewares, and automobiles. Fashion causes changes in consumer goods and at the same time makes people want the new products, since the thought of being unfashionable is a fate worse than death to many people.

Fashion has also become a drawing power for art museums worldwide. Fashion showcases are multiplying and attendance is surging. Harold Koda, curator of the Costume Institute of the Metropolitan Museum of Art, said, "What is endlessly fascinating about fashion is that it can be approached and interpreted from so many different angles. . . . In the end it is about the object: its transformational originality, its details of unequaled technical virtuosity and its incomparably compelling aesthetic."[4]

Curators agree that fashion archives were considered a burden to fashion houses until the eighties, when Diana Vreeland, then a special consultant to the Costume Institute, decided to do an exhibition on Yves Saint Laurent, which turned into a blockbuster for the Metropolitan Museum. According to Koda, Saint Laurent recognized the value of maintaining an archive of his life's work. "Since then, many design houses have begun to keep and actively seek past examples of their most important works. This is helpful in preserving objects that had not been especially valued after they had passed their moment of fashionability." Permanent museums for brands are the latest expression of the trend (Figure 2.1).[5]

The Fashion Business

Fashion today is big business; millions of people are employed in fashion-related activities. The **fashion industries** are those engaged in manufacturing the materials and finished products used in the production of apparel and accessories for men, women, and children. Throughout this book, references to fashion industries mean the manufacturing businesses, unless others are specifically mentioned. The broader term **fashion business** includes all the industries and services connected with fashion: design, manufacturing, distribution, marketing, retailing, advertising, communications, publishing, and consulting—in other words, any business concerned with fashion goods or services.

Marketing

Marketing is a major influence in the fashion business. What does marketing mean? Most people think of marketing only as promotion and selling. However, promotion and selling are only two aspects of marketing. The **marketing** process includes diverse activities that identify consumer needs to plan, price, distribute, and promote products effectively so that they will sell easily. "The aim of marketing is . . . to know and understand the customer so well that the product or service hits him [or her] and sells itself."[6]

Fashion Marketing and Merchandising

In the past the fashion business was rather slow in adopting the marketing techniques that were so successful in the growth of consumer goods such as automobiles,

FIGURE 2.1 Fashion is everywhere. This is a scene from the Costume Institute's Alexander McQueen exhibition at the Metropolitan Museum of Art.

packaged foods, and health and beauty aids. Fashion producers were concerned only with what was economical and easy to produce. They spent considerable time and money trying to convince the consumer that their products were what the consumer wanted and needed. The producer had little or no interest in the wants and needs of the consumer.

However, today the total marketing process has been adopted by the fashion business and is being applied to the products and services of the fashion industries. The result is called *fashion marketing:* that is, the marketing of apparel, accessories, and other fashion-related products to the ultimate consumer.

We are also concerned with **fashion merchandising**, which is the *planning* required to have the right fashion-oriented merchandise at the right time, in the right place, in the right quantities, at the right prices, and with the right sales promotion for a specified target customer.

Misconceptions About Fashion

As the power of fashion to influence our lives grows, three misconceptions about it continue to be widely held. The first and most common misconception is that designers and retailers dictate what the fashion will be and then force it upon helpless consumers. It has been said that the industry is composed of "obsolescence ogres." In reality, consumers themselves decide what the fashion will be by influencing new designs and by accepting or rejecting the styles that are offered. Consumers are, in truth, "variety vultures."

The second misconception is that fashion acts as an influence on women only. Men and children are as influenced by and responsive to fashion as women. Fashion is the force that causes women to raise or lower their skirt lengths from minis to maxis, straighten or frizz their hair, and change from casual sportswear to dressy clothes. It also influences men to grow or shave off their mustaches and beards, choose wide or narrow ties and lapels, and change from casual jeans into three-piece suits. And fashion is the force that makes children demand specific products and styles.

The third misconception is that fashion is a mysterious and unpredictable force. Actually, its direction can be determined and its changes predicted with remarkable accuracy by those who study and understand the fundamentals of fashion. Fashion was once considered an art form controlled by designers, who dictated its content (Figure 2.2). But fashion has now evolved into a science that can be measured and evaluated.

FIGURE 2.2 From wild to wacky: This Surrealist-inspired dress from Christian Dior is sent down the runway not to sell to the public, but rather to get "press buzz."

The Terminology of Fashion

What is the difference between fashion, style, and design? Just what do *high fashion, mass fashion, taste, classic,* and *fad* mean? To avoid confusion when discussing fashion, we must first understand the meanings of these terms. The definitions that follow are based on the work of Dr. Paul H. Nystrom, one of the pioneers in fashion merchandising.[7]

Style

The first step in understanding fashion is to distinguish between *fashion* and *style,* words that most people use interchangeably despite the immense difference in their meanings. In general terms, a style is a characteristic or distinctive artistic expression or presentation. Styles exist in architecture, sculpture, painting, politics, and music, as well as in popular heroes, games, hobbies, pets, flirtations, and weddings.

In apparel, **style** is the characteristic or distinctive appearance of a garment—the combination of features that makes it unique and different from other garments. For example, T-shirts are as different from polo shirts as they are from peasant blouses. Riding jackets are as different from safari jackets as they are from blazers.

Although styles come and go in terms of acceptance, a specific style always remains a style whether it is currently in fashion or not. Some people adopt a style that becomes indelibly associated with them and wear it regardless of whether it is currently fashionable. Carmen Miranda's platform shoes, Katharine Hepburn's pleated trousers, the Duchess of Windsor's jewelry, Marilyn Monroe's white halter dress, Michael Jackson's glitter glove, Madonna's lace tops and fishnet stockings, Jennifer Lopez's signature hip-huggers, Lady Gaga's daily extremism, Victoria Beckham's tailored look with oversize sunglasses, and Katy Perry's glitter and glam (Figure 2.3) are all examples of personal style.

Some styles are named for the period of history in which they originated—Grecian, Roman, Renaissance, Empire, Gibson Girl (early 1900s), flapper (1920s). When such styles return to fashion, their basic elements remain the same. Minor details are altered to reflect the taste or needs of the era in which they reappear. For example, the flapper-style clothing of the 1920s was short, pleated, and body-skimming. That style can be bought today but with changes for current fashion acceptance.

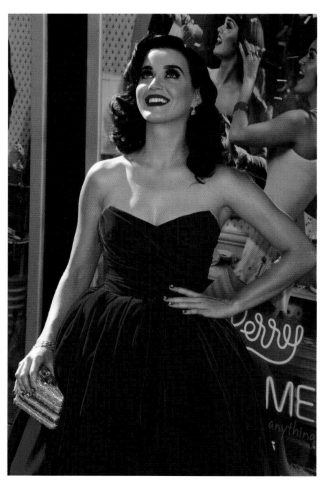

FIGURE 2.3 Katy Perry expresses her glitz and glam choice of style.

Fashion

Fashion is a style that is accepted and used by the majority of a group at any one time, no matter how small that group. A fashion is always based on some particular style. But not every style is a fashion. A fashion is a fact of social psychology. A style is usually a creation from an artist or a designer. A fashion is a result of social emulation and acceptance. A style may be old or new, beautiful or ugly, good or bad. A style is still a style even if it never receives the slightest acceptance or even approval. A style does not become a fashion until it gains some popular acceptance. And it remains a fashion only as long as it is accepted. Miniskirts, square-toed shoes, mustaches, and theatrical daytime makeup have all been fashions. And no doubt each will again be accepted by a majority of a group of people with similar interests or characteristics—for example, college students, young career men and women, or retired men and women.

Fashions appeal to many different groups and can be categorized according to the group to which they appeal. **High fashion** refers to a new style accepted by a limited number of fashion leaders who want to be the first to adopt changes and innovation in fashion. High-fashion styles are generally introduced and sold in small quantities and at relatively high prices. These styles may be limited because they are too sophisticated or extreme to appeal to the needs of the general public, or they are priced well beyond the reach of most people. However, if the style can appeal to a broader audience, it is generally copied, mass-produced, and sold at lower prices. The fashion leaders or innovators who first accepted it then move on to something new.

To contrast with high fashion, **mass fashion**, or **volume fashion**, consists of styles that are widely accepted. These fashions are usually produced and sold in large quantities at moderate to low prices and appeal to the greatest majority of fashion-conscious consumers. Mass fashion accounts for the majority of sales in the fashion business. Mass fashion is the bread and butter of the fashion banquet.

Design

There can be many variations of detail within a specific style. A **design** is a particular or individual interpretation, version, or treatment of a style. A style may be expressed in a great many designs, all different, yet all related because they are in the same style. A sweatshirt or a trench coat, for example, is a distinctive style, but within that style, variations may include different types of necklines, pockets, and sleeves (Figure 2.4). Another example is a satchel handbag, which may be interpreted with different closures, locks, or handles. These minor

FIGURE 2.4 This London Fog trench coat is a more traditional design (left), while Burberry Prorsum's design adds a twist with variations of the sleeves and details (right).

variations are the different interpretations that change the design of a style.

In the fashion industries, manufacturers and retailers assign a number to each individual design produced. This is the **style number**. The style number of a product identifies it for manufacturing, ordering, and selling purposes. In this instance, the term *style number* is used rather than *design number*, even though a design is being identified.

Taste

In fashion, **taste** refers to prevailing opinion of what is and what is not attractive and appropriate for a given occasion. Good taste in fashion, therefore, means sensitivity not only to what is artistically pleasing but also to what is appropriate for a specific situation. A style, such as an evening gown, may be beautiful. But if it is worn to a morning wedding, for example, it may not be considered in good taste.

Many styles are beautiful, but because they are not in fashion, good taste prevents their use. On the other hand, a present-day fashion may be inartistic or even ugly, but its common acceptance means that it is in good taste.

Nystrom described the relationship between good taste and fashion this way: "Good taste essentially is making the most artistic use of current fashion . . . bridging the gap between good art and common usage."[8]

Even during the height of acceptance of a particular fashion, it is considered in good taste only if it is worn by people on whom it looks appropriate. For example, miniskirts, tight pants, bikinis, and halter tops are considered in good taste only for people in good physical shape.

Timing, too, plays a part in what is considered good or bad taste. British costume authority James Laver saw the relationship between taste and fashion in terms of its acceptance level. A style, he said, is thought to be:

"indecent"	10 years before its time
"shameless"	5 years before its time
"outré"	1 year before its time
"smart"	in its time
"dowdy"	1 year after its time
"hideous"	10 years after its time
"ridiculous"	20 years after its time[9]

While the time an individual fashion takes to complete this course may vary, the course is always a cyclical one. A new style is often considered daring and in dubious taste. It is gradually accepted, then widely accepted, and finally gradually discarded.

FIGURE 2.5 The classic Chanel cardigan suit jacket is used as a giant backdrop at the 2008 couture show (left). The classic style is still integrated in today's fashion, as seen in Chanel's Spring 2013 collection (right).

For many decades, Laver's cycle has been accepted as the movement of most fashions. However, in the past few decades, some fashions have deviated from this pattern. The fashion cycles have become shorter and have repeated themselves within a shorter space of time. For the student of fashion, this shorter cycle presents an interesting challenge. What factors determine which fashions will follow the accepted cycles and which fashions will not? To understand the movement of fashion, it is important to understand that fashions are always in harmony with the times in which they appear.

A Classic

Some styles or designs continue to be considered in good taste over a long period of time. They are exceptions to the usual movement of styles through the fashion life cycle. A **classic** is a style or design that satisfies a basic need and remains in general fashion acceptance for an extended period of time (Figure 2.5).

Depending on the fashion statement a person wishes to make, he or she may have only a few classics or may have a wardrobe of mostly classics. A classic is characterized by simplicity of design that keeps it from being easily dated. The Chanel suit is an outstanding example of a classic. The simple lines of the Chanel suit

have made it acceptable for many decades, and although it reappears now and then as a fashion, many women always have a Chanel suit in their wardrobes. Other examples of classics are blue denim jeans, blazer jackets, cardigan or turtleneck sweaters, and button-down oxford shirts. Among accessories, the pump-style shoe, the loafer, the one-button glove, the pearl necklace, and the clutch handbag are also classics. For young children, overalls and one-piece pajamas have become classics.

A Fad

A fashion that suddenly sweeps into popularity, affecting a limited part of the total population, and then quickly disappears is called a **fad**. It comes into existence by the introduction of some feature or detail, usually exaggerated, that excites the interest of the customer. The fad starts by being quickly accepted and then quickly imitated by others.

Fads often begin in lower price ranges, are relatively easy to copy, and therefore flood the market in a very short time. Because of this kind of market saturation, the public tires of fads quickly and they end abruptly.

Fads follow the same cycle as fashions do, but their rise in popularity is much faster, their acceptance much shorter, and their decline much more rapid than that of a true fashion. Because most fads come and go in a single season, they have been called *miniature fashions*. We have seen the King Tut design fad, the Urban Cowboy, punk multicolored hair, grunge, and geek chic. Some specific examples include mega shoulder pads, ponchos, bell-bottoms, jeggings, crocs, harem pants, and feather accessories. Fads, like fashions, invade every field: sports, literature, religion, politics, and education.

However, many things that begin as fads become fashions and can carry over for several seasons. In fact, it is very difficult to draw the line between fads and fashions. The chemise, or sack dress, is probably the outstanding example of this phenomenon. After an instant rise to popularity in the late 1950s, it quickly passed from the fashion scene. A few years later, the chemise reappeared as the shift. In 1974, the chemise again appeared in the Paris collections, modified to eliminate its former disadvantages. American manufacturers quickly reproduced it in several versions and in a wide price range. That the chemise, in its various manifestations, again appeared in the late 1980s and the mid-1990s, and flourished again in 2007 with the swingy shift dress by Elie Tahari, provides strong evidence that the chemise has become a fashion classic (Figure 2.6).[10]

FIGURE 2.6 Starting out as a fad, the chemise dress has turned into a fashion classic.

A Trend

A **trend** is a general direction or movement. For example, if you read in fashion magazines that "there is a trend toward shorter skirts," it means that several designers, including some leading ones, are showing shorter skirts, leading retailers are buying them, and fashion-forward customers are wearing them (Figure 2.7). It is often difficult to tell a trend from a fad; even the experts get confused. However, marketers always want to know whether a new development is going to be a trend or a fad—because they want to cash in on trends but avoid getting burned by fads. A trend can originate anywhere and has a solid foundation that supports its growth; a fad does not.[11]

Components of Fashion

Fashion design does not just happen, nor does the designer wave a magic wand to create a new design. Fashion design involves the combination of four basic elements or components: silhouette, detail, texture, and

FIGURE 2.7 Even the experts are unsure whether the miniskirt is a trend or a fad.

FIGURE 2.8 Silhouettes belong to one of three basic groups: (a) bell-shaped or bouffant, (b) bustle or back fullness, and (c) straight or tubular. Variations of the straight silhouette are (d) slim, (e) rectangle, (f) wedge, and (g) A-line.

color. Only through a change in one or more of these basic components does a new fashion evolve. This is true of any fashion-influenced product, from kitchen appliances to automobiles, from apartment houses to office buildings, and from accessories to apparel.

Silhouette

The **silhouette** of a costume is its overall outline or contour. It is also frequently referred to as *shape* or *form*. It may appear to the casual observer that women have worn countless silhouettes throughout the centuries. In the 1930s, Agnes Brooke Young's research showed that there are actually only three basic forms—straight or tubular; bell-shaped or bouffant; and the bustle, or back fullness—with many variations.[12] We now see most fashion experts include four variations on the tubular silhouette: slim, rectangle, wedge, and A-line (Figure 2.8).

Details

The individual elements that give a silhouette its form or shape are called **details**. These include trimmings; skirt and pant length and width; and shoulder, waist, and sleeve treatment.

Silhouettes evolve gradually from one to another through changes in detail. When the trend in a detail reaches an extreme, a reversal of the trend takes place. For example, dresses and suits featured wide shoulders with much padding in the 1940s and 1950s. This detail was reversed in the late 1960s and 1970s, when the look became casual and unstructured. This casualness reached such extremes that by the start of the 1980s, structured clothing was back in fashion and dress and suit shoulders began once again to grow wider as padding was inserted. By the 1990s, the unstructured look was predominant again; and entering the 2000s, structured suits and wide shoulders were again seen on the runways. By 2007, this look was softened and more unstructured, only to swing back toward more tailored designs today.

Variations in detail allow both designer and consumer to express their individuality freely within the framework of the currently accepted silhouette. To emphasize a natural-waistline silhouette, for example, a slender woman might choose a simple wide belt, a decorated belt, or a belt in a contrasting color. To express his individuality, a man might emphasize the wide-shoulder look with epaulets or heavy shoulder pads.

Texture

One of the most significant components of fashion is texture. **Texture** is the look and feel of material, woven, knit, or nonwoven.

Texture can affect the appearance of a silhouette, giving it a bulky or slender look, depending on the roughness or smoothness of the materials (Figure 2.9). A woman dressed in a rough tweed dress and a bulky knit sweater is likely to look larger and squarer than she would in the same dress executed in a smooth jersey and topped with a cashmere sweater.

Texture influences the drape of a garment. Chiffon clings and flows, making it a good choice for soft, feminine styles, while corduroy has the firmness and bulk suitable for more casual garments.

Texture affects the color of a fabric by causing the surface to either reflect or absorb light. Rough textures absorb light, causing colors to appear flat. Smooth textures reflect light, causing colors to appear brighter. Anyone who has tried to match colors soon discovers that a color that appears extremely bright in a shiny vinyl, satin, or high-gloss enamel paint seems subdued in a rough wool, suede, or stucco wall finish.

FIGURE 2.9 The different layers of texture in this Né-net design produce a rough and bulkier look.

Color

Historically, certain colors denoted rank and profession. Purple, for instance, was associated with royalty, and in some periods could be worn only by those of noble birth. Black became customary for the apparel of the clergy and for members of the judiciary.

Color has always been a major consideration in women's clothing. Since World War II, color in men's clothing has regained the importance it had in previous centuries. Today, color is a key factor in apparel selection for both sexes. It is also important for advertising, packaging, and store decor (Figure 2.10).

Color symbolism often varies with geographical location. While white is the Western world's symbol of purity, worn by brides and used in communion dresses, it is the color of mourning in India.

A fashion designer's color palette changes with consumers' preferences. In some seasons, all is brightness and sharp contrast, and no color is too powerful to be worn. In other seasons, only subdued colors appeal. Fashion merchants must develop an eye for color—not only for the specific hues and values popular in a given season but also for indications of possible trends in consumer preference.

The Fashion Cycle

All fashions move in cycles. The term **fashion cycle** refers to the rise, wide popularity, and then decline in acceptance of a style. The word *cycle* suggests a circle. However, the fashion cycle is represented by a bell-shaped curve (Figure 2.11, top).

Some authorities compare the fashion cycle to a wave, which shows first a slow swell, then a crest, and finally a swift fall. Like the movement of a wave, the movement of a fashion is always forward, never backward. Like waves, fashion cycles do not follow each other in regular, measured order. Some take a short time to crest; others, a long time. The length of the cycle from swell to fall may be long or short. And, again like waves, fashion cycles overlap (Figure 2.11, bottom).

Stages of the Fashion Cycle

Fashion cycles are not haphazard; they don't "just happen." There are definite stages in a style's development that are easily recognized. These stages can be charted and traced, and in the short run, accurately predicted. Being able to recognize and predict the different stages is vital to success in both the buying and the selling of fashion.

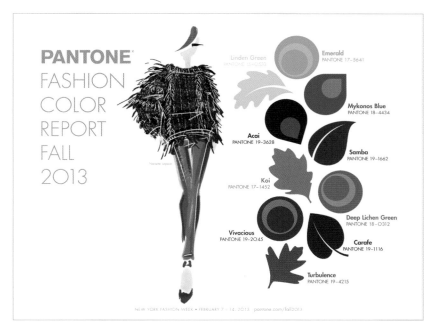

FIGURE 2.10 Each season the color experts at Pantone forecast popular hues for women (top) and men (bottom).

MICHAEL KORS
AMERICAN IDOL:

HE IS THE most irrepressible man in the fashion business. After thirty years, that in itself is an accomplishment. Michael Kors loves fashion and style as much now as he did years ago, when, as a starstruck Fashion Institute of Technology student, the sight of Calvin Klein at Studio 54 made him "long for [his] own banquette there," he told *WWD* in an interview. Today, what gets Kors's heart racing is the sight of women wearing his clothes.

Michael Kors is the golden man of Wall Street. In December of 2011 his company went public, with Kors, chief executive officer John Idol, and partners Silas Chou and Lawrence Stroll ringing the opening bell of the stock exchange. Kors joins a handful of American designers, namely Ralph Lauren, Tommy Hilfiger, and Kenneth Cole, all of whom took their companies public during the last two decades.

As for Kors, the designer has significantly boosted his profile these last few years, in part because of his television exposure as a judge on *Project Runway*, a role he has had since 2004. A key strategy behind Kors's rapid growth has been to reposition the company from primarily a wholesale model to that of a retail one. Furthermore, in recent years, Kors has shifted his emphasis from apparel toward accessories.

Expanding his retail network has been a high priority. The designer has unveiled his largest lifestyle store yet on Madison Avenue in New York, and as of 2012, Michael Kors has a presence in 74 countries. He plans to open between thirty and forty stores in North America, ten to fifteen stores in Europe, and ten more in Japan. Kors continues to push on both the international and domestic front, with store locations in Beverly Hills, Chicago, London, Milan, Paris, Munich, Istanbul, Dubai, Seoul, Tokyo, Hong Kong, Madrid, and Taipei. He also plans to open his largest Chinese flagship store in Shanghai.

It has been more than thirty years since Kors started his namesake line. This anniversary has Kors hitting his stride as he has turned out a series of strong collections that perfectly embody his vision of luxe American glamour. In an article in *Harper's Bazaar*, when asked what his legacy would be, he answered, "My legacy would be that you don't have to give up anything. You can be chic but have a sense of humor, you can be sexy but comfortable, you can be timeless but fresh." He then went on to say, "I think to be empathetic is the greatest gift you can have as a designer. Hopefully, people will look at me and say, 'He really loved women.'"

Michael Kors at the New York Stock Exchange Opening Bell

Fall 2013

Spring 2013

FASHION FOCUS

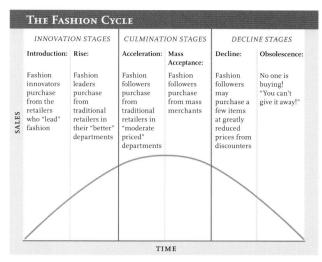

THE FASHION CYCLE

INNOVATION STAGES		CULMINATION STAGES		DECLINE STAGES	
Introduction:	**Rise:**	**Acceleration:**	**Mass Acceptance:**	**Decline:**	**Obsolescence:**
Fashion innovators purchase from the retailers who "lead" fashion	Fashion leaders purchase from traditional retailers in their "better" departments	Fashion followers purchase from traditional retailers in "moderate priced" departments	Fashion followers purchase from mass merchants	Fashion followers may purchase a few items at greatly reduced prices from discounters	No one is buying! "You can't give it away!"

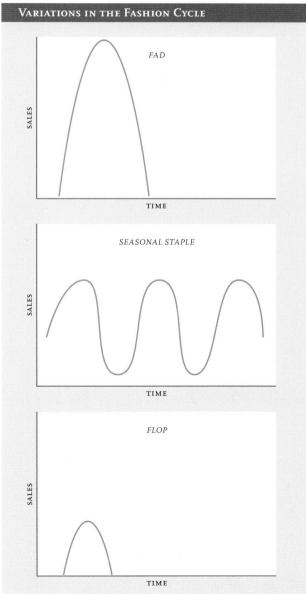

VARIATIONS IN THE FASHION CYCLE

FAD

SEASONAL STAPLE

FLOP

FIGURE 2.11 The basic lifecycle of fashion can be represented by a bell-shaped curve (top). Variations can occur throughout the process as fashion rises and declines (bottom).

Every fashion cycle passes through five stages: (1) introduction, (2) rise, (3) culmination, (4) decline, and (5) obsolescence. A comparison of these stages to the timetable suggested by Laver looks like this:

Introduction	"indecent/shameless"
Rise	"outré"
Culmination	"smart"
Decline	"dowdy/hideous"
Obsolescence	"ridiculous"

The fashion cycle serves as an important guide in fashion merchandising. The fashion merchant uses the fashion cycle concept to introduce new fashion goods, to chart their rise and culmination, and to recognize their decline and obsolescence.

Introduction Stage

The next new fashion may be introduced by a producer in the form of a new style, color, or texture. The new style may be a flared pant leg when slim legs are popular, vibrant colors when earth tones are popular, or slim body-hugging fabrics such as knit jersey when heavy-textured bulky looks are being worn.

New styles are almost always introduced in higher-priced merchandise. They are produced in small quantities, since retail fashion buyers purchase a limited number of pieces to test the new styles' appeal to targeted customers. This testing period comes at the beginning of the buying cycle of fashion merchandise, which coincides with the introduction stage of the fashion cycle. The test period ends when the new style either begins its rise or has been rejected by the target customer. Because there can be many risks, new styles must be priced high enough that those that succeed can cover the losses on those that fail. Promotional activities such as designer appearances, institutional advertising, and charity fashion shows, which appeal to the fashion leaders of the community and also enhance the store's fashion image, take place at this point.

Rise Stage

When the new original design (or its adaptations) is accepted by an increasing number of customers, it is considered to be in its **rise stage**. At this stage, the buyer reorders in quantity for maximum stock coverage.

During the rise stage of a new original design, many retailers offer line-for-line copies or **knockoffs**, as they are called in the fashion industry. Knockoffs are versions of the original designer style duplicated by manufacturers. These copies look exactly like the original except that they have been mass-produced in less expensive fabrics. Because production of the merchandise is now on a larger scale, prices of the knockoffs are generally lower.

As a new style continues to be accepted by more and more customers, adaptations appear. **Adaptations** are designs that have all the dominant features of the style that inspired them but do not claim to be exact copies. Modifications have been made, but distinguishing features of the original, such as a special shoulder treatment or the use of textured fabric, may be retained in the adaptation. At this stage, the promotion effort focuses on regular price lines, full assortments, and product-type ads to persuade the customer of the store's superiority in meeting his or her fashion needs.

Culmination Stage

The **culmination stage** of the fashion cycle is the period when a fashion is at the height of its popularity and use. At this stage, also called the **plateau**, the fashion is in such demand that it can be mass-produced, mass-distributed, and sold at prices within the range of most customers. This stage may be long or brief, depending on how extended the peak of popularity is. The quilted coat, which began as an expensive down-filled style in the late 1970s, reached its culmination stage when mass production in acrylic fill made a quilted coat available to practically every income level. At the culmination stage, the high-price line fashion buyer stops reordering the fashion and begins reducing stock.

The culmination stage of a fashion may be extended in two ways:

1. If a fashion becomes accepted as a classic, it settles into a fairly steady sales pattern. An example is the cardigan sweater, an annual steady seller.

FIGURE 2.12 Recycled magazines and plastic bags are repurposed as clothing to bring about awareness of environmental issues.

2. If new details of design, color, or texture are continually introduced, interest in the fashion may be kept alive longer. Shoulder-strap handbags are a perfect example. Another example is the continued fashion interest in running shoes, fostered by new colors, designs, and comfort innovations.

Decline Stage

When boredom with a fashion sets in, the result is a decrease in consumer demand for that fashion. This is known as the **decline stage**. It is a principle of fashion that all fashions end in excess.

As a fashion starts to decline, consumers may still be wearing it, but they are no longer willing to buy it at its regular price. The outstanding fashion merchandiser is able to recognize the end of the culmination stage and start markdowns early. At this point, production stops immediately or comes slowly to a halt. The leading fashion stores abandon the style; traditional stores take a moderate markdown and advertise the price reduction. A major price-slash clearance or close-out will probably follow in a short while. At this stage, the style may be found in bargain stores at prices far below what the style commanded in earlier stages.

Obsolescence Stage

When strong distaste for a style has set in and it can no longer be sold at any price, the fashion is in its **obsolescence stage**. At this stage, the style can be found only in thrift shops, garage sales, or flea markets. However, in the twenty-first century, *obsolescence* gave rise to new developments: recycled and sustainable fashion (Figure 2.12). Opportunity to recycle clothes that are considered obsolete has become very important. The famous Japanese retail chain UNIQLO, which has become a major success in the United States, has had a recycling program for many years. Its program, All-Product Recycling, allows customers to bring their obsolete UNIQLO apparel to a store for it to be recycled and reused. Because of the many natural disasters around the world—floods, earthquakes, tsunamis, and tornadoes—the recycled clothing has become a major worldwide need.[13]

Lengths of Cycles

Predicting the time span of a fashion cycle is impossible, since each fashion moves at its own speed. However, one guideline can be counted on: declines are fast, and a drop to obsolescence is almost always steeper than a rise to culmination. At the point of obsolescence, as they say in merchandising, "You can't give it away."

The speed with which products are moving through their cycles is accelerating. Rapid technological developments and instant communications have much to do with this speedup, as do fast-changing environmental factors. The result is an intense competition among manufacturers and retailers to provide consumers with what they want and expect—constantly changing assortments from which to choose.

Fast fashion is the retail strategy of keeping fashion fresh, as if it were a perishable good. The model of assortment rotation has been succesful for many retailers, including Zara, H&M, and UNIQLO. For any retailer with variety-seeking customers, some level of fast fashion is important. Retailers using this strategy must manage their inventory accordingly and consider the shorter lifecycles of their products.

Thrift stores, resale shops, and flea markets continue to be destinations for the clothes people no longer like, or just don't wear. Websites like Etsy and eBay are other resources that have expanded the market for reselling clothing. Sellers can easily purge and post merchandise without leaving their homes. On these sites, shoppers can find coveted or unique designer products, adding more variety to their wardrobes. But the price points aren't necessarily cheaper. For example, popular lower-priced clothing from well-known designers, such as Missoni for Target or Versace for H&M (Figure 2.13), can be sold on eBay for prices above their original value because of the demand.

Breaks in the Cycle

In fashion, as in everything else, there are always ups and downs, stops and starts. The normal flow of a fashion cycle can be broken or abruptly interrupted by outside influences. The influence can be simply unpredictable weather or a change in group acceptance. Or it can be much more dramatic and far-reaching—war, worldwide economic depression, or a natural disaster, for example.

Although no formal studies have been made of the phenomenon of the broken cycle, manufacturers and merchants have a theory about it. They believe that a broken cycle usually picks up where it has stopped once conditions return to normal or once the season that was cut short reopens. Consider the effect that a shortage of oil can have on the movement of manufactured fibers. Although the success of manufactured fibers—with all their easy-care attributes—is tremendous, their availability was interrupted by oil shortages in 1973, 1979, the late 1980s, and again through the early 2000s. However, when the oil supply increases, the popularity of these fibers returns to what it had been.

FIGURE 2.13 Versace for H&M is an example of a lower-priced line designed by a well-known high-fashion house.

Widespread economic depressions also temporarily interrupt the normal progress of a fashion cycle. When there is widespread unemployment, fashion moves much more slowly, resuming its pace only with economic recovery and growth.

Wars also affect fashion. They cause shortages that force designers, manufacturers, retailers, and consumers to change fashions less freely or to restrict styles. People redirect their interests, and fashion must take a backseat. When fashion apparel is in a cycle break, interest in cosmetics usually picks up. Women switch cosmetics or use them differently to satisfy their desire for something new. After wars have ended, interest in fashion picks up and flourishes once again.

Long-Run and Short-Run Fashions

The length of time individual fashions take to complete their cycles varies widely. **Long-run fashions** take more seasons to complete their cycles than what might be considered average; **short-run fashions** take fewer seasons.

Some fashions tend to rise in popular acceptance more slowly than others, thereby prolonging their life. Some stay in popular demand much longer than others do. The decline in popular demand for some fashions may be slower than for others.

DAVID LAUREN: THE PRINCE OF POLO

RALPH LAUREN IS one of the most iconic, successful fashion brands on the planet. The company encompasses more than twenty interrelated brands and is engaged in an aggressive global expansion. The Ralph Lauren brand has thrived for decades by bringing to life a classic aesthetic—an appealing, exclusive world that consumers love. However, at some point, people may begin to view this aesthetic as predictable, even old.

Now Lauren's son David is responsible for keeping the brand fresh and for making his father's vision feel relevant in a fast-changing and modern world. Ralph Lauren Corp. may be the retailer of choice for traditional polo players and yacht dwellers, but now the iconic American luxury retailer is, in some ways, more geek than chic. Under David's leadership, the company has transformed itself into a cutting-edge, tech-driven fashion retailer. By associating Ralph Lauren with new digital technology, David has made the company a progressive leader among fashion peers.

A man famously involved in every decision made at his company, Ralph acknowledges his unfamiliarity with the digital world. But David is turning his father's empire into a digital leader—and shaking up the fashion industry. When he debuted a 4-D light show to celebrate the launch of Ralph Lauren e-commerce in the U.K., the project had been months in the planning and making. It relied on architectural light-mapping techniques to create an eight-minute holographic video that was projected onto the storefront. This was a huge success and repeated at the New York store to commemorate the tenth anniversary of ralphlauren.com in the U.S.

To some, it might seem odd that a luxury retailer that sells itself on tradition should be so enthusiastic about holographic light shows and e-commerce. Should anyone question whether these modern bells and whistles actually generate sales, they should look at these figures: In 2011 Ralph Lauren's total sales grew 14.3 percent to $5.5 billion while profits jumped 18.3 percent to $568 million.

David Lauren   Ralph Lauren

Consumer Buying and the Fashion Cycle

Every fashion has both a consumer buying cycle and a consumer use cycle (Figure 2.14). The curve of the consumer buying cycle rises in direct relation to that of the consumer use cycle. But when a fashion reaches its peak, consumer buying tends to decline more rapidly than consumer use. Different segments of society respond to and tire of a fashion at different times, so different groups of consumers continue to wear fashions for varying lengths of time after they have ceased buying them. While each group is using and enjoying a fashion, the producers and retailers serving that group are already abandoning the style and marketing something newer. Their efforts in this direction are most profitable when they anticipate, rather than follow, the trend of consumer demand. Consumer buying is often halted prematurely because producers and sellers no longer wish to risk making and stocking an item they believe will soon decline in popularity. Instead, they concentrate their resources on new items with better prospects for longevity. This procedure is familiar to anyone who has tried to buy summer clothes in late August or skiwear in March.

The Intangibles of Fashion

Fashion itself is intangible. A style is tangible, made up of a definite silhouette and details of design. But fashion is shaped by such powerful intangibles as group acceptance, change, the social forces important during a certain era, and people's desire to relate to specific lifestyles.

Group Acceptance

The fig leaf, the first fashion creation, was widely accepted, and since then we have come a long way. Basically, fashion is acceptance: group acceptance or approval is implied in any definition of fashion. Most people have a deep-seated wish to express themselves as individuals but also to be part of a group. To dress in the latest fashion means that they are trying to be individual yet also to belong.

However, acceptance need not be universal. A style may be adopted by one group while other segments of the population ignore it. A style may also be accepted and become a fashion in one part of the world while it is ignored or rejected elsewhere. Each of the following is considered fashionable by its own inhabitants: the igloo of the Inuit, the thatched hut of some African tribespeople, and the ranch-style house of many American suburbanites. Similarly, many ethnic and religious groups have distinctive styles of dress.

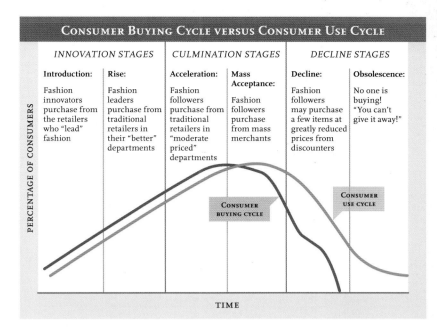

FIGURE 2.14 Consumer use of a fashion product follows a cycle similar to the buying cycle, but the use cycle begins after the buying cycle and endures beyond the buying cycle's decline and obsolescence stages.

The way we dress is a personal signature. The dress or suit we wear is not just a confirmation of the old adage that "clothes make the man [or woman]," but rather an example of the fact that our need for acceptance is expressed largely in the way we dress. Acceptance also means that a fashion is considered appropriate to the occasion for which it is worn. Clothes considered appropriate for big-business boardrooms would not be considered acceptable for casual weekends.

If any of you should doubt the power of acceptance in fashion, try a simple experiment. Put on clothes worn ten or twenty years ago, or totally different in style from what is considered the fashion. Then go out casually among your friends, acquaintances, or even strangers, and note their reactions toward you and then your feelings toward yourself. There will be quizzical looks, doubtful stares, and in some cases smirks and laughter. No one can really belong to a chosen group and at the same time choose to be completely out of present-day fashion. Such is the power of fashion acceptance.

Change

Fashion changes because ideas about politics, religion, leisure, democracy, success, and age change. Fashion is also a complex means for facilitating orderly change within a mass society. This is particularly true when the society is no longer able to provide identity and maintain social order via custom or tradition. In the United States, where different immigrant and ethnic groups must adjust to one another, fashion is one means of providing a social bond.

Fashion is subject to change—both rapid and gradual. Modern communications play a major role in today's accelerated rate of fashion change. The mass media spreads fashion news across the face of the

FIGURE 2.15 DEOS brings fashion and technology together by creating headphones that are encrusted with colored diamonds.

globe in hours, sometimes seconds. Even slight fashion changes are given faster and wider publicity than ever before. Consumers who like these changes demand them from merchants, who in turn demand them from manufacturers.

Each new technological development seems to offer more than the one before and encourages the discarding of the old. In addition to using digital technologies for business purposes, the fashion industry is also decorating them with products such as fashionable headphones (Figure 2.15) and designer cases for tablets and mobile devices.

Another change that is affecting today's fashion world is that a growing number of environmentally conscious consumers are demanding eco-friendly products. The fashion industry is working hard to satisfy this need. With advanced technology, the industry is producing more "green" or sustainable fibers and fabrics. Marketers are also affected by these changes and must rethink how to successfully target these types of consumers. According to a study from *Adweek*, researchers evaluated more than 200 million "green consumers" in the United States and separated these consumers into the following different groups:[14]

- **Alpha Ecos** (43 million adults): Committed to green causes and saving the planet.
- **Eco-Centrics** (34 million adults): Concerned about how environmental products benefit them personally.
- **Eco-Chics** (57 million adults): Understand the cachet of being seen as "green." This younger generation uses social networking to show others how green they are.

- **Economically Ecos** (53 million adults): Less concerned about saving the planet and more concerned about saving money.
- **Eco-Moms** (33 million moms of children under 18): Interested in cost-effective, socially responsible practices and products with an emphasis on kids.

To support the eco-friendly movement, the Sustainable Apparel Coalition formed in 2011 and has worked closely with both manufacturers and retailers to create the Higg Index.[15] This index measures the environmental and social performance of apparel and footwear products, including everything from carbon emissions and chemical usage to conditions in factories. It aims to help companies improve long-term sustainability in the industry, and informs shoppers about their purchases.[16]

The Futility of Forcing Change

Fashion expresses the spirit of the times and in turn influences it. Fashion designers are successful or not depending on their ability to sense and anticipate changes, if not to initiate them. Changes can be initiated, but there are as many examples of failures as there are of successful changes. Efforts have been made from time to time to force changes in the course of fashion, but they usually fail. Fashion is a potent force that by definition requires support by the majority.

As an example, in the late 1960s, designers and retailers decided that skirts had reached their limit in shortness and that women would soon be seeking change. So the designers designed and the retailers stocked and promoted the "midi," a skirt midcalf in length. The designers and retailers were right in theory but wrong in timing and choice of skirt length. Consumers found the midi too sudden and radical a change and did not accept or buy the style in sufficient numbers to make it a fashion. In the late 1980s, designers and retailers did it again—this time they tried to force a change to very short skirts. Again, the public disliked the radical change and refused to buy miniskirts when they were first introduced. In the mid-1990s, however, women were wearing both miniskirts and long skirts. By 2003, the runways were full of miniskirts, and by 2012 hemlines once again fell to midi and maxi lengths.

Occasionally, necessity and government regulation can interrupt the course of fashion. During World War II, the U.S. government controlled the type and quantity of fabric used in consumer goods. One regulation prohibited anything but slit pockets on women's garments to avoid using the extra material that patch pockets require. Skirts were short and silhouettes were narrow, reflecting the scarcity of material.

Meeting the Demand for Change

After World War II, a reaction to these designs was to be expected. A new French designer, Christian Dior, caught and expressed the desire for a freer line and a more feminine garment in his first collection, which achieved instant fashion success. Using fabric with a lavishness that had been impossible in Europe or America during the war years, he created his New Look, with long, full skirts, fitted waistlines, and feminine curves.

Dior did not change the course of fashion; he accelerated it—from an evolutionary course to a revolutionary one. He recognized and interpreted the need of women at that time to get out of stiff, short, narrow, unfeminine clothes and into soft, free, longer, feminine ones. Consumers wanted the change, and the lifting of the very limiting wartime restrictions made it possible to meet their demand.

Another example of a consumer demand for change occurred in menswear just before World War II. Year after year, manufacturers had been turning out versions of a style that had long been popular in England—the padded-shoulder draped suit. A number of young men from very influential families, who were attending well-known northeastern colleges, became tired of that look. They wanted a change. They took their objections to New Haven clothing manufacturers, and the result was the natural-shoulder Ivy League suit that achieved widespread popularity for the next fifteen to twenty years.

A Mirror of the Times

Fashion is a nonverbal symbol. It communicates that the wearer is in step with the times. Because fashions are shaped by the forces of an era, they in turn reflect the way we think and live. Each new fashion seems completely appropriate to its time and reflects that time as no other symbol does. A study of the past and careful observation of the present makes it apparent that fashions are social expressions that document the tastes and values of an era just as the paintings, sculpture, and architecture of the times do. The extreme modesty of the Victorian era was reflected in bulky and concealing fashions. The sexual emancipation of the flappers in the 1920s was expressed in their flattened figures, short skirts, sheer hosiery (it was the first time the bare leg was exposed), and short hair. The individualistic fashions of the 1990s and 2000s have been a true reflection of the current freedom of expression and lifestyle.

Social Class

Fashions mirror the times by reflecting the degree of rigidity in the class structure of an era. Although such ideas are difficult to imagine today, throughout much of history certain fashions were restricted to the members

FIGURE 2.16 Lady Gaga freely chooses how she dresses wherever she goes.

of certain rigidly defined social classes. In some early eras, royal edicts regulated both the type of apparel that could be worn by each group of citizens and how ornate it could be. Class distinctions were thus emphasized. Certain fashions have also been used as indications of high social standing and material success. During the nineteenth century, the constricted waists of Western women and the bound feet of high-caste Chinese women were silent but obvious evidence that the male head of the household was wealthy and esteemed.

Today, social classes are far more fluid and mobile than ever before. Because there is no universal way of life, people can choose their own values and lifestyles—and their dress reflects that choice (Figure 2.16). Many fashions exist simultaneously, and we are all free to adopt the fashions of any social group. If we do not wish to join others in their fashion choices, we can create our own modes and standards of dress. The beatniks of the 1950s and the hippies of the 1960s had their typical fashions, as did the bohemians of the 1920s and the liberated groups of the 1970s. In the 1980s, the phenomenon of the punk rockers existed side by side with the yuppies. In the 1990s, hip-hop fashion coexisted with Ralph Lauren's Polo Sport. Now in the 2000s, vintage has found a home alongside celebrity glamour.

Lifestyle

Fashions also mirror the times by reflecting the activities in which people of an era participate. The importance of court-centered social activities in seventeenth- and eighteenth-century Europe was in evidence in men's and women's ornately styled apparel. Fashions became less colorful and more functional when a new working class was created by the industrial revolution.

Currently, our clothes also vary according to lifestyle. More casual and active sportswear in wardrobes reflect our interest in active sports and leisure pastimes. The difference in the lifestyle of an urban, career-oriented woman and that of a suburban housewife is totally reflected in their choice of wardrobes.

Principles of Fashion

Diversification of fashion has added new dimensions to the interpretation of the principles of fashion. While the intangibles of fashion can be vague and sometimes difficult to predict and chart, certain fundamental principles of fashion are tangible and precise. For many decades these principles served as the solid foundation for fashion identification and forecasting—they still do—but the astute student of fashion recognizes that in today's vibrant and changing atmosphere, the application of these principles becomes a more intricate and challenging task.

The five principles we discuss are the foundations upon which the study of fashion is based.

1. **Consumers establish fashions by accepting or rejecting the styles offered.** The popular belief that designers create artistic designs with little regard for the acceptance of these designs by the public is quite false. No designer can be successful without the support and acceptance of the customer.

    It is true that new fashions can be introduced by famous designers, but it is relatively rare. A few examples are the loose, boxy jacket of the Chanel suit, the famous bias-cut clothes designed by Vionnet, and the New Look by Christian Dior. However, the designers who are considered to be the "creators" of fashion are those who have consistently given expression to the silhouette, color,

fabric, and design that are wanted and accepted by a majority of the **consumers**. Current examples include the looks introduced by Marc Jacobs, Calvin Klein, Donna Karan, and Ralph Lauren.

A **customer** is a patron or potential purchaser of goods or services. Thus, a retail store's dress buyer is a customer of a dress manufacturer, and the dress manufacturer is a customer of a fabric producer. The consumer is the ultimate user, the person who uses the finished fashion garment. Designers create hundreds of new styles each season, based on what they think may attract customers. From among those many styles, manufacturers choose what they think will be successful. They reject many more than they select. Retailers choose from the manufacturers' offerings those styles they believe their customers will want. Consumers then make the vital choice. By accepting some styles and rejecting others, they—and only they—dictate what styles will become fashions.

2. **Fashions are not based on price.** Just because something is expensive, it does not follow that it will be successful. Although new styles that may eventually become fashions are often introduced at high prices, this is happening less and less today. What you pay for an item of apparel is not necessarily an indication of whether the item is considered to be fashionable. In the fashion diversity offered to consumers today, successful fashions are to be found at every price level. Upper-income consumers will accept fashions at very low prices, and consumers at the opposite end of the income scale will often splurge and buy a very expensive item—if it is in fashion. In many cases, consumers coordinate fashions that are both inexpensive and expensive with little regard to the price. For example, an expensive piece of jewelry can be pinned to an inexpensive T-shirt, or conversely, a fashionable piece of costume jewelry can be pinned to an expensive designer suit.

3. **Fashions are evolutionary in nature; they are rarely revolutionary.** In these days of rapid cultural and national revolutions, it is hard to believe that a worldwide phenomenon such as fashion is evolutionary in nature—not revolutionary. To the casual observer it appears as though fashion changes suddenly. Actually, fashion change comes about as a result of gradual movements from one season to the next. Throughout history, there have probably been only two real revolutions in fashion styles. One of these occurred during the twentieth century: the Dior New Look of 1947. The other was the abrupt change

FIGURE 2.17 Fashion is evolutionary, as seen in Christian Lacroix's pouf skirt from 1987 (left) and then again with this reinvented pouf skirt from 2008 (right).

of styles brought about by the French Revolution, when the fashion changed overnight from elaborate full skirts, low-cut daring bodices, and ornate and glamorous fabrics to simple, drab costumes in keeping with the political and moral upheaval.

Fashions usually evolve gradually from one style to another (Figure 2.17). Skirt lengths go up or down an inch at a time, season after season. Shoulder widths narrow or widen gradually, not suddenly. It is only in retrospect that fashion changes seem marked or sudden.

Fashion designers understand and accept this principle. When developing new design ideas, they always keep the current fashion in mind. They know that few people could or would buy a whole new wardrobe every season, and that the success of their designs ultimately depends on sales. Consumers today buy apparel and accessories to supplement and update the wardrobe they already own, some of which was purchased last year, some the year before, some the year before that, and so on. In most cases, consumers will buy only if the purchase complements their existing wardrobe and does not depart too radically from last year's purchases.

4. **No amount of sales promotion can change the direction in which fashions are moving.** Promotional efforts on the part of producers or retailers cannot dictate what consumers will buy, nor can they force people to buy what they do not want. The few times that fashion merchants have tried to promote a radical change in fashion, they have not been successful.

As the women's liberation movement grew in the late 1960s, women rebelled against the constriction of girdles and bras. The overwhelming majority stopped wearing girdles and began wearing pantyhose instead. Various counterculture looks were adopted by some, and a more relaxed look was adopted by nearly everyone. Reflecting this change was the reemergence of the soft, no-seam natural bra. Regardless of promotion by the intimate apparel industry, nothing could persuade the majority of American women to submit again to the rigid control of corsets and girdles. Also,

FIGURE 2.18 This see-through design by Yiqing Yin proves that all fashion ends in excess.

5. **All fashions end in excess.** This saying is sometimes attributed to Paul Poiret, a top Paris designer of the 1920s. Many examples attest to its truth. Eighteenth-century hoopskirts ballooned out to over eight feet in width, which made moving from room to room a complicated maneuver. The French tried to accommodate these skirts and designed doors that could be opened to a width far beyond that of regular doors. They became known as "French doors" and can still be found in architecture today. Similarly, miniskirts of the 1960s finally became so short that the slightest movement caused a major problem in modesty. This same trend toward excess can be found in menswear. Just think of the growth of the width of a tie. It will start as a thin string tie and become wider and wider until it becomes as wide as a bib.

Once the extreme in styling has been reached, a fashion is nearing its end (Figure 2.18). The attraction of the fashion wanes, and people begin to seek a different look—a new fashion.

Summary and Review

In its narrow sense, fashion is the prevailing way a group of people at a particular time and place dress themselves. The fashion industries, which manufacture the materials and finished products of clothing, also produce related goods, including cosmetics, fragrances, and home fashions. Fashion designers attempt to determine what styles—characteristic appearances of garments and other fashion items—will appeal to their target group of consumers. The designs that are offered to the public are versions of a style that are distinguished by their silhouette, details, texture, and color.

Public acceptance of a fashion follows a course called the fashion cycle, which includes the following stages: introduction, rise, culmination, decline, and obsolescence. A fashion that quickly reaches the culmination stage and then declines over a brief period of time is called a fad. A classic, on the other hand, may not necessarily reach its peak of popularity very quickly, but its decline is gradual, and it never reaches the obsolescence stage.

Typically, the fashion leaders who buy a fashion at the introductory stage are the wealthy clientele of high-fashion designers. These consumers can afford to experiment with their wardrobes. When a fashion appears to gain acceptance, it can be mass-produced with less expensive materials for fashion followers. Some fashions have broad appeal, and others attract a smaller segment of the public, for example, a particular

promotional effort cannot renew the life of a fading fashion unless the extent of change gives the fashion an altogether new appeal. This is why stores have markdown or clearance sales. When the sales of a particular style start slumping, stores know they must clear out as much of that stock as possible, even at much lower prices, to make room for newer styles in which consumers have indicated interest.

age group, an ethnic group, or people with a common lifestyle, such as casual suburbanites or more formally dressed businesspeople.

Any fashion evolves according to the demands of its market. Neither pricing nor promotion by the producers can force consumers to embrace a new fashion.

Usually changes evolve gradually, building up to an extreme and then reversing and moving toward the other extreme. The success of fashion merchandisers depends on their ability to predict the changing tastes of their public with scientific accuracy and to use their artistic creativity to satisfy those tastes.

For Review

1. What group ultimately decides whether a style will be fashionable or not? Explain your answer.
2. Apparel styles are often named for the period in history in which they were introduced. Name three such styles and the historic period in which they originated.
3. Give two examples of classics that are in style today for each of the following groups: (a) men, (b) women, and (c) children.
4. Distinguish between (a) style, fashion, and design, and (b) classic and fad.
5. List and briefly explain the interrelationships among the four components of fashion.
6. Fashion apparel change has accelerated during the past 100 years. Which factors, in your opinion, have had the greatest influence on change? Why?
7. Fashions go through a five-stage life cycle. Name and explain each stage.
8. In what respects does the consumer buying cycle differ from the consumer use cycle? How is such information useful to fashion merchants?
9. Can designers, manufacturers, or retailers force unwanted fashion on consumers? Explain your answer.
10. What are the five basic principles relating to fashion? What are the implications for fashion merchants?

For Discussion

The following statements are derived from the text. Discuss the significance of each, giving examples of how each applies to merchandising fashion goods.

1. Men today are as influenced by and responsive to fashion as women.
2. Predicting the time span of a fashion cycle is impossible, since each fashion moves at its own speed.
3. Because there is no universal way of life, people are free to choose their own values and lifestyles.

Trade Talk

Define or briefly explain the following terms:

adaptations
classic
color
consumer
culmination stage
customer
decline stage
design
details
fad
fashion
fashion business
fashion cycle
fashion industries
fashion merchandising
fast fashion
high fashion
knockoffs
long-run fashions
marketing
mass or volume fashion
obsolescence stage
plateau
rise stage
short-run fashions
silhouette
style
style number
taste
texture
trend

Chapter Three

THE ENVIRONMENT
OF FASHION

KEY CONCEPTS

- The four major factors affecting fashion
- How research is used by fashion producers and retailers to help them with market segmentation
- The five basic psychological factors that motivate human behavior—and how each affects fashion

A cardinal rule in any business is "know your customer." This rule is especially true in the fashion business. To satisfy the greatest number of customers and make them want to buy their products, every designer, manufacturer, and retailer must know the answers to the following questions:

- How many potential customers for your products and services are there in a given community?
- How old are these customers?
- How much are they willing to spend on your product?
- What level of service do they expect?
- Are they married or single, homeowners or renters?
- How many children do they have?
- What kind of work do they do?
- What is their annual income?
- What is more important to them: value or style? Prestige or price?
- How much do they have to spend on extras?
- Do they like to shop early or late in the day? Weekdays or weekends?

- Do they use e-commerce?
- What motivates them to shop in a particular store?
- How do they spend their leisure time?

In other words, *Who are your customers?*

Accurate facts about customers, properly interpreted, help designers, manufacturers, and retailers make important decisions about what to offer them. Guesswork and misinterpreted facts can lead to major business failures.

One major source of information about the consumer market is the U.S. Census Bureau, www.census.gov. The U.S. Census produces more than three billion separate statistics about how many Americans there are, what work they do, where they live, and how they are doing as measured by income and creature comforts. These seemingly dull statistics are a treasure trove of vital information, not only for the government but also for every business. They help businesspeople who are interested in translating the data and projections drawn from them into new product and profit opportunities.

Used properly, census data provide us with all-important information about conditions that affect our lives and influence our actions. Collectively, the conditions under which we live are called our **environment**. Just as the environment of one nation or society differs from that of another nation or society, so the environment of one neighborhood differs from that of another. In fashion merchandising, it is important to be aware of the conditions that affect a particular customer's environment and to know how the environment differs from one group to another.

Four major environmental factors that affect fashion interest and demand, which will be discussed in this chapter, are:

1. Market segmentation by geographics, demographics, psychographics, and behavior.
2. The degree of economic development and well-being of a country or society.
3. The sociological characteristics of the class structure.
4. The psychological attitudes of consumers.

Market Segmentation

Both manufacturers and retailers try to identify and select target markets for their goods. **Target markets** are specific groups of potential customers that a business is attempting to turn into regular customers. Businesses attempt to determine who their customers are, what those customers want, how much the customers are willing to pay for goods, where potential customers are located, and how many targeted customers there are. Geographic, demographic, psychographic, and behavioral research studies are vital to determining these important factors.

Most manufacturers and designers are concerned with national trends. Retailers, however, must consider the impact of statistics in their local areas as well as statistics from national studies. **Market segmentation** is the separation of the total consumer market into smaller groups known as **market segments**. By identifying and studying each market segment, producers and retailers can target their goods and services to their special markets. Markets are divided or segmented in four main ways: geographics, demographics, psychographics, and behavior.

Geographics

Geographics are population studies that focus on where people live. These studies organize data by region of the country, by county or city size, by population density, and by climate. See Table 3.1 for geographic data on apparel spending.

TABLE 3.1 *Estimated Household Spending on Apparel and Services*

GEOGRAPHIC AREA	AVERAGE YEARLY SPENDING
Northeast	$1,996
West	$1,928
South	$1,561
Midwest	$1,549

Source: "2010–2011 MSA Tables," Consumer Expenditure Survey, U.S. Bureau of Labor Statistics, September 2012, http://www.bls.gov/cex/csxmsa.htm#y1011. Accessed February 2013.

Demographics

Demographics are population studies that divide broad groups of consumers into smaller, more homogeneous market segments. The variables covered in a demographic study include:

- Age
- Sex
- Family size
- Stages in family life cycle
- Income
- Occupation
- Education
- Religion
- Race and ethnicity or nationality

Psychographics

Psychographics are studies that develop fuller, more personal portraits of potential customers and their lifestyles. Psychographic studies more fully predict consumer purchase patterns and distinguish users of a product. The variables covered in a psychographic study include social class, values and lifestyle, and personality.

Sometimes researchers request information about the actual product benefits desired by consumers. These studies help greatly in matching the image of a company and its product with the type of consumer using the product.

Many research firms combine geographic and demographic studies for retailers and manufacturers. One such firm, Nielsen, produces the PRIZM system, which groups each U.S. household into one of sixty-six segments based on zip code, demographics, consumer behavior, shopping habits, media preference, socioeconomic rank, and urbanization. See the interesting group names in Table 3.2.[1]

PRIZM reveals *what* people buy, not *why*. To get closer to that information, many people turn to another

TABLE 3.2 *Marketing Segments*

Group	Segments
Urban Uptown	Money & Brains, Young Digerati, Bohemian Mix, The Cosmopolitans, American Dreams
Midtown Mix	Urban Achievers, Close-In Couples, Multi-Culti Mosaic
Urban Cores	Urban Elders, City Roots, Big City Blues, Low-Rise Living
Elite Suburbs	Upper Crust, Blue Blood Estates, Movers & Shakers, Winner's Circle
The Affluentials	Executive Suites, New Empty Nest, Pools & Patios, Beltway Boomers, Kids & Cul-de-Sacs, Home Sweet Home
Middleburbs	Gray Power, Young Influentials, Suburban Sprawl, Blue-Chip Blues, Domestic Duos
Inner Suburbs	New Beginnings, Old Glories, American Classics, Suburban Pioneers
Second City Society	Second City Elite, Brite Lites, L'il City, Upward Bound
City Centers	Up-and-Comers, Middleburg Managers, White Picket Fences, Boomtown Singles, Sunset City Blues
Micro-City Blues	City Startups, Mobility Blues, Park Bench Seniors, Hometown Retired, Family Thrifts
Landed Gentry	Country Squires, Big Fish, Small Pond, God's Country, Fast-Track Families, Country Casuals
Country Comfort	Greenbelt Sports, Traditional Times, New Homesteaders, Big Sky Families, Mayberryville
Middle America	Simple Pleasures, Red, White & Blues, Heartlanders, Blue Highways, Kid Country, USA, Shotguns & Pickups
Rustic Living	Young & Rustic, Golden Ponds, Crossroads Villagers, Old Milltowns, Back Country Folks, Bedrock America

Sources: Claritas Inc., www.claritas.com and Nielson, http://www.claritas.com/MyBestSegments/Default.jsp?ID=30&menuOption= segmentexplorer&pageName=Segment%2BExplorer. Accessed February 2013.

widely used research system that uses demographics and psychographics: the **VALS** system. The VALS 2 (Values and Life Styles) system sorts customers into eight major categories based on psychological attributes. The categories are arranged into a framework that puts consumers with the most resources on the top and those with the least on the bottom (Figure 3.1). It also arranged consumers into three groups horizontally: principle-oriented, status-oriented, and action-oriented. The main dimensions of the segmentation framework are primary motivation (the horizontal dimension) and resources (the vertical dimension).

Primary Motivation

According to Strategic Business Insights (SBI), "The combination of motivations and resources determines how a person will express himself or herself in the marketplace as a consumer."[2]

SBI identifies three primary motivations that drive consumers' buying decisions: ideals, achievement, and self-expression. Consumers who are primarily motivated by ideals are guided by knowledge and principles. Consumers who are primarily motivated by achievement look for products and services that demonstrate success to their peers. Consumers who are primarily motivated by self-expression desire social or physical activity, variety, and risk.[3]

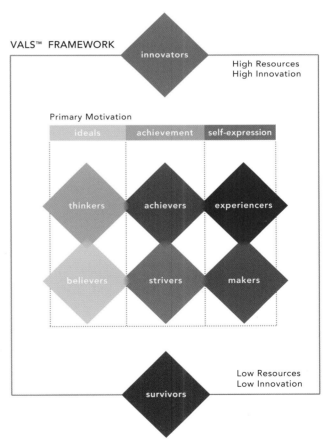

FIGURE 3.1 In the VALS System, each diamond-shaped box represents one of the eight consumer markets.

WHY FASHION NEEDS ECCENTRICS

THE LATE, GREAT British fashion editor Isabella Blow wore any one of her Philip Treacy hats—a jeweled lobster or a giant set of red satin lips—with an ease more customary to people when they put on their daily undergarments.

Regardless of time or place, there has always been a special group of women who are united in their universal need to buck convention. Their early embrace of the odd, the ugly, or the weird often blooms into a full-blown fashion trend. In today's cookie-cutter, keeping-up-with-the-celebrities world, the future of fashion is in the hands of the designers who dare to dream outside the box and the women brave enough to wear their designs. Among these women, Isabella Blow was notable. Her choice of clothing embodied her flagrant disregard for social dictates and put her in the rare category of women whose fearlessness

in dressing transcends trends and notions of good taste. Blow once said the whole point of her job was to make bad clothes look good. She also had a fantastic talent for discovering and then helping many young designers become famous. Among her most notable discoveries are Alexander McQueen and Phillip Treacy.

People like Isabella Blow were considered in their time to be eccentrics, and today we look back and understand their influence on fashion. Among the most well known and influential were Luisa Casati, a Milanese marchesa in the 1800s; Elise De Wolfe and Diana Vreeland in the 1940s; Peggy Guggenheim and Edith Sitwell in the 1950s; Cher in the 1980s; and, of course, the new-century eccentrics like Björk, Lady Gaga, Amanda Harlech, Dodie Rosekrans, and Zandra Rhodes. And then there's Iris Apfel, who's been leading the way from the 1940s through today and beyond.

Isabella
Blow

Zandra
Rhodes

Resources

Personality traits influence the way people use their resources. Conversely, consumers' level of resources—their income—influences the degree to which they can express, through purchasing decisions, their personality traits.

A person's tendency to consume goods and services extends beyond age, income, and education. Energy, self-confidence, intellectualism, novelty seeking, innovativeness, impulsiveness, leadership, and vanity play critical roles. These personality traits in conjunction with key demographics determine an individual's resources. Different levels of resources enhance or constrain a person's expression of his or her primary motivation.[4]

Behavior

In an attempt to gather even more insight into customer preferences, some retailers and manufacturers use research on **behavior**. These studies group consumers according to (1) their opinions of specific products or services and (2) their actual rate of use of these products or services. Behavioral studies help companies understand and predict the behavior of present and potential customers. If you segment your market by behavior, you might be able to identify the reasons for one group's refusal to buy your product. Once you have identified the reason, you may be able to change the product enough to satisfy their objections. An extension of VALS, GeoVALS, estimates the proportion of the eight VALs segments across residential zip codes, enabling users to find their best potential customers.

To keep up with the global economy, SBI has also developed international VALS systems, which reflect cultural differences in language, consumer behavior, and attitudes. As of this writing, VALS systems exist in Japan and the United Kingdom, but other countries are in the works.

The Economic Environment

The growth of fashion demand depends on a high level of economic development, which is reflected in consumer income, population characteristics, and technological advances. In his book *On Human Finery*,[5] Quentin Bell underscores the relationship between economics and fashion. He explains that most economically sophisticated countries discard their national costumes long before other nations begin to abandon theirs. England, for example, which led the Western world into the industrial revolution, was the first country to stop wearing traditional national dress. Bell points out that Greece, Poland, and Spain,

FIGURE 3.2 Asian fashion has embraced a contemporary style of dress. From top to bottom: A traditional look to fabulous new fashions.

countries with little in common except for being in similar stages of economic development, retained their national costumes when countries with more industrialized economies—Germany, Belgium, Denmark, and Japan—were abandoning theirs.

A striking example of how countries with swift economic development also move ahead in fashion is the People's Republic of China. Long restricted to the traditional blue Mao jacket and pants for both sexes, the Chinese have increased their interest in contemporary fashions over the years, as can be seen in the growth of fashion shows and boutiques (Figure 3.2).

Consumer Income

Consumer income can be measured in terms of personal income, disposable income, and discretionary income. Many groups of people use the amount of one's personal income as an indicator of "arriving" in their particular social set. The more personal income these groups have, the more socially acceptable they consider themselves to be. We will also discuss how the purchasing power of the dollar affects consumer income later in this chapter.

Personal Income

The total or gross income received by the population as a whole is called **personal income**. It consists of wages, salaries, interest, dividends, and all other income for everyone in the country. Divide personal income by the number of people in the population and the result is **per capita personal income**.

Disposable Personal Income

The amount a person has left to spend or save after paying taxes is called **disposable personal income**. It is roughly equivalent to take-home pay and provides an approximation of the purchasing power of each consumer during any given year. Disposable income per household and per capita varies according to age groups and sex. As of January 2013, disposable income climbed 2.8 percent after adjustments for inflation, the biggest gains since May 2008.[6]

Discretionary Income

The money that an individual or family can spend or save after buying necessities—food, clothing, shelter, and basic transportation—is called **discretionary income**. Of course, the distinction between necessities and luxuries or between needs and wants is a subjective one. Americans spend nearly 1.5 trillion dollars per year on discretionary goods.[7] See Figure 3.3.

One definition of "middle class" is the middle 60 percent of U.S. households, ranked by income. The most commonly cited figures from the census data are from all households mixed together. Median household income in 2011 was $50,054.[8] Although the economic gap between classes often fluctuates, it is imperative to keep the middle class strong, for they are the key factor in fueling the American economy and fashion business.

The lucky few are like consumer royalty, able to buy a wide variety of goods and services. Although marketers like to target these consumers, it may not be a wise long-term strategy. The superrich have greater purchasing power, but they are declining in number. While middle-class households have less money, they still have overwhelming strength in numbers.

Purchasing Power of the Dollar

Average income has been increasing each year, but people have not gained an equivalent increase in purchasing power because the value of the dollar—its

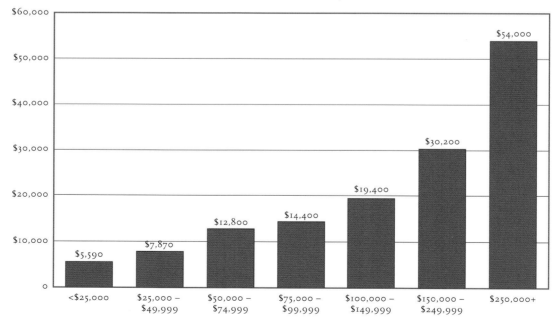

MEAN ANNUAL DISCRETIONARY SPENDING, BY HOUSEHOLD INCOME

FIGURE 3.3 Discretionary spending can vary depending on annual household income. This figure shows how households with incomes of $250,000+ a year spend nearly 10 times more on nonessential goods and services than the lowest income group. Source: Based on data from Experian, "2011 Discretionary Spend Report," p. 6.

purchasing power, or what it will buy—has steadily declined since 1950.

A decline in the purchasing power of money is caused by inflation. **Inflation** is an increase in available money and credit, with relative scarcity of goods, resulting in a significant rise in prices.[9] Inflation, therefore, is an economic situation in which demand exceeds supply. Scarcity of goods and services, in relation to demand, results in ever-increasing prices. Table 3.3 shows the changes in the purchasing power of the consumer dollar from 1950 to 2010.

When income taxes increase, the purchasing power of the family income drops; a decrease in income taxes has the reverse effect. With an inflationary economy, the working time required to acquire the necessities of life—basic food, clothing, transportation, and shelter—increases. The increase is not, however, uniform among all items.

In a **recession**, which represents a low point in a business cycle, money and credit become scarce, or "tight." Interest rates are high, production is down, and the rate of unemployment is up. People in the lower-income groups are the hardest hit; those with high incomes are the least affected. Yet these groups are small when compared with the middle-income group. It is the reaction of these middle-income people to any economic squeeze that is the greatest concern of the fashion merchant. Not only is the middle-income group the largest, it is also the most important market for fashion merchandise.

Consumer spending in the United States took a hit in 2009, due to the recession. However, as incomes grew by the end of December 2012, so did spending.[10]

Both inflation and recession affect consumers' buying patterns. Fashion merchants in particular must thoroughly understand the effects of inflation and recession when planning their inventory assortments and promotional activities. Manufacturers must also understand how consumers are affected by economic factors.

Population

The majority of the population of the United States has some discretionary income and thus can influence the course of fashion. Two factors relating to population, however, have an important bearing on the extent of fashion demand:

1. The size of the total population and the rate of its growth
2. The age mix of the population and its projection into the future

TABLE 3.3 *Purchasing Power of the Dollar: 1950–2010*

YEAR	AVERAGE AS MEASURED BY CONSUMER PRICES
1950	$4.15
1955	$3.73
1960	$3.37
1965	$3.16
1970	$2.57
1975	$1.85
1980	$1.21
1985	$0.92
1990	$0.76
1995	$0.65
2000	$0.58
2005	$0.51
2010	$0.46

Source: *Statistical Abstract of the United States—2011*, "Prices," p. 473.

Size of Population

The size of the population relates to the extent of current fashion demand. The rate of population growth suggests what tomorrow's market may become. In 1920, the United States had a population of about 106 million. By 1950, that figure had reached 151 million, and by 1980, 227.6 million. According to the U.S. Census Bureau, the U.S. population reached 315.3 million in 2013. It projects that the nation's total population will increase beyond 400 million by 2050. Other projections show that the U.S. population will be considerably older and more racially and ethnically diverse by 2060.[11]

Age Mix

The age mix and its projection into the future affect the characteristics of current fashion demand and suggest what they may be in the future. While the overall population continues to grow, the growth rate is not the same for all age groups or for both sexes. Since each group has its own special fashion interests, needs, and reactions, changes in the age mix serve as vital clues to future fashion demand.

For example, children born between 1946 and 1964 are known as the **baby-boom generation**, because they are the largest group ever recorded. The first baby boomers reached age 55 in 2000, at which point, the largest and fastest-growing age group in the United States was graying. They were followed by the much smaller "baby bust" or **generation X** group. This group was in turn followed by the slightly larger "baby boomlet" or "echo-boom" group, known as **generation Y**, or **millennials**. **Generation Z** is the name for those born from the early 2000s to the present. They are known as

TABLE 3.4 *Guide to the Generations*

GENERATION	BORN	LABELS OF THE TIMES	GENERATION TALK	FAMOUS PEOPLE AND THEIR GENERATION
G.I. Generation	1900–1924	War generation	They are high achievers; fearless, but not reckless; patriotic; idealistic; and morally conscious.	Christian Dior, Claire McCardell, Bonnie Cashin, Walt Disney
Silent Generation	1925–1945	Depression generation	They are categorized as being conventional, expecting disappointment but desiring faith; for women, there is the desire for both a career and a family.	Liz Claiborne, Sonia Rykiel, Betsey Johnson, Ralph Lauren
Baby Boomers	1946–1964	Love generation, the hippies	The end of World War II brought a baby boom to many countries, which gave this generation its name; they were the first to have televisions in their homes, which exposed them to news, shows, music, and marketers in a whole new way.	Diane von Furstenberg, Donna Karan, John Galliano, Marc Jacobs, Tom Ford
Generation X	1965–1979	Gap generation	This generation was originally known as "baby bust;" however, later in the U.K. the term Generation X was used and stuck. Generation X thinking has significant overtones of cynicism against things held dear to the previous generations.	Alexander McQueen, Nicolas Ghesquière, Kate Moss, Stella McCartney, Naomi Campbell
Generation Y or Millennials	1980–2000	iGeneration, the MyPod generation	This generation is described as "the digital age that heralded in its birth;" they grew up with more family breakdowns and divorces, which causes them to be more peer-oriented.	Zac Posen, Clare Tough, Christian Siriano
Generation Z or New Silent Generation	2000–present	Internet generation	This generation numerically was the smallest of any other living generation. They are known to grow up faster, and are exposed to education earlier. They are also known as the Internet-savvy, technologically literate generation.	Who will the world see next?

Source: http://geography.about.com/od/populationgeography/qt/generations.htm and the U.S. Census Bureau, http://www.census.gov. Accessed March 2008.

the most tech-savvy generation thus far. (See Table 3.4 for information about generations.)

Because both men and women are living longer, the over-age-65 group is steadily growing. Those 50 years old and older account for over one-half of all discretionary spending power. This mature group becomes increasingly important in the fashion world as their earlier retirement—and in many cases, increased retirement incomes—allows them to spend many active years wherever and however they choose. They are healthier, better educated, more active, and will live longer than the generations before them. Their interests and discretionary purchases vary radically from those of their younger counterparts, offering a real challenge to businesses to meet the demands of the "new old." The demand of older consumers for items such as package travel tours, cosmetic aids, and apparel that suits their ages and retirement lifestyles offers growth opportunities for marketers, especially in fashion.

The Sociological Environment

To understand fashion, we must understand the sociological environment in which fashion trends begin, grow, and fade away. The famous stage and screen designer Cecil Beaton saw fashion as a social phenomenon that reflects "the same continuum of change that rides through any given age." Changes in fashion, Beaton emphasized, "correspond with the subtle and often hidden network of forces that operate on society. . . . In this sense, fashion is a symbol."[12]

Simply stated, changes in fashion are caused by changes in the attitudes of consumers, which in turn are influenced by changes in the social patterns of the times (Figure 3.4). The key sociological factors influencing fashion today are leisure time, ethnic influences, status of women, social and physical mobility, instant communications, and wars, disasters, and crises.

Leisure Time

One of the most precious possessions of the average U.S. citizen today is leisure time, because it is also one of the most scarce. The demands of the workplace compete with the demands of family and home for much of people's waking hours, leaving less and less time for the pursuit of other activities, whether those activities be a fitness regimen, community work, entertainment, relaxation—or even shopping.

The ways in which people use their leisure time are as varied as people themselves. Some turn to active or spectator sports; others prefer to travel. Many seek self-improvement, while growing numbers improve their

FIGURE 3.4 What a difference a decade makes! Top row from left to right: the covered-up 20s, the sturdy 40s, the flirty 50s; bottom row from left to right: the wild 60s, the "anything goes" 90s, and today, back to covering it up!

standard of living with a second job. The increased importance of leisure time has brought changes to people's lives in many ways—in values, standards of living, and scope of activities. As a result, whole new markets have sprung up. Demand for larger and more versatile wardrobes for the many activities consumers can now explore and enjoy has mushroomed.

Casual Living

A look into the closets of the American population would probably reveal one aspect that is much the same from coast to coast, in large cities and in small towns: most would contain a large selection of

casual clothes and sportswear. The market for casual apparel developed with the growth of the suburbs in the 1950s and has had a continual series of boosts in the years since. The "do your own thing" revolution of the 1960s made a casual look for men and women acceptable in what had been more formal places and occasions. The 1970s saw a tremendous surge in the number of women wearing slacks and pantsuits and in the number of men and women wearing jeans just about everywhere.

Even with the return to more formal styles for many occasions in the 1980s, comfortable styling and casual dress continue to strongly influence all segments of

TOMMY HILFIGER: IT'S ALL ABOUT THE TEAM

DESPITE BEING THE face and driving force of a $5.6 billion dynasty, Tommy Hilfiger has seen the dark side of doing business. He faced bankruptcy by age twenty-three, and says it's still one of the best lessons of his life.

Hilfiger's career started in high school with his dream of being a rock musician. His music career didn't take off, but his designs did. When his peers started to take an interest in his rock 'n' roll style, he and a friend began selling jeans out of the back of his car at school. With some savings and a lot of motivation, this eventually morphed into a store, which grew to ten locations. While they had some success, too much partying and not enough knowledge about running a business forced them to declare bankruptcy.

Hilfiger says, "After that I decided that I would teach myself to understand and maintain the business part of the business." He urges aspiring designers to do the same. He says, "So many young designers are bankrupt, broke, running on empty, hanging on by a thread. They have good ideas but no business sense. You really have to understand the business part of the business yourself. And if you're not geared that way, get a partner who knows what you don't know how to do...." When Hilfiger talks about the partners he's been in business with, he says, "I couldn't have done it without them. I've met people who credit themselves with all of the success, but that's not the way it works. It's all about the team."

Fall 2012

Tommy Hilfiger

Fall 2013

society. In the 1990s, dress-down or casual Fridays at work became popular from coast to coast. The choice as to what clothing is suitable for an activity is still largely left to the individual, and now a shift in the direction of casual dress has begun a reverse trend as an interest in dressing up starts to grow again.

Active Sportswear

There is no doubt about it: the superstar of the fashion market in the 1970s, the 1980s, and the 1990s was sportswear. Its growth was phenomenal! While sports clothes have been around since the turn of the century, when they first appeared they were not particularly distinctive. Women's sport dresses for playing tennis or golf were not much different from their regular streetwear, and men's outfits similarly varied little from business suits. By the 1920s, consumers began demanding apparel that was appropriate for active sports or simply for relaxing in the sunshine. But it is the emphasis on health and self in the past three decades that has caused the fantastic growth of the active sportswear market.

Today, sports-minded people play tennis in specially designed tennis fashions. Golfers want special golf-wear. Runners want only jogging outfits. And cyclists seem able to bike only in spandex bike shorts and high-tech helmets. Inline skaters also want helmets, wrist and knee guards, and appropriate fashions. The same goes for ice skaters, skiers, skateboarders, hang gliders, sky divers, and climbers. Health clubs, exercise classes,

and workout gyms exploded in popularity in the 1980s, and today memberships at health clubs and gyms are considered an important part of life for many. A whole new and vast world of activewear and other self-improvement-based fashions and accessories was born. Whatever the activity, the specialized fashions—from high-tech running apparel to bike shorts—quickly followed and became de rigueur. Even those who do not participate in a particular sport beyond watching the pros on television sometimes dress the part!

Ethnic Influences

Minority groups in the United States have experienced vast population increases and sociological changes. The future holds even more change (see Figure 3.5). By 2005, African Americans had slipped from the largest minority group in the United States to the second largest. Hispanics now outnumber African Americans, and the Asian population exhibits a rapid rate of growth. Additionally, according to the 2010 Census, more than nine million Americans identify as belonging to two or more race groups.[13]

This historic shift in the racial and ethnic composition of the U.S. population has many long-range implications. For example, the growth of the Hispanic and Asian populations has brought about an increased demand for clothing in smaller sizes, because both men and women in these groups are typically smaller in stature than people whose ethnic heritage is Northern European.[14]

DISTRIBUTION OF U.S. POPULATION BY RACE/ETHNICITY, 2010 AND 2050

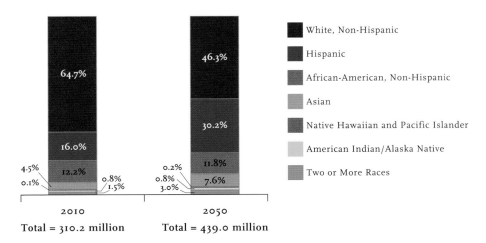

NOTES: All racial groups non-Hispanic. Data do not include residents of Puerto Rico, Guam, the U.S. Virgin Islands, or the Northern Marina Islands. Totals may not add to 100%.

FIGURE 3.5 Projections for 2050 show there will be an increase in the diversity of ethnic groups.
Source: Kaiser Family Foundation, based on data from the U.S. Census Bureau, 2008, Projected Population by Single Year of Age, Sex, Race, and Hispanic Origin for the United States: July 1, 2000 to July 1, 2050.

Hispanics

The Spanish-speaking market within the United States is growing so fast that market researchers cannot keep up with it. In 1987, there were an estimated eighteen million Hispanics in the United States. In addition, six to ten million undocumented Hispanics were estimated to be in the United States. By 2010, the documented Hispanic population of the United States had increased to 50.5 million, making them the largest minority group in the nation.[15] Between 2000 and 2010, this group accounted for more than half of the 27.3 million increase in the total population of the United States.[16] The Hispanic population has made its impact on the fashion scene with the introduction of fiery colors and prints reminiscent of lush South American rain forests.

African Americans

African Americans were the second-largest minority in the United States in 2010.[17] Many black people show the pride they feel in their African heritage by wearing African styles, fabrics, and patterns. Other ethnic groups have adopted these styles as well. Fashion companies have acknowledged the changes that have occurred among the African American population and have reflected these changes in the products they market and the models they use. Cosmetics are available that emphasize rather than hide the beauty of dark skin. African American men and women have become world famous through modeling clothing and advertising various items in magazines and on television.

Asians

Asian Americans are the fastest-growing minority group in the United States, with a population that reached 17.3 million in 2010. Over the years, the Asian population has increased more than four times faster than the total U.S. population, growing by 43 percent from 2000 to 2010.[18] But Asian Americans are not one homogeneous group. They come from more than a dozen countries and speak at least forty-one different languages!

Asians in the United States are more geographically concentrated than African Americans or Hispanics. The states that account for roughly half of the Asian population are New York, California, and Texas.[19]

The end of the Vietnamese war and the influx of thousands of refugees from Cambodia and Vietnam brought additional traditions and costumes to be shared. This stimulated interest in some of the more exotic fashions of the East and in the everyday comfort of the Chinese sandal and quilted jacket.

Immigration from many Asian countries to the United States continues to rise. Chinese Americans are the largest Asian group, followed by Asian Indians, Filipinos, Vietnamese, Koreans, and Japanese. The Asian Indian population is growing at the fastest rate.[20]

Status of Women

In the early 1900s, the American woman was, in many ways, a nonperson. She could not vote, serve on a jury, earn a living at any but a few occupations, own property, or enter public places unescorted. She passed directly from her father's control to her husband's control, without rights or monies. In both households, she dressed to please the man and reflect his status.

Profound changes began to occur during World War I and have accelerated ever since. The most dramatic advances have happened since the mid-1960s, propelled by the women's movement. Women's demands for equal opportunity, equal pay, and equal rights in every facet of life continue to bring about even more change. These changes have affected not only fashion but also the entire field of marketing.

Jobs and Money

In 2009, the number of women ages 16 and over who participated in the labor force was about 72 million.[21] Although this figure has steadily increased during the past few decades, women's salaries in 2009 were still, on average, only 77 percent of men's salaries. Both financial pressures and career satisfaction should keep the number of working women growing (Figure 3.6).

The dramatic increase in the number of working women has led to a surge in fashion interest, because a woman who works is continuously exposed to fashion. It is everywhere around her, as she meets people, shops during her lunch hour, or is on her way home. As a member of the workforce, she now has the incentive, the opportunity, and the means to respond to fashion's appeal.

Finally, women in general today have more money of their own to spend as they see fit. These women and their acceptance or rejection of offered styles have importance in the fashion marketplace.

Education

As of 2009, more women than men have a bachelor's degree or higher—29.9 million women versus 28.7 million men.[22] Often, the better educated a woman becomes, the more willing she is to learn new things. She is also more willing to try new fashions, which of course serves to accelerate fashion change. And with more women today receiving more education than ever before, the repercussions on fashion are unmistakable. Today's educated women have had wider exposure than

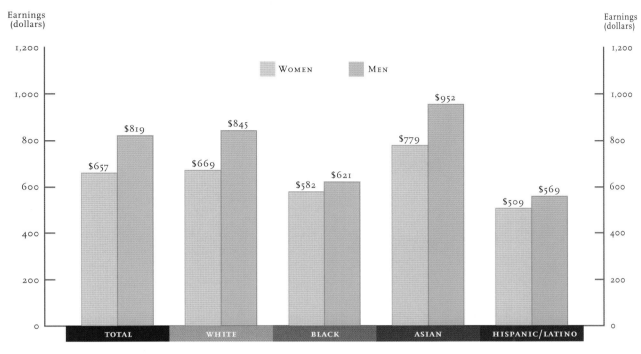

MEDIAN WEEKLY EARNINGS OF FULL-TIME WAGE & SALARY WAGES

(BY SEX, RACE, & HISPANIC OR LATINO ETHNICITY 2009 ANNUAL AVERAGES)

NOTE: Persons whose ethnicity is identified as Hispanic or Latino may be of any race.

FIGURE 3.6 According to the U.S. Census Bureau, Asian women and men earned more than their White, Black, and Hispanic counterparts.

their mothers or grandmothers to other cultures and to people of different backgrounds. Consequently, they are more worldly, more discerning, more demanding, and more confident in their taste and feel for fashion.

No wonder Edward Sapir, a leading social scientist, considered education a major factor in fashion change. "Fashion is custom in the guise of departure from custom," said Sapir.[23] To him, fashion is a resolution of the conflict between people's revolt against adherence to custom and their reluctance to appear lacking in good taste.

Social Freedom

Perhaps the most marked change in the status of women since the early 1900s is the degree of social freedom they now enjoy. Young women today are free to apply for a job and to earn, spend, and save their own money. They are free to go unescorted to a restaurant, theater, or other public place. Women travel more frequently than they did in the past. They travel to more distant locations at a younger age and often alone. Many own their own cars. They may maintain an apartment or share one with others. It is difficult to imagine that the social freedoms and responsibilities that today's young

women accept as normal were considered unfeminine or outrageous as recently as forty years ago.

Short skirts, popular in the 1920s, the early 1940s, the 1960s, and the 2000s, are commonly interpreted as a reflection of women's freedom. So, too, is the simplicity of the styles that prevailed in those periods: chemises, sacks, tents, shifts, other variations of loose-hanging dresses, and pants.

Different theories exist about why these changes came about. Some people believe that stiff, unyielding corsets went out with a stiff, unyielding moral code. Others believe that the changes had no particular social significance. They believe that women rejected inflexible corsets not because of a change in the moral code but because the new materials were simply more comfortable. Similarly, pants may be viewed as an expression of women's freedom or merely as suitable garments for hopping in and out of the indispensable car.

Whatever the reasons, the lifestyles of American women and their opinions and attitudes about fashion have changed radically in the past three decades. American women have gained hard-won freedoms in their social and business lives. They are just as definite about their freedom of choice in fashion (Figure 3.7).

FIGURE 3.7 American women have more freedom today to express their own personal styles and fashion choices.

The thought of today's independent women accepting uncomfortable and constricting clothing or shoes just to follow the dictates of some fashion arbiter, as they did years ago, is ludicrous. Busy, active women, whether at home or at the office, have very carefully defined preferences for fashions that suit their own individual needs and comfort. Successful designers recognize these preferences and make sure that their drawing boards reflect them.

Social Mobility

Almost all societies have classes, and individuals choose either to stand out from or to conform to their actual or aspired-to class. Bell viewed fashion as the process "whereby members of one class imitate those of another, who, in turn, are driven to ever new expedients of fashionable change."[24]

Bell considered the history of fashion inexplicable without relating it to social classes. He is not alone in his thinking. Other sociologists have related fashion change to changes in social mobility and to the effort to associate with a higher class by imitation.

The United States is sometimes called a classless society, but this concept is valid only in that there are no hereditary ranks, royalty, or untouchables. Classes do exist, but they are based largely upon occupation, income, residential location, education, or avocation, and their boundaries have become increasingly fluid. They range from the immensely wealthy (millionaires such as Bill Gates and Donald Trump, or the Vanderbilts, Whitneys, and Rockefellers, for example) at the top to the very wealthy (mostly nouveau riche) to the many middle-income levels and finally to the low-income and poverty levels. At the very bottom are the so-called hard-core unemployed and the homeless.

Middle-Class Influence

Most fashion authorities agree that there is a direct relationship between the growth and strength of the middle class and the growth and strength of fashion demand. Because it is the largest class, it has the majority vote in the adoption of fashions. Members of the middle class tend to be followers, not leaders, of fashion, but the strength of their following pumps money into the fashion industry. And the persistence of their following often spurs fashion leaders to seek newer and different fashions of their own.

Physical Mobility

Physical mobility, like social mobility, encourages the demand for and response to fashion. One effect of travel is cross-pollination of cultures. After seeing how other people live, travelers bring home a desire to adopt or adapt some of what they observed and make it part of their environment.

Marco Polo brought gunpowder, silks, and spices from the Orient, introducing new products to medieval Europe. In the nineteenth century, travelers brought touches of Asian and African fashions to Western dress and home furnishings. In the twentieth century, Latin American and pre-Columbian influences were introduced into North America, dramatically changing the direction and emphasis of fashion in this country.

In the United States, people enjoy several kinds of physical mobility. For example, the daily routine for many people involves driving to work, often in a different city from that of their home.

A second form of physical mobility popular among Americans is vacation travel. Whether travelers are going to a nearby lake or around the world, each trip exposes them to many different fashion influences, and each trip itself demands special fashions.

A third form of physical mobility is change of residence, which, like travel, exposes an individual to new contacts, new environments, and new fashion influences.

Faster Communications

Related to physical mobility is faster communications. In the past, news of every sort traveled more slowly. This meant that life moved more slowly and fashions changed more slowly. It took weeks or months for people in one section of the country to learn what was being worn in another part of the country. Fashion trends moved at a pace that was as leisurely as the news.

Our electronic age has changed all that. Today, we enjoy rapid communication in ever-increasing quantities and infinite varieties. By means of satellites, round-the-clock broadcasting, television, Twitter, Facebook, apps, YouTube, and blogs, we have the world at our fingertips. We can access the latest looks of our favorite celebrities, musicians, and personalities within minutes. Fashion bloggers and tweeters from all over the globe can send the newest designs and fashion updates straight from the runways to electronic devices. For example, in 2013 IMG Fashion partnered with Rightster to live-stream the runway shows from Mercedes-Benz Fashion Week at Lincoln Center. It also provided on-demand videos of every event, making it the first time in history that all shows were instantly accessible to viewers.[25]

Another popular pastime among fashionistas is creating and posting online "haul" videos. These online clips mostly feature young women showing off their shopping purchases. While they make their fashion statement to the world, retailers can also gain from the benefits of free marketing.[26]

Popular movies and television shows also influence fashion. Back in 1983, *Flashdance* caught the fancy of millions of young people. Soon the one-bare-shoulder look was seen everywhere. A few years later, *Top Gun* and its star Tom Cruise helped to popularize aviator-style sunglasses. *Sex and the City* introduced women everywhere to Manolo Blahnik pumps and made quirky accessories such as oversize flower pins and gold name-plate necklaces trendy, while *Mad Men* brought the slim suit back into style.

War, Disaster, and Crisis

War, widespread disaster, and crisis shake people's lives and focus attention on ideas, events, and places that may be completely new. People develop a need for fashions that are compatible with changes in their attitudes and also changes in their environment.

Such changes took place in women's activities and in fashions as a result of the two world wars. For example, World War I brought women into the business world in significant numbers and encouraged their desire for independence and suffrage. World War II drew women into such traditionally masculine jobs as riveting, for

which they previously had not been considered strong enough. It even brought women other than nurses into the military services for the first time in the country's history. All these changes gave rise to women's fashions previously considered appropriate only for men, such as slacks, sport shirts, and jeans.

The Depression of the 1930s was a widespread disaster with a different effect on fashions. Because jobs were scarce, considerably fewer were offered to women than had been before. Women returned to the home and adopted more feminine clothes. And because money also was scarce, wardrobes became skimpier. A single style often served a large number of occasions. Women who did hold jobs felt pressure to look younger so they could compete with younger applicants, which encouraged an increased use of lipstick and cosmetics.

The Psychological Environment

"Fashion promises many things to many people," according to economist Dr. Rachel Dardis. "It can be and is used to attract others, to indicate success, both social and economic, to indicate leadership, and to identify with a particular social group."[27] Fashion interest and demand at any given time may rely heavily on prevailing psychological attitudes (Figure 3.8).

The five basic psychological factors that influence fashion demand are boredom, curiosity, reaction to convention, need for self-assurance, and desire for companionship.[28] These factors motivate a large share of people's actions and reactions.

1. **Boredom.** People tend to become bored with fashions too long in use. Boredom leads to restlessness and a desire for change. In fashion, the desire for change expresses itself in a demand for something new and satisfyingly different from what one already has.
2. **Curiosity.** Curiosity causes interest in change for its own sake. Highly curious people like to experiment; they want to know what is around the next corner. There is curiosity in everyone, though some may respond to it less dramatically than others. Curiosity and the need to experiment keep fashion demand alive.
3. **Reaction to Convention.** One of the most important psychological factors influencing fashion demand is the reaction to convention. People's reactions take one of two forms: rebellion against convention or adherence to it. Rebellion against convention is characteristic of young people. This involves more than boredom or curiosity: it is a positive rejection

FIGURE 3.8 People's surroundings and desire for companionship can be the starting point for an outrageous fashion trend.

of what exists and a search for something new. However, acceptance by the majority is an important part of the definition of fashion. The majority tends to adhere to convention, either within its own group or class or in general.

4. **Need for Self-Assurance.** The need for self-assurance or confidence is a human characteristic that gives impetus to fashion demand. Often the need to overcome feelings of inferiority or of disappointment can be satisfied through apparel. People who consider themselves to be fashionably dressed have an armor that gives them self-assurance. Those who know that their clothes are dated are at a psychological disadvantage.

5. **Desire for Companionship.** The desire for companionship is fundamental in human beings. The instinct for survival of the species drives individuals to seek a mate. Humans' innate gregariousness also encourages them to seek companions. Fashion plays its part in the search for all kinds of companionship. In its broader sense, companionship implies the formation of groups, which require

conformity in dress as well as in other respects. Flamboyant or subdued, a person's mode of dress can be a bid for companionship as well as the symbol of acceptance within a particular group.

Summary and Review

Fashion marketers determine their customers' wants and needs by examining various market segments, identified by geographics, demographics, psychographics, and behavior. Each marketer identifies the group or groups within the general population that are its target customer. Determining the average customer's personal income helps marketers make pricing decisions and estimate sales, especially when population trends are matched with income figures. For example, businesses that target middle-age and retirement-age consumers know that their customers are increasing in number and that the average income for consumers in these age groups is also increasing. The teenage and young adult markets are a smaller portion of the population than they were earlier in the century, but they are an influential market segment, often spending their discretionary income on fashion merchandise. The growing value placed on leisure time and leisure-time activities has increased the market for casual clothing and active sportswear.

Marketers also track trends in the population of targeted ethnic groups. Changing patterns of immigration bring with them new influences from different parts of the world. The Hispanic market has become the largest ethnic-minority market in the United States in the twenty-first century, superseding the African American market in size. The Asian American market is the fastest-growing minority. The non-Hispanic Caucasian population is expected to remain the majority, but by a reduced percentage.

The role of women in society changed dramatically in the twentieth century, and their increased freedom, better education, and growing presence in the labor force increased their average income and changed their buying habits.

Other social forces that affect business include greater mobility and more rapid communications, which bring individuals wider choices in their purchases. Political, economic, and natural upheavals also affect fashion marketing, often leading to trends that last beyond the crisis. As consumers become more knowledgeable about their growing choices in their buying behavior, marketers are paying more attention to psychographic factors as they attempt to identify and meet the demands of their target customers.

For Review

1. Name the four major environmental influences on fashion interest and demand in any era.
2. Market segmentation is vitally important to producers and retailers of fashion merchandise. Explain why, giving at least two examples of how such information could be used by the fashion industry.
3. How does the size and age mix of a population affect current fashion demand? What does information about size and age mix today tell us about the future of fashion demand?
4. In what ways has increased availability of leisure time affected the fashion market?
5. How has the changing status of ethnic groups affected fashion interest and demand? Cite at least two examples.
6. How does a higher level of education affect fashion interest and demand?
7. What is social mobility? How does the degree of social mobility affect fashion interest and demand? Illustrate your answer with examples.
8. Upon what factors are classes in the United States usually based? Why is it more difficult to identify an individual's social class in this country than it is in other countries?
9. Describe three kinds of physical mobility that people in the United States enjoy today, explaining how each influences fashion demand.
10. Five basic psychological factors motivate much of human behavior. List them, explaining how each affects fashion interest and demand.

For Discussion

1. Is discretionary income or disposable personal income the more significant figure to fashion producers and marketers? Why?
2. How did the status of women change during the twentieth and twenty-first centuries? How have these changes affected fashion interest and demand?

Trade Talk

Define or briefly explain the following terms:

baby-boom generation
behavior
demographics
discretionary income
disposable personal income
environment
generation X
generation Y
generation Z
geographics
inflation
market segmentation
market segments
millennials
per capita personal income
personal income
psychographics
purchasing power
recession
target market
VALS

Chapter Four

THE MOVEMENT OF FASHION

KEY CONCEPTS

- Influencing and predicting the movement of fashion
- Theories of fashion adoption
- Identifying fashion leaders and fashion followers

Fashion is, in many ways, like a river. A river is always in motion, continuously flowing—sometimes it is slow and gentle, at other times rushing and turbulent. It is exciting, and never the same. It affects those who ride its currents and those who rest on its shores. Its movements depend on the environment.

All of this is true of fashion, too. The constant movements of fashion depend on an environment made up of social, political, and economic factors. These movements, no matter how obvious or how slight, have meaning and definite direction. There is a special excitement to interpreting these movements and estimating their speed and direction. Everyone involved in fashion, from the designer to the consumer, is caught up in the movement of fashion.

The excitement starts with the textile producers. Fully twelve to eighteen months before they offer their lines to manufacturers, the textile people must choose their designs, textures, and colors. From three to nine months before showing a line to buyers, the apparel manufacturers begin deciding which styles they will produce and in which fabrics. Then, two to six months before the fashions appear on the selling floor, the retail buyers make their selections from the manufacturers' lines. Finally, the excitement passes on to the consumers, as they select the garments that are versatile, appropriate, and suitably priced for their individual needs and wants.

How can all these people be sure their choices are based on reliable predictions? Successful designers, manufacturers, buyers, and consumers have a good understanding of basic cycles, principles, and patterns that operate in the world of fashion. Their predictions are based on this understanding.

Factors Influencing Fashion Movement

At the beginning of this chapter, the movement of fashion was likened to the movement of a river. As James Laver said, in comparing the fashion cycle to a force of nature, "Nothing seems to be able to turn it back until it has spent itself, until it has provoked a reaction by its very excess."[1] However, just as a river can swell to turbulent flood stage or be slowed or diverted by a dam, so the movement of fashion can be accelerated or delayed by a variety of factors.

Accelerating Factors

There are seven general factors that speed up fashion cycles. These influences are, themselves, ever growing and accelerating in the twenty-first century as the pace of life becomes increasingly rapid and geographically all-encompassing. The accelerating factors are:

1. Widespread buying power
2. Leisure time
3. Increased education
4. Improved status of women
5. Technological advances
6. Sales promotion
7. Seasonal change

Widespread Buying Power

Widely diffused discretionary income means there are more people with the financial means to respond to a fashion change. The more consumers flock to a new fashion, the sooner it will reach its culmination. The more widespread the financial ability of consumers to turn to yet a newer fashion, the sooner the current fashion will plunge into obsolescence.

Leisure Time

In the past, long hours of work and little leisure time permitted scant attention to fashion for the great majority of the population. More leisure time usually means more time to buy and enjoy fashion of many kinds. Since 1900, decreases in working hours and increases in paid vacations have encouraged more use of at-home wear, casual clothes, sports apparel, travel clothes, and different types of ordinary business dress. Increased purchases of these types of apparel give impetus to their fashion cycles.

One result of today's fast pace has been e-retail spending. According to the industry news website Internet Retailer, the increased popularity of tablets and smartphones lead users to spend more leisure time online, which means more shopping. Research shows that the tablet retail experience encourages an increase in impulse buys.[2]

In addition to websites and social media, retailers continue to bring shopping into consumers' homes with catalogs and cable TV shopping channels. These allow consumers to place their orders at any time of day.

Increased Education

The increasingly higher level of education in the United States helps to speed up fashion cycles in two ways. First, more people's horizons have been broadened to include new interests and new wants. And second, more people are equipped by education to earn the money to satisfy those wants. These two factors provide significant impetus to the adoption of new fashions.

Improved Status of Women

In a society with few artificial social barriers, women with discretionary income can spend it as they choose. No law or custom prevents any woman from buying the newest and most prestigious styles in dresses, hats, or shoes if she can afford to—thus giving impetus to a fashion cycle in its earliest phases. Sex discrimination in the job market has steadily decreased, and social acceptance of women who manage both homes and jobs has steadily increased. As a result, today's women have more discretionary income and are influencing the speed of fashion cycles in the way they use that income. However, women still earn only about 80 cents on the dollar compared with men—a gap that results in the loss of about $380,000 over a woman's career.[3]

Technological Advances

Today we live in an "instant" world. The stunning advances in technology in almost every area have put us in immediate possession of facts, fantasies, and fashions. We see news as it happens around the world. Goods are sped to retail stores by land, air, and sea more rapidly than would have been dreamed of just a few decades ago.

You no longer have to be at the catwalk shows at Lincoln Center to see New York fashion. Designers are live streaming their shows, designs, and backstage interviews in 3-D on the Web. Audiences around the world

FIGURE 4.1 Sometimes different accelerating factors work together. Here, Nicole Miller's website uses technology for its sales promotion.

can enjoy the feeling of being at the show—and in the front row.

New fibers, finishes, and materials with improved qualities are continually being developed. Technology has improved production techniques and statistical control and analysis for more efficient product marketing. The result has been control of price increases, and in many cases, reduced prices on fashion goods. All of these advances combine to make goods available almost at the instant the consumer is psychologically and financially ready to buy (Figure 4.1). Thus, the cycle of fashion becomes more and more accelerated.

Sales Promotion

The impact of sales promotion is felt everywhere in the fashion world today. Magazines, newspapers, websites, social media, television, billboards, and direct mail all expose the public to new fashions in a never-ending procession. While there is no way to force consumers to accept new fashions, nor any way to save a fashion if consumers reject it, sales promotion can greatly influence a fashion's success by telling people it exists. Sales promotion can help to speed up acceptance of a new fashion or sometimes extend its peak or duration. Promotion, therefore, can frequently help a fashion reach its culmination more speedily.

Seasonal Change

Nothing is so consistent in bringing about change in fashions as the calendar. As the seasons change, so do consumer demands. After months of winter, people want to shed their heavy clothing for lightweight spring and summer fashions. In climates where there are radical seasonal changes, this is only natural, even though our homes, schools, cars, and places of business are kept at desired temperatures through central heating and air conditioning. However, even in areas such as Florida and Hawaii, where the weather is moderate year-round, people change their wardrobes with the seasons. Even if the twenty-first century brings complete climate control, people will never accept the boredom of a year-round wardrobe.

Because people travel at all times of the year to all types of climates, the seasonal changes are accelerated and a kind of preseason testing can go on. Resort wear appears in retail stores in time for selection by the public for winter vacations in tropical areas. The late-June appearance of the first fall fashions in leading stores makes it possible for the style-conscious to make their selections well in advance of the first cold wind. Consumer responses to these early offerings allow manufacturers and retailers alike to know what does and does not appeal.

Delaying Factors

Factors that retard the development of fashion cycles either discourage people from adopting incoming styles or encourage them to continue using styles that might be considered on the decline. Retarding factors include the opposites of the accelerating factors—for example, decreased buying power during recessionary periods. Major retarding factors are habit and custom, religion and sumptuary laws, the nature of the merchandise, and reductions in consumers' buying power.

Habit and Custom

By slowing acceptance of new styles and prolonging the life spans of those already accepted, habit and custom exert a braking effect on fashion movement. Habit slows the adoption of new skirt lengths, silhouettes, necklines, or colors whenever shoppers unconsciously select styles that do not differ perceptibly from those they already own. It is easy for an individual to let habit take over, and some consumers are more susceptible to this tendency than others. Their loyalty to an established style is less a matter of fashion judgment than a natural attraction to the more familiar.

Custom slows progress in the fashion cycle by permitting vestiges of past fashions, status symbols, taboos, or special needs to continue to appear in modern dress. Custom is responsible for such details as buttons on the sleeves of men's suits, vents in men's jackets, and the sharp creases down the front of men's trousers. Custom usually requires a degree of formality in dress for religious services. The trend toward similarity of dress for men and women in the United States has permitted women to wear trousers, but custom still discourages men from wearing skirts.

A classic example of the influence of custom is the placement of buttons. They are on the right side for men, possibly originating with the need to have the weapon arm available while dressing and undressing. Another theory is that they are on the left for women, who tend to hold babies on that side and can more conveniently use the right hand for buttons. The stitching on the backs of gloves is another example; it dates back to a time when sizes were adjusted by lacing at these points.

Religion

Historically, religious leaders have championed custom, and their ceremonial apparel has demonstrated their respect for the old ways. In the past, religious leaders tended to associate fashion with temptation and urged their followers to turn their backs on both. Religion today, however, exerts much less of a restraining influence on fashion. Examples of the new relaxation may be found in the modernization of women's dress in most religious orders and the fact that most women no longer consider a hat obligatory when in church.

A countertrend to religion's diminishing impact on fashion has occurred, as well. It is particularly evident in the adoption of ancient dress in countries such as Afghanistan and Iran that are ruled by religious fundamentalists; and with the growth of the Muslim population in the United States and Europe, Muslim religious leaders have decreed that wearing modern fashions leads to temptation and corruption.

Sumptuary Laws

Sumptuary laws regulate what we can and cannot purchase. There are sumptuary laws that, for example, require children's sleepwear to be flame-retardant. In the past, sumptuary laws have regulated extravagance and luxury in dress on religious or moral grounds. Height of headdress, length of train, width of sleeve, value and weight of material, and color of dress have all at times been restricted by law to specific classes. Such laws were aimed at keeping each class in its place in a rigidly stratified society.[4]

Other laws, such as those of the Puritans, attempted to enforce a general high-mindedness by condemning frippery. An order passed in 1638 by the General Court of Massachusetts stated,

> No garment shall be made with short sleeves, and such as have garments already made with short sleeves shall not wear same unless they cover the arm to the wrist; and hereafter no person whatever shall make any garment for women with sleeves more than half an ell wide.[5]

And in the eighteenth century, a bill was proposed (but rejected) that stated,

> All women of whatever age, rank, profession, or degree, whether virgin, maid, or widow, that shall impose upon, seduce, and betray into matrimony any of His Majesty's subjects by scents, paints, cosmetic washes, artificial teeth, false hair, Spanish wool, iron stays, hoops, high-heeled shoes, or bolstered hips, shall incur the penalty of the law now in force against witchcraft and the like demeanours, and that marriage, upon conviction, shall stand null and void.[6]

In New York in the 1920s and 1930s, fines could be imposed on individuals who appeared on the streets

FIGURE 4.2 In the 1920s, women were stopped on the beach to check that their bathing suits were not more than six inches above their knees.

wearing shorts, or whose bathing-suit shoulder straps were not in place on public beaches. At the Washington Bathing Beach, bathing suits could not be shorter than six inches above the knee (Figure 4.2). People have a way of ignoring local ordinances, however, if they conflict with a fashion cycle that is gathering strength. What was considered indecent exposure then is commonplace today.

School uniforms and standardized attire in public schools have come a long way from their early significance prior to the 1960s and their reemergence in the 1990s. They continue to be worn because of the positive effects they have had on both the schools and the students (Figure 4.3).

Bullying continues to be a concern nationwide, and school uniforms and standardized dress codes are helping to combat the issue. According to a 2011 survey of members of the National School Board Association, the use of school uniforms is on the rise, and 85 percent

FIGURE 4.3 School uniforms are increasing globally. Some students oppose them but others are relieved that they don't have to worry about what to wear.

of respondents with standardized dress programs are focusing on countering bullying.[7]

The debate over uniforms in public schools encompasses many larger issues than simply what children should wear to school. It touches on issues of school improvement, freedom of expression, and culture wars. It is no wonder the debate rages on.

Nature of the Merchandise

Not all merchandise moves at the same pace through a fashion cycle. Often, the very nature of the merchandise is responsible for the rate of movement. Over the years, it has been accepted as normal that men's fashion cycles move more slowly than women's fashions. However, the changing lifestyles of the male population have resulted in accelerating menswear cycles. Women's apparel generally moves in slower cycles than accessories, though some accessories now have full-run cycles comparable to those of apparel.

Reductions in Consumers' Buying Power

Consumers' buying power has a powerful effect on the movement of fashion cycles. When buying power increases, fashion cycles often speed up. Decreased buying power, conversely, can retard the movement of fashion cycles. During economic recessions and resultant high unemployment, consumers' buying power is sharply reduced. Many people make do with clothes they have, buying only necessities. A similar caution is shown by consumers affected by strikes, inflation, high taxes, or high interest rates. All these factors have a slowing influence on fashion cycles. The poorer people are, the less impact they have on fashion's movements. They become bystanders in matters of fashion, and as a result do not keep cycles moving. Laver emphasized the importance of buying power when he said that nothing except poverty can make a style permanent.[8]

Recurring Fashions

In the study of fashion history, we see that styles recur, with adaptations that suit the times in which they reappear. Occasionally, an entire look is reborn. The elegant, simple look of the late 1940s and early 1950s, for example, was born again for the generation of the 1980s. Nostalgia influenced choices not only in apparel but also in hairstyles and makeup.

Sometimes a single costume component or a minor detail that had exhausted its welcome stages a comeback. At other times, a single article of clothing, like the sandals of the ancient Greeks, returns to popularity.

An outstanding example of a recurring men's fashion is the T-shirt. T-shirts originated in France as cotton

FIGURE 4.4 Today's T-shirt puts ego into fashion and announces to the world what the wearer stands for. Here, a sketch of Karl Lagerfeld's face and signature are displayed.

underwear. They were discovered during World War I by American soldiers who preferred them to their own itchy wool union suits. In the 1940s, they reemerged as "tee" shirts for golfing and other active sports. In the 1960s they became part of the women's fashion scene as well, and they are still popular today (Figure 4.4).

Research indicates that in the past, similar silhouettes and details of design in women's apparel have recurred with remarkable regularity. In *Recurring Cycles of Fashion*,[9] Agnes Brooke Young studied skirt silhouettes and their variations in connection with her interest in theatrical costumes. From data she collected on the period from 1760 to 1937, she concluded that despite widely held opinions to the contrary, there were actually only three basic silhouettes—bell-shaped, back fullness, and straight—which always followed each other in the same hundred-year sequence. (See Chapter 2 for variations on this theory.) Each silhouette with all its variations dominated the fashion scene for a period of approximately thirty-five years. Having reached an excess in styling, it then declined in popularity and yielded to the next silhouette in regular sequence.

The anthropologist A. L. Kroeber studied changes in women's apparel from the early 1600s to the early 1900s. His conclusions confirm Young's findings that similar silhouettes recur in fashion acceptance approximately once every hundred years. In addition, Kroeber

BIRTH OF A NOTION

Designers say there is no rhyme or reason to when and how inspiration will strike—and that's half the fun! Here are some sketches by famous designers that show their designs and what inspires them.

" WO-MAN II. "
—DONNA KARAN

" AMERICAN OPTIMISM. "
—TOMMY HILFIGER

" The collection is called Palazzo. Think Rome, Marrakech, Jaipur; she is an aristocratic dreamer, sophisticated but also rebellious and provocative. "
—DIANE VON FURSTENBERG AND YVAN MISPELAERE

FIGURE 4.5 Andrew Gn's design reveals just enough of the neckline and shoulders, while playing with a longer-length dress.

FIGURE 4.6 Full-skirted and colorful, summer dresses from the 1950s showed off a woman's waistline.

found that similar neck widths recurred every hundred years, and similar skirt lengths every thirty-five years.[10]

Playing the Apparel Fashion Game

According to Madge Garland, a well-known English fashion authority, "Every woman is born with a built-in hobby: the adornment of her person. The tricks she can play with it, the shapes she can make of it, the different portions she displays at various times, the coverings she uses or discards" all add up to fashion.[11]

Many clothing authorities read a clear message into the alternate exposure and covering of various parts of the body—sex. J. C. Flügel cited sexual attraction as the dominant motive for wearing clothes.[12]

Laver explained fashion emphasis in terms of the sexuality of the body. "Fashion really began," he said, "with the discovery in the fifteenth century that clothes could be used as a compromise between exhibitionism and modesty."[13] Laver also suggested that those portions of the body no longer fashionable to expose are "sterilized" and are no longer regarded as sexually attractive. Those that are newly exposed are **erogenous**, or sexually stimulating. He viewed fashion as pursuing the emphasis of ever-shifting erogenous zones but never quite catching up with them. "If you really catch up," he warned, "you are immediately arrested for

indecent exposure. If you almost catch up, you are celebrated as a leader of fashion."[14]

Men's apparel has long played the fashion game, too—but, since the industrial revolution, in a less dramatic manner than women's. Women's fashions have tended to concentrate mainly on different ways to convey sexual appeal. Men's fashions have been designed to emphasize such attributes as strength, power, bravery, and high social rank. When a male style does emphasize sex, it is intended to project an overall impression of virility.

Pieces of the Game

The pieces with which the women's fashion game are played are the various parts of the female body: waist, shoulders, bosom, neckline, hips, derriere, legs, and feet, as well as the figure as a whole (Figure 4.5). Historically, as attention to a part of the anatomy reaches a saturation point, the fashion spotlight shifts to some other portion.

The trend of the 1950s and early 1960s was more conservative full skirts and dresses (Figure 4.6). However, the late 1960s and early 1970s brought about the "youth cult" and its attendant revolt against conventional sexual and political attitudes. The "triumph of personal publicity" achieved during this time broke all records for calling attention to just about every area of the human body. This differed from earlier fashion eras that centered attention only on parts of the body. It was, indeed, an allover feast for the eye of the observer.

Rules of the Game

In the game of emphasizing different parts of the female body at different times, as in any game, there are rules.

The first and strongest rule is that fashion emphasis does not flit from one area to another! Rather, a particular area of the body is emphasized until every bit of excitement has been exhausted. At this point, fashion attention turns to another area. For example, when miniskirts of the 1960s could go no higher and still be legal, the fashion emphasis moved on.

The second rule of the fashion game is that only certain parts of the body can be exposed at any given time. There are dozens of examples throughout fashion history that back up this theory: floor-length evening gowns with plunging necklines, high necklines with miniskirts, turtlenecks on sleeveless fashions.

A third rule of the fashion game is that, like fashion itself, fashion attention must always go forward.

Predicting the Movement of Fashion

Designing and selling fashion merchandise to consumers at a profit are what fashion merchandising is all about. To bring excitement and flair to their segment of merchandising, producers, designers, and retailers must have a well-defined plan and follow the movement of general fashion preferences.

The success of fashion merchandising depends on correctly predicting which new styles will be accepted by the majority of consumers. Suggested steps in developing a fashion forecast are as follows:

1. Identify facts about past trends and forecasts.
2. Determine the causes of change in the past.
3. Investigate the difference between past forecasts and actual behavior.
4. Analyze the factors likely to affect trends in the future.
5. Apply forecasting tools and techniques, using accuracy and reliability.
6. Study the forecast continually to determine reasons for significant deviations from expected plans.
7. Revise the forecast when necessary.

With information on these points, projections—a prime requisite in successful fashion merchandising—become possible.

Identifying Trends

A fashion trend, as discussed in Chapter 2, is a direction in which fashion is moving. Designers, manufacturers, and merchants try to recognize each fashion trend to determine how widespread it is and whether it is moving toward or away from maximum fashion acceptance. They can then decide whether to actively promote the fashion to their target customers, wait, or abandon it.

For example, assume that wide-leg pants have developed as a fashion trend. At the introduction and rise stages, retailers will stock and promote more wide-leg pants. When customer response begins to level off, retailers will realize that a saturation point is being reached with this style and will begin introducing narrower pants into their stocks in larger and larger numbers. If the retailers have correctly predicted the downturn in customer demand for wide-leg pants, they will have fewer on hand when the downturn occurs. And while some customers may continue to wear the wide-leg style, they will not be buying new wide-leg pants and certainly not at regular prices. One of the outstanding trend and forecasting companies is Tobé Reports, a division of Henry Doneger Associates, Inc.

Sources of Data

Modern fashion forecasters bear little resemblance to the mystical prognosticators of old. Their ability to predict the strength and direction of fashion trends among their customers has almost nothing to do with what is often called a "fashion sense." Nor does it depend on glances into the future through a cloudy crystal ball. Successful fashion forecasters depend on a most valuable commodity: information. Good, solid facts about the willingness of customers to accept certain goods are the basis of successful merchandising decisions.

Merchants keep records on sales, inventories, new fashion testing, and myriad other contributing factors that aid the fashion merchandising process. In addition, wise merchants keep their eyes open to see what is being worn by their own customers as well as by the public as a whole. They are so familiar with their customers' lifestyles, economic status, educational levels, and social milieu that they can determine at just what point in a fashion's life cycle their customers will be ready to accept or reject it. Merchants turn to every available source for information that will help ensure success. They use their hard-earned sales experience but do not rely just on their own judgment. They learn about the buying habits of customers from the producers of fashion; resident buying, merchandising, and developing offices; and special fashion groups (Figure 4.7).

FIGURE 4.7 Regional shows and seminars are a reliable source of information for retailers—and provide opportunities for networking and fun.

Successful merchants look at the larger fashion picture to better predict just where their local scene fits in.

Interpreting Influential Factors

In fashion forecasting, all the data in the world can be collected by merchants, producers, or designers, but this is of little importance without interpretation. That is where the forecasters' knowledge of fashion and fashion principles come into the picture. From collected data, they are able to identify certain patterns. Then they consider the factors that can accelerate or delay a fashion cycle among their target group of customers. Among these factors are current events, the appearance of prophetic styles, sales promotion efforts, and the standards of taste currently in vogue. Analysts estimate that crowdsourced and customized products could eventually make up as much as 10 percent of the total market for apparel, accessories, and footwear. Sometimes, trends remake design in the following ways:[15]

- Crowdsourcing: This generally means using the many social possibilities of the Web to either create something or solve a problem. Examples of fashion open-source sites that use crowdsourcing are Lookbook.nu, Chictopia.com, and Threadless.com.
- Mass customization: Levi's, Selve, Timberland, Kenneth Cole, and Lori Coulter Swimwear are some of the companies that have used technology and factory production rather than traditional craftsmanship to produce a custom product at a popular price.

- Desktop manufacturing: Digital printers can create three-dimensional objects, such as eyeglasses, jewelry, and electronics, by fusing layers of plastic or metal.

Current Events

The news of what is going on in the country or the world can have a long-term or short-term influence on consumers and affect their response to a fashion (Figure 4.8). For example, in the mid-1980s, many newspapers,

FIGURE 4.8 Fashion shows came to a halt and organizers raised the American flag after the September 11th terrorist attacks on the United States in 2001.

magazines, and TV shows were discussing opportunities for women at mid- and upper-management levels. Success in responsible positions in the business world demanded "dressing for success," and career-minded women responded by adopting the severely tailored business-suit look. By their very appearance, these women indicated their determination to succeed in the still male-dominated world of business. A reaction to this strictly tailored look occurred in the early 1990s, when women turned to a softer, less tailored look and many men abandoned the business suit uniform that had been the standard for generations. Today, men and women choose what fashion is right for them.

Prophetic Styles

Good fashion forecasters keep a sharp watch for what they call **prophetic styles**. These are particularly interesting new styles that are still in the introduction phase of their fashion cycle. Taken up enthusiastically by the socially prominent or by the flamboyantly young, these styles may gather momentum very rapidly or may prove to be nonstarters. Whatever their future course, the degree of acceptance of these very new styles gives forecasters a sense of the directions in which fashion may go.

Sales Promotion Efforts

In addition to analyzing the records of past sales, fashion forecasters give thought to the kind and amount of promotion that helps stimulate interest in prophetic styles. They also consider the kind and amount of additional sales promotion they can look forward to. For example, a fiber producer's powerful advertising and publicity efforts may have helped turn slight interest in a product into a much stronger interest during a corresponding period the previous year. The forecaster's problem is to estimate how far the trend might have developed without those promotional activities. The forecaster must also assess how much momentum remains from the previous year's push to carry the trend forward in the current year, and how much promotional support can be looked for in the future. The promotional effort that a forecaster's own organization plans to expend is only one part of the story; outside efforts, sometimes industrywide, also must be considered in forecasting fashions.

Importance of Timing

Successful merchants must determine what their particular target group of customers is wearing now and what this group is most likely to be wearing one month or three months from now. The data these merchants collect enable them to identify each current fashion,

who is wearing it, and what point it has reached in its fashion cycle.

Since merchants know at what point in a fashion's cycle their customers are most likely to be attracted, they can determine whether to stock a current fashion now, one month from now, or three months from now.

Theories of Fashion Adoption

Fashions are accepted by a few before they are accepted by the majority. An important step in fashion forecasting is isolating and identifying those fashion leaders and keeping track of their preferences. Once these are known, the fashion forecaster is better able to forecast which styles are most likely to succeed as fashions, and how widely and by whom each will be accepted.

Three theories have been advanced to explain the "social contagion" or spread of fashion adoption: the downward-flow theory, the horizontal-flow theory or mass-market theory, and the upward-flow theory. Each attempts to explain the course a fashion travels or is likely to travel, and each has its own claim to validity in reference to particular fashions or social environments (Figure 4.9).

Downward-Flow Theory

The oldest theory of fashion adoption is the **downward-flow theory** (or the *trickle-down theory*). It maintains that to be identified as a true fashion, a style must first be adopted by people at the top of the social pyramid. The style then gradually wins acceptance at progressively lower social levels.

This theory assumes the existence of a social hierarchy in which lower-income people seek identification with more affluent people. At the same time, those at the top seek disassociation from those they consider socially inferior. The theory suggests that (1) fashions are accepted by lower classes only if, and after, they are accepted by upper classes, and (2) upper classes will reject a fashion once it has flowed to a lower social level.

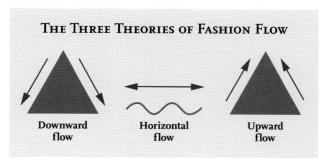

THE THREE THEORIES OF FASHION FLOW

Downward flow Horizontal flow Upward flow

FIGURE 4.9 The three theories of fashion flow.

Thorstein B. Veblen, an economist at the turn of the twentieth century, was among the first to observe this type of social behavior and its effect on fashion. In 1903, the French sociologist Gabriel Tarde described the spread of fashion in terms of a social water tower from which a continuous fall of imitation could descend.[16] The German sociologist George Simmel, one of the first of his discipline to undertake a serious study of fashion, wrote in 1904:

> Social forms, apparel, aesthetic judgment, the whole style of human expression, are constantly being transformed by fashion in [a way that] . . . affects only the upper classes. Just as soon as the lower classes begin to copy their styles, thereby crossing the line of demarcation the upper classes have drawn and destroying their coherence, the upper classes turn away from this style and adopt a new one. . . . The same process is at work as between the different sets within the upper classes, although it is not always visible here.[17]

The downward-flow theory has had among its twentieth-century proponents such authorities as Dwight E. Robinson, Laver, Edward Sapir, and Flügel. Flügel, in fact, suggested that sumptuary laws originated with the reluctance of upper classes to abandon the sartorial distinctiveness that to them represented superiority.

Implications for Merchandising

To some extent, the downward-flow theory has validity. Some fashions may appear first among the socially prominent. Eager manufacturers then quickly mass-produce lower-priced copies that many consumers can afford, and the wealthier consumers seek newer styles.

Because our social structure has radically changed, this theory has few adherents today. The downward-flow theory of fashion dissemination can apply only when a society resembles a pyramid, with people of wealth and position at the apex and followers at successively lower levels. Our social structure today, however, is more like a group of rolling hills than a pyramid. There are many social groups and many directions in which fashion can and does travel.

This altered pattern of fashion acceptance is also a result of the speed with which fashion news now travels. All social groups know about fashion innovation at practically the same time. Moreover, accelerated mass production and mass distribution of fashion goods have broadened acceptance of styles. These goods are available at lower prices and more quickly than ever before.

Industry Practice

For the reasons given above, those who mass-produce fashion goods today are less likely to wait cautiously for approval of newly introduced styles by affluent consumers. As soon as significant signs of an interesting new style appear, the producers are ready to offer adaptations or even copies to the public.

Horizontal-Flow Theory

A newer theory is the **horizontal-flow theory** (or mass-market theory) of fashion adoption. This theory claims that fashions move horizontally between groups on similar social levels rather than vertically from one level to another.

One of the chief exponents of this theory was Dr. Charles W. King. He proposed that the social environment, including rapid mass communications and the promotional efforts of manufacturers and retailers, exposes new styles to the fashion leaders of all social groups at approximately the same time. King noted that there is almost no lag between the adoption of a fashion by one social group and another.[18] Paris fashions, for example, are now copied for mass distribution sometimes even before the originals are available to the more affluent markets. The designers themselves are bringing out their ready-to-wear lines at the same time as their more expensive custom designs.

This horizontal flow has also been observed by some modern supporters of the older downward-flow theory. Robinson, for example, said that any given group or cluster of groups takes its cues from contiguous groups within the same social stratum. He claimed that fashions therefore radiate from a center of each stratum or class.[19]

Implications for Merchandising

The theory of horizontal fashion movement has great significance for merchandising. It points out the fallacy of assuming that there is a single, homogeneous fashion public in this country. In reality, a number of distinctly different groups make up the fashion public. Each group has its own characteristics and its own fashion ideas and needs. The horizontal-flow theory recognizes that what wealthy society people are wearing today is not necessarily what middle-class suburbanites, college students, or office workers will either wear tomorrow or wait until tomorrow to accept. This theory acknowledges that there are separate markets in fashion goods as in any other type of merchandise.

Retailers who apply the horizontal-flow theory will watch their own customers closely rather than be guided solely by what more exclusive stores are selling. They will seek to identify the groups into which

THE LADIES WHO LUNCH

IN THE EARLY years of the twentieth century, when upper-class New York ladies began to venture out for lunch, they met at two newly established clubs: the Colony Club and the Cosmopolitan Club, both of which are still thriving. Although men's social clubs had existed for decades, the idea of women having their own clubs was very controversial. The most extravagant, beautiful, and expensive restaurants in New York were given life by the "ladies who lunch." Besides the Colony and the Cosmopolitan, women like Babe Paley, C. Z. Guest, and Jacqueline Kennedy Onassis helped launch Le Cirque, Le Pavillon, Le Côte Basque, La Caravelle, La Grenouille, Lutèce, and Mortimer's.

By the 1990s, the "power lunch" had replaced the "ladies' lunch," and media mavens replaced society swans. Diane Sawyer is the new Babe Paley, Anna Wintour the modern Gloria Guinness, and women like them started lunching with the "Big Boys" in the Grill Room of the Four Seasons.

Le Cirque Restaurant

Anna Wintour

customers can be divided in terms of income, age, education, and lifestyle. Among their customers, they will look for the innovators and their style choices as well as the influentials and their selections. King defined a **fashion innovator** as a person who is quicker than his or her associates to try out a new style. A **fashion influential** is a person whose advice is sought by associates. A fashion influential's adoption of a new style gives it prestige among a group. The two roles may or may not be played by the same individual within a specific group.

The news that socially prominent women are wearing plunging necklines in exclusive New York restaurants will have less significance for the retailers in a small midwestern city than the observation that the leader of the country club set in their community is abandoning bright colors for black on formal occasions. If the latter is a fashion influential in the community, she is a more important bellwether for them than the New York socialites.

Industry Practice

King drew a distinction between the spread of fashion within the industry itself and its adoption by consumers. A vertical flow definitely operates within the industry, he conceded: "Exclusive and famous designers are watched closely and emulated by lesser designers. Major manufacturers are studied and copied by smaller and less expert competitors."[20] And, as any reader of *Women's Wear Daily* knows, the hottest news in the industry concerns what the top designers and producers are showing.

King pointed out, moreover, that the innovation process in the industry represents a "great filtering system." From an almost infinite number of possibilities, manufacturers select a finite number of styles. From these, trade buyers select a small sampling. Finally, consumers choose from among retailers' selections, thereby endorsing certain ones as accepted fashions.

This process, King maintained, is quite different from the consumer reaction outlined by Simmel and other proponents of the downward-flow theory. The difference lies in the fact that today the mass market does not await the approval of the "class" market before it adopts a fashion.

Upward-Flow Theory

The third theory reflects the enormous social changes that have occurred in the past five decades. Because the process of fashion dissemination that evolved in the decades of the 1950s through the 2000s was the exact opposite of that which prevailed throughout much of recorded history, this theory has important implications for producers and retailers alike.

This theory of fashion adoption is called the **upward-flow theory**. It holds that the young—particularly those of low-income families and those in higher-income groups who adopt low-income lifestyles—are quicker than any social group to create or adopt new and different fashions. As its name implies, this theory is exactly the opposite of the downward-flow theory. The upward-flow theory holds that fashion adoption begins among the young members of lower-income groups and then moves upward into higher-income groups.

The decades of the fifties through today have outstanding examples of the upward-flow theory. In the 1950s, young people discovered Army/Navy surplus stores and were soon wearing khaki pants, caps, battle jackets, fatigues, and even ammunition belts. In the 1960s, led by the Hell's Angels, the motorcycle clubs introduced the fashion world to black leather—in jackets, vests, and studded armbands. Soon the jet set was dressed in black leather long coats, skirts, and pants. Meanwhile, other young people were discovering bib overalls, railroad workers' caps, and all-purpose laborers' coveralls that were soon translated into jumpsuits. Peasant apparel, prairie looks, and styles and designs from various minority groups followed the same pattern. They began as part of a young and lower-income lifestyle and were then quickly adopted among older people with different lifestyles and incomes.

One of the more dramatic illustrations of this pattern has been the T-shirt. In its short-sleeved version, it has long been worn by truckers, laborers, and farmworkers. In its long-sleeved version, it was the uniform of softball teams. In the 1970s, the T-shirt became a message board and sprouted a brand-new fashion cottage industry. The ultimate T-shirt was the Chanel No. 5; first the perfume, then the T-shirt. Actually, the Chanel T-shirt was a logical application of a tenet long held by the late Coco Chanel, who believed that fashion came from the streets and was then adapted by the couture.

In the 1980s, sources of inspiration for fashion styles representing the upward-flow theory were everywhere, especially in the world of rock music. By following the fashion statements of rock-and-roll idols, America's youth were arrayed in worn denim, metal, leather, lace, bangles, spandex, and glitter. Colors ranged from Cyndi Lauper's peacock looks to Roy Orbison's basic black. Madonna became a style-setter and introduced the country to her underwear worn on the outside.

In the 1990s, rap artists not only composed lyrics that spoke of ghetto life in street language; they also introduced and popularized hip-hop clothing styles.

Today, everything goes, but the new sources of inspiration are the celebrities seen on TV, magazine covers, and any other mode of media: the Lady Gagas, Kardashians, Katy Perrys, and others who become part of the reporting of celebrity fashions.

Implications for Merchandising

For producers and retailers, this new direction of fashion flow implies radical changes in traditional methods of charting and forecasting fashion trends. No longer can producers and retailers look solely to name designers and socially prominent fashion leaders for ideas that will become tomorrow's best-selling fashions. They also must pay considerable attention to what young people favor, for the young have now become a large, independent group that can exert considerable influence on fashion styling.

As a result, today fewer retailers and manufacturers attend European couture showings, once considered fashion's most important source of design inspiration. Now producers and retailers alike are more interested in ready-to-wear (prêt-à-porter) showings. Here they look for styles and design details that reflect trends with more fashion relevance for American youth.

Industry Practice

Apparently, fashion will never again flow in only one direction. Of course, customers will always exist for high fashion and for conservative fashion. But producers and retailers must now accept that they will be doing a considerable proportion of their business in fashions created or adopted first by the lower-income young and by those who choose to be allied with them.

Fashion Leaders

As different as they may be, the three theories of fashion flow share one common perspective: they recognize that there are both fashion leaders and fashion followers. People of social, political, and economic importance here and abroad are seen as leaders in the downward-flow theory. The horizontal-flow theory recognizes individuals whose personal prestige makes them leaders within their own circles, whether or not they are known elsewhere. Finally, the important fashion role played by young, lower-income groups in the last half of the twentieth century is recognized in the upward-flow theory.

The theories of fashion adoption stress that the fashion leader is not the creator of the fashion; nor does merely wearing the fashion make a person a fashion leader. As Quentin Bell explained, "The leader of fashion does not come into existence until the fashion is itself created . . . a king or person of great eminence may indeed lead the fashion, but he leads only in the general direction which it has already adopted."[21] If a fashion parade is forming, fashion leaders may head it and even quicken its pace. They cannot, however, bring about a procession; nor can they reverse a procession.

Innovators and Influentials

Famous people are not necessarily fashion leaders, even if they do influence an individual style. Their influence usually is limited to only one striking style, one physical attribute, or one time. The true fashion leader is a person constantly seeking distinction and therefore likely to launch a succession of fashions rather than just one. People like Beau Brummell, who made a career of dressing fashionably, or the Duchess of Windsor, whose wardrobe was front-page fashion news for decades, influence fashion on a much broader scale.

What makes a person a fashion leader? Flügel explained: "Inasmuch as we are aristocratically minded and dare to assert our own individuality by being different, we are leaders of fashion."[22] King, however, made it clear that more than just daring to be different is required. In his analysis, a person eager for the new is merely an innovator or early buyer. To be a leader, one must be influential and sought after for advice within one's coterie. "A fashion influential," said King, "sets the appropriate dress for a specific occasion in a particular circle. Within that circle, an innovator presents current offerings and is the earliest visual communicator of a new style."[23]

Royalty

In the past, fashion leadership was exclusively the province of royalty. New fashions were introduced in royal courts by such leaders as Empress Eugenie and Marie Antoinette. In the twentieth century, the Duchess of Windsor, although an American and a commoner by birth, was a fashion innovator and influential from the 1930s through the 1960s. When the King of England gave up his throne to marry "the woman he loved," style and fashion professionals throughout the world copied her elegance. The Sotheby auction in the late 1980s of the Duchess of Windsor's jewelry sparked new interest in her style, and designers are still showing copies of her jewelry.

Until Princess Diana and Sarah Ferguson married into the British royal family, few royal personages in recent years had qualified as fashion leaders. However, this all changed when Catherine Elizabeth Middleton married Prince William and became Her Royal

FIGURE 4.10 Kate Middleton is recognized as an influential royal and international fashion icon.

FIGURE 4.11 Often in the fashion spotlight, trendsetters Kendall and Kylie Jenner are well-known socialities who became models and clothing designers.

Highness, the Duchess of Cambridge. Today, Catherine (or Kate, as she is known) is well regarded for her sense of fashion and has appeared on countless best-dressed lists (Figure 4.10).

Despite the belief held by some that kings and queens wear crowns and ermine, the truth is that modern royalty has become a hardworking group whose daily life is packed with so many activities that sensible and conservative dress is necessary for most occasions.

The Rich

As monarchies were replaced with democracies, members of the wealthy and international sets came into the fashion spotlight. Whether the members of "society" derive their position from vast fortunes and old family names or from recent wealth, they bring to the scene a glamour and excitement that draws attention to

everything they do. Today, through the constant eye of television, social media, magazines, and newspapers, the average person is able to find fashion leadership in a completely new stratum of society—the jet set.

What these socialites are doing and what they are wearing are instantly served up to the public by the media (Figure 4.11). As far as fashion is concerned, these people are not just in the news; they *are* the news. Any move they make is important enough to be immediately publicized. What they wear is of vital interest to the public. The media tell us what the social leaders wear to dine in a chic restaurant, to attend a charity ball, or to go shopping. Because they are trendsetters, their choices are of prime interest to designers and to the world at large.

Of course, this inundation of news about what social leaders wear influences the public. The average person is affected because so many manufacturers and retailers of fashion take their cue from these social leaders. Right or wrong, fashion merchants count on the fashion sense of these leaders. They know that the overwhelming exposure of these leaders in the media encourages people of ordinary means to imitate them—consciously or unconsciously.

FIGURE 4.12 Music sensation Kanye West is in the public eye not only for his music but also his role in the fashion world.

The Famous

Fashion today takes its impetus and influence from people in every possible walk of life. These people have one thing in common, however: they are famous. Because of some special talent, charisma, notoriety, or popularity, they are constantly mentioned and shown on television, in fashion magazines and newspapers, and on the Web. They may or may not appear in the society pages.

In this group can be found presidents and princesses, movie stars and musicians, sports figures and recording stars, politicians and TV personalities (Figure 4.12). Because these people are seen so frequently, the public has a good sense of their fashions and lifestyles and can imitate them to the extent of the public's means and desires.

Prominent individuals have been responsible for certain fashions that continue to be associated with them. Many times, however, these individuals are not what would be considered fashion leaders. Although the cornrow braiding of hair had been practiced among blacks in Africa and America for decades, it was adopted by many young black women only after Cicely Tyson appeared with the hairstyle in the movie *Sounder* in 1972. In 1979, Bo Derek wore cornrows in the film *10* and gave the style new impetus. In the 1930s, a tremendous impact was felt by an entire menswear industry when Clark Gable appeared without an undershirt in the film *It Happened One Night*. Practically overnight, men from all walks of life shed their undershirts in imitation of Gable. In the late 1930s, women dared to wear slacks after seeing Greta Garbo and Marlene Dietrich wearing them in the movies. In the early 1960s, when First Lady Jacqueline Kennedy appeared in little pillbox hats, both the style and the hat

market blossomed under the publicity. Some styles are so closely associated with the famous people who wore them that they bear their names (Table 4.1). First Lady Michelle Obama is a prominent fashion leader in the twenty-first century, wearing everything from younger designers like Jason Wu to J.Crew.

Athletes

Today, there is strong emphasis on sports, and what prominent sports figures wear is of great importance to the people who seek to imitate them. For example, the names and styles of Eli Manning, Shaun White, Hidetoshi Nakata (Figure 4.13), and Serena Williams are known to most Americans. Television has increased the public acceptance of several sports. For example, people have enjoyed going to baseball, football, or basketball games for years. But sports of a more individual nature, such as tennis and golf, were of minor interest. Now these sports are brought into the living rooms of an increasing number of viewers. As a result, fashions for participating in these sports have grown remarkably

FIGURE 4.13 Athletes, such as Hidetoshi Nakata, are often used in advertisements and as spokespersons to sell sportswear.

TABLE 4.1 *Fashion Styles Named for the Famous*

TRENDSETTERS	STYLES
Amelia Bloomer	Bloomers
Earl of Chesterfield	Chesterfield Jacket
Dwight D. Eisenhower	Eisenhower Jacket
Geraldine Ferraro	"Gerry Cut" (Hairstyle)
Mao Tse Tung	Mao Jacket
Jawaharlal Nehru	Nehru Jacket
Madame de Pompadour	Pompadour (Hairstyle)
Nancy Reagan	"Reagan Plastics" (Costume Jewelry), Color Red
Duke of Wellington	Wellington Boots
Earl of Cardigan	Cardigan Sweater
Duke of Windsor	Windsor Knot (Tie)
Duke of Norfolk	Norfolk Jacket
Nelson Mandela	Madiba Smart (Shirt)
The Beatles	Hairstyle

MADAME DE POMPADOUR

AMELIA BLOOMER

THE BEATLES

DWIGHT D. EISENHOWER

in importance. Tennis is also a very popular participation sport and has given rise to an entire specialized fashion industry. Aspiring tennis players have endless fashion styles, colors, and fabrics from which to choose. A wide selection of fashion is also available for golf, running, swimming, skating, cycling, snorkeling, snowboarding, skiing, and other sports.

Fashion Followers

There is a story about a father filling out forms for his daughter's college entrance application, and he wrote the following to describe his daughter's leadership qualities: "To tell the truth, my daughter is really not a leader, but rather a loyal and devoted follower." The dean of the college admissions responded: "We are welcoming a freshman class of 100 students this year and are delighted to accept your daughter. You can't imagine how happy we are to have one follower among the ninety-nine leaders!"

Most people want to be thought of as leaders, not followers. But many people are followers, and good ones. In fact, followers are in the majority within any group. Without followers, the fashion industry would certainly collapse. Mass production and mass distribution can be possible and profitable only when large numbers of consumers accept the merchandise. Although they may say otherwise, luckily, more people prefer to follow than to lead. The styles fashion leaders adopt may help manufacturers and retailers in determining what will be demanded by the majority of consumers in the near future. Only accurate predictions can ensure the continued success of the giant ready-to-wear business in this country, which depends on mass production and distribution. While fashion leaders may stimulate and excite the fashion industry, fashion followers are the industry's lifeblood.

Reasons for Following Fashion

Theories about why people follow rather than lead in fashion are plentiful. Among the explanations are feelings of insecurity, admiration of others, lack of interest, and ambivalence about the new.

Feelings of Insecurity

Flügel wrote, "Inasmuch as we feel our own inferiority and the need for conformity to the standards set by others, we are followers of fashion."[24] For example, high school boys and girls are at a notably insecure stage of life. They are therefore more susceptible than any other age group to the appeal of fads. A person about to face a difficult interview or attend the first meeting with a new group carefully selects new clothes. Often a feeling

FIGURE 4.14 The public admires Taylor Swift for her celebrity status and style.

of inadequacy can be hidden by wearing a style that others have already approved as appropriate.

Admiration

Flügel also maintained that it is a fundamental human impulse to imitate those who are admired or envied. A natural and symbolic means of doing this is to copy their clothes, makeup, and hairstyles. Outstanding illustrations of this theory have been provided by movie stars and models—Mary Pickford, "America's Sweetheart" of the 1910s; Clara Bow, the It girl of the 1920s; Ginger Rogers, Katharine Hepburn, and Rosalind Russell of the 1930s; Veronica Lake and Ann Sheridan, the "Oomph Girls" of the 1940s; Doris Day and Marilyn Monroe in the 1950s; Twiggy in the 1960s; Farrah Fawcett in the 1970s; Christie Brinkley in the 1980s; Elle MacPherson and Cindy Crawford in the 1990s; Lady Gaga, supermodel Gisele, Beyoncé, Taylor Swift, Sarah Jessica Parker, and Rachel Zoe in the twenty-first century (Figure 4.14). Their clothes and hairstyles were copied instantly among many different groups throughout this country and in many other parts of the world. On a different level, the young girl who copies the hairstyle of her best friend, older sister, or favorite aunt demonstrates the same principle, as do college students who model their appearance after that of a campus leader.

Lack of Interest

Edward Sapir, anthropologist, suggested that many people are insensitive to fashion and follow it only because "they realize that not to fall in with it would be to declare themselves members of a past generation, or dull people who cannot keep up with their neighbors."[25] Their response to fashion, he said, is a sullen surrender, by no means an eager following of the Pied Piper.

Ambivalence

Another theory holds that many people are ambivalent in their attitudes toward the new; they both want it and fear it. For most, it is easier to choose what is already familiar. Such individuals need time and exposure to new styles before they can accept them.

Varying Rates of Response

Individuals vary in the speed with which they respond to a new idea, especially when fashion change is radical and dramatic. Some fashion followers apparently need time to adjust to new ideas. Merchants exploit this point when they buy a few "window pieces" of styles too advanced for their own clientele and expose them in windows and fashion shows to allow customers time to get used to them. Only after a period of exposure to the new styles do the fashion followers accept them.

Fashion and Individuality

In the early part of the twenty-first century, a strange but understandable trend became apparent across the nation. People were striving, through their mode of dress, to declare individuality in the face of computer-age conformity.

People had watched strings of impersonal numbers become more and more a part of their lives—zip codes, bank and credit card account numbers, employee identification numbers, department store accounts, automobile registrations, social security numbers, and so on. An aversion to joining the masses—to becoming "just another number"—began to be felt. So while most people continued to go along with general fashion trends, some asserted their individuality. This was accomplished by distinctive touches each wearer added to an outfit. A new freedom in dress, color and texture combinations, use of accessories, and hairstyles allowed people to assert their individuality without being out of step with the times. Most social scientists see in this a paradox—an endless conflict between the desire to conform and the desire to remain apart.

We have all known people who at some point in their lives found a fashion that particularly pleased them. It might have been a certain style of dress, a certain shoe, or a hairstyle. Even in the face of continuing changes in fashion, the person continued to wear that style in which she or he felt right and attractive. This is an assertion of individuality in the face of conformity.

Although superbly fashion conscious, the actress Joan Crawford never stopped wearing the open-toed, sling-back, wedge shoe of the 1940s. When the pointed toe and stiletto heel of the 1950s gave way to the low, chunky heel of the 1960s, she continued to wear the same style. She was perfectly in step with fashion when the wedge shoe finally returned to popularity in the early 1970s. Woody Allen achieved special recognition for wearing—anywhere and everywhere—sneakers! At formal occasions, he conforms by wearing appropriate formal attire. But his feet remain sneakered, and Woody retains his individuality.

Most people prefer to assert their individuality in a less obvious way, and today's ready-to-wear fashions lend themselves to subtle changes that mark each person's uniqueness. No two people put the same costume together in exactly the same way.

The Paradox of Conformity and Individuality

For decades, experts have tried to explain why people seek both conformity and individuality in fashion. Simmel suggested that two opposing social tendencies are at war: the need for union and the need for isolation. The individual, he reasoned, derives satisfaction from knowing that the way in which he or she expresses a fashion represents something special. At the same time, people gain support from seeing others favor the same style.[26]

Flügel interpreted the paradox in terms of a person's feelings of superiority and inferiority. The individual wants to be like others "insofar as he regards them as superior, but unlike them, in the sense of being more 'fashionable,' insofar as he thinks they are below him."[27]

Sapir tied the conflict to a revolt against custom and a desire to break away from slavish acceptance of fashion. Slight changes from the established form of dress and behavior "seem for the moment to give victory to the individual, while the fact that one's fellows revolt in the same direction gives one a feeling of adventurous safety."[28] He also tied the assertion of individuality to the need to affirm one's self in a powerful society in which the individual has ceased to be the measure.

One example of this conflict may be found in the off-duty dress of people required to wear uniforms during working hours, such as nurses, police officers, and mail carriers. A second example is seen in the clothing worn by many present-day business executives. Far from the days when to be "The Man in the Gray Flannel Suit" meant that a man had arrived in the business world, today executives favor a much more diversified wardrobe. While suits of gray flannel are still worn, so are a wide variety of other fabrics and patterns. And some top executives favor a more relaxed look altogether, preferring to wear appropriately fashioned separate jackets or blazers with their business slacks.

Retailers know that although some people like to lead and some like to follow in fashion, most people buy fashion to express their personality or to identify with a particular group. To belong, they follow fashion; to express their personality, they find ways to individualize fashion.

Self-Expression

Increasing importance is being placed on fashion individuality—on expressing your personality, or refusing to be cast in a mold. Instead of slavishly adopting any one look, today's young person seeks to create an individual effect through the way he or she combines various fashion components (Figure 4.15). For instance, if a young woman thinks a denim skirt, an ankle-length woolen coat, and a heavy turtleneck sweater represent her personality, they may be considered acceptable by others in her group.

FIGURE 4.15 Musician Nicki Minaj expresses her personality and style, regardless of social acceptance.

Forward-looking designers recognize this desire for self-expression. Designers say that basic wardrobe components should be made available, but consumers should be encouraged to combine them as they see fit. For instance, they advise women to wear pants or skirts, long or short, according to how they feel, not according to what past tradition has considered proper for an occasion. They suggest that men make the same choice among tailored suits, leisure wear, and slacks, to find the styles that express their personalities.

Having experienced such fashion freedom, young people may never conform again. Yet despite individual differences in dress, young experimenters have in common a deep-rooted desire to dress differently from older generations.

Summary and Review

It is the nature of fashion to change, but the speed and direction of its changes are difficult to predict. Some factors that accelerate the pace of change are widespread buying power, increased leisure time, increased education, the improved status of women, technological advances that bring new and improved products to the market, and seasonal changes. However, the pace of change can be slowed by habit and custom, religious restrictions, and sumptuary laws (laws placing limits or requirements on the construction of apparel).

Some types of fashion merchandise change more slowly than other types. For example, historically, men's fashions have changed more slowly than women's fashions. Some fashion historians have tracked the basic shapes of apparel, particularly women's wear, and concluded that three basic silhouettes dominate fashion in turn, each for about thirty-five years, creating a cycle that lasts about a hundred years. Other details of line, such as sleeve shape and skirt length, have similar cycles.

Fashion also focuses on different parts of the body at different times, accentuating the seductive appeal of each part in turn. For fashion merchandisers, success depends on the accuracy of predictions of trends and judging when and to what degree a fashion will be adopted by the producer's or retailer's target market. Inventory and sales records and a careful following of current events, the reception of new styles at the introductory stage of the fashion cycle, and sales promotion help forecasters make accurate predictions.

Three theories attempt to explain the movement of fashion: the downward-flow, horizontal-flow, and upward-flow theories. The acceptance of a fashion depends on innovators, who are the first to wear it, and influentials, whose personal style is copied by others.

On a broad scale, public figures are often innovators and influentials. The buying public watches the fashions of royalty, high society, athletes and other entertainers, and other celebrities. On a smaller scale, individual communities have their own fashion innovators and influentials, but a fashion's acceptance ultimately depends on fashion followers. They are the people who spread a fashion and account for the number of sales. Each person adjusts his or her wardrobe to balance a sense of belonging to a group and being an individual.

For Review

1. Describe the theory of fashion cycles and explain why it accelerated in the twentieth century.
2. List the pieces of the women's fashion game, according to Madge Garland. What happens to these pieces?
3. According to leading fashion authorities, what are the three basic rules that govern the fashion game?
4. What basic resources are available to the fashion merchant to predict fashion?
5. Explain the term *prophetic style.*
6. Is the downward-flow theory of fashion adoption as valid today as it was in years past? Explain your answer.
7. How does the horizontal-flow theory of fashion adoption affect fashion merchants today? How are merchants today affected by the upward-flow theory?
8. Explain why (a) rich people, (b) famous people, and (c) athletes are prime candidates for positions of fashion leadership.
9. Give four reasons why most people follow, rather than lead, in regard to fashion. Explain each.
10. How can fashion be used as a means of expressing individuality?

For Discussion

1. Give at least one current example of each of several factors that are accelerating the forward movement of fashions today.
2. Certain factors tend to delay the development of fashion cycles by discouraging the adoption of newly introduced styles. List these factors and give at least one example of how each factor exerts a braking influence on fashion development.
3. Why do people today seek both conformity and individuality in fashion? How does this affect the fashion designer or manufacturer? The fashion retailer?

Trade Talk

Define or briefly explain the following terms:

downward-flow theory
erogenous
fashion influential
fashion innovator
horizontal-flow theory
prophetic styles
sumptuary law
upward-flow theory

THE BUSINESS OF FASHION

KEY CONCEPTS

- The four levels of the fashion business
- The three common forms of business ownership
- The role of franchising and licensing
- The role of the designer, the manufacturer, and the retailer in the fashion business

Fashion is a business, affected by the same technological advances, investment patterns, and economic forces that affect other major businesses in the world. Fashion is not limited just to apparel; it influences our complete lifestyle as well as the products we buy. Fashion influences the automobile, housing, and entertainment industries, and like these industries, it is shaped by the basic principles of business and economics.

What is business? Business is the activity of creating, producing, and marketing products or services. The primary objective of business is to make a profit. **Profit**, or net income, is the amount of money a business earns in excess of its expenses. Consequently, in the United States, business can be defined as the activity of creating, producing, and marketing products or services for a profit.

Economic Importance of the Fashion Business

The business of fashion contributes significantly to the economy of the United States through the materials and services it purchases, the wages and taxes it pays,

and the goods and services it produces. The fashion business is one of the largest employers in the country. However, employment has declined by almost half since the industry boom in the early 1970s. As of 2013, approximately 149,000 people in the United States are employed in apparel manufacturing.[1] More people are employed in the production of jewelry and cosmetics, and millions more are employed by the retail organizations that distribute these goods. When we add to this number a share of the total number of jobs in finance, transportation, advertising, computers, electronics, and other services that devote part of their efforts to the fashion industry, it becomes obvious that the fashion industry has a tremendous impact on our economy.

The growth and development of mass markets, mass-production methods, and mass distribution have contributed to the creation of new job opportunities in the fashion industry—not only in the production area but in design and marketing as well. Young people are entering the fashion business in greater numbers each year and are having a marked effect on the business. Innovation and change have become increasingly important factors in the economic growth of the fashion business.

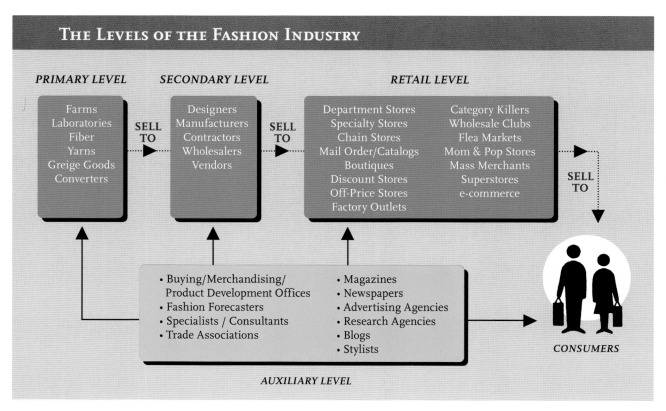

THE LEVELS OF THE FASHION INDUSTRY

PRIMARY LEVEL

Farms
Laboratories
Fiber
Yarns
Greige Goods
Converters

SELL TO

SECONDARY LEVEL

Designers
Manufacturers
Contractors
Wholesalers
Vendors

SELL TO

RETAIL LEVEL

Department Stores
Specialty Stores
Chain Stores
Mail Order/Catalogs
Boutiques
Discount Stores
Off-Price Stores
Factory Outlets

Category Killers
Wholesale Clubs
Flea Markets
Mom & Pop Stores
Mass Merchants
Superstores
e-commerce

SELL TO

- Buying/Merchandising/ Product Development Offices
- Fashion Forecasters
- Specialists / Consultants
- Trade Associations

- Magazines
- Newspapers
- Advertising Agencies
- Research Agencies
- Blogs
- Stylists

CONSUMERS

AUXILIARY LEVEL

FIGURE 5.1 The fashion industry operates collaboratively on four levels to serve the customer.

Scope of the Fashion Business

The fashion business is composed of numerous industries all working to keep consumers of fashion satisfied (Figure 5.1). A special relationship exists among these industries that makes the fashion business different from other businesses. The four levels of the fashion business—known as the primary level, the secondary level, the retail level, and the auxiliary level—are composed of separate entities, but they also work interdependently to provide the market with the fashion merchandise that will satisfy consumers. Because of this unique relationship among the different industries, the fashion business is unusually exciting.

The Primary Level
The **primary level** is composed of the growers and producers of the raw materials of fashion—the fiber, fabric, leather, and fur producers who function in the raw-materials market. The earliest part of the planning function in color and texture takes place on the primary level. It is also the level of the fashion business that works the furthest in advance of the ultimate selling period of the goods. Up to two years' lead time is needed by primary-level companies before the goods will be available to the consumer. Primary-level goods may often be imports from third-world emerging nations, where textiles are usually the earliest form of industrialization.

The Secondary Level
The **secondary level** is composed of industries—manufacturers and contractors—that produce the semifinished or finished fashion goods from the materials produced on the primary level. On the secondary level are the manufacturers of women's, men's, and children's apparel and also legwear, bodywear, and underwear; accessories; cosmetics and fragrances; and home furnishings.

Manufacturers who function on the secondary level may be based in the United States or overseas. Fashion goods are now produced in the Far East, the Caribbean, South America, and Europe. Secondary-level companies work from six to eighteen months ahead of the time that goods are available to the consumer.

The Retail Level
The **retail level** is the ultimate distribution level. On this level are the different types of retailers who buy their goods from the secondary level and then supply them directly to the consumer (Figure 5.2). In many cases, the retail level works with both the primary and secondary levels to ensure a coordinated approach to consumer wants. The interrelationship among the primary, secondary, and retail levels is vertical. The further removed a level is from the consumer, the further in advance it must plan. Retailers make initial purchases for resale to customers from three to six months before the customer buying season.

FIGURE 5.2 The retail level includes nonstore retailers such as the virtual multifashion, design, and art store yoox.com.

The Auxiliary Level

The **auxiliary level** is the only level that functions with all the other levels simultaneously. This level is composed of all the support services that are working constantly with primary producers, secondary manufacturers, and retailers to keep consumers aware of the fashion merchandise produced for ultimate consumption. On this level are all the advertising media—print, audio, and visual—and fashion consultants and researchers.

Diversity and Competition

The enormous variety and diversity that exist in the kinds and sizes of firms that operate on each level of the fashion industry make it a fascinating and competitive business. There are giant firms, both national and international, and small companies with regional or local distribution, doing business side by side as privately or publicly owned corporations, partnerships, or sole proprietorships. Fashion-producing companies may also be part of conglomerates, which also own, for example, entertainment companies, oil wells, professional sports teams, or consumer foods and products divisions.

Whether large or small, the different types of producers have one need in common—the need to understand what their ultimate customer will buy. Only through complete understanding and cooperation can the four levels of the fashion business be aware of new developments in fashion and apply them to satisfy the wants of their customers. This cooperation allows them to have the right merchandise at the right price, in the right place, at the right time, in the right quantities, and with the right sales promotion for their customers.

However, when you begin to try to sell a product or service in our economic system, chances are that someone else will be trying to sell something similar. No matter what the size of the firm involved, potential customers are free to buy where they please and what they please. Each company must compete with the others for those customers' business. A company can choose to compete in one of three ways: price, quality, or innovation.

Competition and Price

Selling blue jeans for less than your competition may bring you more business. However, you are taking in less money than your rival does on each pair sold, and you still have to cover the same cost and expenses. The hope is that your lower price will attract more customers, sell more jeans than your competition, and so come out with a good overall profit. Head-to-head competition like this tends to keep prices down, which is good for the buying public. At the same time, it allows a company to look forward to a promise of profits if it can sell more of its product or service than competitors do (Figure 5.3).

FIGURE 5.3 These three coats are similar in style but different in price: Banana Republic's coat is about $195 (left), the Gap's coat is about $70 (middle), while Old Navy sells its coat for about $40 (right).

Competition and Quality

Rather than sell your jeans for less than your competition, you may choose to compete for customers by offering higher-quality goods. Although you may charge more for your jeans, you offer a better fit, more durable fabric, or better styling. This possibility provides a practical incentive for businesses to maintain high standards and increases the choices available to consumers.

Competition and Innovation

Our economic system not only encourages variations in quality and price, it also encourages immense variety in the types of merchandise and services offered to the public. Changes in taste and new technology bring about innovation, so that your jeans could be trimmed or untrimmed, designer made, or French cut. The economy and the competitive environment are constantly creating new business opportunities. The result is an astonishing diversity of businesses.

Government Regulation of Business

The right of government to regulate business is granted by the U.S. Constitution and by state constitutions. There are two basic categories of federal legislation that affect the fashion industry: (1) laws that regulate competition, and (2) labeling laws designed to protect consumers. Table 5.1 lists the key federal laws that affect and/or regulate the fashion industry.

Forms of Business Ownership

Ownership of a fashion business—or of any business— may take many different legal forms, each carrying certain privileges and responsibilities. The three most common forms of business ownership are the sole proprietorship, the partnership, and the corporation. Corporations tend to be large-scale operations that account for the greatest share of the profits earned by U.S. business. However, sole proprietorships are more numerous, accounting for more than 72 percent of all business.

Each form of ownership has a characteristic structure, legal status, size, and field to which it is best suited. Each has its own advantages and disadvantages and offers a distinctive working environment with its own risks and rewards (Table 5.2).

Business Growth and Expansion

For the past few years, business activity has focused on the change in forms of business growth and expansion.

TABLE 5.1 *Key Federal Laws Affecting the Fashion Industry*

LAWS AFFECTING COMPETITION	PURPOSE AND PROVISIONS
Sherman Antitrust Act—1890	Outlawed monopolies. Outlawed restraint of competition.
Clayton Act—1914	Same purpose as Sherman Act but reinforced Sherman Act by defining some specific restraint—for example, price fixing.
Federal Trade Commission (FTC) Act—1914 (Wheeler–Lee Act of 1938 amended the FTC Act.)	Established the FTC as a "policing" agency. Developed the mechanics for policing unfair methods of competition—for example, false claims, price discrimination, price fixing.
Robinson–Patman Act—1936	Designed to equalize competition between large and small retailers (i.e., to reduce the advantages that big retailers have over small retailers—outgrowth of 1930 Depression and growth of big chain retailers in 1920s.) *Examples of provision of law:* 1. Outlawed price discrimination if both small and large retailers buy the same amount of goods. 2. Outlawed inequitable and unjustified quantity discounts (e.g., discounts allowable if (a) available to all types of retailers and (b) related to actual savings that vendor could make from quantity cuttings or shipments.) 3. Outlawed "phony" advertising allowance monies—that is advertising money must be used for advertising. 4. Outlawed discrimination in promotional allowances (monies for advertising, promotional display, etc.)—equal allowances must be given under same conditions to small and large retailers alike.
Cellar–Kefauver Act—1950	This law made it illegal to eliminate competition by creating a monopoly through the merger of two or more companies.
Product and Labeling Laws Designed to Protect Consumers Wool Products Labeling Act—1939; amended in 1984	Protects consumers from unrevealed presence of substitutes or mixtures. FTC responsible for enforcing law.
Fur Products Labeling Act—1951	Protects consumers and retailers against misbranding, false advertising, and false invoicing.
Flammable Fabrics Act—1954; revised in 1972	Prohibits manufacture or sale of flammable fabrics or apparel.
Textile Fiber Identification Act—1960; amended in 1984	Protects producers and consumers against false identification of fiber content.
Fair Packaging and Labeling Act—1966	Regulates interstate and foreign commerce by prohibiting deceptive methods of packaging or labeling.
Care Labeling of Textile Wearing Apparel Ruling—1972; amended in 1984, 1997	Requires that all apparel have labels attached that clearly inform consumers about care and maintenance of the article.

TABLE 5.2 *Advantages and Disadvantages of Each Form of Business Ownership*

FORM OF OWNERSHIP	ADVANTAGES	DISADVANTAGES
Sole proprietorship (single owner)	• Ability to keep all profits • Simple to form and easiest to dissolve • Ownership flexibility	• Unlimited financial liability • Limited capital • Management deficiencies • Lack of continuity
Partnership (a few owners)	• Ease of formation • Complementary management skills • Greater financial capacity than sole proprietorship • Less red tape than corporation	• Unlimited financial liability • Interpersonal conflicts • Lack of continuity if partner dies • Harder to dissolve than sole proprietorship
Corporation (Inc.) (many owners)	• Limited financial liability • Specialized management skills • Greater financial capacity than other forms of ownership • Economies of larger-scale operation • Easy to transfer ownership	• Difficult and costly form to establish and dissolve ownership • Tax disadvantage • Legal restrictions • Depersonalization

SARAH BURTON: SAVAGE BEAUTY REFASHIONED

SARAH BURTON JOINED Alexander McQueen as an intern while she was still in school. At that time, the fashion house was the talk of London, and its designer, Lee Alexander McQueen, was on the verge of becoming the new couturier at Givenchy. Burton's responsibilities grew as McQueen's small team evolved. After working on menswear, accessories, and footwear, she eventually became design director of womenswear. Burton had never wanted to be in the spotlight, but with that much talent, it was hard not to.

Burton describes the early days of Alexander McQueen as inspiring. She says, "You had the freedom to be creative." Her devotion to McQueen's design vision and to his talented team made her want to take over as creative director. She has since been devoted to honoring and building on McQueen's legacy, even righting some wrongs: "Lee had these incredible shows, but always, under that there were amazing pieces you could wear, but somehow nobody ever believed it was wearable. There's this myth that it's an unwearable house, but that's not true."

Burton maintains that Alexander McQueen will always be centered in "tailoring, incredible dresses, embroideries, prints—and the sexiness of its original designer." She says, "There will always be this McQueen spirit and essence." Yet, she will put her own spin on the designs from a woman's point of view. And what a point of view it's been! Since taking over the helm, Alexander McQueen is on its way to becoming one of the biggest British ready-to-wear brands, with profits of $5.2 million in the first year since Burton took over. And the whole world is noticing Sarah Burton's successes. She was named Designer of the Year at the 2011 British Fashion Awards; received an OBE (Order of the British Empire) from Queen Elizabeth II for her services to the British fashion industry; designed Kate Middleton's wedding gown; and has created dresses for Michelle Obama, Lady Gaga, Naomi Campbell, Gwyneth Paltrow, and Björk.

FASHION FOCUS

Spring 2012

Sarah Burton

Spring 2013

The news media is filled with reports of businesses buying and selling other businesses and seeking new methods to make themselves more efficient and competitive.

One of the most distinct changes in the fashion business has been the rise of corporate giants, which grew through mergers, acquisitions, and internal expansion. The growth of these giants has changed the methods of doing business, and has led to the demise of old-time famous-name sole proprietorships, partnerships, and small companies that could no longer compete.

Growth and expansion are fundamental to today's business world. Corporate growth has become a major economic, political, and social issue in recent years. Growth and expansion can occur in a variety of ways—internal growth, mergers, and acquisitions. Many large corporations grow by more than one of these methods. For example, cosmetics giant Estée Lauder developed the Prescriptives brand to expand to a more upscale consumer market and the skincare line La Mer to appeal to the luxury market. The company also acquired several smaller companies that cater to a younger market, including Bobbi Brown, MAC, and Smashbox.

Internal Growth

A company's ability to grow internally determines its ability to offer more service and broader assortments of merchandise, and to increase profits. This is true because internal growth is real growth in terms of creating new products and new jobs. Internal growth can be accomplished through horizontal means, vertical means, or both. When a company has **horizontal growth**, it expands its capabilities on the level on which it has been performing successfully (Figure 5.4). An apparel company could add new lines to diversify its product offerings; a retail store could open new branches. When a company has **vertical growth**, it expands its capabilities on levels other than its primary function. An apparel company could begin to produce its own fabric or could retail its manufactured goods in stores that the apparel company owns.

Mergers and Acquisitions

In a **merger** (or acquisition), a sale of one company to another company occurs, with the purchasing company usually remaining dominant. Companies merge to form a larger corporate organization for many reasons. They may wish to take advantage of a large corporation's greater purchasing power, or they may want to sell stock to obtain the financial resources needed for expansion. The desire to increase sales is often able to be fulfilled by a merger. At the retail level, for example, the acquisition of the May Department Stores Company

FIGURE 5.4 An example of internal growth is Donna Karan's expansion of its DKNY line.

by Federated Department Stores extended the conglomerate's market. In 2007, Federated Department Stores then changed its name to Macy's Inc.

Operating economies can often be achieved by combining companies. Many times duplicate facilities can be eliminated, and marketing, purchasing, and other operations can be consolidated. **Diversification**, the addition of various lines, products, or services to serve different markets, can also be a motive for a merger. For example, the acquisition of Banana Republic by Gap broadened Gap's market to reach customers for clothing at higher price points. Then Gap started Old Navy to reach to even lower price points. Now the company covers three price points. It also acquired Athleta, a women's activewear apparel company, which helped to expand Gap's online sales and presence.[2]

The Franchise

A rapidly growing business arrangement is the **franchise** (Figure 5.5). This arrangement is a contract that gives an individual (or group of people) the right to own a business while benefiting from the expertise and reputation of an established firm. In return, the individual, known as the franchisee, pays the parent company, known as the franchisor, a set sum to purchase the franchise and royalties on goods or services sold. Franchises may be organized as sole proprietorships, partnerships, or corporations, although the form of business organization that the franchise must use may be designated in the franchise contract.

Franchises are responsible for one in eight jobs in the United States[3] and are steadily growing in volume, according to industry reports. Although the franchise

FIGURE 5.5 Lululemon is a popular designer franchise across the globe.

arrangement is most widespread among fast-food restaurants, convenience stores, and automobile dealers, franchises can be found at many levels of the fashion business, especially in retailing.

The growth in the number of manufacturer-franchised shops is phenomenal. Although we will learn much more about designer-name franchising when we cover the apparel industries, it is important to note this part of the fashion business. For example, Ralph Lauren, Donna Karan, and Oscar de la Renta are all involved in designer-franchised boutiques and shops in major cities throughout the United States, Europe, and Asia.

Advantages

Franchising offers advantages to both the franchisee and the franchisor. The franchisee can get into business quickly, use proven operating methods, and benefit from training programs and mass purchasing offered by the franchisor. The franchisee is provided with a ready market that identifies with the store or brand name, thus assuring customer traffic. The franchisor has a great deal of control over its distribution network, limited liability, and less need for capital for expansion. Expansion is therefore more rapid than would be possible without the franchising arrangement. Royalty and franchise fees add to the profits of the parent company, and the personal interest and efforts of the franchisees as owner-managers help to assure the success of each venture.

Disadvantages

Franchising also has drawbacks for both parties. The franchisee may find profits small in relation to the time and work involved, and often has limited flexibility at the local level. In addition, there is the risk of franchise

arrangements organized merely to sell franchises rather than for their long-range profitability to all parties involved. The franchisor may find profits so slim that it may want to own stores outright rather than franchise them. Attempts to buy back franchises often lead to troubled relations with the remaining franchises.

Licensing

Licensing is an increasingly popular method of expanding an already existing business. **Licensing** is a legal arrangement whereby firms are given permission to produce and market merchandise in the name of the licensor for a specific period of time. The licensor is then paid a percentage of the sales (usually at the wholesale price) called a **royalty fee**. The royalty fee usually ranges from 2 to 15 percent.

Licensing grew tremendously in the late 1970s and continued to increase over the next few decades. Retail sales of licensed merchandise based on fashion labels in the U.S. and Canada were up 6.3 percent in 2011, totaling $18.04 billion.[4] Licensing is an increasingly global business, with the biggest growth opportunities in emerging markets such as Brazil, China, India, the Middle East, and Turkey.[5]

The first designer to license his name to a manufacturer was Christian Dior, who lent his name to a line of ties in 1950. Today, many of the best-known women's and men's apparel designers are licensing either the use of their original designs or just their names without a design for a wide variety of goods, from apparel to luggage. Many fashion labels—Ralph Lauren and Betsey Johnson, for example—also extend into home furnishings through licensing. Among the many American designers involved in licensing are BCBG Max Azria,

Joe (Joseph Abboud), Michael (Michael Kors), Bill Blass, Calvin Klein, Ralph Lauren, and Oscar de la Renta. Most customers are not aware that some of the fashion merchandise they buy is licensed. For example, to customers every Kenneth Cole product is made by Kenneth Cole. In fact, this licensor manufactures no merchandise in house.

The licensing phenomenon is not limited to name designers. Manufacturers of athletic shoes expand their business enormously by licensing their logos and names to producers of active sportswear. Nike, Reebok, and Adidas have been particularly successful. Popular movies and TV shows have spawned apparel and other products based on their themes or characters. Disney saw an 11 percent increase in operating income in the first quarter of 2013, which the company attributes to its merchandise licensing and retail business.[6] Comic or movie characters like Spider-Man, Dora the Explorer, Hello Kitty, and Curious George are also frequently licensed, as are most professional sports teams and many players or athletes. Even the U.S. Army is a licensor. They deal with nearly ninety licensees that offer everything from apparel and watches to cutlery and camping equipment with reported retail sales of more than $30 million in 2010.[7]

The advantage of a licensing arrangement to a manufacturer is that the merchandise is identified with a highly recognizable name, which also generally connotes high quality and produces sales (Figure 5.6). Of course, the manufacturer also risks the designer's popularity fading. However, many manufacturers produce licensed goods for several designers.

The recognition factor can be valuable to retailers in presenting their own fashion image. And to consumers, the designer name not only indicates a certain quality of merchandise but symbolizes status or achievement as well. Because of that built-in appeal, stores have stocked up on designer goods from socks to fragrances and jewelry.

> ### TOP 5 GLOBAL LICENSORS
>
> 1. Disney Consumer Products
> 2. Iconix Brand Group
> 3. Phillips-Van Heusen
> 4. Mattel
> 5. Warner Bros. Consumer Products

FIGURE 5.6 Global retail sales of licensed fashion merchandise has increased over the years. Source: LicenseMag.com, "Global License: The Source for Licensing and Retail Intelligence," May 2011, 14 (2).

Designers' Retail Programs

A famous designer name is a strong selling point at retail. Licensing spreads a designer's name while giving the financial responsibility—and risk—to licensees who are specialists in their respective product categories. For example, Phillips-Van Heusen (PVH), originally a men's shirt manufacturer, today has a portfolio of licensed brands. From designer labels such as Geoffrey Beene, Kenneth Cole, Calvin Klein, DKNY, Joseph Abboud, Michael Kors, and Tommy Hilfiger to those with celebrity appeal, which include the Sean John and Donald Trump licenses, PVH is currently looking into licensing luggage and watches across all their brands.

PVH consumers can shop for their licensed products in more than ninety different countries, including Australia, the Netherlands, France, Denmark, India, United Kingdom, Portugal, China, and South Africa.[8]

Birth of a Fashion

But how do fashions generally begin? Who starts them, who sponsors them, and what influences customers to accept them? Answers to these questions are complex and involve designers, manufacturers, retailers, and—most of all—customers.

The myth that every change in fashion is caused by a designer seeking a new way to make money is, of course, not true. As we saw in Chapter 1, it is consumers who bring about changes in fashion. The needs and wants of consumers change. Their ideas about what is appropriate and acceptable change, as do their interests in life. These are all motives that influence fashion designers and manufacturers to produce new and different styles for consumers' consideration. The charting, forecasting, and satisfaction of consumer demand are the fashion industry's main concerns.

Current trends in consumers' purchasing, lifestyles, and attitudes are noted and analyzed. Subsequently, the trends are interpreted and presented to consumers in the form of new styles. Designers and manufacturers influence fashion by providing an unending series of new designs from which consumers choose how best to express their individual lifestyles.

Many precautions are taken to ensure that designers are presenting what customers want. Even so, at least two-thirds of the new designs introduced each season by the fashion industry fail to become fashions. Some designs are introduced too early, before the public is ready to accept them. Other designs fail because they are too extreme for consumer acceptance. Still other designs fail to become fashions because although they are commonly accepted in many places, they meet pockets of resistance in certain areas of the country. What is worn in New York is not necessarily what consumers in less urban areas of the United States are ready to accept. Only a trend that reflects a nationwide mood will successfully cross the United States from ocean to ocean and affect the lives and wardrobes of all those in between.

The Designer's Role

The days when the design world was populated by a few visionaries whose ideas produced all the designs for the public are long gone. There are now unlimited opportunities in the field of design for those who have the special talents, both artistic and practical, that are needed to shape the consumer's world. Designers are everywhere, and they design everything—fashions, furnishings, housewares, and office equipment. Their tools range from pencil and sketchpad to computer programs.

Designers must continually study the lifestyles of those consumers for whom their designs are intended. Because designers work far in advance of their designs' final production, they must be able to predict future fashion trends. Designers must be aware of the effects of current events, socioeconomic conditions, and psychological attitudes on fashion interest and demand.

In creating designs that not only reflect consumer attitudes and needs but also give expression to artistic ideas, fashion designers are continually influenced and limited by many factors. Of particular importance are practical business considerations. All designs must be produced at a profit and within the firm's predetermined wholesale price range. Consequently, designers must consider the availability and cost of materials, the particular image that the firm wants to maintain, available production techniques, and labor costs. Great designers use their creativity to overcome all these limitations and to produce salable, exciting designs.

Types of Designers

Most designers can be classified in one of the following three categories:

1. *High-fashion or "name" designers* are responsible for the full range of decisions of a fashion house as well as for establishing the image and creating designs for the company. They design ready-to-wear lines as well as custom designs, and many license the use of their prestigious names to manufacturers of accessories, fragrances and cosmetics, and home fashions. Some, like Ralph Lauren in the United States, run houses that bear their own name. Others take over a design company at the death or retirement of its founder. For example, Karl Lagerfeld took over the designing reins at Chanel, in addition to running his own studio.

2. *Stylist-designers* work for manufacturers and adapt the designs of others, typically of name designers. Usually they create variations in less expensive fabrics to appeal to a market for lower-priced merchandise at the late rise or early culmination stage of the fashion cycle.

3. *Freelance designers* sell sketches of their original designs or adaptations to manufacturers. Freelancers typically work out of design studios. They are not involved in the selection of fabrics and colors or in the business decisions required to manufacture the products based on their designs. Donna Karan, now an internationally recognized name designer, got her start designing for Anne Klein.

Insight and Intuition

A designer takes a fashion idea and embodies it in new styles. Even the most creative designers, however, disclaim any power to force acceptance of their styles. Few have said so more effectively than Paul Poiret, one of the twentieth century's great Parisian couturiers. He once told an American audience:

> I know you think me a king of fashion. . . . It is a reception which cannot but flatter me and of which I cannot complain. All the same, I must undeceive you with regard to the powers of a king of fashion. We are not capricious despots such as wake up one fine day, decide upon a change in habits, abolish a neckline, or puff out a sleeve. We are neither arbiters nor dictators. Rather we are to be thought of as the blindly obedient servants of woman, who for her part is always enamoured of change and has a thirst for novelty. It is our role, and our duty, to be on the watch for the moment at which she becomes bored with what she is wearing, that we may suggest at the right instant something else which will meet her taste and needs. It is therefore with a pair of antennae and not a rod of iron that I come before you, and not as a master that I speak, but as a slave . . . who must dive into your innermost thoughts.[9]

Insight and intuition always play a large part in a designer's success. Constant experimentation with new

FIGURE 5.7 Museum exhibitions, such as the Schiaparelli and Prada exhibit at the Metropolitan Museum of Art, often inspire new trends or reinvent old ones.

ideas is a must. As one fashion reaches the excess that marks its approaching demise, a designer must have new styles ready and waiting for the public.

Sources of Design Inspiration

Where does the designer get ideas and inspiration for new fashion? The answer, of course, is everywhere! Through television, the designer experiences all the wonders of the entertainment world. By watching films, the designer is exposed to the influences of all the arts and lifestyles throughout the world. Because consumers are exposed to movies through international distribution, films prime their audiences to accept new fashions inspired by the costumes they see. Museum exhibits, art shows, world happenings, expositions, the theater, music, dance, and world travel are all sources of design inspiration to fashion designers (Figure 5.7). The fashions of the past are also a rich source of design inspiration.

While always alert to the new and exciting, fashion designers never lose sight of the recent past. They know that consumers need to anticipate something new each season. But they also recognize that whatever new style is introduced will have to take its place with what consumers already have in their wardrobes. No one starts with all new clothes each season. Rarely does a revolutionary new style succeed. Instead, it is the evolutionary new style that so often becomes the best-selling fashion.

The Manufacturer's Role

Manufacturers would agree with Dwight E. Robinson that "every market into which the consumer's fashion sense has insinuated itself is, by that very token,

subject to [the] common, compelling need for unceasing change in the styling of its goods."[10]

Even in such mundane items as writing paper, the need for change has produced rainbows of pastels, brilliant deep shades, and the traditional white with dainty or bold prints. Similarly, in basics such as bedsheets or men's dress shirts, the once traditional white has yielded to a variety of colors, stripes, and prints. There is scarcely an industry serving consumers today in which the manufacturer's success does not depend, in part, on an ability to attune styling to fashion interest and demand. A current trend is to hire merchandisers who do market research for the manufacturer, specializing in identifying the correct customer and his or her needs and wants.

Types of Manufacturers

In general, manufacturers of fashion goods can be divided into five groups, differentiated by styling and price.

1. *High-fashion apparel:* This group of designers and firms produces innovative apparel that is very expensive.

2. *Bridge market:* This group bridges the price range between custom designs and high-quality but less expensive merchandise; hence the name **bridge market**. Some high-fashion designers also produce bridge lines.

3. *Better market:* This group is usually identified as the **better market** because its price range is just below that of the bridge lines.

4. *Moderate-priced market:* This group of firms, usually identified as the **moderate-priced market**, sometimes produces originals but usually turns

THE NEW CEO: IT CAN BE YOU

ACCORDING TO MANAGEMENT psychologists, executive recruiters, and consultants, chief executive officers need to be as well-versed in the profit and loss and balance sheets as they are in merchandising, marketing, Facebook, Twitter, Pinterest, and mobile technology. As a result, it has become increasingly difficult to find top talent that not only has the vision, leadership, execution, and interpersonal skills necessary to successfully lead a global organization, but also an understanding of technological supply chain logistics and international know-how.

Fashion companies in particular, and retailing in general, are characterized by a highly entrepreneurial spirit. The leadership model is changing because the brick-and-mortar retailer now has to focus on its brand as well as its Web presence. On top of this, retailing has become a global endeavor. The classic merchant-and-operator leadership mode has to be adjusted to account for this enormous change.

Over recent years, retail and fashion companies have thinned the ranks of management, cutting back on training programs and leadership development programs. Therefore, it is necessary to stay ahead of the game and competition. Skills that have always been in demand are functional ones, such as finance and marketing, and attributes such as leadership, intellect, integrity, and vision. However, in a global economy, new skills are needed—particularly cross-cultural communications. It is also necessary to stay current in education and industry trends. So whom can we hire and train to become the next fantastic CEO? How about you?

out adaptations of styles that have survived the introduction stage and are in the rise stage of their fashion life cycle.

5. *Budget market:* This group of manufacturers, usually identified as the **budget market**, makes no attempt to offer new or unusual styling. Rather, these firms mass-produce close copies or adaptations of styles that have proved their acceptance in higher-priced markets.

In the field of women's apparel, manufacturers are committed to producing several new lines a year. A **line** is an assortment of new designs with a designated period for delivery to the retailer. Some of these may be new in every sense of the word and others merely adaptations of currently popular styles. Producers hope that a few of the designs in a given line will prove to be "hot"—so precisely in step with demand that their sales will be profitably large.

For the most part, the fashion industries are made up of manufacturers whose ability to anticipate the public's response to styles is excellent. Those who do badly in this respect, even for a single season, usually reap small sales and large losses. Unless they are unusually well financed, they quickly find themselves out of business. In the fashion industry, the survival of the fittest means the survival of those who give the most able assistance in the birth and growth of fashions that consumers will buy.

The Retailer's Role

Although retailers do not usually create fashion, they can encourage or retard its progress by the degree of accuracy with which they anticipate the demands of their customers. They seek out from manufacturers styles that they believe are most likely to win acceptance from these target groups.

Some large retailers work directly with manufacturers and firms at the primary level to develop styles for exclusive sale at their stores. Thus, retailers such as Gap and The Limited can stock only their own labels. Others, such as Federated Department Stores, sell private-label merchandise along with national brands. (We examine the practice of product development by retailers in more detail in Chapter 16.)

Types of Retailers

There are many ways to classify retail firms. However, when firms are evaluated on the basis of their leadership positions, they tend to fall into three main categories.

First, there are firms that are considered *fashion leaders* (Figure 5.8, top). They feature newly introduced

FIGURE 5.8 The different types of retailers include the fashion leaders, such as Neiman Marcus (top); traditional retailers, such as Macy's (middle); and mass merchants, such as Target (bottom).

styles that have only limited production and distribution. These styles, called *designer collections*, are usually very expensive. Examples of these firms include Bergdorf Goodman, Neiman Marcus, and Nordstrom.

A second group, called *traditional retailers*—by far the largest in number—features fashions that have captured consumer interest in their introduction stage and are in the late rise or early culmination stage of their life cycles (Figure 5.8, middle). These styles are from designers' *bridge collections* or from better or moderate-priced manufacturers. Since these styles are usually widely produced by this time, they are most often offered at prices that are more moderate. Examples of these firms include Macy's and Dillard's. The distinction between traditional retailers and fashion leaders is somewhat blurred in that the fashion leaders may also carry "traditional" merchandise, and the traditional retailers may have designer departments.

A third group of retailers, often called *mass merchants*, features widely accepted fashions that are well into the culmination phase of their life cycles (Figure 5.8, bottom). Since fashions at this stage of development are usually mass-produced, mass merchants can and do offer fashions at moderate to low prices. Examples of these firms include J.C. Penney, Sears, and Kohl's. At the low end of the mass market are the *discounters*, such as Walmart, Kmart, and Target.

Fashion Influence

Sometimes, because of their constant and intimate contact with their customers, retailers are so intuitive or creative that they lead their suppliers in anticipating the styles their customers will accept (Figure 5.9). Such retailers accelerate the introduction and progress of new fashions by persuading manufacturers to produce styles that answer an upcoming need or demand. Because of this ability, retailers are doing increasingly more product development for their own customers. (This trend is discussed in detail in Chapter 17.)

However, most retailers simply select from what is offered to them by producers with whom they have been successful in the past. There is a constant flow, back and forth, of information about the styles that the customer is buying. The systems that producers and retailers have today for this purpose are rapid and accurate. Because of these instantly available and

FIGURE 5.10 Retailers can monitor the preferences of their customers based on sales and demand.

accurate records, retailers can monitor sudden or gradual changes in the preferences of their own customers. The variations in what consumers are buying at a particular store are reflected in what the store buys from the manufacturers of fashion merchandise (Figure 5.10). From these manufacturers comes information about customer preferences that flows in several different directions. One flow is back to the retail stores to alert them to trends they may not have noticed themselves.

Retailers can influence fashion by failing to stock styles that consumers are ready to buy if given the opportunity. Conversely, retailers can make the mistake of exposing new styles prematurely. No amount of retail effort can make customers buy styles in which they have not yet developed interest or in which they have lost interest. The more accurately a retailer understands his or her customers' fashion preferences, the more successful the operation will be. And the more successful the operation, the more important the retailer's fashion influence will be.

Summary and Review

The fashion industry is a major business sector in the United States and around the world. It employs people at four levels: (1) producers of materials, such as natural and manufactured textiles, leather, fur, and materials used in decorative trimmings; (2) manufacturers of apparel, accessories, cosmetics and fragrances, and

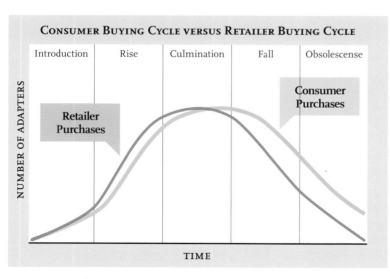

FIGURE 5.9 Retailers have to stay just a step ahead of their target customers. Retailers must have sufficient stock available when customers are ready to buy a new fashion, but they must also avoid being overstocked when customers' interest shifts to a new fashion.

home fashions; (3) fashion retailers; and (4) auxiliary services to the other three levels, including market research and forecasting and promotional services. Businesses at all four levels collaborate to capture their share of the market.

Companies compete with others at their level by offering advantages of price, quality, and innovation. The federal government regulates the production and sale of fashion goods to ensure safe, functional products for consumers and fair marketing practices among competitors.

Like other businesses, fashion businesses at all levels may be sole proprietorships, partnerships, or corporations. Fashion companies grow horizontally by getting into new markets or vertically by expanding into levels beyond the level of their original business. They may expand internally, acquire or merge with other companies, or franchise or license a part of their business. Licensing is an important part of virtually every major designer's business strategy, and businesses outside the fashion industry license their names and logos to apparel producers.

At all levels, fashion business executives must be able to predict the tastes of the consumers who wear and use their merchandise. Depending on level, a company must anticipate consumer demand from six months to more than a year in advance of the day a new fashion becomes available at retail.

For Review

1. What is the primary objective of all businesses? Explain your answer.
2. Describe the four levels of the fashion business; give examples.
3. How does the auxiliary level differ from the other levels?
4. Compare the advantages and disadvantages of a sole proprietorship and a partnership as a form of business for a fashion retailer.
5. Why do companies seek growth through mergers and acquisitions?
6. What are the practical obstacles that limit fashion designers? What additional factors must be considered in developing each fashion design?
7. List the three types of designers commonly serving the U.S. fashion industry today. Give the responsibilities of each.
8. If you were the president of a national chain of shoe stores, what are five laws and regulations that would affect how you do business? Which of these laws would not affect a small, privately owned bridal shop?
9. Differentiate between a license agreement and a franchise.
10. How is a licensed designer name an advantage to the manufacturer? To the consumer? To the retailer?

For Discussion

1. What initial decisions must be made by an individual or group of individuals who plan to form a company with regard to the form of ownership that will be most beneficial to all?
2. What does the statement "You're only as good as your last collection" mean in regard to fashion designers?

Trade Talk

Define or briefly explain the following terms:

auxiliary level
better market
bridge market
budget market
diversification
franchise
horizontal growth
licensing
line
merger
moderate-priced market
primary level
profit
retail level
royalty fee
secondary level
vertical growth

Unit Two
THE PRIMARY LEVEL: THE MATERIALS OF FASHION

All good stories have a terrific beginning. So it is with fashion—all good fashions have good beginnings. They are the fibers, fabrics, leather, and fur industries known in fashion as the primary markets. In this unit, you will examine the primary market suppliers—the growers and producers of the raw materials of fashion. You will begin to develop a basic vocabulary and a working knowledge of the following:

- Chapter 6: The history, manufacturing, and uses of natural and manufactured fibers.
- Chapter 7: The history, processing, and politics of manufacturing leathers and furs.

The earliest part of the planning function—in both color and texture—takes place on the primary level. It is also the level of the fashion business that works the furthest in advance of the ultimate selling period for the finished goods. The primary level is the foundation upon which the merchandisers and marketers of fashion products build their ideas and designs that will answer the needs and wants of the consumer.

Chapter Six
TEXTILES: FIBERS AND FABRICS

KEY CONCEPTS

- The difference between natural fibers and manufactured fibers
- The major steps in the production of most fabrics
- The effect of imports on the U.S. fiber and fabric industries
- The effects of new technology on textiles
- "Going green" with fibers and fabrics

So important is the material or fabric a garment is made of that Christian Dior, the world-famous haute-couture designer, once said of it, "Fabric not only expresses a designer's dream, but also stimulates his own ideas. It can be the beginning of an inspiration. Many a dress of mine is born of the fabric alone."[1]

The enormous appeal of fabric—and the fibers of which it is composed—lies in its many varied textures, finishes, uses, and colors. These are created, as we shall learn, by the fiber and fabric industries, which work closely together to produce an end product, called fashion textiles.

The production of fiber and fabrics is the first step in the manufacture of clothing, accessories, and home fashions. The makers of **trimmings** are also at the primary level of the fashion business. (Other primary suppliers who create fur and leather are explored in Chapter 7.)

The Fiber Industry

A **fiber**—an extremely fine, hairlike strand almost invisible to the eye—is the smallest element of a fabric. It is also the starting point of a fabric. Fibers can be spun or twisted into continuous threads called **yarn**, and yarns can be knitted, woven, or bonded into **fabrics**. Although tiny, fibers have enormous influence on fashion. They are what give a fabric its color, weight, texture, and durability.

Fibers are either natural or manufactured. **Natural fibers** are found in nature; that is, they come from plant or animal sources. In contrast, **manufactured fibers** are made in a chemist's laboratory. They may be made from substances that occur in nature, such as wood pulp, air, petroleum, or natural gas, but these natural substances must be converted into fibers before they can be made into fabric. Manufactured fibers are sometimes called *man-made* or *synthetic* fibers. Because manufactured fibers are invented in the laboratory, they are more plentiful than natural fibers. Currently, twenty-five manufactured fibers are available. Some of the manufactured fibers whose names you may recognize are rayon, nylon, acetate, acrylic, spandex, and polyester.

History and Development

The use of natural fibers is ancient, whereas most of the manufactured fibers have been invented in the past sixty-five years. Despite their relatively short life span, however, very rapid advances have been made in the use of manufactured fibers. In contrast, the natural fiber industry has developed much more slowly. In fact, many of the recent developments in natural fibers are actually advances made in the manufactured fiber industry that were transferred to the natural fiber industry.

Natural Fibers

The use of natural fibers predates written history. Prehistoric humans are known to have gathered flax, the fiber in linen, to make yarns for fabrics (Table 6.1). There are four major natural fibers: cotton, wool, silk,

FIGURE 6.1 Ostrich feathers, a natural luxury animal fiber, are used in high-fashion apparel.

TABLE 6.1 *Natural Luxury Animal Fibers*

NAME	SOURCE	CHARACTERISTICS AND USES
Alpaca	Member of llama family found in Andes Mountains in South America	Fine, hollow-core fleece; annual shearing yields 6–12 lbs of fibers; 22 natural shades; strongest, most resilient wool; scarce
Angora	Rabbit hair	Soft fiber; dyes well; sheds easily
Camel hair	Camel	Usually left in natural tones; used in coats, jackets, artists' brushes
Cashmere	Kashmir goat (60% found in China but also bred in United States)	Rare (1/100 of wool crop); sheared annually; one goat produces enough for one-quarter of a sweater
Goose down (often mixed with feathers to cut cost)	Goose	Most compressible insulation; lightweight warmth for jackets, with goose vest, comforters, pillows, sleeping bags, feather beds
Llama	Llama found in Andes Mountains of South America; United States, Canada, Australia, and New Zealand	Coarser, stronger than alpaca; used in utilitarian items such as sacks
Marabou	African marabou stork or turkey	Soft, fluffy material from feathers
Mohair	Angora goat, originally from Turkey, now from South Africa, Texas, and New Zealand	Twice-yearly shearing; 2 1/2 times as strong as wool; less allergenic than sheep's wool
Ostrich feathers	Ostrich	Used in high-fashion apparel, feather dusters
Pashmina	Mountain goats from Himalayas	Softer than cashmere; fiber equivalent to merino
Qiviut	Musk ox down from Canada, Alaska	Natural taupe color; soft, light, 8 times warmer than sheep's wool; rare ($20–$25/oz)
Vicuna	Rare llama-like animal from Peru	World's finest natural fiber

FIGURE 6.2 A textile worker weaves cotton into cotton fibers on a traditional multiple-harness frame loom.

FIGURE 6.3 Yiqing Yin's colorful silk dress flows down the runway.

and flax (linen). Two other natural fibers are ramie and hemp. In addition, there are many other natural fibers that are in short supply and therefore limited to luxury items (Table 6.1 and Figure 6.1).

Cotton, the most widely used of all the natural fibers, is the substance attached to the seed of a cotton plant (Figure 6.2). Cotton fibers are composed primarily of cellulose, a carbohydrate that especially lends itself to the manufacture of fibrous and paper products. Cotton fibers are soft, comfortable, absorb moisture quickly, and have a cooling effect that makes cotton a good fiber for hot or warm weather. Cotton is also strong and durable. Usually the fluffy cotton boll is white, but new growing methods have brought about naturally colored cotton. This new cotton can be grown in at least twenty-two colors, thus reducing the need for dyes. Long and extra-long cotton fibers (or staple) produce the finest fabrics. When it comes to the export of raw cotton, the United States is the leader, accounting for over one-third of the global trade.[2] While more than eighty countries produce cotton, China, India, and the United States account for two-thirds of its total production.[3]

Wool is the fiber that forms the coat of sheep. Sheep produce one of the few replenishable natural commodities. Shear a sheep's coat time after time, and it quickly grows a new one. An animal fiber, wool is composed mostly of protein. Wool fiber is a natural insulator and is used to make warm clothes. Wool fiber, in fact, has a natural crimp that is ideal for the production of bulky yarns that trap air to form insulating barriers against the cold. Wool absorbs moisture more slowly and dries more slowly than cotton. A lightweight summer wool has been developed to be machine washable.

Silk comes from the cocoon formed by a silkworm. The silkworm forces two fine streams of a thick liquid out of tiny openings in its head. These streams harden into filaments, or fibers, upon contact with the air. Silk, best known for its luxurious feel, is a breathable fabric that can be worn year-round (Figure 6.3). For many years silk required dry cleaning, but much of today's silk is washable.

Flax, used to make linen, comes from the stem of a flax plant (Figure 6.4). Only after the flax fiber is spun into yarn and woven or knit into fabric is the product called **linen** (Figure 6.5). Flax is the strongest of the vegetable fibers (it is twice as strong as cotton), and like cotton, it absorbs moisture and dries quickly. These features make linen an excellent fabric for warm-weather apparel. However, even with new technology that makes linen less apt to wrinkle, it still has a tendency to wrinkle and is harder to iron than cotton. Flax

FIGURE 6.4 The stem of this flax plant is used to make linen.

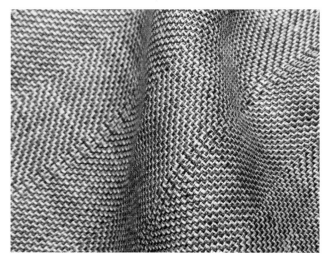

FIGURE 6.5 Flax fiber is spun into yarn and woven or knit to create this lightweight linen look.

is grown in many parts of the world, but top-quality flax is primarily grown in Western Europe.

Ramie comes from a woody-leafed Asian plant grown mostly in China. It has been available in the United States only since 1979, when the United States and China reopened trade with each other. A linen-like fabric suitable for warm-weather apparel, ramie is also inexpensive.

Hemp is a fibrous plant with an interesting history in the United States. It was an agricultural staple in America for hundreds of years. In fact, the Declaration of Independence was written on hemp paper. The crop was so important then that three colonies had laws requiring farmers to grow hemp. Today, it is illegal to grow hemp under federal law in the United States. Raising it in the United States (and most industrialized nations) has been illegal since 1938, because lawmakers feared that growers would plant illegal marijuana, which looks very similar to industrial hemp (although industrial hemp lacks hallucinatory power), making

the illegal weed harder to find. Imports of finished hemp garments are allowed, however, and demand is soaring. Not only are its ecological, or "green," properties high selling points, but its aesthetic, comfort, and performance have made it a very popular and viable fiber for home furnishings and fashion.[4]

Manufactured Fibers

Manufactured or synthetic fibers have been improving the quality of our lives since rayon, the first synthetic fiber, went into production in 1910. Since then, many other manufactured fibers have been introduced in thousands of new apparel, upholstery, and industrial applications (Table 6.2).

Manufactured fibers offer a variety of characteristics that are mostly unavailable in natural fibers. Each year, manufactured fibers find new uses in our wardrobes, homes, hospitals, and workplaces. Designers like Armani, Calvin Klein, and Joseph Abboud all use high-tech, stretch, and classic fabrics to illustrate the constant innovation of their product lines.

All manufactured fibers start life as thick liquids. Fibers of continuous, indefinite lengths are produced by forcing the liquid through the tiny holes of a mechanical device called a **spinnerette** (Figure 6.6). This is similar to the way pasta dough is pushed through a pasta machine to make spaghetti.

Fibers are then cut into short lengths and spun into yarn, as is the case with natural fibers, or they are chemically processed into yarn directly. In the latter case, the production of fiber and yarn occurs simultaneously.

There are two basic types of manufactured fibers: cellulosic and noncellulosic.

FIGURE 6.6 Manufactured fibers of varying lengths are produced by forcing thick liquids through the tiny holes of a device known as a spinnerette.

TABLE 6.2 *Manufactured Fibers*

Date	Fiber	First Commercial Production
1910	Rayon	Rayon fiber was the first manufactured fiber. The first commercial production of rayon fiber in the United States was in 1910 by the American Viscose Company. By using two different chemicals and manufacturing techniques, two basic types of rayon were developed: viscose rayon and cuprammonium rayon. Today, only viscose rayon is produced in the United States.
1924	Acetate	The first commercial production of acetate fiber in the United States was in 1924 by the Celanese Corporation.
1938	Nylon	The first commercial production of nylon in the United States was in 1939 by the E. I. Du Pont de Nemours & Company, Inc. It is the second most-used manufactured fiber in this country, behind polyester.
1950	Acrylic	The first commercial production of acrylic fiber in the United States was in 1950 by E. I. Du Pont de Nemours & Company, Inc.
1953	Polyester	The first commercial production of polyester fiber in the United States was in 1953 by E. I. Du Pont de Nemours & Company, Inc. Polyester is the most used manufactured fiber in the United States.
1954	Triacetate	The first commercial production of triacetate fiber in the United States was in 1954 by the Celanese Corporation. Domestic triacetate production was discontinued in 1985.
1959	Spandex	The first commercial production of spandex fiber in the United States was 1959 by E. I. Du Pont de Nemours & Company, Inc. It is an elastomeric manufactured fiber (able to stretch at least 100 percent and snap back like natural rubber). Spandex is used in filament form.
1961	Polyolefin/ polypropylene	The first commercial production of an olefin fiber manufactured in the United States was by Hercules Incorporated. In 1966, polyolefin was the world's first and only Nobel Prize–winning fiber.
1993	Lyocell	The first commercial production of lyocell in the United States was in 1993 by Courtaulds Fibers, under the Tencel trade name. Environmentally friendly, lyocell is produced from the wood pulp of trees grown specifically for this purpose. It is specially processed, using a solvent spinning technique in which the dissolving agent is recycled, reducing environmental effluents.
2002	Polyatide	The first commercial production of PLA in the United States was in 2002 by Cargill Dow Polymers. PLA is a plastic derived from natural plant sugars, bridging the gap between natural fibers and conventional synthetic fibers.

NYLON	RAYON	POLYESTER

Source: Adapted from Fabric Link/Fabric University, www.fabriclink.com/University/History.cfm, and www.Fibersource.com.

Cellulosic Fibers

Cellulose, the same fibrous substance found in the natural fibers of plants, is also used to manufacture **cellulosic fibers**. The cellulosic fibers are made with a minimum of chemical steps. They include rayon, acetate, triacetate, and Lyocell. (Triacetate is now produced only in small quantities in Europe.) The cellulose used to make these fibers comes mostly from soft woods, such as spruce.

Noncellulosic Fibers

Petroleum, coal, natural gas, air, and water are used to make **noncellulosic fibers**. They are produced from various combinations of carbon, hydrogen, nitrogen, and oxygen. Fiber chemists working in laboratories link the molecules into long chains called **polymers**. Nylon, acrylic, and polyester (Figure 6.7) are in this category.

FIGURE 6.7 Carmen Marc Valvo's embellished silk organza and polyester gown has a flattering drape that is luxurious and breathable.

Levi's Vintage Denim

DKNY Denim 1991

Calvin Klein Jeans

DENIM THROUGH THE DECADES:
THE AMERICAN WAY—JEANS

ALTHOUGH JEANS HAD their roots in Europe, they found their true home in America. Fashion historians agree that jeans came to the U.S. not long after the country declared its independence from Great Britain, giving them an American life span as well as an American heritage.

Jeans spent their first 150 years in America as a rugged workhorse. In the West, gold prospectors and ranch hands took to the sturdy bottoms, which were just as popular among farmers and factory workers in the East. But jeans were destined for a larger role than the workwear function that originally was assigned to them.

Bavarian immigrant Levi Strauss expanded his San Francisco business in 1873 during the California Gold Rush with riveted workpants made from denim with a button front. These pants remain in fashion today as Style 501. Enterprises similar to Levi's developed in other parts of the country. The Mercantile Co. in Salina, Kansas, introduced a fly-front jean in the 1920s, and Wrangler Jeans in North

Carolina debuted styles that appealed to cowboys in the 1940s.

Looking for a piece of the denim action, retailers rushed to capitalize on the trend. Real estate executive Donald Fisher built a specialty store business dedicated to selling Levi's. The Gap, named for the growing divide between the generations, opened in San Francisco in 1969 and would eventually grow into the largest U.S.-based specialty store.

Once the basic jean makers laid the foundation, fashion designers rushed in, armed with sexier fits, alternative looks, and—beginning in the late 1970s— big advertising budgets. Calvin Klein, Jordache, Sasson, Gloria Vanderbilt, Guess, and Sergio Valente were among the first to put marketing muscle behind their "designer jeans," pushing retailers to buy in and avail themselves of presold customers. Since then, jeans have evolved from dark washes to faded and worn, to color and novelty—only to return to their darker, more basic roots today. What began as a relatively small trend has endured. Jeans are worn everywhere from the office to the opera these days.

TABLE 6.3 *Generic Names and Trade Names of Manufactured Fibers Used in the United States*

GENERIC NAME	TRADENAMES
Acetate	Celanese, Chromspun, Estron, Microsafe
Acrylic	Acrilan, Bio Fresh, Bounce-Back, Creslan, Cystar, Cystar AF, Duraspun, Fi-lana, Pil-Trol, Sayelle, So-Lara, Smart Yarns, Wear-Dated, Wintuk
Aramid	Kevlar, Nomex
Lyocell	Lenzing Lyocell, Tencel
Modacrylic	SEF Plus
Nylon	A.C.E., Anso, Antron, Assurance, Avantige, Cantrece, Capima, Caplana, Caprolan, Captiva, Cordura, Creme de Captiva, Crepeset, DuraSoft, DyeNAMIX, Eclipse, Hardline, Hydrofil, Hytel, Matinesse, Microsupplex, No Shock, PowerSilk, Resistat, Shimmereen, Silkey Touch, Solution, Sportouch, Stainmaster, Stay Gard, Supplex, Tactel, Tru-Ballistic, Ultra Image, Ultra Touch, Ultron, Wear-Dated, Wellon, Wellstrand, WorryFree, Zefsprot, Zeftron
Olefin	Alpha, Essera, Impressa, Inova, Marvess, Patlon III, Polystrand, Spectra, Synera, Trace
Polyester	A.C.E., Ceylon, Comfort Fiber, Compet, Coolmax, Corebond, Dacronfi, ESP, Fortrel, Hollofi, Kodaire, Kodel, KodOfill, KodOsoff, Pentron, Premafill Plump, Premafill Soft, Trevira, Trevira Finesse, Trevira Microness, Universe
PBI	PBI Logo
Rayon	Beau-Grip, Fibro, Galaxy
Spandex	Lycra
Sulfar	Ryton

Adapted from www.fibersource.com. Washington, D.C.: American Fiber Manufacturers Association.

Generic Names for Manufactured Fibers

The Federal Trade Commission has assigned **generic names**, or nontrademarked names, to twenty-five manufactured fibers. Within any of these broad generic categories, fiber producers can modify the composition to produce a new fiber, called a **variant**. The variant is then given a brand name by the producer. There are hundreds of **brand names**, or trademarks, that are registered with the U.S. Patent Office; only the manufacturer of a variant is allowed to use the registered name. For example, polyester is the generic name, and Dacron is the DuPont trademark for polyester (Table 6.3).

The properties of these fibers greatly influence the behavior of the finished fabric made from them. Polyester, for example, is strong and wrinkle-resistant, which contributes to its durability and washability. Once scorned as the dull material of inexpensive leisure suits, today's polyester has the subtle sheen of fine silk.

Microfibers

A major technological breakthrough occurred in 1989 with the first commercial production of microfiber in the United States by DuPont. A **microfiber** is a fiber that is two or three times smaller than a human hair— smaller than wool, cotton, or silk fibers (Figure 6.8).

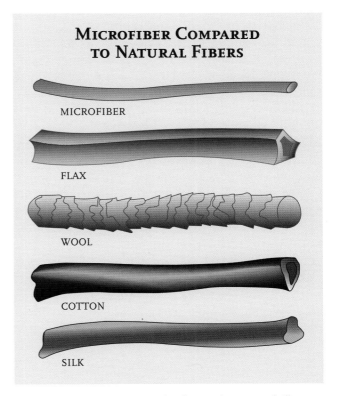

MICROFIBER COMPARED TO NATURAL FIBERS

MICROFIBER

FLAX

WOOL

COTTON

SILK

FIGURE 6.8 A microfiber compared to flax, wool, cotton, and silk.

FIGURE 6.9 Gore-Tex fabric is known for extreme weather protection that keeps the wearer dry and comfortable.

Microfiber is the thinnest and finest of all manufactured fibers. It has a touch and texture similar to silk or cashmere, but is wrinkle-resistant and can usually be machine washed and dried. Microfiber is produced in a number of manufactured fibers—for example, nylon, acrylic, and polyester. Designers use it widely in women's wear, menswear, activewear, outerwear, and home furnishings (Figure 6.9).

Organization and Operation

Because of the differences in the origin and characteristics of fibers, each industry—the natural fiber industry and the manufactured fiber industry—is organized along different lines.

The Natural Fiber Industry

Cotton is produced in four major areas of the United States: the Southeast; the Mississippi Delta; the Texas–Oklahoma panhandle; and New Mexico, Arizona, and California.

Nearly all cotton growers sell their product in local markets, either to mill representatives or, more typically, to wholesalers. The cotton wholesalers bargain at central markets in Memphis, New Orleans, Dallas, Houston, New York, and Chicago.

The wool produced in the United States comes from relatively small sheep ranches in the western states. Boston is the central marketplace for wool, both domestic and imported. Additionally, the U.S. military and the export market are integral to the livelihood of domestic producers of wool.[5]

Linen, silk, and ramie are not produced in any great quantities in the United States. Like hemp, these fibers are imported from foreign sources.

The natural fiber industry in the United States has been greatly affected by the advent of manufactured fibers. The ability to tailor the manufactured fibers to the demands of the ever-changing marketplace has forced the natural fiber industries to become more attuned to the needs of their customers. To compete, the natural fiber industries have become more aggressive about developing new uses for their products and have aggressively promoted themselves. Cotton, usually a warm-weather fiber, is now promoted as a year-round fiber, largely through the use of heavier cotton fibers used to make cotton sweaters. And wool, usually designed for cold-weather wear, is now being treated to make new, lightweight fibers suitable for year-round wear. Through advanced technology and innovative chemical processing, many natural fibers are treated with special finishes to give them care-and-wear properties equal to those of manufactured fibers.

The Manufactured Fiber Industry

Obviously, climate and terrain have nothing to do with the production of a manufactured fiber. Indeed, chemical plants are extremely adaptable, requiring only supplies of raw chemicals, power, and labor. Chemical companies have thus erected their plants in every part of the United States—up and down the East Coast, in the South, the Midwest, and increasingly on the West Coast. Operations are located wherever companies have found raw materials or railroads and waterways for convenient shipment of those materials. Most of these plants are huge.

With manufactured fibers, it is also possible for the producing plant to serve as its own market. It purchases fibers from chemical companies, spins them into yarn, and then knits or weaves the yarn into fabric. International Textile Group is one of the giants that consolidate all operations, from spun yarn manufacture to finished fabric.

Fiber Production

Limited quantities of a new or modified manufactured fiber are usually first produced in a pilot plant on an experimental basis. If research indicates that both industry and consumers will accept the new product, mass production begins. New applications of the fiber are then explored and new industries are consulted and encouraged to use it.

While this procedure is going on in one chemical company, there is always the possibility that another company may be working along similar lines to develop a competitive fiber. The company that is first to develop a new fiber has no assurance that it will have the field to itself for long. There are many brands of such manufactured fibers as nylon, rayon, and acetate on the market, and a roster of companies is producing various acrylics and polyesters (Table 6.3).

The fierce competition among various producers of manufactured fibers is tied to the fact that in one

FIGURE 6.10 Even unbranded fibers must be carefully identified on labels, along with International Care Symbols, bar codes, and, of course, the manufacturer's name and logo.

season, a need may arise for fiber that is stretchable, offers warmth without weight, and is also wrinkle-resistant. Armed with a list of customer preferences, competing laboratories go to work to develop new products. It is no wonder that several of them come up with the same answer at the same time.

Under the Textile Fibers Products Identification Act of 1960, consumer products that use textile fibers are required to label their products by the country where the fibers are processed or manufactured and by the generic names and percentages of each fiber that is used, assuming that it is more than 5 percent, in order, by weight (Figure 6.10). Brand names or trademarks may also be used on the label, but they are not required by law.

Fiber Distribution

Producers of manufactured fibers sell their fibers to fabric manufacturers in one of three ways:

1. As unbranded products, with no restrictions placed on their end use and no implied or required standards of performance claimed
2. As branded or trademarked fibers, with assurance to consumers that the quality of the fiber has been controlled by its producer, but not necessarily with assurance as to either implied or required standards of performance in the end product
3. Under a licensing agreement, whereby the use of the fiber trademark is permitted only to those manufacturers whose fabrics or other end products pass tests set up by the fiber producer for their specific end uses or applications

Licensing programs set up by different fiber producers and by processors of yarn vary considerably in scope. The more comprehensive programs entail extensive wear testing to back up the licensing agreement. The fiber and yarn producers exercise considerable control over fabric products that have been licensed, sometimes specifying blend levels, and offer technical services to help correct a fabric that fails to pass a qualifying test. The trademarks used under such licensing agreements are referred to as **licensed trademarks**. Fiber Industries' Fortrel is an example of a licensed trademark.

Merchandising and Marketing

No matter how familiar producers and consumers may be with the qualities of each fiber, there is always the need to disseminate information about the newest modifications and their application to fashion merchandise. To do this, producers of both natural and manufactured fibers make extensive use of advertising, publicity, and market research. They also extend various customer services to manufacturers, retailers, and consumers.

The American Fiber Manufacturers Association, Inc. is the trade association for U.S. companies that manufacture synthetic and cellulosic fibers. The industry employs twenty-seven thousand people and produces more than six billion pounds of fiber in the United States.[6]

So that they can better promote their new products (and themselves), the natural fiber industries also have organized trade associations that carry their messages to the textile industry as well as to the customer (Table 6.4).

TABLE 6.4 *Natural Fiber Trade Associations*

FIBER	ORGANIZATION
Cotton	Cotton Incorporated National Cotton Council
Linen	Masters of Linen (European)
Mohair	The Mohair Council of America
Wool	America Wool Council The Woolmark Company

Source: Hemp Industries Association, 1999. Available at www.thehia.org.

COLUMBIA SPORTSWEAR:
A DIFFERENT KIND OF ADVENTURE IN FIBERS, FABRICS, AND FASHION

COLUMBIA SPORTSWEAR KNOWS a thing or two about adventure. The outdoor apparel brand has been in business for more than seventy years, developing new and better products that help improve the way its customers enjoy the outdoors. For eleven consecutive seasons, this company of innovators has launched apparel technology that ranges from shirts that repel bugs to boots that feature rechargeable heating systems.

Columbia Sportswear's ingenuity continues today as it focuses on new ways to deliver products that promote comfort and increase performance. Three new developments—Omni-Freeze ICE, Omni-Wick EVAP, and Omni-Wind Block—resulted from studying the body's natural thermal regulation process. Omni-Freeze ICE capitalizes on the sweat that your body naturally produces to deliver "aggressive heat management," says Woody Blackford, vice president of global innovation. "The moment the moisture hits the fabric's surface the temperature of the fabric is lowered, creating an immediate cooling sensation," he says.

Omni-Wick EVAP is a wicking technology that proactively manages sweat and moisture. EVAP uses moisture management technology that disperses sweat across a broad surface, allowing moisture to spread out and evaporate quickly. The company's launch of Omni-Wind Block offers a technology that provides protection from one of "nature's harshest invisible obstacles." "Wind chill can substantially lower the perceived air temperature, making you even colder in windy conditions," says Blackford. Omni-Wind Block styles, including the Triteca Softshell, feature a technologically advanced membrane that provides ultra-breathable wind protection—the wind chill is kept from coming in, but perspiration is allowed to escape. The technology uses an ultra-light membrane that is windproof, waterproof, extremely lightweight, and breathable.

So say hello to bad weather. Thanks to Columbia Sportswear, you can battle the outdoors while maintaining comfort.

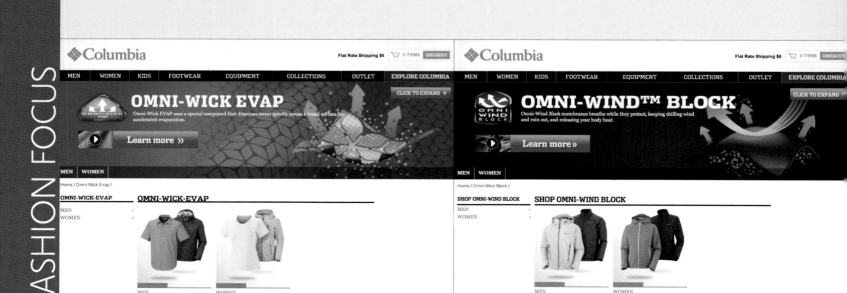

FASHION FOCUS

FIGURE 6.11 Invista uses advertising to promote their swimwear products that have Lycra.

Advertising and Publicity

As you might suspect, given their greater potential for competition, the manufactured fiber industries spend considerably more money on advertising than do the natural fiber industries (Figure 6.11). They maintain a steady flow of advertising and publicity directed at both the trade and consumer markets. Sometimes an advertising campaign promotes an entire range of textile fibers; at other times, it concentrates on only a single fiber. Fiber companies give most of their advertising dollars to support the manufacturers who use their fibers.

Some natural fiber groups are putting more effort and money into campaigns to combat the growing domination of manufactured fibers. Because these campaigns are mainly handled by trade associations, they promote the fiber itself, not the products of an individual natural fiber producer. One of the most eye-catching campaigns is that of Cotton Incorporated (Figure 6.12). The ads and posters not only emphasize cotton's advantages as a fiber but also point to the cotton industry's importance in the economy and to cotton's ecological appeal. Cotton Incorporated started a campaign to improve its environmental image and market cotton as a natural fiber.

Fiber sources also provide garment producers and retailers with various aids that facilitate mention of their fibers in consumer advertising, adding to the recognition already achieved by the fiber producer's name, trademark, slogan, or logo. For example, the Woolmark Company encourages the use of its ball-of-yarn logo in producer and retailer advertising of all wool merchandise as well as in displays.

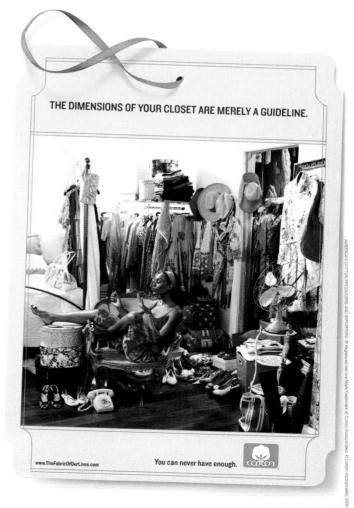

FIGURE 6.12 This campaign from Cotton Incorporated focuses on its products and its importance in the economy.

Fiber industry producers and trade associations continually provide the press with new information, background material, and photographs for editorial features. Some of this publicity effort is accomplished by direct contact with the press; some of it is done by supplying garment producers and retailers with materials they can use for promotion.

Advertising undertaken by fiber producers in cooperation with fabric and garment manufacturers and retailers benefits the fiber industry in two ways. First, consumers begin to associate the fiber name with other names that are already familiar, such as the name of the fiber source or the name of the retail store selling the garment. This is particularly important in introducing a new manufactured fiber. Second, fabric and garment producers, as well as retailers, are encouraged to use and promote the fiber because the fiber producer's share of advertising costs subsidizes its local or national advertising.

Customer Services

All major producers of manufactured fibers and many smaller firms offer a number of services to direct and secondary users of their products. Producers of natural fibers, working through their associations, also offer many such services. These include:

- Technical advice as well as technical know-how on weaving and knitting techniques
- Assistance to textile and garment producers and retailers in locating supplies
- Fabric libraries that include information about sources, prices, and delivery schedules (research in a fabric library saves precious time spent shopping the market for trend information)
- Fashion presentations and exhibits for the textile industry, retailers, garment manufacturers, the fashion press, and occasionally, the public
- Extensive literature for manufacturers, retailers, educators, and consumers about fiber properties, use, and care
- Fashion experts who address groups of manufacturers, retailers, or consumers, staging fashion shows and demonstrations
- Educational films, audiovisual aids, and webinars for use by the trade, schools, and consumer groups

Trends in the Fiber Industry

The most dramatic trend in the fiber industry is the increasing use of blends of natural and manufactured fibers. This trend is discussed in more detail in the next section of this chapter, as is the second most widespread trend, the use of microfibers.

The U.S. fiber industry is fighting hard to overcome a major problem: the encroachment of imports into its domestic markets. Since manufactured fibers account for more than 75 percent of fiber usage annually in the United States, it is evident that this will be a continuing problem. The U.S. fiber industry will have to fight harder than ever for its share of the international and even the domestic market. Added to this challenge is consumers' tremendous interest in "going green" (see page 122).

To many observers, the manufactured fiber story is just beginning, and the next half-century promises to be even more exciting than the previous one. Productivity is expected to increase, with profit levels expected to rise by 3 to 5 percent from 2014 to 2016. There are also fascinating new products emerging from the laboratories. According to *Textile World*, there is growth ahead for all the textile and apparel subsectors—basic mill products, fabricated mill products, and clothing. Additionally, U.S. companies are likely to become even stronger.[7]

The Textile Fabric Industry

Midway between the fiber and the finished apparel, accessory, or home furnishing product is the fabric. **Textile fabric** is any material that is made by weaving, knitting, braiding, knotting, laminating, felting, or chemical bonding. It is the basic material from which most articles of apparel, accessories, and home fashions are made (Figure 6.13).

Americans use a lot of textile fabric. Each person consumes nearly eighty-six pounds of textile fabric annually. We use fabric for clothing and home furnishings: in transportation, industry, defense, recreation, and health care.

The production of most fabrics begins with the creation of yarn from fibers. With the exception of felted fabric and a few other nonwoven fabrics, fibers cannot be made into fabrics without first spinning or twisting them into yarn. Yarns are then woven or knit into greige (pronounced—and sometimes spelled—"gray") goods, or unfinished fabrics. **Greige goods** are converted into finished fabrics for consumer or industrial use.

History and Development

The earliest step toward the mechanization of the textile fabric industry was the introduction of the spinning wheel. Not until the eighteenth century did the British

FIGURE 6.13 A hand-shuttle loom is used by many designers to create unique fabrics.

FIGURE 6.14 Early cotton textile mill.

develop mechanical methods of spinning cotton fibers into yarn. The result of mechanized spinning—large quantities of yarn—increased the need for better looms to weave the yarn into fabric. The first power loom was invented by an English clergyman, Dr. Edmund Cartwright, and patented in 1785. It used water as a source of energy.

In 1813, Francis Cabot Lowell, a New Englander, and a team of Boston merchants built the first successful power loom and the first textile fabric mill in the United States. The demands of a rapidly growing country provided an eager market for the output of American textile mills, and the young industry flourished. Even more automation and mechanization followed (Figure 6.14).

One of the biggest changes in the U.S. textile industry has been the massive shift to shuttleless looms. These looms are much faster and quieter. They are also wider and less likely to break the yarns.

Today it is possible for a single operator to oversee as many as a hundred weaving machines, if the fabric is not too detailed. Similarly, dyeing and finishing plants can produce more than one million square yards of finished textiles per week.

Organization and Operation

For decades, there was no pattern of organization in the textile fabric industry. Some textile fabric companies were large corporations employing thousands of people, but many remained small operations with only a few dozen employees.

Textile mills today are widely dispersed throughout the country. The industry has tended to seek areas where labor and land costs are low. There has also been little advantage in concentrating production in any one area through the construction of giant mills or complexes. Textile mills used to be concentrated in the northeastern states, but today the southeastern part of the country offers cheaper labor and land.

Because commitments to specific weaves, colors, and finishes must be made six to eighteen months in advance, the textile fabric industry is extremely well informed about fashion and alert to new trends (Figure 6.15). Information about these trends comes from fashion designers, predictive services, fashion directors for fiber or yarn companies, and advance textile shows throughout the world. But because they are geared to mass-production methods, most mills were reluctant to produce short experimental runs for individual designers. This is changing as new technology becomes available.

The market centers for textile fabrics are not at the mills but in the fashion capital of the country, New York City. There, on the doorstep of the garment industry, every mill of importance has a salesroom. A fabric buyer or designer for a garment maker, or a retail store apparel buyer or fashion coordinator, does not have to go far to obtain firsthand information on what the fabric market offers.

FIGURE 6.15 Fabrics come in a wide variety of weaves, colors, and finishes and follow the latest fashion trends.

The Converter

It is probably correct to say that the textile converter is the real middleman of the textile industry. **Textile converters** buy greige goods from the mills, have the goods processed to order by the finishing plants, and then sell the finished goods to garment makers. Therefore, textile converters must be on top of trends in colors, patterns, and finishes. They must fully understand fashion and must be able to anticipate demand. Converters work very quickly, because they come on the production scene toward the end of the operation and are primarily interested in the finish and texture applied to the greige goods.

In recent years, converters' know-how has helped U.S. textile producers meet the competition from foreign textile producers, who offer more fashion-oriented goods in small yardages. Converters can supply apparel producers with fewer yards of selected fabrics than can larger fabric mills. The latter must produce tremendous yardages of a designated pattern or design in order to maintain a profitable operation. While many converters are small operators, others, such as Springs Global, are large. As the industry continues to consolidate, the converter function is still important, but it is done within the corporation rather than by an outside firm.

Merchandising and Marketing

Many designers let the fabric act as the creative impetus for their designs. Good designers respond to new fabrics and search for that special fabric that will drape in the way they want or that has just the color or texture they need. It is the job of the fabric industry to introduce designers to the particular fabric needed.

The textile industry works several seasons ahead. Fiber producers usually work two years ahead of a season. They must present their products this early to textile mills and converters so they will have enough lead time to plan their color and fabric lines. The fabric market presents its products a year ahead of a season. Their first presentation is to the manufacturers of apparel and accessories, after which they present their finished products to retail stores and the press—all ahead of season—so they can publicize upcoming trends.

Because the textile industry must work several seasons ahead of consumer demand, it must also take the lead in recognizing new fashion directions.

The Industry's Fashion Experts

To guide them in future planning, textile firms employ staffs of fashion experts. These experts work with textile designers to create fabrics in the weights, textures, colors, and patterns that they anticipate consumers will want. Since most of the early decisions in both the fiber and the fabric market are based on color, the industry's fashion experts also work closely with specialized associations within the fashion industry that provide advance research and trend information.

Most prominent among these groups are the ones that work exclusively with color, such as the Color Association of the United States, the International Color Authority, and Pantone (Figure 6.16). One of Pantone's partnerships includes Clariant International, one of the largest colorant and chemical companies in the world. The Pantone Fashion and Home Color System uses SMART colors, which are more environmentally friendly.

Color forecasting services provide their clients with reports and newsletters, color swatches, palette predictions, and color-matching services—all geared to each of the apparel markets (men's, women's, children's).

In addition to making decisions about color, the fabric industry must also consider fabrication and texture. If the trend is toward structured clothing, firm fabrication will be necessary, but when a soft, layered look is in, fabrication can be lightweight and soft.

Since trends must be spotted so far in the future, the fashion experts play an important role as they work with fiber and fabric mills as well as designers and buyers.

Textile Trade Shows and Fairs

New trends are also introduced at trade shows and fairs held throughout the world. Usually semiannual events, these shows are attended by designers, manufacturers, and retailers. The most important of these shows are the following:

- Interstoff Textile Fair in Asia
- Première Vision (First Look) in Paris, France
- Première Vision Preview in New York
- Ideacomo (Ideas from Como) in Como, Italy
- Pitti Filati (Pitti Yarns) in Florence, Italy
- China (Guangzhou) International Trade Fair for Home Textiles
- China International Trade Fair for Apparel Fabrics and Accessories
- Techtextil India
- Spin Expo in New York City
- TexWorld USA in New York City

The failure to identify and act on a trend seen at a major textile show, for example, would mean that retailers and apparel manufacturers would be unable to supply the fashions that consumers want.

PANTONE fashion color report SPRING 2012

NEW YORK FASHION WEEK • SEPTEMBER 8 – 15, 2011

Tangerine Tango PANTONE 17-1463

Solar Power PANTONE 13-0759

Cabaret PANTONE 18-2140

Bellflower PANTONE 18-3628

Sodalite Blue PANTONE 19-3953

Sweet Lilac PANTONE 14-2808

Margarita PANTONE 14-0116

Driftwood PANTONE 18-1210

Cockatoo PANTONE 14-5420

Nanette Lepore

Starfish PANTONE 16-1120

FIGURE 6.16 Pantone's fashion color report, Spring 2012.

Advertising and Publicity

Unlike fiber producers, fabric manufacturers rarely advertise these days. But when they do, their advertising usually features the brand names of their products and frequently the names of specific apparel manufacturers that use their goods. Either with the cooperation of fiber sources or on their own, these fabric houses run advertisements in a wide variety of mass-circulation and business-to-business magazines and newspapers, sharing the cost of brand advertising run by retail stores. Their advertising generally makes consumers aware of new apparel styles, the fabrics of which they are made, and often the names of retail stores where they may be purchased.

Fabric producers compete among themselves for the business of apparel producers. They also compete for recognition among retail store buyers and for consumer acceptance of products made of their goods. They publicize brand names and fabric developments, and they stage seasonal fashion shows in market areas for retailers and the fashion press. They provide hangtags for the use of garment manufacturers. These tags may bear not only the fabric's brand name but also information relating to its care. In accordance with federal regulation, fabric producers supply manufacturers with the instructions for the required care labels that must be permanently sewn into all garments. Many fabric firms supply information to consumers and the trade press and make educational materials available to schools, consumer groups, and retail sales personnel.

Research and Development

Fabric producers, like fiber producers, now devote attention to exploring the market potential of their products and anticipating the needs of their customers. Success in the fashion industry depends on supplying customers with what they want. Swift changes are the rule in fashion. Anticipation of such changes requires close attention to the market and a scientific study of trends. Market research is used to identify changing lifestyles as well as geographic demands.

Many of the large fabric producers maintain product- and market-research divisions. Their experts work closely with both the trade and consumer markets in studying fabric performance characteristics. Many fabric producers provide garment manufacturers with sample runs of new fabrics for experimental purposes. The market researchers conduct consumer studies relating to the demand for or acceptance of finishes, blends, and other desired characteristics. Such studies

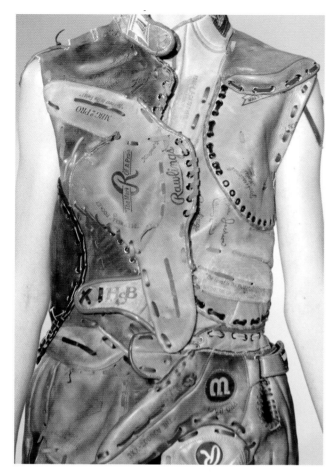

FIGURE 6.17 Maison Martin Margiela's innovative design uses recycled baseball gloves to create an eye-catching look.

also help fabric and garment producers to determine what consumers will want in the future, where and when they will want it, and in what quantities.

The Green Scene

Being eco-friendly in the production of fibers and fabrics is at the forefront of customer concerns. Textile manufacturers are collecting plastic bottles, used clothing, and cotton and wool scraps, then turning them into first-quality garments (Figures 6.17 and 6.18).

The public is being asked to recycle waste, fly less frequently, and drive smaller cars. While textile production uses large amounts of energy, water, and chemicals, the industry has made an effort to reduce its impact on the environment through recycling.[8] After the recycling process, very little is left over to be thrown into landfills. Recycled cotton can be reused as rags or in high-quality paper; wool gets incorporated into car insulation and seat stuffing; and other natural fibers can be used to create building materials, upholstery, and compost.[9]

In 2006, Cotton Incorporated started the Cotton From Blue to Green Campaign (www.cottonfromblue togreen.org). This innovative program encourages consumers to donate their old denim through participating retailers, colleges, and other drop-off locations. The old denim is then recycled into UltraTouch Natural Cotton Fiber Insulation, a product that is used in commercial buildings and residential homes throughout the country.[10] Another example is Gap. In 2010, more than 320,000 denim pieces were collected through Gap stores alone.[11]

Encouraging consumers to buy fewer clothes, choose eco-friendly materials like organic cotton or hemp, wash them less often, keep them longer, and recycle them could dramatically reduce the industry's environmental impact.

Repreve, a company in North Carolina, produces yarns made from 100 percent recycled materials, including reclaimed fabric. Their eco-friendly product meets the same quality standards as polyester or nylon yarns and can be used in everything from dress pants and socks to home and hotel furnishings. Other well-known companies that offer recycling programs include DuPont; Foss Manufacturing Company, Inc.; Polartec; Toray Industries, Inc.; Patagonia; and the Carpet America Recovery Effort.

The U.S. floor-covering industry has responded to the issue of decreasing space in existing landfills. Interface, known globally in the floor-covering industry, set up a carpet recycling program called ReEntry to produce recycled materials from old carpets.

Synthetic Fabrics Going Green

During the 1930s, 1940s, and 1950s, nylon's durability, polyester's UV protection, and spandex's stretch were developed. Activewear textiles have been characterized by their performance capabilities—and their extremely negative impact on the environment—ever since.

Synthetic or man-made fibers are derived from petroleum, one of the earth's finite and most environmentally problematic resources. A fiber called Ingeo offers the best properties of natural and synthetic fibers without the use of petroleum. One of Ingeo's remarkable characteristics is that it is completely biodegradable and compostable. Ingeo completes the cycle of production, consumption, disposal, and reuse.[12]

Today, we have access to a crop of textiles with exceptional properties. Along with a promise to work hand-in-hand with Mother Nature, mills are developing some of the most comfortable, sanitary performance materials ever, including the following:

- Hemp, which is known for moisture absorption, antibacterial properties, and reutilization
- Soy, which has excellent moisture absorption and transmission, making it more sanitary than cotton;

the fiber is versatile enough to make everything from cashmerelike sweaters to faux fur

- Bamboo, a fiber that comes from refined bamboo pulp made of the plant's stems and leaves; bamboo fabrics, which are soft and inhibit the growth of bacteria, are perfect for yoga, aerobics, and activewear[13]

While these original materials are considered more eco-friendly, it is important to note that some manufacturing processes may not be. The overall process and chemicals that are used must be evaluated to determine if the finished product really is green.

Customer Services

Fabric companies speak with great fashion authority. They also employ merchandising and marketing staffs whose expertise in fashion trends is available to apparel manufacturers, retailers, the fashion press, and frequently to consumers. Fashion staffs attend fashion forecasts. They conduct in-store sales training programs, address consumer groups, and stage fashion shows for the trade and press. They help retail stores arrange fashion shows and storewide promotions featuring their products, and they assist buyers in locating merchandise made from their fabrics.

Trends in the Textile Fabric Industry

A dramatic change in the mind-set of the textile producers and marketing managers has broadened the product mix, quickened the response time required to meet customer demand, and made possible shorter runs of more innovative and fashionable fabrics. Currently, retailers, apparel manufacturers, and the fiber and fabric industries are working together to explore new and innovative ways to move textile products through the pipeline to the ultimate consumer more quickly and efficiently.

The role of the textile fiber and fabric industries in the U.S. economy is an important one, and forecasters predict that the consumption rate of textiles will continue to increase. Some of the major trends that affect both the fiber and fabric industries are:

- Global competition
- Increasing exports
- Increased government regulations
- Greater diversification of products
- Environmental concerns
- New technology in equipment

Lifecycle of EcoSpun

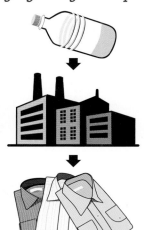

Picked up at curbside and community recycling centers, PET containers are sorted by type and color, cleaned, crushed and chopped into flake.

These tiny pieces are then liquified and extruded from shower head-like spinnerettes creating fibers for crimping, cutting and baling.

The knit or woven fabric is made into a variety of products for apparel and home.

FIGURE 6.18 From garbage to garments: This diagram demonstrates how attractive shirts have been made from recycled plastic bottles.

Global Competition

While a major concern of the U.S. textile industry is the growth of global competition, this has been changing during the past few years. In 2011, textile and apparel imports to the United States fell 8.4 percent, with China, Indonesia, South Korea, Bangladesh, and Pakistan all posting significant declines.[14] Domestic fiber and fabric mills are still adversely affected by overseas competition, as U.S. apparel makers continue to turn to such countries as Vietnam and Mexico for cheap fabrics and labor. The Central American Free Trade Agreement, which passed in 2005, has also helped open the doors for the export market in Central America.[15]

Not surprisingly, another trend, limited to fabric producers, is toward the acquisition or establishment of mills abroad. Such foreign-based mills may be wholly owned by a U.S. firm or jointly owned by a U.S. firm and a host-country firm. Most mills are located close to the fiber sources. The engineers may be American or American-trained, but the rest of the staff are local workers who are paid according to local wage scales. Advantages to the host-country firm are the availability of the facilities, the fashion knowledge gained, the technical skill of the U.S. owners or part owners, and increased employment opportunities for its citizens. By producing some goods abroad, domestic manufacturers

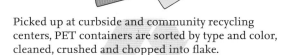

are able to defend themselves against the competition of foreign-made fabrics.

Another trend involves foreign business firms buying into fabric or finishing plants here. Some of these firms are becoming partners in, or sole owners of, new facilities being built in the United States. An example is Hoechst, a West German company that bought Celanese, a major U.S. producer.

Despite these trends, domestic producers, particularly given their closeness to their customers, still have a number of important advantages over importers. They can react more quickly, provide shorter lead time, structure shorter production runs, and in general remove much of the guesswork that used to hinder the industry.

Increasing Exports

The U.S. domestic textile industry has helped boost export numbers for overall goods and services. Textile exports increased 20 percent to $15.2 billion in 2010 compared to 2009.[16] The textile industry continues to direct more of its efforts toward capturing a share of the global market. A number of corporate strategies for the years ahead include the following:

- Increasing the focus on foreign markets and operations for apparel fabrics, since most studies indicate that the major growth in apparel markets will be outside the United States
- Developing overseas and U.S. manufacturing operations, or exploring licensing in conjunction with foreign mills, to attain a stronger foothold on the international scene
- Devoting increased resources to market research and technological advances

According to World Trade Organization statistics, the United States textile industry is the third largest exporter of textile products in the world, primarily exporting yarns and fabrics. Textile exports in 2011 totaled more than $17 billion.[17]

A concern for U.S. companies that want to export to European countries is the ISO 9000 standards. These are a set of international standards that companies must meet to be "ISO certified." These standards are generic and apply to any industry. Basically, in order to be certified, companies must have systems in place to judge quality. Many European companies will not buy from a company that is not ISO certified.

The ISO 14000 was a set of standards that was developed after the success of the ISO 9000. It was designed to assess the need for international environment management standards.

Production of High-Tech Fabrics

We live in a high-tech age, when almost every new product is a result of combined effort and sophistication in research and development. Fabric is no exception, as evidenced by the frequent introduction of new textiles endowed with some novel and valuable property, characteristic, or performance.

A fabric that has been constructed, finished, or processed in a way that gives it certain innovative, unusual, or hard-to-achieve qualities not normally available can be defined as **high-tech fabric**.

Protective Uses of High-Tech Fabrics

Many common fabrics have been transformed into high-tech fabrics (Figure 6.19) by coating or laminating them, or by making them with innovative yarns such as Kevlar, Nomex, Spectra, and so on. These fabrics are engineered to resist extreme temperature changes, or to have superior strength, or to have resistance to radiation, corrosive chemicals, and other stresses.

A bright future is forecast for these high-tech fabrics in a variety of situations:

- *Activewear*—Apparel for running, golfing, cycling, skating, sailing
- *Rainwear*—Raincoats, capes, hats
- *All-weather wear*—Apparel for hunting, fishing, skiing, mountaineering, and so forth
- *Swimwear*—Bathing suits, bodysuits for diving, life vests
- *Protective clothing*—Garments to protect the wearer from hazardous waste; medical contamination; bullets or shrapnel; radiation; cutting or abrasion; electronic, computer, and pharmaceutical manufacture
- *Heat and fire protection clothing*—Occupational clothing for firefighters, blast furnace workers, race car drivers, tank crews
- *Chemical protection clothing*—Occupational clothing for chemical workers and workers at toxic waste sites and spills

FIGURE 6.19 Roxy Athletix's high-performance top keeps you warm while blocking moisture.

FIGURE 6.20 Michael Sontag uses Teflon® coated silk in this sleek design.

Use of High-Tech Fabrics for Apparel

Designers at all price points are incorporating a range of materials besides natural fibers—metallic threads, plastic, vinyl, rubber, and reflective material. In one of his early collections, the late Alexander McQueen attracted a lot of attention when he cut out pieces of lace, backed them with latex, and splattered them on nude chiffon. Gianni Versace had used clear vinyl extensively, as well as a chain-mail fabric that drapes easily. "I have always been in love with antique armors," Versace said. "I wanted to use metal in a dress as though it were fabric." Helmut Lang adopted the reflecting strips commonly found on backpacks, running shoes, and firefighters' uniforms into reflective jeans. Frederic Molenac, designing for the Madame Grès collection, used Lycra with neoprene, a rubberlike fabric. Cynthia Rowley incorporated stainless steel organza into some of her designs. Miuccia Prada uses mostly synthetics in her Miu Miu line; some of her jackets have Velcro fastenings. As the expanding field of new fabrics grows, more and more designers are finding inspiration and aesthetic value in high-tech fabrics.

Greater Diversification of Products

Today, the textile industry produces a more diversified range of fibers and fabrics than ever before. The specialization that once divided the industry into separate segments, each producing fabrics from a single type of fiber, has all but faded. To meet the needs of consumers, it is often necessary to blend two or more fibers into a yarn or to combine yarns of two fibers. Mills are learning to adjust their operations to any new fiber or combination of fibers. The high cost of cotton in recent years has pushed weavers to create alternative fabrics, mixing natural and artificial fibers. Cotton has been blended with linen, viscose, synthetics, and cellulose-based fibers such as Lyocell, Modal, and Tencel.[18]

Another bright spot for the domestic textile market is **geotextiles**, or manufactured permeable textiles that are currently used in reinforcing or stabilizing civil engineering projects. Two examples of industrial fabrics are Kevlar and Tyvek, which are used for diverse applications such as book covers and house wrappings to prevent moisture penetration.

An example of an industrial protective coating is Teflon (Figure 6.20)—yes, the coating used on nonstick frying pans—which is now used to protect delicate fabrics. With fashion designers searching for new fabrics every day, can apparel applications for industrial and geotextiles be far behind?

Increased Government Regulation

One of the biggest impacts on the textile industry in the past decade has been the intervention of the federal government in every aspect of the industry: health and safety, noise levels and chemical pollution, consumer product liability, environmental impact, and hiring practices.

Until recently, federal regulation of the textile industry was mainly concerned with the fiber content labeling of fabrics and products made of those fabrics. In 1953, the Flammable Fabrics Act was passed, but it served to ban from the market only a few very ignitable fabrics and apparel made from them. The increasing strength and direction of the consumerism movement, however, resulted in more government regulation of the textile industry on both the federal and state levels.

In July 1972, two important changes in federal textile regulations took effect: the ruling by the Federal Trade Commission (FTC) on Care Labeling of Textile Wearing Apparel and the revision of the Flammable Fabrics Act. The FTC's care-labeling rule requires that all fabrics—piece goods as well as apparel and accessories made of fabric—be labeled to show the type of care they require. In 1997, the FTC again changed the rules by introducing new care label symbols. They indicate whether

FIGURE 6.21 A textile manufacturing plant.

the fabric can be hand washed or machine washed or should be dry-cleaned. In 2000, this rule was updated to clarify requirements, and the definitions of "hot," "warm," and "cold" water were changed to harmonize with the definitions used by the American Association of Textile Chemists and Colorists (AATCC).[19] The symbols also indicate whether ironing is required, and if so, at what temperature. The manufacturer must sew a permanent label with these care symbols into each garment. Other trends in the textile industry that are a result of government environmental and consumer regulations include the following:

- Fibers and textile products will be made by larger producers with a resulting decrease in the number of small concerns and marginal operations. This will result primarily from the higher production costs related to complying with the new government regulations and the greater capital investment required to stay competitive in a period of continually rising costs.
- Manufacturing operations will function at higher efficiencies, recycling as much material as possible and converting waste to energy.
- New chemical processes will be developed to recover, recycle, and reuse fibers, dyes, and other chemicals.
- Fibers with built-in environmental disadvantages will slowly give way to more suitable replacements, or new processing techniques will be devised to allow their continued use.
- Transfer printing may be an important way to reduce some of the dye-house stream-pollution problems.
- Consumers will be increasingly protected, with particular emphasis on children's apparel and home furnishings.
- Consumers will be better advised on the characteristics of their purchases.

New Technology in Equipment

"New technology is totally revolutionizing the textile industry," says Jack Lenor Larsen, an eminent textiles designer in the home furnishings industry. The trend toward increased mechanization and automation is clearly apparent throughout the industry, as it has changed from one that is labor intensive to one that is equipment intensive.

Over the years, the textile industry has experienced a number of technological developments, such as the shuttleless loom and computer design of fabrics. In the mills, new machines combine higher production speeds with lower energy consumption (Figure 6.21). Automated weaving and knitting machines produce more with fewer operators.

The industry is also experimenting with printing techniques. In the past decade, the use of digital technology has increased in the textile printing industry, and it is growing at the fastest rate among other traditional printing methods. It supports versatility, quick delivery, short printing runs, and cost effectiveness to fulfill the needs of the fast-fashion market. Moreover, it promotes green manufacturing production with less pollution compared with conventional printing processes.[20]

The development of closed-loop production systems, as used by Leipzing Fibers in the production of the cellulosic fibers Modal and Tencel, has also helped reduce waste. "It takes 700 gallons of fresh water to make one cotton T-shirt," says Ann Gillespie, director of Industry Integrity at Textile Exchange.[21] Recently, more innovative systems are being introduced to reduce water consumption and increase dye consumption during the manufacturing process.[22]

Additionally, new technology promotes improved communication among fiber, fabric, apparel, and retail businesses. It shortens the time between the placement of orders by retailers and the delivery of goods. (See Chapter 8 for more information on supply chain management.)

U.S. textile plants are characterized by computer-run looms that feed a mile of yarn per minute, as well as completely automated yarn-spinning plants that can run twenty-four hours a day, seven days a week. Advancements and new equipment are introduced at shows like the SPESA Expo (short for Sewn Product Equipment and Suppliers of the Americas), which is held in Atlanta in conjunction with Techtextil North America and ATME-I Megatex. Other shows include the Garment Technology Expo, ITMA, and the Japanese International Apparel Machinery Show.

Summary and Review

Textiles begin with fibers, which may be natural (cotton, wool, flax, and silk) or manufactured. Manufactured fibers are either cellulosic (made of cellulose, which is also the substance of natural plant fibers) or noncellulosic (made by combining chemicals in a laboratory). Variants of generic manufactured fibers bear the trade name of the manufacturer. For example, Dacron is DuPont's brand of polyester.

The main market for fibers is the textile fabric industry, which weaves, knits, or otherwise turns fibers into greige goods. These goods are then finished by either the textile mill or converters, who add such treatments as dye, waterproofing, fire protection, and permanent-press finishes. Finishes added to natural fibers allow them to compete more effectively with manufactured fibers by taking on some of the properties that consumers demand in apparel and other textile products.

Textiles are sold primarily to manufacturers of apparel and home fashions, but marketing of fibers and textiles is directed at retailers and consumers, too, to build demand. U.S. textile manufacturers compete with foreign imports through technological advances that speed production, minimize pollution, and improve the performance of fabrics in terms of colorfastness, insulation, and other desirable features. New technology and systems expedite order fulfillment.

For Review

1. What is the difference between a natural and a manufactured fiber? Give five examples of each, and indicate the source of each natural fiber you name.
2. What has the natural fiber industry done to counteract the effects of manufactured fibers in the marketplace?
3. Trace the steps through which a new or newly modified manufactured fiber passes as it goes from conception to general availability.
4. Name and explain the three ways in which producers of manufactured fibers usually sell their products to fabric manufacturers.
5. Describe the three major merchandising and marketing activities of natural and manufactured fiber producers.
6. Describe the major steps in the production of most fabrics.
7. What is the function of the textile converter? What are the advantages of dealing with a converter for (a) a fabric mill and (b) an apparel producer?
8. How do textile fabric producers keep informed about new fashion trends?
9. How have increased fiber, yarn, and fabric imports affected the American textile industry?
10. What are the provisions of the Flammable Fabrics Act of 1953 and the FTC's rule on Care Labeling of Textile Wearing Apparel of 1972?

For Discussion

1. What is the role of trade associations in the marketing of fibers and textile fabrics?
2. When a major designer designed his collection for a mass merchandiser, he went directly to the textile mills with specifications for his fabrics in regard to width, pattern repeats, and so on. Can most designers do this? Why or why not?
3. Discuss the relationship of environmentally green fibers/fabrics and manufactured fibers/fabrics by a manufacturer and retail customer.

Trade Talk

Define or briefly explain the following terms:

brand names
cellulosic fibers
cotton
fabrics
fiber
flax
generic names
geotextiles
greige goods
hemp
high-tech fabric
licensed trademarks
linen
manufactured fibers
microfiber
natural fibers
noncellulosic fibers
polymers
ramie
silk
spinnerette
textile converters
textile fabric
trimmings
variant
wool
yarn

Chapter Seven
LEATHER AND FUR

KEY CONCEPTS

- The three major types of companies in the leather industry and their functions
- The nine different categories of leather and the special finishes used on leather
- The history and development of the fur industry in the United States
- The functions of the three major groups in the fur industry
- The steps in transforming fur pelts into finished garments

The most glamorous and sought-after textiles—leather and fur—are also the two oldest. Prehistoric people discovered that the animals they killed for food could serve another purpose, that of providing them with warmth and protection from the elements. One side of an animal skin could be worked into leather; the other furnished fur. Today leather and fur are vital to the apparel, home furnishings, and automotive industries, contributing the raw materials for coats and jackets, handbags, shoes, gloves, and an ever-widening range of fashion products.

The leather industry continues the process of expanding its markets. New processing methods have created leathers so thin and supple that designers can use them for everything from bikinis to shirts to evening wear—all available in an incredible array of colors.

After several years of decline because of environmental concerns over the use of scarce or rare animal skins, furs are making a comeback, especially with the young, first-time customer. The demand for furs has never been greater, at the very time when the fur industry is experimenting with new colors and styles.

The Leather Industry

Making leather is a highly specialized and time-consuming operation. Because of the time involved, the leather industry must anticipate and predict trends far in advance of other textile suppliers. Leather producers typically decide what production method, textures, finishes, and colors they will use eight to sixteen months before a leather reaches apparel and accessory manufacturers. As a result, those in other fashion industries often look to the leather industry for leadership, particularly in terms of color and texture.

Since leather is a by-product of the meatpacking industry, it is not the target of environmentalists as is the fur industry. Few animals are raised specifically for their hides. Most animals are raised to feed people, and their skins and hides, which have no food value, are then sold to the leather trade.

FIGURE 7.1 Working with leather dates back to 1550 B.C. in ancient Egypt. The figure on the left is soaking the hide in a large jar; the figure on the right is stretching and kneading a skin on a trestle to soften it. The figures at the center bottom are cutting a skin with a knife. At the top right is the completed skin of an animal.

History and Development

Archaeologists have found leather thong sandals in the tombs of ancient Egypt. They were the prized possessions of priests and pharaohs more than 5,000 years ago (Figure 7.1). From the earliest times, leather was valued as clothing, but as tanning methods improved, leather became important for armor, helmets, and saddles. In Europe in the Middle Ages, leather was considered a luxury product within the reach of the rich and nobility only.

In the many years that Indian tribes roamed the North American continent, long before the arrival of the first European colonists, the tanning of leather was an important part of tribal life. Indians used deerskins to make clothing, soft yet sturdy moccasins, and tepee homes. By today's tanning standards, their methods would be considered limited and primitive, yet the techniques they used to transform raw animal hides into a variety of products certainly served them well.

In 1623, not long after the arrival of the Pilgrims in Massachusetts, the first commercial tannery in the American colonies was established in Plymouth by an Englishman with the fitting name of Experience Miller. Later, Peter Minuet, governor of New Amsterdam, invented the first machinery used for tanning in the colonies. His invention was a horse-driven stone mill that ground the oak bark then used to convert animal skins into leather.

Many years passed before more important mechanization of the leather industry occurred. But in 1809, a giant step was taken. Samuel Parker invented a machine that could split heavy steer hides twenty-five times faster than people could do it by hand. The machine also produced a lighter and more supple leather: just what people wanted for their shoes, boots, and other clothing.

Today, machines do much of the manual work formerly required to stir hides and skins as they soak. Other machines dehair and deflesh them. Still others split the skins and emboss patterns on them. Machinery has taken much of the human labor out of the processing of leather. In addition, chemistry has provided new tanning agents that reduce the time required to transform hides and skins into leather. These new tanning agents also help achieve a greater variety of finishes. This variety is possible in spite of restrictions on the commercial use of the skins of some animals that have been placed on endangered-species lists.

Organization and Operation

Although tanning was once a cottage industry in the United States, it quickly became, relatively speaking, big business. By 1870, there were over 6,600 small tanneries in the United States. By 1979, only 4,500 tanneries operated in the United States. Like the textile industry, the leather business has been subjected to its share of mergers since the late 1970s. A combination of factors hit the American tanning industry then: overwhelming shoe imports, stronger environmental regulations, and sharply increased exports of hides. As of 2008, there were 673 businesses in the United States "engaged in tanning, currying, and finishing raw or cured hides and skins into leather valued at $1.01 billion." Most are located in California, New York, Texas, and Wisconsin, with Wisconsin producing $646.8 million for the industry.[1] In recent years, the trend toward environmentally friendly products has led consumers to demand faux (or fake) leather instead of genuine leather, hurting revenue. (*Faux* is the French word for "false.") It is projected that the industry will stabilize over the coming years, particularly in the global footwear market.[2]

The American leather industry is divided into three major types of companies: regular tanneries, contract tanneries, and converters. **Regular tanneries** purchase and process skins and hides and sell the leather as their finished product. **Contract tanneries** process the hides and skins to the specifications of other firms (mainly converters) but are not involved in the final sale of the leather. **Converters** buy the hides and skins from the meatpackers, commission the tanning to the contract tanneries, and then sell the finished leather. In recent years, converters have been buying finished leather from both regular and contract tanneries.

The leather industry has remained specialized. Calfskin tanners do not normally tan kidskin, and gloveskin tanners do not work with sole leather.

Like textile producers, most leather firms maintain sales offices or representatives in New York City for the convenience of their customers.

Categories of Leather
Almost all leather comes from cattle. But the hides and skins of many other animals from all parts of the world are also used in fashion apparel and accessories. There are nine major categories of leather (Table 7.1).

The Equine Group
Horses provide a rugged leather. Some horsehide is tanned into cordovan leather, which makes extremely durable and sturdy shoe uppers. The hide is also used for leather jackets. But it is important to know that most of what is called "pony skin" is actually stenciled calfskin, which is used because it is more pliable than real pony skin. Real top-quality pony skin comes from wild horses in Poland and Russia.

The Exotic Leathers
Supplies of the so-called exotic leathers are diminishing worldwide, driving prices up sharply. There is some good news, however. From 1967 to 1987, the American alligator was listed as an endangered species.

Today, the alligator is out of danger because of a policy called **sustainable use**, an environmental program that encourages landowners to preserve alligator eggs and habitats in return for the right to use a percentage of the grown animals.

In a related development, the Native American Ponca Tribe of Nebraska is raising bison (American buffalo) and has opened a tannery in Nebraska to tan the hides with the hair on them to make buffalo robes. They use an environmentally friendly process known as brain tanning, which leaves the hides softer than chemical tanning and makes them easier to sew.[3]

Leather Processing
Animal pelts are divided into three classes, each based on weight. Those that weigh fifteen pounds or less when shipped to the tannery are called **skins**. This class consists mostly of calves, goats, pigs, sheep, and deer. Those weighing from fifteen to twenty-five pounds, mostly young horses and cattle, are called **kips**. Those weighing more than twenty-five pounds, primarily cattle, oxen, buffalo, and horse skins, are called **hides**.

The process of transforming animal pelts into leather is known as **tanning**. The word is derived from a Latin word for oak bark, which was used in early treatments of animal skins. Tanning is the oldest known craft.

Three to six months are needed to tan hides for sole leather and saddlery. Less time is required for tanning kips and skins, but the processes are more numerous and require more expensive equipment and highly trained labor. The tanning process involves minerals, vegetable materials, oils, and chemicals, used alone or in combination. The choice of a tanning agent depends on the end use for which the leather is being prepared.

Tanning Methods
Two tanning methods use minerals. One uses alum; the other uses chrome salts. Alum, used by the ancient Egyptians to make writing paper, is rarely used today. Chrome tanning, introduced in 1893, is still used to process nearly two-thirds of all leather produced in the United States. This is a fast method that takes hours rather than weeks. It produces leather for shoe uppers, garments, gloves, handbags, and other products. Chrome-tanned leather can be identified by the pale, blue-gray color in the center of the cut edge. It is slippery when wet. It is usually washable and can be cleaned by gentle sponging.

Vegetable tanning, which is also an ancient method, uses the tannic acids that naturally occur in the bark, wood, or nuts of various trees and shrubs and in tea

TABLE 7.1 *Nine Major Categories of Leather*

CATEGORIES	HIDES FROM	PRODUCING LEATHER FOR:	
Cattle	Steer Cow Bull	• Shoe and slipper outsoles, insoles, uppers, linings, counters, welts, heels, etc. • Traveling bags, suitcases, briefcases, luggage straps, etc. • Gloves and garments • Upholstery for automobiles, furniture, airplanes, buses, decoration • Handbags, purses, wallets, waist belts, other personal leather goods	• Harnesses, saddles, bridles, skirting (for saddles), etc. • Machinery belting, packings, washers, aprons, carders, combers, pickers, etc. • Footballs, basketballs, volleyballs, and other sporting goods • Laces, scabbards, holsters, etc.
	Kips or kipskins (from large calves or undersized cattle)	• Shoe and slipper uppers and linings • Handbags and other personal leather goods • Gloves and garments • Sweatbands for hats	• Rawhide and parchment • Athletic helmets • Bookbindings • Handicrafts, etc.
Sheep and Lamb	Wooled Skins, Hair Skins (cabrettas), Shearlings	• Shoe and slipper uppers and linings • Gloves and garments • Chamois • Handbags and other personal leather goods • Moutons and shearlings (skins with wool on) • Parchment	• Textile rollers • Hats, hat sweatbands, millinery, and caps • Bookbindings • Piano actions • Sporting goods (balls, gloves, etc.)
Goat and Kid	Goat and Kid	• Shoe and fancy uppers, linings • Gloves and garments	• Fancy leather goods, handbags • Bookbindings
Equine	Horse, Colt, Ass, Mule, and Zebra	• Shoe soles and uppers • Luggage • Gloves and garments • Belts	• Aviator's clothing • Sporting goods (baseball covers and mitts, etc.)
Buffalo	Domesticated Land and Water Buffalo (not American Bison, whose hide is not tanned for their leather)	• Shoe soles and uppers • Handbags • Fancy leather goods, luggage • Buffing wheels	
Pig and Hog	Pig, Hog, Boar, Peccary, Carpincho (a brazilian rodent)	• Gloves • Innersoles, contours, etc. • Fancy leather goods, luggage	• Saddlery and harnesses • Shoe uppers • Upholstery
Deer	Fallow Deer, Reindeer, Elk, and Caribou skins	• Shoe uppers • Gloves • Clothing • Piano actions	• Moccasins • Mukluks • Fancy leather goods
Kangaroo and Wallaby	Skins producing very strong leather	• Shoe uppers, including track and basketball shoes	

Exotic Leathers
  Aquatic
 	
  Land
 	
  Reptile
	• Frog, Seal, Shark, Walrus, and Turtle
	• Camel, Elephant, Ostrich, and Pangolin
	• Alligator, Crocodile, Lizard, and Snake		

CATTLE   GOAT   KANGAROO

Source: Leather Industries of America, *Dictionary of Leather Terminology*, 8th ed. (Washington, D.C.: Leather Industries of America).

leaves. Vegetable tanning is used on cow, steer, horse, and buffalo hides. The product is a heavy, often relatively stiff leather used for the soles of shoes, some shoe uppers, some handbags and belts, and saddlery. Vegetable-tanned leather can be identified by a dark center streak in the cut edge. It is resistant to moisture and can be cleaned by sponging. Vegetable tanning is the slowest tanning method and takes months to complete. Because it is so labor intensive, relatively little vegetable tanning is done in the United States.

It is also possible to combine tanning agents. For example, a vegetable and mineral combination is used to "retan" work shoes and boots. Combinations of alum and formaldehyde or oil and chrome are common. The most widely used and quickest method of tanning relies primarily on formaldehyde.

Processing with oil is one of the oldest methods of turning raw animal skins into leather. A fish oil—usually codfish—is used. Oil tanning is still used today to produce chamois, doeskin, and buckskin—relatively soft and pliable leathers used in making gloves and jackets.

Finishing

The finishing process gives leather the desired thickness, moisture, color, and aesthetic appeal (Figure 7.2). Leather can be dyed in nearly five hundred different colors. Dyed leather is also sometimes finished with oils and fats to ensure softness or strength, or to waterproof it. Special color effects include sponging, stenciling,

FIGURE 7.2 The drying out (top) and finishing processes (bottom) give leather the desired thickness, moisture, color, and aesthetic appeal.

spraying, or tie dyeing. Other finishes include matte, luster or pearl, suede, patent, or metallic. It is important to note that suede is a finish, not a kind of leather. Table 7.2 describes the characteristics of different leather finishes.

TABLE 7.2 *Special Finishes for Leather*

FINISHES	CHARACTERISTICS
Aniline	Polished surface achieved with aniline dyes
Matte (mat)	Flat eggshell-surface look
Luster or pearl	Soft, opaque finish with a transparent glow
Antiqued	Subtle two-toned effect like polished antique wood
Burnished	Similar to antiqued but with less shadowing
Metallic	Surface look of various metals—copper, gold, silver, bronze
Waxy	Dulled, rustic look, as in waxy glove leathers
Patent	Glossy, high-shine finish
Napped	Buffed surface such as in suede or brushed leather
Suede	Leather finish that can be applied to a wide variety of leather
Washable	Waterproof finish that can be applied to some leathers

Source: William A. Rossi, "What You Should Know about Leathers," *Footwear News Magazine,* June 1982, p. 16; and Rohm-Hass, *Leather Technicians Handbook of Furnishings,* 1994.

Merchandising and Marketing

Because of the lead time needed to produce leather, the leather industry not only must stay abreast of fashion, it must be several steps ahead of it. Months before other fashion industries commit themselves to colors and textures, leather producers have already made their decisions. They have started the search for the right dyes and treatments to meet expected future demand. As a result, the leather industry's forecasters are considered the best and most experienced in the fashion industry.

Fashion Information Services

Because the leather industry makes their assessments of fashion trends so far in advance, others in the industry look to them for information. Like other fashion industries, the leather industry retains experts to disseminate information about their trends and new products. They often produce booklets that forecast trends, describe new colors and textures, and generally promote the leather industry. Samples of important textures and looks are included.

Fashion experts also work directly with retailers, manufacturers, and the press to help crystallize their thinking about leather products. One-on-one meetings, seminars, and fashion presentations are used to educate the fashion industry and consumers about leather.

Despite all this activity, individual tanners are not known by name to the public. Nor is a fashion editor, in describing a leather garment, likely to mention its manufacturer. Leather producers are not named in retail stores or in leather manufacturers' advertising. Consumers who can name several fabric and fiber producers would have a difficult time naming any leather tanners.

Trade Associations and Trade Shows

Much of the information collected and disseminated by the leather industry comes through trade associations, such as the Leather Industries of America and the United States Hide, Skin and Leather Association.

Trade shows are another important source of information within the leather industry. Two years before the ultimate consumer sees finished leather products in retail stores, the leathers are introduced in several industry trade shows (Figure 7.3). The Asia Pacific Leather Fair (APLF; formerly known as the Hong Kong Leather Fair) began twenty-six years ago. Over the years APLF has expanded its scope and currently organizes six premium events in Hong Kong, China, and India, covering a wide range of industry sectors.[4] There is also Shoes and Leather Guangzhou, which is held in May or June, and the India International Leather Fair, which is held each year.

Research and Development

The leather industry retains and expands its markets by adapting its products to fashion's changing requirements. Before World War II, relatively few colors and types of leather were available in any one season, and each usually had a fashion life of several years. Today, a major tannery may turn out hundreds of leather colors and types each season, meanwhile preparing to produce more new colors and textures for the next season.

To protect and expand their markets, leather producers constantly broaden their range of colors, weights, and textures. They also introduce improvements that make leather an acceptable material where it formerly had either limited use or no use at all. Recent innovations in the industry include everything from experimenting with new finishes and creating new types of dyes to using laser cutting for more advanced patterns and precise cuts and developing more environmentally friendly leather fabric using recycled scraps.

Leather has the weight of tradition behind it; people have regarded fine leather as a symbol of luxury for centuries. However, leather shares its hold on the fashion field with other and newer materials. Through product research and development, producers are attempting to meet the competition not only among leathers but also from other materials.

Trends in the Leather Industry

Until just a few decades ago, the leather industry concerned itself primarily with meeting consumer needs in relatively few fashion areas—mainly shoes, gloves, belts, handbags, luggage, and small leather goods. The use of leather for apparel was restricted largely to a few items of outerwear, such as jackets and coats. These were stiff, bulky, and primarily functional in appeal. Now designers offer colorful, supple leather vests, jeans, pants, blazers, anoraks, skirts, and suits of every description, in addition to jackets and coats (Figure 7.4).

FIGURE 7.3 Different materials, garments, accessories, and patterns showcased at a trade show in Moscow.

FIGURE 7.4 The beauty and versatility of soft leather is a hit on the runway. Neil Barrett's look from his 2013 collection (left), and Robert Rodriguez's white leather pants and jacket (right).

FIGURE 7.5 An exotic, snakeskin leather jacket by Gucci.

The leather industry has changed as a result of three trends: enlarging market opportunities, increased competition from synthetics, and increased foreign trade.

Enlarging Markets

Improved methods of tanning are turning out better, more versatile leathers with improved fashion characteristics. In general, these improvements include the following:

- Softer and more pliable leathers. Tanners' ability to split full-grain leather thinner and thinner creates suppleness.
- Dyed leathers. The methods for dying leathers are more successful and offer a greater variety of colors.
- Washable leather finishes and improved cleaning techniques. Techniques are now easier for consumers to care for leather garments.
- Sustainable leathers. Increased research and manufacturing methods produce more eco-friendly leather.

In cowhide leathers, the demand is high for the lighter-weight, mellow, natural-looking, full-grain leathers. Especially desirable are the glazed, rich-colored, aniline-dyed types that accentuate the natural beauty of the grain. These leathers are used predominantly in luggage, portfolios, and furniture.

Sheep and lamb tanners produce lighter-weight shearling for coats, jackets, and vests. The nonwool side is traditionally finished as suede, but it can also have a napped finish.

Prada and Gucci (Figure 7.5) are two upscale fashion companies built on leather. They continue to expand their offerings season after season. Other designers working with leather include Vakko, Donna Karan, Ralph Lauren, Escada, Michael Kors, and Calvin Klein.

Increased Competition from Synthetics

In the past few decades, the leather market has been eroded by synthetics. Leather heel lifts, which used to be commonplace, are now more often than not replaced with plastic. Synthetics that look and feel like leather but are less susceptible to scratches and easier to maintain are used to make handbags and other small leather goods.

Since most synthetic leather products were not as attractive as leather, synthetics did not offer leather any real competition for a long time. However, imitation leathers and suedes that were true substitutes began to be marketed. The most important one, Ultrasuede, quickly became a fashion classic. Although a washable synthetic, Ultrasuede does not have an image of being fake or cheap, and it is used by high-fashion designers. Vinyl is widely used for shoes, handbags, and other accessories, and its appearance has improved over the years.

Increased Foreign Trade

An increased worldwide demand for leather has enabled American hide dealers to obtain higher prices for their products in countries where demand outstrips supply.

The United States is the world's largest exporter of hides, so trade is critical to the prosperity of the U.S. hide industry. For this reason it is essential that U.S. hide exporters continue to gain access to foreign markets. New and expanded market access through trade agreements is the most important catalyst for increased hide exports.[5]

LOEWE: HIDE & CHIC

IN THE MIDST of a global recession, when luxury companies have been concentrating on diversification to retain or regain their high-end status, Loewe has returned to its very old roots with resounding success.

Loewe's leather goods was founded in 1846 in Madrid, Spain. The city was awash with royal wedding fever in anticipation of the marriages of Isabel II and her sister, the Infanta Maria Luisa Fernanda. Leather artisans worked day and night to meet the demand for tobacco pouches, coin purses, boxes, bags, and cigar cases—everything made to order and customized to the whims of the ladies and gentlemen of the royal court. By 1905, Loewe was named the official "Supplier to the Royal Court," and over the years it gained popularity among celebrities, including Ernest Hemingway, Maria Callas, Cary Grant, and more recently, Penelope Cruz.

Today, Loewe is famous for its light-as-air trench coats, body-skimming blazers, leather wallets and picture frames, and their perennial, top-selling Amazonia bag. Equally famous are Loewe's coveted golden gift boxes, which trigger the same excitement in Spaniards as a little blue box from Tiffany's does for Americans.

Loewe's advantage is the centuries-old Spanish tradition of leather craftsmanship. Spain is internationally renowned for the quality of its lambskin and Loewe uses only the best of the best. Ultra-soft, organically dyed skins only 0.7mm thick are achieved by a unique combination of painstaking hand-buffing, followed by a final polishing with glass cylinders. Every hand-crafted item from Loewe is intended as an heirloom; garments coming in for repair are rarely less than twenty years old and are often brought in for resizing, so a daughter can wear her mother's still-cool jacket.

Despite Spain's currently dire economy, Loewe has seen double-digit sales growth, is doubling its production facility, expanding the number of stores in Spain and Japan, and scouting a New York City location following success with boutiques at Bergdorf Goodman, Jeffrey, and Hirshleifer's. While its parent company LVMH does not release earnings, they are estimated at $327.9 million.

Industry Growth Factors

Several factors point to overall industry growth. Foremost among these is the trend toward a classic and elegant fashion look with an emphasis on quality. When quality is desired, consumers want real leather with all its mystique and will not settle for substitutes. Additionally, foreign demand continues to build in developing countries.[6] Another hopeful sign is that the supply of raw hides is large enough to allow for growth in production.

The Fur Industry

Long before prehistoric people learned how to plant crops, weave cloth, or build shelters, they figured out how to use fur. They spread it on the floor and used it as rugs. They used it to cover and create walls, perhaps bringing some warmth into an otherwise cold and drafty cave (Figure 7.6).

By the Middle Ages, the wearing of fur announced one's wealth and status. Sable, marten, ermine, and fox were the favored furs of nobility (Figure 7.7). Italian cardinals wore ermine as a symbol of purity; English nobles wore it as a sign of power. Fur was also a valued commodity used in trading. For centuries in Northern Europe, furs were valued more than gold and silver. Fur was still as good as gold in 1900 when Chile banked chinchilla skins as security for a loan.

Fur is still big business in America, with fur retail sales totaling $1.34 billion in 2011—up 34 percent since 1990.[7] According to the Fur Information Council of America, the fur industry has seen a rapid increase in designers, who now number well over 500, choosing to use fur in their fall/winter and even spring/summer collections. Mark Oaten, chief executive officer of the International Fur Trade Federation, states, "The bold and innovative fur designs of these young designers confirms that fur is, and will continue to be, a hot trend moving toward the future."[8] Men and women of all ages are buying fur today. It can be found in designer boutiques, specialty retailers, sporting goods stores, accessories shops, and boutiques for men and women, as well as at the more traditional fur salons and department stores.

History and Development

The search for a northwest passage that would shorten the route between Europe and the Orient led to the establishment of the fur trade in North America. When French explorer Jacques Cartier arrived at the mouth of the Saint Lawrence River in 1534, he traded furs with the Indians. The next year, when he sailed even

FIGURE 7.6 Eskimos have been wearing fur for years as a source of warmth.

FIGURE 7.7 Louise Cromwell poses in fox furs, c. 1911.

FIGURE 7.8 Luxurious furs find themselves in the fashion spotlight throughout changes in seasons and trends, such as these fur coats by Viktor & Rolf (left) and Fendi (right).

Ironically, just as beavers were becoming scarce, the fashion changed. Abraham Lincoln wore a silk top hat to his inauguration, and men stopped wearing beaver hats and began to buy hats made of silk and felt. The demand for beaver ceased almost overnight.

The interest in women's furs remained strong, however, and during the Civil War, the first mink ranch was established by T. D. Phillips and W. Woodstock. In 1880, silver fox fur farming began on Prince Edward Island, off the eastern coast of Canada. Fur farming and ranching have undergone renewed expansion in the past half century.

Fashions in furs (Figures 7.8 and 7.9) do change, although they change less quickly than do other apparel styles because furs are expensive. While mink coats account for half of all furs sold today, fifty years ago, a woman who wanted to look glamorous chose an

farther up the river, he realized what a vast wealth of fur-bearing animals existed on the continent. English and Dutch explorers soon joined the French in setting up trading posts. The first posts were situated along the Saint Lawrence and Hudson rivers, but they soon dotted the continent. Early fur-trading posts played a role in establishing such cities as Saint Louis, Chicago, Detroit, Saint Paul, and Spokane.

The plentiful supply of furs helped the colonists in other ways. They were able to export furs and use the money to bring European necessities—and even some luxuries—to the New World. Furs were an important source of clothing and furnishings. For a while in the mid-eighteenth century, furs were virtually the currency of North America.

It is the beaver, in particular, that truly deserves a special place in North American history. The discovery of this fur led to a fur rush that rivaled the Gold Rush. Beaver was used mostly to make men's hats, but in Canada in 1733, one beaver pelt could also buy a pound of sugar, two combs, six thimbles, or eight knives. Settlers pushed west in search of beaver, leaving behind communities with names like Beaver Creek, Beaver Falls, and Beaver Lake. Fortunes were made. John Jacob Astor was among the first to become a millionaire in the beaver trade. He dreamed of a beaver-fur empire stretching from New York to the Northwest Territory.

FIGURE 7.9 Zac Posen's colorful fur cape complements the design of his silk faille halter gown.

TABLE 7.3 *Selected Popular Furs and Their Characteristics*

FUR	CHARACTERISTICS	LOOK FOR	FUR	CHARACTERISTICS	LOOK FOR
Beaver Sheared	Soft, plushy texture.	Silky texture. Well-matched pelts, evenly sheared.	**Lynx**	Russian lynx is the softest and whitest of these long-haired furs, with the most subtle beige markings. Canadian lynx is next, while Montana lynx has stronger markings. Lynx cat or bobcat is reddish black fading to spotted white on longer belly hairs.	Creamy white tones and subtle markings.
Natural	Long, lustrous guard hairs over thick underfur.	Lustrous sheen of guard hairs and thickness of underfur.			
Calf	Short, sleek, flat hairs. Comes in many natural colors and patterns and may be dyed.	Lustrous, supple pelt with bright luster. Marking should be attractive.	**Marten** American	See also sable. Long, silky guard hairs and dense underfur. Color ranges from blue-brown to dark brown.	Texture and clarity of color.
Chinchilla	A short, dense, very silky fur. Originally from South America but now wholly ranch raised.	Lustrous slate-blue top hair and dark underfur, although mutation colors are now available.	Baum	Softer, silkier, and shinier than American marten.	
			Stone	The finest marten has soft, thick guard hairs and a bluish-brown cast with pale underfur.	
Coyote	A long-haired fur, often pale gray or tan in color. Durable and warm.	Long guard hair and thick, soft underfur.	**Mink**	Soft and lightweight, with lustrous guard hairs and dense underfur.	Natural luster and clarity of color. Fur should be full and dense.
Ermine	A fur with very silky white guard hairs and dense underfur.	Clear white color.	Mutation	Most colors of any natural ranched fur, from white to grays, blues, and beiges.	
Fox	The widest range of natural mutation colors of any fur except mink; silver, blue, white, red, cross, beige, gray, and brown. Can also be dyed in a wide variety of colors.	Long, glossy guard hairs and thick soft underfur; clarity of color.	Ranch	Color ranges from a true, rich brown to a deep brownish black.	
			Wild Pieced*	Generally brown in color. Color and pattern depend on pieces used. This is the least expensive mink.	Pattern and well-made seams.
Lamb American processed	Pelts of fine wool sheep sheared to show the pattern near the skin. Naturally white but may be dyed.	Silky, lustrous moire pattern, not too curly.	**Nutria**	Similar to beaver, often sheared for a sporty, more lightweight feel. Popular for linings and trims. Often dyed in a variety of colors.	Clarity of color.
Broadtail	A natural (unsheared) flat moire pattern. Color may be natural browns, gray, black, or dyed in more exotic colors.	Silky texture and uniformity of pattern.	**Rabbit**	Generally long hair in a variety of natural colors, including 14 natural mutation colors in ranch rabbit. May be sheared and grooved. Not very durable, shed easily.	Silky texture and uniformity of colors.
Mongolian	Long, wavy, silky guard hair. May be natural off-white, bleached, or dyed in more exotic colors.	Silky texture, with wavy—not frizzy—hair.			
Mouton	Pelts are sheared; hairs are straightened for soft, water-repellent fur, generally dyed brown.	Uniformity of shearing.	**Raccoon**	Long silver, black-tipped guard hairs over wooly underfur. May also be plucked and sheared and dyed.	Silvery cast. Plenty of guard hair with heavy underfur.
Shearling	Natural sheepskin (lamb pelt), with the leather side sueded and worn outside. The fur side (or inside) is often sheared.	Softness of leather side and even shearing.	**Sable**	Member of marten family. Russian sable has a silver cast, the most expensive. Crown sable is brown with a blue coat. Canadian golden sable, an amber tone, is less expensive.	Soft, deep fur in dark, lustrous brown, with silky guard hairs.
Persian lamb	From karakul sheep raised in Southwest Africa or central Asia. Traditionally black, brown, and gray, new mutation colors available; also dyed.	Silky curls or ripples of fur and soft, light, pliable leather.	**Tanuki**	Also called Japanese raccoon. Color is light amber brown with distinctive cross markings.	Clarity of color and dense, full texture.

LAMBSWOOL   FOX   LYNX   MINK

*The same piecing technique can be used for almost any fur. The most common pieced furs are mink, sable, marten, fox, Persian lamb, raccoon, and beaver.

Adapted from a number of sources, including the booklet *Choosing Fur* published jointly by the Fur Council of Canada and the Fur Information Council of America, Herndon, Virginia, pp. 4–5.

ermine cape. Today, an ermine cape would be valuable only as a theatrical prop—and it could be picked up fairly cheaply in a secondhand store.

More than at any other time in the history of fur fashion, the current list of furs is long and varied. Mink is the overwhelming favorite among consumers. Sable is a distant second, followed by fox and beaver. A new category, called sport or contemporary, includes such furs as raccoon, fox, beaver, coyote, muskrat, tanuki (Japanese raccoon), and nutria (a South American beaverlike animal). Table 7.3 lists furs and their characteristics.

In addition to the use of newer furs such as tanuki and nutria, fur manufacturers often reintroduce older ones. Persian lamb, shunned by fur buyers for more

than two generations, has now made a comeback. Remembered as a fur that was used for grandmother's conservative coat, Persian lamb, which is flat enough to be cut almost like cloth, is now being put to new uses. It is a prime choice in new fur garments such as scarfs, sweaters, and jackets.

Sometimes an interest in a fur comes about because fur manufacturers invent a finishing technique that makes a fur seem new. A renewed interest in raccoon can be traced to a technique that eliminated much of its bulkiness. In the 1940s, beaver was invariably sheared to look like a short fur; today it is sometimes left unplucked, giving it a totally new look. Or beaver may be sheared and given multicolored insets.

FUR?

I'd rather go naked

—Eva Mendes for PETA PETA.org

FIGURE 7.10 PETA's demonstrations and antifur campaigns attract media attention.

Animal Rights Groups

Over the past forty years, animal rights groups have protested the wearing of animal fur as cruel and inhumane. Some groups are opposed to trapping fur-bearing animals in the wild. Others also protest **fur farming**. Some groups, such as **PETA** (People for the Ethical Treatment of Animals) and the Friends of Animals have staged confrontations and demonstrations to get media attention (Figure 7.10). Long-standing activists Carnie Wilson, Pamela Anderson, Kim Basinger, Tyra Banks, and Joaquin Phoenix were all used as endorsements in

PETA antifur campaigns that coincided with the New York Fashion Week. Some activists have thrown paint at women wearing furs. Others have picketed fur stores and industry trade fairs. Still other groups, such as the Animal Liberation Front, have raided mink and fox farms and let the animals loose. They also destroyed pedigree cards containing irreplaceable genetic data.

The industry response has been strong on a number of fronts. It is working with the U.S. and Canadian governments and the International Standards Organization to develop global humane trapping standards. Fur farmers are proposing legislation to make the crime of releasing fur-bearing animals a felony. Associations of American and Canadian fur farmers have also offered rewards for information leading to the arrest of fur raiders. Fur auction houses are offering farmers vandalism insurance. The industry has done a great deal of consumer education to stress that today's farmed furs come from only nonendangered species. They also stress the following points:

- Fur farms do not remove animals from the wild.
- An overwhelming majority of U.S. mink production comes from farms certified as humane.
- Unlike manufactured faux fur, real fur does not use nonrenewable petroleum by-products.

Manufactured Furs

Manufactured, synthetic, or faux furs were long regarded as beneath the notice of serious designers and were limited to inexpensive garments. Technological developments and animal rights activism changed that view, and manufactured furs are accepted as fashionable.

The improved synthetic furs are used by a wide range of designers for higher-priced garments that still cost less than real fur. In 1999, Oleg Cassini unveiled a hundred-piece fake fur line in a show sponsored by the Humane Society. The event was videotaped so that many people could view the show. Named the Evolutionary Fur, the fake fur line retailed from $500 to $1,000 and was carried in major department stores. Since then, some designers still shun real fur as a matter of principle and use fakes instead. However, many industry observers feel that the fur industry has profited from the popularity of both real and manufactured fur.

Real Fur Versus Faux Fur

Imitation is the greatest form of flattery. The proliferation of fake or faux fur only proves that fur is in! But, no matter how good the fake (Figure 7.11, top), it will never have the warmth, the feel, or the durability of

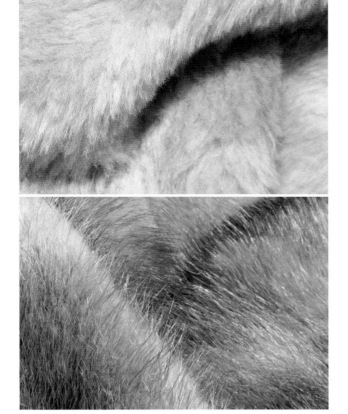

FIGURE 7.11 No matter how good the fake fur looks (top), it will never have the warmth, the feel, or the durability of real fur (bottom).

real fur (Figure 7.11, bottom). In 2013 the Federal Trade Commission found that several retailers were selling and marketing real fur as faux fur. These legal cases sparked interest about labeling laws among consumers and in the fashion industry. It also resulted in the fashion industry paying closer attention to labeling laws and the marketing of fur products.[9] (See also "Restrictive Legislation" on page 146.)

A strong argument against faux fur, from an environmental standpoint, is that most of it is made from natural resources (such as oil) that are limited in availability, while fur is a renewable resource. The manufacture of fake fur also releases harmful chemicals into the atmosphere.

Organization and Operation

The fur industry in the United States is divided into three groups, which also represent the three stages of fur production: (1) the trappers, farmers, and ranchers who produce the pelts and sell them at auction; (2) the fur-processing companies; and (3) the manufacturers of fur products.

Pelt Production

The first step in the production of fur is to obtain the necessary pelts. A **pelt** is the skin of a fur-bearing animal.

Trappers are the primary source of wild-animal pelts, which must be taken only during the coldest season of the year in order to be of prime quality. Trappers sell pelts to nearby country stores or directly to itinerant buyers. In some areas, collectors or receiving houses accept pelts for sale on consignment from trappers or local merchants. When enough pelts have been gathered, a fur merchant exports them or sends them to an auction house, or they are sold at a private sale through a broker.

Most furs come from farms or ranches, where fur-bearing animals are bred and raised strictly for their fur. Almost all mink, rabbit, fox, and more recently, chinchilla, Persian lamb, and broadtail are ranched. Fur farming offers two important advantages. First, animals can be raised under controlled conditions. Second, they can be bred selectively. When wild mink roamed North America, they came in one color, a dark brown with reddish highlights. Today, many beautiful colors, some of which are trademarked and denote a manufacturer's private label, are available. Among the better-known names are Azurene, Lunaraine, Rovalia, Lutetia, Jasmin, Tourmaline, Cerulean, and the most recognizable name of all, Blackglama.

Fur Auctions

Fur pelts are sold at auctions today, much as they were in the thirteenth century. Fur buyers and manufacturers bid on the pelts, which are sold in bundles. Buyers look for bundles that are matched in quality and color (Figure 7.12). This enables a manufacturer to make up a garment of uniform beauty.

FIGURE 7.12 When buyers purchase pelts, they look for bundles that are matched in quality and color.

FUR
IS FLYING AGAIN:
FASHION, FUR, AND THE NEXT GENERATION

FUR IS LEGENDARY. Its glamour and sense of old-world luxury made it the chosen material of Hollywood's screen sirens and iconic starlets for decades. Yet, today, fur is playing a starring role on fashion's runways, adorning shoes, slung over shoulders, and appearing in a host of new styles, shapes, and colors. Innovative designs are reinventing the rules and making the presence of fur in fashion stronger than ever.

The average age of consumers looking for fur has shifted—it has gotten younger, and designers are noticing. In 2011, more than 500 designers showed fur as part of their collections. Their new, fresh approach toward designing with fur lends it the casual air of a wardrobe staple, rather than a luxury item. Now that fur is being colored and cut differently, people can even wear it with jeans and sneakers.

Without a doubt, the future of fur is being written by the young, fashionable consumers who are demanding it; however, the increased interest in fur has triggered regulations. The Truth in Fur Labeling Act was passed in 2010 after a number of retailers were fined for selling real fur masquerading as faux, or trying to pass off ferret as mink. In 2011, the city of West Hollywood approved a ban on the sale of real fur—the first of its kind—slated to take effect in Fall 2013. The Fur Information Council of America is planning to challenge the ban in court, citing the limits it would put on the city's fashion industry. "You cannot be a fashion destination if you cannot represent the designers' full collections of designs in retail establishments," says FICA executive director Keith Kaplan. "There's no truer determination of consumer attitudes than the cash register."

Dries Van Noten's
Fall 2012

Roberto Cavalli
Fall 2012

Serkan Cura
Fall 2012

Jean Paul Gaultier
Fall 2012

Buyers compete to purchase a "top bundle"—that is, an unusually beautiful bundle that goes for an unusually high price. This, in turn, results in a much-touted coat—often costing $100,000 or more—that is made from the top bundle.

The auction trail is an international one, although except for England, Tokyo, and more recently, Beijing, each market sells indigenous furs. Fur buyers from the United States travel to Canada, Scandinavia, China, and Russia. To buy North American furs, fur buyers travel to auction houses in New York, Seattle, Toronto, and North Bay, Canada.

Fur Processing

After manufacturers of fur goods buy the pelts, they contract with fur-dressing and fur-dyeing firms to process them.

The job of fur dressers is to make the pelts suitable for use in consumer products. The pelts are first softened by soaking and mechanical means. Then a flesher removes any unwanted substances from the inner surface of the skin. For less expensive furs, this is done by roller-type machines. At this point, the pelts are treated with solutions that tan the skin side into pliable leather. The fur side may be processed at the same time. This involves either plucking unwanted guard hairs or shearing the underfur to make the fur more lightweight. Although fur dressing has traditionally been a handcraft industry, modern technology is turning it into a more mechanical process.

After dressing, the pelts may go to a dyer. Fur dyes were once made from vegetable matter but are now mostly derived from chemical compounds. New dyes are constantly being developed, making it possible to dye fur more successfully and in more shades than ever before.

Fur Manufacturing

Most fur manufacturers are small, independently owned and operated shops, although a few large companies have emerged largely as a result of the explosion in the number of fur products.

The production of fur garments lends itself neither to mass production nor to large-scale operations. Skill and judgment are required at every stage of manufacturing. Doing each step by hand lets a worker deal with each pelt's color, quality, and peculiarities.

The following steps transform pelts into finished garments:

1. A design of the garment is sketched.
2. A paper pattern is made of the garment.

FIGURE 7.13 This worker is letting out this short-skin fur to make a longer garment.

3. A canvas pattern is made.
4. The skins are cut to conform to the designer's sketch, exhibit the fur to its best advantage, and minimize waste.
5. The cut skins are sewn together.
6. The skins are wetted and then stapled to a board to dry, a process that sets them permanently.
7. The garment sections are sewn together.
8. The garment is lined and finished.
9. The garment is inspected.

For some luxurious furs, the cutting operation becomes extremely complex. Short skins must be **let out** to a suitable length for garments (Figure 7.13). Letting out mink, for example, involves cutting each skin down the center of a dark vertical line of fur (the grotzen stripe). Each half skin must then be cut at an angle into diagonal strips one-eighth to three-sixteenths of an inch wide. Then each tiny strip is resewn at an angle to the strips above and below it to make a long, narrow skin. The other half skin is sewn in a similar manner.

The two halves are then joined, resulting in a longer, slimmer pelt that is more beautiful than the original. Considerable hand labor is required to do all of these operations. Ten miles of thread and more than 1,200 staples can be used in a single coat.

Retail Distribution of Furs

There are more than fifteen hundred retail stores across the United States that specialize in furs. While some are chain operations, 85 percent of fur retailers are small, family-owned businesses. That said, the line between manufacturing and retailing is less clear in the fur industry than in most other industries. Retail fur merchants, for example, typically make up an assortment of garments to sell off the rack to customers, but they also maintain a supply of skins in their workroom for custom work.

In retail stores, fur departments are either leased or consignment departments. Both operations permit a retail store to offer its customers a large selection without tying up a lot of capital in inventory.

A **leased department** is situated in the store but run by an independent merchant (such as Maximilian at Bloomingdale's), who pays a percentage of sales to the store as rent. The operator either owns or leases the stock. Lessees often run several similar departments in many stores and can, if necessary, move garments and skins from one location to another. Lessees, who are a unique kind of retailer, are usually well capitalized and have expert knowledge in both furs and retailing.

In **consignment selling**, a fur manufacturer supplies merchandise to a retail store, which has the option of returning unsold items. In effect, the manufacturer lends stock to a store. Consignment selling is influenced by the state of the economy. When interest rates are high, stores tend to buy less stock.

Merchandising and Marketing

Fur traders, dressers, producers, and their labor unions all work through their various trade associations to encourage the demand for fur.

Trade Associations

Trade associations mount their own campaigns to promote furs, and they also work with retailers. The leading trade association is the Fur Information Council of America, which represents fur retailers and manufacturers. It has placed ads in various fashion magazines to counter some of the animal rights arguments.

The ranch mink association, American Legend, is a nonprofit cooperative formed through the combination of two major mink-producing groups: Emba Mink Breeders Association and Great Lakes Mink

Association. With more than 220 member owners, American Legend markets more than 70 percent of the total North American mink crop annually.[10] It has a program to protect its trademarks from infringement. The association supplies labels and other point-of-purchase materials only to retailers and manufacturers who can prove they purchased the group's pelts at an American Legend auction.

Trade associations not only monitor the industry but also help to educate consumers. Fur is a product that is most successfully purchased when the consumer has some specialized knowledge about what he or she is buying. Consumers need to know, for example, that the rarer the breed, the more expensive the fur. According to the Fur Council of Canada, here are some things for consumers to watch for when purchasing fur:[11]

- The pelts should be lustrous, supple, and well matched.
- There should be a dense, soft underfur that is evident to the touch.
- Seams should be tightly sewn and hems should fall straight.
- A well-made fur should have balance and fall evenly and comfortably from the wearer's shoulders.
- There should be give to the leather side of the fur.

Another important factor in the quality of fur is whether the pelts are female or male. Most female skins are softer and lighter. Although there are exceptions, such as fitch, for which the male skins are preferred, a coat of female mink costs more than one of male skins.

International Fur Fairs

As the demand for fur increases, people are traveling all over the globe to get the best buys. Designers, manufacturers, retailers, importers and exporters, wholesalers, and the media all attend one or more of the leading international fur fairs listed in Table 7.4.

TABLE 7.4 *Leading International Fur Fairs*

SITE	NAME OF FAIR	MONTH HELD
Tokyo	Japan International Fashion Fair Outerwear	February
Hong Kong	Hong Kong International Fur & Fashion Fair	February
Milan	Mifur Fur & Leather Exhibition	March
Lausanne	Comispiel	March
Moscow	Moda Spring & Mexa Fall	March, October
Frankfurt	Frankfurt International Outerwear Fair	March, October
Montreal	North American Fur & Fashion Outerwear Expo	May

Labeling

The Fur Products Labeling Act of 1952 requires that all furs be labeled according to:

1. The English name of the animal
2. Its country of origin
3. The type of processing, including dyeing, to which the pelts have been subjected
4. Whether or not parts have been cut from a used garment or from the less desirable paw or tail sections

Years ago, such labeling would have been helpful, for example, to prevent a customer from buying a less expensive, dyed muskrat that was touted as the much rarer and more expensive Hudson seal. Today, labeling is helpful in distinguishing one fur from another in an industry that, without intending to defraud, has learned to capitalize on fashion trends by treating less expensive furs to look like more expensive ones.

Trends in the Fur Industry

As a general rule, the demand for furs is related to the economy. During the Depression, fur sales dropped off dramatically. After World War II, when the economy was expanding, fur sales boomed. In the early 1970s, conservationists' concerns about the diminishing wildlife species put a temporary damper on fur sales, but the industry rebounded in the 1980s. Mid-1987 saw the highest point, the $2 billion mark. But in the early 1990s, a combination of antifur activism and mild winters brought a rapid downturn in fur sales. Synthetic fur sales also rose rapidly. Industry experts say the outlook for the fur industry continues to be good, despite the fact that pelt prices are currently rising. In the 2011/2012 auction season, record prices were obtained for mink and fox pelts.[12]

Growth will be affected by the following four major trends:

- Renewed fashion interest in furs
- Increased foreign trade
- Restrictive legislation that actually helps the industry
- New channels of retail distribution

Renewed Fashion Interest

Once worn only by the rich or for formal occasions, furs are now bought and worn by many kinds of consumers for many occasions. The average customer no longer buys one conservatively cut coat, either. Furs are now sporty and casual, elegant and classic, or faddish and

FIGURE 7.14 Elegant or casual, furs come in all colors and shapes. This look is from Jean Paul Gaultier's Fall 2012 collection.

trendy (Figure 7.14)—and with such choices, many customers have been persuaded to buy more than one.

Not only have older women—the traditional market—continued to buy furs, but the market has expanded to young and working women as well. In the 1970s and 1980s, a new market opened up for fur—namely, women themselves. For many years, women received fur coats only as gifts. They seldom bought this luxury item for themselves. But in the 1970s and 1980s, when more women started working and also began to get paid more for their work, they started buying furs for themselves, thus creating, in effect, a new market—one that the fur industry has been quick to recognize and expand upon. Odd as it seems today, fur advertising had always been directed at men buying fur coats as gifts for women.

Fur manufacturers are exploring other new markets as well. For most of history, men as well as women wore furs, but in the past one hundred years, the fur coat became almost exclusively a woman's garment. In the early 1980s, men once again began wearing fur coats. The fur industry continues to expand into new products, using fur to make garments such as vests, sweaters, and dresses that have not traditionally been

FIGURE 7.15 A fur accessory can be a unique accent for any outfit.

made of fur. Fur is also used in accessories and trims on garments (Figure 7.15).

Finally, the growing excitement and sales of fur have led to big-name designers entering the field or expanding their collections with fur. Over the years the fashion industry has seen innovative techniques from designers such as Christian Dior, Dennis Basso, Marc Jacobs, Byron Lars, and Fendi. American designers like Oscar de La Renta and Jerry Sorbara have produced fur collections for years. Younger designers like Zac Posen and Alexander Wang are incorporating fur in their collections, too. Canadian designers have traditionally worked with fur. D'Arcy Moses presents themes of Canada's indigenous peoples in furs inset with patterns of trees and eagle feathers. Fellow Canadian Paula Lishman is famous for her knit fur and washable fur-with-cotton knits. And Zuki made waves with his astonishing op-art sheared beaver coats.

The fur industry—from breeders and manufacturers to retailers and customers—has changed drastically in the twenty-first century. This is most evident from a style and design standpoint, where more youth-oriented styles are being paraded down the runways.

Increased Foreign Trade

The export market is strong for the American fur industry, not only because of the variety of furs that are available but also because of the reputation for quality in U.S. pelt dressing. The United States produces innovative, high-style furs that are in great demand around the world. China is currently the world's largest importer of fur. Demand is also strong in North America, Europe, Russia, and the rest of the Far East. Developing markets such as Ukraine, Turkey, and Kazakhstan are showing a steady growth in demand.[13]

Restrictive Legislation

The Federal Trade Commission and the fur industry are constantly engaged in talks about fur labeling. The Endangered Species Act of 1973 forbade the sale of furs made from endangered species such as leopard, tiger, ocelot, cheetah, jaguar, and a few types of wolf.

In 2012 the European Parliament put a labeling law into effect for textiles that include less than 20 percent animal products (such as fur, leather, or bone). The label must be clearly marked and contain the phrase "contains non-textile parts of animal origin" in the language of the country where it is sold.[14]

New Channels of Retail Distribution

Fur manufacturers have sought other distribution channels in addition to the retail outlets that they have opened.

Hotel, armory, and arena fur sales are held almost every fall and winter weekend in New York City and other large cities. Fur manufacturers can conduct these sales for a fraction of the cost in wages and rent that would be required if they were to maintain comparable facilities year-round. Even better, the average hotel ballroom, armory, or arena showroom is suitable for displaying thousands of coats, far more than the average fur salon can attractively exhibit. These sales appeal to customers, who like the hands-on approach and lower prices. The same customers who frequent weekend sales can also shop in manufacturer-leased discount and off-price stores.

Summary and Review

In America, the tanning of leather for clothing and footwear dates back to the precolonial Native American populations. Today, the industry consists of three major types of businesses: regular tanneries, contract tanneries, and converters.

Most leather comes from cattle as an offshoot of the meatpacking industry, but leather is also produced from the pelts of eight other animal groups. Tanneries tend to specialize according to the end use of the leather. Tanning may involve one or more processes using minerals, vegetable materials, oils, and chemicals, alone or in combination, to achieve the desired color and textural finish.

Leather industry trade associations, like Leather Industries of America and the United States Hide, Skin and Leather Association, advise their members on fashion and technical issues and promote the industry to its markets.

Fur has been used for warmth in clothing and shelter since prehistoric times. Fur trading, especially in beaver skins, was a major industry in the European colonization of America, and it remained so well into the 19th century. For much of the 20th century, fur was considered a luxury fashion item for women, but in recent years, fur has been used as a trim for various types of apparel, and men's furs have become a growing market. The efforts of animal rights activists, periods of economic downturn, and competition from imports and from faux furs have challenged the industry, but most recently, economic prosperity and industry campaigns to educate the public about humane industry practices have had a positive effect on sales.

The fur industry is made up of three groups: (1) trappers, farmers, and ranchers, (2) fur-processing companies, who buy furs at auctions, and (3) manufacturers of fur products. Processing pelts and turning them into fashion products requires skilled labor, although some mechanization has been introduced into processing. The distinction between levels in the fur industry is less precise than in other segments of the fashion industry. Because of the specialized knowledge and the financial investment required, furs are often sold to consumers by consignment or leased departments in retail stores, at manufacturers' shows, or in hotels and other large spaces.

For Review

1. In what ways have technological advances in machinery and chemistry benefited the leather industry?
2. Name and describe the three major types of companies in the leather industry.
3. What are the nine major groups of fur-bearing animals?
4. What has Leather Industries of America done to broaden the leather market and soften the impact of competition from synthetics?
5. What factors point to growth for the leather industry?
6. Describe the history and development of the fur industry in the United States.
7. Into what three groups is the fur industry divided? Briefly describe the function of each.
8. What are the advantages of fur farming over trapping?
9. Outline the steps in the process of transforming processed fur pelts into finished garments.
10. Differentiate between leased departments and consignment selling as these terms apply to retail distribution of fur garments. What major advantages does each have for retail merchants?

For Discussion

1. Discuss the following statement from the text and its implications for leather merchandising: "The leather industry not only must stay abreast of fashion, it must be several steps ahead of it."
2. Discuss current trends in the leather industry that relate to (a) enlarging markets, (b) competition from synthetics, and (c) increased foreign trade.
3. Discuss the pros and cons of trapping and raising animals for their fur. Explain your support or rejection of the arguments advanced by animal rights activists and by the fur industry.
4. Discuss current trends in the fur industry as they relate to (a) fashion interest, (b) increased foreign trade, (c) new channels of retail distribution, (d) imports, (e) rising overhead, and (f) lack of skilled workers.

Trade Talk

Define or briefly explain the following terms:

consignment selling
contract tanneries
converters
fur farming
hide
kips
leased department
let out
pelt
PETA
regular tanneries
skins
sustainable use
tanning

Unit Three THE SECONDARY LEVEL: THE PRODUCERS OF APPAREL

Fashion has many faces—different faces for different places, different looks for different years. Fashion also consists of products, and products have a past. The history of a product includes all the designers and manufacturers who have watched their customers and are always trying to give them what they want. This is quite an extraordinary challenge for the producers of fashion.

In this unit, you will learn how the fashion apparel manufacturing business has changed from an industry of many small companies into an industry dominated by a growing group of giants. You will begin to develop a basic vocabulary and a working knowledge of the following:

- Chapter 8: The six-stage process of developing and producing a line and the major industry practices of licensing, private labels, specification buying, off-shore production, the use of factors, chargebacks, SIC/NAICS codes, and supply chain management.
- Chapters 9–11: The history of women's, men's, children's, and teen's apparel industries and the categories, size ranges, and price zones, as well as the roles of brand names and designer names in the marketing process.

Chapter Eight

PRODUCT DEVELOPMENT

KEY CONCEPTS

- The major advantages and disadvantages of the contractor system
- The six-stage process of developing and producing a line
- The major industry practices of licensing, private-label and specification buying, offshore production, CAD/CAM, the use of factors, chargebacks, and SIC/NAICS codes
- The supply chain management movement and the mass customization theory
- How bar codes, scanners, and RFID are integral to product development and supply chain management

The level of activity in textile and apparel product development has been steadily increasing. This increase in activity, together with the global manufacturing and assembly practices, has integrated product development into the mainstream business-decision structure of all fashion industry firms, from manufacturers to retailers.

If new apparel and fashion-related products are not developed, sales and profits decline, technology and markets change, or innovation by other firms makes the original product obsolete. All of this points to the importance of product development for the continued success of a company.

Product development is the teaming of market and trend research with the merchandising, design, and technical processes that develop a final product. Product development is used by both wholesale manufacturers, who develop products for a signature brand, and retailers, who use it for private-label development for their own stores.

Whether making plain T-shirts or elaborate evening gowns, the men's, women's, and children's apparel industries in the United States have managed to settle into a basic cycle of design and production that repeats itself more or less unchanged from season to season. However, before an article of clothing reaches the retail store racks, a great deal of work and planning are involved. (There are similar cycles for accessories, beauty, and home fashions; they are discussed in Unit Four.) This chapter focuses on the design and production of apparel for men, women, and children; subsequent chapters examine each area in detail.

What Is a Product Line, and Who Develops It?

Product lines of apparel are created and styled for wholesale presentation several times, or seasons, per year. In the fashion industries, a product line is simply called a *line*. A line not only encompasses the individual item of apparel or accessories but the entire season's production

FIGURE 8.1 Jitrois's collection at the Fall 2013 show is linked together by a common theme of colors, fabrics, and style.

from that manufacturer as well. The term **line** is used for moderate- and popular-priced apparel. The term **collection** describes an expensive line in the United States or in Europe. Lines are divided into **groups** of garments, linked by a common theme like color, fabric, or style (Figure 8.1). Each garment is known by a style number or simply "number," such as 401 or 57.

At the present time, fashion designs cannot be copyrighted in the United States. However, fabric designs and artwork on clothing are protected. The American Apparel and Footwear Association and the Council of Fashion Designers of America are sponsoring legislation that would protect fashion designers and apparel brands from knockoffs. The bill is known as the Innovative Design Protection and Piracy Prevention Act. Copying from creative designers is common and often seen throughout the fashion industry; it is not considered piracy. At some firms, few if any designs are original; rather, they are copied **line-for-line** in a similar fabric, or adapted from another designer in a cheaper fabric (knockoffs), or reworked from a previous season in a different color or fabric, creating designs known as **anchors**.

Designers typically work on three seasonal lines at a time. They monitor the sales of the current season's line, put the finishing touches on next season's line, and meanwhile begin to develop the new line for the *following* season. Clearly, this is a challenging balancing act!

Clothing manufacturers produce between four and six lines every year. For women's wear, these are Spring, Summer, Transitional or Fall I, Fall or Fall II, Resort, and Holiday (Table 8.1).

Many firms, however, add new styles to lines throughout the year to keep buyers shopping their lines to see what is new. Or, at a minimum, they update styles or change the fabrics used in the line. Conversely, as new styles are added, old ones are dropped.

Manufacturers start work on their new lines anywhere between three and twelve months before presentation to retail buyers. This means clothes are planned and designed as much as a year before customers see them in the stores.

Now we examine the roles played by the merchandiser, the designer, and the producer.

Role of the Merchandiser

The merchandiser is the person who channels the creativity of the designer and design staff so that the six "rights" of merchandising can be successfully accomplished. These rights are the right merchandise, at the right price, at the right time, in the right place, in the right quantity, with the right promotion. To these rights must be added another one—the right customer! Because this customer is so important, the merchandiser is given the responsibility to research who the right customer is.

Some people in the industry have described the merchandiser as the glue that holds the whole product development concept together. In fact, the merchandiser is the liaison among the design staff, the production facilities, and the sales staff. The merchandiser has to view the line from the design point of view and also has to be knowledgeable about production and sales efforts.

Role of the Designer

Designers can create by sketching (croquis), by drawing on a computer (computer-aided design, or CAD), or by draping cloth on a model. In addition to looking for artistic excellence, designers must keep practical

TABLE 8.1 *Seasonal Lines*

NAME OF LINE	WHEN SHOWN
Spring	September (New York), October (Los Angeles and Dallas)
Summer	Early January
Transitional or Fall I	February
Fall or Fall II	February
Resort	June (New York), July (Miami), August (Dallas)
Holiday	July (New York), August (Dallas)

business considerations in mind. All designs must be produced at a profit and within the firm's wholesale price range. Consequently, designers must keep in mind the availability and cost of materials, the cost of cutting and sewing the garment, and labor costs.

Most U.S. designers who use their artistic and innovative talents to design fashion-oriented merchandise fall into one of three categories:

1. High-fashion or "name" designers
2. Stylist-designers
3. Freelance artist-designers

High-fashion designers are usually referred to in this country as "name" designers. Because of the success and originality of their designs, name designers are well known to fashion-conscious customers. High-fashion designers are responsible not only for creating the designs but also for the choice of fabric, texture, and color in which each design is to be executed (Figure 8.2). They may often be involved in development of the production model as well as in plans for the promotion of a firm's line. Some name designers work for fashion houses, as does Francisco Costa for Calvin Klein. Others, like Oscar de la Renta and Anna Sui, own their own firms or are financed by a silent partner outside the firm. Still others, like Ralph Lauren and Donna Karan, are publicly owned corporations that are listed on a stock exchange.

Designer names were once associated only with original, expensive designs in apparel. Then, beginning in 1922 with Chanel, many designers licensed their names to fragrances. Today, most name designers also license their names to manufacturers of accessories and home furnishings.

Stylist-designers use their creative talents to adapt or change the successful designs of others. A stylist-designer must understand fabric and garment construction as well as the manufacturing process, because designs are usually adapted at lower prices. Stylist-designers usually create designs at the late rise or early culmination stages of the fashion cycle. They are usually not involved in details relating to the production of the firm's line or in the planning of its promotional activities. Rather, their focus is on designing within the limits of the firm's production capacity and capability. Stylist-designers who work in a firm that sells to major retail store chains often accompany the firm's salespeople to define the look or to learn firsthand what the retail store buyer wants.

FIGURE 8.2 Tropical birds and other flights of fancy grouped in clusters on the inspiration board for Jonathan Saunders's collection.

Freelance artist-designers sell their sketches and CAD (computer-aided design) drawings to manufacturers. They may work independently at home or from a design studio. These sketches may be original designs by the freelancer or adaptations of a design furnished by the manufacturer. The sketches may reflect the freelancer's own ideas or the manufacturer's detailed specifications. With the delivery of a sketch to the manufacturer, a freelancer's job ends, and he or she goes on to another project.

Role of the Producer

The fashion apparel industry consists of three types of producers: manufacturers, jobbers, and contractors. An **apparel manufacturer** is one who performs all the operations required to produce apparel, from buying the fabric to selling and shipping the finished garments. An **apparel jobber** handles the designing, the planning, the purchasing, usually the cutting, the selling, and the shipping, but not the actual sewing operation. An **apparel contractor** is a producer whose sole function is to supply sewing services to the industry, where it is sometimes called an **outside shop**. Contractors that specialize in the production of one product are sometimes called **item houses**. Increasingly, the term manufacturer is being used more loosely to describe any firm that handles any part of the cutting or sewing process, and the terms jobber and contractor are used less often.

Manufacturers

A **manufacturer**, by definition, is a producer who handles all phases of a garment's production. The staff produces the original design or buys an acceptable design from a freelance designer. Each line is planned by the company executives. The company purchases the fabric and trimmings needed. The cutting and sewing are usually done in the company's factories. On certain occasions, however, a manufacturer may use the services of a contractor if sales of an item exceed the capacity of the firm's sewing facilities and if shipping deadlines cannot otherwise be met. The company's sales force and traffic department handle the selling and shipping of the finished goods. One great advantage of this type of operation is that close quality control can be maintained. When producers contract out some part of their work, they cannot as effectively monitor its quality.

Apparel Jobbers

Apparel jobbers handle all phases of the production of a garment except for the actual sewing and sometimes the cutting. A jobber firm may employ a design staff to create various seasonal lines or may buy sketches from freelance designers. The jobber's staff buys the fabric and trimmings necessary to produce the styles in each line, makes up samples, and grades the patterns. In most cases, the staff also cuts the fabric for the various parts of each garment. Jobbers, however, do not actually sew and finish garments. Instead, they arrange with outside factories run by contractors to perform these manufacturing operations. The sales staff takes orders for garments in each line, and the shipping department fills store orders from the finished garments returned by the contractor. (Note that apparel jobbers are involved in manufacturing, whereas in other fields jobbers buy finished goods and sell them to small users who are not able to place large orders.)

Contractors

Contractors usually specialize in just one phase of the production of a garment: sewing. In some cases contractors also perform the cutting operation from patterns submitted by a jobber or a manufacturer. Contractors developed early in the history of the fashion industry, with the beginning of mass-production techniques. Contractors serve those producers who have little or no sewing capability of their own as well as those whose current business exceeds their own capacity. Sometimes a subcontractor is used by the initial contractor for specialized work that the initial contractor is not equipped to perform, such as beading or embroidery. When there is a very large order, a subcontractor may be used to produce the overbooked production.

If a contractor is used, cut pieces of the garment are provided by the manufacturer. For an agreed price per garment, the article is sewn, finished, inspected, pressed, hung, or packaged, and returned to the manufacturer for shipment to retail stores.

In the mass production of ready-to-wear apparel, a single sewing-machine operator rarely makes a complete garment. Each operator sews only a certain section of the garment, such as a sleeve or a hem. This division of labor, called **section work** or **piecework**, makes it unnecessary for an operator to switch from one highly specialized machine to another or to make adjustments on the machine. Any change or adjustment in equipment takes time and increases labor costs. In the fashion trade, time lost in making such changes also causes delays in getting a style to consumers. Delays in production could mean the loss of timeliness and sales appeal before an article reaches market.

A contractor may arrange to work exclusively with one or more jobbers or manufacturers, reserving the right to work for others whenever the contractor's facilities are not fully employed. Such agreements are necessarily reciprocal. If a contractor agrees to give preference to a particular jobber's or manufacturer's work, the jobber or manufacturer gives preference to that contractor when placing sewing orders.

The advantages and disadvantages of the contractor system for the manufacturer are as follows:

Advantages:
- Large amounts of capital are not required for investment in sewing equipment that may soon become obsolete.
- Difficulties in the hiring and training of suitable workers are minimized.
- The amount of capital necessary to meet regular payrolls is greatly reduced.
- By providing additional manufacturing facilities in periods of peak demand, contractors help speed up delivery of orders.
- It is unnecessary to keep one factory busy year-round.

Disadvantages:
- No individual has full responsibility for the finished product.
- Other manufacturers (jobbers) may use the same facilities and get preferential treatment, because they place larger orders, offer repeat business, or even guarantee future business.
- The quality of workmanship and inspection tends to be uneven.

The Product Development Process

In a study published in the Journal of Textile and Apparel Technology and Management, the authors listed the following functions for an effective integrated system of product development:[1]

- Marketing
- Forecasting
- Merchandising
- Product line development
- Product design and specifications
- Material requisition planning
- Inventory control
- Costing
- Production planning and scheduling
- Sourcing and manufacturing
- Quality control
- Human resources
- Purchasing
- Logistics
- Warehouse inventory movement systems
- Finance
- Sales
- Field sales support
- Performance measurement
- External communication

Currently there are many variations in the product development process. We discuss a simple six-stage process that covers the functions performed at every firm, regardless of size. The major differences are the number of people involved and how they communicate and interact (Figure 8.3).

The six-stage product development process is outlined in the following pages (Figure 8.4):

- Stage 1. Planning the line
- Stage 2. Creating the design concept
- Stage 3. Developing the designs
- Stage 4. Planning production
- Stage 5. Production
- Stage 6. Distributing the line

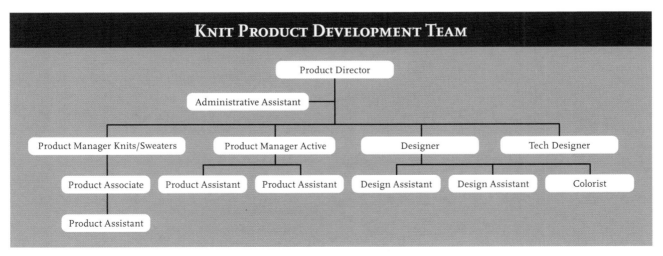

FIGURE 8.3 This organizational chart outlines the hierarchy of a product development team.

FIGURE 8.4 From top to bottom: The product development process includes planning a line, creating the design concept, developing the design, and production.

Stage 1: Planning the Line

The first step of the product development process involves the work of a designer or a product development team, working under the direction of a merchandiser. These people are charged with creating a line. Their first task is research. They review information on trends, colors, fabrics, and other materials, often using fashion forecasting services, such as the Doneger Group, Stylesight, Promostyl, or Fashion Snoops. Of course, team members must keep in mind previous fashion successes or failures, so past sales records as well as markdown reports are reviewed. Some firms develop trend boards that contain visual or graphic representations of developments that are affecting their target customer. All of this research helps designers or product development teams formulate some idea of what the new line will contain.

Using all their merchandising and marketing skills, merchandisers or designers help to form and maintain a positive image in the marketplace for the manufacturer. It is this image that influences a specific consumer group to buy a particular line at the retail level.

In most cases, design has to be disciplined and directed so that the particular image of the manufacturer and the merchandise that is produced will continue to fit the needs and wants of a specific consumer group.

There are three major types of firms that develop a line of apparel:

1. *Large Manufacturers.* In a large apparel firm, such as VF Corporation and Levi Strauss & Co., merchandisers are responsible for developing new lines. Merchandisers plan the overall fashion direction for the coming season and direct a design staff about the kinds of garments to be designed. They may also determine color choices. The design staff is generally not known to the public. Together with the marketing and sales departments, the merchandiser and designer form a product development team, which is responsible for a particular product line or brand.

2. *Designer-Owned Firms.* In firms at which the designer is also the owner (or part owner), the designer may design all or part of a line, using other designers to fill out the line. Examples of this kind of firm are Ralph Lauren, Vera Wang, and Oscar de la Renta.

3. *Small Manufacturers.* In small firms, all the activities in the product development process may be done by the owner, with one or more assistants.

Stage 2: Creating the Design Concept

Next come designs for individual garments. Each one is sketched or developed in muslin. At this stage, the designer or design staff considers his or her work and weighs it on two points: first, on its own individual merit, and second, for its suitability in the line as a whole. Many designs are discarded at this point.

Price is also a critical factor in determining whether or not a design is deleted from a line. A cost analysis is often done at this stage, and designs that are too expensive to produce profitably at the desired price point are rejected.

Stage 3: Developing the Designs

Those designs that seem most likely to succeed are made up as finished sample garments. A patternmaker creates a production pattern in the garment size the company uses to produce its samples. From this pattern, one or more samples are cut. Finally, the garment is sewn by a designer's assistant, who is also a seamstress. This person is called a **sample hand**.

Now the design is presented to various executives and managers of the company—people in sales, purchasing, production, and cost accounting. Both the cost of the fabric and the cost of producing the garment are carefully analyzed. Many designs are discarded at this point, while others are sent back to the design department for modification. A few are accepted. The accepted design is assigned a style number. At this point, it is officially part of a manufacturer's line.

Computer-Aided Design

Although the day has not yet arrived when designers will throw away their sketch pads and pencils, **computer-aided design (CAD)** gives designers the freedom to explore and manipulate their designs in relatively easy, quick, and inexpensive ways. A designer no longer has to take a chance that he or she is having a sample made up in the best color. CAD is used to test various colors and color combinations, fabrics, and styles. It allows three-dimensional (3-D) contouring of objects on screen (Figure 8.5). Folds, creases, and textures are simulated so that CAD-generated garments drape and hang accurately. Once the design is set on the computer, the computer image is used to create a pattern complete with darts, seams, and tailor's markings. Because the computer can create the design in 3-D, the computer image can be rotated to see all sides of the garment. Many companies are thus reducing the number of costly sample garments that they produce. Instead of a physical sample, they can use the computer image in merchandising and sales presentations.

FIGURE 8.5 Many designers use CAD systems to change, clarify, and perfect their designs.

Computer-aided manufacturing (CAM) works with CAD to increase efficiency and regulate manufacturing processes. This is part of Product Lifecycle Management (PLM), which we will discuss more later in this chapter.

Stage 4: Planning Production

This stage of the product development process begins with sourcing, or determining where the components of a garment (fabric, thread, linings, facings, buttons, trim, etc.) will be purchased and, in some cases, where the garments will be cut and sewn. It is now that the vital question of domestic or foreign manufacture must be decided. (This is discussed in more detail later in this chapter.) Reservations for production must be made so that the garments will be available when needed. The fabric must be ordered, along with the other components of the garment. Finally, each garment must be costed out so that the exact cost and selling price can be set. See Figure 8.6 for an illustration of how a typical garment is costed. The samples are used to determine the cost of producing the garment. The money needed to finance production must be obtained. Only when all of these steps have been completed can actual production begin.

The samples, each with its style number, are then presented to retail buyers at the manufacturers' seasonal shows. The retail buyers either accept or reject parts of the line, or more rarely, the entire line. The buyers usually place orders for some of the individual designs. Sometimes they test a line by buying a small number of styles in small quantities. If these styles sell, they reorder them. Most manufacturers have set **minimum orders** for the quantity, number of styles, and/or dollar amount required to accept the retail buyer's order.

MANUFACTURER'S COSTS

Materials		
Wool-blend fabric	$14.60	
Lining	1.90	
Thread	.20	
Zipper	.20	
Button	.40	
Total Materials	17.30	
Labor		
Direct: cut/sew/finish	5.00	
Factory burden	6.25	
FG warehousing, & distribution	2.60	
Total Labor	13.85	
Packing costs	1.95	
(tags, labels, hangers, pins, bags)		
Overhead		
Sewing expense	2.54	
Administrative expense	5.62	
Financing (interest)	.60	
Returns & allowances	2.62	
Total Overhead	11.38	
Trade discount	3.40	
(8% off for prompt payment)		
Taxes	2.20	
Net profit	2.87	

Wholesale $52.95

WOOL-BLEND SKIRT:
Wholesale price $52.95
Retail price $118.00

RETAILER'S COSTS

Initial cost	$52.95
$56.35 less discount for prompt payment	
Markdowns	13.50
(10.6% average over all sportswear)	
Shortage	2.36
(2% of retail price)	
Store/retailing expense	42.48
(36% of retail price) Salaries, sales, promotions, rent, utilities, receiving, marking, administrative costs, insurance.	
Taxes	2.80
Net profit	3.91

Retail Sales Price $118.00

FIGURE 8.6 A costing sheet for a garment includes each component and its cost.

Because the manufacturer usually has not yet begun production when a line is shown to the buyers, it may be possible to fine-tune production to the buyers' orders. When a particular style receives a lot of attention from buyers, it is then scheduled for production. Items that generate little or no enthusiasm are dropped from the line.

Production contracts are often being finalized while the manufacturer's representatives are selling the line to retail accounts. If these two things can be done simultaneously, the manufacturer has a better chance of moving to the next step or "cutting as close to paper as possible," which means limiting the risk of investing in fabric, trim, and production costs while negotiating quantity discounts.

Stage 5: Production

Cutting

One of the most important steps in the mass production of apparel is the cutting of the garment pieces. Once a garment is slated for production, it is **graded**, or sloped, to each of the various sizes in which it will be made. After a pattern has been graded into the various sizes, the pieces are laid out on a long piece of paper called a **marker**. The success of cutting depends on the accuracy with which each of the many layers of material are placed on top of one another. A **spreader**, or laying-up machine, carries the material along a guide on either side of the cutting table, spreading the material evenly from end to end. The marker is laid on top of these layers.

In many companies, cutting is still a manual process, although with the evolution of computer-aided equipment, we are seeing more facilities employing these technologies. Computers are programmed to feed instructions to laser, blade, or high-speed water-jet machines that do the actual cutting.

Once the cutting is completed, the pieces of each pattern—the sleeves, collars, fronts, and backs—are tied into bundles according to their sizes. This process is called **bundling**; it must be done by hand. The bundles are then moved to the manufacturers' sewing operators, who may be on the premises or in contractors' shops.

Sewing

Technology has dramatically changed the sewing stage of production. The industrial sewing machine sews

FIGURE 8.7 Threading and embroidery require both great care and skill. This embroidery machine helps to speed up production.

much faster than a home sewing machine because it has an engine with a clutch and brake rather than a motor. Home sewing machines perform many functions, while industrial machines perform specialized functions. Some sew only seams, while others sew blind hems. Button machines sew on buttons. Computerized sewing machines that have capabilities for embroidery can be set up to stitch whole patterns (Figure 8.7).

Meanwhile, **single-hand operations** still exist, in which one operator sews the entire garment. These are used for very high-priced garments that are produced in very small quantities. Today, most manufacturers use a combination of mass-production systems, including the popular **modular manufacturing system**, in which teams of seven to nine workers produce entire garments, passing them on to each other until the garment is complete. This system requires extensive cross-training, so each team member can learn all the tasks involved and do them as the flow of work demands.

Finishing the Product

The sewn garment is still far from ready for the retail floor. Pants, for example, are sewn with the legs inside out. They must be turned right side out. A label must be sewn in. Buttons and buttonholes may be added at this stage.

Some fabrics are washed at this stage to prevent shrinkage. Others have a wrinkle-resistant finish applied. Still others are dyed at this point, called garment-dyeing, which gives the manufacturer last-minute control of color.

The garment is then pressed and folded or hung on a hanger with a plastic bag over it. Some manufacturers also offer services that make their apparel **floor ready**— that is, with bar-coded price tickets attached, cartons labeled, and shipping documents attached. Of course, this service adds to the cost, but many retailers find that this strategy makes up in speed for the cost. See "Stage 6: Distributing the Line."

Inspecting the Product

Garments are inspected many times during the production process. First the fabric and the dye quality are checked. Cutting is checked for pattern matching and size specs, among other things. Sewing is also checked repeatedly along the way for stitch length, seam type, buttonhole stitching, and hem stitching. **Quality assurance**, or **QA**, which refers to the product meeting the standards established for it, includes the inspection of each ingredient of the garment: fabric, thread, buttons, snaps or zippers, hem tape, linings, shoulder pads, and so forth.

Stage 6: Distributing the Line

Once the line is completed, it still requires more work before the retailer can sell it. Sales tickets and bar codes must be added; these time-consuming tasks are frequently done by the manufacturer, except for the smallest stores. Then shipments must be consolidated and finally sent to retailers by truck, rail, or air.

As the season progresses, manufacturers remain sensitive to retail sales. For example, when reorders come in, they recut only the garments that are most in demand—and therefore, the most profitable. Manufacturers may also recut "hot sellers" in different fabrics and colors to maximize the sales generated by high customer demand.

Specializing by Product

Apparel producers have typically been specialists, producing apparel for a particular gender and age, a particular size range, and a specific price range. A women's blouse manufacturer, for example, seldom makes dresses, and a dress manufacturer usually does not turn out dresses in both women's and junior sizes. A coat and suit manufacturer does not usually produce both expensive and popular-priced lines.

By Gender, Age, and Size Categories, and by Classification

Historically, the U.S. apparel industry has been divided into three major categories: women's, men's, and children's. These three categories are discussed in detail in Chapters 9, 10, and 11. Within these three categories are smaller subcategories, divided by age. For example, children's wear is subdivided into infants', toddlers',

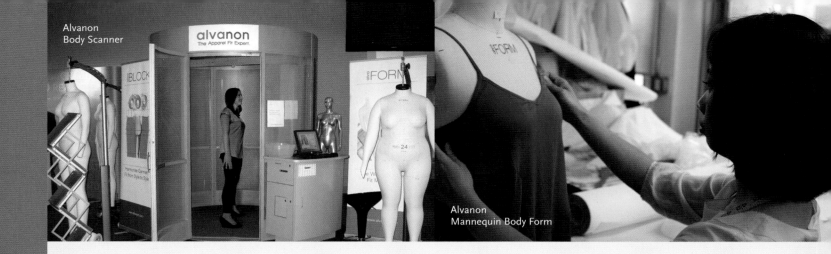

Alvanon Body Scanner

Alvanon Mannequin Body Form

VANITY SIZING

ARE YOU A size 4? A 6? An 8? Often women shoppers don't know and they can actually be all these sizes without gaining or losing an ounce! This is because the retail world is flooded by a sea of clothing sizes. To find the right one, women must tread through "misses," "petites," "pluses," "juniors," "women's," and "one size fits all." And after discovering a favorite fit in one brand, the same woman may need to go one or two sizes larger or smaller when shopping another designer and manufacturer.

Vanity sizing is the culprit behind this seesaw in sizes. Even though a standard measurement chart exists, the U.S. government doesn't enforce standardized sizes for women's clothing because it is next to impossible to require designers and manufacturers to stick to them. Standardizing sizing can complicate transactions between domestic and foreign designers whose countries sometimes have different measurement charts. Also, many brands view their sizing not as a mind game, but as a way to better relate to shoppers' needs, wants, and body types. For designers, the flexibility to come

up with their own sizes helps them create and market clothes for their target customers—and their egos. But studies have found that the public wants clothing labels with more sizing information on them, and stores such as Macy's have launched Web components with tips on what sizes, brands, and styles may be best suited for their customers.

Ed Gribbin, president of Alvanon, the largest maker of mannequin body forms in the world, says everyone has a number in their head. "Every brand looks at their fit as something that's proprietary, like their 'secret sauce,' and none is willing to share that info with anyone else." Alvanon works with brands to expand the number of people they can dress by focusing not only on size numbers but also body shapes. "Every one of our mannequins is based on thousands of body scans of real people," Gribbin says. "There is no perfect anything. We are so diverse that in any given size, there are probably four or six different body types that are represented." Gribbin says color may be the number one reason shoppers gravitate toward a garment, "but fit is the number one reason people buy it or return it, and it's the number one reason they go back to a particular brand."

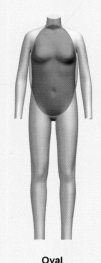

Oval

Rectangle

Modified Hourglass

Hourglass

Spoon

Inverted Triangle

girls' and boys', preteen (girls), and young men's. Within infants' wear, sizes include 0 to 3 months, 6 months, 12 months, 18 months, and 24 months.

Another way that apparel is organized is by the type of garment produced, or classification. Examples for girls' wear include the following:

- Outerwear—coats, jackets, raincoats
- Dresses
- Blouses
- Sportswear—pants, sweaters, shirts
- Active sportswear—swimsuits, skiwear, bike shorts
- Underwear
- Sleepwear
- Socks
- Tights
- School uniforms

Despite a move toward greater diversification, producers and retailers still have to think and work like specialists. For instance, a producer must choose an inexpensive fabric for a popular-priced line and a more expensive fabric for a better-priced line. Retail buyers still shop one group of producers for sportswear, another for coats, and still another for bridal wear—and this practice is not likely to change in the near future.

Brands and Labels

A special supplement to *Women's Wear Daily* listed distinct kinds of brands or labels used by apparel industry insiders:[2]

1. National/designer brand
2. Private label
3. Retail store brand
4. Nonbrands

Customers, of course, realize few of these distinctions; they think of them all as "brands" or "nonbrands." But to retailers and manufacturers, these distinctions are vital, impacting heavily on their profits and offering differentiation in an era when customers complain of the sameness of many stores and the goods they offer.

National/Designer Brands

National brands are those that are owned by a manufacturer who advertises them nationally. Some of the first apparel brands to gain national recognition were the Arrow Shirt Company and the BVD Company, a maker of men's underwear, in the 1930s. National brands continued to grow in number over the next five decades, but the 1980s and 1990s saw a tremendous leap in sales for national brands. In part, this growth resulted from

FIGURE 8.8 J.C. Penney sells the national brand Levi's.

a huge increase in the number of national advertising campaigns directed at consumers. National brands are expected to continue to predominate in the industry, while private labels fill in the cracks.[3] Examples of national brands include Pendleton, Fruit of the Loom, Levi's (Figure 8.8), Carter's, Reebok, Hanes, Revlon, and Juicy Couture.

Designer labels carry the name of a designer; they have grown enormously in number and importance since the 1940s. The four U.S. megadesigners are Ralph Lauren, Calvin Klein, Donna Karan, and Tommy Hilfiger. Hundreds more are working in the United States today. Many other designer names continue to be featured, although the original designer has retired or died; examples include Anne Klein, Liz Claiborne, and Halston.

Designer labels are no longer limited to apparel; they are frequently found on accessories of every kind, on fragrances and cosmetics, and on home furnishings.

Private Labels

A **private label** is one that is owned by a retailer and found only in its stores. For decades, the private label occupied a comfortable but unspectacular niche in U.S. apparel retailing. Starting about thirty years ago, things began to change. Specialty chains, most notably Gap, began to put their names on the clothes they sold.

Examples of private-label apparel are the Jaclyn Smith line sold by Kmart, American Rag sold by Macy's (Figure 8.9), and the Original Arizona Jean Company line sold by J.C. Penney. Today, it is standard practice for specialty chains to sell merchandise only under their own brand's programs. "Everyone is trying to get directly to the consumer with as few middlemen as possible," says Tom Burns, senior vice president of the Doneger Group, the trend analysts and forecasters who work with dozens of stores in the United States and abroad. "Retailers feel they understand consumers and their lifestyles better than anyone and feel that by creating lifestyle brands, whether created, licensed, or bought, they can better control the product and the direction of the product."[4]

At Macy's, private-label lines have been growing three times as fast as wholesale lines—making private-label clothes the fastest growing product category in American department stores.

Terry Lundgren, chairman, president, and CEO of Macy's Inc., says, "Last year [2009], more than 40 percent of Macy's sales came from private labels. This percentage will be growing in the years ahead, particularly with Madonna's Material Girl, Sean John, and other exclusives." At Kohl's, the private-label brands are Simply Vera Vera Wang, Dana Buchman, LC Lauren Conrad, Elle, and Aldo.[5]

Retail Store Brands

A **retail store brand** is the name of a chain that is used as the exclusive label on most of the items in the store or catalog. Examples of retail store brands for apparel and accessories include Gap, The Limited, Ann Taylor, Victoria's Secret, Talbots, L.L.Bean, and J.Crew (Figure 8.10). Examples of store brands for home furnishings include Pier 1, Crate and Barrel, and Williams-Sonoma. Few, if any, national or designer brands are carried by these stores or catalogs.

FIGURE 8.9 Macy's sells the private label American Rag.

FIGURE 8.10 J.Crew is an example of a retail store brand that uses its own label on merchandise.

Nonbrands

This is a label to which customers attach little or no importance. These labels are usually used by firms that manufacture low-priced goods and do little or no advertising to consumers. These labels are found in discount and off-price stores.

Industry Practices

Every industry has its own particular way of conducting business; the apparel industry is no exception. Some of the practices discussed in this section grew as responses to specific industry problems. These practices were once considered trends but are so established now that they are no longer trends but business as usual. The major industry practices that we discuss are manufacturers acting as retailers, licensing, private-label and specification buying, offshore production, the use of factors, chargebacks, and SIC/NAIC Codes.

Manufacturers Acting as Retailers

An increasing number of clothing manufacturers are opening their own stores. Disappointed by the sales, service, and space allotted to them in retail stores and wanting to create the right atmosphere for their clothing, they are choosing to enter the retail business themselves. Of course, larger profits are also part of the attraction. The manufacturer can sell the product to consumers at full retail price rather than at the wholesale price required by retail customers.

Designer Ralph Lauren was the first to take this step. Frustrated by the way department and specialty stores were selling his clothes, he opened the first Polo/Ralph Lauren shop on Rodeo Drive in Beverly Hills in 1971. Since then, he has built an empire of Polo/Ralph Lauren shops that stretches coast to coast in the United States and across the oceans to Europe and Asia. Calvin Klein, Donna Karan, Adrienne Vittadini, Marc Jacobs, and Vivienne Tam have also opened their own retail outlets. Besides designer stores, manufacturing giants VF Corporation, Liz Claiborne, Inc., The Jones Group, Inc., and Kellwood Company are mutating into multi-headed beasts, with direct-to-consumer sides becoming an increasingly large part of their businesses.

But whether all manufacturers and designers will be successful retailers remains to be seen. A producer first has to compete for good retail talent, as well as retail space in a prime location, both of which can be expensive. The risks escalate if the manufacturer franchises, which many must do when they cannot personally oversee their retail empire.

FIGURE 8.11 Outlet malls, like Woodbury Common Premium Outlets, feature factory outlets for stores such as the Gap, Banana Republic, and Polo Ralph Lauren.

Another problem is the reaction of the department and specialty stores that carry the manufacturers' lines. They feel such competition is unfair, and many have decided to stop carrying lines that are sold in manufacturers' own outlets. Other stores have learned to live with the new outlets.

Manufacturers' outlet stores, called factory outlets, have also grown at a rapid rate (Figure 8.11). They allow manufacturers to dispose of poor sellers, overstocks, and seconds and still make more money on them than they could by selling them to discount retailers as closeouts.

The opposite of manufacturers acting as retailers is retailers acting as manufacturers, through the private-label programs of department stores and discounters, and through the retail store brands of specialty chains like Gap and Talbots. These strategies are discussed in depth in Chapter 19.

Licensing

Licensing, which was described in Chapter 5, experienced a boom in the United States in the 1980s and 1990s, largely because of the emergence of an important new market segment—working women. As a group, they are not quite in the income bracket to buy designer clothes, but designers have learned that they can capitalize on the market these women represent through licensing ventures.

The great appeal of licensing is that merchandise is identified with a highly recognizable name. Licensed products in the United States are estimated at $104 billion annually.[6] The advantages for designers include the royalties they receive on the sale of each product (usually from 2 to 15 percent), greater exposure of their

WHEN DO DESIGNERS REACH THE NEXT LEVEL?: THE MAGIC NUMBER

WHEN NEW DESIGNERS send their collections down the runway, they are preoccupied with many thoughts. Are their designs on-trend? How will their new styles be received? When will their companies be ready for the next level? For that last question, at least, there is an answer: The magic number is $25 million!

That is the sales volume that indicates when a brand is on its way to going corporate. But even then, there's no guarantee of success. Many brands lose money in their first few years and very few designer businesses get even close to earning $25 million in sales. Instead, many designers must simply get by with smaller businesses. But there are many ways for smaller brands to generate business that may help them reach the $25 million mark. These designers learn to make money by hustling and being creative—for instance, they get sponsors for their fashion shows or work with as few samples as possible. Buzz and editorial exposure can also help defray a lot of expenses. Some designers earn fees for designing a capsule collection for a mass merchant chain; others open their own retail stores.

But what about those designers who have hit the $25 million level and are now trying to get to the next step up? Brands that have reached $25 million usually have enough notoriety to help them secure a lucrative licensing deal. Then, the sky is the limit. Companies that keep growing beyond $60 million to $100 million, then $200 million and up are able to gain the interest of the public market and join the ranks of other publicly traded fashion companies like Prada, Ferragamo, and Michael Kors.

name, and little investment in product development and manufacturing.

The disadvantages in licensing are few. When designers turn over control to a manufacturer, as they do when they license a product, they may lose some quality control. A bigger concern is that a designer may move too far afield for his or her more exclusive customers, but considering the potential profits in licensing, this is unlikely to worry many designers.

Christian Dior was a pioneer in licensing, having granted his first license in 1949. Even though Dior died in 1957, his name still appears on many products. Besides the Christian Dior shoe, jewelry, perfume, and cosmetic products that are owned and produced under the umbrella of Dior's parent company, LVMH, the brand also has a license with Safilo Group. Pierre Cardin used licenses to create a fashion empire—the largest of its kind—with more than 800 products, from perfumes to pencil holders!

The first landmark deal in licensing in the United States occurred in the 1930s when Mickey Mouse products flooded the market. Later in the 1930s, Shirley Temple was the first human to find a windfall in selling her name for use on dresses, dolls, and an assortment of other products.

One of the pioneers of designer apparel licensing in the United States was Bill Blass, who had forty-two licenses for men's and women's apparel and accessories and home fashions. Anne Klein has many licenses for accessories, such as with Swank for jewelry and other manufacturers for eyeglasses, watches, and coats.

Valentino, another fashion pioneer, was among the first to enter into product extension licensing, and explains it as follows: "Licenses allowed us to expand our business, maintain the couture collection, open boutiques, but in hindsight, a number of those licenses backfired because there was not enough couture. Licenses work if they are under a partnership format." Stefano Sassi, Valentino's current CEO, added that licenses are "key for anyone with goals to develop new projects, expand one's visibility, and complete the brand's perception," and that "it's fundamental to create the right balance between licenses, accessories, and clothing, which should remain Valentino's core business."[7]

A final note on the importance of a company's brand name: **corporate licensing**, or the use of a company's name on related merchandise, is the fastest growing segment of licensing today. Overall, corporate licensing reached $19.7 billion in sales in 2010, according to the International Licensing Industry Merchandisers' Association.[8] The Nike swoosh is seen worldwide. Harley Davidson has licensed its name for T-shirts and

children's wear, Dr. Scholl's has expanded from foot care to pillows, and Jeep even has a line of sunglasses.

Private Label and Specification Buying

The terms private label and specification buying may be used to describe the same items of merchandise, but the meanings are slightly different. If the retailer agrees, the manufacturer may design private-label merchandise for the retailer. Macy's private labels include Alfani, Charter Club, and JM Collection. On the other hand, **specification buying** is a type of purchasing that is done to the store's, rather than the manufacturer's, standards. J.C. Penney and Gap are two examples of stores that make extensive use of specification buying. These retailers provide the standards and guidelines for the manufacture of clothes they order. Standards cover everything from the quality of materials and workmanship to styling and cost.

Specification buying has become so specialized that many stores now employ a **specification manager** or **product manager** who is trained in specification buying. While keeping an eye on industry and government standards, specification managers work closely with manufacturers to ensure that their products will be economically successful for both the retailer and the manufacturer.

As they grow more successful with specification buying, stores have begun to use it for their private-label lines. Initially intended as a way to keep production at home, a growing amount of private label is now purchased offshore. (See also the following section.)

Because retailers often place large orders for a few related lines, the private labels are a growth area for the manufacturers and may account for 20 to 45 percent of the manufacturer's output. According to the individual agreement between retailer and manufacturer, product development can be in the hands of either party. To maintain the separate, distinctive images of their retailer clients' private brands and their own national brands, some manufacturers have separate teams of designers. The manufacturer can achieve economies of scale by sourcing both their national brand and their retailer clients' brands from the same offshore supplier.

Offshore Production

Offshore production is the manufacturing of goods abroad where labor is cheaper. Offshore production is often viewed as a way to reduce costs and therefore compete more effectively with low-cost imports. In the United States, some industry insiders view this practice as a threat to the health of American labor; others regard it as a necessity in order for U.S. manufacturers to remain competitive.

Offshore production is appealing under certain conditions because the federal government gives domestic producers a special tariff advantage, provided only part of the production is done offshore. Under Section 807 of the Tariff Classification Act, for example, manufacturers can cut and design their own garments and finish them domestically, sending only the sewing to a labor-cheap offshore country. Duty is paid only on the value added to the garment by the work done abroad. A substantial amount of offshore production has been in Asia, India, Vietnam, and areas where wages are low and shipping costs less. However, brands and retailers in the United States are now reassessing the value of manufacturing more products domestically.

Use of Factors

Apparel manufacturers and contractors need cash or credit to produce garments the season before they are sold. Some banks have been reluctant to lend money to apparel companies because of the high risks involved. So an alternate system of financing has developed for the apparel industry. Called **factors**, these companies either purchase a manufacturer's accounts receivable or advance cash on the basis of the accounts receivable. Their interest rates are generally higher than those of a bank.

Another practice is the use of credit insurance by firms that do not use factors. Credit insurance, used for decades in Europe, protects the insured company from losses as a result of a customer's bankruptcy or very late payment. Credit insurance is also useful for a U.S. manufacturer with international business, since it is cheaper than international letters of credit.[9]

Chargebacks

As retail chains have grown in size, their power over their suppliers has also increased. Apparel manufacturers are increasingly hit with demands for **chargebacks**, which are financial penalties imposed on manufacturers by retailers. The reasons for chargebacks include errors like mistakes in purchase orders or ticketing. Sometimes retailers request chargebacks for partial or late shipments, or even for poor-selling products. Chargebacks are also used for cooperative advertising. Naturally, chargebacks can cause financial problems for designers and manufacturers, especially small ones.

SIC/NAICS Codes

Another reflection of globalization is the change from the Standard Industrial Classification (SIC) codes to the North American Industry Classification System (NAICS). SIC was originally developed in the 1930s to classify U.S. establishments by the type of activity in which they primarily engage and to create a database of comparable information that would describe the parts of the U.S. economy. Over the years, the SIC was revised periodically to reflect the changes in the businesses that make up the U.S. economy, with the last major revision in 1987. In 1997, the SIC was replaced by the NAICS, which is also being used by Canada and Mexico. The NAICS provides industrial statistics produced in the three countries that are comparable for the first time, reflecting the interrelated nature of these economies. This data is extremely useful for businesses, and the fashion industry is at the forefront of those using the information to aid in decision making. Table 8.2 shows comparisons of the SIC and NAICS codes. (The new codes are much simpler.)

Advanced Technologies and Strategies

A number of advanced technologies and the strategies used to harness them have been implemented by the U.S. apparel industry. These technologies have already had a profound impact on the profitability of the business. They include the use of product lifecycle management (PLM); supply chain management (SCM); bar codes, scanners, and radio-frequency identification (RFID); electronic data interchange (EDI); mass customization; and body scanning.

Product Lifecycle Management

Stand-alone computerized equipment is a big part of most manufacturers' plants. Known as computer-aided manufacturing (CAM), it includes such things as programmable sewing machines, patternmaking machines, and cutting machines.

But the enormous power of the computer lies in its ability to be linked to other computers, so that technology can direct the entire production process from design to finished garment. **Product Lifecycle Management** or **PLM** is a strategic system that links information within a manufacturing company to increase efficiency and manage the life of a product. This technology has the potential for cost savings, optimized lead times, and improved speed to the market. Fashion companies that have implemented extended PLM typically see margin improvements ranging from 5 percent to 20 percent and have reduced cycle times of up to 40 percent.[10]

PLM not only helps the bottom line but also allows for more accurate planning, which reduces markdowns and closeouts. Apparel companies are also incorporating other integrated solutions into their processes, such as enterprise resource planning (ERP). ERP is a system that creates stronger communication among

TABLE 8.2 *Comparison of Selected NAICS and SIC Codes*

NAICS Codes		SIC Codes	
315	Apparel Manufacturing		
3152	Cut and Sew Apparel Manufacturing		
31521	Cut and Sew Apparel Contractors		
315211	Men's and Boys' Cut and Sew Apparel Contractors	2311	Men's and Boys' Suits, Coats, and Overcoats (contractors)
		2321	Men's and Boys' Shirts, Except Work Shirts (contractors)
		2322	Men's and Boys' Underwear and Nightwear (contractors)
		2325	Men's and Boys' Trousers and Slacks (contractors)
		2326	Men's and Boys' Work Clothing (contractors)
		2329	Men's and Boys' Clothing, NEC (contractors)
		2341	Women's, Misses', Children's, and Infants' Underwear and Nightwear (boys' contractors)
		2361	Girl's, Children's, and Infants' Dresses, Blouses, and Shirts (boys' contractors)
		2369	Girl's, Children's, and Infants' Outerwear, NEC (boys' contractors)
		2384	Robes and Dressing Gowns (men's and boys' contractors)
		2385	Waterproof Outerwear (men's and boys' contractors)
		2389	Apparel and Accessories, NEC (contractors)
		2395	Pleating, Decorative and Novelty Stitching, and Tucking for the Trade (men's and boys' apparel contractors)
315212	Women's, Girls', and Infants' Cut and Sew Apparel Contractors	2331	Women's, Misses', and Juniors' Blouses and Shirts (contractors)
		2335	Women's, Misses', and Juniors' Dresses (contractors)
		2337	Women's, Misses', and Juniors' Suits, Skirts, and Coats (contractors)
		2339	Women's, Misses', and Juniors' Outerwear, NEC (contractors)
		2341	Women's, Misses', Children's, and Infants' Underwear and Nightwear (contractors)
		2342	Brassieres, Girdles, and Allied Garments (contractors)
		2361	Girls', Children's, and Infants' Dresses, Blouses, and Shirts (girls' and infants' contractors)
		2369	Girls', Children's, and Infants' Outerwear, NEC (girls' and infants' contractors)
		2384	Robes and Dressing Gowns (women's, girls', and infants' contractors)
		2385	Waterproof Outerwear (women's, girls', and infants' contractors)
		2389	Apparel and Accessories, NEC (contractors)
		2395	Pleating, Decorative and Novelty Stitching, and Tucking for the Trade (women's, girls' and infants' apparel contractors)

various departments by placing all information in one location.[11]

Supply Chain Management

A well-known business strategy that was used in the late 1990s was **Quick Response (QR)**. QR shortened time frames from raw materials to design to production to finished product to the consumer. It was developed to give U.S. manufacturers a potent weapon against imports and foreign competitors. The necessary partnerships and electronic high-tech mechanisms are in place to link all parts of the supply pipeline directly to the nation's retailers. What it really means is a far closer association between manufacturer, supplier, retailer, and customer. It requires the development of trust and communication, and that goes all the way from the cash register to the apparel people and the textile suppliers. Simply put, it aims at delivering the right product at the right time.

A similar concept is called **supply chain management (SCM)**. Supply chain management has the same benefits as QR, but takes the process one step further. SCM allows companies to share forecasting, point-of-sales data, inventory information, and the supply and demand for materials or products. Companies are continually seeking to improve these processes to ultimately increase sales.

Bar Codes, Scanners, and Radio-Frequency Identification

Bar coding, scanning, and **Radio-Frequency Identification (RFID)** communications have become integral parts of supply chain management. Bar coding makes tracking merchandise—from fabric rolls to designer dresses—easier, faster, and more accurate (Figure 8.12).

The **universal product code (UPC)** is one of a number of bar codes used for automatic identification of items scanned at retail cash registers. UPC is the symbol that has been most widely accepted by retailers and manufacturers.

Bar codes are made up of a pattern of dark bars and white spaces of varying widths. A group of bars and spaces represents one character. **Scanners** read the bar code. The UPC symbol does not contain the price of the merchandise; that information is added by the retailer to the store's computerized cash registers. It can be easily changed.

RFID (Figure 8.13) is an item-level tagging device that stores data. It uses a unique serial number that allows the tracking of products, cartons, containers, and individual items as they move through the supply chain. RFID tags hold more data than bar codes and

The Role of Technology in Getting the Right Product to the Right Place at the Right Time

1. SCANNING AT THE POINT OF PURCHASE
   Instant inventory monitoring
2. USING LOCATOR COMPUTER PROGRAM
   Find nearest supply when product runs low
3. TRANSMITTING DATA BY SATELLITE
   Stores can track and order changes
4. USING SUPPLIER/RETAILER COMPUTER LINKS
   Sales history is available to supplier
5. FORECASTING BY COMPUTER
   Improves coordination between retailers and suppliers.

FIGURE 8.12 Bar codes give vital product information.

FIGURE 8.13 RFID tags increase accuracy for recording products and inventory.

can be read many times faster. With this technology, companies have the ability to increase efficiency and accuracy in counting inventory.[12]

Electronic Data Interchange

Electronic data interchange (EDI) is the electronic exchange of machine-readable data in standard formats between one company's computers and another company's computers. It replaces a large number of paper forms that were the primary link between manufacturers and their retailer customers. These included forms like purchase orders, invoices, packing slips, shipping documents, and inventory forms.

EDI is faster than mail, messenger, or air delivery services. By eliminating paper-based transactions, large companies save clerical time, paper, and postage. EDI includes the use of handheld laser scanners, satellite links, and wireless systems. This technology results in both increased productivity and improved customer service.

Mass Customization

For nearly a century, we have lived in a world where mass production has been the model for products and services, because standardized products mean lower costs. And yet every time a customer takes home an attribute that he or she really does not want in the product, it is a form of waste. In **mass customization**, the idea is to tailor the product to fit one particular customer—not one size fits all—and to supply thousands of individuals at mass prices, not custom-made prices.

Women often have a harder time than men finding clothes that fit. Today, mass customization is not technically true customization, but rather an automated form of made-to-measure apparel.

Since Levi's introduced its now-discontinued Personal Pair jeans in 1995, more than a dozen fashion companies have tried mass customization, so named because it combines advanced technology with factory production, instead of old-fashioned craftsmanship, to make something unique yet affordable. Among the companies who are using mass customization are Lands' End, Tommy Hilfiger, Target, Ralph Lauren, J.C. Penney, Nike, Timberland, Atelier, and Brooks Brothers.

Body Scanning

Currently, more than one-third of the apparel returned by American women is brought back to stores because it doesn't fit well. Body shapes tend to change significantly three times in a woman's life—around ages 20, 35, and 55—and those variations, along with the 60-year-old sizing system that hasn't evolved with women's changing body types, has made a good fit harder to find.

Body-scanning technology has evolved to help manufacturers, retailers, and customers to get a better fit. An example of a 3-D body scanner system in use today is Intellifit (Figure 8.14). Within seconds, the scanner takes a snapshot of the human form and produces a 3-D replica with complete measurement data. As more apparel companies discover 3-D body-scanning technology, the fitting room as we know it could become a thing of the past.

FIGURE 8.14 Intellifit allows shoppers to get better-fitting clothing, without having to waste too much time in the dressing room.

FIGURE 8.15 Calvin Klein extended its apparel brand with handbags and shoes.

Industry Trends

The fashion industry is moving closer to traditional marketing models for consumer goods. We focus on three trends that prove this point: brand extensions, industry cooperation, and globalization.

Brand Extensions

A common technique in consumer goods marketing is **brand extension**, a strategy in which a company uses a successful brand name to launch new or modified products. Brand extension saves the company the high cost of promoting a new name and creates instant brand recognition of the new product line (Figure 8.15). It is one way in which a company can diversify its product line. This is a common strategy of packaged goods manufacturers; for example, the Dial brand of the Armour conglomerate was used on a variety of products beyond the original bar soap. One fashion company that extended its line is Fossil, which was successful with watches and then branched out into handbags and belts.

In the apparel industries, a move into a related category of apparel is the easiest and cheapest way to diversify. A company that makes T-shirts may add a line of cotton sweatshirts, which are also sized small, medium, large, and extra large. A designer of men's suits may add coats. A children's wear manufacturer may add an infants' line. A women's shoe manufacturer may add matching handbags.

The move to an unrelated line has traditionally been more difficult—and more costly. One of the first brand extensions by apparel designers was expanding into fragrances and cosmetics. Other examples of brand extensions include adding accessories, men's and women's wear, children's wear, and home furnishings.

Industry Cooperation

It is necessary for companies in the fashion industry to harness technology as they strive to push costs out of the entire product distribution pipeline rather than to just push costs onto their trading partners. The issue of partnerships, or strategic alliances, between textile producers, apparel and accessories manufacturers, and retailers is discussed in more detail in Chapter 19.

Globalization

Globalization of the marketplace—finding both foreign competitors and foreign customers—has happened to a wide range of U.S. heavy manufacturing industries; for example, cars, televisions, electronics, steel, and computers. Starting in the 1970s, globalization occurred in the apparel industries and is still flourishing today. The globalization of the fashion business has made it necessary for companies both large and small to have a worldview, a global perspective that helps them to see the possibilities for their businesses. Today, a U.S. apparel company might source fabric from China, manufacture garments in Vietnam, send them to Italy for custom design work, and ship the final product to a U.S. warehouse for retail delivery. There is no way this can be done without a worldview and some sophisticated logistics technology. (See Chapter 17 for further discussion on this topic.)

Summary and Review

The men's, women's, and children's apparel industries develop and produce lines of apparel following a standard cycle. The six-stage process of developing and producing a line involves (1) planning a line, (2) creating the design concept, (3) developing the designs, (4) planning production, (5) production, and (6) distributing the line.

Types of producers include manufacturers, apparel jobbers, and contractors. Producers specialize by gender, age, and size categories, as well as by classification. While consumers generally do not know the differences, industry insiders distinguish between the major types of brands and labels: (1) national/designer brands, (2) private labels, (3) retail store brands, and (4) nonbrands.

Major industry practices that directly affect profitability include manufacturers acting as retailers, licensing, private label and specification buying, off-shore production, the use of factors, chargebacks, and SIC/NAICS codes.

Advanced technologies affecting product development of apparel include product lifecycle management (PLM); supply chain management (SCM); bar codes, scanners, and radio-frequency identification (RFID); electronic data interchange (EDI); mass customization; and body scanning.

Product development is also affected by the major industry trends of brand extensions, industry cooperation, and globalization.

For Review

1. How does a jobber differ from a manufacturer?
2. What are the major advantages of the contractor system? What is the key disadvantage?
3. What are the six stages of the product development process?
4. What is a chargeback?
5. What is the goal of supply chain management?
6. Why do most fashion producers sell directly to retail stores rather than through wholesalers?
7. What is the difference between a national brand and a private label?
8. What role does offshore production play in the fashion industry?
9. What are the benefits of PLM?
10. Discuss the major problems facing a manufacturer who is also a retailer.

For Discussion

1. Compare and contrast the roles of the designer, the merchandiser, and the product manager in developing a line.
2. Give current examples of brand extensions in apparel, accessories, beauty, and home furnishings.

Trade Talk

Define or briefly explain the following terms:

anchor
apparel contractor
apparel jobber
apparel manufacturer
bar code
body scanning
brand extension
bundling
chargeback
collection
computer-aided design (CAD)
computer-aided manufacturing (CAM)
corporate licensing
electronic data interchange (EDI)
factor
floor ready
freelance artist-designer
graded
group
high-fashion or name designer
item house
line
line-for-line
manufacturer (apparel)
marker
mass customization

minimum order
modular manufacturing system
national brand
offshore production
outside shop
piecework
private label
product development
product lifecycle management (PLM)
product manager
quality assurance (QA)
Quick Response (QR)
Radio-Frequency Identification (RFID)
retail store brand
sample hand
scanner
section work
single-hand operation
specification buying
specification manager
spreader
stylist-designer
supply chain management (SCM)
universal product code (UPC)

KEY CONCEPTS

- Categories, size ranges, and price zones of women's apparel
- Roles of brand names and designer names in the marketing of women's wear
- Advertising and promotional activities in the marketing of women's apparel
- Trends in the women's apparel industry

The manufacturing and merchandising of women's apparel is a giant multibillion-dollar industry employing hundreds of thousands of people. Its influence on the economy is so strong that retail sales figures are one indicator of the health of the nation's economy.

Of necessity, the industry exists in a constant state of change, reacting on an ongoing basis to women's tastes and styles, to an increasingly global economy, and to new technology (Figure 9.1). It is an industry that truly thrives on change and novelty.

History of the Women's Apparel Industry

For thousands of years, people made their own clothes, often producing their own raw materials and converting them into textiles with which they could sew. A farmer might grow cotton, for example, and his wife would spin and weave it into cotton fabric, which she then used to make the family's clothes. Until the mass manufacturing of clothing began, sewing was considered women's work, except for the clothing of the wealthy man, who

"bespoke" handmade garments from a male tailor who specialized in men's high-fashion apparel.

The first step in moving the manufacture of clothes out of the home came around 1800, when professional male tailors began to make more men's clothing. These clothes were still **custom-made**, that is, fitted to the individual who would wear them, and then sewn by hand. A few professional dressmakers began to make women's clothes, but only rich women could afford these custom-made designs. Most women still sewed their own clothes at home.

Growth of Ready-to-Wear

The mass production of clothing did not begin until the mid-nineteenth century. After the Civil War, some manufacturers began to mass-produce cloaks and mantles for women. These garments were not fitted, so they could be made in standard sizes and produced in large numbers.

By the turn of the century, limited quantities of women's suits, skirts, and blouses were being made in factories. Around 1910, someone had the idea of sewing a blouse and skirt together in what was called a shirtwaist, and the women's ready-to-wear dress business was born.

FIGURE 9.1 The "ups and downs" of fashion and skirt lengths from the 1900s–1960s. Source: Courtesy of H.W. Gossard Co.

In contrast to custom-made clothes produced by professional dressmakers or tailors or made by home sewers, **ready-to-wear (RTW)** clothes are produced in factories to standardized measurements. In the first decade of the twentieth century, growing numbers of women began to substitute store-bought clothes for home-sewn ones.

Acceptance of Ready-to-Wear in the Twentieth Century

By the 1920s, most women shopped for their wardrobes in department and women's specialty stores. Mass production and distribution through retail outlets accelerated the fashion cycle of styles produced in the following three decades and made the latest fashions available to the vast middle and working classes. With technological improvements in machinery and the development of synthetic fabrics, fashion producers were able to respond quickly to the changing needs of women for clothing that suited changing social, economic, and political conditions.

Growth of the Fashion District

Crucial in the evolution and success of the American ready-to-wear business is New York's fashion district. This fashion center was created early in the twentieth century by a committee of clothing manufacturers working with investors and a major real estate developer. The manufacturers had outgrown their small shops and factories on the Lower East Side and needed to expand. They wanted to move into a new, mostly undeveloped area of the burgeoning city. Between 1918 and 1921, fifty to sixty manufacturers moved uptown to Seventh Avenue, along the west side of Manhattan. With more room for expansion in the new area, these entrepreneurs were able to parlay a baby business into a mature industry.

New York City, already a major industrial center, was well positioned to capitalize on the ready-to-wear boom. A large pool of cheap immigrant labor was available. In addition, New York was ideally located near the textile producers in New England and the South. It was also a port city, so imported textiles could be brought in when needed. By 1923, the city was producing 80 percent of all women's apparel, with 20 percent still being done by home sewers and custom tailors. The 1920s and 1930s saw the emergence of several large clothing manufacturers.

Although New York remains the fashion capital of the United States and an international fashion center, sportswear and activewear manufacturers are now booming in California, especially in Los Angeles.

Unionization

The history of the women's apparel business cannot be told without also describing the growth and influence of the clothing unions. The success of the industry in the early twentieth century came about largely because the manufacturers were able to draw upon a substantial supply of immigrant labor. The industry was dominated by Jewish and Italian workers. In 1910, 55 percent of garment workers were Jewish, 35 percent were Italian, and 10 percent were from other groups. Many of the immigrants had no skills, but a sizable number had trained as dressmakers or tailors in their homelands. Skilled and unskilled labor was needed in the garment industry, which seemed to have gotten big overnight. The opportunity to turn a large and quick profit was enormous, at least for the owners.

At the other end of the scale, unfortunately, were the workers, who worked long hours for very little pay under conditions that were totally unregulated. A typical garment factory was dark, overcrowded, unsanitary, and unsafe.

In 1900, the workers began to unionize, a move they saw as their only chance to improve their working conditions. The International Ladies Garment Workers Union (ILGWU) was formed, and it remained the major garment industry union for many years.

Unionization did not happen overnight, and employers resisted the new union's demands as much as they could. Strikes in 1909 and 1910 paved the way for collective bargaining (Figure 9.2), but public sympathy for the ladies' garment workers was not aroused until the devastating Triangle Shirtwaist Factory fire in 1911. One hundred forty-six workers, most of them young women, were killed. A tragedy of massive proportions, it nonetheless lent strength to the union movement.

At last people began to realize that the union stood for more than collective bargaining, that indeed many of its demands revolved around matters of life and death. The union's new strength opened the door to many concessions that helped the workers, such as strict building codes and protective labor laws. Child labor was outlawed.

The ILGWU managed to survive the Depression years. Under the guidance of David Dubinsky, who took the helm in 1932 and held it for thirty-four years, the ILGWU enjoyed a period of expansion, and the garment industry underwent a period of innovative growth. ILGWU negotiated a thirty-five-hour, five-day work week and paid vacations. It instituted health, welfare, and pension programs and financed housing projects and recreation centers.

From 1975 until 1995, the ILGWU fought imports—the first real threat to the American women's apparel

FIGURE 9.2 Women picketed in the early 1900s to improve their unsatisfactory working conditions.

industry in several decades—with its Look for the Union Label campaign. As part of the Union of Needletrade, Industrial, and Textile Employees (UNITE), it actively supports the current Crafted with Pride in U.S.A. campaign and the movement to abolish sweatshops at home and abroad (see Chapter 17).

In 1995, the ILGWU merged with the Amalgamated Clothing and Textile Workers Union. UNITE, as the new union was known, represented the majority of workers in basic apparel and textiles, as well as millinery, shoes, and gloves.

However, in 2004, because of waning union membership in the apparel and textile industries, UNITE and HERE (Hotel Employees and Restaurant Employees International Union) merged, forming UNITE HERE. In 2009, as a result of disagreements within the union, UNITE HERE broke up and formed Workers United, a new union that represents a diverse membership of apparel manufacturing employees.

Organization and Operation of the Women's Apparel Industry

For many decades, the typical women's apparel company was a small, independently owned, and often family-run business. Unlike the automobile industry, no Ford or General Motors dominated the women's apparel industry. In the early 1970s, about 5,000 firms made women's dresses. The industry's power came from its collective size. Its 5,000 firms did $3 billion in business every year.

All this changed in the 1970s. An expanding economy led to increased demand for everything, including clothing. Many of the textile companies had grown into huge businesses, as had several major retailers. Pushed from both directions, the clothing manufacturers responded by merging to create large, publicly owned corporations.

Within a few years, it became obvious that many of the large corporations and conglomerates were not

THE SISTER ACT

1. If I said "The Row," what would you say?
2. If I said "Rodarte," what would you say?

The answers:
1. The Olsen Twins
2. The Mulleavy Sisters

Good for you! You got all the right answers—and if you didn't, read on and learn.

THE ROW'S OLSEN twins and Rodarte's Mulleavy sisters all started in showbiz before they took their talent to the fabulous world of fashion. The Olsens got their start in TV, the Mulleavys in opera, movies, and art. This experience gave both duos the knowledge they needed in order to start and maintain very successful fashion enterprises.

Mary Kate and Ashley Olsen made the transition from child actresses to fashion designers, avoiding the "fast-luck" stigma of some celebrity brands. Their serious approach to business has earned them what some other "celebrity" lines have lacked—industry respect. Certainly, fame opened the door for them, but their close connection to their core audience—mostly through marketing via social media—has been at the heart of their success. Today, the Olsens' company, Dualstar Entertainment Group LLC., oversees their multimedia ventures, including The Row designer line; the contemporary brand, Elizabeth and James; Olsenboye, the junior line exclusive to J.C. Penney;

and the members-only, highly personalized retail venture, Stylemint.com. In 2012, their success received industry recognition when the sisters were awarded the prestigious CFDA Award for Women's Wear Designer of the Year.

Kate and Laura Mulleavy, the inseparable sisters behind the Rodarte label, have taken couture down roads of their own choosing: horror movies, Renaissance painting, and opera. A typical creative meeting with the sisters goes something like this: "Well, let's dress the chorus all in white. No, let's not dress them at all. Yes, let's dress them, but let's dress them in paper and we'll project things onto them." Clearly, the Mulleavy sisters' unconventional approach to fashion resonates with other artists. Their avant-garde creations have won them nearly every fashion accolade, and they have a cult following among A-list actresses like Cate Blanchett, Natalie Portman, Reese Witherspoon, Keira Knightley, Kirsten Dunst, Chloe Sevigny, and Elle and Dakota Fanning. That is an achievement we can all appreciate.

Mary Kate & Ashley Olsen

The Row Fall 2011

Laura & Kate Mulleavy

Rodarte Fall 2013

as successful as the smaller companies had been. The major problem was that the giants lacked the ability to respond quickly, a necessity in the fashion industry. Those that have survived and prospered have combined the advantages of large and small size by having divisions and subsidiaries function independently within the larger structure.

Regardless of whether a company is part of a conglomerate or a family-owned shop, the way in which clothes are produced does not vary. The operation of the apparel industry remains remarkably similar from business to business. The organization of the industry is currently undergoing changes, however. After years of specialization, giant apparel producers have emerged, bringing diversification. A number of the giants have divisions manufacturing menswear, children's wear, home fashions, and accessories. Other fashion businesses branched *into* women's wear. Ralph Lauren, who began his career designing neckties, subsequently began a women's line to parallel his menswear designs. Nike and Reebok expanded from manufacturing athletic footwear to producing men's and women's activewear to go with their lines of shoes.

Size of Producers

The legacy of the mergers and acquisitions of the 1980s is a bottom-line mentality. The trend toward giantism shows no signs of letting up. It will continue if for no other reason than that the economy demands it. This means that as some firms strive to become giants, many small- and medium-sized firms will be swallowed up or will go out of business because they cannot compete. But those giants that give their subsidiaries and divisions the autonomy needed to serve their markets and thereby get to the bottom line can expect to continue to prosper. One example of a giant apparel firm that is growing is the VF Corporation, which designs, manufactures, and markets apparel for women, men, and children, with the following brand names: 7 For All Mankind, Lee, Wrangler, Riders, Rustler, Vans Off the Wall, and JanSport, among others.

The Role of Designers

Designers, too, must balance diversification with specialization. From superstars to the new generation struggling to be recognized, all designers specialize to the extent that they are marketing their own artistic identity to a segment of the population that shares their vision.

Today, as designers from the United States show in Paris and Milan, and European and Japanese designers show in New York, fashion-conscious consumers have a virtually limitless choice of looks they can adopt. There

FIGURE 9.3 Oscar de la Renta shows off his unique designs in women's apparel.

is the gentrified elegance of Ralph Lauren; the clean, crisp silhouettes of Derek Lam; the eye-catching prints of Prabal Gurung; and the luxury and sumptuousness of Oscar de la Renta (Figure 9.3). The established designers of upscale lines not only cater to the people who can afford their clothing but also lead the way for producers of more moderately priced fashion in interpreting trends in fashion and popular culture.

Categories in Women's Apparel

The following are the basic categories in women's apparel, and the types of garments generally included in each are organized in Table 9.1.

The categories of outerwear, suits, dresses, and blouses have been fixtures in the women's ready-to-wear industry from the beginning, and sportswear and separates has been an important category since the 1930s. Jeans are considered a separate category by many manufacturers and retailers because of their unique position in Americans' wardrobes. The uniforms and aprons category fills a consumer need but does not set fashion trends. The same is true of the category for special needs.

Increasing attention to the categories of activewear, formal or after-five wear, bridal wear, and maternity deserve further discussion. Along with apparel for the physically challenged, these categories may be thought of as small market segments or niche markets that can be grouped by lifestyle and interests.

TABLE 9.1 *Basic Categories in Women's Apparel and the Types of Garments Included in Each Category*

CATEGORY	TYPES OF GARMENTS	CATEGORY	TYPES OF GARMENTS
Outerwear	Coats, rainwear, jackets	Activewear	Clothing for participatory sports and athletic activities such as swimwear, tennis dresses, running suits, cycling shorts, exercise apparel, and skiwear
Dresses	One- or two-piece designs and ensembles (a dress with a jacket or coat)	Uniforms and aprons	Aprons, smocks, housedresses, and a variety of uniforms
Blouses	Dress and tailored	Maternity	Dresses, sportswear, evening clothes, suits, and blouses designed to accommodate the special needs of pregnant women
Suits	Jacket/skirt and jacket/pants combinations	Innerwear	Brassieres, panties, shapewear, bodywear, sleepwear, and other intimate apparel (see Chapter 12)
After-5 and evening clothes	Formal and prom gowns, and other dressy apparel; this is often called "special occasion"	Special needs	Dresses, slops, nightgowns, hosiery, and other intimate apparel designed with snaps or Velcro for ease of use by elderly or physically challenged women
Bridal wear	Gowns and dresses for brides, attendants, and mothers of the bride and groom		
Sportswear and separates	Town-and-country and spectator sportswear, such as pants, shorts, tops, sweaters, skirts, shirts, jackets, casual dresses, and jumpsuits		

OUTERWEAR    DRESSES    AFTER-5 AND EVENING    UNIFORMS

Activewear

Two-thirds of women dedicate at least half of their closets to activewear. **Activewear** is apparel made for specific sports and exercise activities, but it has also become part of many people's everyday wardrobes. More people are embracing yoga pants and hoodies in and out of the gym. Women's activewear alone has doubled in the last ten years to a $14 billion industry, according to research firm the NPD Group.[1]

Demand for high-tech performance apparel, from weekend warriors and world-class athletes alike, helped drive up sales of sports apparel. Although prices have been steadily rising in the active apparel area, they have not deterred customers, because the performance products today deliver more than is traditionally expected of fashion, such as moisture management and temperature control. Still, fashion and lifestyle play a big part of consumers' choices.

As the country becomes more casual and the gym rats become more fashionable, the lines between sportswear and activewear are blurring. As sportswear companies enter the athletic area and customers look to active companies to dress them outside the gym, athletic apparel companies are examining the balance between performance and fashion (Figure 9.4). One company that has blended fashion and function to great success is luxury brand retailer Lululemon. With sales topping $1 billion in 2011, Lululemon has a devout following of women who wear their signature activewear—retailing at approximately $90 and up—and other apparel inside and outside of the studio or gym.[2]

Another way that sportswear companies are making activewear fashionable is by enlisting big-name designers from the fashion world. Some fashion-focused lines, particularly big-name collaborations, are Adidas with Stella McCartney and Emporio Armani with Reebok.

Swimwear has been an important segment of the women's apparel industry for decades, and the business has evolved somewhat differently from other activewear. Stodgy swimsuits just won't cut it anymore. Newer brands are among those companies picking up the slack. However, manufacturers jumping into the swimwear market beware: adjusting to rapid fashion trends that have kept contemporary apparel whirling has become critical for success in swimwear as well.

FIGURE 9.4 Puma's activewear is both functional and fashionable.

FIGURE 9.5 Ski wear is on the rise. Here, skier Lindsey Vonn wears a specially designed look from Under Armour at the Olympics.

Old and young women are getting bigger in one area: cup size. Some brands are cutting cups up to DD and E, and Lauren by Ralph Lauren is increasing the number of swimsuit groups that feature D cups.

Some of the fabrics that are used in other activewear are also used in swimsuits, but for a different purpose. Lycra, for example, provides control that improves the appearance of the fit. The biggest U.S. manufacturers of swimwear continue to be such specialists as Jantzen and Catalina, which produce designer brands through licensing agreements and also produce their own lines.

The ski and snowboarding industry has been slow to adapt to wider fashion trends over the years, but this is another area of activewear on the rise (Figure 9.5). New technology provides better-fitting clothing and movement on and off the slopes. Robert Yturri, senior vice president of product and brand management at Obermeyer, says, "Silhouettes are becoming a lot more form fitting. That versatility of having a ski jacket that goes from slope to street is what we're seeing." The gap between ski wear and snowboarding apparel is also narrowing. Companies are now more open to expanding their products and image, whereas in the past they were strictly known as either ski or snowboarding producers.[3]

Formal Wear

Despite the growing casualness of everyday apparel, people all over the world still like to mark special occasions by wearing formal clothing. Elegant fabrics, trim,

and silhouettes—worn with more elaborate jewelry, watches, and other accessories—mark most formal wear. This category is often called "after-five" or "special occasion."

Designers like Marchesa, Roberto Cavalli, among others, specialize in dressing Hollywood stars for opening nights and awards ceremonies; thousands of women across the country want similar looks for weddings, dances, and formal dinners.

It is interesting to note that evening wear gets more media coverage than any other category, especially at the Oscars, the Tony Awards, the Grammy Awards, and similar events.

Picking out a prom dress has become a coming-of-age ritual in many parts of the United States, not unlike the formal "coming out" party ritual for debutantes—as well as a solid source of income for many manufacturers and retailers.

Bridal Wear

Bridal wear has always been a category for a personal fashion statement, both for brides and designers. The tradition of the haute couture runway shows in Paris is to conclude with the modeling of a bridal gown, and some designers are known primarily for their work in this category. Weddings of movie stars, royalty, and other celebrities often inspire trends in bridal fashions, but the range of available styles runs from modern interpretations of Victorian designs to unadorned slip dresses. Hemlines range from the traditional floor length to street length to mini, and variety appears even in color. The rising age of first-time brides and the increase in the number of second weddings in recent years has contributed to the popularity of sophisticated styles.

In 2011, more than 2.1 million couples were married in the United States, and the average cost for the wedding expenses was estimated at $27,021.[4] The wedding reception with food, liquor, music, photographs, and so on costs most of the money. But what about the wedding dress? For many brides, the wedding dress is really the top priority, and they spend an average of $1,099 for their gown. Designers like Vera Wang, Carolina Herrera, Reem Acra, Badgley Mischka, and Nicole Miller cater to these brides each year (Figure 9.6). Shrugs, jackets, and shorter dresses are all trends that have been seen on the bridal runways. Are there ways to cut the dress costs? Mainstream retailers such as J.Crew and Ann Taylor are bringing bridal gowns into their stores at lower prices. And of course there's always eBay. More than 5,000 dresses were sold on the auction site in a six-month period in 2007, with winning prices ranging from $50 to $5,200. There is also

FIGURE 9.6 Fashion designers offer a wide range of fashionable gowns for the modern bride. From left to right: Dresses from Kenneth Pool and Carolina Herrera.

Size Ranges

Women's apparel is divided into several size ranges. Unfortunately, the industry has not yet developed standard industry-wide size measurements for each of these ranges, although exploratory work has been undertaken in this direction. In many cases, the manufacturer has the pattern made to fit its targeted customer's approximate size measurement. This is why one manufacturer's misses' size 12 is likely to fit quite differently from another manufacturer's misses' size 12. With licensing agreements and offshore production playing an increasing role in apparel manufacturing, even two different styles bearing the same label in the same size may fit differently.

Women's wear is produced in the following size ranges:

- *Misses*—Includes regular even-numbered sizes 4 to 22, tall sizes 12 to 20, and sometimes sizes as small as 0 to 2.
- *Juniors*—Includes regular sizes 5 to 21 and petite sizes 1 to 15.
- *Petites*—Includes misses' even-numbered sizes usually in 2P to 22P.
- *Women's*—Includes even-numbered sizes and range from sizes 14 to 24, with half sizes, such as 14½. Women's Petite includes even-numbered sizes 12WP to 26WP.
- *Plus*—Includes sizes 14W to 28W, and XL to 5X.

Misses

Misses' sizes are cut to fit the average adult woman's figure. Most women who are between five feet five inches and five feet nine inches tall and of average weight can find suitably proportioned sizes in this range. You may hear the term "missy" used to describe this size range.

Juniors

The juniors range was introduced in the 1950s by Anne Fogarty, whose Anne Fogarty Five was

FIGURE 9.7 Customers can find comfort, sophistication, and style in today's maternity wear, such as this look from Jessica Simpson's line for Destination Maternity.

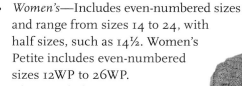

the option of borrowing a dress from a friend—which is widely accepted today. Besides, each bride needs "something borrowed," doesn't she?[5]

Maternity

Providing quality, comfort, and fit, maternity wear is so popular, some moms admit they were better dressed when they were pregnant than after their babies were born. The influx of ready-to-wear designs joining the maternity sector has changed the image of maternity wear. The designers are translating current trends and bringing them into the maternity industry faster than they did in the past (Figure 9.7).

In the last few years, there has been a new image of the state of pregnancy, and many retailers credit Hollywood for the change. Celebrities have been influencing fashion through celebrity clothing lines, and what they wear becomes very popular.

Destination Maternity Corporation is the world's leading maternity apparel retailer. As of May 2011, Destination Maternity operates 2,361 retail locations, including 663 stores predominantly under the trade names Motherhood Maternity®, A Pea in the Pod®, Destination Maternity®, and Oh Baby by Motherhood® (exclusively for Kohl's). They also sell its products through their brand-specific websites.[6]

designed to fit a slimmer, shorter-waisted figure than the misses' size 6, which was the smallest readily available size at the time. Because the juniors figure is more common among teenagers than fully developed women, much of the apparel in this range has youthful styling, and many of the customers in juniors departments and stores are teenagers. Companies like Wet Seal, Rampage, and XOXO are responding to the growth of the juniors market, as is the specialized juniors catalog and store dELiA*s. Clearly, this segment of the market promises great opportunities for producers and retailers.

Petites

Proportioned for short, small-boned women who mostly wear sizes 0 to 8, petite sizes are worn by both junior and misses customers. Not only are the skirts and pant legs shorter than in regular-sized apparel, but the sleeves are shorter as well, and details such as collars and pockets are scaled down. Some companies that offer petite sizing include J.Crew, Banana Republic, and Ann Taylor.

Women's

Approximately one-third of all women in the United States wears women's sizes 16 through 20, 26 to 52, XL to 5X, and women's petites sizes 12WP to 26WP, which are designed to fit shorter women with a fuller bust and shorter waistline. However, in the past, apparel in these sizes made up only a small percentage of production and was notable for its lack of style. This has all changed! Designers and manufacturers got on the bandwagon, and labels like Liz Claiborne, Dana Buchman, and Eileen Fisher began making stylish clothes for larger-sized women.

Plus Size

The plus-size market, as it is now known, does $35 billion annually. Industry watchers say the plus-size apparel market for women is one of the fastest-growing sectors in retail (Figure 9.8). Department stores took the lead, moving larger sizes to their main apparel shopping floors. It is estimated that 30 percent of clothes in larger sizes are private-label or store brands.

Many specialty retailers have also begun to woo this customer. Talbots started "Talbots Woman" as a store dedicated to larger sizes, Gap offers clothing through size 20, and Old Navy's online-only Women's Plus collection includes sizes 16 through 30. Lands' End and L.L.Bean, leading catalog companies, have devoted special catalogs to these customers, and their business has been overwhelming. Both Catherines and Lane Bryant, which are part of Ascena Retail Group, Inc., have become popular plus-size businesses.

With celebrities like Mo'Nique, Queen Latifah, Chenese Lewis (who was the first woman crowned Miss Plus America), and Toccara Jones (the first plus-size supermodel appearing on television regularly), the new look of the stylish and sophisticated plus-size woman has been reinforced. Mass and midtier stores are the top destinations for plus-size fashions. Kmart, Sears, and Dress Barn are some examples of the most popular shops, but retailers like Wal-Mart and Kohl's are taking their trendy lines, such as Jennifer Lopez Collection, Daisy Fuentes, and Apt. 9, into plus sizes. A popular online plus-size fashion website is Pasazz.net, which features many plus-size merchants and offers fashion-conscious, plus-size women around the world a welcoming community where they can share their joys and frustrations about being full-figured in a "thin is in" world.

Wholesale Price Points

Women's apparel is produced and marketed at a wide range of wholesale prices. Major factors contributing to the wholesale price of a garment are:

- The quality of materials
- The quality of workmanship
- The amount and type of labor required in the production process
- The executive and sales position structure of the organization
- Showroom rent and business overhead

Major Price Zones

Within the wide range of prices, however, there are certain traditional **price zones**, or series of somewhat contiguous price lines that appeal to specific target groups of customers. The women's ready-to-wear market has six major price zones. In order from the most to least expensive, they are as follows:

1. *Designer Signature.* The highest price zone includes lines by such name designers as Ralph Lauren, Oscar de la Renta, Calvin Klein, Donna Karan, and Jean Paul Gaultier. A jacket alone costs more than $1,500.
2. *Bridge.* This zone is so named because it bridges the price ranges between designer and better prices.

FIGURE 9.8 Lucky Brand provides stylish apparel for the plus-size consumer.

Look Book

FIGURE 9.9 Price determines which customers are buying what products. Ellen Tracy's merchandise is an example of a bridge price point.

Bridge merchandise usually costs one-third to one-half of designer prices, or $800 to $1,000 for a three-piece outfit. A jacket alone costs about $300. Some designers who produce lines at the designer signature zone or at lower zones also have bridge lines. Examples include Tommy by Tommy Hilfiger, Donna Karan's DKNY, Calvin Klein's CK, and Theory's Premise.[7] Ellen Tracy (Figure 9.9), Tahari, Dana Buchman, Eileen Fisher, and Andrea Jovine are positioned as bridge companies.

3. *Contemporary.* This zone is favored by young designers who want to enter the market with innovative, designer-quality lines but, at the same time, seek a broader market than that of the designer signature zone. By using less expensive fabrics and locating their stores in lower-rent spaces, they can offer their lines at lower prices. Jackets wholesale from $90 to $120. Labels in this zone include Laundry by Shelli Segal, Vivienne Tam, and Cynthia Rowley.

4. *Better.* Apparel in this zone is usually medium to high in price. New labels in the better category include RACHEL, by Rachel Roy, which is sold exclusively at Macy's and ranges in price from $89 to $149. Other labels found in better departments include Liz Claiborne, Ellen Tracy, Jones New York, Nautica, and Chaus.

5. *Moderate.* As the name suggests, this zone includes lines of nationally advertised makers, such as Guess, Esprit, Levi Strauss, and Jantzen, that have less prestige than lines with designer names but still appeal to middle-class consumers. However, more designer firms are moving into this price zone. Moderate merchandise is sold mostly in chain stores or in main-floor departments in department stores.

6. *Budget.* The lowest price zone is sometimes referred to as the "promotional" or "mass" market. It includes some national brand names such as Wrangler and Donnkenny but refers primarily to mass-market retailer private labels, such as J.C. Penney's Arizona line of jeans, Sears's Canyon River Blues line of jeans, or Kmart's Jaclyn Smith line.

There is also a seventh price zone, the *high end*, for the superrich. Some designers are trading up, offering special pieces in very limited quantities and at astronomical prices. This range is aimed at people who crave exclusivity and have the means to afford it. Carolina Herrera, Bill Blass, and Oscar de la Renta are known for developing exclusive designs for special customers.

Multiple Price Zones

Some producers offer merchandise in several price zones to capture a share of the business in each of several market segments. Manufacturer/retailer firms such as The Limited and Gap cater to different price-zone markets in each of their member store chains. Merchandise at The Limited stores appeals to a higher-income customer than that at New York & Company.

Gap's stores have a somewhat overlapping price zone structure, with Banana Republic merchandise at its highest zones, Gap catering to the middle of its market, and Old Navy at its low end.

Designers also produce lines segmented by price zone. For example, DKNY is the label of Donna Karan's bridge collection; the Donna Karan label is reserved for her lines in the designer price zone, and the Limited Edition label is used for her custom-made collection. Ralph Lauren is another designer with lines in several different price zones. Some of his brands include Lauren, RLX, Black Label, Blue Label, Denim & Supply, and Golf, which target a variety of customers.

Off-price apparel stores, which sell name-brand and designer merchandise at prices well below traditional department-store levels, are putting increasing pressure on all the traditional price zones, especially moderate to better. These outlets, such as Marshalls, T.J.Maxx, and Loehmann's, are thriving because customers are aware of the price zones associated with the labels and realize they are getting a bargain, though perhaps not this season's look. Factory outlets offer prices similar to those found in off-price stores, but the merchandise is limited to the goods of a single producer.

Perhaps the most compelling reason a consumer would be willing to pay full retail price at a traditional department or specialty store is the availability of a broad assortment of styles, sizes, and colors from the beginning of each season. Generally, the stock in off-price and factory outlets is limited to merchandise that was not ordered earlier by stores charging full retail price.

Private Labels

Traditional department and specialty stores can also compete in pricing by developing their own private labels. Much of this merchandise is priced in the better price zone, but the quality is comparable to that of designer signature or bridge apparel. Some of the same manufacturers who produce the name-brand merchandise that a store is selling at higher prices also make the store's private-label goods. Private-label merchandise is vigorously promoted to develop brand recognition, and some customers do not distinguish between private and national brands when they shop.

Seasonal Classifications

In addition to classifying women's apparel by function, size, and price zone, retailers and producers also pay attention to season. This classification is different from the others, however, in that few businesses specialize in just one season. Even swimwear is sold in the winter Resort season as well as the summer.

FIGURE 9.10 A look from Jean Paul Gaultier Fall/Winter 2012 show (left) and a Spring/Summer outfit featuring Carven's shorts and Reed Krakoff's light cotton and nylon jacket (right).

The major apparel seasons correspond to the calendar, with the semiannual designer runway shows introducing Fall/Winter and Spring/Summer collections (Figure 9.10), each a half year in advance of the time when the new fashions appear on the retail selling floor. Within the Fall season are the holiday season, which features evening wear for New Year's Eve, and the resort season when cruise wear and swimsuits are the focus of attention. The Spring/Summer season has its emphasis on summer. In temperate climates with seasonal temperature changes, spring weather does not last long. Therefore, lightweight topcoats and linen suits in dark colors have less of a market than apparel designed for warmer weather.

Merchandising and Marketing

Most fashion producers sell directly to retail stores rather than through intermediaries. The pace of fashion in all but a few staple items is much too fast to allow for the selling, reselling, or warehousing activities of wholesale distributors or jobbers.

As a result, women's apparel producers aim their sales promotion efforts at both retailers and consumers. Such efforts take the form of advertising (Figure 9.11),

Paul &
Maurice
Marciano
(left to right)

GUESS AT 30:
AMERICAN DREAMERS
PAUL AND MAURICE MARCIANO

WHEN THE MARCIANO brothers, newly arrived in California, opened their first U.S. store in 1977, their customers were still listening to ABBA and Queen on their cassette players and just getting a handle on credit cards. Today, Guess retail customers are smart-phone toting, social-media hounds, rocking out to Flo Rida and Katy Perry, shopping at nearly 1,600 stores spanning eighty-seven countries and online, and experimenting with paying for merchandise on their mobile devices.

In the three decades since Paul and Maurice Marciano founded Guess as an American-flavored jeanswear line, it has evolved into an international lifestyle brand with revenues of over $2.69 billion. Its brand-defining ads evoke a mood of vintage Hollywood glamour and maintain an active role within the current art scene. "Guess is a brand and not just a shopping destination," said Nancy Shachtman, Guess president of North America. "We don't follow every trend, we focus on our aesthetics." Guess is not only concerned with expanding its audience country by country, but it is also pursuing different age groups. "Our strategy is to capture the customer young, stay with her when she graduates, and then stay with her the rest of her life," explained

Shachtman. While Guess's original retail concept may focus on women in their twenties and thirties, its Guess by Marciano concept widens Guess's demographics to forty-somethings while G Guess draws teenagers.

Despite unquestionable success, the Marciano brothers maintain a long list of corporate objectives. These include far deeper penetration of an Internet and social media presence, further expansion of their retail network in the U.S. and abroad, and developing the more youth-oriented, lower-priced G by Guess brand—all while they continue to fine-tune the flagship Guess label. Guess continues to look to the future. As Paul Marciano concluded, "At the end of the day, you have to stay true to your heritage, to your roots, and bring it to the digital world."

FIGURE 9.11 Advertisements, such as this one for Tommy Hilfiger, bring in publicity and sales for designers.

publicity, and sales promotion. Chapter 20 discusses the collaborative marketing efforts of producers and retailers from the retailers' perspective.

Advertising

Most retail advertising of women's fashion apparel carries the name of the manufacturer. But this was not always the case. Until the 1930s, many retailers refused to let manufacturers put any tags or labels on the clothes they made. Merchandise shortages during World War II, coupled with government regulations, helped to reverse this situation. Most merchants are now happy to capitalize on the producers' labels that are attached to clothes. They feature manufacturers' names in their own advertising and displays and set up special sections within stores that are exclusively devoted to individual producers' lines.

The 1980s saw a tremendous growth in sales for national brands and nationally known designer labels. In part, this growth resulted from national advertising campaigns directed at consumers. National brands and designer labels have continued with no signs of a change in this trend.

Fashion Shows, Press Weeks, and Trade Shows

The major public relations effort in women's wear goes into the presentations and fashion shows at which designers present their new collections to retailers and fashion media.

The shows provide reporters and bloggers with the opportunity to examine the newest designer collections as well as those of leading European manufacturers.

Editors are deluged with press releases, photos, and interviews that will help them tell the fashion stories to their readers. Initially, there were "press weeks" following the formal line openings, at which designers exhibited merchandise lines in all price categories specially to the press rather than to buyers. Gradually, however, the lower-priced merchandise was eliminated. Press weeks as exclusive showcases for high-priced fashion continued; then, as a result of cost and timing factors, they too were eliminated. Now the press sees the collections at the same time as the retailers do.

To coordinate shows of their new lines during market weeks, the manufacturers who lease permanent or temporary showroom space at the major regional markets in Los Angeles, Dallas, Miami, Atlanta, and Seattle depend on the services of the management of their market buildings. New York designers (including foreign designers with New York showrooms) are not housed in a single site. However, they join together during the fashion week shows that are staged in New York City at Lincoln Center. IMG sponsors an annual awards show that attracts international press and broadcast coverage (Figure 9.12). The company was also the first to live-stream every runway show from Mercedes-Benz Fashion Week. The giant MAGIC show for women's wear is held semiannually in Las Vegas. Also in Las Vegas is the WomensWear in Nevada show (formerly the Big and Tall Woman's Show or B.A.T.WOMAN) for plus and tall sizes, which has become an international hit. Other major international women's wear shows include those held semiannually in Paris, London, Milan, Tokyo, and Hong Kong. These shows are discussed in more detail in Chapter 16.

NEWS | 04/15/2013: IMG GOLF STRENGTHENS GLOBAL RESOURCES, AND FLORIDA PRESENCE, WITH ACQUISITION OF IGP SPORTS & SEARCH

IMG

ABOUT US | SERVICES | NEWS | CAREERS — CONTACT US

British Eurosport Signs Three-Year Speedway Deal

Global leader in sports, fashion and media.

NEWS: 04/15/2013

IMG GOLF STRENGTHENS GLOBAL RESOURCES, AND FLORIDA PRESENCE, WITH ACQUISITION OF IGP SPORTS & ENTERTAINMENT GROUP

Acquisition of South Florida company, led by industry veteran Kenneth R. Kennerly, adds high-profile event, corporate hospitality and client representation resources as industry leader opens offices in North Palm Beach, Florida

NEWS: 04/15/2013

IMG SIGNS JINGDONG AS EXCLUSIVE ONLINE RETAIL PARTNER OF THE CHINESE SUPER LEAGUE

IMG Worldwide and Jingdong (JD.com) jointly announced today that IMG Worldwide, the global sports, fashion and media company has signed Jingdong, China's leading direct B2C e-commerce company, as the exclusive online retail partner of the Chinese Super League (CSL) for the next five years.

SERVICES BY CAPABILITY

Consulting
Event Management
Hospitality
League Development
Licensing
Media Distribution
Media Production
Performance Training
Speakers
Sponsorships
Strategic Initiatives
Talent Representation
Venue Services
Video Archive

SERVICES BY CATEGORY

Action Sports
Baseball
Basketball
College Sports
Cricket
Entertainment
Fashion
Figure Skating
Football - Soccer
Football - US
Global Institutions
Golf
Mass Participation
Motorsports
Olympics
Poker

FIGURE 9.12 IMG is well known for reporting the latest fashion events and trends.

Trunk Shows

Trunk shows are another excellent form of publicity for the women's apparel industry. **Trunk shows** present a manufacturer's line to a retail store's sales staff and its customers (Figure 9.13). A representative of the company, sometimes a designer, typically mounts a fashion show of sample garments. After the show, he or she meets with customers to discuss the styles and their fashion relevance. The retail store's customers may review items they have seen and order them.

Everyone benefits from trunk shows. Customers see clothes as the designer planned them and coordinated them, and they experience some of the glamour of the fashion industry. The retailer enjoys the dramatic influx of customers who come to such personal appearances and shows and any profits that result as

clothes are ordered. The manufacturer tests the line on real customers in order to understand real consumers' needs *firsthand!* If customer response is enthusiastic, the designer achieves new status—and bigger orders—from the retailer than otherwise expected.

Although trunk shows may mean headaches for designers, they still pack a punch when it comes to selling high-priced clothes. Designers say that trunk shows account for anywhere from 20 to 43 percent of a line's business. These shows also give the designer an opportunity to make a personal statement directly to the consumer.

Donna Karan joined the trunk show circuit when she began designing under her own name. Besides being good for profits, trunk shows seem to have a great effect on the designer's designs. Being able to see his or her clothes on the women who wear them, in the part of the country where they live, helps the designer find out what works and what does not.

Most of these clothes retail for more than $500, making them investment dressing. Many designers say that store buyers have a limit on how much they may purchase from any one designer. At a trunk show, the consumer can see almost everything that the designer has created and is given a much larger choice and selection.

Promotion Aids

Manufacturers provide retailers with an assortment of other promotional aids designed to assist them and speed the sale of merchandise. A firm may offer any or all of the following:

- Display ideas, displays, and stock fixtures
- Reorder forms and assistance in checking stock for reordering purposes
- Educational and sales training assistance for salespersons and customers

FIGURE 9.13 Customers gather for Derek Lam's trunk show.

DEREK LAM

- Promotional talks by producers' representatives
- Assistance in giving in-store fashion shows
- Statement enclosures or other ads designed to reach customers by mail
- Special retail promotions to tie in with national advertising campaigns
- Advertising mats for smaller stores
- Cooperative advertising funds from the manufacturer or the fiber association
- Webinars and online videos

Industry Trends

Over the past few decades, American designers have succeeded in rivaling designers from Paris and Milan as definers of high fashion. The United States has also seen an increase in competition in the global marketplace. While U.S. manufacturers currently outsource labor to foreign countries, there has been a shift to domestic apparel production. There are also developments in automation of production, processes, and technology that will allow for more growth in this industry. See also Chapter 8, Product Development, and Chapter 17, Global Sourcing and Merchandising.

Summary and Review

Women's wear is the largest segment of the fashion industry, and it sets the trends for other segments. Merchandising of ready-to-wear apparel in the United States has been centered in the fashion district of New York City, with other major markets in Los Angeles, Dallas, and Atlanta. Mass production has depended on a unionized labor force, represented by Workers United.

The production of women's wear is segmented in several ways, and companies may specialize according to use categories, such as activewear or bridal wear; sizes, including misses, juniors, petite, women's, and half sizes; price zones, ranging from designer signature to bridge to better and contemporary to moderate and budget. Manufacturers and designers change their goods by selling season.

Merchandising and marketing activities include advertising; publicity; fashion shows, market weeks, and trade shows; trunk shows; and other promotion aids.

Industry trends in the United States show an increase in domestic manufacturing. There are also developments in automation of production, processes, and technology, which will create more growth.

For Review

1. Why did New York City become the center of the garment industry in the United States?
2. Discuss the growth and contributions of UNITE to the apparel industry.
3. Name some specialized market segments served by apparel manufacturers.
4. List the traditional basic categories of women's apparel, giving types of garments in each category.
5. Into what size ranges is women's apparel traditionally divided?
6. List and describe the six major price zones into which women's apparel is divided. What are the major factors contributing to the wholesale price of garments?
7. Why do most fashion producers sell directly to retail stores rather than through wholesalers?
8. Discuss the merchandising activities of women's fashion producers today.
9. How does a manufacturer or designer benefit from attending a trunk show in a retail store?
10. What kinds of promotional aids do manufacturers provide to retailers to sell merchandise?

For Discussion

1. Discuss the advantages and disadvantages of standardization of women's apparel sizes.
2. What are the repercussions of a name-brand or designer manufacturer selling current-season apparel to off-price outlets as well as to department and specialty shops?

Trade Talk

Define or briefly explain the following terms:

activewear
custom-made
price zones
ready-to-wear (RTW)
trunk show

KEY CONCEPTS

- The history of the menswear industry
- Categories of men's apparel
- Roles of brand names and designer names in the marketing of menswear
- Advertising and promotional activities in the marketing of men's apparel

Clothes have been part of the story of man—yes, "man"—because most of the world's great clothes have been worn by men to express power, wealth, and glory. Such male clothes are shown in museums around the world. These clothes represented the tribal chief, the warrior, the cleric, and the monarch—in a word, the male (Figure 10.1).

In fact, the men's business outfit in the twenty-first century has retained a somewhat conservative style that evolved in the late 1700s. Over the years, neutral colors have prevailed, and changes in style have occurred mostly in the details. Jackets are longer or shorter, with wider or narrower lapels; jacket vents and trouser cuffs come and go. Shirt collars mutate into various shapes, and ties are invented and reinvented. But overall, men's clothing has changed very little (Figure 10.2).

History of the Men's Apparel Industry

The oldest of the domestic apparel industries, the menswear industry gave birth to the women's and children's wear industries. It got its start in the late 1700s. Prior to that, the rich patronized tailor shops, where their clothing was custom-made or fitted to them. Everyone else wore homemade clothing.

Birth of Ready-to-Wear

The first ready-to-wear men's clothing was made by tailors in port cities along the Atlantic coast. Seamen arrived in these cities in need of clothes to wear on land but without the time to have them tailor-made. To meet their needs, a few astute tailors began anticipating the ships' arrivals by making up batches of suits in rough size groupings. Sailors, who could put on the new clothes and walk away in them, liked the idea. These early ready-to-wear stores were called **slop shops**, a name that was appropriate to what they sold. Ready-to-wear clothing offered none of the careful fit or detail of custom-tailored clothes. But the price was right and the convenience was important, so ready-to-wear clothing gradually gained acceptance in ever-widening circles.

Although never considered slop shops, some distinguished menswear retail operations got their start on waterfronts. Brooks Brothers' first store opened in 1818 in downtown New York, and Jacob Reed's Sons' first store opened in 1824 near the Philadelphia waterfront.

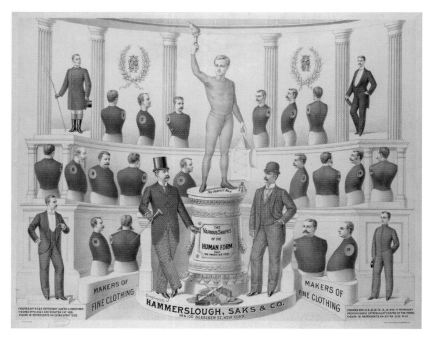

FIGURE 10.1 The various shapes of the male form.

FIGURE 10.2 Over the years, there have been minimal changes in men's apparel. From left to right: men's sportswear looks from 1955 and 2013.

Role of the Industrial Revolution

The market for ready-to-wear clothing was further increased by the industrial revolution. Ironically, though, the industrial revolution also helped to create the new conservative look that prevailed for so long. The industrial revolution led to the introduction of machinery in all areas of production and replaced the absolute dependence on human hands in the making of goods. Clothing, like much else, could be mass produced. This, in part, led to standardization in people's tastes. Mass-produced clothes were made for the lowest common denominator, which in menswear led to a conservatively cut, dark-colored suit.

The look, however, was not entirely the result of mass production. The idea of conservative men's suits also had its origins in a new role model that emerged during the industrial revolution—the industrialist. On the one hand, these newly rich tycoons had working-class roots and were not about to dress like the rich peacocks. On the other hand, they had finally gained access to something long denied them—power and money—and they wanted this distinction to show in their dress. Sober and conservative themselves, they chose to wear clothes that embodied these values.

The industrial revolution also helped to create a managerial class made entirely of men who were happy to emulate the look of the rich industrialists. Soon all men who worked in offices wore the look, and the tailored, dark-colored work suit that men would wear for the next 150 years was born.

The industrial revolution helped to move the production of clothing out of the home. The demand for people to operate the new machines was so great that entire families often went to work. This left no one at home to sew and further boosted the demand for ready-to-wear clothing.

Mid- to Late 1800s

As late as the mid-1800s, rich people still did not consider buying their clothes off the rack in shops that had once been slop shops. The middle class, usually the most important element in making a style acceptable, patronized these stores.

Advances in Production Techniques

The introduction of the sewing machine in 1846 was another important advance in men's apparel; it sped up production. During the Civil War, when manufacturers scrambled to make uniforms according to specification, standardized sizes for a variety of figure types developed. The invention of paper patterns by Ebenezer Butterick and his wife in 1863 improved the consistency of the sizing, assuring a better fit in ready-to-wear clothing—the last thing that was necessary to make them popular with all classes.

Use of Contractors

As the men's ready-to-wear business grew, so did its attractiveness as a profitable investment. But going into business as a menswear manufacturer required considerable capital in terms of factory construction, equipment, and labor costs. This situation led to the birth of the contractor business, described in Chapter 8. By hiring a contractor to do the sewing and sometimes the cutting as well, manufacturers eliminated the need for their own factories, sewing machines, or labor force. They could function with just a showroom or space for shipping.

Early contractors of menswear operated in one of two ways. Usually, they set up their own factories where the manufacturing was done. But sometimes they distributed work to operators who would work at home, either on their own machines or on machines rented from the contractors. These workers were paid on a piecework basis.

Right after the Civil War and for the next two decades or so, menswear was manufactured in three different ways:

1. In inside shops, or garment factories, owned and operated by manufacturers
2. In contract shops, or contractors' factories, where garments were produced for manufacturers
3. In homes, where garments were made usually for contractors but sometimes for manufacturers

The Rise of Unions

As the menswear market and industry grew, so did competition among manufacturers. To produce ready-to-wear clothing at competitive prices, manufacturers and contractors demanded long hours from workers, yet paid low wages. In addition, factory working conditions, which had never been good, deteriorated further. Contractors were particularly guilty, and their factories deserved the names "sweatshops," or "sweaters," that were given to them. According to an official New York State inspection report of 1887:

> The workshops occupied by these contracting manufacturers of clothing, or "sweaters" as they are commonly called, are foul in the extreme. Noxious gases emanate from all corners. The buildings are ill smelling from cellar to garret. The water-closets are used by males and females, and usually stand in the room where the work is done. The people are huddled together too closely for comfort, even if all other conditions were excellent.[1]

What happened next was inevitable. Workers finally rebelled against working conditions, hours, and pay. Local employee unions had existed in the industry since the early 1800s, but none had lasted long or wielded much power. The Journeymen Tailors' National Union, formed in 1883, functioned mainly as a craft union. A union representing all apparel industry workers, the United Garment Workers of America, was organized in 1891, but it had little power and soon collapsed. Finally, in 1914, the Amalgamated Clothing Workers of America was formed. It remained the major union of the menswear industry until the 1970s, when it merged with the Textile Workers of America and the United Shoe Workers of America to form the Amalgamated Clothing and Textile Workers Union (ACTWU). Then, in 1995, the ACTWU joined with the International Ladies Garment Workers Union to form UNITE, the Union of Needletrade, Industrial, and Textile Employees, and in 2004 its name changed to UNITE HERE.

UNITE HERE represented the workers in virtually all domestic plants in the tailored-clothing segment of menswear manufacturing. The common beginnings of both the union and the factories in the Northeast may account for this strong presence. However, its influence in factories producing men's work clothes, furnishings, and sportswear in other parts of the country was almost nonexistent until the famous strike during the early 1970s at the El Paso, Texas, factory of the Farah Company, one of the largest manufacturers of men's pants and work clothes. The company had resisted the attempt of the ACTWU to organize the Farah workers for many years, and only after a long court battle were the plant and its workers unionized. However, the influence of UNITE HERE was still not as strong in other segments and regions as it was in tailored clothing in the Northeast.

In 2009, as a result of disagreements within the union, UNITE HERE broke up. Workers United, a new union representing apparel manufacturing employees, formed as a result. However, disputes surrounding the breakup of UNITE HERE continued for years. In 2011, the union was successful in its fight to keep a Hugo Boss plant open in Cleveland, preventing outsourcing to Turkey.[2]

Acceptance of Ready-to-Wear

Store-bought clothes finally broke the class barrier during the last half of the nineteenth century. Financial crises such as the panics of 1869, 1873, and 1907 sent men who had formerly worn only custom-tailored clothes into the ready-to-wear clothing stores. Even though custom tailoring remained a vital part of the menswear industry far longer than it lasted in women's wear, it was dealt a final blow during the Great Depression. Today, it represents only a small segment of the industry.

World War II

The Great Depression of 1929 brought about a decline in demand for all consumer products, and the economy did not get back on its feet again until World War II.

During the war, of course, the entire apparel industry was given over to the war effort. The menswear

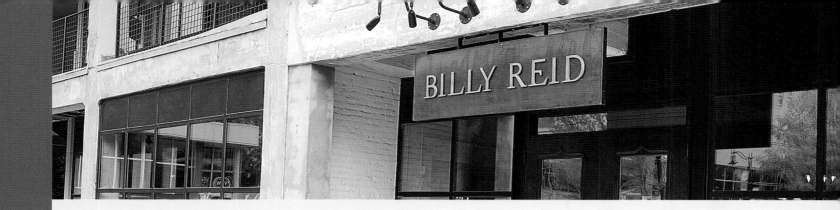

BILLY REID:
EVERYTHING THAT COULD GO WRONG, WENT WRONG

BILLY REID'S **2012** win for CFDA Menswear Designer of the Year was sweet vindication for a designer whose business had been a roller coaster of highs and lows over the past fifteen years. In that time, Reid launched two labels and saw one go out of business in the aftermath of September 11, 2001. Referring to his CFDA win, he said, "It's terrific, but we're right back at work. We have to make samples and get production made. We have to keep running our stores. We've got to continue to grow our company."

If Reid remains more focused on production than his prestigious prize, it is because he learned the hard way that while awards are nice, they hardly guarantee profits. In 2001, he won the CFDA Perry Ellis award for best new menswear designer for his previous William Reid label—but a year later, he was out of business! "Everything that could go wrong, went wrong," he said. After the closure of his first

label, Reid supported himself working freelance jobs for companies including Fruit of the Loom underwear and Taylor Made golf apparel.

In 2004, Reid relaunched his brand as Billy Reid. E-commerce has been an important sales driver. "We see retail as a huge growth opportunity for us. However, we do not want to be in the malls. I don't like going to malls, my friends don't like going to malls, and I don't think men in general like malls."

Today, Reid is building a flourishing menswear business and is on a retail expansion kick with the opening of his eighth store. The new store joins existing stores in New York; Nashville; Dallas; Houston; Charleston, South Carolina; and Florence, Alabama. Because of his talent, his interest, and the pure joy he gets from making and selling clothes that make his customers happy, Billy Reid has proven that no matter what has gone wrong, so many things have gone right.

Billy Reid

Fall 2012

industry ground to a halt and turned its attention to making uniforms. Restrictions were placed on the design and use of fabric. Trouser cuffs, which required extra fabric, disappeared. Once the war ended, however, the restrictions were lifted, and even more important, a long era of postwar prosperity began.

The returning servicemen were eager to get out of their uniforms. The demand for "civvies," or civilian clothes, was so great that for a few years clothing manufacturers worked—with little thought for changing styles—simply to keep up with the demand. By the late 1940s, manufacturers were meeting demand and could even stand back and consider style.

The Postwar Era

The major change in the menswear industry in the postwar period was the emergence of a new class of clothes called sportswear. It originated in Southern California in the late 1940s, where suburban living and a climate conducive to leisure created a demand for clothes to be worn outside work.

For a while, the demand for sportswear was filled by a group of former New York manufacturers who had gravitated to the West Coast. They gave sportswear not only to California but to the entire nation. The California market, as sportswear came to be known in the business, gained further momentum when buyers from major department stores such as Marshall Field, Hudson's, Macy's, and Lord & Taylor traveled to the West Coast to attend the spring sportswear show held every October in Palm Springs. New York clothing manufacturers wasted no time cashing in on the trend. By the mid-1960s, men's sportswear was as much a part of the East Coast market as tailored clothing.

What later become known as designer clothes also got their start in California in the 1940s. Hollywood motion-picture costume designers such as Don Loper, Orry-Kelly, Howard Greer, and Milo Anderson created lines for California sportswear manufacturers. Oleg Cassini and Adrian began licensing agreements with New York neckwear producers.

Designer clothes à la California proved to be an idea born before its time, a rare occurrence in the trendy fashion world. The designer sportswear could not compete with the new Ivy League or continental look that emerged on the East Coast. Designer clothes faded away and did not reemerge until the 1960s, when designers like Pierre Cardin and John Weitz would try again, with much greater success.

Fashions of the 1960, 1970s, and 1980s

Little happened in men's fashion until the 1960s, when suddenly menswear blossomed, cultivated by the

FIGURE 10.3 This Edwardian look was popular for men in the late 1960s and 1970s.

costuming of such British rock groups as the Beatles and the Rolling Stones. The mod look brought color to menswear after a 150-year absence. It was followed by the Edwardian look, which changed the shape of menswear for the first time in decades (Figure 10.3). Other styles, such as the Nehru jacket, were little more than fads.

Revolutionary Fashion. The social revolution of the 1960s was reflected in the hippies' all-occasion dress code. For men, it prescribed long hair and beards; jeans; a choice of tie-dyed T-shirt, denim work shirt, or colorfully flower-powered shirt with no tie; love beads; and, weather permitting, sandals. The civil rights movement was expressed in fashion by the adoption of African clothing, especially the dashiki, a colorfully printed, loose-fitting, collarless woven shirt.

In Europe, Pierre Cardin's Peacock look, with its peaked shoulders, fitted waist, and flared pants, transformed the male uniform and blazed the trail for current men's fashions.

Revolutionary Fabrics. For the first time since the development of the sewing machine, technology influenced menswear fashions. Knits, made from synthetic fibers, enjoyed a boom in the 1970s. Suddenly a man could outfit himself entirely in knit clothes—a double-knit suit, circular knit shirt, interlock knit underwear, a knit tie, and jersey-knit socks.

The overexposure of knits, often in poorly designed and constructed clothing, gave polyester a bad image. Its use fell off in the women's apparel industry, but menswear manufacturers continued to use it in a low-key way in woven fabrics. Today, 95 percent of men's tailored clothing is made with polyester, most typically blends combining polyester with wool or cotton. Sixty-five percent of men's finer quality suits are made of a 55/45 polyester/wool blend; it is the most popular suiting fabric in the United States.

Another technological development of the period that has had staying power is the permanent-press finish of cotton. Home laundering of no-iron shirts has made a difference in the maintenance of men's wardrobes.

In the 1980s, men's fashion took on new life once again, as it had in the 1960s. For the first time, magazines devoted exclusively to men's fashion appeared. Men's fashion types emerged, and a variety of styles became acceptable. A man could be the continental type or the Ivy League type; he could be Edwardian, if he chose.

For those who did not trust their own judgment, scientifically confirmed "dress for success" guidelines were suggested in John Malloy's book of the same name. The book prescribed style and color details to create the right combination of authority and friendliness for a

variety of business negotiations. Intentionally conservative in its advice, it promoted what came to be known in the 1980s as the "power suit" and "power tie" for "power lunches" (Figure 10.4).

The Casual Look

The look that really took off among more self-confident dressers was one of casual elegance, personified by the stars of the popular television show *Miami Vice*. The clothes were designed by big designer names, which ensured their elegance, and they were casual, which basically added up to T-shirts worn under Italian sports jackets, classic loafers with no socks, and ever-present designer sunglasses. For the first time, the American menswear market was segmented as the women's market always had been by age, education, and income.

Dress-Down Fridays

In the 1990s, the casual look was officially welcomed to the corporate office, sometimes without the elegance. It began with dress-down Fridays in the summer, when companies made allowance for the quick weekend getaway to the beach. Gradually, the trend expanded to the cooler months and to other days of the week. Each firm that followed the trend had to make up its own rules—or decide not to.

Since the 1990s, men's buying patterns have been changing. "Men aren't shopping just out of need anymore," says Tom Kalenderian, executive vice president and General Merchandise Manager of menswear

FIGURE 10.4 From left to right: Power suits from 1797, 1897, and 2012.

FIGURE 10.5 Tailored clothing, like these designs by Ralph Lauren, comes in a variety of options and is a popular part of the menswear industry.

at Barneys New York. "The shopping experience has become one of entertainment, and that creates a naturally fertile ground for more impulse buying."[3]

Trends in the Twenty-First Century

In the twenty-first century, male executives are thinking and talking more about fashion because greater numbers of men are buying their clothes themselves. This trend represents a huge change from when women purchased 75 percent of men's clothing. Today, 84 percent of men are taking the reins to outfit themselves.[4]

In 2011, the sale of men's clothing outpaced women's clothing.[5] Tailored clothing made big gains, with double-digit increases in the sales of dress shirts (14 percent), suits (23 percent), and sport coats (20 percent).[6] Experts speculate that men are dressing better to land new jobs and are starting to shop again after the economic downturn of 2008. "It goes back to the 'Frugal Fatigue' phenomenon we have been watching," says Marshal Cohen, the NPD Group's chief industry analyst. "It seems to have materialized for apparel in 2011 as consumers finally got back to building their wardrobes again."[7]

Demographic Influences

The popularity of casual business wardrobes may be attributable to the coming of age of the baby boomers. Many male baby boomers have been worrying more about aging and are doing something about it. The baby boomer generation is not only the most celebrated of generations but also presents a lucrative opportunity for the grooming market, as aging men become concerned with retaining a youthful and distinguished appearance.

Style is expected to remain an important factor in menswear. It should be noted, however, that in the midst of the interest in new styles, there has been a return to classic, clean, almost preppy American sportswear—even among younger men. Gothic looks and streetwear covered in logos are becoming a thing of the past. For formal business and social occasions, the conservative men's suit remains the outfit of choice, and not only for the president.

Organization and Operation of the Industry

The menswear industry traditionally has been divided into firms making different kinds of clothing:

1. *Tailored clothing*—Suits, overcoats, topcoats, sports coats, formal wear, and separate trousers (Figure 10.5)
2. *Furnishings*—Dress shirts, neckwear, sweaters, headwear, underwear, socks, suspenders (Figure 10.6), robes, and pajamas

FIGURE 10.6 Furnishings, like these suspenders, can add a touch of style to a look.

3. *Outerwear*—Raincoats, coats, jackets, and active sportswear (Figure 10.7)
4. *Work clothing*—Work shirts, work pants, overalls, and related items
5. *Other*—Uniforms and miscellaneous items

The federal government uses these five classifications. Although it is not an official classification, sportswear (including active sportswear) has become a vital portion of the business and should be considered a menswear category.

Size and Location of Manufacturers

Key players in the U.S. menswear and boys' wear manufacturing sector include Levi Strauss, VF Corporation, and PVH (Phillips-Van Heusen). Although there are menswear manufacturers in almost every section of the country, the greatest numbers of plants are in the mid-Atlantic states. New York, New Jersey, and Pennsylvania form the center of the tailored-clothing industry. More than 40 percent of all American menswear manufacturers are located in this area.

However, the industry's center is gradually moving. A number of northeastern manufacturers have set up plant facilities in the South, where both land and labor are less expensive. These include not only apparel manufacturers from the mid-Atlantic states but also some men's shoe manufacturers, who were once found almost exclusively in New England. Some menswear manufacturers have always been located in the South, which has long been a center for manufacturers of men's shirts, underwear, and work clothes. For instance, one of the largest firms manufacturing separate trousers—a segment of the tailored-clothing industry—is Haggar in Dallas. The number of firms located in the West is also steadily growing. For example, Guess and L.A. Gear are located in Los Angeles, and Levi Strauss, Nautica, and Patagonia are headquartered in San Francisco. In

FIGURE 10.7 Viktor & Rolf incorporate fur trim in their outerwear for men.

the Pacific Northwest, Portland, Oregon, is the home of Pendleton, while Eddie Bauer and REI are located in Seattle, Washington. Most of these companies produce sportswear or casual attire. The upper Midwest (home to Lands' End, in Wisconsin) is also important for sports outerwear and activewear such as parkas, ski wear, and hunting and fishing gear.

Dual Distribution

It is far more common in the menswear industry than in women's apparel for clothes to be distributed on a two-tier system called **dual distribution**. In dual distribution, apparel is made available through both wholesale and retail channels; that is, the manufacturer sells it in its own retail stores as well as to retail stores owned by others. The practice got its start in the first half of the nineteenth century when the ready-to-wear business, along with the country's population, was expanding.

Designing a Line

For generations, tailored-clothing manufacturers in the United States were known as slow but painstakingly careful followers, rather than leaders, in menswear styling. The typical tailored-clothing manufacturer had a staff of tailors to execute existing designs or bought freelance designs. Designers' names were known only within the trade and were seldom considered important by consumers.

Traditionally, the leading fashion influence was English styling. Designers in this country would study the styles currently popular in England (specifically Savile Row), decide which might be acceptable here, and gradually develop a line based on those styles. Production was a slow process because of the amount of handwork involved in making tailored clothing. Usually, a full year passed from the time a style was developed until a finished product was delivered to a retail store.

The first signs of male rebellion against traditional styling came during the late 1940s and early 1950s. As described earlier, year after year manufacturers had been turning out versions of a style that had long been popular on Savile Row—a draped suit with padded shoulders, based originally on the broad-chested uniform of the Brigade of Guards. A number of young men attending well-known northeastern colleges became tired of the traditional look. They took their objections to New Haven clothing manufacturers, and the result was the natural-shoulder Ivy League suit.

A radical shift in attitudes in the 1960s finally made men willing to wear suits as fashion. The antiwar protests, student activism, black power, and other political movements encouraged American men to express themselves in a nonmainstream manner. They led to the era of the "Peacock revolution," when men once again took great pride in their appearance, as they had done in days long ago. Some favored long hair, bold plaid suits, brightly colored shirts, wide multicolored ties, and shiny boots. Others dressed, even for work, in Nehru and Mao jackets, leisure suits, white loafers, polyester double knits, and the "Las Vegas look"—shirts unbuttoned to the waist and gold necklaces in abundance around their necks.

Importance of Name Designers

By the late 1960s, designer names in the menswear industry mushroomed. Most of them were women's wear designers, often from Europe, who decided to exploit their renown by trying out their creativity in the men's field. So popular was the European designer image that even an American designer like Bill Kaiserman gave his firm an Italian name, Raphael.

Among the first American designers who made no bones about being American were Oleg Cassini, John Weitz, Bill Blass, and Ralph Lauren. In fact, Bill Blass won the first Coty Award ever given for menswear design, in 1968.

Since most of these designers were famous as designers of women's apparel, there was a question about whether men would buy their designs. The movement of men into fashion during the 1960s and 1970s dispelled that doubt. *The New York Times* reported:

> The idea that men would wear clothes designed by a woman's apparel designer was never considered seriously, and one thing that men have arrived at today is that being interested in clothes does not carry a stigma.[8]

The fact that much of menswear, particularly furnishings and sportswear, was bought by women for men also aided in the acceptance of name designer styles. Women were familiar with the names and had confidence in the designer's taste.

Although the first foreign country that influenced the design of menswear was England, French and Italian designers became as important in menswear as the traditional English. Pierre Cardin signed his first contract for men's shirts and ties in 1959 and did his first ready-to-wear men's designs in 1961. Christian Dior, Yves Saint Laurent, and other famous women's designers followed his example. One important menswear designer who did not come from the ranks of women's wear is Ralph Lauren. He began his career in

George Zimmer

GEORGE ZIMMER: MEN'S WEARHOUSE

OVER THE PAST forty years, George Zimmer has built Men's Wearhouse into America's largest men's facility retailer, but he still calls himself "an old hippie." Since opening in Houston in 1973, Zimmer has systematically built the largest men's specialty store chain, a $2.1 billion giant with more than 1,200 stores in the U.S. and Canada. Today, one in every five suits sold in the U.S. is bought in one of his stores. Reinforcing the company is the tagline: "You're going to love the way you look, I guarantee it."

Men's Wearhouse has guided American consumers into casual and formal dress with a touch of style by providing an extensive assortment of brands and silhouettes to accommodate every body type and fashion sensibility. At one time, Men's Wearhouse struggled to buy well-known brands; however, today, Calvin Klein, Ralph Lauren, and other top designer labels are part of its assortment.

For nearly four decades, Zimmer has proven that people can enjoy what they do and still be successful. Men's Wearhouse has landed on *Fortune*'s list as one of the one hundred best companies to work for, a ranking that is determined by surveying a firm's employees. "Wardrobe consultants," the company's term for salespeople, often enjoy greater opportunity for advancement than is the industry standard.

On a national scale, the Men's Wearhouse has focused on helping to dress men struggling to enter or reenter the workforce. It has spearheaded a national suit drive where customers donate used suits, shirts, ties, shoes, sportswear, and outerwear. More than 88,000 pieces of apparel were donated and Men's Wearhouse matched the number of suit donations with the same number of dress shirts. "It is the goal of Men's Wearhouse to make sure that no men are denied the opportunity to be good providers, responsible citizens, and positive role models because they lack the appropriate wardrobe to land a job," the company said.

Zimmer sums up his philosophy simply: "[There is] more to business than formulas," and "following the Golden Rule is the best way to ensure success."

In June 2013, the Men's Wearhouse Board terminated Zimmer. While this may have come as a surprise to many in the industry, this is a reality that happens in businesses. It may also lead him to begin a new chapter in menswear.

menswear, designing for women only after he became successful and famous designing for men.

Currently, an entirely new world of menswear has emerged in which designer labels are promoted as heavily as well-established brand names used to be. A designer who licenses his or her name in suits may also license men's jeans, shirts, jackets, sportswear, active-wear, or ties. The manufacturer pays for the design or name of the designer in royalties based on gross sales.

Manufacturing companies that license name designers usually establish separate divisions and in many cases allocate separate manufacturing facilities for them. In licensing agreements, the extent of designer involvement varies; designers are not necessarily responsible for all the designs that bear their name. Some licensing agreements simply pay for the use of the designer's name, and the name designer has no design input at all.

Today the "name game" is big business in all segments of the menswear industry. While there are no hard figures on the amount of designer business alone at the wholesale level, the best market estimates for retail sales are over $1 billion for all categories combined.

One reason for the continuing popularity of designer names is that they are so easily promoted. Consumers associate them with prestige and fashion and recognize them when they see them (Figure 10.8). Designers have helped by becoming highly visible. Their names are household words, and their faces frequently appear in newspapers and magazines. They lend themselves to the fantasies of the customer who longs for wealth and excitement.

Leading Italian designers of menswear include Armani, Brioni, Donatella Versace, Dolce & Gabbana, Romeo Gigli, Kiton, and Ermenegildo Zegna. Four Belgian designers achieved widespread popularity in the late 1990s: Raf Simons, Wim Neels, Dries Van Noten, and Walter Van Beirendonck. This trend continued in 2013 with Christian Wijnants, winner of the International Woolmark Prize. Other influential European designers include Helmut Lang, Paul Smith, Hedi Slimane, Comme des Garçon, Yohji Yamamoto, and Jean Paul Gaultier.

American designers of menswear include, of course, the "Big Four": Ralph Lauren, Calvin Klein, Donna Karan, and Tommy Hilfiger. Other popular designers include Michael Kors, Marc Jacobs, Perry Ellis, Mossimo, Gene Meyer, John Bartlett, Alexander Julian, and Jhane Barnes.

High-end fashion designers are edging into the booming market for specially made men's suits. Retailers including Brooks Brothers are getting customers to pay more for so-called made-to-measure suits. Luxury

FIGURE 10.8 Vivienne Westwood redefines tailored American style with her playful and fashionable plaid designs.

labels, including Tom Ford, Versace, and Jil Sander, are producing their own options that start at 20 to 30 percent higher than their off-the-rack lines. In the United States, the custom and made-to-measure market accounts for more than 20 percent of suits costing more than $1,200. "One of a kind is the ultimate luxury," says Milton Pedraza, chief executive of consultant Luxury Institute.[9]

Market Segments

Most market segments are based on style differences, but some exist because they involve different production methods. The five main market segments in menswear are (1) tailored clothing, (2) sportswear, (3) activewear, (4) contemporary apparel, and (5) bridge apparel.

Tailored Clothing

Tailored-clothing firms produce structured or semi-structured suits, overcoats, topcoats, sports coats, formal wear, and separate slacks that involve hand-tailoring operations. While this kind of clothing once dominated the market, the demand for tailored clothing has steadily declined. The higher price of tailored clothing makes the difference all the more striking. Despite the decline, tailored suits have long been—and still are—considered the backbone of the menswear industry.

A tailored suit is structured, or three-dimensional, which gives it a shape even when it is not worn. Until very recently, tailored clothing was graded according to the number of hand-tailoring operations required to make it. The grades were 1, 2, 4, 4½, 6, and 6½, with a grade 1 suit representing the lowest quality.

At the top of the quality scale, the number of hand-tailoring operations has been reduced by machinery that can produce stitching of a similar caliber. However, the finest suits still have hand-sewn details representing hours of work by skilled tailors.

Designer Suits. Another difference between an inexpensive, low-grade suit and an expensive designer suit is the way each is cut. Designer suits are typically sized on a "seven-inch drop." **Drop** refers to the difference in inches between the chest measurement of a suit jacket and the waist of the pants. Some jackets designed for young men and other customers who keep in shape may have an even greater drop. The most common is the six-inch drop.

Differences also exist between traditional suits, which have a natural shoulder, and suits with **European styling**, which feature a more fitted jacket, built-up shoulders, and a higher armhole.

Production. The production of tailored clothing, as you have probably guessed, is a long, complicated process, although it does parallel the production process for women's apparel. Styles are selected for a new line, after which a manufacturer orders fabrics for the line. Delivery of the fabric may take up to nine months, so it must be ordered far in advance of when it will be used. Next, the line is presented to buyers. Manufacturers do not start to cut suits until enough orders have accumulated to make production of a style worthwhile.

Men's tailored clothing is produced in the following proportioned sizes, with the number ranges representing chest measurements:

- Short (36–44)
- Regular (35–46)
- Long (37–48)
- Extra long (38–50)
- Portly short (39–48)
- Large (46, 48, 50)

Not every style is cut in every size range, but the most popular styles are made up in at least half the size ranges.

Suit Separates. The steady decline in structured and semistructured tailored menswear has been offset by an increased demand for **suit separates**—sports jackets and trousers that are worn much as the tailored suit used to be. Tailored suits are now the business uniform only in large, sophisticated cities, and even there, only in some firms and industries and for some levels of management. Elsewhere, suit separates are often worn to work—or for almost any occasion except where formal wear is required.

Although an attempt was made in the 1960s to sell menswear consumers on the idea of coordinated sportswear, that is, jackets, vests, and pants that could be mixed and matched with one another, the idea never took hold. Today, suit separates refers to sports jackets and trousers.

Suit separates are usually machine-made and, as a result, can be significantly lower-priced than tailored garments. When they are made for better-priced lines, they can also be expensive. Because each item is bought separately, the expensive alterations that manufacturers and retailers must often make on tailored clothes are avoided. One industry expert believes that men who buy separates are more fashion-aware than those who need the reassurance of a preassembled look.

Sportswear

Sportswear, or casual wear, which runs the gamut from unconstructed jackets, knit and woven sports shirts, slacks, and leisure shorts to coordinated tops and bottoms, has been the fastest growing segment of the menswear industry since the 1970s. Changes in lifestyle, plus men's growing interest in having more variety and fashion in their wardrobes, have created a demand for leisure clothes.

A generation ago, tailored clothing was office or formal wear, and sportswear was strictly weekend or vacation wear. Today, the real difference between the two lies in the construction rather than the occasion or the styling, colors, or fabrics of the garments.

Sportswear is unstructured, or at minimum, less structured than tailored clothing. Few if any hand-tailoring operations, for example, are required to make a sports jacket. Sportswear lacks padding, binding, and lining and takes its shape (if indeed it has any shape these days) from the person who is wearing it.

Sportswear production also differs from that of tailored wear. Unlike tailored-wear manufacturers, who want staying power for their styles and a lot of lead time, sportswear manufacturers are interested in short runs and a quick response to customer demand. A **short run** is the production of a limited number of units of a particular item, fewer than would normally be considered an average number to produce. Producers of men's sportswear sometimes rely on contractors to keep up with the fast-moving fashion cycles of this market segment. The quality of workmanship is much less important than the quick production of the styles, colors, and fabrics that customers want.

In addition, unstructured sportswear, regardless of the kind of firm producing it, is likely to be made up in a much narrower size range than tailored clothing. For instance, a sport shirt is not produced in the wide variety of neck sizes, sleeve lengths, and collar and cuff styles in which a dress shirt is made. Instead, a sport shirt is usually produced in four basic sizes (small, medium, large, and extra large), with a choice between short and long sleeves.

This is the kind of production work that contractors handle most successfully. When contractors are used, the sportswear manufacturer may be the designer, a designer may be hired, or a design may be bought from a freelancer. The manufacturer buys the needed fabric. Then sometimes the cutting and all of the sewing are done by the contractor, as in the women's apparel field. Finally, the finished goods are returned to the manufacturer, who handles the distribution.

Activewear

Another phenomenon that emerged in the 1980s and continues today is the rapid growth of the activewear market, which consists of clothing worn during active sports participation as well as during leisure time (Figure 10.9). In fact, the larger segment of this market is men who want to look as if they are doing something athletic, even when they are ambling to the store for the Sunday paper or flopping down in front of the television set to watch a ball game. As a result, the active sportswear producers make running suits for men who run and for men who do not but want to look as if they do. Sportswear was also responsible for making color a permanent part of men's wardrobes. Colorful ski and snowboarding apparel dominates the slopes. Golf wear has become popular on and off the links, with licensed apparel and accessories by players like Tiger Woods for Nike. Major brand names in athletic shoes have become big names in activewear as well.

Contemporary Apparel

Contemporary menswear refers to a special type of styling that provides high quality and fashion. Contemporary menswear, which produces clothing in all categories, can often be distinguished by its use of bright colors.

FIGURE 10.9 Activewear is a major part of the menswear industry. This image shows Usain Bolt wearing the official uniform by Puma for the 2012 London Olympics.

Initially, the typical consumer was a young, educated man with the verve to look fashionable. Today, contemporary menswear no longer belongs exclusively to the young but is worn by elegant, style-conscious men of all age groups.

Contemporary merchandise is produced by both tailored-clothing and sportswear firms. It is usually produced under a name designer's licensing agreement rather than being styled by a manufacturer's in-house or freelance designer. When this type of merchandise is produced by a firm already making other types of apparel and furnishings, new operating divisions are usually created to handle the product, give it identity, and enhance its marketability.

Bridge Apparel

The term **bridge apparel** came into play in the menswear industry to define clothing that spanned the style gap between young men's and men's collections, and the price gap between contemporary and designer apparel. In broad terms, bridge customers are usually between 25 and 40 and have sophistication and style.

Unlike the bridge concept in women's sportswear, for which certain manufacturers and designers have developed collections specifically created as bridge lines, men's bridge apparel is defined much more by retailers than by manufacturers. Each retailer may interpret bridge differently in order to fit its own customer profile. Therefore, one store might have bridge lines while another might call them contemporary. Whatever their definition of bridge apparel, retailers that identify a portion of their menswear assortment as bridge apparel are seeking to balance fashion with price.

FIGURE 10.10 Recycled polyester ski wear at Pyua is on display at the International Trade Fair in Germany.

Merchandising and Marketing

Like the women's wear producers, menswear producers back their lines with advertising and publicity. Menswear fiber and textile producers sometimes promote their products. The largest percentage of promotion is done, however, by the menswear producers, who rely on agencies, freelancers, and less often, on an in-house department for advertising and publicity.

Advertising

Men's apparel producers began advertising in the late 1800s. Initially, they used trade advertising to establish contact with retailers. Strong, stable relationships were built, and in many large towns and small cities, major manufacturers maintain an exclusive arrangement with one retailer. Not surprisingly, the producers tend to put a lot of their advertising money into cooperative advertising for their long-term retail accounts. Brand-name and designer name producers also sponsor national advertising campaigns. See Chapter 20 for more details on advertising, publicity, and public relations.

Trade Associations

The major publicity efforts, however, are still undertaken by the trade associations, which sponsor market weeks, trade shows, and other promotions designed to publicize individual producers and the industry as a whole (Figure 10.10). New York is the largest U.S. market center for all kinds of menswear, including tailored clothing, sportswear, contemporary lines, and furnishings. Regional markets in other parts of the country—Chicago, Los Angeles, and Dallas, for example—are growing in importance, but the largest number of permanent showrooms is still located in New York.

A number of trade associations support the menswear industry. The following have a major role:

- Men's Apparel Guild of California (MAGIC). This group was founded in 1933 as the Los Angeles Men's Wear Manufacturers Association to promote California-style men's sportswear. It has since expanded beyond California to an international show and to other segments of the menswear industry. Currently, it includes women's and children's trade shows in addition to its semiannual extravaganzas in Las Vegas.
- Big and Tall Associates. Founded in 1972 for manufacturers and retailers who cater to men over five feet, eleven inches tall and/or with chest measurements over forty-eight inches, this organization conducts semiannual market weeks.

Table 10.1 lists the major menswear trade shows in the United States. As the market for imports and exports has grown in size and importance, more and more domestic manufacturers now attend the important

TABLE 10.1 *Major U.S. Trade Shows for Menswear*

WHO	WHERE	WHEN
ENKNYC	The Tunnel/La Venue, NYC	January & July
Chicago Collective & BATA	The Merchandise Mart, Chicago	January & August
The Cobb Show (organized by Atlanta Exhibition Apparel Group)	Cobb Galleria, Atlanta	January, March, May, July & October
MAGIC MENSWEAR	The Mandalay Convention Center and the Las Vegas Convention Center, Las Vegas	February & August

international shows, most notably Pitti Uomo in Italy, IMBEX in London, and SEHM in France.

Industry Trends

The dynamics of population growth as well as lifestyle changes and developments in the economy are bringing about changes in all segments of the menswear industry. Some of the most noteworthy trends include a diversification of products on the part of producers, the automation of production processes, an increase in foreign production and sales, and a proliferation of specialty stores. Consumers are showing greater interest in style and are demanding quality in fabric and construction.

Specialty Trends in Retailing

From the very beginning, independent specialty stores such as Brooks Brothers were important to the growth and impact of fashionable menswear. Although many small retailers have closed over the years, others, such as Mitchells/Richards in Connecticut; Mario's in Portland, Oregon; and Coffman's in Greenville, North Carolina, have found a formula that has allowed them to survive. They all attribute their success to an unwavering devotion to the customer. In fact, Mitchells/Richards CEO Jack Mitchell wrote a book called *Hugging Your Customers* that details to what lengths retailers need to go to in order to take care of their loyal customers.

One of the country's largest menswear retailers is The Men's Wearhouse. Opened in 1973, the company continued to grow, and founder and former executive chairman George Zimmer became known for his now-famous tagline, "You're going to like the way you look. I guarantee it," on radio and TV. The company boasts the flagship Men's Wearhouse chain; Moores, in Canada; and K&G Superstores, in the United States. As of 2013, Men's Wearhouse reports annual sales of over $2.3 billion and operates more than 1,200 stores in the United States and Canada (see page 198).[10]

Catalog sales are another specialty trend. Despite an increase in online marketing, major retailers, as well as specialty stores, send out catalogs geared exclusively to men, and stores such as L.L.Bean, which have always sold by catalog, report an increase in business. Catalogs are typically slated for a specific market; that is, they specialize in low prices; certain styles or fashions, such as golf or western; a certain size range, such as big and tall; or exclusivity. Those specialty catalogs that have done thorough market research and have offered their customers exactly what they want have been quite successful.

Style and Lifestyle

A former vice president and director of men's clothing at Neiman Marcus summed up the men's market, saying, "The clothing business hasn't changed, but the lifestyle has."[11] The first half is debatable: many of the major players remain the same today, but their continuing success has been correlated with their ability to adapt to the changes in the buying behavior of the ultimate consumer. Because men are now interested in fashion, they are buying different kinds of clothes. Most men's wardrobes today can be divided into three categories according to use: suits for formal business and social occasions, activewear for sports (spectator as well as participatory) and for the most casual situations, and slacks and sports coats for everyday office wear and after-work socializing. Matching the category to the occasion is not always a clear-cut, easy decision, however. Separates may be acceptable for client meetings, depending on the firm and the client, for example. And at some social events, men dressed in the three categories may mingle comfortably.

The daily decision about what to wear to work is probably the most important wardrobe choice because of its relationship to career success. The question plagues employers as much as employees. When dress codes began to be relaxed, the certainty about image that was associated with the business suit faded. Deliberately or by chance, new dress codes are being created. Savvy menswear marketers among both producers and retailers are coming to the rescue with seminars and brochures.

When men do wear traditional tailored clothing these days, they favor quality in fabric and workmanship and styling that flatters their build and expresses their taste. Spending $700 to $1,200 for a tailored suit is not unusual. Since many men no longer need an assortment of suits for business wear, they can afford to invest more in each suit they do buy. And they want value for their money.

Separates

Although the popular-priced blazers, vests, and slacks produced by such companies as Levi Strauss and Haggar have found a permanent place in the menswear market, with the renewed emphasis on quality, better-priced tailored clothes are once again selling well. They are unlikely, however, to edge out separates. HMX Group, the giant maker of men's suits, introduced sportswear lines under the Hickey Freeman and Hart Schaffner Marx names. Colors are lighter and brighter in these new lines, and the items are meant to be mixed and matched, as women have done for decades with separates.

Shirt Styles

Producers have recently made some changes in shirt sleeve sizes. Men's long-sleeved dress shirts are made in neck sizes fourteen to seventeen inches, graduated in half inches. In each size, the sleeve length has, until recently, also been graduated from thirty-two to thirty-five inches. In an effort to reduce inventories and increase stock turnover, however, producers have begun making dress shirts in two sleeve lengths. The lengths include both regular (32–34 inches) and long (34–35 inches). Over 50 percent of all men's dress shirts are now produced only in regular and long-sleeve lengths.

Whether this trend will prevail is unclear. Not all shirtmakers have converted to the new sizing, and with the renewed interest in quality, there has also been a reverse trend among some producers toward making exact sleeve sizes again.

Fitted dress shirts, tapered through the torso, or with darts to make them fit close to the body, resurfaced in the late 1990s after an absence of more than a decade. They were widely supported by designers, led by Ralph Lauren and including Perry Ellis and Tommy Hilfiger. The sales of men's dress shirts are on the rise, along with the accessories that go with them. Eric Jennings, fashion director for menswear at Saks Fifth Avenue, says, "Men are feeling more confident to experiment and [are] realizing that they do have more options."[12]

Designer and Brand-Name Labels

When Michael Bastian announced in 2006 that he was leaving his post as men's fashion director at New York's Bergdorf Goodman to design a line of men's clothing, he said he saw a niche in American menswear no one was filling—upscale versions of classic styles.

A number of other designers had the same idea. Among them, Tim Hamilton, an alumnus of Polo Ralph Lauren and J.Crew; Jurgen Oeltjenbruns, previously of Versace and DKNY; and Tony Melillo, a former *Esquire* magazine style director, launched lines that are updates of classic American menswear. So have Isaac Mizrahi, Narciso Rodriguez, and Elie Tahari, designers known for their women's wear. Shopping for men's clothing is no longer as simple as choosing among Ralph Lauren, Calvin Klein, and Tommy Bahama. Shoppers now face a large choice of brands, some from designers whose names are familiar only to the fashion-oriented consumer.

The proliferation of new labels is seen as an attempt by designers and retailers to use strategies that have worked successfully in the women's apparel department. By pushing new lines and fresh looks more often, they hope to generate excitement and continue the increase of sales.

More traditional menswear labels are targeting younger customers by making their retail spaces fresh and hip. In 2011, Brooks Brothers opened a concept store in New York City that aims to bring the brand to a newer generation. "You won't find a shirt-and-tie wall here," says Lou Amendola, chief merchandising officer of Brooks Brothers.[13] The store focuses more on sportswear than tailored clothing. It also has free Wi-Fi with a retro feel to the decor, complete with exposed brick and vintage video games.

Joining the push for fashion-forward menswear in the luxury market, traditional American menswear brands are going after younger customers, taking lessons from designers like Ermenegildo Zegna, Giorgio Armani, and Hugo Boss, who have successfully reached younger customers by producing juniors' lines with slimmer-fitting jackets and pants. The Joseph Abboud brand launched Joe Joseph Abboud, a line aimed at twenty-two- to thirty-year olds. Jos. A. Bank Clothiers, Inc., introduced Joseph. HMX Group's Hickey Freeman started selling Sterling, and the group's Hart Schaffner Marx and Oxxford clothes have lines aimed at young men who don't want to look like their dads or grandfathers. By launching these new labels, the companies hope to build brand loyalty among men who will eventually trade up to their pricier lines, where similar items can cost hundreds of dollars more.[14]

National brands, which have already had considerable impact, are expected to remain strong in the foreseeable future. In tailored menswear, brand names are seen as a sign of quality. Private-label merchandise is also making inroads. As is the case with women's private labels, they provide menswear retailers with exclusivity and higher profit margins (Figure 10.11). Retail operations strive to provide their customers with a mix of designer names, brand names, and private labels.

FIGURE 10.11 J.Crew offers updated American classics to its men and women customers.

Summary and Review

Designer and brand names are part of the push to provide men with up-to-date fashion. And while there will always be a market for classic or traditional men's clothes, industry forecasters predict that menswear will continue to be ever more fashion oriented. The Europeanization of the American tailored-clothing market has brought an appreciation of quality and fit. Comfort and convenience remain important to the average man, especially in casual wear and activewear.

While in the past menswear has changed more slowly than women's wear, the industry saw dramatic change and growth in the 1990s, as dress-down Fridays were adopted by most businesses in the United States. The activewear category also saw dramatic growth as firm, toned bodies became the goal of tens of thousands of men. As the baby boomers aged, more and more men became interested in enhancing their style and gaining a more youthful look. There has recently been a big boost in menswear sales, specifically for separates, suits, accessories, and sportswear.

The industry has been quick to capitalize on the growing interest in menswear, offering increasingly diverse products by using increased automation. Retailers jumped on the bandwagon, offering improved visual merchandising and increased advertising in newspapers, magazines, and on the Internet.

For Review

1. What effect did the industrial revolution have on male apparel? What socioeconomic factors were responsible for the drastic changes that occurred?
2. What three developments in the mid-nineteenth century were largely responsible for the development of the men's ready-to-wear industry in this country? How did each help to accelerate those developments?
3. Discuss the development of sportswear and casual wear in the men's market and the influence they have had on the menswear industry as a whole.
4. For what three reasons did early manufacturers of men's tailored clothing give up the use of contractors?
5. What role have unions played in the production of menswear? Why were unions formed in the nineteenth and early twentieth centuries? What role do they play in the industry today?
6. Name the different segments into which the menswear industry is subdivided on the basis of the type of product lines each produces. What specific products are produced by each segment?
7. How has the sizing of men's suits and dress shirts been simplified in recent years?
8. What is the role of trade shows in promoting men's fashions? Name and describe five trade shows that command national attention.
9. Name key players in the U.S. menswear manufacturing sector.
10. Describe two menswear style trends that are likely to continue.

For Discussion

1. Is the conservative men's suit dying out, or is it taking on a new life in the wake of more casual business dress codes? In what situations are tailored suits commonly worn in your community? What local trends do you see?
2. What is the role of designer names in menswear? Which men's designer fashions are currently popular?

Trade Talk

Define or briefly explain the following terms:

bridge apparel
contemporary menswear
drop
dual distribution
European styling
short run
slop shop
sportswear
suit separates
tailored-clothing firm

Chapter Eleven
CHILDREN'S AND TEENS' APPAREL

KEY CONCEPTS

- The impact of demographics on the children's apparel industry
- The history of the children's apparel industry
- Size categories of children's wear
- Unique features of infants' and toddlers' wear
- Merchandising and marketing of children's apparel
- Licensing in the children's apparel industry
- Industry trends and responses to social issues

We are all familiar with the phrase "out of the mouths of babes." Today, as media bombards children with grown-up images, new demands are heard out of the mouths of babes—demands for all things that are presented to them on television, in movies, and in books. Gone are the days when children were seen and not heard—producers of products such as soft drinks, candy, food, music, movies, and apparel heed the newly acquired sophistication of children. Everything presented to children is entertainment, and children want it all! This gives designers and producers of children's apparel a wonderful opportunity to adapt to the wants of these savvy new customers. Burberry, the famous London fashion house, is a classic example of a company that extended its brand to children's wear. Burberry produced two new products featuring its famous signature plaid—a luxury children's line featuring shearling coats, plaid duffel bags, and a Burberry Barbie. Burberry outfitted this legendary doll icon with a plaid skirt and classic trench coat, plus a plaid messenger bag. Ah, to be young, fashionable, and in love with Barbie (Figure 11.1).[1]

Making clothing fun for pint-size consumers and the adults who pay for their wardrobes is a serious business, and the global market for children's wear is projected to reach \$156.8 billion by 2015.[2]

Psychological Importance of Children's, Tweens', and Teens' Clothes

The apparel industry is not the only potential beneficiary of the growing interest in dressing children well. Psychologists believe that clothes play an important role in shaping and guiding a child's self-image. As parents understand the role that clothes play at various stages of a child's growth, they can help to ensure that a child's appearance will enhance his or her striving to become a mature, self-confident adult.[3]

FIGURE 11.1 Barbie, the famous fashion doll, has a wide variety of clothing and style—much like today's teens.

Proponents of the idea of school uniforms argue that uniforms foster a sense of belonging to a group and encourage neatness. Their opponents point out that selecting one's own attire is a form of self-expression. Both views recognize the importance of clothing to a child's self-identity.

Demographics and the Children's, Tweens', and Teens' Apparel Industry

This apparel industry is unusual in the extent to which it has been shaped by demographics. Patterns of childbearing tend to be cyclical. Although the birthrate had been steadily declining since the end of the nineteenth century, the aftermath of World War II brought about a baby boom. Women who had been working to support the war effort turned over their jobs to the returning soldiers and went home to become full-time housewives—and mothers. The birthrate soared. Three to four children per family was not unusual. Between 1953 and 1964, a whopping four million births occurred every year.

In the 1970s, many people became concerned that the world population was growing too rapidly and advocated that families have fewer children. More women began to work outside the home again. The birthrate declined, and the average number of children per family sank to fewer than two.

The 1980s did not bring about another baby boom, with three to four children per family, but because the baby boom generation had themselves reached childbearing age, the number of babies born increased for the first time since the 1960s. This increase occurred even though women continued to have a statistical average of 1.5 children, and many postponed motherhood to continue their careers. Over 3.5 million babies were born in 1987, and almost 3.9 million were born in 1988. Besides the increasing number of children, the culture of spending in the 1980s contributed to the success of the children's apparel industry. The number of mothers who worked soared, and two-income families generally had more discretionary income. People not only bought more for each child, but they also purchased more expensive goods than in the past.

In the 1990s, parents reined in their family clothing budgets. For single mothers and for couples whose sense of job security was diminished by mergers and downsizing, the mother's income came to be viewed as essential to the family's financial well-being rather than extra money. But parents' more cautious spending behavior has not caused a downturn in the children's apparel industry. What has happened instead is that new markets for children's wear have emerged. In 1996, the first wave of baby boom babies turned fifty, and the population of their elders was growing, thanks to life-prolonging improvements in health care. All those doting grandparents have made the over-fifty age group the top spenders on children's retail clothing. Toward the other end of the age spectrum, children themselves, especially those over age twelve, have become a formidable group of shoppers. Their style- and brand-consciousness contributes significantly to the success of such brands as Tommy Hilfiger, Calvin Klein, Guess, Levi's, and Gap.

The teen market is steadily growing and has been successfully impacted by fashion apparel and accessories. A growing number of well-known designers and retailers are cashing in on the trend by getting into the teen and tween business, which is constantly growing. On average, thirteen-year-olds spend approximately $54 on clothes each month, while teens age fourteen to eighteen spend $64, according to Cotton Incorporated's Lifestyle Monitor Survey. And since tweens usually rely on an adult to make the purchase, 71 percent say they plan most of their apparel purchases, rather than impulse shop.[4]

A baby boom birthrate occurred during the first few years of the twenty-first century, with the number of babies born in the U.S. reaching an all-time high in 2007. However, the onset of the recession may have forced twentysomethings to delay starting families, as there was a plunge in 2012 to its lowest level in twenty-five years.[5] Despite economic effects of the recession, research shows that parents have continued to spend money on apparel, shoes, and accessories for their children at a constant rate.[6]

History of the Children's Apparel Industry

Although boys' wear is considered part of the men's apparel industry, for our purposes, it is considered as part of children's wear and described in this chapter.

As a commercial activity, the children's wear industry is a phenomenon of the twentieth century. For most of history, children were dressed like miniature adults. Study a portrait from the Renaissance or the American colonial era, and you will see children wearing the same low necklines, bustles, and pantaloons that were currently stylish with adults.

When children's clothes finally began to look different from those that adults wore, toward the end of the 1800s, they took on the look of uniforms. All little girls, for example, dressed in a similar drab outfit—dark, high-button shoes, a midcalf-length skirt, and dark stockings.

Clothes were made extra large so children could grow into them. Their construction was sturdy so they could be handed down to younger children. Many children's clothes were hand-sewn or made by a few apparel manufacturers who seldom offered any variations on the clothes or, for that matter, experienced any growth in their businesses. It did not matter that children's clothes were dull and unattractive because no child would dare to protest what parents wanted him or her to wear. One 1800s success story was the William Carter Company, which began in 1865 and became one of the largest children's underwear companies. It is still in business today and is known as Carter's. The company also owns OshKosh, in addition to several other children's brands.

Although a few designers specialized in high-priced children's wear in the early 1900s, it was not until after World War I that the commercial production and distribution of stylish children's wear began. Not surprisingly, the growth of the children's wear industry followed in the wake of the developing women's wear industry. When women stopped making their own clothes, they also stopped making their children's clothes.

The children's wear industry also grew because manufacturers found ways to make factory-produced clothing sturdier than homemade clothes. The development of snaps, zippers, and more durable sewing methods were important contributions.

Another important step in the manufacture of children's clothes occurred after World War I, when manufacturers began to standardize children's wear sizes. What began as a very primitive method of sizing children's clothing has since turned into a highly sophisticated sizing operation, with many categories and subdivisions.

The next major change in the children's wear industry was the introduction of radio and movies into Americans' lives in the 1920s, 1930s, and 1940s. All across the country, mothers dressed their little girls like Shirley Temple and their boys like cowboy western heroes. Teens wanted to dress like Judy Garland and Mickey Rooney, stars of countless teen musicals.

In the 1950s, another change—really a revolution—was brought about by the introduction of television into Americans' homes. It did not take advertisers long to discover that children, among the largest group of consumers of television, could be targeted directly. From *Howdy Doody* to *The Mickey Mouse Club*—and the innumerable shows that have followed—kids loved television, shows and commercials alike. Then it was a short step to gear the advertising in other media—radio as well as magazines and newspapers—toward children.

Television programs geared to audiences of different ages help to establish the popularity of clothing styles for each age group, from the preschoolers playing on *Sesame Street* to the high school students on *iCarly* and *Glee*.

Organization and Operation of the Children's, Tweens', and Teens' Apparel Industry

There are close to one thousand companies that make children's apparel. Despite the prominence of such giant companies as Carter's, Gerber Children's Wear, and Healthtex, most children's clothes are still made by small, family-owned businesses. Notable among them

GapKids

GapKids + DVF
Collection at Gap

THE KIDS
ARE NOW IN CHARGE

ONCE UPON A time, children were seen but not heard. Now, they are at the center of the universe. It is hard to imagine, but for long stretches in Western history, children were treated badly. As recently as the Victorian era, "spare the rod and spoil the child" was the definition of child rearing, and child labor was a staple of the economy.

Today, children can be seen *and* heard all over town and they are no longer viewed as secondary to adults. The needs and rights of children are now carefully taken into account and their individuality and self-esteem are promoted as never before.

Children have become their own viable market—and the fashion industry has responded. Designers like Stella McCartney, Ralph Lauren, Isaac Mizrahi, and Diane Von Furstenberg have had great success with their children's wear collections, and top couture designers such as Oscar de la Renta, Alber Elbaz, and Versace have happily joined the ranks. Certainly, these designers recognize that the kids will be "in charge" for many more years. By providing for these young customers now, it's their hope that these designer-clad infants will most likely choose designer labels when they begin shopping for themselves.

are the following multigenerational firms: Quiltex, Celebrity International, Will'beth, and Vitamins Baby.

Many adult apparel producers, including Levi Strauss, Patagonia, Old Navy, Gap, and Reebok, also operate children's apparel divisions. Many adult apparel designers have also begun children's divisions.

Like adult clothing, children's wear is divided into categories based on price, size, and type of merchandise. Children's clothes are produced in designer, better-priced, moderate, and budget price ranges. Most children's clothes bought by parents are in the budget and moderate price ranges, while better-priced and designer merchandise is a common gift purchase by grandparents and other adults.

Size Categories

A super-sophisticated marketplace makes sizing little customers more challenging than ever before. The industry debates whether the traditional size categories really reflect a child's age and maturity level—particularly in the sophisticated state of today's market. Across the country, retailers and manufacturers are questioning and reimaging the size standards, each with their own idea of what would constitute the ideal size categories.[7]

According to the National Centers for Disease Control and Prevention, about one-third of children and adolescents in the United States are overweight or obese.

Some retailers and vendors do offer plus-size clothing selections, but the availability of attractive, flattering plus-size offerings for children is scarce. J.C. Penney has carried extended sizes for children for more than fifteen years.

Although the actual size range is the same, the **preteen sizes** for girls offer more sophisticated styling than the **girls' sizes**. Similarly, the **young men's** category (also called **prep**, **student**, or **teen**) stresses sophisticated styling more than **boys' sizes**.

Special Features of Infants' and Toddlers' Wear

Clothing in **infants'** and **toddlers' sizes** is designed to meet needs that are unique to the youngest children. For example, pants are available with snaps along the inseams to facilitate diaper changes. Undershirts may have snaps to open at the front so that they don't have to be pulled over the baby's head. Elasticized waistbands—rather than buttons or zippers—make changing pants or skirts easier for adults and for toddlers who are learning to dress themselves. Stretchy suits and snowsuits for infants and sleepwear for infants and toddlers may be fitted with soft-soled feet to offer extra warmth and protection. Mittenlike flaps on newborns' sleepwear help to prevent babies from scratching themselves with their fast-growing fingernails. Bonnets and caps tie under the chin, and bootees have elastic around the ankles to keep these clothing items on the baby.

Layettes—collections of crib and bath linens, sleepwear, and underwear for infants—include some unique items, such as sleeping sacs with drawstrings at the bottom. A one-piece undergarment known as a "onesie," consisting of a shirt with a long tail that extends under a diaper and snaps to the front of the shirt, is another item designed specifically for infants.

Product Specialization

Children's wear manufacturers typically specialize by product. One producer will make only girls' knits, while another makes only girls' dresses, and another makes only preteen sportswear. But unlike the producers of adult wear, children's wear producers often make a single type of clothing in several size ranges. For example, a producer may make boys' sportswear in sizes 8 through 20, while a producer of girls' dresses may make a product in toddlers' through girls' sizes.

A few observations about the fabrics used in children's wear are worth keeping in mind. One is the enduring popularity of knits for infants' wear and for tops in the everyday wardrobes of girls and boys through the larger size ranges. Another is the demand for natural fibers, especially cotton. Anyone interested in the children's apparel industry should be aware of the Flammable Fabrics Act of 1972 and its subsequent modifications, which require that sleepwear for children be treated with flame-retardant finishes.

The same design and production methods that are used in the manufacturing of adult apparel are used in children's wear, although these methods are often simplified. While children's garments require less fabric, they are usually more expensive to make because they require more labor.

The Role of Fashion in Children's Wear

Even the most basic lines of children's clothing reflect attempts to make the clothes fashionable, and the demand for style, once primarily an urban phenomenon, is now felt in most geographic areas in the country (Figure 11.2).

The demand for stylish children's clothes, which has escalated every year, has culminated in designer clothing for children. Children's wear, however, must still be viewed as a business that is a *fashionable* rather

FIGURE 11.2 Fashion consciousness starts with the very youngest.

world, and typically lagged a year or more behind adult fashions. Today, however, the lag is shrinking.

Increasingly, children look to their own peers and to the group just ahead of them, young adults, for pace-setting styles and trends. Successful children's wear producers have learned that they, too, must look to the young adult fashion world for inspiration. This means watching fads as well as trends. Popular young adult fads and styles are increasingly being translated into children's wear lines (Figure 11.3).

The industry has also begun to use fashion-forecasting specialists to enable manufacturers to incorporate new styles into their lines as soon as a trend is spotted. At this point, the smaller (and trendier) manufacturers are still quicker to incorporate new styles and fashion than are the larger companies. The leading designers of adult fashion who have developed lines of children's apparel and the retailers whose store brands

than a *fashion* business. The difference is that while the children's wear industry produces fashionable clothing, the styles adapt men's and women's styles. They are not in and of themselves innovative, nor does new fashion start in children's wear lines. However, the backpack is one exception.

The children's wear industry also does not operate with the intensity of the adult clothing industry. Children's clothes, for example, do not follow a ready-to-wear production and design schedule.

Producers of children's clothing have typically operated on a one-line-per-season production schedule, and four lines—Spring, Summer, Winter, and Fall—are typical. Lines are not updated during a season. Once a line has been shown and accepted, that is all the manufacturer produces. An exciting and very hot new look might appear at midseason, but only rarely. Most manufacturers cannot produce a new look until the following season, at which point demand may even have begun to decline.

The children's wear business has begun to make the kinds of operational changes necessary to permit it to stay more on top of changing fashion. Styles in children's wear used to trickle down from the adult fashion

FIGURE 11.3 Harajuku clothing and perfume by Gwen Stefani is available for kids, as well as young adults.

extend to the children's market—Gap and GapKids, for example—can bring out corresponding lines of adults' and children's fashion concurrently.

The Role of Fashion in Teens' and Tweens' Wear

Today's teens and tweens are the first age groups for which television has not been the primary entertainment; it is but one technology of many at which they spend their leisure hours. Their top leisure activity: surfing the Web.

There are distinct differences between teens and tweens in attitudes, buying habits, and other consumer behaviors, as reported in *Marketing to Teens & Tweens*, published by EPM Communications, owner of *The Licensing Letter*.[8] The report looks at the trends shaping these consumers with an eye toward where these trends will lead in the future. Teens and tweens both like to be defined as individuals yet still fit in with peers. But teens in general show more individualistic qualities, while tweens tend more toward the group.

A growing number of well-known designers and retailers hope to benefit by getting into the teen and tween business. The idea of families sharing a clothing label has long been the foundation for apparel empires such as Polo/Ralph Lauren, Rocawear, and Gap. Moms and daughters are shopping the same racks. To satisfy this new trend, specialty chain J.Crew Group started selling tiny versions of its popular adult apparel. The kids' line, called CrewCuts, has done so well that J.Crew expanded into freestanding stores for CrewCuts.

Merchandising and Marketing

Many of the features and activities of the children's wear industry are similar, if not identical, to those of the women's and men's apparel industries. For example, eco-friendly fashions are seen in children's fashions, too (Figure 11.4). However, sales promotion and advertising activities for children's wear are considerably more limited. The giants in the industry—Carter's and Healthtex—advertise aggressively to consumers. Smaller firms—the majority of firms producing budget and moderately priced children's wear—leave most consumer advertising to retailers. Firms producing higher-priced, name-designer merchandise do a limited amount of consumer advertising. The high cost of this advertising is often shared with textile firms.

In general, the industry uses the trade press for its advertising. Specialized publications concerned with children's wear include *Earnshaw's* and *Childrenswear Buyer* magazine (in the U.K.). Trade publications that report on adult fashions, such as *Women's Wear Daily*, also carry children's wear advertising and news reports of interest to retailers on a regular basis. More companies are using Twitter, Facebook, and mobile devices as marketing channels to reach out to both teens and their parents, often combining information about the company with a catalog.

Market Centers

Most of the children's wear firms are located in the North Atlantic states, particularly in New York City. As is the trend in the women's and men's apparel industries, some factories have moved farther south in order to obtain lower production costs. Many goods are produced in foreign countries—outerwear, jeans, woven shirts, and sweaters primarily in the Far East, and infants' knits and apparel items in Greece, Spain, and Israel. These countries offer lower production costs than do France, Italy, and Switzerland, which produce prestige merchandise. But the design, sales, and distribution centers of such firms remain in New York City. While New York continues to be the most important market center for children's wear, many producers maintain permanent showrooms in the large regional apparel marts, especially in Miami, and schedule showings there. Los Angeles, too, has emerged as a children's apparel center not only because of its

FIGURE 11.4 Sustainable clothing is available for children, too. These dresses from Kicky Pants are made out of bamboo.

FIGURE 11.5 Trade show booths are an important place for children's apparel manufacturers to reach retail store buyers.

enormous manufacturing base but also for the fashion trends that originate there.

Trade Shows

The California Market Center in Los Angeles promotes through direct mail, floor displays, and caravans that bring in retailers from surrounding counties. It also sponsors L.A. Kids Market. Dallas KidsWorld Market is another trade event for baby, children's, and juvenile products held at the Dallas Market Center. Other popular children's wear trade shows (Figure 11.5) include the Children's Club trade show in New York City, produced by ENK International; and an annual Women's and Children's Apparel Market in Chicago.

Designer Labels

Children's designer-label clothing and accessories are highly visible in stores across the country. The appeal of these items seems to rise above income levels. Designer labels are available in stores geared to middle-income as well as high-income customers. Although designer wear for children has been around for a while—Izod introduced a boys' line in the late 1960s—the explosion in designer-label children's wear took off in the late 1970s with the designer jean craze.

Designer labels are expected to continue to grow in children's wear. Lanvin, Burberry, Fendi, Dolce & Gabbana, Donna Karan, and Versace are some examples of designers who have already expanded their designs to the children's market (Figure 11.6). Several companies, including Esprit, Guess, Patagonia, and Ralph Lauren, have created separate divisions for their children's wear designs.

Well-known brand names in children's wear include Flapdoodles, Gymboree, Little Me, Absorba, Joe Boxer, Cotton Caboodle, and, of course, Guess and Gap. Because they have designer-name status, some children's wear designers, following in the pioneering footsteps of Florence Eiseman and Ruth Scharf, have acquired celebrity status, such as Hanna Andersson.

Status names are also changing the shape of the boys' wear industry. It is difficult to tell which came first, though—the boys' demand for designer clothes or the designers' efforts to enter the boys' wear market. Whatever the case, well-known fashion designers are

FIGURE 11.6 Designers like Marc Jacobs have expanded into the children's wear market.

now competing for space alongside traditional branded merchandise in boys' wear departments. Boys' wear, in fact, has become a prime area for designers such as Ralph Lauren, Tommy Hilfiger, and Calvin Klein. Of course, not all designers actually design and manufacture all the products sold under their labels.

Licensing

Like designer labels, other kinds of licensed names provide a sense of fashion rightness, in addition to giving a garment or line instant identification in consumers' minds. As a result, as the children's wear industry became more fashion-conscious, manufacturers were quick to produce licensed goods. In addition to designer names, the ever-popular cartoon and toy character licenses share the spotlight with a growing number of sports and corporate licenses.

Character Licensing

The first licensed cartoon character was Buster Brown in 1904. Licensed cartoon and toy characters, long a staple with children, are still thriving in the twenty-first century. Younger children especially enjoy wearing representations of their favorite characters. A widespread example is Dora the Explorer, whose picture adorns children coast to coast.

Character licenses dominate in children's T-shirts, sweatshirts, and sleepwear and are also strong in accessories and sportswear (Figure 11.7). Their impact is not as great in dresses, suits, and outerwear, but some of

FIGURE 11.7 Character licenses are everywhere in the children's apparel industry. Vans creates more kid-friendly designs by incorporating Hello Kitty in their products.

these items are available. Children's character licenses, especially those associated with feature-length movies, tend to be short lived. Only a few reached the ranks of true stardom (and big profit). As a result, many retailers, particularly department store buyers, have become cautious about overinvesting in them. Department stores, whose promotion is necessary if a licensed character is to be truly successful, tend to stick with classics like Pooh, Snoopy, and Mickey Mouse. In the popular-priced lines of children's apparel, a licensing agreement between Kmart and Children's Television Workshop, creators of *Sesame Street*, has proven to be very successful over the years.

Disney has its own retail outlets, where the mix of apparel, accessories, and toys may help to extend the lives of the movie characters. Warner Brothers owns more than 3,700 active licenses worldwide and sells merchandise through its online store. These licenses include DC Comics' Batman, Superman, Green Lantern, Wonder Woman, Supergirl, Harry Potter, and Looney Tunes characters. Warner Brothers also own Hanna-Barbera properties, including Yogi Bear and Tom & Jerry.[9]

Sports Licensing

Sports licensing is another prospering area of licensing. Sports figures and teams both have high media visibility and thus enjoy instant recognition among children and young adults. In areas with professional or school teams, college stores, airport shops, and stadium concessions increase the availability of licensed apparel at retail. Sports figures add their names to running apparel, tennis clothes and accessories, as well as less active casual and sportswear lines, with great success. And producers of athletic shoes, sweatshirts, and sports equipment feature their names and logos on active sportswear.

Professional hockey, football, basketball, and baseball teams, as well as college and university athletic teams, now routinely license their names for use on clothes, mostly T-shirts and sweatshirts. Sportswear companies are also quick to capitalize on trends. Over the past decade, soccer has been the fastest-growing sport among young Americans. Nike, Adidas, and Reebok are among the many brands that offer soccer apparel for children.

Industry Trends

Like women's apparel manufacturers, children's wear producers are constantly on the lookout for ways to increase productivity and reduce—or at least minimize—costs while still maintaining quality.

MADONNA: THE ORIGINAL MATERIAL GIRL

MADONNA BURST FROM the New York City club scene to national fame in 1982 with her first album. Hailed as one of the greatest pop musicians, her music and style were lauded and criticized, depending on who you asked. Her thrift-store mash-up of visible inner wear; blue jeans; bracelet-lined arms; tousled highlighted hair; and infamous "boy toy" belt buckle was the aspiration of every teen girl and the nightmare of parents.

Looking back today, what was considered shocking then now seems innocent, but at the time, her lyrics, videos, and style were unlike anything that had been seen before. Madonna was a 180-degree turn from the tidy, well-groomed pop stars who preceded her. She sparked the imagination of people around the world and has been a muse for designers like Jean Paul Gaultier, Jeremy Scott, Alexander Wang, Dolce & Gabbana, Philip Treacy, and Givenchy's Riccardo Tisci ever since.

Always the trendsetter and fashion icon, Madonna hurtled from muse to creator, along with daughter Lourdes, with whom she began designing the Material Girl juniors clothing line in 2010. In 2012, Madonna launched her lifestyle brand Truth or Dare, aimed at women 27-50. It featured her first signature scent and footwear collection, followed by intimates, handbags, and accessories.

Madonna takes great care that her brands convey her style and sensibility. "I don't take creating anything, whether it's fragrance, or beauty products, or clothes lightly, and I need a lot of time to do stuff. I don't like it when other people create for me [because] if I'm not going to wear it, I'm not going to sell it."

Madonna's enterprises, whether in music, film, or fashion, will continue to expand and surprise us because that is what allows her to thrive. "To have fun, that's the main issue," she says. "To continue to be a provocateur, to do what we perceive as the realm of the young people, to provoke, to be rebellious, to start a revolution."

Material Girl Launch

MATERIAL GIRL

Lourdes Leon, Georgia May Jagger, and Madonna (left to right)

FIGURE 11.8 H&M launched a children's wear collection in collaboration with UNICEF to benefit the poorest areas in the world.

E-commerce continues to thrive for suppliers, manufacturers, and retailers of children's wear. Carter's launched two e-commerce sites, www.carters.com and www.oshkoshbgosh.com, in 2010. Each website features a shopping cart that collects items from both sites, enabling consumers to only have to check out once.[10] The e-commerce sites that attract the most traffic are already attached to a major retail brand, like the Disney Store (www.disneystore.com) for younger children and Abercrombie and Fitch (www.abercrombie.com) for teens.

Specialty Retail Outlets

Increasing attention is being given to children's wear by apparel retailers whose main lines are men's and women's clothing (Figure 11.8). A related trend is the prominence of clothing in the merchandise mix of retail outlets carrying a broader array of children's goods. Even among clothing stores that have not opened freestanding children's outlets, distinctive stores-within-stores are now selling children's wear exclusively. Carrying the trend to its logical conclusion, the infants' and toddlers' departments of the children's stores and stores-within-stores are being set up as separate outlets.

Separate Stores

Typical of this trend are Gap's GapKids and BabyGap. Begun in 1969 as a retailer of jeans for adults, Gap expanded into a private-label specialty store featuring casual wear for men and women. In 1986, the first GapKids store opened, offering Gap customers basic but fashionable children's wear that catered to the same tastes as the adult lines. The BabyGap line, begun in 1990, became a separate department within GapKids

stores and departments, and in 1996, the flagship freestanding BabyGap store opened in New York. GapKids later expanded its products by featuring designer lines from Stella McCartney and Diane von Furstenberg.

Gymboree is a successful children's wear retailer that used a different concept to build its business. Its Outlet division, started in 2005, now operates 150 stores. The Janie and Jack stores, which sell clothing at higher prices than the company's original Gymboree children's stores, now number 120 stores since their 2002 launch.

Catalogs

Major catalog retailers such as Lands' End, Eddie Bauer, and L.L.Bean have also increased their offerings for children's wear. Marketing clothes to a group which, for the most part, is too young to drive or hold down full-time jobs is a risky proposition. But who said dealing with teenagers was easy? dELiA*s, Inc. is a multi-channel retail company with two lifestyle brands—dELiA*s and Alloy—that primarily target teenage girls and young women. The company sells apparel, accessories, and footwear to consumers through their direct-mail catalogs. Additionally, they market their brands and sell products through their website, which includes a digital edition of their catalog.

Resale of Children's Wear

Another important trend in children's wear retailing is the growth of secondhand resale or consignment stores. For parents who are concerned about the price of their children's wardrobe basics, secondhand clothes received as hand-me-downs or purchased at garage sales or nursery school bazaars have always been a good

FIGURE 11.9 Children's Orchard, a franchiser for resale shops for children's clothing and accessories, supplies its franchisees with ads they can run in local newspapers. The franchisee just needs to add the store's address, phone number, and business hours.

source of clothing. Since children—especially infants and toddlers—so quickly outgrow their clothes, budget-minded parents are using this kind of outlet.

Resale shops have emerged as a popular source of "lightly used" children's wear. One retail franchise chain, Once Upon a Child, has become a prominent resale outlet, with more than 240 locations throughout the United States and Canada. Another big resale chain is the Children's Orchard (Figure 11.9).

The appeal of these stores to budget-conscious parents is twofold: they can sell their children's outgrown clothing and get paid for it immediately. This practice distinguishes resale shops from consignment shops, which pay a percentage of the retail price only when the item is sold.

Once Upon a Child (www.ouac.com), Children's Orchard (www.childrensorchard.com), and similar stores also have successful online businesses. Interestingly, resale of children's clothing has become a very popular form of online shopping. There are hundreds of small and large websites that offer "gently used" children's clothing.

School Uniforms

In 2008, the U.S. market for school uniforms reached $490 million.[11] School officials believe uniforms have contributed to improved behavior, including reductions in lateness, class cutting, bullying, fighting, robberies, and other crimes.

Back in 1996, President Clinton's State of the Union address included a pitch for school uniforms. The U.S. Department of Education sent every school district in the United States a *Manual on School Uniforms*, which began with a section called "School Uniforms: Where They Are and Why They Work." Uniforms have become

so common at elementary and middle schools that in many areas of the country they are the rule, not the exception.

Supporters of uniforms point out that uniforms can help students identify with their school and make intruders not in uniform easier to spot. They cite the positive associations of children with other uniformed groups, such as scouts, teams in children's athletic leagues, children in private and parochial schools, and children in public schools in other countries. Stylish but functional uniforms (Figure 11.10) are presented as a superior alternative to the unofficial uniforms of street gangs.

Answering the objections of opponents, supporters point out that uniforms equalize affluent and low-income students and that a set of uniforms need not be more expensive than an ordinary school wardrobe. Children can be encouraged to participate in the selection of uniforms as a way of expressing their tastes.

As uniforms have become more common, many schools have updated the traditional (and itchy) blue blazers, plaid skirts, and white knee socks. An increasing number of students are sporting "business casual" clothes like pants, jumpers, and denim shirts from brands like Lands' End, Old Navy, Target, and Walmart instead.

J.C. Penney, in partnership with IzodEd, is the year-round headquarters for school uniforms. Through izoded.com and select J.C. Penney stores, customers can receive school uniform specifications and purchase

FIGURE 11.10 There are now more comfortable and fashionable options for school uniforms.

their local school district–approved apparel that is promoted as stylish, comfortable, and easy to care for. In addition, J.C. Penney can accommodate all special-size uniform needs with its vast assortment of fits for all kids and teens in stores and at jcp.com.[12]

For manufacturing, some stores are turning to French Toast (which is also available for purchase through J.C. Penney), whose large presence and experience in the market allows for a broad assortment of styles and colors and good depth in sizing. Some schools are using traditional dealers/distributors of adult uniforms, since these companies have long made quality clothes designed and constructed for daily wear.[13]

Summary and Review

The children's wear market is segmented by gender and by size categories. The special features of infants' and toddlers' apparel must be taken into consideration by designers and manufacturers.

Designer labels, which are often licensed to manufacturers that specialize in children's products, are becoming increasingly important in this industry, as are character and sports licensing.

Established trends that bear watching are multiple price lines offered by manufacturers and steady offshore production. Retail trends include establishing separate stores, the widespread use of catalogs, and establishing Internet sites. The trend toward school uniforms for grade school students and some high school students also demands attention.

Most experts are optimistic that the two prevalent trends—a move toward greater fashion in children's and teens' wear and another move toward buying better children's and teens' wear—are unlikely to reverse themselves in the coming years. This situation should make this industry one of the more stable divisions in the fashion industry. The segment that has simply been called children's wear can now rightly be called children's and teens' fashion.

For Review

1. How did the children's wear industry adjust to demographic changes between the 1980s and the 1990s?
2. What three developments occurred after World War I to cause the growth of the children's wear industry?
3. Name and briefly describe the seven size categories of children's wear. What distinguishes girls' from preteen sizes and boys' from young men's sizes?
4. Explain the statement "Children's wear . . . must still be viewed as a business that is fashionable rather than a fashion business." Do you agree with this statement? Explain your reasons.
5. How is consumer advertising handled by different types of firms in the children's wear business?
6. What accounts for the popularity of character licensing in children's wear?
7. What is the appeal of designer-label children's clothing?
8. Describe the current trend toward specialty retail outlets for children's wear.
9. Explain the popularity of resale shops for children's wear.

For Discussion

1. Discuss the importance of licensing in today's children's wear market. How does the licensing system work? Why is it particularly popular with children?
2. Discuss the pros and cons of school uniforms. What impact does this issue have on the children's wear industry?
3. What trends do you see in the young adult market today that have filtered into the design of children's clothing?

Trade Talk

Define or briefly explain the following terms:

boys' sizes
children's sizes
girls' sizes
infants' sizes
preteen sizes
teens' sizes
toddlers' sizes
young men's, prep, student, or teen sizes

THE SECONDARY LEVEL: THE OTHER PRODUCERS

No matter how chic, exquisite, or hip your apparel may look, it is the finishing touches that make your outfit something special, something that says . . . you! For years, intimate apparel, accessories, and beauty were not necessarily the most important part of your fashion look. Things have really changed. What we choose for our intimate apparel, accessories, beauty, and the items we surround ourselves with at home, all add up to our own personal fashion feel and look. The four chapters in this unit explore the activities of these other producers:

- Chapter 12: The history, merchandising, and marketing of innerwear, bodywear, and legwear.
- Chapter 13: The transformation of accessories throughout history and a discussion about how the industry has become a thriving market.
- Chapter 14: The different categories and major market segments of the beauty industry (formerly known as Cosmetics and Fragrances).
- Chapter 15: The growing trends in home fashions, and how top apparel designers have influenced this market.

Chapter Twelve

INNERWEAR, BODYWEAR, LEGWEAR

KEY CONCEPTS

- History of the women's intimate apparel industry
- Categories of intimate apparel
- Merchandising and marketing of intimate apparel
- Merchandising of men's and children's underwear and sleepwear
- History and organization of the hosiery industry
- Branding of women's legwear
- Trends in the hosiery industry

Innerwear, bodywear, and legwear used to be personal and secret choices, hidden from everyone except our closest and dearest. What supported our bodies, glorified our figures, and made us feel wanted was a secret weapon we shared with no one. Today, all that has changed! Men, women, and children flaunt the "intimate apparel" that was once hidden from view. What is hidden under clothing can never make a name for itself, so innerwear, bodywear, and legwear designers decreed that it should all "hang out." Today, bras, corsets, slips, nightgowns, underwear, and hosiery are a very important part of a person's total fashion look. People enjoy the luxurious array of styles and colors provided by these industries and consider them an important part of their wardrobes. The importance of designer names in these industries has helped to ensure that the interpretation of changes in silhouette, fabrication, and color is reflected in the innerwear, bodywear, and legwear industries.

When you shop for boxers, do you think of Calvin Klein or Joe Boxer? Do you associate Nike or Russell with activewear? And is Hanes or Donna Karan your choice for hosiery? If you are looking for a leotard, do you think of Danskin or Capezio? Do you buy "no brand" socks or Gold Toe? All these manufacturers are vying for your business. They and their competitors also want their names in the forefront of your mind. Manufacturers and retailers have long recognized that the intimate apparel and hosiery segments of the fashion industry operate in support of the women's, men's, and children's apparel segments. Consumers maximize the versatility of their wardrobes and enhance the look of each outfit by coordinating their underwear and legwear with their clothing. Therefore, the way for a designer, manufacturer, or retailer to grow is to provide the components of a total fashion statement.

Overview of the Underwear and Innerwear Industries

In the past, the manufacturing and marketing of men's and children's underwear was driven by considerations of practical functionality, but lately, these segments of the apparel industry have also felt the impact of fashion. Through mergers and acquisitions, producers of men's and children's underwear have become divisions of more diversified apparel firms. This trend is discussed later in this chapter.

Women's underwear or **innerwear**, sometimes called "inner fashions," "intimate apparel," or "body fashions," is the trade term for women's underwear, usually divided into foundations (bras, shapewear, lingerie, and loungewear). Originally these groups of products were separate industries, but a single industry called **intimate apparel** evolved as a result of business mergers, diversification of products, technological advances in fibers and fabrications, and a growing relationship between these industries and women's ready-to-wear.

FIGURE 12.1 Shapewear has transformed throughout history. An advertisement for the Warner Brothers' Coraline corset shows the early types of foundations (top) compared with Spanx, the more flexible shapewear used today (bottom).

Innerwear or Intimate Apparel

The wearing of undergarments probably grew out of practical need as people sought something to protect their skins from the chafing of harsh animal skins. And indeed, for many years the purpose of underwear was primarily utilitarian. Foundation garments were for shaping and support, lingerie provided warmth and protection, and loungewear marked the boundaries of propriety for at-home entertaining. As the distinctions among these categories have blurred, new fashion features of intimate apparel, new types of undergarments, and new uses of innerwear as outerwear have emerged—literally.

History and Development

The foundations industry began after the Civil War with the opening of the Warner Brothers' corset factory in Bridgeport, Connecticut (Figure 12.1, top). The bell-shaped silhouette was then at the height of its popularity. To achieve the tiny waist demanded by the bell and its successors, the bustle-back and Gibson Girl silhouettes, women wore corsets made of sturdy, unyielding cotton. Reinforced with vertical stays of whalebone or steel, the corsets laced up the front or back. They were tightly laced to achieve the extreme (in many cases) constriction of the waist and internal organs that fashion required.

Variations on these stiff corsets were worn by all women until the 1920s, when the rounded and bustled silhouettes that had prevailed for decades gave way to the straight, loose styles of the boyish flappers. Stiff, full-torso corsets were no longer required. The new silhouette demanded that the bosom and hips be minimized. Bandage-like bras were created to flatten the bust, and new girdle-like corsets controlled any conspicuous bulges below the waist.

By the 1930s, soft, feminine curves were back in style. Rubberized elastic was introduced, and the corset became known as the "girdle." Women now coaxed their bodies into two new types of foundations, the two-way stretch girdle and the cup-type brassiere, both of which were more comfortable than any of their predecessors.

These innovations set a precedent in the foundations industry and in women's lives. Women would henceforth wear inner garments that molded the figure more gently. Undergarments would now permit freedom of movement.

The 1930s also marked the introduction of rayon, changing the face of the intimate apparel industry. Until then, most mass-produced lingerie and loungewear were made of cotton, with wool being used in extremely cold climates. Silk, which was expensive and tedious to care for, appeared in custom-made, luxury

FIGURE 12.2 Women protesters took off their bras to place on the bra-burning pile in honor of the social revolution of their time.

styles affordable only for the rich. Rayon had the luxurious feel of silk, but it was washable and inexpensive.

Similar fibers followed in the 1950s with the reintroduction of nylon, a synthetic fiber that was softer and longer wearing than rayon and even more easily maintained. (Its use had been limited during the war years—1940 to 1945.) Innovations in fabrics continued over the next four decades, with the introduction of polyester, acrylics, microfibers, Tencel, and Lyocell. Stronger sheer fabrics, more pliable leathers, and Ultrasuede also helped transform the intimate apparel industry, especially loungewear.

Repeated improvements in elasticized fabrics have led to softer, more comfortable, and increasingly lightweight foundation garments that retain their shape even after many washings. Spandex body shapers mixed with nylon or polyester microfibers are the latest episode in this ongoing saga, and Nancy Ganz, whose Lycra Bodyslimmers were introduced in 1990, is the heroine. Depending on the area they wanted to reshape, women were able to rely on her hipslip, thighslimmer, buttbooster, or knee beater.

In the twenty-first century Sara Blakely reinvigorated shapewear with her creation of Spanx (Figure 12.1, bottom). In an effort to find a blemish-free look under her white pants, Blakely started a revolution. She created an array of problem-solving products for every body type and budget. The Spanx brand now houses more than 200 products ranging from slimming apparel and swimsuits to bras, activewear, and men's undershirts.[1]

Brassieres offer the best example of the massive style changes that the intimate apparel industry has undergone in the past half century. They have evolved from the original bandage-type bra to a cup form; from plain-weave cotton to polyester fiber-filled, to spandex; from the "no-bra" (unconstructed) look to the molded (unseamed) bra.

An important development of the 1940s was the introduction of padded bras to enhance the figure. In the 1960s, feminist activists rebelled against this focus on creating a standard of female beauty, which they characterized as treatment of women as sex objects. Bra burning became a symbol of the social revolution of the decade (Figure 12.2). As the movement matured and women felt less compelled to demonstrate their independence from physical stereotypes in such dramatic ways, they adopted natural-looking soft cups and seamless styles of bras that became available in the 1970s. Gradually, more structured styles of foundations were reintroduced to support the power dressing of the businesswoman of the 1980s.

In 1986, the Wacoal Company of Japan, a leading manufacturer of foundations, pioneered the computer mapping of the female body, which permitted them and other manufacturers to design undergarments that truly supported and enhanced the female figure. The push-in-and-up bra, introduced in 1994 by Sara Lee Foundations as the Wonderbra, was the foundation fashion story of the 1990s.

In 2006, the Barely There brand conducted a survey in which 75 percent of the women respondents claimed that wearing a bad bra can result in a bad mood. This became known as the Bad Bra Syndrome (BBS), and according to the survey, it was affecting three out of four American women. To help remedy the problem, Barely There Intimates introduced the Invisible Look bra collection.

"Starting with the right intimate apparel, and specifically a great-fitting bra, is one of my number one fashion tips for women," says Stacy London, style expert and cohost of TLC's *What Not To Wear*. "With the Invisible Look Bra, women can wear anything from a tight-fitting white tank top to a strapless black dress and feel completely confident that how incredible they look in their clothes is the only thing people will notice."[2]

Chapter Twelve *Innerwear, Bodywear, Legwear* 225

Sara Blakely

POWER PANTIES®
SPANX®
BY SARA BLAKELY®

sugg. retail $30.00

look slimmer &
feel comfortable

no more
panty lines

invisible under clothe
(no leg band!)

SARA BLAKELY:
UNDERWEAR BILLIONAIRE

THE IRONY OF Spanx is that its inventor didn't even need them . . . she was a size 2 when the idea hit her. With just $5,000 and a great idea, she proved that you don't need expensive research and millions of dollars to know what women want and how to market it.

Obsessed with creating comfortable, slimming garments that minimize figure flaws, Blakely reinvented shapewear with innovative designs and won the hearts of fashion-loving women from Oprah Winfrey to Beyoncé and Gwyneth Paltrow. Spanx has developed and launched more than one hundred styles with names like Bra-llelujah, Hide and Sleek, Power Panties, and Slim-Cognito—all designed to be innovative, comfortable, slimming, and stylish.

Spanx started as a one-woman show. In her first year in business, Blakely sold her new inventions from a folding table in the foyer of Neiman Marcus. Her marketing consisted of a giant before-and-after photo that showed how different her derriere looked in cream slacks when she wore her $30 Spanx Power Panties versus regular bikini briefs. Thus, she began a shapewear revolution!

As her business continues to grow, Blakely looks for ways to share her slimming secrets with even more women. One such effort is her launch of ASSETS by Sara Blakely, a brand for Target. Blakely is thrilled to give better underwear options to women everywhere—and to give back. A portion of each Spanx and ASSETS purchase goes to the Blakely Foundation, which is dedicated to supporting and empowering women around the world.

Innerwear has become increasingly luxurious over the decades. And fashion has finally invaded this segment of the market, so much so that some beautifully designed undergarments are now worn as outer garments. A lacy silk camisole can be used as a dressy top to wear under a suit jacket—or alone. A sexy slip can become an evening garment, and lounging pajamas are elegant components of any ensemble. Driving the market are teenage and young adult shoppers, who demand variety to meet their disparate needs, from sports bras for the gym to body shapers for form-fitting fashions. The market also meets the needs of aging baby boomers, who want to retain a shapely, sexy look.

Categories of Intimate Apparel

Items traditionally classified as **foundations** support either the bust (brassieres) or the lower torso (girdles, which have evolved into shapewear). **Lingerie** is the term for less structured innerwear and sleepwear, and **loungewear** refers to the loose-fitting apparel designed for home entertaining and, more recently, an evening out.

Bras

Brassieres are the most important foundation item for the bust. Their practical features are designed to fit different body types and suit a variety of purposes and occasions. Wide straps, banding or underwires under the cups, and closures with three or more hooks offer extra support and comfort for buxom women. Padding adds shaping and increased size for women with smaller bustlines, and the push-up bra, known as the Wonderbra, lifts the bust, creating a different silhouette. Cups cover the breasts completely or not, sides are wide or narrow, and straps are positioned strategically or removed so that the bra will not show unintentionally under the top.

In addition, materials and design accommodate special needs: training bras gently support the developing breasts of young teens; sports bras move with the body, give support, and absorb perspiration (Figure 12.3, left); nursing bras have cups that unfasten to allow a mother to breast-feed without undressing; and mastectomy bras have pockets for prostheses. A bustier is a foundation garment that extends over the waist or hips. It serves more often as outerwear, making a provocative fashion statement for evening wear when covered with satin, crushed velvet, or sequins.

Bras are complicated to make, and their production requires careful management. They may contain twenty pieces and come in more than a dozen sizes and colors for each style. Fit is critical; no one wants to

FIGURE 12.3 Bras come in all shapes and sizes, from the Hanes sports bra (left) to the Victoria's Secret jeweled push-up bra (right).

have a bra altered. Bra manufacturers have to wring the most they can out of each component—such as getting the same kind of strap to work for five different bras. The major offshore bra production center is the Philippines, followed by Costa Rica.

For more than ten years, Victoria's Secret Fantasy Bras collection has been a sensation on the runways (Figure 12.3, right). Although its ability to provide actual support as a bra is debatable, who cares, if one's décolletage can get a $2.5 million lift? That was the estimated value of Victoria's Secret's 2011 Fantasy Treasure Bra.[3]

Continuing the trend of taking lingerie beyond simple foundation garments, in 2011, French designer Yasmine Eslami started designing shirts to match the bras in her collection, a step toward building a complete wardrobe from the inside out. Eslami also offers a personalization surface, where initials can be embroidered onto garments.[4]

Shapewear

Girdles, corsets, and corselettes (one-piece combinations of a brassiere and girdle) are traditional foundation items designed to smooth and flatten the lines of the stomach, buttocks, hips, and thighs. As with *garter belts*, they also have fasteners to hold up a woman's stockings. With the advent of pantyhose and a growing casualness in everyday dress, these items have been replaced in many women's wardrobes by **shapers**, or shapewear, lightweight undergarments that control problem areas with spandex. Control briefs serve the purpose of the old-fashioned girdle; and for more focused control, waist-cincher briefs, butt boosters, tummy toners, and thigh trimmers are available.

Lingerie

The lingerie segment of intimate apparel has typically been divided into daywear (slips, petticoats, camisoles, and panties) and nightwear (nightgowns, sleep shirts, nightshirts, chemises, baby-dolls, pajamas, wraps, and robes) (Figure 12.4). **Chemises** are sleep gowns with no waistlines, while *baby-dolls* are short, sheer gowns with matching panties. *Wraps* are short robes that cross and tie in front.

The latest revolution in lingerie is the rise of the thong panty. Thongs have come a long way from being a slightly scandalous item that could be found only on showgirls and Brazilian carnival dancers: today they have become a mainstream lingerie basic worn by women of all ages. Clever products, like the "control thong" from Donna Karan, hold in the tummy and eliminate bumps and lumps of underwear lines.

In the nightwear classification, styles also range from sporty and casual to romantic and seductive. Chenille robes, seemingly dead since the 1950s, revived

FIGURE 12.4 The fabrics in glamorous sleepwear can often resemble evening wear.

in the late 1990s, as TV sitcom stars began wearing updated versions decorated with amusing motifs, such as coffee cups and cats with fish bones. At the elegant end of the style spectrum are the *peignoir* (a sheer robe, often with lace detail) and gown set, popular as a Valentine's Day gift, and the *kimono*, an adaptation of the traditional Japanese garment. The Westernized version is often made of rich silk or less expensive synthetics that imitate silk's luxurious appearance; the kimono can also serve as loungewear.

This market is also expanding with added styles and better-fitting lingerie for plus-size women and women who are categorized as wearing in-between sizes. Since 2005, the average dress size in the United States has gone from 12 to 14. The average bra cup size has increased to a 36C from the average size of 36B ten years earlier. In response, major bra brands have started manufacturing a broader range of sizes in a wider variety of styles, also adding to the D, DD, or larger range.[5]

Loungewear

Loungewear is the trade term for robes, lounging pajamas, hostess gowns, bed jackets, and housecoats or dusters. *Dusters*, which usually have buttons or snaps down the front, are especially popular with the elderly and handicapped, because they are easy to put on and take off. Leggings and fleece pants and tops are also popular attire for at-home wear for women of all ages, especially in cold areas. Activewear is also increasingly worn as leisurewear (Figure 12.5), especially by the young and fashionable.

Designs from other cultures are also popular, such as the Hawaiian *muumuu* or float, a short-sleeved garment that slips on over the head and comes in several lengths. *Caftans*, ankle-length garments with long sleeves, came originally from Turkey and are widely worn throughout the Middle East. The African *dashiki*, a loose-fitting pullover garment, is also seen increasingly in the United States.

Market Centers

New York City is the principal market center for the intimate apparel industry. The major firms maintain permanent showrooms there, as well as in most of the regional apparel marts, like Dallas, Chicago, Los Angeles, and Atlanta. Market weeks are held five times a year:

- Early Spring—August
- Summer—January
- Fall and Holiday—May
- Spring—November
- Early Fall—March

FIGURE 12.5 Activewear is also worn as leisurewear.

The Intimate Apparel Council is a trade group that is part of the American Apparel and Footwear Association, which organizes subsidiary, promotional activities for market weeks. One of their endeavors is Intimate Apparel Market Week, which is held four times a year and has greatly increased business. The Intimate Apparel Council also organized the first-ever industry-sponsored lingerie fashion show at the Mercedes-Benz Fashion Week in September 2001. In recent years, the August market in New York has become the focal point for many buyers. Currently, the two main intimate apparel trade shows in the United States are CURVENY (New York City) and CURVENV (Las Vegas), held in February and August each year. In 2013, the first Lingerie Fashion Week dedicated exclusively to intimate apparel made its debut in New York. Six emerging brands unveiled collections: Affinitas & Parfait, FYI by Dani Read, NaïS, Nevaeh Intimates, Rouge Séduire, and Uye Surana. Innerwear categories included bras, undies, loungewear, sleepwear, hosiery, and men's underwear.[6]

Merchandising and Marketing

In the merchandising and marketing of innerwear, an emphasis on brand names is concurrent with a trend toward greater promotion of individual styles, colors, fabrics, textures, and designer names (Figure 12.6). Producers and designers aim to coordinate their innerwear and outerwear lines and to offer a range of images that offer a complete look for a variety of occasions and moods. Market segmentation by age groups enables producers and retailers to target their merchandising and marketing efforts.

Brand Names

Since Warner Brothers opened its first factory in 1874, brand names have been important in the intimate apparel industry. (Warner's is now one of the brands of Warnaco, which also produces Olga and Calvin Klein Underwear.) Many of its merchandising and marketing activities, such as cooperative advertising with retailers in consumer publications and advertisements in trade publications, are geared toward promoting brand names.

These strategies have met with considerable success, as women have identified intimate apparel as a category in which they rely on brand names as an indicator of durability and consistency of fit. As mergers, acquisitions, and licenses of designer names join several brands under a corporate umbrella, parent companies are retaining the individual names to keep their loyal customers. Jockey, the men's and boys' underwear firm, started Jockey for Her in 1982. In 1997, it

FIGURE 12.6 Revealing the latest fashions in intimate apparel, the Victoria's Secret Fashion Show is one of the biggest in the industry.

acquired Formfit seamless panties and the Formfit name, relaunching Formfit in the summer of 2000 under the slogan "Fashion, Fit, Comfort." The company now offers a wide variety of seamless panties for women, including Seamfree, Modern Micro, Naturals, and No Panty Line Promise.

Market Segments

Teenagers and young adults are a very influential segment of the intimate apparel business. In leisurewear, their interest in working out—or looking as if they do—has popularized such fabrics as fleece, jersey knit, flannel, and flannelette, all of which inject a sportswear attitude into these casual styles. The trend is carried out in underwear in cotton crop tops and matching boy-leg briefs or boxers, and in sports bras. Such companies as Natori, with its popular Josie line, cater to this segment.

The under-twenty-five shopper has also supported body shapers. Despite increasing interest in health food and exercise, many women find it easier, faster, and more comfortable to shape up with the help of spandex. The plus-size woman is a focus of many designers, who are creating attractive and form-fitting leotards, sports bras, and shorts for this emerging market. Playtex offers both the Eighteen Hour Comfort Strap bra and the Cross Your Heart bra with side shaping as part of its very successful lines to appeal to the plus-size woman.

Visual Merchandising

In-store displays for innerwear departments and specialty stores demonstrate the importance of brand names and the close connections between product classifications. In contrast to earlier eras, when intimate apparel was stocked in closed drawers rather than displayed, contemporary fixtures allow for the grouping of bras and panties by brand and, within a brand display, by style and color. Price tags color-coded by size help the customer select her size within each style and color grouping. Although bras and panties are sometimes displayed by size, with different brands and colors on the same rack, this practice is giving way to the more visually appealing displays arranged by brand, style, and color, which promote the fashion features of the merchandise (Figure 12.7).

Victoria's Secret stores are a good example of the role of visual merchandising in producing a coordinated fashion image. The interior design of the stores, with elegantly appointed alcoves, allows for separate displays of related items in an intimate space, and the Victorian-style dressers that serve as storage and display fixtures reinforce the upscale, feminine look of the merchandise.

FIGURE 12.7 Organized displays for intimate apparel help to promote the fashion features of the merchandise.

Industry Trends

Variety is the watchword in every aspect of the intimate apparel industry. Not only are firms that once specialized in foundations, lingerie, or loungewear joining together to produce complete and complementary lines of intimate apparel, but these companies are becoming part of larger firms with other holdings in related segments of the apparel industry. For example, Playtex, Bali, and Wonderbra are siblings of Champion activewear and hosiery manufacturers Hanes and L'eggs, under the umbrella of the parent corporation of Hanes Brands, Inc. Limited Brands operates 1,799 specialty stores through the Victoria's Secret and Bath and Body Works brands, in addition to Victoria's Secret's tremendous catalog business.

These alliances allow the parent corporation to coordinate its appeals to different market segments, offering styles and price points that attract different age and income groups and retain brand loyalty.

Market Expansion

Intimate apparel producers are expanding their markets in aggressive and innovative ways, including launching crossover product lines and licensing. Crossover products include the Hanes Her Way brand of underwear, which was spun off the Hanes men's underwear brand in 1986. The equally famous Jockey for Her (Figure 12.8) underwear crossover eventually evolved into additional Jockey products for women, which now range from their signature underwear to activewear and sleepwear.

FIGURE 12.8 Jockey sells a variety of products in the intimate apparel category, including underwear, sleepwear, and activewear.

Through the licensing of designer names, producers are coordinating their products with ready-to-wear. Licensing is equally advantageous to the designer in associating his or her name and fashion image with this apparel category. For example, American innerwear company Komar's licensed brands include Ellen Tracy, Hello Kitty, Betsey Johnson Intimates, Kensie, Company (Ellen Tracy), and LizWear by Liz Claiborne. As in the ready-to-wear departments, sections of intimate apparel departments feature the lines of individual designers and manufacturers such as Vanity Fair, Chantelle, La Perla, and Calvin Klein Intimates.

Paradoxically, as conglomerates are expanding through acquisitions and mergers of producers that serve various segments, the brands, whether part of a larger organization or not, are focusing on precisely defined segments to increase market share. Rapidly changing selections of colors and prints appeal to the desire for something new among their young customers.

Manufacturers and designers continue to use TV home shopping channels like QVC and the Home Shopping Network to sell their products. Retailers like HerRoom (Figure 12.9) and True&Co offer online tools that provide women with privacy and convenience for finding a bra that fits.[7]

Junior Innerwear Departments

Recognizing the growing influence of teenage and young adult shoppers (ages thirteen to thirty-two) on the intimate apparel market, department stores as well as national chains and discounters are starting to merchandise junior innerwear as collection concepts, much like the shops-within-a-shop for designer-label outerwear. Although consumers in this segment typically have less income than their elders, they are more prone to impulse buying of items they consider "fun." They want merchandise they will not find in their mothers' wardrobes. Growing up with the idea that fashion features as well as functionality are important criteria for their innerwear buying decisions, young shoppers are responding favorably to the junior innerwear departments.

Catalogs and Online Promotion

Manufacturers such as Vanity Fair are marketing their brands directly to retail customers through catalogs. Many department stores send out special intimate apparel catalogs, and they regularly include high-fashion intimate apparel in their seasonal catalogs. The Victoria's Secret catalog, with its provocatively

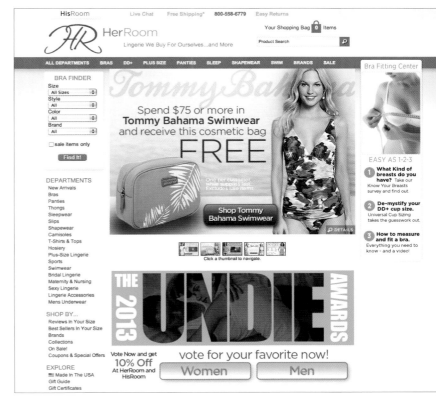

FIGURE 12.9 HerRoom offers online tools for customers to find the best-fitting intimate apparel.

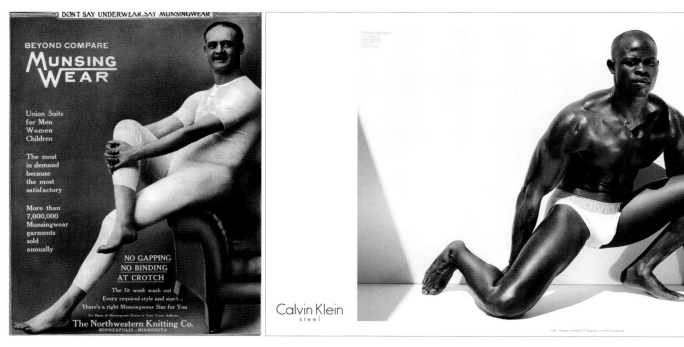

FIGURE 12.10 Men's underwear styles have changed more slowly than women's over the years, but they are now under the influence of fashion.

posed models, is a separate company from the stores of the same name. It has a distribution of 365 million and releases fifteen to twenty catalogs a year. Even L.L.Bean, with its focus on the great outdoors, features silk and thermal long underwear for men and women in its winter catalogs.

Another major source of nonstore retailing for intimate apparel involves online sales. Even the smallest producer cannot afford to be without a website or social media presence through which it can sell or promote its products.

Men's and Children's Underwear and Sleepwear

Even more than women's intimate apparel, men's and children's underwear have been considered utilitarian rather than fashion apparel categories. Today, however, the fashion influence has taken hold.

Men's and Children's Underwear

Much of the history of men's underwear is the history of the biggest name in the industry, Fruit of the Loom. Founded as Union Underwear in 1926, the company began with one-piece underwear known as "union suits." The company was one of the finished-garment licensees of the Fruit of the Loom textile company, and it introduced boxer shorts and knit underwear under that label in the 1940s.

The knit styles of briefs and undershirts were also produced by two famous manufacturers of men's and boy's underwear: Jockey, founded in the late 1800s, and Munsingwear, founded in 1909. Undershirt styles were limited to short-sleeved crew- and V-necks and sleeveless, U-necked ribbed vests. Virtually all men's knit underwear was white, and woven boxers were made in limited colors and patterns (Figure 12.10, left).

Not until the 1970s did a wide choice of colors and patterns become available. About the same time, bikini styles in briefs were introduced to the newly fashion-conscious male shopper. In 1982, Calvin Klein's men's underwear collection made white seem boring. By the mid-1990s, casual pants styles with low-slung waists allowed men to show their allegiances to their favorite designers and brands by revealing the elastic waistbands of their underpants, inscribed with such names as Calvin (Figure 12.10, right), Tommy Hilfiger, or Jockey.

Young men have also adopted loose-fitting, comfortable boxer shorts and have made them a fashion item for at-home and sleepwear. Boxers are made in a limitless variety of colors and prints and in woven silks, cotton flannel, and jersey knit cotton/polyester blends, as well as the traditional lightweight woven cotton. Women have incorporated boxers into their own wardrobes. In addition to the established men's underwear brands, Joe Boxer enjoys a large market for this item, as does the licensed Tommy Hilfiger Intimates at Bestform, a unit of VF Corporation.

Men's underwear is making a new and dynamic name for itself as a wired community. One of its largest players is Freshpair.com, an online-only underwear site for men and women that carries major brands, including Hanes, Emporio Armani, Diesel, 2(x)ist, and Calvin Klein. The balance of its large men's inventory comprises new boutique, fashion-oriented brands such as C-IN2, Frank Dandy, and Papi that specialize in technical fabrics, sexier cuts, and whimsical colors and fabrics. Online retail also provides shoppers with two key commodities: privacy and simplicity.

The marketing of men's underwear as a fashion item benefits retailers' private-label merchandise as well as national and designer brands. A study of men's shopping habits found that 24 percent of dollar sales and 15 percent of unit sales of men's underwear, sleepwear, and loungewear went to private-label brands. Since customers see the merchandise as a brand, comparable to national brands but available exclusively through a particular store, loyalty to private labels translates into store loyalty.

Children's underwear has also evolved from merely functional to fashionable. Girls' panties were available in pastel colors for decades, but the range of colors and prints has exploded to match the variety available to adult women. Thanks to Fruit of the Loom's Underoos line, which first appeared in 1978, little boys also have the chance to express their tastes and to sport the images of favorite cartoon characters, like Batman and Superman. Today, Fruit of the Loom, working under a licensing agreement with Marvel Entertainment, manufactures children's underwear lines based on several premier Marvel character franchises. Fruit of the Loom products are inspired by a diverse range of Marvel heroes and villains including Spider-Man, Wolverine, Captain America, Iron Man, and Thor. Other manufacturers have joined this trend; for example, Hanes features *Toy Story* characters on its briefs for boys. Little girls also have cartoon characters, like Dora the Explorer, Olivia, and Angelina Ballerina.

The website Ecobaby (www.ecobaby.com) exemplifies another trend in children's underwear: parents' preference for natural, environment-friendly products for infants. Companies such as Ecobaby and Peau-Ethique are paving the way for organic innerwear (Figure 12.11).

Men's and Children's Pajamas and Robes

Cotton, batiste, flannel, and silk, all in a variety of colors and patterns, have added a fashion element to men's sleepwear. Perhaps the most ubiquitous robe of the last fifty years is the terry-cloth robe—worn by men, women, and children and as famous for its comfortable cotton fabric as for its loose fit and easy belt. At the other end of the price spectrum is the classic men's silk robe, by designers such as Fernando Sánchez and by private labels such as Saks Fifth Avenue.

Children's sleepwear, like adults', includes pajamas, nightgowns, and nightshirts, as well as Dr. Denton's. This brand name for sleepers with feet—and sometimes with a back flap for convenience in using the toilet—has come to be used as a generic term for such garments. Special finishes are applied to children's sleepwear to improve its flame resistance, in compliance with the Flammable Fabrics Act. However, the Consumer Products Safety Commission loosened its regulation in 1996, allowing the use of cotton and cotton blends and holding tight-fitting sleepwear in sizes 9 months to 14X and infants' sizes 0 to 9 months to general apparel standards rather than the more stringent children's sleepwear standards.

Bodywear

The physical fitness boom of the 1980s and 1990s, which lured millions of Americans into aerobics classes and bodybuilding activities, also was responsible for producing a new fashion category, **bodywear.** It encompasses coordinated leotards, tights, unitards, wrap skirts, sweatsuits, leg warmers, shorts, T-shirts, and crop tops. The line between bodywear and activewear is constantly shifting—especially as stretch fabrics find their way into more and more activewear.

Originally, bodywear was sold in hosiery departments, but most stores are now selling it in separate shops or boutiques. Some department stores, such as Nordstrom and Dillard's, have focused even more attention on bodywear by staging fashion shows, scheduling personal appearances by designers, and even sponsoring in-store exercise and dance classes. More sporting goods stores and specialty stores are adding bodywear, especially if it has performance features, such as moisture-wicking fabric. Some gyms have become bodywear retailers as a sideline to their exercise businesses.

FIGURE 12.11 An organic baby look from Peau-Ethique's permanent collection. A crop of emerging brands is paving the way for innerwear's green future.

DAVID BECKHAM'S UNDIES GETTING A LITTLE EXTRA ATTENTION

SOME THINGS ARE fashion and some things are necessity. Where do men's undergarments belong? Right in the middle.

The market for boxers, briefs, and undershorts is guaranteed no matter what the economy is doing. But innovation in style and technology has turned men's undergarments—once considered an afterthought—into a buzz-worthy category of men's clothes. Even designer-name companies such as Diesel, Emporio Armani, Hugo Boss, and Calvin Klein have entered the new undergarment category, whose sales currently total more than $3.3 billion.

Marshall Cohen, chief industry analyst with market research for the NPD Group said men's underwear is a growth category, but it took the right conditions to get on the fashion industry's radar. Streamlined design, comfortable stretch fabrics, and the idea that dressing starts at the base layer have all added to the popularity of "extra attention" undergarments for men.

Swedish retailer H&M garnered its own attention by signing a contract to sell David Beckham boxers, briefs, and T-shirts, as well as vests, pajamas, and long johns. Beckham said in a statement that it takes him and his design team eighteen months to come up with just the right styles. Their plan is to introduce new products that expand on the basics each season. Men's underwear has never been so posh!

David Beckham's Emporio Armani Underwear Campaign

Many fashion-conscious women insist on being stylish while they stretch, strain, and sweat to get in shape. Longtime bodywear manufacturers, such as Danskin, capitalized on this market by creating new, exciting leotards with coordinating tights, cover-ups, and other workout apparel necessities (Figure 12.12). Many designers and retailers, such as Ralph Lauren and Gap, sell bodywear products in addition to apparel.

Yoga has become increasingly popular. This trend has naturally launched new lines of yoga wear, with garments like cotton tank tops and stretchy pants. The upscale activewear retailer Lululemon has enjoyed great success since opening its first store in a yoga studio in Vancouver in 1998. Revenue for the company reached $1 billion in 2011.[8]

In the dancewear category, Capezio, long famous as a manufacturer of ballet and pointe shoes, is known also for its leotards, unitards, dance dresses, tights, body warmers, and leg warmers. Capezio products, available in more than 3,000 stores, have been expanded to include lines for figure skating, ballroom dancing, yoga and Pilates, and drill team and cheerleading.

Legwear

The ancient Greeks were among the first to wear cloth **legwear**. By the late 1500s, European men and women wore stockings made from a single fabric width that was knitted flat, with the two edges sewn together to form a back seam. This technology remained essentially unchanged for centuries. Because of wear at the heels and toes, socks often developed holes that had to be mended, a process called darning. For centuries, darning socks was an everyday task for women.

New generations of teenagers and young adults who never wore hose are discovering legwear. Marshal Cohen, chief industry analyst at the NPD Group, says, "The industry needs to take advantage of that. It's a gift from the fashion gods to get a young consumer who will embrace this for the first time in her life, and could be a customer for the rest of her life if the industry responds properly."[9]

The Evolution of Women's Hosiery

Until World War I, women's legs were concealed under floor-length skirts and dresses. When skirt lengths moved up and women's legs became visible, interest in adorning them increased, and the hosiery industry began to grow. Hanes, Trimfit, Berkshire, and Round the Clock were all introduced in the 1920s. But it was not until the introduction of nylon that hosiery as we know it today became a fashion accessory. Before the introduction of nylon in 1938, women wore seamed

FIGURE 12.12 This advertisement features actress and singer Hilary Duff wearing Danskin's shorts, sports bra, and jacket.

silk, cotton, or rayon stockings. Because of its easier care and greater durability, the new nylon hosiery was eagerly accepted despite its high price. Still, a "run" or "ladder" in a nylon stocking was an expensive accident, and women went to great lengths to prevent them. Saleswomen routinely donned gloves before showing stockings to a customer.

Fashion first entered the hosiery picture in the 1950s with the introduction of colors other than black or flesh tones. But it was not until the 1960s that hosiery became a major fashion accessory. To accessorize the shorter skirt—eventually evolving into the miniskirt and micromini—colors, textures, and weights of stockings were created in great variety. Women wore "pettipants" in the early 1960s to cover the garters of their garter belts or girdles—and to show a bit of lace under the shorter skirts. Then pantyhose were introduced and became a fantastic success. In turn, their popularity led to the introduction of seamless pantyhose and figure-control or support pantyhose (Figure 12.13, top).

In the 1970s, when women began wearing pants to work, knee-high and ankle-high hosiery were introduced. Together with pantyhose, they captured the major share of the hosiery business. The sale of stockings plummeted and has never recovered. In addition, with elasticized bands on knee-high and over-the-knee hosiery, garters became unnecessary, and garter belts and pettipants became passé.

FIGURE 12.13 A group of girls who work in a hosiery factory try on stockings for a waterproofing test for nylon's introduction in 1938 (top). Today's hosiery comes in a wider variety of colors and patterns (bottom).

In the 1980s, changes in lifestyle produced a new set of customer needs and wants that were met with textures in pantyhose and tights. Socks in ribs and knits, leg warmers, and many kinds of athletic socks revitalized the industry.

The 1990s saw a drop in the sales of pantyhose, brought about in part by the advent of casual dress days in 90 percent of U.S. businesses. Even with more tailored pants, women may opt for trouser socks, a type of knee-high hosiery that is slightly heavier than sheer knee-highs and is available in a variety of colors and textures. In the early 2000s, another influence was the impact of teenage customers, who shop for hosiery more frequently than adult women. Reacting to the latest fashion news on MTV, young shoppers boosted the sales of brightly colored tights and designer brands. Today, hosiery in a wide variety of hues and patterns, ranging from opaque and eye-catching to sheer and romantic, remains hugely popular with consumers (Figure 12.13, bottom). Legwear also serves as a relatively inexpensive way for women to update their wardrobes.

Hosiery continues to evolve away from the basic item it was thirty years ago. Consumers are seeking and willing to pay more for the right product. Hosiery is considered an accessory as important as shoes and handbags.

Socks

The influence of teenage shoppers has also boosted the women's sock business. Women of all ages have responded well to the combination of fashion design and comfort features offered in socks for casual wear and for extensive physical activity, such as sports (Figure 12.14). Women's socks generally come in three lengths: ankle, crew, and knee.

For work and athletic socks, the comfort features are emphasized. Cushioning may be designed for very specific activities, with differences between, say, tennis and running. **Wicking**, the ability to carry the moisture of perspiration away from the skin, is offered by various synthetic fibers. Cotton and wool are often combined with nylon, acrylic, and spandex to add elasticity, shape retention, and ventilation.

These comfort features are also an important selling point for men's athletic socks. A new development to reduce blister-causing friction is the interloping of Teflon fibers with polyester and cotton at pressure points in socks. Inventor Bob Gunn has worked with DuPont's Teflon and Chipman Union, a sock-making firm, to market Blister Guards socks.

Tube socks, which are knit without a defined heel, are popular as a functional everyday sock. The one-size-fits-all design is almost impossible to outgrow. Tube socks are less expensive to produce than conventional socks, and the savings are passed on to the consumer. Packaging of three or six pairs at a reduced per-pair price also appeals to the budget-minded shopper.

More expensive ragg socks, which are very thick, warm socks designed for wear with boots or sandals, are increasingly popular for work or winter sports.

FIGURE 12.14 Socks come in a variety of styles and colors.

Similarly, Polarfleece socks in various lengths are also good for keeping the feet warm, even when wet.

In the 2000s, socks stepped to the forefront of their category. The reemergence of legwear as a fashion item is allowing designers to branch out and be more creative. Many manufacturers are expanding their sock collections and using new materials. For now, to tie socks in with their fashion-forward hosiery collections, they have added metallic threads and also moved toward texture with ribs, pointelles, and cables that stretch out to reveal design elements. Today, socks can be a key part of putting one's best foot forward!

Here's a sock alert: pity the sock that becomes separated from its mate. Pity the sock that says farewell to its match in the overflow of the washer or is sucked into a black hole by the exhaust vent in the dryer. Well, pity the stray sock no more! LittleMissMatched, a San Francisco–based company, embraced the dilemma of the missing sock. The company started out selling prepackaged whimsical socks that encouraged little girls to mix and match. Since launching in 2004, LittleMissMatched has expanded to sell clothing, furniture, and even bedding. In 2010, the company generated $55 million in revenue and has stores in Disney World, Disneyland, Chicago, and Manhattan.[10]

Organization and Operation

The hosiery industry consists primarily of large firms, many of which are divisions of huge textile or apparel conglomerates. The largest concentration of hosiery plants is found in the southern states, with more than half of them in North Carolina.

Since hosiery is knitted in the greige (unfinished) state, most manufacturers can produce branded and unbranded hosiery in the same mill. The greige goods are then dyed, finished, stamped, and packaged to specification for national brand, private brand, or unbranded hosiery.

Merchandising and Marketing

Traditionally, the women's hosiery industry concentrated its merchandising activities almost exclusively on the promotion and sale of nationally advertised brands. Recently, however, the industry has been merchandising its products for private labeling or for sale from self-service displays in supermarkets and drugstores. Designer labeling has also become increasingly important. The world's largest hosiery manufacturer, Hanes Brands, Inc., has the Hanes and L'eggs brands. At Dillard's, Spanx and other upscale shapewear lines have eclipsed more moderate, promotional resources to become "the backbone of the intimate apparel business," says William Dillard III, vice president of

intimate apparel, accessories, and shoes. "Spanx has revolutionized undergarments and the way clothes fit."

National Brands

Major hosiery producers sell their brand lines to retail stores across the country. Producers aggressively advertise their lines in national magazines and newspapers and on television. They also usually supply cooperative advertising, display aids, and fashion assistance to help promote these national brands at the store level. Major national brands include Hanes, Round the Clock, and Kayser-Roth.

Designer-Label Brands

Because designer labeling adds an aura of couture and prestige to any item, designer labels have appeared on a variety of hosiery items, including pantyhose, socks, and leg warmers. Almost all of the designer-label hosiery is the result of licensing agreements between the designer and manufacturers of national brands. In hosiery and pantyhose, Kayser-Roth uses Calvin Klein, and GBT Group uses Givenchy. Legwear Resource (the name-brand division of Leg Resource, Inc.) holds exclusive licenses for Anne Klein, New York, AK Anne Klein, Betsey Johnson, and Nicole Miller.

In 2011, DKNY Legwear tapped Eric Daman, costume designer of *Gossip Girl*, to design a capsule collection of patterned legwear that included textured dots, opaque and sheer stripes, and jacquards. The artwork on the packaging featured a New York City landscape, which paid homage to Donna Karan's hometown. DKNY hosiery has been one of the main legwear brands used on *Gossip Girl* since the show first aired.[11]

Private Brands

Chain organizations, retail stores, and some individual stores have developed their own private or store brands that compete with nationally advertised brands. A private label offers many advantages for the retailer. The cost of the hosiery is usually less because there is no built-in charge for advertising as there is for national brands. The private brand can be made up in colors and construction that will match customer profile specifications. Because the private brand is not available elsewhere, price promotions are easier. Customer loyalty can also be built upon the exclusivity of the private brand. Charter Club hosiery, tights, and socks, for example, are the private label of Macy's, Inc.

Mass-Merchandised Brands

For self-service stores such as supermarkets, discount stores, and drug chains, hosiery manufacturers have developed low-priced, packaged hosiery. Each mass-merchandised brand offers a good choice of styles and colors. Each manufacturer supplies attractive, self-service stock fixtures and promotes its brand through national advertising. When L'eggs pantyhose, made by Hanes, were introduced, their distinctive packaging in plastic eggs brought immediate name recognition, but by the early 1990s, a more conventional package was adopted to become more environmentally friendly. By then, the name was nationally established as one of the best-selling mass-merchandised brands, along with competitor Kayser-Roth's No Nonsense pantyhose. Surprisingly, nearly half of the stores that distribute No Nonsense are food stores, drugstores, and other mass merchandisers.

Industry Trends

Trends in the legwear industry are similar to those in the innerwear industry. As discussed earlier, licensing agreements enable designers and manufacturers to produce and market lines of legwear that coordinate with a designer's ready-to-wear lines. Special packaging also promotes brand loyalty. Manufacturers assist retailers with visual merchandising to help them stimulate sales. In manufacturing, the trend is toward offshore production.

Fashion Trends

Fashion trends have a tremendous influence on sales in the hosiery industry. For example, when skirts are shorter or have leg-revealing silhouettes, texture and color in hosiery become important. Apparel manufacturers work with hosiery manufacturers to design pantyhose that are both texture- and color-coordinated to their sportswear. The hosiery is displayed with the apparel to promote a total fashion look.

The inventory of most hosiery departments includes ankle-length, knee-high, and over-the-knee stockings; sheer and opaque pantyhose; leg warmers; bodywear; and casual footwear. Bodywear and casual footwear are relatively high-priced retail items, while packaged hosiery is low-priced. As a result, some stores have made separate departments out of these two different categories.

The needs and wants of customers prompt hosiery manufacturers to design entirely new items. Control-top pantyhose (Figure 12.15), spandex, support hose, and queen-size pantyhose cater to the demands of an aging population that is also growing heavier. Lycra hosiery provides a more comfortable fit and keeps out moisture.

Men's, women's, and children's sock sales are predicted to increase steadily in the next decade. Athletic, sport, and work socks are the sources of growth in the men's area. New textures, colors, and patterns are fueling the market in women's socks. Children are emulating their sports heroes and requesting their specific brand of sport socks.

Special Packaging

Manufacturers turn to special packaging as a way to make their products stand out in this very competitive industry. For example, Wigwam Socks created specialized packaging that classifies the style of each sock to a certain function, including trail, snow, sport, work, and health.[12]

Bonuses are popular in sock merchandising. Hue marketed its sport socks through a three-for-twelve program, which allowed customers to pick and choose three pairs of socks at a discounted price. While each pair retailed for $5, a selection from any of the sport sock lines cost $12. Some of the special packaging success stories include the Gold Toe (Figure 12.16) gift-with-purchase program of Gold Toe Brands. The company packaged a one-ounce radio with a six-pair pack of boy's crew socks. This promotion was so successful that the package was prominently displayed at the entrance of many legwear stores.

FIGURE 12.16 Gold Toe uses visual merchandising and special packaging strategies to help promote its products.

Visual Merchandising

In-store displays and other point-of-purchase materials are being offered by manufacturers to retailers to add some color to hosiery departments. While increasingly casual dress codes among office workers have caused a decline in sales of sheer pantyhose, the women's sock market has blossomed. Fishnets, animal prints, luxury yarns, and novelty styles, such as the super-low sock traditionally used only by athletes, have given new life to the category. This lighthearted approach has also inspired sock vendors to promote holiday- and Halloween-themed socks with matching retail displays.

Summary and Review

The categories of women's intimate apparel, men's and children's underwear and sleepwear, and hosiery for all three market segments were long considered strictly utilitarian, but today all of these categories have taken on fashion features. A consumer can develop a wardrobe that is coordinated from the inside to the outside and from head to toe.

Women's intimate apparel includes foundation garments (bras and shapewear), lingerie (such as panties, camisoles, slips, and sleepwear), and loungewear. These formerly separate categories are now coordinated and are often promoted as distinctive designer or producer lines.

Men's underwear and sleepwear also features a broad choice of colors and a variety of styles, ranging from bikini briefs to loose boxers, and children's underwear and sleepwear are decorated with favorite cartoon characters.

The growing awareness of the need for exercise to be physically fit has generated the development of a separate apparel category called bodywear, which includes spandex shorts and tops for both women and men, leotards, and other apparel suitable for wearing while working out.

Hosiery categories include women's pantyhose and tights and a variety of styles of socks for men, women, and children. Through licensing, apparel designers have gained customer loyalty for brands of hosiery coordinated with their apparel lines. Private labels and mass-merchandised brands also have their adherents among consumers, who identify brand names with a particular fashion and quality image. Hosiery manufacturing is carried out wholly or partly overseas by many producers.

For Review

1. How does the foundations industry respond to trends in ready-to-wear?
2. How does the intimate apparel industry relate to the ready-to-wear industry?
3. How does the display of women's underwear and intimate apparel demonstrate the growing influence of fashion features? How do current visual merchandising practices differ from those of the past?
4. Why is the juniors market important to the women's intimate apparel industry?
5. What fashion features have been emphasized in the merchandising and marketing of men's underwear?
6. What is bodywear, and how did it grow into a separate apparel category?
7. Why is the development of new fibers so important to the women's hosiery industry?
8. Identify and describe four categories of brands of women's hosiery.
9. What is the influence of fashion trends in ready-to-wear on the fashion features of women's, men's, and children's hosiery?
10. How does special packaging help hosiery producers increase market share?

For Discussion

1. Discuss current trends in the intimate apparel industry as they relate to (a) mergers, (b) diversification of product lines, and (c) styling.
2. How have the apparel trends of the twenty-first century affected the innerwear and hosiery industries?

Trade Talk

Define or briefly explain the following terms:

bodywear
chemise
foundations
innerwear
intimate apparel
legwear
lingerie
loungewear
shapers
wicking

Chapter Thirteen
ACCESSORIES

KEY CONCEPTS

- History and development of the accessory industries
- Organization, operation, merchandising, and marketing of the footwear and jewelry industries
- Manufacturing, merchandising, and marketing of handbags, belts, gloves, hats, neckwear, and eyewear
- Trends in the various classifications of accessories

Accessories in the twenty-first century continue to create excitement and sizzle at retail, and whether in the luxury, midtier, or mass markets, they provide customers with a jolt of fresh fashion, instant access to the latest trends, and in many cases, a piece of a designer dream.

The manufacturers of accessories must constantly forecast the changes in cycles of fashion so that their accessories are perfect for new fashions. These changes include the variations not only in silhouette but also in fabrications and color. The marketing of accessories gained an enormous boost with the entrance of well-known designers' names into the business. Today, the fame of the accessories designer is as important as the fame of the clothing designer; and in many cases, it is the same famous name. It is only through constant alertness to trends and degrees of customer acceptance that fashion accessory designers succeed. They must be prepared to design and produce styles that blend, follow or lead, and innovate. The fashion accessories category includes footwear, handbags, gloves, hats, neckwear, eyewear, and jewelry.

Footwear

Footwear has always conjured up exciting, glamorous, and amusing times in history and literature. We read about gallant heroes in seven-league boots, princesses in glass slippers, Mercury with winged feet, and, of course, the magic red shoes that took Dorothy from the land of Oz back home to Kansas.

Feet, the base upon which our bodies stand, have been wrapped, covered, or left exposed since the beginning of time (Figure 13.1). Primitive people wrapped their feet in fur, and later people strapped them into sandals. Chinese women bound their feet. Footwear often was—and still is—dictated by profession: Arctic trappers wore snowshoes, while ballet dancers wore pointe or toe shoes; cowboys wore leather boots, and firefighters wore rubber boots.

Making shoes was once a painstaking handicraft. But the commercial production of shoes has developed into an industry providing over 300 variations in shoe lengths and widths and over 10,000 different shapes and styles. The footwear category includes shoes, slippers, athletic shoes, and boots. Most shoe styles

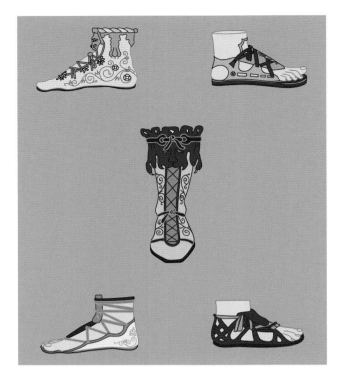

FIGURE 13.1 Ancient Roman styles of sandals.

originated in Europe, keeping pace with the growth of European fashion. However, a classic shoe style that originated in America is the moccasin. Favored by both men and women and adored by most children, the moccasin style of shoe still retains its popularity and stands as one of the first examples of unisex fashion.

Organization and Operation

Footwear production was once a major industry in New England, but many of that region's factories have downsized or closed (Figure 13.2). Timberland of Stratham, New Hampshire, best known for its work boots, and Converse, which is owned by Nike, still maintain corporate offices in North Andover, Massachusetts, but no longer manufacture there. The shoe industry moved west when the Midwest became an important source of hide supplies and cheaper labor, and another large center of production grew around Saint Louis, Missouri. Brown Shoe Company, producer of Naturalizer, Ryka, Via Spiga, Avia, and Dr. Scholl's, is based there.

The largest shoe producer in the United States today is Nike. Nike actually does not own any of the manufacturing facilities that produce the shoes and apparel it sells; rather it acts more like a wholesaler and focuses on marketing its products.

Imports are also a factor in dress shoes at higher price points. A longstanding reputation for quality craftsmanship and styling has contributed to the success of Italian manufacturers such as Ferragamo, Prada, Gucci, and Tod's. Italy is the number one producer of high-end designer shoes, with world-famous designs

and quality craftsmanship. The bulk of less expensive imported shoes comes from Asia, mainly China. As of 2011, footwear was one of the top five import categories from China, reaching \$16.7 billion.[1] Other countries that export low-priced shoes are Brazil, Vietnam, Indonesia, the Dominican Republic, and India. The United States has also recently seen an increase in domestic production, after decades of declines.[2] Many of the U.S. manufacturers in the twenty-first century that have been successful have turned to niche markets.

Shoe production begins with a last. Lasts were originally wooden forms in the shape of a foot, over which the shoes were built. Most modern factories, American and foreign, make lasts of plastic or aluminum. Lasts made from these materials provide more exact measurements and are easier to handle than the old wooden ones.

The variety of lasts, the quality of materials, and the number and type of manufacturing operations required determine the quality and price of the finished shoe. As many as 200 to 300 operations performed by highly skilled workers are required to make an expensive, high-quality shoe. Shoe manufacturers produce shoes in an enormous range of sizes. The normal range of women's shoe sizes involves 103 width and length combinations. And this does not include sizes shorter than 4, longer than 11, or wider than E.

FIGURE 13.2 Lining stitcher in an old Massachusetts shoe factory, 1895.

FIGURE 13.3 Styles of women's shoes run the gamut from pointed to open toes, d'Orsay to stiletto heels, and sandals to ankle boots.

Inventories, production problems, and capital investments in the shoe business are tremendous compared with those of other fashion-related industries. Thus, it is not surprising that giant companies dominate the industry. Among the fashion industries, only cosmetics has a higher percentage of production by giant companies.

Women's Shoes

For centuries, little attention was paid to the styling of women's shoes. Their purpose was regarded as purely functional. Since the 1920s, however, women's feet have been plainly visible, and shoes have developed both in fashion importance and variety. After World War II, the black or brown all-purpose shoes designed to be worn with any wardrobe disappeared. New and varied leather finishes, textures, plastic and fabric materials, and ranges of colors provided shoe styles that not only kept pace with changes in fashion but in many cases originated fashion trends.

Styles have run the fashion gamut from pointed to square toes, from high to flat heels, and from naked sandals to thigh-high boots (Figure 13.3). Typically—but not always—broad toes and low, chunky heels go together, and narrow, pointed-toe shoes are more likely to have stiletto heels. The slim, elegant designs have been popular when apparel fashions have emphasized formality, and the heavier, more down-to-earth styles have been the rage in seasons when more casual clothing styles prevailed.

Stiletto heels made a huge comeback in the late 1990s as young fashion-conscious women eagerly followed the example of Sarah Jessica Parker's character, Carrie, in the popular TV series *Sex and the City*. Today, high heels are still immensely popular, and some women wear fragile stiletto shoes as their everyday footwear, regardless of weather and temperature (Figure 13.4). Similarly, boots are often worn in warmer temperatures. On the other end of the spectrum, comfortable flats can be dressed up with adorned toe-cap leather and woven materials. The details of the toe cap are also seen in heels and can add something extra to the basic work shoe.

FIGURE 13.4 A look from Walter Steiger's "Unicorn" collection for Spring 2013.

TORY BURCH: WHAT'S NEXT? THE MOON?

Tory Burch is an American fashion designer who has hit the business in a fantastic swirl of success. Born and educated in Philadelphia, she began her career in New York City, working with fashion designers such as Ralph Lauren and Vera Wang, in addition to *Harper's Bazaar* magazine. Burch began her fashion label in her New York Upper East Side apartment in February 2004. TRB by Tory Burch—later known as Tory Burch—was an immediate success, quickly spreading to freestanding boutiques and endorsed by Oprah Winfrey the following year. When Burch opened her flagship store in the NoLita neighborhood of Manhattan, the store was almost completely sold out on the first day! Today, Tory Burch fashions are available at freestanding Tory Burch boutiques across the U.S.,

Europe, the Middle East, Asia, and South America. Her designs are also available online at toryburch.com and at more than 1,000 select department and specialty stores worldwide.

The Tory Burch style is described as preppy-bohemian luxe. Her clothing has appeared on television shows like *Gossip Girl*, which increased her popularity among young women, but her style transcends generations and lifestyles. Burch's clothing is versatile enough to be in the wardrobes of a wide range of women—from working women to soccer moms to socialites.

Burch's popularity isn't limited to her customer base. She's been recognized within the fashion industry as well. Her honors and awards started in 2005 when she won the Rising Star Award for best new Retail Concept from the Fashion Group International. In 2007, she won the Accessory Branch Launch of the Year from the Accessories Council of Excellence, and in 2008 she beat Marc Jacobs and Michael Kors for the CFDA's Accessories Designer of the Year. What's next for Burch? Only time will tell, but her future will likely be as bright as her signature prints.

Fall 2012

Tory Burch

FIGURE 13.5 To keep up with the mainstream of fashion, manufacturers of men's dress shoes (left) have branched into casual styles (right).

Men's Shoes

A shift in thinking and lifestyle on the part of American men has had a dramatic effect on the merchandising of men's shoes. Dress shoes were once the most important sales category in men's shoe departments in retail stores. They are now being replaced by dress/casual and casual shoes, which were once considered appropriate only for the eighteen-to-twenty-five age group but now are preferred by men of all ages (Figure 13.5). The dress shoe business is now considered a niche market.

Timberland, Sebago, and Rockport are examples of casual shoe manufacturers whose reputation for durable work shoes has benefited from this trend. Sperry Top-Siders, made by Collective Brands, were once limited to boat owners; today they are much more widely worn for casual wear. Red Wing Shoes of Red Wing, Minnesota, continues to grow in its niche: specialized work shoes for letter carriers, loggers, welders, firefighters, and electrical linemen.

Well-known U.S. brand names for men's dress and casual shoes include Florsheim, Johnston & Murphy, Allen Edmonds, and Alden. L.B. Evans has been making slippers and sandals in New England since 1804. At the high end of the market are Gokey boots and shoes, which are handmade in the United States to customers' exact specifications; they are sold by Orvis through its catalog and stores.

American designer dress and dress/casual shoes are also predominately produced abroad. High-end imports from Europe include Clark's of England, Bally of Switzerland, and Ferragamo, Gucci, and Bruno Magli of Italy.

Children's Shoes

From an early age, both boys and girls take a serious interest in their shoe wardrobes (Figure 13.6). Perhaps they are influenced by stories about shoes with magical powers, as in "Cinderella," "Puss in Boots," and "The Twelve Dancing Princesses."

Shoes, especially everyday shoes, are subject to wear and tear, so even though they are outgrown as quickly as apparel, they are not as suitable for handing down or buying secondhand. Furthermore, a professionally fitted new pair of shoes is more likely to ensure health and comfort than are used shoes. Children thus must be active participants in the purchase decision. Having a deciding vote on the comfort of their shoes, children can easily make the next step to expressing opinions on appearances. The styles of children's dress shoes are

FIGURE 13.6 Even though they grow out of them quickly, kids take a big interest in their shoe wardrobes.

adaptations of adult styles, with oxfords being popular for boys and the classic Mary Janes for girls. The use of leather distinguishes higher-priced lines from less expensive lines of vinyl and other leather substitutes.

As athletic shoes evolved from canvas sneakers, they became the preferred shoe for school wear. Practical features, such as Velcro fastenings; purely decorative features, such as the popular light-up shoe; and brand and style identification, such as that provided by Nike's Air Jordans, all influence children's preferences. But the trend toward school uniforms for public school students is slowing the switch to athletic shoes for school wear, and leather oxfords or T-straps are reemerging.

Athletic Shoes

Sneakers, the original athletic shoe, were made possible by Charles Goodyear, who invented the vulcanizing process for rubber in the late 1800s. Concurrent to Keds in 1917, the Converse Rubber Shoe Company created what became known as the rubberized shoe, the Converse All-Star. This shoe is still very popular today—the company has sold more than 500 million

FIGURE 13.7 Whether you are walking, running, jumping, or hiking, there are fashionable athletic shoes for every activity.

pairs! From these humble beginnings, a huge industry has grown—and shod the world (Figure 13.7).

Perhaps the most significant development in shoes since the 1980s—affecting men's, women's, and children's shoes—has been the proliferation of athletic footwear. Spurred by the trend toward more casual dressing, this separate category is now considered a mature market.

Athletic shoes have become ever more specialized. Manufacturers make special shoes for virtually any sports activity—walking, running, climbing, aerobics, racquetball, biking, hiking, and golf. Most of the "super-specialty" shoes are carried in specialty sporting goods stores, while department stores and other general retailers stock a less specialized and more fashion-oriented range of athletic shoes.

Merchandising and Marketing

As with most fashion industries, New York City is the major U.S. market center for shoes. It is there that most producers maintain permanent showrooms, and the city is also home to the industry's trade shows. The Fashion Footwear Association of New York, with a membership of more than 300 manufacturers representing over 800 brand names, stages the international footwear trade show New York Shoe Expo four times a year.

The American Apparel and Footwear Association (AAFA) was formed in 2000 through the merger of two highly regarded trade associations: the American Apparel and Manufacturers Association and Footwear Industries of America. Drawing from a broad, strong membership base, AAFA is the national trade association representing apparel, footwear, and sewn products companies, which compete in the global marketplace.[3]

Brand names are important in the footwear industry, and manufacturers advertise extensively in fashion magazines (Figure 13.8), on television, and online. Designer names are also growing in importance, especially at the midprice to high end of the market. In 2007, three shoe companies came together through Payless Shoe Source's acquisition of Collective Licensing International, a brand management and global licensing company, and the acquisition of the Stride Rite Corporation, the leader in lifestyle and athletic branded footwear and high-quality children's footwear. Since forming, Collective Brands, Inc. continues to grow, with brands reaching consumers in nearly 100 countries and territories around the world through retail, licensing, franchising, and e-commerce platforms.[4] In contrast with most other fashion industries, many of the large shoe manufacturers operate retail chain organizations of their own.

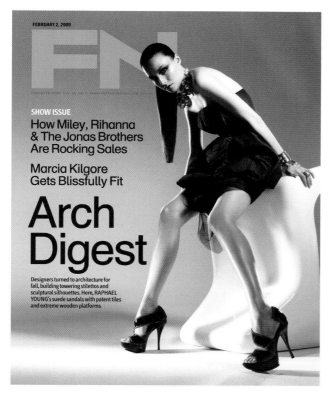

FIGURE 13.8 *Footwear News* provides inside perspective on news, fashion trends, and the business strategies relating to the footwear industry.

Some shoe manufacturers also operate in the retail field through leased departments in retail stores. Because of the tremendous amount of capital required to stock a shoe department and the expertise needed to fit and sell shoes, many department and specialty stores lease their shoe departments to shoe manufacturers. Surveys by the National Federation of Retailers have repeatedly shown that women's shoe departments are among those most commonly leased by its member stores. Macy's, Saks, and Nordstrom are a few examples of department stores that have had much success selling a wide variety of footwear styles and brands.

For most men's shoe retailers, space limitations make meeting consumer demands a challenge. Even stores that deal exclusively in men's shoes tend to be small, with less than 1,700 square feet of space for both selling and stocking. The manufacturers' retail outlets that predominate among freestanding units cannot compete on availability of many brands. Online retailers such as Zappos and Piperlime, which have less of a space problem, have realized a golden opportunity to attract customers, so long as they maintain an easy return policy.

Because of the tremendous consumer demand for athletic shoes, many retailers have begun paying extra attention to this category, often creating a separate department for athletic shoes. Athletic shoe stores, such as the Athlete's Foot, Foot Locker, and Foot Action chains, which carry a variety of brands and related fashion-oriented merchandise, have sprung up across the country.

Industry Trends

Americans purchased 2.27 billion pairs of shoes in 2010.[5] NPD Group reports that while more consumers have shopped online for apparel than for footwear, footwear comes out ahead in terms of sales. Regardless of gender, multibrand retailer sites are the most preferred websites for online footwear shopping.[6]

Whether in athletic or other footwear, there is a strong relationship between shoes and the clothes with which they are worn. Increased emphasis on fashion continues to be the major trend in the footwear industry. Shoe designers and manufacturers regularly attend the MICAM Shoevent, in Milan, Italy, or the GDS International Event for Shoes and Accessories, in Germany. They also attend European apparel openings, as do shoe buyers from retail stores, gathering information on international trends in styling. More and more, apparel fashions influence both the styling and color of footwear. Skirt lengths, silhouette, pants, and sporty or dressy clothes are the fashion keys to women's shoe designs. It is therefore essential for retailers to coordinate shoes and apparel wherever and whenever they can.

Clothing designers designing shoes is a growing trend. Back in 1986, Donna Karan launched her own label, and she was one of the first clothing designers to make a statement about having their own shoes to finish off the total look. On the heels of Donna, designers Tom Ford and Marc Jacobs also put their design stamp on influential footwear collections.

While the shoe market is a very lucrative one, it's also highly competitive. The new *garmentos*-cum-cobblers are up against massive shoe brands, including Gucci, Prada, Louis Vuitton, and Ferragamo, as well as older shoemakers like Manolo Blahnik and Christian Louboutin.[7]

Additionally, like apparel manufacturers, some U.S. shoe companies rely on factories overseas, particularly in developing countries where the labor is cheaper. However, there is a notable rise of U.S. domestic production.

Handbags

Handbags are continuing their reign as the best-selling classification within the accessories industry. Once again, many retailers have expanded their space to accommodate more and/or new brands. Fashion continues to drive handbag sales, both in branded and private-label product. Consumers show little price resistance for the "right design"—especially at luxury level. Designer "it" bags drew even more attention to the classification—even with retail prices exceeding $1,000 and higher.

As fashion statements, handbags are used to dramatize, harmonize, or contrast with whatever else one is wearing. Styles vary from the most casual, used for sportswear, to the more formal, used for dress-up evening occasions. A handbag may be small or large; its shape, a pouch or a tote, draped or boxy. So important are handbags as fashion accessories that many women own a wardrobe of them. The late Princess Grace of Monaco favored the Hermès bag, now called the Kelly bag in her honor. The late Princess Diana was often photographed with one of her more than twenty Ferragamo clutch purses. Perhaps the most-copied handbag of this century was Chanel's "2.55" diamond-quilted bag, with the shoulder strap that slides through golden chains.

As personal statements, handbags also send a message. A woman who chooses to carry a leather briefcase, for example, sends a professional message, while a woman who uses a backpack sends one of functionalism. Whether a woman opts for a small, delicate beaded handbag at night or something far more exotic, perhaps a gold box set with unusual jewels, says something about her. The woman who carries a tailored, expensive leather purse creates an image that is more chic than that of the woman who settles on a vinyl tote.

Organization and Operation

Compared with other fashion industries, the handbag industry is small. The number of domestic firms producing handbags diminishes each year, as imports made in Europe, South America, and the Far East increase. Although U.S. manufacturers' brand names are relatively unimportant in the handbag industry (except for certain classics such as Coach Bags, LeSportsac, and Dooney & Bourke), designer handbags have become popular (Figure 13.9). Famous names like Anne Klein, Ralph Lauren, Donna Karan, and Marc Jacobs have entered licensing agreements with handbag manufacturers. Judith Leiber is still famous for her handmade beaded bags in animal shapes and her metal **minaudières** (small evening bags). Kate Spade has won several awards for her striking handbag designs. Today, not all quality handbags are made of leather; microfiber and nylon are key materials.

Several foreign manufacturers, such as Louis Vuitton, Hermès, Ferragamo, Bottega Veneta, and Gucci, have always enjoyed enormous status at the high end of the market, and the names of Chanel and, more recently, Prada are associated with distinctive styles of handbags.

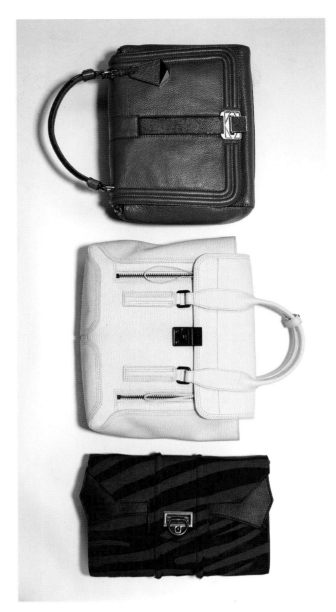

FIGURE 13.9 Some customers will pay top dollar for a designer bag. From top to bottom: Rebecca Minkoff's leather handbag, 3.1 Phillip Lim's cowhide leather bag, and Reece Hudson's calf hair and leather clutch.

Backpacks

Some of the larger manufacturers have recently diversified their lines, reaching out to men, who have flirted with the idea of carrying handbags since the 1960s. The backpack has gained favor with men who do not have enough room in their pockets or briefcases for everything they want to carry. Perhaps the backpack's acceptance is a carryover from its use as a school bookbag. For that purpose, it remains popular with boys and girls from kindergarten through college (Figure 13.10). The messenger bag is also a popular alternative choice for the men's market.

Small Leather Goods/Personal Goods

The category called **small leather goods** or **personal goods** includes wallets, key cases and chains, jewelry cases, briefcases, and carrying cases for cell phones

FIGURE 13.10 Backpacks are a popular way for students, and even adults, to transport valuables.

Merchandising and Marketing

Few handbag manufacturers are large enough to advertise on a national basis in newspapers and television. The customer's impression of what is new and fashionable in handbags is mostly gleaned through store displays and advertising online and in magazines. Catalogs and home shopping networks are also popular ways of reaching customers.

Industry Trends

Faced with severe competition from foreign imports, many domestic handbag manufacturers have themselves become importers of foreign-made handbags. These importers employ American designers to create styles and then have the handbags made in countries with low wage scales.

The industry's trade organization—the Fashion Accessories Shippers' Association (FASA)—has worked closely with government agencies to promote the domestic handbag industry both here and abroad. FASA supports the interests of importers as well as manufacturers of handbags and related accessories (including belts, small leather goods, gloves, and luggage).

The leather goods trade fair, Mipel, held in spring and autumn in Milan, attracts handbag buyers from all over the world.

and laptop computers (Figure 13.11). Similarly, men and women with busy schedules are increasingly seen with leather-covered appointment books or organizers. Of course, despite the name, not all of these items are made of leather. Fabrics, particularly nylon and microfibers, have assumed great importance in this category. Leading manufacturers of these items in the United States include Coach, Nine West, and Dooney & Bourke. More and more designers have moved into this category; among them are Kate Spade and Anne Klein.

Belts

For dressing an outfit up or down to suit the occasion, a belt is an easy solution. Since belts are not absolutely essential—if you need one to hold up your pants, you can have your pants altered or buy a better-fitting pair—their appeal as a fashion accessory is of primary importance (Figure 13.12). Although belts are categorized and sold with small leather goods, they are also

FIGURE 13.11 Whether you are carrying a little or a lot, Ellie Tahari's line of matching leather clutches and handbags meets the needs of every customer.

FIGURE 13.12 The right belt can dress up any outfit.

Coach
Legacy
Collection
Fall 2012

COACH:
FROM LOCAL LEATHER SHOP
TO GLOBAL FASHION POWERHOUSE

COACH BEGAN IN 1941 as a family-run workshop in a Manhattan loft with six craftspeople who made small leather goods such as men's wallets and billfolds by hand. Today, Coach operates as a global brand with sales of more than $4 billion. Known for its craftsmanship, Coach enjoys its status as an "accessible luxury" brand. Its products cover a range of categories—from handbags and women's and men's accessories to footwear, briefcases, jewelry, eyewear, travel bags, fragrances, and watches. The company learned early on that it was important to control its destiny by opening and operating its own stores; today, these stores represent the lion's share of its business.

Through the effort of its CEO Lew Frankfort, Coach has always been on the lookout for people who see new venues for its business. Currently, it is Reed Krakoff who has marched with Frankfort to turn Coach into one of fashion's most powerful names. As president and executive creative director, Krakoff is a brand architect and his creative control extends from product design to advertising and store concepts.

Krakoff had a fashion design background, working with Narciso Rodriguez at Anne Klein and later at Polo Ralph Lauren and Tommy Hilfiger, but he had no background in accessories. With Frankfort's support, Krakoff amped up the fashion factor in Coach's collections. He also set out to release new accessory designs with the same frequency as ready-to-wear apparel in order to encourage consumers to buy Coach products more regularly. Krakoff wants Coach to be the go-to brand for accessories that women can carry to work and into the evening. He also wants shoppers to be drawn to the brand, not because they need a new bag, but because they desire a particular style he created.

Now, let's hear it for the boys: The men's business represents an enormous growth opportunity for Coach. By expanding its product offerings, opening freestanding stores, and increasing the penetration of men's merchandise in existing stores, Coach's men's line is on track to be an overall growth contributor for the company. Ironically, men's is where Coach got its start, reinforcing the saying "what goes around, comes around!"

made of a host of other materials including cloth, plastic, metal, and straw.

The price of a belt can be less than $10 or more than $500, depending on the materials, the precious metals or jewels used in the belt buckle, and the amount of hand-craftsmanship involved in its production. Designer names and logos—often appearing on the buckle or other metal trim—add to the fashion status of a belt and often to its price.

The fashion district of New York City is the home of belt manufacturing, though manufacturers like Tandy Brands in Dallas, Texas, can be found across the country. Manufacturers who produce belts to be sold as separate fashion accessory items are said to be in the **rack trade**. They are distinguished from the **cut-up trade**, which manufactures belts to be sold as part of a dress, skirt, or pair of trousers. **Self belts**, with bands and sometimes buckles covered in the same fabric as the apparel item with which they are sold, are produced by this segment of the industry.

In the rack trade, most men's and women's belts are sized according to waist measurements, with women's belts ranging from twenty-two to thirty-two inches and men's from twenty-eight to forty-four inches. Sometimes they are grouped as small, medium, large, and extra large. Plus sizes in belts have become more important. Belts manufactured for the cut-up trade are made in lengths to fit the size of the garment.

Gloves

Crude animal-skin coverings were the forerunners of mittens, which, in turn, evolved into gloves with individual fingers. Gloves are not new, though; leather gloves were discovered in the tombs of ancient Egyptians.

Gloves have enjoyed a long and varied history, at times even taking on symbolic value. To bring them luck, knights once wore their ladies' gloves on their armor as they went into battle. So long as women wore modest dress, men often cherished the gloves of their beloved as erotic objects. Gloves were once exchanged when property was being sold as a gesture of good faith. And in dueling days, one man would slap another across the face with his glove as an invitation to a duel. Gloves have also been used to denote rank or authority. Until the sixteenth century, only men of the clergy or of noble rank were allowed to wear them.

For centuries, gloves were coordinated in styling, detail, and color with current apparel styles. To be specific, glove styles correlated to the currently popular sleeve length, especially in coats and suits.

In the first half of the twentieth century, the glove business flourished largely because no self-respecting,

FIGURE 13.13 Leather gloves were discovered centuries ago but are still a trendy and functional accessory.

let alone fashionably dressed, woman went out without wearing gloves. The untrimmed, white, wrist-length glove was de rigueur for dress occasions, as was the suit glove, which extends a few inches above the wrist, often made up in leather and used for general wear. The 1960s, which saw the onset of a long period of casual dress, also saw the end of gloves as a requirement for a well-dressed woman. White cotton gloves as an accessory for dress or business wear disappeared. When leather became expensive in the 1980s, manufacturers began to make gloves of knit and woven fabrics, which now dominate the market. Currently, in winter, when gloves are worn for warmth, they are coordinated with dress or casual outfits (Figure 13.13).

Organization and Operation

The production of gloves varies, depending upon whether they are made of leather or fabric. Leather gloves are among the most difficult accessories to manufacture. Most leather gloves are made, at minimum, with hand-guided operations, and some are still made entirely by hand.

Leather gloves are typically made in small factories, since few machines and workers are required to run such a factory. Glove producers tend to specialize, performing only one manufacturing operation, such as cutting or stitching. Other operations are farmed out to nearby plants, each of which, in turn, has its own specialty.

In contrast to the methods used to make leather gloves, the fabric-glove industry is much more mechanized. The cheapest gloves and mittens have only two parts—a front and a back—sewn together. More expensive gloves have separate small pieces that fit the fingers and thumbs. Most fabric gloves are made of some kind of double-woven fiber, because this gives them great durability. Knit gloves and mittens are made of wool, acrylic, and cotton—even cotton string—usually in one-size-fits-all. Chenille and Polarfleece are popular for cold weather wear, along with fake fur.

New York City was once the center of the glove-manufacturing industry. Today, glove manufacturers have turned to offshore production, and most gloves are made in China, the Caribbean, and the Philippines. One well-known specialist glove manufacturer in the United States is the Totes ISOTONER Corporation, which makes the Isotoner line of fabric and leather gloves. Other fashion glove makers in the United States are Fownes, Grandoe, and LaCrasia.

Merchandising and Marketing

Compared with the dollars spent on consumer advertising for other accessories, the industry outlay for glove advertising is quite modest. Only a few large producers with nationally distributed brand names actively promote their products or offer even limited merchandising support services to retail stores.

Manufacturers have learned to make gloves more creatively. Gloves are lined with—and sometimes even made of—a wide array of knitted fabrics, lace, cashmere, fur, and silk. Wonderful colors—like orange, purple, acid yellow, and lime green—are often matched to winter hats or scarfs.

Finally, while many fashion industries have turned to diversification, the glove industry has moved in the opposite direction, toward specialization. Glove manufacturers, for example, have created markets for gardening gloves, driving gloves, and gloves for specific sports. Men and women can choose from an array of gloves designed for use at tennis, baseball, bicycling, and golfing—to name just a few. Gloves for skiing and winter gloves and mittens are made of high-tech materials, like Gore-Tex, Thinsulate, and Polartec, to maximize their insulating properties.

Industry Trends

The industry is trying to improve manufacturing procedures in order to reduce costs. Manufacturers have reduced the number of glove sizes, preferring to sell gloves in only small, medium, and large. Stretch-fabric gloves, in which one size fits all, are made as well. In addition, improved materials are resulting from product research and development in the leather industry. These are expected to increase the market potential of domestically produced leather gloves. For example, many leather gloves today are hand washable and come in a wide range of fashion colors.

The fabric-glove industry has incorporated technology into their products with speciality features like touch-screen fingertips. The industry continues to explore innovative packaging techniques, such as packaging matching hats and gloves (or mittens) together, or matching scarfs and gloves, or matching headbands or earmuffs with gloves for winter wear.

Millinery

According to an old saying, whatever is worn on the head is a sign of the mind beneath it. Since the head is one of the more vulnerable parts of the body, hats do have a protective function. But they are also a fashion accessory (Figure 13.14).

The man's hat of the nineteenth and twentieth centuries in Europe, which was derived from the medieval helmet, protected its wearer both physically and psychologically. The heavy crown kept the head safe from blows, and the brim shaded the face from strong sunlight and close scrutiny. In nineteenth-century America,

FIGURE 13.14 A milliner fitting and adjusting a glamorous hat.

the cowboy hat became an enduring national icon. Late in the century, the top hat was a status symbol of a special kind. This was the time of European immigration, and those who wanted to distinguish themselves from the immigrant peasants took care to wear hats.

After decades of prosperity and popularity, the men's hat industry began to collapse in the years following World War II. This was soon true for the women's hat industry, called the **millinery** industry, as well. Because of the more casual approach to dressing and the popularity of women's beehive and bouffant hairstyles, men's and women's hat sales hit bottom in 1960. During the freewheeling 1960s and 1970s, a hat was worn only on the coldest days—strictly for warmth, not for fashion.

During that time, the millinery industry and its active trade association, the National Millinery Institute, researched, publicized, and campaigned in an extensive effort to reverse the trend, with little success. This was not surprising, since, as we have already learned, no amount of sales promotion can change the direction in which fashion is moving.

However, the pendulum has begun to swing back toward the popularity of hats for men, women, and children. Several factors have contributed to this development. One was the fierce winters of the late 1990s, which led to the increased popularity of all types of winter hats and caps. David Chu of Nautica designed a polyester fleece cap and scarf that provide warmth while wicking away moisture. The fleece stocking cap for kids was a runaway best-seller. On the ski slopes and city streets, a variation of a jester's cap was also popular. Today, a range of headwear, from streetwise Kangol hats, berets, and caps to elegant fedoras, have become must-haves among young fashion addicts (Figure 13.15). Many leading luxury houses like Gucci, Louis Vuitton, and Burberry are enjoying tremendous success with their logo-embellished newsboy caps, bucket hats, and fedoras.

Another factor was the featuring of flamboyant hats in designer shows, especially on the runways of Paris and Milan. Although these extreme styles are presented more as a display of the designer's imagination than as

FIGURE 13.15 Women and men are increasingly conscious of their accessory choices, including hats in different shapes and sizes.

FIGURE 13.16 Philip Treacy design on the runway.

an attempt to introduce a trend, they remind fashion arbiters and consumers that hats can be a fun accessory and can make or break an outfit. Philip Treacy, a well-known British hat designer, has designed hats for the runway shows of Chanel, Valentino, and Versace (Figure 13.16). Treacy has also expanded into handbags.

Well-known U.S. millinery designers include Patricia Underwood, Eric Javits, and, at a lower price point, Betmar. Makins Hats designs for both men and women; its clients include Denzel Washington, Brad Pitt, Carlos Santana, and Madonna. August Accessories of Oxnard, California, uses neoprene in a line of reversible, weather-proof hats.

The third factor contributing to the increased popularity of hats is the awareness of the dangers of overexposure to the sun. Dermatologists recommend wearing hats for protection in all seasons. Straw and canvas hats with large bills or brims offer shade without undesired warmth. Also available are hats made of

fabrics with an SPF (sun protection factor). Baby hats that tie under the chin, or bonnets, have long been popular for infants; they are now widely used for toddlers as well. Along with the popular safari hat for men, hats with neck guards, once seen only in French Foreign Legion movies, have become popular in retirement communities across the country.

As with many fashion trends, the growing popularity of baseball caps as a fashion accessory started with young consumers. In this instance, boys and young men have worn them as a mark of support for their favorite teams. Soon the caps became promotional items for businesses, clubs, and other organizations. Designers took up the trend, putting their names and logos on this activewear accessory, often adding sequins, beading, or braid trims. Caps have proliferated, worn backward or forward, by men, women, and children.

The men's felt hat industry in the United States is still alive and well. Cowboy hats and "Indiana Jones" hats are popular styles, though porkpies and fedoras have experienced a resurgence in popularity thanks to television shows such as *Mad Men* and *Boardwalk Empire* and the celebrities who are big fans of wearing hats, like Johnny Depp and Bruno Mars. The largest manufacturer is RHE Hatco of Garland, Texas. It owns the famous Stetson brand of cowboy or western hats as well as the Dobbs and Resistol brands. A few men's custom hatters can still be found; among them are Colorado Mountain Hat Company in Fairplay, Colorado; Rand's Custom Hats in Billings, Montana; and The Custom Hatter in Buffalo, New York. Well-known European brands for men include Kangol and James Lock & Co., of England, and Borsalino, of Italy.

The center of the women's millinery industry is in New York City with some smaller firms in Los Angeles and Saint Louis. One-person millinery shops can be found in many cities, since millinery involves a great deal of handwork and is ideal for custom work.

Neckwear

The introduction of foreign designers' signature scarfs began in the 1970s. Customers are wearing scarfs to change the look of an outfit. Squares and oblongs of varying sizes can be tied in different ways, sometimes with the help of specially designed scarf clips. Neckerchiefs, the hottest trend in the late 1990s, energized the scarf category by bringing women from twenty to thirty-five years old into the department. Often entire walls were devoted to displays—much like socks and tights.

Echo is one of the largest manufacturers of scarfs in the United States. In addition, a number of leading

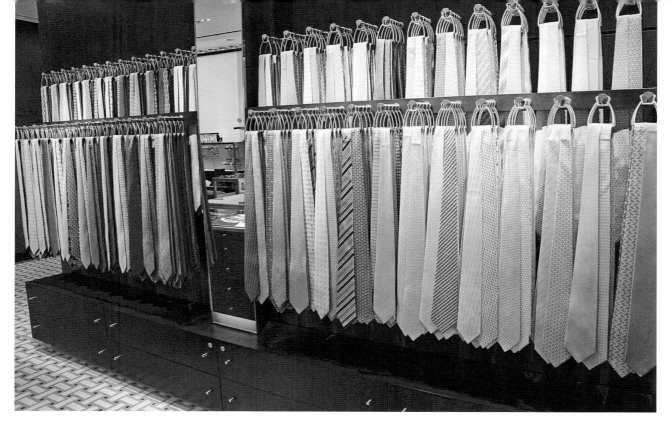

FIGURE 13.17 A colorful or patterned tie can brighten up any business suit.

American designer names have become associated with neckwear, further enhancing the category's appeal. Among them are Perry Ellis and Anne Klein, Ellen Tracy, Oscar de la Renta, and Liz Claiborne. Some high-end imported scarfs, like those of Hermès (France) and Pucci and Gucci (Italy), are famous worldwide.

For men, ties have been a standard accessory for business suits for more than a century. They have provided an opportunity to brighten the business uniform with a small splash of bright colors and lively patterns (Figure 13.17). The necktie, or four-in-hand, and the bowtie are the two most common styles. The bolo, or string tie, is popular in the southwestern United States. The ascot, or broad neck scarf, is rarely seen today.

Among patterns, the regimental stripes have been popular for decades; they began with military regiments in England. Club ties have small embroidered emblems. Today most ties are made of woven silk or polyester. Knit ties and ties of leather or other specialty fabrics account for only a small percentage of total production.

At the height of power dressing in the late 1970s and 1980s, the color, print, and fabric of a necktie became a silent language, communicating the wearer's status. In more casual office environments where ties are not always required, there may be "conversational" or whimsical ties—shaped like a fish or printed with cartoon characters.

Top names of licensed neckwear in the United States include Sean John, Ralph Lauren (who began his career designing ties), Perry Ellis, and Calvin Klein. In addition to neckties, men wear neck scarfs of wool in winter. The knit variation of these scarfs is called a muffler. Some men wear silk neck scarfs with formal dress coats.

Eyewear

In recent years, consumers have become increasingly aware of the need to protect their eyes from the sun's harmful ultraviolet rays. Even for children, sunglasses are now considered more than a cute, wearable toy.

At the same time, manufacturers of sunglasses have made a concerted effort to produce styles that are high fashion. Wraparound frames, clear frames, and lenses that are reflective or tinted different colors are some of the distinctive design features. Combine these factors with the high visibility of sunglasses on prominent celebrities, and it is no wonder that sales in this category have exploded.

Italian firms dominate the world of eyewear. The biggest of them, Luxottica, had annual sales of over six billion euros in 2011, which is equivalent to more than $8 billion.

"Ten years ago, sunglasses were a functional device," says Andrea Guerra, chief executive of Luxottica. Today, sunglasses have colored lenses, oddly shaped frames, and all kinds of adornment, including loud logos in silver and gold, and clusters of diamonds. Oversized frames remain popular, along with retro preppy styles and classic silhouettes.

Luxottica attributes its success to the strength of its in-house brands and to its control of the retailers where they are sold. Luxottica bought Lens Crafters in 1995,

FIGURE 13.18 At Sunglass Hut the in-store photo booths allow customers to take photos of themselves wearing different sunglasses. They can then e-mail friends and family for advice on which products to choose.

FIGURE 13.19 Eyewear is functional and fashionable.

and then acquired Sunglass Hut. The brands it owns, such as Ray-Ban, acquired in 1999, are the backbone of the business. In 2007, Luxottica announced the purchase of another portfolio of brands with the takeover of Oakley, a California-based maker of sunglasses. Other house brands include Vogue, Persol, Oliver Peoples, Arnette, and REVO. Luxottica's licensed brands include Bulgari, Burberry, Chanel, Dolce & Gabbana, Donna Karan, Polo Ralph Lauren, Paul Smith, Prada, Stella McCartney, Tiffany, Tory Burch, Versace, and Coach.

The company operates 2,700 retail locations worldwide, mainly through the Sunglass Hut brand (Figure 13.18). In 2010, Luxottica distributed approximately 20.4 million pairs of prescription glasses and 38.4 million sunglasses.[8]

Prescription eyeglasses are another important segment of the fashion eyewear category. Despite the popularity of contact lenses, optometrists now fit their customers to improve their looks as well as their vision. Aging baby boomers have spurred growth in the market for nonprescription reading glasses, or **readers**. The industry has responded with fashionable styles available at different price points (Figure 13.19). Designer readers are available from such famous names as Donna Karan, Hugo Boss, Perry Ellis, and Calvin Klein. Lower-priced readers are available in drugstores.

Marchon Eyewear is the largest manufacturer and distributor of prescription and sunglasses frames in the world. The firm has stayed ahead of the curve, accurately predicting when eyeglasses would move from the directly functional to the glamorously fashionable and sporty. They acquired licensing agreements with globally recognized brands such as Calvin Klein, Chloé, Michael Kors, Valentino, Lacoste, Emilio Pucci, Diane von Furstenberg, Nike, and Nine West. The company sells more than sixteen million frames annually.[9]

Jewelry

Jewelry has always played a significant and varied role in people's lives. In ancient times, some articles of jewelry were worn as amulets to ward off evil. Jewelry was popular among ancient Greeks, Romans, and Africans. The beautiful Roman women featured in the old frescoes wore long, thin necklaces that encircled their necks two or three times, strands of pearls braided in their hair, and engraved belts decorated with precious stones.

A symbol of wealth and importance, jewelry was at certain times worn only by nobility. Laden with gold chains, their clothing adorned with gems, their fingers covered with rings, they carried on their persons the fortunes of their ruling houses. Medieval noblemen displayed elaborate heraldic emblems symbolizing their knighthood, and military men, another privileged class, used to make a great display of their decorations, which were once jewel-encrusted. Jeweled tiaras were in vogue among the upper classes in the Napoleonic era, because they simulated the laurel wreaths of antiquity. Tiaras saw an unexpected revival among brides in the early 1980s when Lady Diana Spencer wore a Spencer family heirloom tiara at her wedding to Prince Charles. Tiaras resurfaced again in the late 1990s, when designers like John Galliano and Vivienne Westwood featured them in their fashion shows. Suddenly tiaras were seen at proms and debutante balls around the United States.

Organization and Operation

Methods of making jewelry have changed little over time. Modern jewelers melt and shape metal, cut and carve stones, and string beads and shells much as jewelers have been doing for centuries (Figure 13.20). Jewelry designers have always used enamel, glass, ceramic, and natural mineral formations as their raw materials.

Based on the quality of their products, the jewelry industry in the United States can be divided into two primary groups: fine jewelry and costume or fashion jewelry. A third group, bridge jewelry, has gained in importance, as has a fourth group, ethnic jewelry.

Fine Jewelry

Fine jewelry is the counterpart of haute couture. Only precious metals such as gold and platinum are used to make fine jewelry. Sterling silver is also considered a precious metal, although its intrinsic value is far less than that of gold or platinum. Too soft to be used alone, these precious metals are **alloyed**, or combined, with one or more other metals to make them hard enough to be fashioned into jewelry.

Platinum (which includes palladium, rhodium, and iridium) is the most expensive metal. It was first used for jewelry by Cartier and became a hallmark of the Art Deco movement of the 1920s and 1930s.

The gold content of jewelry is measured by weight in **karats**, abbreviated as K. An item called **solid gold** actually has only twenty-four karats of gold, or 1/24 gold to 23/24 alloy. Less costly 14K gold is popular in the United States, while 18K gold is popular in Europe, and 22K gold is popular in India. Gold-filled jewelry is made of an inexpensive base metal with a heavy layer of gold on top. White gold is a substitute for platinum; it is an alloy of gold and another metal, usually nickel. **Vermeil** (pronounced "ver-MAY") is a composite of gold over **sterling silver**. The term *sterling silver* is used for jewelry (and flatware) with at least 92.5 parts of silver; the remaining 7.5 parts are usually copper. Not all sterling silver is equal; thicker items are generally more valuable than thin ones.

The stones used in fine jewelry are called gemstones to distinguish them from lower-quality stones that are used for industrial purposes. Gemstones, which always

FIGURE 13.20 An elaborate statement necklace, like this design by Badgley Mischka, can add style and elegance.

FIGURE 13.21 Gemstone necklaces by Astley Clarke Gemstones.

come from natural mineral formations, have traditionally been classified as either precious or semiprecious. Precious stones include diamonds, emeralds, rubies, and sapphires (Figure 13.21). Stones are measured by weight, in a unit of measure called a **carat**, which equals 200 milligrams, or 1/142 of an ounce. Carats are subdivided into points; there are one hundred points to a carat. Thus a half-carat stone is a fifty-point stone.

Diamonds are the hardest substance known and are in limited supply (Figure 13.22). From 250 tons of ore, only one carat of rough diamonds can be recovered, and only 20 percent of them are suitable for gemstones. Diamonds are found in South Africa, Siberia, Australia, and Arkansas. The world supply is dominated by the De Beers cartel of South Africa. It has spent millions to promote the romance of diamonds with its ad slogan "A diamond is forever."

Diamonds are usually cut into fifty-eight facets, which are small, polished planes that are precisely placed to reflect the maximum amount of light. Traditional cuts or shapes of diamonds are round, emerald, marquise, pear, oval, and heart (Figure 13.23). The radiant cut, which was developed in 1976, has about seventy facets and was originally created to hide flaws.

Advanced technology in the new millennium has unleashed a new crop of innovative cuts. Among them is the square-shaped Context cut, which is not cleaved but based on the natural twelve-sided rough diamond crystal. Other cuts include the circular Spirit Sun cut and

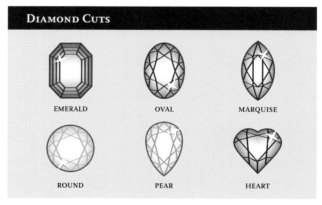

FIGURE 13.22 Even though there is a limited supply, diamonds are still a girl's best friend. This ring is from Ivanka Trump's sustainable diamond collection.

the triple-brilliant Gabrielle cut, which has 105 facets (compared with the traditional 58) and is available in a wide range of classic shapes.[10] For centuries, diamond briolettes and faceted diamond heads were used in some of the world's most famous jewelry. Historians believe the **briolette** cut, an oval or pear-shaped gemstone cut in triangular facets, originated in India. The Crown Jewels of Iran and the tiara worn by the Grand Duchess Xenia Alexandrovna of Russia were both made with briolette diamonds.

Briolettes began to regain popularity in commercial jewelry designs in the 1990s and remain a hot trend today. Laser-cutting and drilling tools make it easier for jewelry designers to use them, and, with color on the frontline of fashion, designers are using these fancy-colored diamond briolettes. Most of these colored, diamond briolettes are one of a kind, and designers cannot guarantee that shapes and colors will always be available.[11]

A solitaire is the mounting of a single gemstone; a diamond solitaire is the traditional engagement ring. A Tiffany setting refers to a four- or six-prong setting that flares out from the base to the top, with long slender prongs that hold the stone. A baguette is a rectangular-shaped small stone used with a larger stone. A pavé setting is one in which a number of small stones are set as closely together as possible, so that no metal shows between them, and they appear as an all-stone surface.

Real, or oriental, pearls are of animal origin but are still considered precious stones. Tahitian and South Sea pearls are the most expensive real pearls. Cultured pearls are pearls formed by an oyster around an irritant placed in the oyster's body by a person. They are not considered precious stones, although they can be raised only in limited parts of the world's oceans. Freshwater pearls are nugget-shaped pearls that grow in lakes or rivers; they are more abundant and less expensive than real or cultured pearls.

DIAMOND CUTS		
EMERALD	OVAL	MARQUISE
ROUND	PEAR	HEART

FIGURE 13.23 Traditional diamond cuts.

Pearls are measured in millimeters of circumference and length. Size contributes to the value of pearls; large pearls are hard for oysters to grow and so are more expensive. Pearls cannot be cut or shaped like other gems. The more symmetrical the pearl, the more expensive it is. Pearls with irregular and asymmetrical shapes are called baroque pearls. The rarest—and most expensive—pearls are black; other natural tints are cream, a pinkish hue, or a bluish one.

The so-called semiprecious stones include a host of other natural stones that were once more costly and less rare than precious stones but are still quite beautiful (Table 13.1). The Jewelers of America association holds that the division of gems into precious and semiprecious is invalid, because discoveries have added new varieties that are higher priced, because of their rarity, than the better-known gems. For example, fine jade is more valuable than a lesser-quality emerald. Tanzanite, first discovered near Mount Kilimanjaro in 1967, is a deep purple gemstone that Tiffany & Co. has popularized. Although it is considered a semiprecious stone, it is being used by fine-jewelry designers in very expensive pieces.

Chemists have succeeded in creating **synthetic stones** that are chemically identical to real stones. Synthetic stones are now used in combination with 14K gold and sterling silver. The most popular of the synthetics is zirconia, which offers the dazzle of diamonds at a fraction of the cost. Other synthetic stones include synthetic spinel, which looks like emeralds or aquamarines, and synthetic corumdum, which looks like amethysts.

Fine-jewelry production is still a handcraft industry. A lapidary, or stonecutter, transforms dull-looking stones in their natural states into gems by cutting, carving, and polishing them. Then the jeweler creates a setting for the stones to bring out their brilliance.

In the established fine-jewelry houses, as in haute couture houses, design, production, and retail sales typically take place under one roof—and one management. Many fine-jewelry firms sell only the jewelry they create, much of which is custom designed for them. Names such as Cartier and Tiffany have always been used to sell jewelry, but in the past, the designers, who were in the employ of these companies, were not well known. In the past few decades, though, individual designers have taken on new importance, and customers now look for jewelry designed by their favorite designers.

Paloma Picasso and Elsa Peretti designs are sold at Tiffany & Co. Other leading independent designers with large followings include Barry Kieselstein-Cord,

TABLE 13.1 *Fine Gemstones*

Alexandrite	
Amber*	
Amethyst	
Aquamarine	
Chrysoberyl	AQUAMARINE
Citrine	
Garnet	
Iolite	
Jade	
Kunzite	GARNET
Lapis lazuli	
Moonstone	
Opal	
Peridot	
Rubellite	OPAL
Spinel	
Tanzanite	
Topaz	
Tourmaline	
Tsavorite	
Turquoise	
Zircon	TOURMALINE

*Vegetable, not mineral, in origin.
Source: Jewelers of America, *What You Should Know about Gems.* New York: Jewelers of America, Inc.

Robert Lee Morris, David Yurman, and Steven Lagos. As another example, Bergdorf Goodman's fine-jewelry department carries the work of eight designers: Diamond in the Rough, Gurhan, Henry Dunay, Judith Ripka, Paolo Costagli, Roberto Coin, Stephen Webster, and Yossi Harari.

Costume Jewelry

Costume or **fashion jewelry** is like mass-produced apparel. A wide range of materials—wood, glass, and base metals such as brass, aluminum, copper, tin, and lead—are used to make it (Figure 13.24). Base metals are sometimes coated with costlier precious metals such as gold, rhodium, or silver. The stones and simulated (fake) pearls used in costume jewelry are made from clay, glass, or plastic. While they are attractive and interesting in their surface appearance, they are less costly and lack the more desirable properties (durability, for one) of natural stones.

Before the 1920s, costume jewelry as we know it did not exist. Most jewelry was made from gold or, more rarely, silver set with precious or semiprecious stones. Jewelry was worn for its sentimental or economic value and was never used to accessorize one's clothing.

FIGURE 13.24 Heidi Klum models her own costume jewelry line that she sells on QVC.

The age of costume jewelry began with designer Coco Chanel. In the 1920s, she introduced long, large, and obviously fake strands of pearls to be worn with her clothes. This new accessory was called costume jewelry because it was meant to coordinate with one's costume. The pearls were called *simulated* in English and *faux* in French.

Chanel, it might be noted, not only helped to create an industry but also continued to wear her trademark pearls for the rest of her life. Today, simulated pearls—indeed Chanel-style pearls—are a staple of the costume jewelry industry. Two first ladies also contributed to the popularity of pearls: Jackie Kennedy Onassis (Figure 13.25) and Barbara Bush.

Costume jewelry has always gone through phases. At times, it is intended to look like fine jewelry; at other times, frankly fake-looking jewelry is in style. Beginning in the 1960s and continuing to today, Kenneth Jay Lane designed costume jewelry so real-looking that socialites and other fashion leaders favored it over their own authentic jewels.

There is always a market in costume jewelry for products that look like the real thing; most mass-produced jewelry, in fact, falls into this category. Large, popular-priced costume jewelry houses employ stylists who design seasonal lines or adapt styles from higher-priced

FIGURE 13.25 When the estate of the late Jacqueline Kennedy Onassis auctioned the set of simulated pearls she wore in this widely reproduced photograph, they fetched the amazing price of $211,500! Copies were made by Carolee Jewelry; they sold for $300.

lines. Much of mass-produced costume jewelry is made in Providence, Rhode Island, where small jewelry manufacturing firms are still located, though the industry there has shrunk considerably. Facilities are geared toward producing jewelry to the specifications of individual firms, much as apparel manufacturers contract out their work and use jobbers.

Mass-production methods are employed in contrast to the handwork that exemplifies the making of fine jewelry. While a fine jeweler pounds and hand-shapes metal, manufacturers of costume jewelry cast metal by melting it and then pouring it into molds to harden. Designs are applied to the hardened metal surface by painting it with colored enamel or embossing it by machine. **Electroplating** is the name of a process that coats inexpensive base materials with a thin coat of silver or gold.

Large firms dominate the industry. Examples are Fifth and Pacific Companies and Carolee. While most large firms work with multiple price lines and many different materials, some companies do specialize. An example is Swarovski Jewelry U.S., which specializes in crystal jewelry, made under the company name.

Still, more than 90 percent of U.S. jewelry producers are small, family-owned companies. Individuals with creative talent often open successful small retail or wholesale operations that cater to customers who are interested in individualized styling and trendsetting fashions. Such operations are an outgrowth of the handcraft movement of the 1960s and 1970s. Handmade jewelry had a major comeback at the beginning of the new millennium, which launched a rise of small, independent jewelry designers across the country.

Bridge Jewelry

Dramatic increases in the price of gold and silver in the early 1980s left jewelers seeking new ways to meet the public's demand for reasonably priced authentic jewelry. The solution was **bridge jewelry**, that is, jewelry that forms a bridge—in price, materials, and style—between fine and costume jewelry. Prices at retail range from about $100 to $2,500 for bridge jewelry. (Also see the discussion of bridge apparel in Chapter 9.)

The development of bridge jewelry led to increased use of sterling silver and its subsequent elevation to a precious metal. The boom in Native American jewelry in the early 1970s also helped to create interest in bridge jewelry. Many department stores and specialty stores created bridge departments to handle sterling silver and Native American jewelry, and when interest in it faded, they were open to other kinds of bridge jewelry that would help them keep the customer base they had developed.

Bridge jewelry departments at such stores as Neiman Marcus now carry gold-filled, vermeil, sterling silver, and some 14K gold fashion jewelry set with semiprecious stones. Sterling silver jewelry continues to grow rapidly in popularity. Bridge designers include Zina and Janis by Janis Savitt. Judith Jack specializes in marcasite (crystallized mineral) jewelry, which attracts both costume and fine-jewelry customers.

Ethnic Jewelry

The category of **ethnic jewelry** includes pieces from all over the world at all price points, although some of these items are not made of intrinsically valuable materials, but rather of shells, stones, wood, or fabric. The artistry is so remarkable that these items can command a higher price than costume jewelry. As previously mentioned, Native American jewelry in silver and turquoise has been popular for decades. Two famous styles of silver necklaces, the squash blossom necklace and the liquid silver necklace, continue to be reinterpreted by modern Native American designers.

Ralph Lauren popularized African jewelry with his 1997 collection that was inspired by the Masai of Kenya; it included arm cuffs, bead chokers, and hoop earrings. Similarly, traditional ethnic jewelry from India, made from 22K gold and decorated with ornate patterns and precious gemstones, became popular in the late 1990s after Nicole Kidman and Goldie Hawn began wearing these styles. Most people, however, buy far less expensive designs in glass, brass, and silver. Chinese-inspired jewelry made of jade, coral, and mother-of-pearl is perennially popular, as is the yin-yang symbol. Moroccan beads, the Egyptian ankh, Guatemalan string figures, Greek worry beads, Caribbean shell necklaces, Peruvian hammered copper earrings—all have fans worldwide.

Another category of ethnic jewelry involves wearing religious or spiritual symbols in necklaces, earrings, rings, or pins, such as the Jewish Star of David, the Christian cross, the Buddhist lotus blossom, the Native American eagle feather, and the New Age crystal. The famous Indian Navratan Haar ring is made of nine gems with astrological significance: a diamond in the center, circled by eight rainbow-colored stones: ruby, emerald, cinnamon, coral, cat's-eye, blue and yellow sapphires, and pearl.

Designers must show sensitivity when adapting these powerful symbols into jewelry. A storm of protest arose when Madonna wore a cross as part of her onstage costume during the early part of her career; it was interpreted by many as irreverent, even blasphemous.

Many people wear their so-called birthstone, to which folklore attributes good luck, according to their sign of the zodiac. In fact, the concept of the birthstone was introduced in the United States in 1912 by the predecessor of the Jewelers of America association and is matched to calendar months rather than the zodiac.

Another interesting development in ethnic jewelry is the growing number of firms making licensed copies or reproductions of museum pieces of jewelry. Museums around the world, from the State Historical Museum of Moscow, to the Vatican Library, to the Metropolitan Museum of Art in New York, are selling vast amounts of inexpensive reproductions of museum pieces in their stores and through catalogs. These pieces come from many different eras and many different cultures; what they have in common is that they have been preserved because of their beauty and power.

Watches

The useful, dependable wristwatch is a relative newcomer to the 500-year history of mechanical timepieces. Nineteenth-century craftsmen made the pocket watch efficient—and a thing of beauty. In 1904, Louis Cartier introduced the first modern wristwatch, the Santos-Dumont, named for a Brazilian aviator. By 2004, on its one-hundredth anniversary, Cartier was selling more than 100,000 Santos-Dumonts a year.[12]

There are three basic types of watches made today: the mechanical, the self-winding, and the quartz movement. Mechanical watches are driven by a balance wheel and powered by a spring, which must be hand wound. Automatic or self-winding watches wind themselves as the wearer moves a wrist. The quartz movement, invented in the 1970s, offers very accurate timekeeping at a low cost. Most quartz watches have removable batteries that last about one year.

Analog watches have faces with hands that sweep around the numbers "clockwise." Digital watches display the time in numbers, generally using a liquid crystal display. Extra features available in some watches include night-light buttons, calendars, moon-phase indicators, stopwatch (or chronograph) features, alarms, and chimes. Some watches also give the time in other countries or time zones. But watches have always been a fashion statement as well as a useful device.

The inexpensive Timex watch of the 1960s, which "took a licking, but kept on ticking," broadened the market to include a huge number of people who could not afford even the mass-market watches of previous decades. Today, the Timex Group includes brands such as Guess, Marc Ecko, Timex, Versace, Valentino Timeless, and Salvatore Ferragamo Timepieces.

During the 1980s, Swatch (Figure 13.26) made a splash in the market with its casual watches and spread its name and contemporary look into a number of other product categories such as jewelry. The Swatch Group

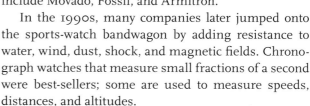

FIGURE 13.26 Swatch's Breguet Tradition watch displays visible gears.

brand Omega was the official timekeeper for the Olympics in 2012. The increased marketing opportunities aided in an increase of their gross sales by 14 percent.[13] Other well-known watch companies include Movado, Fossil, and Armitron.

In the 1990s, many companies later jumped onto the sports-watch bandwagon by adding resistance to water, wind, dust, shock, and magnetic fields. Chronograph watches that measure small fractions of a second were best-sellers; some are used to measure speeds, distances, and altitudes.

With the rising cost of gold and other raw materials during recent years, the luxury watch market has been strong. "[Customers] want something that not only provides gratification at the time of purchase, but is also going to stand the test of time," says Nicholas Bos, vice president and worldwide creative director of Van Cleef & Arpels, a maker of luxury watches.[14] Other leading manufacturers of luxury timepieces include Rolex, Omega, Patek Philippe, Cartier, Tag Heuer, Bulgari, Chanel, Harry Winston, David Yurman, and Montblanc, to name a few. The vintage market is also gaining steam, with Christie's auction house reporting record sales in 2010.[15]

At the other end of the market are children's watches. The Mickey Mouse watch for children was introduced in the 1930s. Armitron is another maker of branded watches such as Hot Wheels, Batman, Barbie, and Star Trek.

But, have cell phones made watches obsolete? Many speculate that the widespread use of cell phones has reduced the interest in watches, but manufacturers and retailers believe the watch business will withstand the test of time. A watch is still an accessory that can add a bit of fashion to any outfit.

Merchandising and Marketing

Jewelry manufacturers present their new styles and, in the case of costume jewelry manufacturers, their new lines at semiannual shows, such as JA New York, sponsored by the industry's trade association, the Jewelers of America. One of the largest trade shows is Accessories The Show, held in New York in January, February, and May. Other major trade associations include the American Gem Society, the Diamond Council of America, the Fashion Jewelry and Accessories Trade Association, and the Gemological Institute of America.

Fine-jewelry manufacturers traditionally have concentrated on providing a wide range of basic pieces, most notably diamond rings and watches. They support their lines with a variety of services offered to stores. Some advertising assistance is offered, but this has not been common in a business where brand names have been relatively unknown. However, with the emergence of designer jewelry names, this is changing.

For all types of jewelry, but especially diamond rings, the month of December and Valentine's Day are especially busy. Birthdays and anniversaries provide a steady year-round business, while watches show a sales spurt around graduation time. Today, the popularity of vintage clothing has led to a renewed interest in estate pieces, or fine jewelry of earlier eras, still in its original settings.

Costume jewelry firms offer seasonal lines designed to coordinate with what is currently fashionable in apparel. Most costume jewelry is produced on a contract basis, which offers the advantage of fast turnaround on individual items. When a particular item is suddenly in demand, costume jewelry manufacturers can switch gears and produce it quickly in a large quantity. For example, as the popularity of statement necklaces increased, they were manufactured for the masses.

The larger firms also market their goods under their nationally known brand names and advertise widely in national consumer publications. In addition, they offer cooperative advertising to retail outlets. Some manufacturers provide guidance and sales training to retailers.

Major jewelry-store chains include the mall-oriented Zale's, Helzberg Diamonds, and the Fred Meyer chain. Tiffany's, Cartier, and Gumps occupy the high end of the market. Ross-Simons is a leading retailer-cataloger. Most department stores have extensive jewelry departments, carrying fine, bridge, and costume lines, with varying amounts of ethnic specialty items. Many thousands of small jewelry stores also exist across the country.

Industry research reveals that the largest segment of the jewelry market is women buying it for themselves. This has led the World Gold Council, among others, to advertise directly to women. Retailers have also begun to focus their advertising on women, especially in diamonds. Ross-Simons, among others, promotes one solitaire diamond ring that can be worn on the right hand regardless of marital status. The romantic ads that promote diamond anniversary gifts that "tell her you'd marry her all over again" are directed at men—and subliminally at women.

All retailers report increasing problems with balancing the need for displaying jewelry with the need for keeping it secure. Shoplifting and armed robbery are real threats. Special locked display cases, drawers, and vaults have been used increasingly in major cities worldwide, as have a number of small antitheft tags attached to the merchandise.

Industry Trends

All branches of the jewelry industry emphasize the production of designs that complement currently fashionable styles. For example, when turtlenecks are popular, jewelry companies make long chains and pendants that look graceful on high necklines. When sleeveless dresses are in fashion, bracelets become an important piece of jewelry. When French cuffs are in fashion, both men and women wear cufflinks. When prints are popular, jewelry styles become tailored; but when solid or somber colors are popular, jewelry often moves to center stage with more complex designs and bright colors.

Masculine and unisex designs in gold chains, earrings, rings, shirt studs, nose studs, and fashion/sports watches are popular. To compete with costume jewelry, which has gained broad acceptance over the past few decades, fine-jewelry companies have begun to diversify. Some have broadened their lines by moving into bridge jewelry. Others have also diversified into complementary nonjewelry areas. For example, Swank, Inc., a division of Randa Accessories Leather Goods LLC, produces travel accessories, men's gifts, women's belts, and leather goods in addition to their jewelry line. They also have licensing agreements with lifestyle brands like Guess, Kenneth Cole, Pierre Cardin, Nautica, and Donald Trump.[16]

Designer jewelry is another major market force, especially in costume jewelry. Designers are thought to have been a major contributing factor to expanding sales. Chanel, Kenneth Cole, Anne Klein, Donna Karan, Yves Saint Laurent, Dior, Liz Claiborne, Givenchy, Pierre Cardin, and Ralph Lauren are some of the apparel designers who have been successful in licensing jewelry lines.

Other Accessories

There are many categories of accessories—and much variation within categories—from dress shoes to flip flops, from briefcases to lunch boxes, from hard hats to snoods, from anklets to ankhs. Other ornaments, like ribbons, bows, feathers, and fabric flowers, come and go in popularity. The accessory maker needs to move quickly in and out of these trends. Three other categories of accessories deserve mention; they are handkerchiefs, umbrellas, and hair ornaments.

That most functional of accessories—the handkerchief—has had its main function usurped by paper

FIGURE 13.27 New accessories lines debut at Moda Las Vegas and AccessoriesTheShow.

tissues. Today most women's handkerchiefs are produced in China or Japan, where they are a fashion item. Most men's handkerchiefs are packaged by the dozen (or baker's dozen—thirteen) in all cotton or cotton-polyester blends. Some high-end stores provide monogramming for an additional charge. Silk "show" handkerchiefs, called pocket squares, are produced for both men and women. They are puffed casually, not worn square, like standard cotton handkerchiefs. Children's handkerchiefs are a novelty item.

Trends in the Fashion Accessories Industries

For accessory manufacturers, being supporters of apparel fashions does not necessarily mean being followers. In fact, accessory manufacturers must often be fashion leaders. In the fashion business, which always moves in the fast lane, accessory manufacturers must move in a faster lane than anyone else. They have to be able to adapt or change a style in midseason if that is what is required to stay on top of current trends.

Market Weeks and Trade Shows

New accessory lines are shown during the five major fashion market weeks in New York so that merchants can buy a coordinated look. These include:

- Summer, January
- Transitional, March
- Fall, May
- Holiday, August
- Spring, November

In the United States, the MAGIC and WWDMAGIC shows held in Las Vegas in February and August are the largest trade shows for accessories. The International Fashion Jewelry and Accessory Show takes place in New York and Rhode Island. Paris Premiere Classe, the Fashion Accessories Trade Show, is held in Paris in March and October. These shows are a reflection of the growing importance of accessories to retailers and consumers (Figure 13.27).

Retailing Accessories

Accessories are sold in every kind of store, ranging from the largest department stores to smaller boutiques to specialized stores carrying only one kind of accessory or a limited array of related accessories. Retailers have traditionally viewed accessories as impulse items—products that customers typically buy on the spur of the moment. Additionally, a person who may not want to or who is not able to update a wardrobe with the latest apparel styles each season can use accessories to look fashionable.

Also, less expensive accessories are still purchased when there is price resistance to costlier items of apparel. Accessories are chosen because of their color, style, and newness, or simply because one wants to give one's wardrobe—and spirits—a lift.

In recognition of this impulse-buying pattern, most department stores position accessories on the main floor, or near the door or cash register in the case of small stores. More recently, they have experimented successfully with **outposts**, small accessory departments located next to apparel departments, and with movable kiosks, or large carts.

Some stores feature one-stop shopping, with boutiques (often stocked exclusively by one designer) that allow customers to buy everything they need—apparel and accessories—in one department. One-stop shopping has proven especially successful with working women who have little time to shop. It also appeals to the women who are a little unsure of themselves and like the added help that one-stop shopping provides in coordinating their outfits. Forever 21 is an example of a retailer that offers both apparel and accessories in one location—and at affordable prices. Designer signature stores featuring apparel have become a mainstay.

Some chains, like Icing and Claire's, sell only accessories. Other chains sell only subspecialties, like Tie Rack, which sells men's ties, or Sunglass Hut. Many stores, of course, sell only shoes, or only jewelry. Every major apparel catalog also offers selected accessories. Specialty catalogers include Nature's Jewelry, Coldwater Creek, and Horchow. Other general merchandisers, from L.L.Bean to Spiegel to Talbots to the giant Service Merchandise, also offer substantial selections of accessories online. Etsy, Amazon, and eBay are popular online-only retailers where customers can find a wide range of accessories.

Summary and Review

Specific accessories wax and wane in popularity, but some accessories are always popular, because most people do not consider themselves fully dressed until they have accessorized an outfit. Over the years, the business has boomed overall. Many people feel the accessory business, like many other fashion categories, has been given a boost by its association with designer names.

And the benefits are mutual. At the haute couture shows of Paris and Milan, the clothing has become the designer's fashion statement, and accessories have generated the financial support—as well as supporting the look of the season—to allow designers to experiment. Made-to-order gowns and ensembles are individually produced by hand, whereas accessories can be machine-made in larger numbers and sold at higher margins. Similarly, American ready-to-wear designers literally display their names or logos on licensed accessories such as belts, scarfs, caps, handbags, and sunglasses. For the purveyors of fashion as much as for the consumer, accessories support a complete, coordinated image. In addition, they are the source of a more attractive bottom line.

For Review

1. Why have U.S. shoe producers moved their factories offshore? How has this trend affected the footwear industry?
2. How do changes in lifestyle and activities affect the shoe industry? Give examples.
3. Describe the merchandising and marketing of handbags in the United States today.
4. What are the current trends in the millinery industry?
5. What are the major types of neckties sold today?
6. Why are shoe and fine-jewelry departments often leased?
7. What three metals are considered precious? What is the difference between solid gold and 14K gold?
8. What are the major gemstones used in the production of jewelry?
9. Give several examples of how women's apparel fashions influence jewelry fashions.
10. What categories of merchandise are to be found in fashion accessory departments today? In outposts?

For Discussion

1. How have the accessories industries been affected in the last decade?
2. List each of the major fashion accessory items and discuss why they are important to the total fashion look. At which stage of the fashion cycle is each item positioned? Give reasons for your answers.

Trade Talk

Define or briefly explain the following terms:

alloyed
bridge jewelry
briolette
carat
costume or fashion jewelry
cut-up trade
electroplating
ethnic jewelry
karat
millinery
minaudières
outpost
personal goods
rack trade
readers
self belt
small leather goods
solid gold
sterling silver
synthetic stones
vermeil

Chapter Fourteen
BEAUTY

KEY CONCEPTS

- History and development of the beauty industry
- Categories and the major market segments in beauty
- Federal laws and environmental issues affecting products
- Advertising and promotion of beauty products
- Trends in the beauty industry

o be or not to be?—that is the question. Should we be bemused, bothered, and bewildered about our looks? Or should we revel in the beauty that is natural and nurtured? Whichever way you choose, the beauty industry will meet your needs and wants with exciting new colors and potions, in both exotic test-tube creations or drawn from the world's natural fauna and flora. This quest for beauty is hardly new. For thousands of years people have smeared themselves with lotions and potions of every kind in the hope of making themselves as attractive as possible (Figure 14.1). As far back as 100 B.C., Cleopatra rubbed her face with lemon rinds, took milk baths, accentuated her eyes with kohl, and set her hair with mud. When Queen Elizabeth I of England died in 1603, her face was caked with a thick layer of chalk, the foundation of her day, which she wore to cover the pock marks of an early illness. Before modern hygiene dictated daily bathing, natural body odors were masked by perfumes. In the days of the Roman Empire, spices and scents were imported from Africa and Asia. A popular Greek scent called Susinum is evidence of

the existence of brands.[1] In the American colonial era, Caswell-Massey, predecessor of the modern drugstore, sold cologne to then-colonel George Washington.

The beauty industry is big business today and continues to get bigger. It turns out hundreds of new products annually, each of which must compete for a share of the market. These days, the fashion-apparel business plays an important role in building the business of the cosmetics industry. Many designers have introduced their own cosmetic and fragrance lines, and they often work with the cosmetics manufacturers to help them design new products that will coordinate with each season's new styles.

Thanks to the new link to designers' new season's styles, cosmetics, like fashion, are now cyclical. For example, when sports clothes are popular, and a no-makeup look is in, the cosmetics industry, eager to maintain sales, has learned to respond with appropriately low-key cosmetics and fresh, country-like scents. When bright colors and elaborate clothes are in style, the industry touts more makeup, brighter palettes, and heavier scents.

History and Development of the Beauty Industry

For centuries, the pursuit of beauty was the prerogative of the rich. Special beauty aids concocted in temples, monasteries, alchemists' cells, and kitchens were available only to the privileged few. Makeup in French was known as *maquillage*, and used only in court circles—and by the demimonde. Only in the past seventy-five years has the pursuit of beauty found its way into modern laboratories and brought with it an ability to manufacture and distribute cosmetics on a widespread basis for ordinary people (Figure 14.2). Max Factor, the Hollywood makeup artist, is credited with popularizing the terms *lipstick, makeup,* and *eye shadow* in the 1920s.[2]

Although an elite segment of the market has survived, cosmetics and fragrances are now available to anyone who wants to use them. What were once luxuries are now viewed by many as necessities. This perception, in turn, has led to more innovation in mass production, advertising, and package design. The market has also become increasingly segmented as different kinds of cosmetics and scents are made available to customers based on their age, gender, ethnic group, lifestyle, and ability to pay.

Dreams Versus Science

With the move to the laboratory came a new emphasis on the scientific development of cosmetics. Whereas for decades the word *moisturize* alone was enough to sell a skin cream, new, improved creams were now promoted for their abilities to "nourish" and "renew" the skin. Today, one takes a "daily dose" of skin care products, which are likely to be "pH-balanced." Cosmetics salespersons no longer help their customers select a makeup shade; they are trained technicians who can "diagnose" the customer's needs and prescribe the right "formula." Fragrances, too, are regarded with a more scientific approach despite the romantic allure that is attached to their use. One way of keeping down costs of mass-merchandised fragrances is the laboratory production of synthetic substitutes for expensive natural ingredients.

Until the 1960s, most women's use of colored makeup was limited. The development of easy-to-apply powders, gels, and glosses and the marketing of attractive packages brought about a change of buying habits. Estée Lauder's promotional brainstorm, offering a gift sample with a cosmetics purchase, is still a popular way of luring customers to the cosmetics counter.

The 1970s saw the emergence of *natural* products made from such ingredients as aloe vera, honey, musk,

FIGURE 14.1 Egyptians used kohl as eyeliner around the entire eyes and on their brows. Kohl was used to brighten and beautify the eyes as well as protect them from outside contaminants.

FIGURE 14.2 In the 1920s makeup started to become a necessity for most women.

FIGURE 14.3 Today, the choices for designer- and celebrity-branded fragrances continue to grow.

FIGURE 14.4 The iconic bottle of Chanel No.5.

almonds, and henna. Incense moved beyond the head shop into respectability. The trend toward natural cosmetics in the 1980s turned into a full-blown consumer preoccupation with health and self-image. The new emphasis was on the protective aspects of cosmetics. The buying public began to seek products that maintained and protected their skin rather than merely enhancing them cosmetically. Skin care products became the fastest-growing segment of the cosmetics industry. Although fashion and beauty have remained the driving force behind most cosmetics sales in the 2000s, more consumers than ever before are willing to spend money for products that enhance their overall health.

In 2011, a good share of fragrances were celebrity- and designer-branded potions (Figure 14.3). Among them were Beyoncé's Heat Rush, Michael Kors's Island Palm Beach, Reb'l Fleur by Rihanna, and Elie Saab Le Parfum. Mary Ellen Lapansky, executive director of the Fragrance Foundation, says, "We're seeing lush, full-bodied women's fragrances, to focus on the floral, that are heavily concentrated and longer-lasting and make a statement." She drew a distinction between current blends and the sometimes-overpowering scents of the 1980s. "No one should smell you beyond your scent circle," she says.[3]

Legends Versus the New Entrepreneurs

The beauty industry has always been dominated by personalities, a trait that shows little sign of abating. What has changed is the nature of the personalities and their purposes in their businesses.

An early worldwide celebrity associated with fragrance was Coco Chanel. More than ninety years ago, she introduced a perfume that, despite its unpretentious name, became associated with designer fashion: Chanel No. 5 (Figure 14.4). Decades later, another French designer linked fragrance with designer fashion; he was Christian Dior. His Miss Dior accompanied his famous post–World War II New Look.

But the big names in cosmetics and fragrances were not all French. From the 1950s through the 1970s, a few flamboyant personalities in the United States, most notably Elizabeth Arden, Helena Rubinstein, Max Factor, and Estée Lauder, dominated the industry and virtually dictated its shape and scope. Less well known but equally innovative were Dorothy Gray, Hazel Bishop, and Harriet Hubbard Ayer. The drive, intuition, foresight, and promotional ability of these pioneers is still felt in the industry and has rarely been duplicated in other industries. By the mid-1980s, most of the companies founded by these individuals had become public corporations or part of multinational conglomerates.

Only Estée Lauder survived with her beauty empire still intact and run by her personally (Figure 14.5). This famous "nose" personally developed her fragrance lines while overseeing her cosmetics empire. Instead of being swallowed up by a larger organization, she built her own conglomerate with the Aramis, Clinique, and Prescriptives brands. Not until 1995, after she had turned management of the company over to her son,

BOBBI BROWN: REDEFINING BEAUTY

BOBBI BROWN, THE self-made cosmetics mogul, has changed the face of makeup. For more than twenty years, she's made it her mission to reach women with this message: "Beauty isn't about perfection. It's about celebrating your individuality." She not only fulfills her mission with her cosmetics line—seven looks that help women to recognize their own beauty and teach them how to maintain it inside and out—but also through her passionate commitment to charitable causes for women.

Brown was working as a makeup artist when she set out to create cosmetics that flatter a woman's own beauty rather than masking her imperfections. According to Leonard Lauder, "She wants everyone to look like themselves, every woman a queen, and I love that." Brown started with a single lipstick because she was so unhappy with the products that already existed. "I had the idea to create a lipstick that didn't smell, wasn't dry or greasy, and looked like your natural lip color—only better," she said. Thus began an empire.

Her first lipstick was quickly followed by nine other natural-looking shades. When they debuted as Bobbi Brown Essentials at Bergdorf Goodman's department store in 1991, Brown expected to sell one hundred lipsticks in the first month, but instead she sold one hundred in the first day! Clearly, Bobbi Brown Essentials filled an unmet need: There were a lot of unhappy women looking for something other than the heavy, unnatural-looking makeup available at that time. As Brown herself says, "We are living in a world of entrepreneurs, and I think there's much opportunity in the world for a product that doesn't exist or for making something that's better than what is out there."

Bobbi Brown Essentials was so successful that only four years later, in 1995, Estée Lauder bought the company, allowing Brown to maintain full creative control as CEO. Today, her line is sold in more than 400 stores in twenty countries and graces countless numbers of beautiful faces—from celebrities to royalty to athletes to everyday women around the world.

For everyone from Beginner to Pro

BOBBI BROWN MAKEUP MANUAL

From the ends of the earth,
an astonishing discovery.

New. Re-Nutriv Re-Creation

Now, create and sustain a remarkably more youthful appearance, with a renewed look of radiance and striking vitality. From the pristine depths of the Antarctic Ocean comes the inspiration for our exclusively refined, sustainably cultivated Glacial BioExtract,™ proven to help skin boost its natural elastin production.* Re-Creation Face Creme and Night Serum (also availible for eyes).

A stunning breakthrough for beautiful skin.
*In vitro studies at leading research centers in the United States and France.

ESTĒE LAUDER
Re-Nutriv

FIGURE 14.5 Estée Lauder, Inc., was founded by Estée Lauder, one of the first-generation superstars of the American cosmetics industry, and is still flourishing today.

did it go public, and even then, the family retained control of 85 percent of the stock.

The beauty industry seems destined to be run by personalities, and a second generation, with names like Adrien Arpel, Madeleine Mono, Christine Valmy, Georgette Klinger, Merle Norman, Flori Roberts, and Mary Kay Ash soon emerged. Unlike the old stars, though, these new entrepreneurs relied less on personality and more on sound business strategies. In England, Anita Roddick opened her first Body Shop in 1976, making environmental protection the guiding force of her business decisions.

A third generation of personalities in cosmetics includes the late Frank Toskan, of the Canadian firm MAC (Make-up Art Cosmetics), and Bobbi Brown. Besides being makeup artists for the fashion industry who brought their expertise to the public, Brown and Toskan had in common their parent company, Estée Lauder.

Organization and Operation of the Industry

The beauty industry has undergone significant changes in recent years in terms of its organization and operation. Once made up entirely of many small firms, none of which controlled a significant share of the market, it is now dominated by a few huge, global firms that command large market shares. Although the industry still supports hundreds of companies, many are now owned by conglomerates that also produce other consumer goods, such as processed foods, health care products, and household cleaners. The largest companies in the world with holdings in the cosmetics and fragrance industry are L'Oréal, in which Nestlé has a substantial interest; Procter & Gamble; Unilever; and Estée Lauder. Complicating the issues are licensing of designer brands and cosmetics, and the constant changes in mergers, sales, and acquisitions that take place according to changes in the market and the economy. In 2010, there were twenty beauty mergers and acquisitions. Most notable included Shiseido, the fifth-largest cosmetics company in the world, purchasing Bare Escentuals; Coty Inc. acquiring Philosophy; and Estée Lauder purchasing Smashbox.[4] The number of mergers and acquisitions jumped to twenty-seven in 2011 and is expected to increase in the future as smaller companies are struggling to stay in business, and global brands are finding that acquiring established independent brands is less costly than building new ones from scratch.[5]

A Global Business

The joining of cosmetics and fragrance firms in multinational conglomerates is part of the same trend that is manifested in the changing role of heads of companies from product development artists to master marketers. The giant parent companies can offer their cosmetics and fragrance industry subsidiaries clout and expertise in the consumer marketplace. As packaging, promotion, and distribution become as much a part of the product as the ingredients, the giant corporations develop global marketing strategies to get each product line into the hands of its targeted group of consumers.

Western Europe has a global cosmetics and fragrance industry of its own. Their marketing practices are similar to those in the United States, with subsidiaries and lines catering to various market segments.

In other parts of the world, industry experts anticipate major market growth in Latin America—especially Brazil. Also, Japanese and Korean beauty companies are expected to expand their reach to the United States and Europe. "Global players are looking for innovation and an entrepreneurial approach that they can bring to the next level," says investment banker Elsa Berry, head of Houlihan Lokey's cross-border consumer coverage.[6]

The Main Categories

All large, nationally advertised cosmetics firms produce hundreds of items. For sales and inventory purposes, products must thus be divided into broad categories. The typical order form of one large firm, for example, lists all the company's products, in the various sizes or colors available, under end-use categories such as:

- Fragrances
- Color cosmetics (facial makeup, including lip and cheek color, eye makeup, and liquid and powder foundations)
- Skin care
- Sun care
- Nail care
- Hair care

If a firm produces men's as well as women's cosmetics, each of the two lines is given its own distinctive brand name, and, of course, separate sales and inventory records are kept for each brand line. We discuss all but hair care in more detail.

Because of fashion and product obsolescence, as well as customer boredom, manufacturers are constantly updating and shipping new items to keep cosmetics customers buying new products, or new colors, or both. Manufacturers update formulas when they become aware of new technology and new ingredients to improve their products.

A system of product returns, unique to the cosmetics industry, aids the retailer in keeping the inventory current. The industry refers to this system as **rubber-banding**, which means that cosmetic products not sold within a specified period of time may be returned to the manufacturer to be replaced with others that will sell. This guarantees that the cosmetics retailer will never have to take a markdown on this merchandise. Only if a cosmetics company is discontinuing an item does it permit markdowns by a store. (Other industries allow returns to vendors only for damages, overshipments, or wrong shipment.)

Fragrances

The term **fragrance** includes (in increasing order of strength, lasting power, and price) cologne, eau de toilette (toilet water), eau de parfum, and perfume. Other forms of fragrances are spray perfume, aftershave lotion, and **home fragrances**. Scents are also added to other beauty products, such as soap, shampoo, bubble bath, and hand and body lotions, but the items in the fragrance category are designed specifically to enhance the smell of the person wearing them.

The scent of a fragrance is a combination of essential oils, often from plants, including a variety of trees, flowers, grasses, herbs and spices, and edible extracts—like the very popular vanilla (Figure 14.6). Other scents are concocted in the perfumer's laboratory. Each scent is called a **note**, and, like musical notes, they vary in strength and duration. The perfumer, like the composer, combines them in a harmonious whole. Alcohol carries the scent to the skin. The more alcohol, the less concentrated the fragrance.

Fragrances are affected by the body chemistry of the wearer; they may smell differently on different people or even on the same person at different times. For example, diet may make one's skin more or less oily, and fragrance is more intense on oily skin. In addition, the scent of a single application of a fragrance changes over time. Virginia Bonofiglio, who teaches the unique Fragrance Knowledge course at the Fashion Institute of Technology, describes "three major stages in the life of a perfume":

FIGURE 14.6 Fragrances often come from essential oils, herbs, extracts, and plants.

First, the top note—what you smell when you take a whiff from a bottle—usually a citrus or green smell, which lasts about fifteen minutes on the skin. Then the middle note, often a floral or wood, which lasts three to four hours. And finally the bottom note, usually a musk or vanilla, which lasts four to five hours.[7]

Cosmetics manufacturers produce fragrances with their own brand names and, under licensing agreements, the names of designers and celebrities. Tommy and Tommy Girl, Tommy Hilfiger's fragrance lines, are manufactured by Estée Lauder, which also produces, under its own name, such scents as Beautiful, Pleasures, and Youth Dew and, under the names of its subsidiaries, Aramis and Clinique's Happy Aromatics, among others.

Continual innovation in fragrances is necessary to maintain growth in a fashion-conscious market. As many as one hundred new fragrances may be launched in a season in various concentrations. Fragrances are also bottled in a range of sizes, making even expensive perfumes available to a larger market.

Perfumes are worn predominantly by women twenty-five to forty-four years old—a group that is both fashion-conscious and affluent enough to buy this luxury product. Toilet waters and colognes, also worn by the aforementioned group on informal occasions, have great appeal for younger women because they are lower priced. They appeal to men because they are more subtle than most perfumes. The industry offers lower-priced products to entice the male or female customer from any economic level to try a new product. Table 14.1 lists the top five women's and men's fragrances found in department stores.

Color Cosmetics

The term **color cosmetics** usually refers to facial makeup; nail color is categorized with other nail care products. Color is the primary feature of facial makeup,

FIGURE 14.7 Smashbox creates eye shadow palettes to enhance specific eye colors.

but the substance into which the pigment is mixed is also important. The oils, wax, and talc that are used in the bases of color cosmetics affect the wearer's skin and the finish of the makeup. The pigments also interact with the ingredients in the bases, so manufacturing products that are consistent from batch to batch require a well-equipped factory staffed by experts.

Lip coloring is produced in the form of lipstick and solid or gel-like glosses. It may be opaque or transparent, and the finish may be matte, glossy, or even glittery. This variety and the range of colors allows for mixing to achieve a look suitable to the occasion and the colors in one's outfit. In 2010, rich and retro colors made a big splash, while neutrals gained in popularity in 2011.

Liquid, gel, and powder blushes, in addition to the more traditional rouge, provide similar variety in cheek color cosmetics. Liquid and powder foundations not only give the skin an even surface and color; the various formulations also provide skin care for dry, oily, and normal skin.

Eye makeup, especially eye shadow, is available in a broad range of colors, not all of them natural, to set off this most expressive facial feature (Figure 14.7).

Estée Lauder, Lancôme, and Clinique are called the Big Three because they dominate color cosmetics. In addition to these prestige lines, mass-market color

TABLE 14.1 *Top 5 Scents for Men and Women*

TOP MEN'S SCENTS	TOP WOMEN'S SCENTS
1. Giorgio Armani Acqua di Giò Pour Homme	1. Chanel Coco Mademoiselle
2. Giorgio Armani Armani Code	2. Estée Lauder Beautiful
3. Chanel Bleu de Chanel	3. Dolce & Gabbana Light Blue
4. Dolce & Gabbana The One for Men	4. Chanel No. 5
5. Dolce & Gabbana Light Blue Pour Homme	5. Donna Karan Cashmere Mist

Source: http://racked.com/archives/2011/05/20/wwd-ranks-the-topten-womens-and-mens-fragrances-in-america.php. Accessed February 2013.

TABLE 14.2 *Top 5 Cosmetic Companies*

COMPANY	SUBSIDIARIES/MAIN BRANDS
L'Oréal Clichy, France	L'Oréal Paris, Garnier, Maybelline New York, SoftSheen Carson, Essie, Le Club des Créateurs de Beauté, Lancôme, Biotherm, Helena Rubinstein, Kiehl's, Shu Uemura, Giorgio Armani Parfums and Cosmetics, Parfums Cacharel, Ralph Lauren Fragrances, Diesel, Viktor & Rolf, Yves Saint Laurent, Stella McCartney, Maison Martin Margiela, Yue-Sai, Paloma Picasso, Parfums Guy Laroche, Vichy, La Roche-Posay, SkinCeuticals, Roger & Gallet, Sanoflore, The Body Shop.
Procter & Gamble Co. Cincinnati	Pantene, Head & Shoulders, Clairol, Herbal Essences, Nice 'n Easy, Natural Instincts, Wella, Wella Koleston, Sebastian Professional, Nioxin, Vidal Sassoon, Aussie, Rejoice, Frédéric Fekkai (hair care), Cover Girl, Max Factor (makeup), Hugo Boss, Gucci, Old Spice, Lacoste, Escada, Puma, Anna Sui, Ghost, Dunhill, Christina Aguilera, Rochas, Replay, Bruno Banani, Mexx (fragrance), Dolce & Gabbana (fragrance, makeup), Venus, Olay, SK-II, DDF, Gillette, The Art of Shaving (skin care), Secret (deodorant)
Unilever London/ Rotterdam, Netherlands	Axe/Lynx, Impulse, Rexona/Sure, Degree, Dove, Lux, Pond's, Suave, Sunsilk/Seda/ Hazeline, Timotei, Clear, Mods, Vaseline, Tigi, Monsavon, Radox, Duschdas, Brylcreem, Black Pearl, Clean Line, 100 Recipes of Beauty, Silky Hands, Tresemmé, Motions, Kalina, Nexxus Salon Hair Care, Consort, St. Ives, Soft & Beautiful, Just for Me, TCB, Simple (skin care)
The Estée Lauder Cos. New York	Estée Lauder, Aramis, Clinique, Prescriptives, Lab Series, Origins, MAC Cosmetics, Bobbi Brown, Tommy Hilfiger, Kiton, La Mer, Donna Karan, Aveda, Jo Malone, Bumble and Bumble, Darphin, Michael Kors, Sean John, Missoni, Tom Ford Beauty, Coach, Ojon, Smashbox, Ermenegildo Zegna, American Beauty, Flirt, Good Skin Labs, Grassroots Research Labs
Shiseido Co. Tokyo	Shiseido, Clé de Peau Beauté, Sea Breeze, Carita, Decléor, Nars, Joico, Aupres, Senka, Urara, Pure & Mild, Za, D'ici Là, Ipsa, Ayura, Ettusais, Shiseido Professional, Zotos, Serge Lutens, Bare Escentuals, Tsubaki, Parfums Issey Miyake, Parfums Jean Paul Gaultier, Parfums Narciso Rodriguez, Parfums Elie Saab

Source: "WWD Beauty Inc.'s Top 100: The Top Ten," WWD.com, August 20, 2012, www.wwd.com/beauty-industry-news/financial/wwd-beauty-incs-top-100-the-top-10-6142686. Accessed February 2013.

cosmetics manufacturers are influential in certain product categories, although most produce the full range. For example, Cover Girl, a division of Procter & Gamble, is noted for foundations, while Maybelline, a subsidiary of L'Oréal, is a big name in eye makeup. See Table 14.2 for a list of the top five cosmetics companies.

Skin Care

Soap, long the basis of skin care, is no longer the only product used for bathing. In a market that is constantly demanding new choices, alternatives to the familiar bar of soap have turned a bath or shower into a new experience. Bar soap is still the largest selling product for bathing, but the growth of sales is challenged by liquid soap, syndet bars (Dove, among others), and body washes and gels. The washes and gels are marketed as a way of avoiding the skin-drying effects of soap; both women and men rely on mild detergents for cleansing.

Perhaps because bathing is a routine daily activity rather than a luxury, mass-merchandise products sold at low price points are at the forefront of the market. Some popular brands of washes are Softsoap and Suave. Prestige products are also being marketed. Dove Men + Care and Axe (both by Unilever) are two popular body washes targeted to men.

Of course, the skin care category is wider than just soap or soap substitutes. It includes hand, face, foot, and body lotions, as well as creams, scrubs, masks, moisturizers, and anticellulite treatments. The enormous impact of alpha hydroxy acids on these products cannot be overestimated. This emerging segment of skin care products is based on dermatology and promises to correct the visible signs of aging and promote new cell growth. (See the discussion under Federal Laws, later in this chapter.) The addition of antibacterial agents to skin care products is discussed later in this chapter, as are the antiallergenic versions of these products.

Sun Care

Sun care has become a major category of the cosmetics industry, as consumers have become increasingly aware of the health dangers—and aging effects—of the sun's rays. As a result, even the prestige manufacturers have rushed to produce a wide range of scientifically formulated sun products (Figure 14.8).

FIGURE 14.8 Neutrogena's Wet Skin spray product is specially formulated to be applied to wet skin and provides protection from the sun.

An important feature of a sunscreen is its SPF, or sun protection factor. The SPF number, which indicates how long the screen will protect the wearer from burning, may go higher than one hundred. Most people are adequately protected by a sunscreen with an SPF of 15, but SPF 30 is now becoming the norm. There is also a market for post-sun products, items that are intended for use immediately after sun exposure. These products often contain botanicals, such as aloe, which have anti-inflammatory effects that help soothe burned skin.

What once was a category dominated by drugstores and mass merchants has now become a major business for department stores as well. Despite the efforts of the medical community, most consumers continue to get too much sun.

Product innovation, in conjunction with consumers' growing concern about sun damage, has fueled the sunless tanner market in the United States and will continue to do so over the next few years. Driving the growth in the sunless tanner category is an increase in consumer awareness that dangerous rays not only can be deadly but also can damage the skin and cause signs of aging. It is no secret that today's beauty shopper desperately wants to ward off future wrinkles and diminish the ones she already has. To keep them protected, marketers have rolled out an array of products: sunless tanning lotions and sprays, in addition to waterproof, hypoallergenic, quick-drying, nongreasy, and oil-free products that claim to provide broad-spectrum UVA/UVB protection.

Nail Care

Nail care products really took off in the 1990s, and they are exploding today: nail polish sales reached $710 billion in 2011.[8] These products are more diverse than ever, with colors ranging from subdued neutrals and clear enamels to dramatic blues, greens, and yellows. Nail art has also become hugely popular, allowing consumers to decorate their nails with cheetah spots, snakeskin prints, jewels, and many other quirky and even outrageous designs that would have been unheard of merely five years ago. "Nails come in any way, shape or form," says Karen Grant, a senior analyst with the NPD Group, which tracks cosmetics trends. "They've become a fashion accessory."[9] Experts also see nail color as a recession-proof cosmetic enhancer much like lipstick was in the past.

Packaging

Packaging plays a vital role in marketing fragrances and cosmetics (Figure 14.9). Often it is the package rather than the contents that leads the customer to

FIGURE 14.9 Some customers may purchase Justin Bieber's Someday fragrance for the packaging alone.

buy one product over another. Manufacturers have historically tried for unique packaging. In the early 1900s, when Coty perfume was the most expensive in France, Coty tried to get the exclusive rights to a newly invented—and enormously expensive—packaging material: cellophane.[10]

It often seems that the bottle and packaging take on incredible significance. According to the Fragrance Foundation, for every $100,000 in expected gross sales, a manufacturer should plan to spend $20,000 on the bottle (and the perfume in it) and $35,000 on advertising and promotion. An interesting example of a successful perfume marketing concept in which the bottle played a vital role is Parfums Christian Dior's blockbuster scent J'Adore. Launched in 1999, at a time when best-selling fragrances were packaged in minimalist bottles like CK and cK One, J'Adore set a new trend with a voluptuous amphora-shaped bottle with a golden Masai-like collar around the neck. Patrick Choel, president of the Perfumes and Cosmetics Division at LVMH, which released J'Adore, claimed that the bottle was actually more important than the fragrance itself.[11]

Efforts to preserve natural resources by recycling packaging materials have had a mixed influence on the packaging of cosmetics and fragrances. (See Recyclable Packaging later in this chapter.) The use of sustainable packaging for cosmetics has become more popular in the twenty-first century, but it still lags behind other industries. Some beauty companies, such as Lush, have made a concerted effort to reduce or eliminate packaging for many of their products.

Private-Label Manufacturers

Although dominated by giant producers of nationally advertised brand lines, the industry has many **private-label manufacturers**, producing merchandise to specification under the brand names of chain stores,

BEAUTY
IS A SCIENCE

MOST PEOPLE KNOW the name L'Oréal but many are unaware that it is the largest cosmetics company in the world, with operations in 130 countries, twenty-seven internationally known brands, and annual sales of more than $28 billion. With product lines that run the gamut from mass-market to luxury to professional, L'Oréal is the company behind many brands you may already love—like The Body Shop, Essie, Garnier, Maybelline, Lancome, Kiehl's, Helena Rubenstein, and La Roche-Posay—just to name a few.

This global colossus grew from an unlikely beginning: in the kitchen of an unstoppable chemist named Eugene Schueller. While he was teaching at the Sorbonne in Paris, Schueller was approached by a hairdresser who was searching for reliable hair dye. Unable to resist a challenge, Schueller quit his job and used his kitchen as a laboratory to formulate the very first synthetic hair dye. This dye, perfected in 1907, was the first product of The Safe Hair-Dye Company of France, which became L'Oréal a year later.

Before L'Oréal, beauty products were usually handmade and untested. As a result, many products were unreliable, made bogus claims, or had harmful effects on consumers. L'Oréal was the first company whose products were based on science and promised consistent results. This commitment to science remains the company's mission: "Since its creation by a researcher, [L'Oréal] has been pushing back the frontiers of knowledge. Its unique research arm enables it to continually explore new territories and invent the products of the future, while drawing inspiration from beauty rituals all over the world."

Today, L'Oréal spends 3.5 percent of its sales—just over $1 billion—on Research and Development at nineteen research centers and sixteen evaluation centers around the world. Through this effort, L'Oréal stays on the cutting-edge of both science and beauty, exploring how recent discoveries in genetics or the antiaging effects of stem cells can improve its products. According to a company spokesman, this next frontier includes "cosmetics used on the surface but also those taken orally or via the use of a device to maximize effects or modify the skin.... L'Oréal is in a position to anticipate these changes and remain the beauty market leader in these categories."

mass merchants, department stores, small independent stores and hair salons, and direct-to-the-home marketers. The famous scent Giorgio was born in the Rodeo Drive Giorgio store. It was such a success that, although an original private label, it is now sold in fine stores from coast to coast. Competitors Avon Products and Mary Kay Cosmetics both sell products produced and packaged for them by the same private-label manufacturer.

Some of the better-known private-label manufacturers are Kolmar Laboratories of Port Jervis, New York, and Private Label Cosmetics of Fair Lawn, New Jersey. Kolmar sells mass quantities to large users, but not all private-label producers are big enough to meet large orders. Small private-label manufacturers supply small distributors. A beauty salon owner can walk into a private-label distributor's office, and in less than ten days and for about $500, have a complete private-label line in his or her shop. Or a dermatologist may want a private-label line of products to sell to patients. However, this line is based on what the private-label house has already been manufacturing. Private-label manufacturers do not develop new products for individual clients.

Retailers get little help from their private-label suppliers. Private-label firms do not share advertising costs, provide gift-with-purchase offers, or accept returns.

A serious threat to the private-label industry is posed by federal ingredient-label requirements. Packaging is usually kept to a minimum by private-label firms in order to keep prices low. To get the government-required ingredient label on a small lipstick, however, an additional package is required. Through its lobbying group, the Independent Cosmetic Manufacturers and Distributors Association, the private-label industry is fighting labeling requirements.

Copycat Scents

The conspicuous consumption of expensive designer fragrances in the 1980s gave rise to a new industry segment, producers of **copycat scents**. These products are unabashed imitations of the packaging as well as the aromas of popular designer fragrances. Comparison advertising highlights the price difference to assure customers who cannot afford the prestige brand that they are getting value for their dollar. In the more economically cautious 1990s, copycats thrived in mass-merchandise and off-price outlets, flea markets, and direct mail. Knockoff fragrances that appeal to young consumers, such as cK One and Tommy, have fared especially well.

The leading producers of fragrances have been fighting this copycat category. There have been many

lawsuits, and the international courts have upheld copyright lawsuits for the first time. A court in the Netherlands ruled that a fragrance called Female Treasure, marketed by Dutch company Kecofa, is so similar to Lancôme's Trésor that it constituted a deliberate and unlawful copyright infringement. In 2004, a court in Paris handed down a similar judgment against Belgian company Bellure for imitating the composition of twelve L'Oréal fragrances, including Trésor, Miracle, Anaïs Anaïs, Drakkar Noir, Emporio Armani, and Ralph Lauren Romance.

These judgments marked the first time courts in European Union member states—and possibly the world—had ruled that a fragrance could be protected by copyright, just like other original works of authorship, such as music or artwork.[12]

Federal Laws

Because chemicals are the basis for most cosmetic products, the Food and Drug Administration (FDA) is the federal agency that polices and regulates the cosmetics industry. The Federal Trade Commission defines a **cosmetic** as any article other than soap that is intended to be "rubbed, poured, sprinkled, or sprayed on, introduced into, or otherwise applied to the human body for cleansing, beautifying, promoting attractiveness, or altering the appearance without affecting the body's structure or functions."[13]

Manufacturers are prevented by FDA regulations from using potentially harmful ingredients and from making exaggerated claims regarding the effects of their products. An example of the results of these regulations is the use of **alpha hydroxy acids (AHAs)**—which are extracted from fruits, yogurt, and sugarcane. These are found mostly in facial creams intended to prevent wrinkles and improve texture and tone of skin. When they were introduced in 1994, AHAs came under federal scrutiny as the FDA considered whether to regulate their use as a drug. In manufacturers' tests, AHAs showed effectiveness, but while they awaited the FDA's decision, many producers limited the amount of AHAs in their product so that they could sell it as a cosmetic. In 2005, the FDA issued *Guidance for Industry: Labeling of Cosmetics Containing Alpha Hydroxy Acids as Ingredients* to educate consumers about the potential for increased skin sensitivity to the sun from the use of cosmetics with AHAs. It was also meant to educate manufacturers about proper labeling.[14]

The 1938 Federal Food, Drug, and Cosmetic Act was the first federal law controlling cosmetics. It prohibited the adulteration and misbranding of cosmetics. Amendments added to the law in 1952 made it more stringent. More amendments in 1960 required government review and approval of the safety of color additives used in cosmetics.

The Fair Packing and Labeling Act of 1966 prohibits unfair or deceptive methods of packaging and labeling. This act covers many consumer industries in addition to the cosmetics industry. All cosmetics labeled since April 15, 1977, must bear a list of their ingredients in descending order of weight. To help identify potentially dangerous ingredients for manufacturers, the Cosmetic Ingredient Review, an independent research group funded by the industry trade organization, the Personal Care Products Council (formerly the Cosmetic, Toiletry and Fragrance Association), was established in the early 1980s.

In any event, the major ingredients of most cosmetics in any price range do not vary much and mostly consist of fats, oils, waxes, talc, alcohol, glycerin, borax, coloring matter, and perfumes.

Constant surveillance by consumer and industry groups and advisory boards keeps the cosmetics industry sensitive to product liability. The FDA Modernization Act of 1997 focused on modernizing the regulation of medical products, food, and cosmetics. This act includes provisions for global harmonization of standards. Since the European Federation of Associations of Health Products Manufacturers has more stringent standards than the United States does, U.S. manufacturers expect to be required to register their products and formulas and to establish their safety before selling them to the European customer.

The Campaign for Safe Cosmetics, a coalition of health and environmental organizations, has been pressuring personal-care product and cosmetics companies to phase out chemicals they say have been linked to cancer, birth defects, and other health problems for several years. This effort has aided the enactment of the California chemical ingredient disclosure law for cosmetics and a 2007 EU policy requiring all companies, including cosmetics firms that produce or use chemicals, to collect extensive data on possible human health risks of the substances.

Environmental Concerns

Environmentalism, as a major issue of political and social concern, has had a strong effect on consumer buying habits and on industry practices to meet consumers' demands. Attention to health and fitness influences what people are willing to put on their skin and hair, so a demand for natural products and ingredients has arisen in the cosmetics and fragrances industry, just as it has in the food industry. Consumers

FIGURE 14.10 Avalon Organics adheres to natural and organic guidelines—for every one of its products within the line.

are also becoming more educated about the effects of their behavior on natural resources.

Natural or Botanical Products

Although everything on earth has a chemical composition, many people prefer products made from substances grown by nature to products produced by chemists in a laboratory (Figure 14.10). The cosmetic and therapeutic benefits of essential oils derived from plants prove that Mother Nature's recipes are effective, and many consumers do not believe that scientists can improve upon—or even equal—these ingredients. Perhaps there is also a connection in some people's minds between the natural look in today's fashion and natural ingredients in the cosmetics that help them achieve that look.

Table 14.3 lists some oils that are harvested from nature for use in cosmetics. Some companies, notably The Body Shop, Aveda, and Origins, use only natural ingredients in their cosmetics. Adding to the appeal of the products themselves is the satisfaction consumers derive from knowing that their purchases benefit the populations of countries where the ingredients are found.

TABLE 14.3 *Some Popular Oils Used in Cosmetics*

OIL	COSMETICS IN WHICH IT IS USED
Aloe leaf gel	Sun care products, shampoos, hair rinses
Apricot kernel oil	Hair preparations, bath oils
Avocado oil	Burn treatments, shaving cream
Babassu oil	Skin care products, suntan products
Black currant seed oil	Treatments for dry skin
Borage oil	Moisturizers
Castor oil	Lipstick
Cocoa butter	Sun care products
Coconut oil	Shampoo
Djarak oil	Products to treat skin diseases and wounds, products to promote hair growth
Groundnut oil	Skin cleansers
Japan wax	Makeup sticks, mascara
Jojoba oil	Sun care products
Keku nut oil	Treatments for dry skin, sunburn, and acne prevention; conditioning shampoos
Kiwi oil	Products to support cell growth
Macadamia nut oil	Baby oil
Mexican poppy oil	Treatments for dry skin
Sea buckthorn oil	Antiaging preparations
Wheat germ oil	Hair and skin care products

AVOCADO

BLACK CURRANT

COCONUT

MACADAMIA NUT

FIGURE 14.11 Whole Body by Whole Foods Market offers high-quality products that are not tested on animals.

Animal Testing

The issue of testing cosmetic and fragrance formulas on animals to ensure that they are safe for human use reached the height of controversy in the late 1970s when animal rights activists protested the testing of eye makeup on rabbits. Outraged that animals should be subjected to painful and blinding tests so that people could enjoy a luxury product, the protesters threatened boycotts of the offending manufacturers' products and picketing of their headquarters. The tests were eventually suspended when less controversial and equally reliable computerized analyses were developed to acquire the same kind of information.

According to legislation passed in New York State in 2007, cosmetics manufacturers and ingredient suppliers are prohibited from conducting any test that involves the placing of a cosmetic or cosmetic ingredient in an animal's eye or on an animal's skin to measure its irritant effects. Alternatives to the use of animals for eye and skin irritancy tests of cosmetics and their ingredients are widely available and in use by many corporations, including Avon, Noxell, Revlon, Paul Mitchell, Fabergé, Mary Kay, and Whole Foods Market (Figure 14.11).[15] Breakthroughs in science and technology might also help eliminate the need to test cosmetics on animals. In a study funded by L'Oréal, the biotech firm Hurel used lab-grown human skin cells to simulate the body's allergic response to certain chemicals. Traditionally, this type of testing was conducted on mice.[16]

Recyclable Packaging

Packaging of cosmetics has been greatly influenced by interest in recycling. But the elaborate glass bottles used for designer fragrances are not the object of serious recycling efforts because the product is a luxury item, which is often saved as an art object.

The cardboard outer packaging of many luxury cosmetics and fragrances is more of an issue. Many of the coatings used to give the packages an elegant appearance render the cardboard unsuitable for recycling. Cargo Cosmetics has come up with the answer to this problem: the packaging for their PlantLove line of cosmetics is made entirely of corn—a renewable, abundant resource. This environmentally friendly innovation also emits less greenhouse gases.[17]

Mass-merchandised lines of such products as liquid soap, shampoo, and hand and body lotions are typically packaged in recyclable plastic containers. In 2011, Procter and Gamble started shipping products that included sustainable and recyclable plastic made from Brazilian sugarcane.[18]

Market Segments

The success of a perfume or cosmetic depends on accurate identification of the target customer and recognition of the product features, packaging, and promotional activities that will attract that customer's attention. Women have long been recognized as the primary market for beauty products, but six other major market segments have been identified. These segments overlap, but in defining the target for each product or line, the marketer focuses on particular characteristics. Currently, the most promising market segments are the male market, the teen market, the children's market, the ethnic market, the home market, and the export market.

The Male Market

The beauty market for men has expanded and is expected to experience above-average growth in the future. Changing male images are opening up new and larger markets in hair care, face and body care, and fragrances (Figure 14.12). Men are buying more diversified products, such as moisturizers, cleansers, and skin toners.

Men, like women, are concerned about aging. Unlike women, they have done little about it until recently. It has become socially acceptable for men to treat skin to impede the aging process, and there is also a growing trend for male grooming. The demand for male

FIGURE 14.12 Yves Saint Laurent's L'Homme Libre fragrance targets the male market.

grooming products is of increasing importance to the cosmetics industry, and companies are responding by looking beyond shaving foam and razors.

Many market-leading companies targeted the growing male consumer market early on. L'Oréal, for example, launched its comprehensive men's skin care and personal care range, Men's Experts, in the global market in late 2004.

Increasingly sophisticated products that have traditionally catered to female vanities are being marketed to men, with manufacturers like Beiersdorf and Shiseido launching products such as antiwrinkle creams, bronzing products, and toning gels. France-based company L'Occitane launched a mass-market male cosmetic range, Cade Male Cosmetics, in 2005.

Body washes are another addition to this growing category, with companies offering innovative multiuse products aimed at men. For example, in 2011 Nivea launched Platinum Protect Deodorizing 3-in-1 Hair and Body Wash.

The word *metrosexual* has become a term of the twenty-first century, with male role models like David Beckham professing to use products such as concealer and mascara. The launch of the M Cover concealer product by Clinique, its first foray into male cosmetics, pushed the company further into the public eye as a trendsetter. Premium cosmetics company Jean Paul Gaultier launched Le Male Cosmetics, and though the trend has not yet been adopted by the masses, there is customer interest.

Despite the upsurge in male cosmetics in stores, today the Internet has become a prime retail area for the more self-conscious male consumer. Men can browse online and explore products within a nonthreatening environment.

In 2012, sales of men's toiletries and cosmetics in the United States hit $2.6 billion and are estimated to reach $3.2 billion by 2016.[19] All indications show that many men have accepted beauty products as an integral part of their lifestyle.

The Teen Market

Buying a first tube of lipstick has been a rite of passage for teenage girls for generations, but the typical teenager of today has gone far beyond this initial plunge into cosmetic and fragrance purchases. The U.S. youth collectively spends billions of dollars on cosmetics and toiletries annually.

Furthermore, today's typical teen customer has her own tastes—literally. Bonne Bell, the pioneer in cosmetics lines for teens, features Lip Rush clear gloss in flavors ranging from Kiwi Ice to Cool Cotton Candy.

Bonne Bell's success has inspired other producers to offer cosmetics lines specifically for the teen market segment. They go after their target customer by following her into the mass-merchandise store, the apparel specialty store, and the record store. They speak to her on MTV and online. Besides flavored lipstick, they offer her eye makeup and nail enamel in attention-getting colors.

Prestige cosmetics and fragrance producers appeal to the teenage customer with light and unisex scents. The ecologically oriented lines, such as those offered by The Body Shop, are also popular with this segment.

With teenage girls spending a total of more than $100 million per month on beauty products, it is no surprise that this sector of the fashion industry courts their business.[20] And the benefit is mutual: for a fraction of the price of a new dress or pair of jeans, a teen can express her style and indulge her shopping impulses.

Of course, both boys and girls spend heavily on acne treatments and concealers to help them deal with their teenage complexion problems. A success story was Bioré's wildly popular—and quickly imitated—dermal patch designed to remove blackheads.

The Children's Market

The children's market, which has existed since the 1950s, is now expanding. Actually, this segment can be regarded as two markets: parents and the children themselves. Parents, particularly the parents of infants, want only the best to protect their children's sensitive skin. Dual-wage-earner couples who postponed parenthood now have more income to spend on their children and a willingness to invest at least as much on their children's skin and hair care products as they spend on their own.

A proliferation of sunscreens is part of the fashion industry's response to consumers' concern about protection from ultraviolet rays. Parents are now more aware of the dangers of excessive sun exposure, and products geared to infants and children constitute one of the most vibrant segments of the skin care business. Kimberly-Clark Corporation has extended its well-known Huggies Little Swimmers brand by launching a collection of three sunscreen lotions with the only patented self-adhesive sun sensors for measuring exposure to ultraviolet B (UVB) radiation, which causes sunburn.

Whatever influence children have on their parents' purchases is directed toward products that are fun. For two- to eight-year-olds, fun means bubble bath, lip balm, printed bandages, candy-flavored toothpaste, and licensed products featuring their favorite cartoon characters and television celebrities (Figure 14.13).

FIGURE 14.13 Cosmetics and fragrances for kids often come in fun packaging, with bright colors, sparkles, and popular celebrities or cartoon characters.

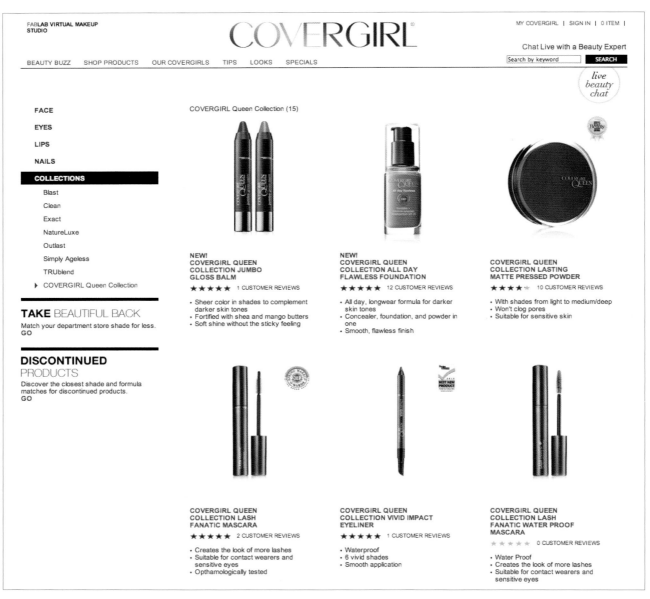

FIGURE 14.14 Cover Girl's Queen Collection designs cosmetics and skincare products specifically for multicultural women with different skin tones.

The Ethnic Market

The complexion of the U.S. population is changing as the birthrates for African Americans, Asian Americans, Hispanics, and Native Americans exceed that of Americans of European ancestry. As of 2012, the minority population under the age of five was nearly 50 percent. More than 36 percent of the total population of the United States is made up of African Americans, Asian Americans, and Hispanics. As a group, they represent $1.6 trillion in collective purchasing power. Recent research shows that ethnic consumers will soon replace baby boomers as a critical demographic in the United States.[21] Thus, retail sales to these groups are one of the fastest-growing segments of the beauty industry.

Differences in skin shades and tones and hair texture among African American women have stimulated the development of special products for this segment of the ethnic market. In the 1960s, companies such as Libra and Astarte pioneered in creating mass-market lines for black women. Another early pioneer, Flori Roberts, produced the first prestige cosmetic line for African Americans. Still a major force in the cosmetics industry, she also introduced the first fragrance within a black cosmetics line, initiated in-store seminars on careers for black women, and began in-store makeup demonstrations. According to research, African American women report spending 80 percent more on cosmetics and almost twice as much on skin care products than the general market.[22]

The multicultural market in the United States presents many opportunities for suppliers to increase their presence in categories as varied as personal care products, cosmetics, and fragrances (Figure 14.14). These are bound to grow as ethnic groups account for an increasingly larger share of the general public and have significant spending power as well. According to the NPD Group, more than three-quarters of women across ethnic groups currently use basic beauty products such as skin care, makeup, bath, and fragrances. According to Karen Grant, vice president and global beauty industry analyst for the NPD Groups:

> In beauty, the future is today—not in ten, twenty, or fifty years from now. Today's ethnic population is already exerting an impact across all beauty categories. That is a fact the beauty industry must recognize right now. And, just as all boomers cannot be lumped together and marketed as one homogeneous group, 'women of color' are diverse, rapidly changing, and defy generalization. To tap into the power of this ever-expanding group, beauty manufacturers and retailers must understand the nuances of differences and adapt strategies to be identified as 'for someone like me.' That is a key statement for leading brands that resonates well with these increasingly important groups of beauty consumers.[23]

The challenge that retailers and product marketers face in coming up with the right product mix and selling strategies is daunting. In the personal care product category, discount stores, chain drugstores, and supermarkets have been at the forefront of finding effective ways to reach them. Ethnic products, once comprising a relatively narrow niche, have now gotten the attention of large consumer product companies eager to capitalize on a growing market.

But, just as chain retailers are getting a firm handle on the ethnic mix of each store, consumers are throwing a wrench into micromarketing by buying items they like rather than those targeted to them. An example is HiP, from L'Oréal, which sources said was initially intended to reach women of color but which had such high appeal in testing that it was launched as a general market line.[24]

For retailers, the challenge now is to determine how to merchandise the blurred categories. Many retailers still want larger selections in stores with a high concentration of ethnic consumers. Others, however, are using these smaller brands as a way to provide shoppers with more choices. Many chains are open to taking on brands with more ethnic heritage and using these niche brands as a point of difference between competitors.

The Home Fragrances Market

The home fragrances market took a major hit during the recession in the twenty-first century. The good news is that the industry is expected to recover, bolstered by consumers' interest in the aromatic benefits of candles, along with potpourri, incense, and air fresheners.

FIGURE 14.15 As founder and CEO of Nest Fragrances, Jason Wu expanded his apparel designs to the home fragrances market, creating luxury-scented candles.

The public's growing awareness of fragrance is not restricted to personal use but includes use in their homes as well. Many consumers are gaining satisfaction from enhancing their environment and are taking in-home activities, such as gourmet cooking and home entertaining, more seriously.

Fashion designers were quick to pick up on the interest in environmental fragrances, and many have already produced scented candles, silk flowers, paperweights, and holiday gifts (Figure 14.15). The pioneer is Ralph Lauren, whose collection has been available since the late 1970s. Donna Karan, Oscar de la Renta, and Marc Jacobs also have designer home fragrance lines.

The green movement has candle manufacturers making consumer education a key marketing priority as arguments for or against the benefits of certain wax ingredients heat up the marketplace. A broadening of other home fragrance delivery methods, such as diffuser reeds, scented oils, and potpourri, also has many manufacturers vying for their share of the market.

Home fragrance today is as much an accessory to interior design as any piece of art, furniture, or lamp placed into a perfectly decorated room. It isn't the price point that matters, but rather how the home fragrance object will complement the environment. As we become aware that these little luxuries help improve our mood and help us to sleep better, the future for home fragrances is very bright.[25]

The Export Market

The export market for U.S. cosmetics has grown in recent years partly because the Westernization of much of the world has made the wearing of cosmetics acceptable. Until 1980, China had a law that banned the wearing of cosmetics, and in what was once the Soviet Union and its Eastern Bloc satellites, American products were hardly known until recently. That has all changed. Japan, China, Western Europe, and South America have emerged as strong markets for U.S. cosmetics and fragrances.

Fortunately, American cosmetics and fragrances usually need little or no adjustment in formulas and packaging in order to succeed in the international market. An exception is Japan, where cosmetics are basically treated the same as pharmaceuticals and require licensing for import and sale. The Japanese list of approved ingredients restricts some formulas and specifies strict labeling requirements. But in the rest of the world, American products have enough variety for marketers to edit their offering to suit the demands of their customers abroad. Superior ingredients, promotion, and distribution work as well abroad as at home, and American companies have the expertise and money to ensure that their products continue to be best sellers around the world.

The U.S. Commerce Department has promoted efforts by small cosmetics companies to export to the more affluent third-world countries where per capita expenditures on cosmetics products are growing rapidly. Direct distribution, private-label products produced for foreign firms, and licensing specialties for foreign production are considered the most productive prospects for this international market.

U.S. companies cashing in on the opening of the vast Chinese market to imported cosmetics include Revlon and direct sellers Avon and Amway. Hong Kong imported an estimated $316 million worth of cosmetics, toiletries, and skin care products from the United States in 2011.[26] As the infrastructure improves and the Chinese become more familiar with these foreign products, demand is expected to increase.

A trade bloc of Asian–Pacific nations is emerging as another potential major market because of the standardization of import rules and the invitation to the United States to join the bloc. In contrast, India, despite its dense population, substantial middle class, and a cosmetics market that is growing at a rate of between 15 and 20 percent per year, has proven to be tough for U.S. companies to break into.[27]

Merchandising and Marketing

The cosmetics and fragrance business is a highly visible one. Its products are used nearly every day by millions of people. In the prestige cosmetics market, competition for restricted distribution to quality department and specialty stores is keen. All of the prestige brand manufacturers want to sell their lines in the most prestigious store in each town. They offer these stores exclusives, specials, and cooperative advertising to guarantee that their products will receive prime locations. Limiting the doors where their products are available adds to the aura of exclusivity and uniqueness the manufacturer of each line wishes to convey to its target customers. Such merchandising techniques are used by most prestigious cosmetics brands, including Chanel, Estée Lauder, Elizabeth Arden, Clinique, Orlane, Lancôme, Borghese, and Ultima II.

Distribution

The structure of distribution techniques in the cosmetics area is both distinctive and complex, involving such elements as class versus mass distribution, limited versus popular distribution, mass-market distribution, and distribution limited to in-store salons. The use of behind-the-counter brand-line representatives or direct selling techniques is also popular in the cosmetics and fragrance industry.

Class Versus Mass

Another name for *class* is "franchise," so when industry insiders talk about "class versus mass," they mean franchise versus mass. In **franchise distribution**, the manufacturer or exclusive distributor sells directly to the ultimate retailer. No wholesalers, jobbers, diverters, rack jobbers, or intermediaries of any kind are involved. Each vending retailer is on the books of the manufacturer or distributor as a direct-receivable account. A good example of this is Estée Lauder, which sells directly to stores such as Neiman Marcus and Saks Fifth Avenue. In contrast, third-party vendors, such as wholesalers, diverters, and jobbers, play a role in mass distribution. These third parties may sell to any one of a number of retailers of any type. No control is exercised over these intermediaries. Manufacturers may not know their retailers. Furthermore, territory or other definable exclusivity does not run from manufacturer to retailer in mass distribution (see page 285) as it does in the franchise or class relationship. A good example of this is Revlon's line, which is sold in mass-merchandise outlets such as variety stores, drugstores, and chain stores.

Limited Versus Popular

The franchise cosmetics business is described as being either limited or popular in its distribution pattern. In the industry, any line distributed to more than 5,000 doors is considered popular; any line distributed to fewer than 5,000 doors is limited.

Counter Brand-Line Representatives

Since a need exists to inform and educate cosmetics customers about the many products that are available to them, prestige cosmetics companies place their own **brand-line representatives** behind the counter as line salespeople. These line salespeople, also called *beauty counselors*, are well equipped to perform this important function. They are trained in the end-use of the hundreds of items carried in each specific line. In many instances, the salaries of these salespeople are paid by the cosmetics company directly. Sometimes, in an arrangement called **joint merchandising**, the store shares in the payment of their salaries. These salespeople are also responsible for stocking inventory. They keep detailed records that show what items are and are not selling. The cosmetics companies constantly keep their brand salespeople informed about new items, new colors, and new promotions through updated training and materials. As might be expected, the limited-door stores have the best-trained salespeople.

Mass-Market Distribution

The **mass-distribution** cosmetics market involves drugstores, discount stores, variety stores, and large national chains such as Sears and J.C. Penney. The volume of business done in these stores is growing. As they have become increasingly interested in distribution to these types of retail outlets, large cosmetics companies have planned and implemented new merchandising activities. Until a few years ago, the mass-distribution outlets were limited to selling lines such as Cover Girl, Maybelline, or a store's own label line. Now large, nationally advertised brands such as Max Factor and Revlon have introduced their medium-priced lines into these outlets, enabling customers to select products more easily and thus increase sales. Mass-market retailers are turning to open-access display systems and mass-marketing displays. Sephora is an example of a beauty-retail company that sells classic and emerging brands across a variety of product categories, including skin care, makeup, fragrance, and hair care, in addition to Sephora's own private label (Figure 14.16).[28]

In-Store Salons

In-store salons that provide a full range of hair, skin, and body services are another trend. Customers can now obtain specialized advice and beauty care right on the department-store floor from such lines as Lancôme, Clinique, Orlane, Payot, and Adrien Arpel. In-store salons have helped to introduce American women to the beauty routines long favored by European women, and in turn, the products and regimens have been simplified to fit in with Americans' fast-paced lives. Regimens will become increasingly personalized as computers tailor them to individual customer's needs.

FIGURE 14.16 Make Up For Ever and Benefit have a shop-in-shop in Sephora.

Direct Selling

A few companies sell their products to consumers only through individual or group presentations by their own salespeople. Three well-known examples are Avon, Mary Kay, and BeautiControl.

Advertising and Sales Promotion

National advertising budgets of cosmetics companies are immense, especially in comparison to sales. Fierce competition for retail shelf space forces companies to spend millions annually to support a single fragrance line, even more if it is a new product. And national advertising is not the only type of sales promotion in which a company must engage.

The expense of promotion and advertising is well worth the effort. A campaign combining direct mail, television, and print exposure often results in three times the usual amount of business generated by a particular product in any given week.

Television is still a vital medium for cosmetics that are sold by mail or phone order. Extended broadcast advertising is accomplished on QVC and the Home Shopping Network, which experienced a nearly 20 percent growth in sales between 2005 and 2010.[29] Infomercials on cable channels have also led to big sales for brands such as Proactiv, Sheer Cover, and Hydroxatone. Magazine ads continue to be the traditional way of reaching a targeted segment of the cosmetics market, while many retail store catalogs regularly push beauty products in their catalogs. According to research firm Kline & Company, brands for cosmetics and toiletries are rapidly moving ahead in the game with their social and mobile strategies. While they are experimenting with various social media platforms to create new consumer relations opportunities, they are not yet dropping traditional marketing efforts.[30]

Premiums

An extensive publicity campaign is often mounted to introduce new products, and they are usually promoted by celebrities. Many companies also use **premiums**, a gift-with-purchase or a purchase-with-purchase offer, to promote their products. This is a concept that originated with Estée Lauder. These premiums range from samples of products to cosmetic "paint boxes," umbrellas, tote bags, scarfs, and even small duffel bags.

Direct Mail

Because of the breadth and depth of its reach, many stores are finding direct mail one of the most successful forms of advertising for both promotions and regular-priced cosmetics. Another advantage to the store is that direct mail campaigns are generally vendor-funded. The most common formats are order forms in four-color vendor mailers, bill insertion leaflets, and remittance envelope stubs. Estimates of sales volume from mail-order average about 2 to 3 percent of all cosmetics sales per year.

Scent and Color Strips

Another promotional tool that has gained a foothold in the cosmetics industry is the use of scent and color strips, sometimes as bill insertions, but more often as part of a company's advertisement in a magazine. Scent and color strips allow consumers to experiment with new eyeshadow colors or try out new fragrances in the privacy of their own homes. Much to the relief of people who are ultrasensitive to odors, scent samples, liquids, and creams can be encapsulated so that they must be opened before the smell is released. Multiple-color samples can also be sealed under a plastic patch that peels away.

Digital Technology

A number of cosmetics companies offer the assistance of technology to give customers personalized advice when shopping for beauty products. Clinique was the first cosmetics brand to use Apple's iPad and Microsoft's Surface in stores. These tools, along with specialized software for Clinique, help consumers identify skin care concerns. With a ninety-second computer-guided analysis, the customer can find products that best suit their needs. The Clinique Experience Bar also allows shoppers to try samples, expedite checkout, and share their virtual browsing basket on Facebook. These advancements not only help customers locate the best products, but they also allow for a more enjoyable shopping experience (Figure 14.17).[31] Less elaborate programs prepare a collection of cosmetics for a customer according to information about her coloring and skin type.

E-Commerce

Between 2005 and 2012, the sales of cosmetics and toiletries via e-commerce sites grew by more than 25 percent.[32] Virtually every cosmetics and fragrance company now has its own website and a presence on social media sites such as Facebook and Twitter to promote and sell its products, as well as offer information about company history, promotions, and locations of retailers.

Daily deal and "flash sale" sites such as Groupon, LivingSocial, HauteLook, Rue La La, and Gilt Groupe have also helped boost online sales. They offer shoppers exclusive deals and discounts that are usually only available for a very limited time—often only a matter of days or hours.

FIGURE 14.17 Clinique Experience Bar uses technology to help customers choose and buy their beauty products.

Trade Associations, Shows, and Publications

The Personal Care Products Council is a major cosmetics trade association. Its membership includes more than 600 companies throughout the cosmetics, toiletries, and fragrance industries. The council coordinates the industry commitment to scientific and quality standards (Figure 14.18). It is the industry vehicle for information exchange about scientific developments among association members, consumers, and those who regulate the industry at federal, state, and local government levels. The council also keeps members informed on government regulations and offers advice on interpretation and compliance. Through its website (personalcarecouncil.org), the council offers members access to government agencies, product safety resources, international trade organizations, and the sites of other members.

Another helpful organization is the Fragrance Foundation in New York (www.fragrance.org), founded in 1949. Manufacturers, suppliers, designers, packagers, retailers, and media and public relations personnel who are involved in the industry are members. The Fragrance Foundation maintains a library of print and video materials and publishes industry reports and educational and sales training materials. It sponsors National Fragrance Week in June and honors fragrances and their designers with FiFi Awards. The

FIGURE 14.18 CosmeticsInfo.org is an information website that includes factual and scientific information on ingredients most commonly used in cosmetics and personal care products in the United States. It is sponsored by The Personal Care Products Council and its members.

Fragrance Foundation also sponsors a program at the Fashion Institute of Technology (FIT), in New York City. It includes mentoring, an internship program, and placement assistance.

International trade shows bring together visitors and exhibitors from all facets of the cosmetics and fragrance industry—manufacturers, suppliers, packagers, retailers, and advertising and promotion specialists. The largest trade show in the United States is the HBA Global Expo, held in the Jacob K. Javits Center in New York. The mammoth Cosmoprof holds trade shows in Bologna, Hong Kong, and Las Vegas; Cosmoprof is the perfect occasion to launch a new line in front of the entire worldwide industry, and many producers do so.

Industry Trends

The cosmetics and fragrance industry continues to accelerate globally. In the United States, sales of skin care products are expected to grow at a fast pace, due to an older and more affluent population and the increasing popularity of men's products.

The market for fragrance will remain strong, in part because of the steadily increasing number of working women, who prefer a lighter fragrance when at work to the heavy perfumes they may wear in the evening. The concept of a **fragrance wardrobe** to suit the various roles a woman (or man) assumes is being promoted and has boosted demand. Men are also adapting (though more slowly) to the idea of one fragrance for the office, another for sports, and another for evening.

Four other sectors predicted to continue solid growth include: (1) antiaging products, (2) antibacterial and antiallergenic products, (3) aromatherapy products, and (4) spa products.

Antiaging Products

In 1996, when the oldest members of the baby boomer generation turned 50, they raced to the cosmetics counter for skin care products to ward off or lessen the appearance of wrinkles. About the same time, laboratory tests confirmed the effectiveness of AHAs for this purpose, and the FDA decided to regulate AHAs as cosmetics rather than as drugs.

Today, America's quest for youth continues. According to recent research conducted by the NPD Group, 75 percent of women use "skin care products to look the best they can for their age."[33]

Aging consumers, particularly female baby boomers, are still the primary force driving sales in the antiaging treatment market. But baby boomer women aren't the only ones driving the growth. Younger women seeking preventative solutions and men who consider antiaging as a regular aspect of their grooming routine also are fueling sales. In a survey conducted by *Prevention* magazine, 35 percent of women in their twenties reported that they were willing to pay a premium for skin care products that had antiaging benefits (Figure 14.19).[34]

Antibacterial and Antiallergenic Products

Antibacterial and antiallergenic cleansing products have been available in both mass-merchandised and prestige lines for a long time, and the market for these products continues to grow. Almay and Clinique exemplify the two ends of the market. Functional cosmetics and targeting beauty from the inside are among the fastest-growing segments in the cosmetics and nutraceuticals market, with antiaging, antiwrinkle, and anticellulite among the top claims made for many products containing a variety of mostly natural substances. As natural and organic beauty items continue to make their way onto the beauty scene, items bearing the U.S. Department of Agriculture organic seal have launched in stores, including items by Origins and Nature's Gate.

What makes these launches so newsworthy is that each brand was able to concoct formulas for lotions worthy of the seal. Mass retailers acknowledge the importance of separating natural and organic items from mainstream items in order to demonstrate their point of difference. Stores such as Target, Whole Foods,

FIGURE 14.19 Dove offers antiaging products that keep skin soft and free of wrinkles, while also taking a more positive approach toward aging.

TABLE 14.4 *The Effects of Scents*

SCENT	EFFECT
Spiced apple, lavender	Lower blood pressure, ward off panic attacks, reduce stress
Plum, peach	Reduce pain
Jasmine, green apple	Lift depression
Geranium	Dispels anxiety
Peppermint, lemon	Restore energy
Chamomile, rose, vanilla	Relax the spirit
Cloves, cinnamon, oriental spices	Increase sensuality
Seashore, cucumber	Combat claustrophobia
Floral scent	Promotes faster puzzle-solving

LAVENDER CHAMOMILE PEPPERMINT

Source: Renee Covino Rouland, "The Bath and Shower Experience," *Discount Merchandiser*; and Maxine Wilkie, "Scent of a Market," *American Demographics*.

Walgreens, Duane Reade, CVS, and Longs are planning to showcase their natural and organic ingredient items separately.[35]

Aromatherapy Products

Aromatherapy involves fragrant oils distilled from plants, herbs, and flowers; these oils have been used for centuries to stimulate or relax. So important has the study of the physiological effects of fragrance on humans become that Annette Green, former executive director of the Fragrance Foundation, coined the term *aromachology* to describe the modern, research-based phenomenon. Dr. Alan Hirsch of the Smell and Taste Treatment and Research Foundation in Chicago explains that specific feelings can be transmitted through odor because the olfactory nerve of the nose attaches directly to the limbic system of the brain, which influences emotions, memory, hormone secretion, appetite, and sexuality. This connection explains the association of smells with memories of people and places. Some scents that promote emotional responses and behaviors are listed in Table 14.4. Notice that food scents are especially influential.

The fragrance industry uses this research in the development of home fragrances, and that segment of the market has consequently been thriving. The association that actively promotes aromatherapy research is the Sense of Smell Institute.

Spa Products

The ultimate indulgence in personal care is a visit to a health spa. The word *spa* originally referred to a European institution built around a thermal spring, where doctors sent the chronically ill for treatments lasting weeks. Today, spas are springing up in health clubs, department stores, and beauty salons across the country, where they offer treatments lasting a day or a few hours (Figure 14.20). Most **spas** offer a wide range of services, including massages, manicures, pedicures, waxings, and facials, which often are combined with aromatherapy. In addition, one can, for a price ranging from $20 to more than $300, be completely covered in a body wrap, which is thought to cleanse and heal the skin and relax the body. In a **body wrap**, herbs, seaweed, or mud is applied directly to the body, which is then wrapped like a mummy to allow the substances to penetrate the pores. In a similar procedure, the wrapping cloths are soaked in the substances and then wrapped around the body. Body wraps date back to biblical times and came to America by way of Europe, where

FIGURE 14.20 Bliss spas offer a full range of facial and body treatments, as well as shops that allow the spa-goer to take a bit of "bliss" home with her or him.

they have been popular for centuries. The muds and other substances used in spa products still have many of the same sources, like the famed Dead Sea salts. The experts who administer these therapies and the special equipment available at spas give them an aura of alternative medicine, providing a rationale for the consumer's investment. Spa products fit in with the trend in cosmetics toward products that promote the health of the skin.

Treatments with fango, a mud rich in minerals, are popular, as are exfoliation treatments, which remove dead cells, smooth the skin, and promote circulation. Anticellulite treatments are frequently available. Many spas also offer **thalassotherapy**, which involves seawater, seaweed, or sea algae and is believed to hydrate and rejuvenate the skin.

Reflections of Trends

The focus of the beauty industry echoes trends in other segments of the fashion industry. Newly popular beauty products respond to the same trends as apparel and accessories, as the examples in Table 14.5 show.

Summary and Review

Over the past few decades, beauty products have proliferated in the global marketplace, sparked by advances in science and technology. Today's consumer selects products not only for its ingredients, but also for its packaging, its promotion, and where it can be bought.

TABLE 14.5 *Fashion Trends in Apparel and Accessories to Beauty*

TREND	APPAREL AND ACCESSORIES	BEAUTY
Health and fitness	Activewear, workout apparel, summer hats, and sunglasses to protect from sun's rays	Skin care products, spas and spa products, sun-protection products, hypoallergenic and antiaging products
Casual lifestyle	Dress-down Fridays and informal office dress codes	Light fragrances, light makeup for no-makeup look
Individuality	Easing of business dress codes, mix-and-match separates, size lines for different figure types, and custom-fit jeans	Light fragrances, light makeup for no-makeup look
Internationalism	International corporations and conglomerates, global marketing, marketing on the Internet, breakdown of trade barriers, international sourcing	Same as apparel and accessories
Multiculturalism	Adaptation of ethnic themes by designers; textiles and patterns from around the world; Native American, Indian, and African jewelry and other accessories	Ethnic cosmetics lines, ethnic hair care products and hairstyles (hair extensions, dreadlocks), shiatsu, reflexology, and thalassotherapy

Some stores are perceived as having higher status, and therefore many product lines are sold only in these types of stores, through a manufacturer's own sales force, through direct mail, or on the Internet.

The main categories in this industry are fragrance, color cosmetics, skin care, sun care, and nail care. The increasingly global nature of the industry will most likely mean increased regulation in the coming decades. Also, environmental concerns like animal testing, recyclable packaging, and natural or botanical ingredients are leading to higher industry standards worldwide.

As the industry continues to expand, new market segments beyond the traditional women's market have attracted increased attention. These segments include the male market, the teen market, the children's market, the ethnic market, the home fragrances market, and the export market.

Trends in beauty follow those in apparel and accessories, and bear close attention. The major trends include antiaging, antibacterial, natural, antiallergenic, aromatherapy, and spa products. The male and ethnic markets are also expected to continue to thrive.

For Review

1. How do the heads of the major cosmetics and fragrance firms today differ from their predecessors in the first decades of the twentieth century?
2. What distinguishes perfume from cologne and toilet water?
3. How does the beauty industry relate to the ready-to-wear industry?
4. Summarize the Food and Drug Administration's laws in regard to cosmetics.
5. Where are the international growth opportunities for beauty producers?
6. Describe the products of the home fragrance market.
7. Outline the major distribution methods used by the cosmetics industry.
8. Describe the various advertising and promotion activities currently engaged in by the beauty industry.
9. Identify the major professional organizations of the beauty industry and describe their activities.
10. Briefly discuss the most significant trends in beauty products today.

For Discussion

1. Discuss current trends in the beauty industry as they relate to: (a) mergers, (b) diversification of product lines, and (c) global marketing.
2. Discuss the recent growth in men's cosmetics and ethnic cosmetics lines.
3. Cosmetics salespersons, or brand-line representatives, exercise much more control over the products carried in their stock than do salespeople in other departments in a store. Discuss the system used and its advantages and disadvantages.

Trade Talk

Define or briefly explain the following terms:

alpha hydroxy acids (AHAs)
aromatherapy
body wrap
brand-line representatives
color cosmetics
copycat scent
cosmetic
fragrance
fragrance wardrobe
franchise distribution
home fragrances
joint merchandising
mass distribution
note
premiums
private-label manufacturers
rubber-banding
spa
thalassotherapy

Chapter Fifteen
HOME FASHIONS

KEY CONCEPTS

- History of the home furnishings industries
- Organization, operation, and product categories of soft goods and tabletop goods industries
- Market segments of the home fashions industry
- Market centers and resources of the home fashions industry
- Fashion influences in the home fashions industry
- Technological advancements and the home fashions industry

I t is said that your home is your castle. Whether that home is a spacious, sprawling mansion or just one room that you can call your own, it is your space. It is a place to relax, be solitary, entertain friends, and establish an environment that supports your lifestyle. Therefore, creating a sanctuary that you look forward to coming home to has become the dream of people in the twenty-first century (Figure 15.1).

As Americans spend more time at home, they are also spending more of their money on home decorating—and redecorating—and less on their personal wardrobes. This trend is especially apparent in the dominant markets segment for fashion goods—baby boom women. So fashion designers, textile manufacturers, and retailers are turning their attention to the home furnishings and home accessories business. **Home fashions** is the umbrella term used frequently today to describe the two fashion-driven industries that have

long been called *home furnishings* and *home accessories*. In this text, we use all three terms, since that is what you will see and hear in the field.

In this market, fashion exerts its greatest influence in the **soft goods** lines, including bed, bath, and table linens; curtains and draperies; upholstery fabric; and area rugs; and in the **tabletop** categories of dinnerware, glassware, flatware, hollowware, and giftware (Figure 15.2). (Furniture, electronic equipment, home appliances, and wall-to-wall carpeting have slower fashion cycles; these items are typically one-time purchases or long-term investments.)

A serious problem for both manufacturers and retailers of home furnishings is the vast amount of product knowledge required to sell these products. The challenge of sales staff education is a great one; the most successful manufacturers share the burden with retailers by providing extensive sales aids.

FIGURE 15.1 Home fashions reflect your personality and style just as much as how you dress.

History of the Home Furnishings Industries

The types of furnishings and household accessories in contemporary American homes are based primarily on models and ideas that the early European immigrants brought with them. Most of our beds and eating utensils, for example, are Western. But many of the fabrics and other material, the decorative patterns, and the objects themselves originated in the East and came to America *through* rather than *from* Europe. The rugs that covered the floors in medieval European castles were imported by the crusaders, and when later Europeans established their own rug factories, the designs evolved from patterns developed in Turkey, Persia, India, and China. China was also the source of the finest quality of clay for ceramic dinnerware. Before there were Wedgwood and Royal Doulton potteries in England, British nobles imported their custom-designed dinnerware with the family crest from China through the British East India Company.

The Role of Linen

From ancient times, linen was used in the Middle East and Europe for clothing and bedding. When medieval Europeans began sitting at a table for meals rather than reclining, they wiped their hands on remnants of linen cloth covering the table. The association of linen with sheets, tablecloths, and towels was so strong that even today, when these household accessories are usually made of other textiles, we still refer to them as bed, table, and bath linens. The history of tabletop goods is more varied than that of linen and so is discussed under each category.

The Evolution of Global Home Fashions

Travelers since Marco Polo have brought home examples of native crafts and handwork to beautify their homes and impress their friends. Today, materials, designs, and finished goods move simultaneously in both directions between East and West and beyond. African kente cloth patterns appear on American bed linens; **sisal** from Brazil and Tanzania is imported into the United States for rugs; Japanese apartments feature Western rooms; and Americans buy their bedding from specialized futon shops. Home fashions retain their distinctive local character, but they are enjoyed in homes far from their point of origin.

Organization and Operation of the Industries

Manufacturers of soft goods and tabletop merchandise can be found all across the country. Their showrooms, however, are centered in New York, like the showrooms for other categories of fashion merchandise. And as in other fashion businesses, the home fashions industry involves the widespread and growing use of licensing agreements.

Soft Goods Manufacturers

As the United States grew from an agricultural nation to a vast industrialized one, textile mills and manufacturers of textile home furnishing products were

FIGURE 15.2 Choices of dinnerware, glassware, and flatware can make a table more vibrant, such as this look by Diane von Furstenberg.

established in the cotton-growing South. The major American textile mills are also the largest manufacturers of goods produced from their fabrics. Some mills specialize in apparel textiles and products or in home furnishing textiles and products, and others manufacture both.

Because household linens are essentially flat sheets of cloth, they require little work beyond the manufacturing of the textiles, perhaps hemming or the addition of decorative trim. Bedspreads, comforters, blankets, and curtains are also manufactured by the same vertically integrated companies and may be coordinated with bed or bathroom linens. Similarly, area rugs are often manufactured by carpet mills.

Tabletop Manufacturers

The fashion influence on the marketing of household linens and other soft goods for the home is also apparent in the hard lines of home furnishings. Everything from furniture to kitchen appliances has a fashion cycle. Our discussion focuses on the categories of tabletop goods because the role of fashion is most apparent in these segments of the home furnishings industry. From the time the medieval Europeans began to use forks instead of fingers, the basic items in a table setting have not changed significantly in function. Design criteria drive the consumer's buying decision. Today, when home entertaining has become a widespread leisure-time activity, the selection of fashionable tabletop goods is part of the fun.

Because the three categories of tabletop goods—dinnerware, glassware, and flatware—are used together, manufacturers in each category have grown through expansion as well as mergers and acquisitions into the other categories. Some large firms also include companies or divisions that produce table linens and products outside of the home furnishings industry. For example, Lenox, the leading U.S. manufacturer of china dinnerware, also produces crystal and giftware. There is no single geographic center in the United States or elsewhere for these companies that manufacture so many different products.

The economic recession also played a role in mergers and acquisitions in the 2000s. In addition to dealing with economic woes, the industry has also grappled with changing consumer attitudes. While entertaining at home remains popular, consumers are now less interested in formal tabletop products. This attitude shift has caused the industry to focus more on functional and giftable products.[1]

Other leading tabletop manufacturers include Fitz and Floyd, Lifetime Brands (Mikasa and Pfaltzgraff),

Villeroy & Boch, and Ralph Lauren. The Homer Laughlin China Company is the largest china manufacturer in the United States. Its Fiesta product line, created in 1936, is one of the most collected china products in the world. Today, it comes in thirty-eight colors, with one new color produced each year.[2] Dozens of the company's other patterns are sold through retail outlets and to numerous restaurants, hotels, and institutions.

Popular imports of tabletop products include WWRD (Wedgwood, Waterford, and Royal Doulton) and the Portmeirion Group (Portmeirion, Spode, Royal Worcester, and Pimpernel) in the United Kingdom. Limoges, Lalique, Baccarat, and Cristal d'Arques are famous French manufacturers. Orrefors crystal from Sweden is world famous. In Italy, Silvestri and Bormioli Rocco e Figlio produce beautiful glassware. Versace and Armani, also from Italy, have a large collection of tabletop products, in addition to their world-famous apparel collections. Rosenthal and Meissen glassware and china come from Germany, while Noritake, Sango, and Morimura are very popular lines from Japan.

Licensing

Designer names are not the only commodity licensed in the home furnishings industry. Colonial Williamsburg presents an example of the stringent conditions of licensing by a cultural institution.

Character licensing is the main form of licensing in the industries that manufacture tabletop goods, and most of the licensed characters appear on lines of dinnerware and glassware for children. Not surprisingly, Disney rules in the licensing of animated movie stars for glasses and dinnerware, as it does for sheets. The marketing campaigns for children's movies typically include a three- to six-month selling period for related merchandise, and the release of the movie in DVD form may add to the life of these products. In addition to sales through conventional retail channels, glassware featuring characters from movies and children's television shows is given away as promotional items by fast-food chains. Classic Disney characters—Mickey, Minnie, Donald, and friends—and classic literary characters like Winnie the Pooh have longer careers as licensed decorations.

Designing a Soft Goods Line

To meet and encourage the demand of cocooning consumers, manufacturers are designing coordinated lines of bedroom accessories. Sheets and pillowcases match or complement bed covers and window treatments; bath linen sets may also be coordinated with the bedroom lines. These fashionable products generate replacement sales long before the replaced items wear out. However, the soft goods fashion cycle is slower than the apparel fashion cycle, lasting years rather than seasons. New colors and designs may be introduced annually or in two seasonal showings, but previous years' fashions are not totally replaced by new offerings. Some lines stop selling only when the producer discontinues them.

The need for color forecasting for home accessories is a twentieth-century phenomenon. Earlier, bed linens were undyed, then they were bleached white, and finally colors and prints began to come on the market. Since the 1990s, the color cycle has been reduced from ten-year periods of recent decades to colors remaining fashionable for just a few years. Ironically, environmentalism has made the neutral hues of undyed textiles one of the hottest new color trends. Trends in color are monitored and predicted by organizations such as the Color Association of the United States and the International Colour Authority and by companies such as the Color Marketing Group.

The success of a new line of household linens depends on accurate forecasting of fashions in prints, weaves, and fabrics, as well as color, and on production processes that ensure timely availability. With computers, textile designers can create decorative prints or translate their hand-drawn designs into repeated patterns. Computer-aided design (CAD) programs allow designers to produce a print design in several color combinations, thereby expanding their lines at a minimal increase in cost. CAD programs even produce decorative stitching patterns for quilts and instruct computerized quilting machines in how to sew them more quickly and accurately than conventional equipment can.

Other consumer demands that manufacturers must consider in designing a line include finishes that enhance the products for their intended purposes. For example, table linens may be treated for stain resistance, and wool carpeting may be treated for protection from mildew, molds, and moths. Filling for pillows and comforters can be treated with chemicals that protect allergy sufferers from bacteria and dust mites. Techniques for decorating linens with print patterns affect the feel—and price—of sheets and bath and kitchen towels.

The demand by ecology-minded consumers for natural products has given rise to lines of 100 percent cotton bed and bath linens not treated with the bleaches that normally set dyes or the formaldehyde in permanent-press finishes. These natural features create a fashion statement with their characteristic limited palette and wrinkles. There are two fronts on which home textiles product developers can best appeal to consumers: environmentally friendly goods and technology. A few items are beginning to appear that claim to employ nanotechnology in their fibers, but for the most part, there is no evidence of how that technology improves the product in a significant and perceivable way. Time to put on your thinking caps, home fashions industry. Here are a few ideas that could really make a difference. What about a comforter or a sheet that could change patterns? What about a reactive window panel that could help heat or cool a room? What about an area rug that could shift sizes? What about a bath towel that could warm itself up?

Importance of Name Designers

Whether the entry of apparel designers into the home furnishings industry made it a fashion business, or if instead consumer interest in home decorating lured the designers into the home accessories market, is a chicken-or-egg question. The important fact is that home fashions from name designers satisfy a consumer need. The designer's name on the label is assurance of a consistent look that the consumer recognizes from the designer's apparel lines (Figure 15.3). This is true even though the designer's involvement may be limited to providing—or merely approving—the print patterns and colors. Many licensing agreements leave textile selection and other production decisions, as well as the marketing plan, to the manufacturer.

Bill Blass was the first major American apparel designer to design a home fashions line in the 1960s. Laura Ashley followed in the 1970s, and Ralph Lauren in the 1980s. Since then, Ralph Lauren has become the largest supplier of sheets, towels, and pillows to department stores. A number of designers have followed, among them Calvin Klein, Liz Claiborne, Ellen Tracy, Donna Karan, Tommy Hilfiger, Josie Natori, and Vera Wang.

Importance of Brand Names

If a designer's name conjures up a particular fashion image, brand names suggest other qualities that consumers also consider when they shop, such as textile selections and price points. The major textile mills that produce household linens are known to the public primarily by the brand names of their sheets and towels because consumers buy these end products more than they buy curtains, upholstery fabric, or bolts of fabric for home sewing.

FIGURE 15.3 Designer labels such as Oscar de la Renta have made their way into the home fashions market.

FROM SUPERMODELS TO ENTREPRENEURS

FASHION DESIGNERS HAVE long had a big influence on the soft goods section of home fashions. Bill Blass, Ralph Lauren, and Donna Karan were some of the first fashion designers to design for the home. But do you have to be a fashion designer to be successful in designing home fashions? Absolutely not! Two of today's most successful designers of home decor are women who made their names as fashion models: Cindy Crawford and Kathy Ireland.

Cindy Crawford started modeling in the late 1980s and by 1995 was named the highest-paid model on the planet by *Forbes* magazine. Over the next decade, she began to shift her professional focus away from modeling and toward other endeavors, including home fashion design. In 2005 the world saw the launch of The Cindy Crawford Home Collection, a furniture line that grosses more than $250 million annually. She followed up that success with Cindy Crawford Style, a partnership with J.C. Penney that includes bedding, bath, table linens, window treatments, dinnerware, lighting, decorative accessories, and outdoor furniture.

Kathy Ireland has also found success beyond the world of modeling. Famous for appearing in the swimsuit issue of *Sports Illustrated* every year between 1984 and 1996, she founded her design and marketing firm, kathy ireland Worldwide (kiWW), in 1993. As Chair, CEO, and Chief Designer, Ireland has declared her company's mission: "Finding solutions for families, especially busy moms." Through her company, she licenses her name to more than 15,000 different products that include home decor items ranging from leather sofas and window treatments to floor lamps and ceiling fans. This effort has certainly paid off—in 2011, annual sales for kiWW reached $1.9 billion, making Ireland a bigger licensor than even Martha Stewart.

FASHION FOCUS

Cindy Crawford and the Cindy Crawford Home Collection

Store brand names are also influential. When the Federated Department Stores conglomerate took over Macy's, one of the major attractions of the acquisition was Macy's expertise in marketing its private brands, such as the Charter Club brand of apparel and home accessories. By circumventing the middleman, retailers can sell their private brands for a lower price than they sell comparable brand-name merchandise, even virtually identical goods manufactured by the same supplier. And the exclusivity of the private brand builds store loyalty.

Two high-end European manufacturers of bed linens are Porthault, of France, and Pratesi, of Italy. Pratesi has nine "salons" in the United States, where a king-size sheet of Egyptian cotton sells for $3,000!

Designing a Tabletop Line

Tabletop goods respond to the same trends that affect other segments of the home furnishings industry and other fashion industries. Producers rely on resources such as the Color Marketing Group for forecasts of color, design themes, and other changing consumer preferences. This information leads to the introduction of new patterns and sometimes the discontinuation of old ones. Public interest in ecology, combined with the promotion of gardening by Martha Stewart and others, has given rise to the decoration of tabletop products with floral patterns and gardening themes.

Producers also base technical production decisions and the allocation of resources to particular product categories on their analyses of trends in the marketplace. When consumers are cautious about investing in high-ticket purchases, manufacturers may promote giftware items and introduce more new pieces in that category rather than focusing on lines of formal china dinnerware or sterling flatware. Another strategy, exemplified in the manufacturing of dinnerware, is to improve productivity and reduce costs through technological advances. A heat transfer process for applying multicolor decorations to ceramic wares has enabled manufacturers to offer a more salable product in moderately priced lines.

Importance of Brand Names

Although manufacturers of tabletop goods produce a variety of products, many of the larger firms are associated with the category that was their initial specialty. Indeed, some names conjure up a particular segment of a category or even the name of a pattern. The name Wedgwood is so closely identified with its most famous design that the background color is called Wedgwood blue (Figure 15.4).

FIGURE 15.4 Wedgwood blue punchbowl, 1928.

Some manufacturers capitalize on their image in one home accessories category by developing coordinated or complementary lines in related categories. Waterford used its reputation for fine lead crystal to gain entry into the market for table linens. It has produced lines at different price points to attract different market segments. At the high end are lines for collectors of its glassware; and for newlyweds who want to own something with the Waterford name, the lower-priced lines are affordable. Lalique (glassware and jewelry) and Puiforcat (handcrafted silverware) also entered the dinnerware market and offer glassware, flatware, and porcelain lines.

Product Categories of Selected Soft Goods

Textile fabrics and other materials, such as fur, leather, straw, cork, paper, and metal wire, are used to decorate walls, floors, windows, and furniture. We focus on the seven main categories of soft goods that bring fashion to the home interior wardrobe (Table 15.1).

TABLE 15.1 *Major Categories of Soft Goods*

Category	Examples
Bed linens	Sheets, pillowcases, bed covers, blankets, pillows
Bath linens	Towels, washcloths, floor coverings
Table linens	Tablecloths, napkins, placemats
Window treatments	Curtains, shades, blinds, valences
Upholstery fabric	Slipcovers, pillows
Miscellaneous	Throws, kitchen towels, appliance covers
Area rugs	Scatter rugs, runners

FIGURE 15.5 Bed linens are one of the most frequently purchased categories of home accessories, and the coordination of sheets and pillowcases encourage replacement purchases.

Bed Linens

For several reasons, bed linens, especially sheets and pillowcases, are one of the most frequently purchased categories of home accessories (Figure 15.5). For a weekly change of freshly laundered sheets and pillowcases, a stock of three sets is recommended: one set on the bed, one in the wash, and one in the closet. Furthermore, a change of bedding is a relatively inexpensive way to achieve a dramatic change in the look of a room, especially if the colors and patterns of various items are mixed and matched. Buying a new bed often means buying new bed linens to fit—for example, when a baby outgrows its crib or adults in the family opt for a larger bed. New mattresses, which may be as thick as fourteen inches, may require new fitted sheets and mattress pads with more generous corner pockets than the bedding designed for older eight-inch-thick mattresses.

Although linen and even silk are used for luxury sheets, most sheets are made of cotton/polyester blends or cotton of a tight, smooth weave called percale. Two criteria are used to judge their quality: thread count and cotton content. Thread count refers to the number of threads per square inch. A higher count indicates a finer, softer sheet. Thread counts range from 180 to numbers higher than 1,000; 200 is considered standard. When it comes to thread count, quality is more important than quantity. Designer Charlotte Moss says:

I feel about thread count the way I feel about SPF. After a certain number, does it really matter? What you're paying for at a Porthault [a purveyor of luxury French linens], for example, isn't just the high thread count—it's the prestige and their beautiful, exclusive patterns, materials, and embroidery.[3]

Cotton/polyester blends are common in mass-merchandised sheets and offer a no-iron finish and moderate price, but 100 percent cotton is preferred for its softness. Pima cotton sheets are woven with at least 8 percent of a high-quality cotton fiber from Arizona. Supima sheets are made of 100 percent pima cotton. The finest cotton for sheets and pillowcases is imported Egyptian cotton. In harsh winter climates, soft flannel (cotton brushed to raise the nap) sheets are often used for additional warmth.

There are many subcategories of bed linens, including sheets, pillowcases, bedcovers, blankets, and pillows. Some of the latest fashions involve the choice of bed covers. Replacing bedspreads with a cozier, less formal look are quilts, comforters, and duvets. The **duvet** (pronounced doo-VAY), a down-filled quilt in a cover, can serve as an all-in-one top sheet, comforter, blanket, and decorative covering. Some bedding sets include coordinated sheets and pillowcases, pillow shams (covers that go over the pillowcase when the bed is not in use), a duvet cover, and a dust ruffle or bed skirt (which tucks between the mattress and box spring and hangs to the floor). Sets of coordinated sheets, pillowcases, comforter, shams, and dust ruffle, called Bed-in-a-Bag, were introduced by Dan River; customers responded enthusiastically to the convenience of this product.

Sheets and pillowcases are sized to fit standard-size mattresses and pillows. Note that a **California king** is an extra-long, extra-wide sheet, and that an extra-long twin sheet is the size usually found in dorm rooms.

A version of traditional Japanese bedding has been adapted to Western use and sizing. In Japan, where people remove their shoes upon entering a home and floors are covered with thick tatami mats, bedding is placed on the tatami for sleeping and rolled up for storage during the day. A densely filled futon serves as a mattress and a top futon as a comforter. The Western version, the heavier bottom or mattress futon, is often sold with a hinged wooden frame. For sleeping, the futon is placed on the flat frame. The frame can be folded, and the futon draped over the back and seat, to convert the bed into a couch.

Bath Linens

The most distinctive characteristic of bath linens is the cotton terry cloth that is used for virtually all towels. The loop construction of the threads creates a spongy fabric that holds water, thus enhancing the natural absorbency of cotton. The base from which the loops project may have a small amount of polyester woven with the cotton to prolong the life of the towel. The fabrication of textiles for other bathroom accessories, such as rugs and covers for toilet seat lids and toilet tanks, typically echoes the texture of terry cloth.

Because towels are a staple item produced in standardized sizes, they are a natural candidate for automated manufacturing. Machinery in some large mills can measure, cut, hem, and even fold towels. The plain-textured towels that make up the largest portion of the market are produced this way. The major manufacturers subcontract to smaller companies to produce towels with decorative features, such as embroidery (Figure 15.6).

Adding fashion to function is the rainbow of choices in single colors and patterns. Sculptured towels provide another design detail. Textures include waffle weave, corduroy-like ribbing, chevrons, and other patterns. Along with the proliferation of soaps, body washes, shampoos, and lotions, giant fluffy bath towels and

FIGURE 15.7 The patterns on this table linen and complementary colors on top create an inviting setting, while protecting the table underneath.

other attractive bath linens add an element of luxury to personal hygiene.

Table Linens

The informality of the contemporary American lifestyle has reduced the everyday use of table linens. Placemats and paper napkins are the norm at many dinner tables. On the other hand, this informality has elevated the dinner party to the level of a state occasion, even when the guests are close friends and the atmosphere is casual. For the sizable segment of the population who enjoy home entertaining as a leisure pastime, attractive table linens lend elegance to the meal.

Tablecloths are manufactured in a variety of sizes and shapes, and matching napkins are usually sold separately so that customers can buy as many as they need. The choices of textiles and weaves range from fine damask and cotton/linen blends, usually in white or off-white, for formal settings to more colorful synthetics for an informally decorated table (Figure 15.7). Stain-resistant and no-iron finishes are especially appealing to customers with small children. Several kinds of table coverings that may be placed over a tablecloth for protection from spills and crumbs (like vinyl cloths) also vary the table setting.

Window Treatments

As the link between a room and the outside world, windows are a focal point of interior design. There are so many ways of accenting a window with textiles—not to mention wooden shutters and plastic, metal, or wooden blinds—that labels like *curtains* or *draperies* are too limited. Interior decorators refer to this vast category as *window treatments* (Figure 15.8), which encompasses many important subcategories and items.

FIGURE 15.6 Bath towels come in a variety of colors and sometimes have decorative features, such as embroidery. They are often coordinated with other merchandise such as soap dishes and furniture.

FIGURE 15.8 Window treatments encompass curtains, draperies, and other window adornments.

Each contributes to the character of the window and the room, creating an atmosphere of openness or privacy, casualness or formality, streamlined simplicity or ornateness.

The main distinction between curtains and draperies is in the weight of the fabric. Draperies are made of heavier, opaque material and are often lined. Typically, they are hung from rods by hooks and can be opened or closed by pulling a cord. Curtains are made of lighter-weight, translucent fabric and are unlined. They may be hung from rods, like draperies, or they may frame the window. Some window treatments combine curtains and draperies. Either may have a matching **valance**, a horizontal strip across the top of the window, or a valance may be used alone.

Today, window treatments are often made of acrylic, polyester, nylon, and other synthetics that are more resistant than some natural fibers to the fading effects of sunlight. Curtains, especially, are easy to maintain; they may be laundered at home and changed to coordinate with bed linens. Draperies and Roman shades are more often selected to match fabric wall coverings or complement the fabrics of upholstered furniture, so these window treatments may be replaced less frequently than curtains.

Upholstery Fabric

Furniture is expensive, making the selection of upholstery fabric an infrequent decision but an important one for fashion-conscious consumers. Whether they are purchasing a single piece or decorating an entire room, they shop for furniture that works well with other pieces and with the window treatments, floor coverings, and other home furnishings to achieve a coherent decor. In response to recent consumer demand for increased decorating options, **slipcovers** have reemerged as a home fashion item. They can protect the permanent upholstery and give a chair or sofa a new look. They are also often machine washable. A wide range of plastic gadgets has been developed to improve the fit of slipcovers.

The choice of material also has a significant influence on the look of upholstery, as well as on its durability and ease of maintenance. In the 1990s, polyester and other synthetics gained the acceptance of interior designers, who for many years favored cotton, linen, and silk. Nontextiles, such as leather and vinyl, are also available for upholstery. Some new nontextiles, such as metallic yarn and thinly sliced cork, are being used in combination with textiles for upholstery, window treatments, and other home decorating purposes.

Miscellaneous Soft Goods

A whole host of miscellaneous items is sold as accessories to the major categories of home furnishings. For example, the firms that manufacture bath linens and the stores and departments that sell them to consumers also produce and sell beach towels, even though they are not intended for use in the home. Other items may be associated with several major categories, such as decorative pillows, which are featured with both bed linens and upholstered furniture.

Throws, small woven blankets about fifty by sixty inches, became hot during the "cocooning" 1990s. An earlier kind of throw, called an *afghan*, is a knitted or crocheted item, often handmade, and frequently displayed over the back of a sofa. Throws are still popular today and come in a wide spectrum of colors, patterns, prints, and materials, including cashmere, pashmina, silk, velvet, and faux fur.

Area Rugs

In the category of soft floor coverings, **area rugs**, which cover most of the floor of a room but are removable, offer greater flexibility in decorating than carpets, which are permanently tacked to the floor (Figure 15.9). The distinction between rugs and carpets is sometimes lost in the common reference to "oriental carpets," which are more accurately referred to as "oriental rugs." The first

FIGURE 15.9 This area rug covers a large portion of the floor but can be easily removed.

rugs were hand-woven and hand-dyed in Asia, and the craft is still practiced in China, India, Turkey, and Iran (formerly Persia). Antique rugs from these countries are highly valued home accessories. Each rug-making region has its own distinctive patterns and colors, but oriental rugs have in common a rectangular shape; an oblong central field; the use of repeated geometric and floral motifs; borders, often a main border and secondary borders; and nearly—but not entirely—symmetrical designs.

In colonial times, most rugs were made at home; hooked or braided styles were made of textile scraps. Rich families had handmade needlepoint rugs and chair covers. Rug manufacturing developed in the United States after the Revolutionary War, and with the invention of a power loom that could weave two-ply ingrain carpets by Erastus Brigham Bigelow in 1839, it became a major industry, expanding its market from the wealthy to lower income levels.

Rug category leader Mohawk Industries reported gains in area-rug sales based on investment in product development for improved color and design capabilities. The company introduced these capabilities to achieve better color and design. Mohawk's products are now found at major retailers throughout the world, ranging from Home Depot and Lowe's to Macy's and Bloomingdale's.

The improved product in the marketplace has demanded better placements and displays in retail that have resulted in gains. Kohl's department stores changed their fixtures to hold and display more products in the same square footage. Macy's has also experienced a growth in the area-rug business over the last decade.

Product Categories of Selected Tabletop Goods

A well-appointed table sets the stage for fine dining and demonstrates the host's mastery of the art of gracious home entertaining. Today's consumers can choose from broad selections of dinnerware, glassware, and flatware to suit their needs, no matter what their taste or budget. Some of the most commonly used items in each category are listed in Table 15.2. Two other important categories—hollowware and giftware—are often combined at the retail level.

Dinnerware

The term **dinnerware** refers to the whole range of serving vessels for presenting food to diners and the cups, bowls, and plates for holding individual portions

IKEA
ISN'T JUST FOR COLLEGE STUDENTS

IKEA WAS FOUNDED in 1943 when Ingvar Kamprad, then seventeen years old, got money from his father for doing well in school. Kamprad used the money to establish his own business. The name IKEA is formed from the founder's initials (I.K.) plus the first letters of Elmyard and Agunnaryd, the farm and village in Sweden where he grew up. Though known today for its minimalist and functional furniture, IKEA originally sold pens, wallets, picture frames, table runners, watches, jewelry, and nylon stockings—meeting basic needs with products at reduced prices.

Furniture was introduced into the IKEA product range in 1948. Produced by local manufacturers in the forests close to Kamprad's home, the furniture was well received by consumers and the line expanded. During the 1950s, IKEA's customers were able to see and touch the furniture before placing orders at the company's first furniture showroom. The innovation was a success and IKEA soon expanded to Norway, Denmark, Switzerland, and France. By the time IKEA opened its first store in the U.S.—in Philadelphia in 1985—the company had 10,000 employees and sixty stores.

In the 1990s, the IKEA Group developed a policy to ensure that the company took environmental responsibility for all activities conducted within the business. The 2000s brought great growth to IKEA, as it entered more countries and built a reputation for successful partnerships regarding social and environmental projects. IKEA reports that most cities are happy to have them there. According to Mike Ward, president of IKEA USA, "An average store will add 450 jobs to the local economy—that's good for the city and it's good for us!" Here in America, IKEA was traditionally seen as a good option for college students, but IKEA's popularity is increasing among more diverse consumer groups, with growth now coming from the main areas of the home—living rooms, kitchens, and bedrooms.

(Figure 15.10). These pieces are sometimes collectively called *dishes*, but that term also has the narrower meaning of plates. The generic term *china* also has a more limited meaning, labeling only one of the materials of which dinnerware may be made. We use the industry term *dinnerware* to avoid confusion.

Categories of Dinnerware

Dinnerware is available in glass and, in response to consumer concerns about breakage and price, in melamine and other plastics. However, most dinnerware is ceramic, that is, made of baked—or *fired*—clay. The quality of the clay is a major factor in the quality of the product. In ascending order of quality, the major clay bodies used for dinnerware are peasant pottery, earthenware, ironstone, stoneware, china (or porcelain), and bone china. Peasant pottery is most often used only for serving pieces or decorative objects. Hand-decorated Delft pottery from Holland and Majolica from Italy are valued as craft objects for display. Stoneware is common for everyday dinnerware, and china and bone china, with more formal decorative patterns, for serving guests.

Glazes and other decorative features of dinnerware also affect their value and durability and raise safety

FIGURE 15.10 Maidenhair Fern table setting by Martha Stewart Home.

issues. In formulating glazes, manufacturers must balance the desired colors against the resistance of the glaze to the chemicals in detergent. Decorative gold trim renders a piece unusable in a microwave, and other aspects of the chemical composition control whether a product is oven-proof, dishwasher-safe, and suitable for the refrigerator or freezer.

TABLE 15.2 *Dinnerware, Glassware, and Flatware*

DINNERWARE	GLASSWARE	FLATWARE
Place Setting	*Stemmed*	*Four-Piece Place Setting*
Dinner plate	Brandy snifter	Knife
Salad plate	Champagne flute	Dinner fork
Cup	Cocktail	Teaspoon
Saucer	Cordial	Salad fork
Bowl	Sherry	
	Water	*Five-Piece Place Setting*
Accessory Pieces	Wine	Soup spoon
Bread plate		
Soup bowl	*Tumblers*	*Accessory Pieces*
Rimmed soup bowl	Iced tea	Iced tea spoon
Mug	Beer mug	Steak knife
	Juice	Butter spreader
Serving Pieces	Double old-fashioned	
Vegetable dish (some covered)		*Serving Pieces*
Platter	*Serving Pieces*	Salad fork and spoon
Coffeepot	Decanters	Salad tongs
Teapot	Pitchers	Serving spoons
Sugar bowl		Meat fork
Creamer		Pie server
Cake plate		Cake rack

Sets of Dinnerware

Dinnerware is usually sold in sets of service for four, eight, or twelve, including serving pieces and basic place settings. Service for four is common in casual patterns for everyday family use. The number of serving pieces may be limited, and the place settings may include only a dinner plate and cup and saucer. Five-piece place settings add a salad plate and a bowl or bread and butter plate to the basic items.

Customers can expand their sets of dinnerware or replace broken pieces by purchasing additional place settings or individual items. Pieces sold individually are called open stock. The most elaborate sets of dinnerware include plates, bowls, and cups that vary in size and shape according to very specific use. For example, a coffee cup is larger than a teacup and has straighter sides. Most modern patterns, however, include fewer types of items, and contemporary consumers, with their informal lifestyle, do not demand such fine distinctions. In fact, a common practice is to build a set of dinnerware from open stock, coordinating items in the same pattern but different colors.

Glassware

Glass has long been recognized as a versatile material with properties suitable for many uses. Essentially, glass is sand, melted in a furnace and molded or blown into the desired shape and allowed to harden. Because the main component is nonporous, glass is ideal for vessels for storing and serving food and beverages. Examples of beautifully colored opaque glass vessels from ancient Egypt, Syria, and Rome have survived for thousands of years.

The English colonists brought the manufacturing of glass to America. In the nineteenth century, Americans made several technical contributions to the industry. A pressing machine, introduced in 1825, allowed for the production of pressed-glass patterns. The production of the first electric lightbulbs by Corning Glass Works in 1879 was an early example of this company's focus on innovations in industrial uses of glass. But later Corning also developed glass products for oven-to-table use, including Pyrex and CorningWare.

At the end of the century, Michael J. Owens of the Libbey Company invented an automatic bottle machine that greatly improved production processes. Now the largest glassware manufacturer in the United States, Libbey makes more than two thousand products, including its popularly priced lines of drinking glasses.

The top quality is leaded glass, which has a minimum of 5 percent lead oxide. Full lead crystal has at least 24 percent lead oxide. The softness of lead crystal makes it easy to hand cut, and it is the most brilliant crystal. Some concerns have been raised, however, about the leaching of lead into wine decanters, because the wine usually remains in the decanter for long periods.

Place Settings

Three types of glassware categorized by shape are **tumblers**, cylindrical glasses; **footed tumblers**, tumblers with a heavy bottom; and **stemware**, bowl-shaped glasses on a stalk or, as the name suggests, stem. The various shapes are designed to hold specific beverages (Figure 15.11). Water may be served in any of the shapes. Milk, fruit and vegetable juices, and sodas are typically served in tumblers or footed tumblers, and cocktails in footed tumblers.

Drinking wine from the correct glass enhances enjoyment because the shape captures the bouquet. At a formal table, appropriate stemware may be set out for red and white wine. But modern society is not strict about the rules. Although manufacturers of fine crystal offer sets in matched patterns, many customers prefer to buy glassware from open stock and to set their tables with just one or two glasses at each place.

Flatware

The use of flatware is a relatively recent phenomenon, and it is not as widespread as the use of dinnerware or glassware. Think of all the Asian countries where chopsticks are used and the not-so-primitive societies that have developed ways of eating neatly without utensils. In fact, hors d'oeuvres, sandwiches, and other finger foods are common in cultures that serve other foods with flatware.

FIGURE 15.11 Glassware comes in various shapes, and each piece is designed to hold a specific beverage.

In medieval Europe, a banquet invitation was a "bring your own flatware" occasion. People of high social status acquired a personal silver knife, fork, and spoon set at birth and used their own utensils—in addition to their hands—wherever they ate. The Italians of the sixteenth century were the first to eat their meat with a knife and fork, and the practice was not widely accepted elsewhere in Europe for a hundred years. But once the idea of having a variety of knives, forks, and spoons took hold, the choices became overwhelming. Different spoons were designed for coffee and tea and for cream soups and clear soups.

Flatware continues to contribute to the style of a table setting. It can be formal or casual, traditional or modern, elegant or utilitarian. Ideally it makes eating easier and more pleasant.

Categories of Flatware

Like "china" that is actually stoneware, "linens" made of cotton, and plastic "glasses," not all "silverware" is silver. Only sterling silver can accurately wear that label. It must be 92.5 percent silver and only 7.5 percent alloy metal (copper, for example, which is added for strength). If the flatware is silver plate, the proportions of silver to alloy are more or less reversed: the silver is a coating over an alloy core. *Vermeil* (pronounced ver-MAY), silver flatware dipped in gold to prevent corrosion of the silver by the chemicals in certain foods, may be made up in whole sets of flatware or in a few pieces. Stainless steel flatware is manufactured for everyday use, but some of it is of high enough quality to be used with fine china. The best-known American manufacturers of flatware—Oneida, Reed & Barton, Gorham, Towle, and Kirk Stieff, among them—offer patterns in all four categories.

Place Settings and Serving Pieces

Like other tabletop goods, flatware is sold in sets for four, eight, and twelve as well as open stock. The typical place setting consists of a knife, dinner fork, salad fork, and teaspoon, and in some sets, a soup spoon. Serving utensils are designed to facilitate transfer of a portion from the serving dish to the individual's plate. Slotted vegetable spoons drain the vegetables; a pie server slides neatly under the slice; and so on.

Hollowware

The term **hollowware** covers a variety of metal service items such as trays, candlesticks, sugar bowls and creamers, coffeepots, and teapots. Common materials for hollowware include sterling silver, silver plate, and pewter. Some items may be kept on display in the living room or dining room and used for buffet service.

TABLE 15.3 *Giftware*

ALL OCCASIONS	BABY GIFTS	DESK SETS
Picture frames	Cups	Blotters
Mirrors	Spoons	Bookends
Vases	Rattles	Pencil holders
Flower pots	Teething rings	Notepad holders
Candlesticks	Porringer	Letter holders
Candles	Comb and brush set	Letter openers
Clocks		Pen holders
Figurines		

Giftware

Giftware is a thriving segment of the home accessories industry because of recurring gift-giving occasions. Some gifts may be made from any of a number of materials. Picture frames in wood, ceramic materials, a variety of metals, and even leather and papier-mâché are all popular. Giftware can be displayed on coffee tables, desks, and shelves, adding decorative accents to a room. Table 15.3 lists some of the more frequently given gift items.

An interesting aspect of the gift market is the proliferation of museum reproductions now available from institutions worldwide. In the United States, reproductions have become available not only from the Museum of Fine Arts, Boston, the Art Institute of Chicago, the Smithsonian, and the Metropolitan Museum of Art of New York, but also from smaller institutions like the Delaware Art Museum, the Columbus Museum of Art, and the Museum of South Texas History. Some of these museums also have set up freestanding stores outside the museum.

All of the cultural institutions named, both great and small, are members of the Museum Store Association (MSA), an organization of retail personnel at cultural institutions across the country. Museum stores offer unique shopping opportunities that can't be experienced anywhere else, and MSA represents more than 1,600 stores in every kind of cultural institution, from art museums and science centers to zoos, botanic gardens, and nature parks to performing arts centers, libraries, halls of fame, historic houses, and other cultural institutions.[4]

Market Segments

New homes, whether they are the first apartment of a newly married couple, the expanded home of a growing family, or the vacation home that is the prize of financial success, provide a dependable market for the home furnishings industry. Replacement purchases, spurred by the cocooning of baby boomers, add a direction for growth. Other huge market segments, beyond the scope of this text, are the institutional and military markets.

Bridal

Marriages are a source of celebration for the home furnishings industry as well as for the newlyweds because they generate spending disproportionate to the small percentage of households—less than 3 percent in the United States—they represent. Many couples experience a sudden surge of money as they combine their incomes and reduce the costs of separate housing. They spend their windfall on setting up their new home, and well-wishers among their friends and family buy them gifts. The fact that half of all purchases of sterling silver flatware and giftware are for the bridal market is a dramatic indicator of the impact of this segment.

Wedding or **bridal registries** in department stores and specialty stores give the retailer an opportunity to establish a good relationship with the customer by offering a service. They provide a record of the customer's taste and attract the business of gift givers who want to be sure of making the right selection. Today, most department stores and mass-market retailers have added online registrations to complement their computerized in-store registry programs (Figure 15.12). The

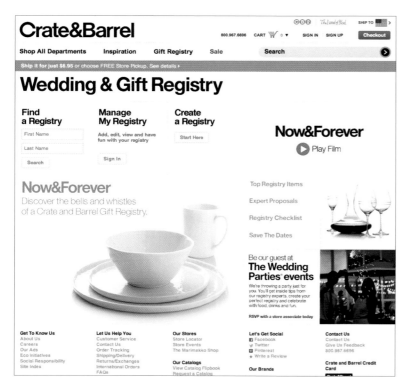

FIGURE 15.12 Brides- and grooms-to-be can browse Crate & Barrel's top registry picks and create their own wish lists.

Knot and WeddingChannel are established sites that already have audiences of over three million.[5]

New Home/Vacation Home

When a family or individual moves into a new home, at whatever stage of the life cycle, possibilities open up for sellers of home furnishings. New housing tends to increase the demand for bedroom and bathroom products because the new homes typically have more bedrooms and bathrooms. Moves to accommodate the growth of a family feed the market for baby giftware as well as the market for bed linens. Going away to college involves buying bed and bath linens, perhaps even window treatments. Even a move into a retirement community involves home furnishing purchases—new window treatments, for example, when the old ones do not fit.

Vacation homes are often initially furnished with castoffs from the main residence. But the informal nature of life at the beach, in the mountains, or at a country retreat usually dictates a less formal style of decorating, with emphasis on easy upkeep. It is the rare vacation home that does not gradually get redecorated!

Replacement

The replacement market exists at many levels. Many young people begin their first apartments with hand-me-downs from relatives and friends. As their earnings grow, they replace the worst of the used items. Some households seek inexpensive replacements for broken or worn items. Many of these people shop at garage sales, flea markets, thrift stores, or discounters. Others trade up to slightly more expensive items. Thanks to cocooning baby boomers, redecorating has expanded the home furnishings market. As life expectancy increases, boomers will continue to have a significant influence on the replacement market.

Market Resources

The producers and marketers of home furnishings have both common and unique interests, and resources are available to meet the needs of the industry as a whole and those of the various segments. As a world fashion capital, New York is the location of manufacturers' showrooms for home textiles and other home furnishings products and the site of major industry trade shows. AmericasMart Atlanta, with 600 showrooms and proximity to the large textile mills, is also important in the international home furnishings scene. North Carolina is the center of the furniture industry in the United States and has

FIGURE 15.13 Maison et Objet, the vast, semi-annual home furnishings trade fair, gives people from around the world a preview of upcoming trends.

showrooms that include upholstery, pillows, and other decorative objects. The vast Merchandise Mart in Chicago is devoted to furniture and various soft goods and tabletop merchandise.

Trade Associations

Organizations that promote all home furnishings industries include the Home Furnishings Independents Association, in Dallas; the National Home Furnishings Association, in High Point, North Carolina; the Home Fashion Products Association, in New York City; and the International Housewares Association, in Rosemont, Illinois.

The home textiles industry is served by trade associations that are also involved in apparel textiles. Cotton Incorporated and the Wool Council promote specific textiles. The Decorative Furnishings Association and the National Association of Decorative Fabrics Distributors focus on home textiles.

Because High Point, North Carolina, is the center of furniture manufacturing, it is also the home of the American Home Furnishings Alliance and the Upholstered Furniture Action Council. Other associations that promote specific industry segments include the Carpet and Rug Institute, in Dalton, Georgia, and the National Association of Floor Covering Distributors, in Chicago.

Trade Shows

New York, Chicago, and Atlanta, with their large numbers of permanent showrooms and vast convention facilities, host the biggest trade shows (Figure 15.13). The New York International Gift Fair and the Gift and Home Textiles Market Week run together at the Javits Center each January and August. The New York Tabletop Market is also a major event.

The International Home and Housewares Show in Chicago attracts thousands of buyers from around the world every March; the Chicago Merchandise Mart also draws buyers all year because of the huge number of showrooms it contains. In Atlanta, the Atlanta International Area Rug Market features exhibitors and products from all over the world.

Trade Publications

Weekly magazines for the home furnishings industry, such as *Home Furnishings News (HFN)*, and *Home Accents Today*, provide broad coverage. *Home Textiles Today* and *LDB Interior Textiles* have a slightly narrower focus on home textiles. Other trade publications, such as *Ceramic Industry*, indicate by their name which segment of the market they serve. See Table 15.4 for a more complete list of trade publications.

TABLE 15.4 *Trade Publications for the Home Furnishings Industry*

BROAD COVERAGE	SEGMENTS OF THE HOME FURNISHINGS INDUSTRY
FDM—Furniture Design and Manufacturing	Ceramic Industry
HFN—Home Furnishings News	Floor Covering Weekly
Home Accents Today	Residential Lighting
Home Furnishings Review	Furniture Today
Interior Design	

Merchandising and Marketing

Home furnishings can take many routes from manufacturer to consumer. Depending on the product, there may be a few or many stops along the way.

The distribution of textile products for the home is particularly complex and involves a number of professionals, each of whom adds service and expertise to the process. The major manufacturers display their household linens in their New York showrooms, and their sales representatives bring sample books with fabric swatches and photos of products to customers.

Retail Channels of Distribution

Consumers have a variety of resources to meet their home furnishings needs. For customized upholstered furniture and window treatments, as well as expert advice and access to goods not otherwise available, consumers can turn to professional interior designers. Some designers have their own firms, and others are on staff at home furnishings and department stores.

Consumers who are making their own selections turn to different types of stores for different categories of goods. For example, mass merchandisers are the main source of household linens.

Some vendors see home centers as the fastest-growing channel. Many home center retailers are moving boldly into soft goods once thought incompatible with their hard lines and building products mix. One example is Home Depot's Home Decorator Collection.

For consumers who are bargain conscious but want more upscale merchandise than is available through the mass merchandisers, the category killer in home furnishings is the discount superstore. The leading chain is Bed, Bath & Beyond. Overlapping their market is Williams-Sonoma, which is primarily a retailer of housewares and appliances but also offers casual tabletop goods and other home fashion products.

HomeGoods is the off-price chain of TJX Companies, which owns Marshalls and T.J.Maxx. Bath & Body Works is owned by Limited Brands, Inc. IKEA, a Swedish superstore chain, offers low-price furniture (some of which the customer assembles), home furnishings, and housewares. Manufacturers' factory outlets also appeal to this segment of the market.

The broad assortments in different product lines offered by the superstores have cut into the business of the traditional department stores. Some of the ways the department stores are holding on to their customers are by offering exclusive merchandise, including private brands; featuring designer lines in model room displays; and matching competitors' prices through periodic "white sales."

In categories in which the superstore discounters do not compete or where their offerings are limited, department stores continue as dominant players. They account for 40 percent of giftware purchases and about one-third of sterling silver flatware sales.

Specialty stores in this market segment compete by offering exclusive merchandise, often imported goods. Well-known examples are Crate and Barrel, Pottery Barn, and Domain. Specialty stores, with almost half the sales in the giftware segment, are the competitors to beat.

Nonstore retailing is another resource for consumers. Some stores, both specialist and general merchandise retailers, do a significant portion of their home furnishings business through catalog divisions (Figure 15.14). Bloomingdale's, Crate and Barrel, Eddie Bauer Home, Tiffany, and Gumps are a few examples that convey the range of retailers who have followed this route. Catalog retailers like Lands' End and L.L.Bean have also added home furnishings to their lines. Specialty catalogs include Williams-Sonoma Home, Ross-Simons Gift & Home Collection, the Horchow Collection, Domestications, Smith & Noble, and Country Curtains. All these companies also have their own websites that showcase and sell their products, as well as provide information

FIGURE 15.14 Anthropologie, Crate & Barrel, and Pottery Barn advertise their home products through catalogs.

about them. Online private-sale site Hautelook.com has more than eight million members. The company, purchased by Nordstrom in 2011, sells home, fashion, beauty, and lifestyle brands. Their home decor makes up about 60 percent of the site's total sales.[6]

NPD found that there is also some evidence of showrooming—researching a product in the brick-and-mortar store first and then buying it online. However, the majority of purchases for home products still happen at the brick-and-mortar stores. The report also notes that two out of three customers research a home-related product online first but then end up purchasing it in the brick-and-mortar store—the opposite of showrooming.[7]

Advertising and Publicity

What could be more natural to cocooners and home decorating enthusiasts than to curl up with a magazine directed right at them? Home decorating magazines, known in the trade as "**shelter magazines**," include *Architectural Digest* (Figure 15.15), *Better Homes and Gardens*, *House Beautiful*, *Country Living*, *Elle Decor*, and *Martha Stewart Living*. They are a great medium for manufacturers to advertise to the public and build

FIGURE 15.15 *Architectural Digest* reaches more customers globally with its French edition.

demand for their brands. Retailers, especially national chains, also advertise in these periodicals. Other magazines that feature ads for home furnishings include the bridal magazines like *Brides*, women's magazines like *Woman's Day* and *The Ladies Home Journal*, and upscale magazines like *Town and Country* and *The New Yorker*. There are also a newer crop of magazines, including *Wallpaper*, *Surface*, and *City*, with content that focuses on avant-garde trends in interior designs as well as fashion.

Magazines are perhaps even more beneficial as a source of publicity than as an advertising medium. They provide favorable mention by a presumably disinterested authority and show attractively photographed examples of a product or line in use.

Newspapers are another advertising medium advantageous to both producers and retailers, who share the costs through cooperative advertising agreements. And local media can provide publicity to retailers for in-store events such as the opening of a new unit of a chain; a lecture by a home furnishings star; a home fashion show, perhaps featuring a designer; or a cooking demonstration that culminates in the presentation of a meal at a beautifully set table.

HGTV uses its television channel, magazine, website, newsletter, blog, and social media sites to offer do-it-yourself (DIY) tips and trends for improving all aspects of a living space. The company also invites interaction with customers via message boards, contests, and giveaways.[8]

Industry Trends

In the home furnishings industry, as in other aspects of daily life, fashion, technology, and environmentalism have been important influences. Responses at all levels to issues in these three areas will continue to affect one another in the future.

Growing Fashion Influence

We have already observed how baby boomers have turned their fashion interests toward their homes and how apparel designers, alert to the trend, have responded.

We have also seen how the life cycle of home fashion products has sped up as consumers spend their money on replacement purchases that can give them a new look at relatively little expense. As producers use new technology to develop faster, more economical ways of manufacturing and delivering goods, their response has generated even greater demand.

FIGURE 15.16 This machine enables manufacturers to produce embossed goods at a high speed.

Design and Production

Advancements in production speed up manufacturing and thereby enable producers to fill orders more quickly (Figure 15.16). Borrowing from the apparel industry, home furnishings manufacturers, especially textile producers, have instituted quick-response procedures (see Chapter 8). The retailer can keep enough stock to meet immediate demand but not be stuck with items that have passed their fashion peak. It is the connection between retailer and supplier that enables both to analyze sales trends and adjust stock levels accordingly. Additionally, the home fashions industry must keep up with trends in apparel.

Improvements in technology not only mean faster and more highly automated production and delivery of products but also define the changes in the very nature of the product. In the manufacturing of bedding, especially pillows, high-tech fibers now protect consumers from allergy-producing molds, mildews, fungi, and dust mites. **Antimicrobials**, compounds that are spun into acetate fibers, break down the cells of microbes that lurk in the moist atmosphere of bedding.

Other treatments of textiles include no-iron finishes on bed linens, antifungal finishes on drapery fabric, and pesticides in wool carpeting.

Green Products

Countering the trend toward the use of high-tech fabrics is a demand for untreated natural materials (Figure 15.17). Manufacturers and retailers have been responsive to the increasing environmental concerns by developing more green products for the home over the past decade. Gaiam, for example, is a company that offers eco-friendly home accessories and decor, as well as information about how to create healthy living solutions. Ecological issues affect both the processes of producing home furnishings and the resulting products.

Growth of Exports

Imports have focused on high-end merchandise, such as Egyptian cotton bed linens, Indian rugs, and fine china and crystal from famous European companies. Many of these products are valued for the tradition of artistry and craftsmanship they exemplify and for their distinctive designs. The demand and prices for lumber are also on the rise globally. Lumber is important for the home category because it is used for products such as furniture, flooring, and plywood products.

Summary and Review

A trend toward spending more leisure time at home has prompted interest in home decorating and has sped up the fashion life cycle of home furnishings in such categories as household linens, window treatments, upholstery fabrics, area rugs, and tabletop goods. Clothing designers have developed home fashions lines, often through licensing agreements with major textile manufacturers. National and store brands of household linens and tabletop goods have taken on distinctive fashion images. Computer-aided drafting has enabled designers and manufacturers to provide consumers with new patterns of soft goods and tabletop items to meet growing demand.

Major market segments for home accessories include the bridal market, the new home and vacation home segments, and a growing market for replacement merchandise. This last segment is propelled by home-centered leisure activity and the availability of relatively inexpensive purchases that can bring new looks to home decor.

FIGURE 15.17 The trend for organic, eco-friendly home products, such as these bed linens by Organic Style, continues to grow.

The home furnishing industry is served by trade associations, trade shows, and trade publications that address both the collective interests of all segments and the specialized interests of the home textiles industry and other product line segments. New York is the main market center, and the Atlanta market is also important. Textile manufacturing and the production of household linens are centralized in the South. The production of tabletop goods is not centralized but is dominated by a few large producers.

Channels of distribution at the retail level include discount superstores, department stores, manufacturers' outlets, specialty retailers, and catalog retailers.

Shelter magazines, newspapers, television, and online sites are major mediums for retail advertising and publicity.

The interplay of fashion, technology, and environmentalism dominates trends in the home furnishings industry. Some fashion trends are a casual lifestyle and a preference for natural fibers and other natural materials. Advancements in production speed up manufacturing and enable producers to fill orders more quickly. Environmentalism is manifested in concern about the environmental impact of production processes and the effect of chemicals in home furnishing products on consumers and the environment.

For Review

1. Why have apparel designers branched out into home furnishing lines?
2. Why are the names of textile mills important in the merchandising of household linens?
3. What benefits do natural fibers offer in household linens? What benefits do synthetics offer?
4. What do window treatments contribute to interior design?
5. Why have slipcovers become fashionable?
6. Name five shelter magazines.
7. What role do stages of the family life cycle play in defining market segments for home furnishings?
8. Name the major trade associations in the home furnishings industry. What services do they provide for their members?
9. Name five retail channels of distribution for home furnishings and describe the market of each of these types of retailer.
10. Identify three trends in the home furnishings industry.

For Discussion

1. Why is the home furnishings industry considered a fashion industry? Discuss the influence of fashion on the manufacturing, merchandising, and marketing of home furnishings.
2. Discuss the influence of computerized manufacturing on the home furnishings industry.
3. Discuss the influence of concern for the environment on the fashion features of home furnishings. What role do ecological issues play in the selection of materials and treatment of textiles?

Trade Talk

Define or briefly explain the following terms:

antimicrobials
area rug
California king
dinnerware
duvet
footed tumbler
hollowware
home fashions
shelter magazine
sisal
slipcover
soft goods
stemware
tabletop
throw
tumbler
valance
wedding or bridal registries

THE RETAIL LEVEL: THE MARKETS FOR FASHION

In this unit, you will learn about the explosion of global fashion markets and marts, manufacturers and retailers, and the elements of policies and strategies in fashion retailing. You will begin to develop a basic vocabulary and working knowledge of the following:

- Chapter 16: The development of fashion markets, marts, and trade shows internationally.
- Chapter 17: The importance of global sourcing and merchandising, including importing, domestic and offshore production, and international trade laws.
- Chapter 18: The history and development of fashion retailing; organization for buying and merchandising in chains, leased departments, and franchises; and the operations of different types of retailers.
- Chapter 19: The trends in merchandising and operational policies and the major strategies used in retailing.

Chapter Sixteen
GLOBAL FASHION MARKETS

KEY CONCEPTS

- Meaning of the terms *market*, *market center*, *mart*, and *trade show*, and the function of each in bringing fashion from producers to consumers
- Locations and activities of markets, marts, and trade shows in the United States
- Locations and activities of foreign fashion markets
- Trends in U.S. and foreign fashion markets

As the children's poem states, "To market, to market, to buy a fat pig; home again, home again, jiggety jig." Going to market can be an exciting and different experience, whether it is to buy food, candy, sporting goods, or clothes. Most of us go to market with great expectations and plans—and once home from market, sometimes the purchase is perfect and other times it is just not right. Regardless of the outcome of the trip, it is your money and can be spent however you wish. However, this is not the case when you spend someone else's money, as is the case for store buyers. When buying for a store, you are using its money, which requires an exhausting amount of planning, organization, and hard work before you can even go to market.

Market Terminology

Markets, market centers, marts—what are they? You will hear these terms used frequently and even interchangeably, which makes them that much harder to sort out.

Market

The word *market* has several meanings. We have already spoken of the market, or demand, for a specific product; for instance, how much people want to buy athletic shoes, dress casual trousers, or coordinated bed linens. In this chapter, the word takes on yet another meaning. A **market** is the place where goods are offered for sale and sold at wholesale prices. It is an important step in the pipeline that takes clothes and other fashion items from manufacturer to customer. Buyers attend markets, in effect, to choose the styles we will all be wearing within a few months.

You may hear the term **domestic market**; it refers to the market in one's own country. For example, in the United States it refers to the places throughout the United States where goods are sold to retail buyers. The **foreign market**, then, refers to places outside the United States. If you live in Canada, Canada is your domestic market, and the United States is considered a foreign market. (Both domestic and foreign markets are discussed in detail later in this chapter.)

Market Center

Actually, there is no one giant shopping mall that serves as a market for the entire American fashion industry. Instead, several **market centers**, or geographic locations, exist throughout the country, and what are—to Americans—foreign market centers dot the globe. A market center is a city where fashion is offered and sold wholesale.

The first market center in the United States that comes to mind is New York City. For many people in and out of the fashion industry, New York City epitomizes the allure and excitement of the fashion world. Indeed, New York is the oldest market center in the United States and in many ways the most challenging to visit.

But in recent years, fashion has become regionalized, and while New York still offers much of America's fashion, it no longer produces all of it. In the past few decades, Los Angeles, Dallas, and Miami all have become flourishing market centers. Other cities that are not major apparel production centers, such as Chicago, Atlanta, and Denver, are considered markets rather than market centers, although the line between the two sometimes blurs. Chicago, for example, has always promoted itself as a market center.

Mart

A **mart** is a building or complex of buildings that houses a wholesale market, that is, an exhibition of fashions that are ready to be sold to retail stores (Figure 16.1). Most marts are owned and operated by independent investors. Some marts are operated either by the cities themselves or by trade associations.

Like convention centers, marts consist almost entirely of exhibition space. Some space is rented out as full-time corporate showrooms, but in many marts, the space is rented only during market weeks. These marts often balance their income by sponsoring other shows and conventions.

FIGURE 16.1 The granddaddy of all the marts is the Chicago Merchandise Mart built in 1930.

New York City, which, despite the rise of regional marts, in many ways still reigns as the country's premiere market center, is ironically the only market center without a mart. Part of the aura of a New York market week is the trek through the city from showroom to showroom.

The granddaddy of marts is the Merchandise Mart in Chicago, which opened its doors in the early 1930s, making Chicago New York's only rival for years. Because the Merchandise Mart was centrally located, buyers from across the country found it convenient to meet in this huge building on the Chicago River several times a year to do their wholesale buying. The Mart is still very much in use today for other goods, such as home furnishings, contract (office/institutional) furnishings, kitchen and bath, and gifts and decorative accessories.

Market Weeks

Buyers can and do travel to market centers and to some marts at any time during the year to visit individual producers, but several times a year, they also gather for market week (Table 16.1). Few buyers are willing to forgo the glamour and excitement of **market week**. During market week, market centers and marts are filled to the rafters with producers and designers, all of whom exhibit their new lines with as much style and panache as possible. The atmosphere is electrifying, heady with new, innovative ideas and the latest trends.

As a purely physical convenience, it is immeasurably easier for buyers to take in new trends and make their buying decisions when they can see lots of clothes all at once. But beyond that, market week also gives everyone a chance to talk to each other and generally take in what is new in the industry.

Trade Shows

Trade shows are periodic exhibits that are scheduled throughout the year in regional market centers and some marts. Smaller than market weeks, trade shows are typically attended by buyers from one region of the country. Exceptions are a few huge trade shows, such as MAGIC, which attract buyers from all over the world.

TABLE 16.1 *A Basic Market Week Calendar*

Month	Merchandise Shown
January	Summer market
Late March–early April	Early Fall market
Late May–early June	Late Fall market
August–early September	Resort market
Late October–early November	Spring market

History and Development of Market Centers in the United States

New York City was the first market center in the United States. When design and production clustered in New York, it followed that it would become a center for buying, too. That New York was the most cosmopolitan and fashion conscious of American cities also helped. Even when travel was a strenuous undertaking, buyers at major stores tried to travel to New York twice a year. To service them, manufacturers set up showrooms near their factories in the garment district.

But for many, twice-a-year buying trips were not enough to service a store properly. And many owners and buyers for small stores across the country could not afford to travel to New York. To handle accounts between New York buying trips and to help those who did not come to New York at all, manufacturers hired **sales representatives**.

The Role of Sales Representatives

Sales representatives played an important role in transforming other cities into market centers. For years, in addition to being the only link between apparel manufacturers in New York and the rest of the country, these jobs were filled by men. Traveling at first by train, and later by car, sales reps, as they were familiarly called, mailed advance notices to key customers in each city to announce the date of their arrival. In the early days of the fashion business, sales reps carried only one line. Later, as the fashion business became more sophisticated, they carried several noncompeting lines so they could offer their clients more variety. Once a rep arrived in a city, he rented one or more hotel rooms, which he used to exhibit his line of apparel.

For company more than anything else (the life of a sales rep was lonely), reps began to travel in groups. Soon, groups of sales reps were jointly renting clusters of adjoining rooms, so their customers could visit not just one but several exhibits at once. When they learned that this was good for business, the next step was to rent a large hotel ballroom or exhibition hall. This gradually led to the development of regional market centers, such as the Chicago Merchandise Mart.

The Role of Marts

The Chicago Merchandise Mart had little competition until the 1960s, when other cities began to build their own marts, and regional markets took a giant step forward in their development. California had become a recognized center for selling sportswear by the 1940s, and it would soon become the second largest market center outside New York City. In 1964, the CaliforniaMart opened in Los Angeles, giving that city the capacity to sponsor a major market show rather than just sportswear shows. That same year, the dazzling Dallas Market Center opened and began servicing the western half of the country. The successes in Dallas and Los Angeles prompted other cities to open their own marts, and throughout the 1970s, Atlanta, Seattle, Miami, Denver, Pittsburgh, Minneapolis, and Charlotte, North Carolina, became important regional market centers.

Sales reps employed by large producers operate out of corporate showrooms in a fashion mart. If the rep can write up $1 million in orders, maintaining a permanent base at a mart is advantageous for the rep, the corporation, and their retail buyer customers. Apparel producers whose sales in a region do not warrant the investment in a corporate showroom often rely on multiline sales reps. These reps rent showroom space at the regional mart during market weeks.

Services of Market Centers and Marts

A market week is organized by manufacturers' associations, in cooperation with the market center or mart staff. It is the prime selling opportunity for market center or mart staffs, fashion producers, and sales reps, all of whom devote themselves to making the visit as easy and convenient as possible for the buyers. Keeping buyers interested, comfortable, and happy encourages them to write orders.

Market weeks are scheduled several months before the clothes will be needed in the stores. Four or five market weeks are held each year for women's and children's wear, three to five for men's and boy's wear, and two to five for shoes. Separate market weeks are held in many market centers or marts for accessories, infants' and children's wear, lingerie, western wear, sportswear, and bridal apparel. (Table 16.1 lists the seasonal fashions shown at market weeks throughout the year.) The chapters in Units Three and Four include more specific market week calendars for the various categories of fashion merchandise.

Physical Facilities

As discussed later in this chapter, the physical facilities vary between New York and the rest of the market centers and marts in the United States. The physical facilities of marts are designed for buyers' convenience. Exhibition space is arranged by fashion category; for example, handbags, small leather goods, and jewelry are typically located together; women's sportswear occupies another area, and lingerie still another.

Marts include an array of meeting rooms, ranging from auditoriums and theaters for fashion shows

FIGURE 16.2 The Moda Manhattan website shows it's the place to be for fashion and accessory trends.

to smaller rooms for seminars and conferences. The newer marts even have office space where buyers can take a quiet moment to relax—and add up what they have spent.

Publicity

A market week is only as successful as the exhibitors it manages to attract, so most regional markets and marts mount an ongoing publicity program to draw interesting and exciting exhibitors (Figure 16.2). So that the chemistry will be mutual, market centers and marts also do what they can to attract buyers.

The most popular form of publicity is the fashion shows that highlight every market week. The shows are hectic because they are so huge and so much activity is going on. They are also among the more extravagant and interesting fashion shows ever staged, primarily

because they are the work of many different designers, all of whom enter their most beautiful or interesting designs. To give some coherence to a market week fashion show, it is often organized around a theme, such as a particular color or, more often, an exciting new trend.

Special Services for Market Week

The market center or mart staff does everything in their power to make viewing and buying of seasonal lines easy for buyers who travel to market week (Figure 16.3). The endless rounds of exhibits are exhilarating but exhausting, and no one wants to lose buyers because they were not offered enough support.

Support services begin even before the buyer leaves home. Buyers are sent information on hotels with special rates, shuttle service to and from the fashion shows, and screening procedures. Only authorized manufacturers and buyers are admitted to market week, and security is high throughout.

Specialized support services are also planned. For example, models are hired to work in the showrooms in case a buyer wants to see someone wearing a particular garment. Beyond this, buyers are provided with an array of information, educational, and between-show services.

Information Services

Once the buyers arrive, they are given a **buyer's directory** and a calendar to help them find their way around and schedule events they want to see. A steady flow of daily publications—trade newspapers, flyers, brochures, and newsletters—continues throughout the week and keeps buyers abreast of breaking market week news.

FIGURE 16.3 Top retailers exhibit new products at the MRket show.

An orientation program is typically scheduled for the first day, and consultants are on call throughout the week to discuss and deal with specific problems. Seminars and conferences are held to supply buyers with the latest information on fashion. Typical topics are new advances in fiber and fabrics, trends in fashion colors, the latest merchandising techniques, advertising and promotion ideas, and sales training hints.

General Services

The level of life and services between market weeks varies from place to place, but the trend is for both market centers and marts to stay open year-round. At the Miami International Merchandise Mart, for example, many tenants operate their showrooms year-round.

The New York Market

As a market, New York belongs in a category by itself, not only because it is the city with the most resources to offer the fashion world but also, as mentioned earlier, because it has no central mart building.

Trading Area and Economic Impact

The lack of a central mart in New York is a minor drawback compared with what many buyers consider the glory of shopping this crème de la crème of markets. New York, after all, is a major fashion leader, and buyers servicing stores of any size often go to New York to do so, regardless of the other markets they add to their schedule.

Textile and fiber companies and home furnishings producers maintain showrooms often in or near the garment district. Most local manufacturers feel they must maintain a New York showroom, and many regional manufacturers sponsor one as well, if only during market weeks. Many foreign manufacturers, high-fashion European designers, and emerging designers participate in the New York market. The Garment Industry Development Corporation's program Showroom New York (funded by the state of New York) also provides showroom space and advisory services to local emerging designers, helping to link brands, retailers, and designers.[1]

Originally, New York Fashion Week was under the auspices of CFDA (Council of Fashion Designers of America) and organized by CFDA's offshoot 7th on Sixth. In September 2001, CFDA sold the 7th on Sixth trademark and operations to the sports management and marketing agency International Management Group (IMG). Within the fashion industry IMG represents the world's top models, leading designers, and most influential photographers, art directors, and stylists.[2]

The New York market is open year-round, but specific times are still set aside for market weeks. (Chapters 6 through 15 contain specific listings of New York market weeks by industry.)

Advantages of the New York Market

Buyers who come to New York can shop not only the market but also the department stores and boutiques for which the city is known. It offers every kind of fashion in every price range, including men's, women's, and children's wear, accessories, intimate apparel, and cosmetics. New York is also home to the flagship stores of Macy's, Bloomingdale's, Lord & Taylor, Barneys, Bergdorf Goodman, and Saks Fifth Avenue. There is also a high concentration of national and international flagship designer stores. Areas like the Upper East Side, SoHo, and the Meatpacking District are brimming with elegant flagship boutiques like Marc Jacobs, Donna Karan, and Ralph Lauren. Because New York is one of the fashion capitals of the world, practically every important international fashion house has a flagship store here.

The city is also the hub of the fashion network. Many national organizations have headquarters here and stand ready to provide assistance and support services to buyers. Even on a personal level, the networking possibilities are good. Local New York buyers attend market weeks, as do buyers from all over the country. Buyers who can attend only a few market weeks each year generally head for New York.

Last but hardly least, part of the draw of New York is that it is the fashion capital of the United States. The fashion publishing industry is located there. The Fashion Institute of Technology (FIT), founded in 1944 and located in the garment district, provides training in fashion design, production, and merchandising, and since the 1940s, its graduates have been making their mark on American design. The Metropolitan Museum of Art houses one of the world's largest archives of historic fashions. New York is also home to opera, theater, and ballet—all sources of inspiration to those in the fashion world. Here, too, are the restaurants and nightclubs where celebrities of the media and the international political scene present their own unofficial fashion shows.

The Regional Market Centers

Each market center has its own unique flavor, as does each city, and buyers look forward to the varied experiences they will have at different markets. Many small retailers prefer to rely on regional market centers that are closer to home. Travel costs are lower, less time is spent away from the stores, and for many, the atmosphere feels more personal. Some popular regional markets include Los Angeles, San Francisco, Dallas, or Miami. Retailers can visit them year-round or during special market weeks.

The California Market

Much of the look and style of California's markets revolves around its casual lifestyle, which it seems to sell almost as much as it sells its clothing.

Los Angeles

Los Angeles's fashion industry alone directly supports 87,000 jobs.[3] Since the 1930s, when California introduced pants for women, the West Coast has been the source of many important trends in sportswear. Los Angeles is also home to some of the country's largest sportswear manufacturers, such as Guess, L.A. Gear, and Speedo. Other Los Angeles successes are BCBG Max Azria and Rodarte. Bob Mackie, who designs for Hollywood stars and is frequently seen on the television home shopping channel QVC, is also based in Los Angeles.

Surf-fashion firms include companies such as Hurley, Billabong, and Blake Kuwahara's KATA Eyewear.

Apparel design, production, and distribution are spread out along the entire West Coast, with a concentration in Los Angeles. The California Market Center, the iconic hub of the style industries in Los Angeles, is an important part of the industry. It holds markets, trade shows, seminars, and events for the fashion, home design, gifts, and textiles industries, in addition to exclusive events and sample sales open to the public (Figure 16.4).[4]

San Francisco

San Francisco is home to about 500 apparel companies, including Levi Strauss, Gap, Old Navy, and Jessica McClintock.[5] There are also more than one hundred retailers that carry locally manufactured merchandise labeled as SFMade. SFMade is a nonprofit that aims to boost the economy by keeping manufacturing in the San Francisco area. Banana Republic is an example of one retailer that carries these products. It has also replicated its popular SFMade pop-up shop in flagship locations in Chicago, Los Angeles, and New York.[6]

Macy's in San Francisco's Union Square has also contributed to the growth of the fashion industry by sponsoring the creation of a program called the Fashion Incubator San Francisco. Its purpose is to educate the city's fashion designers so they can become sustainable entrepreneurs. This initiative is geared toward boosting future employment opportunities in San Francisco and growth in the fashion industry.[7]

FIGURE 16.4 Joy Han's look on the runway at an L.A. trade show.

The Dallas Market

The mood at Dallas market weeks is strongly southwestern. Handcrafted clothes, or clothes that look handcrafted, with bright, vibrant colors are seen here. Once a center for budget garments, Dallas has become an important production and market center. Now the third largest center in the country, it advertises itself as the "marketplace for the Southwest, the nation, and the world." Dallas-produced fashions are shown alongside fashions from New York, California, and around the world. Popular Dallas-based designers include Shirin Askari, Nha Khanh, August Alexander, Prashe, and Abi Ferrin.[8]

The Dallas Market Center is a complete wholesale merchandise resource that holds fifty-plus markets each year. Retailers from around the globe source products ranging from home furnishings, gifts, decorative accessories, and lighting to textiles, fashion accessories, and men's, western, women's, and children's apparel.[9]

The Miami Market

The Miami market weeks have a highly international—mostly Hispanic and South American—flavor. Colors and styles are lively. The Miami market is also known for an outstanding selection of children's wear.

Greater Miami has become one of the most dynamic, cosmopolitan, and international fashion-producing centers in the country. Drawn by the temperate climate and quality labor force, many apparel designers and manufacturers now call South Florida home. Retailers find that Miami-produced clothing is well made, reasonably priced, and perfect for the semitropical weather that prevails in the Sun Belt. In Miami, three strong selling seasons—cruise wear, spring, and summer—are available year-round. In addition to cruise and resort wear, Miami design and production focus on budget and moderate-priced sportswear, swimwear, and children's clothing. Miami-based designers of better-priced daytime and evening wear are becoming known for their work.

The Miami Merchandise Mart, Florida's only wholesale mart, features more than 200 U.S. and international wholesale merchandise showrooms in 286,000 square feet of space, adjacent to Miami International Airport. Established in 1968, it is the premier trade destination for local, national, and international retail buyers.[10]

The Regional Marts

Although they are not major centers of fashion apparel production, several cities, such as Charlotte and Denver, have proven they can hold their own against larger marts. They do so primarily by emphasizing local design and production. Regional marts sponsor market weeks and in other ways operate much as the larger marts do.

Local marts have made inroads in servicing the stores in their trading area, and many department store buyers who regularly go to New York and Los Angeles feel they now must supplement these major buying trips with trips to their local regional market.

Trade Shows in the United States

Trade shows, which are held in market centers throughout the year, are sponsored by **trade associations**—professional organizations of manufacturers and sales representatives. A few of these events are major extravaganzas that attract buyers from across the country and even from abroad. MAGIC International, held twice a year at the Las Vegas Convention Center, has the atmosphere of an apparel mart market week minus the permanent facilities.

The typical U.S. trade show, however, is much smaller than a mart show and lasts two to four days. Regional trade shows are held in hotels and motels, civic centers, and small exhibition halls. Specialized trade shows cover areas of fashion that might otherwise get lost at major market weeks. The Big & Tall Associates shows suits and outerwear for big and tall men, for

example, and the Surf Expo features surf equipment and surf-inspired sportswear.

These small trade shows show every sign of being able to hold their own against the proliferation of marts and market weeks. Trade shows are especially popular with small retailers and exhibitors because they are typically less expensive than market weeks for both groups of participants to attend. Small retailers like to deal with sales reps who are personally familiar with their needs and can cater to them at these smaller exhibits. Buyers from boutiques find that trade shows are their best outlet for the kind of unique and unusual merchandise they seek. Trade shows are known for displaying the work of unusual or small designers who do not ordinarily exhibit at the major marts.

The disadvantage of trade shows is that the exhibitors are limited in number. Buyers have difficulty doing across-the-board buying that is easily accomplished during market weeks at major marts. Trade shows also cannot feature the ongoing service that marts offer, as marts are increasingly open year-round.

Foreign Fashion Markets

For several centuries, the foreign fashion market consisted entirely of French designers' high fashions. In the 1960s, the ready-to-wear market emerged first in Italy and then in France. Today, cultural and economic changes and a renewed interest in nationalism and ethnicity have combined to encourage the development of fashion markets worldwide. American buyers no longer travel abroad exclusively to France and Italy; they journey to fashion markets all over the globe.

At the opposite extreme from the fashion buyers who stick close to home are those who make a twice-yearly ritual of visiting the dazzling and often frenzied foreign fashion markets. As Americans have become increasingly fashion conscious, the foreign shows have taken on greater importance. Particularly for the retailers who cater to an upscale and fashion trendsetting clientele, even faithful attendance at the New York market weeks is not sufficient for staying at the forefront.

Foreign fashion markets are designed to show off the fashion industries around the world. In the leading foreign markets, clothing is typically designed and presented on two different levels. First in prestige and cost are the haute couture clothes. These original designs, which use luxury fabrics and are known for their exquisite detailing, are expensive out of necessity and thus are made in very limited numbers. With prices that start in the thousands of dollars for a single garment, haute couture design is affordable to only a small group of wealthy women and men.

STELLA'S STAR POWER

HAVING A FAMOUS name can bring many blessings, like having your friends Naomi Campbell, Kate Moss, and Yasmin Le Bon model at your senior collection fashion show, or having your father—a former Beatle—write a song especially for the occasion. It can even lead to being asked to head a major Paris fashion house only two years after receiving your degree in fashion design.

A famous name can also be a curse that causes fashion's heavy-hitters to tell every news outlet that you were only hired for your name. People may also imply, once your collections are successful, that you're not really the one doing the work. If you're Stella McCartney, you're able to take it all—good and bad—and make the very best of it.

McCartney was asked to head Paris fashion house Chloé two years after she graduated from Central St. Martins College of Arts and Design. When she accepted, her face was splashed across the front of every newspaper in London, leading many—including Karl Lagerfeld, the man she was hired to replace—to

speculate that it was a publicity stunt. But McCartney proved them wrong. More than fifteen years later, the consensus is that she is indeed a gifted designer in the fashion business.

In 2001, McCartney launched her own fashion house. Stella McCartney, Ltd., has estimated annual retail sales of $120 million, not including her many licensing deals like the wildly popular Stella McCartney for Adidas or L.I.L.Y. perfume with L'Oréal. Her company is successful because she has a deep understanding of her customer: a busy working woman who is looking for well-designed, fashionable, and wearable clothes rather than red-carpet eveningwear. "I like to design things that allow women to be themselves, but at the same time offer something that they might not have thought of or that they wouldn't have dared to do," she says. "For me, it's about finding the correct balance so that it feels comfortable and natural." It is this understanding of the emotion of clothes— of what lies beneath the surface—that propels McCartney's success.

Fall 2012

Stella McCartney

Fall 2013

The next layer of fashion design is called **prêt-à-porter** (pronounced "pret-ah-por-TAY"). A French term meaning "ready-to-wear," prêt-à-porter is produced in far larger numbers than haute couture. Like haute couture, it is introduced in foreign fashion markets at semiannual shows where design collections are revealed to the fashion world. Haute couture and designer prêt-à-porter provide the inspiration for the inexpensive mass-market designs that dominate the fashion market.

France

France first emerged as a fashion showcase during the reign of Louis XIV (1643–1715), often called the Sun King, partly because of his lavish lifestyle. The elaborate clothing worn by his court was widely copied by royalty and the wealthy throughout Europe. The splendor of his court at Versailles created a market for beautiful fabrics, tapestries, and lace. Textile production in Lyons and lace works in Alençon were established to meet these needs. Paris, already an important city and located only a few miles from Versailles, became the fashion capital. Paris is still considered the cradle of the fashion world.

Paris Couture

France has been the center of haute couture since 1858, when the house of Charles Frederick Worth, generally regarded as the father of Paris couture, opened its doors. Beginning about 1907, Paul Poiret became the second great fashion legend of Paris. Poiret was the first to stage fashion shows and to branch out into the related fields of perfume, accessories, fabric design, and interior decoration.

A **couture house** is an apparel firm for which a designer creates original designs and styles. The proprietor or designer of a couture house is known as a **couturier** (pronounced "koo-tour-ee-AY") if male or **couturière** ("koo-tour-ee-AIR") if female. Most Paris couture houses are known by the names of their founders—Yves Saint Laurent, Givenchy, and Chanel, for example. The name may survive even after the original designer's retirement or death, but the signature style changes with his or her successor. In recent years, rapid changes of personnel and licensing of designer names has blurred the identity of the fashion houses and focused attention on individual designers. For example, Karl Lagerfeld designs for Chanel and Fendi, as well as for himself.

In 1868, an elite couture trade association, called the Chambre Syndicale de la Couture Parisienne, came into being. Membership in the Chambre Syndicale (pronounced "shahmbrah seen-dee-KAHL") was by invitation only and was restricted to couture houses that agreed to abide by its strict rules. In 1973,

FIGURE 16.5 Serkan Cura's birdlike design for Spring 2012.

Fédération Française de la Couture, du Prêt-à-Porter des Couturiers et des Créateurs de Mode was established. La Fédération is the executive organ of all the trade associations (or Chambre Syndicales) of each fashion division. Haute couture, ready-to-wear, and menswear each has its own Chambre Syndicale. You can look up fashion show schedules and general information on the federation's website: www.modeaparis.com.[11]

The Chambre Syndicale is a strong force in the French fashion industry. From the foreign visitors' point of view, its most valuable contribution is the organization and scheduling of the twice-yearly market shows. It handles registration and issues the coveted (and limited) admission cards. It also registers and copyrights new fashion designs. It is illegal in France to copy a registered fashion design without making special arrangements and paying a fee. (In the United States, there is no copyright protection for clothing designs.) From its members' point of view, the Chambre Syndicale's most valuable contribution is that it represents its members in arbitration disputes and seeking regulation of wages and working hours.

Couture Shows. The Paris couture house trade shows are held twice yearly: the spring/summer collections (Figure 16.5) are shown in late January, and the fall/winter ones in late July. These shows have evolved into a promotional outlet for the couturiers. Today they are an expense rather than a source of income, as in the past. All the clothes in an haute couture collection are made to measure. Customers select a sample from the runway show, then make an appointment with the fashion house's atelier to get the garment custom made for them. This is, of course, outrageously expensive. The wealthy private customers in the audience, who order the clothes for their personal wardrobes, are too few in number for their purchases to exceed the costs of producing the samples and the show. The fashion press, who comprise the remainder of the audience, perform the mutually beneficial job of publicizing the exciting, glamorous news about the designers' creativity.

Other Couture Business Activities

The sales of haute couture clothing have steadily declined in recent years as prices have risen and customers have turned to designer ready-to-wear lines. To survive, couture houses have expanded into other, more lucrative activities, such as the development of ready-to-wear collections and the establishment of boutiques and the ever-present (and profitable) licensing arrangements.

Couturiers' Ready-to-Wear. Most couturiers' ready-to-wear clothes are sold to department and specialty stores, which often set aside special areas or departments to display these prestige items.

The exclusivity and cost of producing haute couture lines, in combination with declining craftsmanship skills among designers and atelier staff, have changed the Parisian fashion climate. The ready-to-wear business has completely eclipsed haute couture on the French prestige designer market. Ready-to-wear lines are not ordered directly by the customer but are bought in bulk by buyers, who select the styles they like from the runway and then order them in various sizes and quantities. Although some houses still have an haute couture atelier and participate in haute couture fashion shows, it's the ready-to-wear lines that are featured in their advertising, showrooms, and stores. Today, many famous fashion houses, like Balenciaga, Chloé, Louis Vuitton, and Yves Saint Laurent, produce ready-to-wear lines.

Couture Boutiques. The French word for *shop*, **boutique** has come to mean, more specifically, a shop that carries exclusive merchandise. In the past, many couturiers installed boutiques on the first floor or a lower floor of their design houses. Most famous fashion labels also have their own flagship ready-to-wear stores in key cities around the world. Goods sold in these shops are usually designed by the couture house staff and are sometimes even made in the couture workrooms. All bear the famous label.

This was where the haute couture customers made their appointments. Some of these boutiques still exist;

for example, Chanel's ready-to-wear flagship store on Rue Cambon in Paris is still adjoined to the Chanel atelier. Today, most French fashion houses have several flagship boutiques that sell their ready-to-wear collections as well as accessories. These stores are designed to reflect the image of the house and create an atmosphere that expresses the spirit of the label.

Licensing Agreements. The most lucrative business activities for couturiers are the numerous licensing arrangements they establish to sell their accessories and ready-to-wear lines and also a variety of goods produced by others on their behalf. The most popular prestige licenses include perfume, shoes, bags, sunglasses, and watches.

French Ready-to-Wear

The burgeoning French ready-to-wear (or prêt-à-porter) fashion has two distinct sources: designers and mass-market producers. Innovative ready-to-wear designers such as Dries Van Noten, Olivier Theyskens, and Junya Watanabe have added excitement to the French fashion industry over the years. Fast-growing contemporary brands like Zadig & Voltaire (Figure 16.6), Comptoir des Cotonniers, Sandro, Maje, Claudie Pierlot, and The Kooples are reinventing ready-to-wear fashion. Thus,

FIGURE 16.6 Zadig & Voltaire's ready-to-wear look for Fall 2013.

they have changed the image of Paris as the center of French fashion to the French center of international fashion leadership.[12]

To meet the needs of ready-to-wear designers, the Chambre Syndicale created an autonomous section for designers who work exclusively in ready-to-wear, designating them *créateurs* (pronounced "kray-ah-TERS") to distinguish them from couturiers. Among the **créateurs** are such important names as Karl Lagerfeld, Sonia Rykiel, Christian Lacroix, and Jean Paul Gaultier.

Although their prestige is great, the couturiers and créateurs represent only a small part of the French fashion industry in terms of numbers and revenue. The remaining 1,200 companies are mass producers of ready-to-wear apparel.

Prêt-à-Porter Trade Shows. The French ready-to-wear producers present their collections at two market shows a year. The first, for the Fall/Winter collections, is held in March, and the second in October, for the Spring/Summer collections. Actually, two large trade shows take place simultaneously. The runway shows, sponsored by the Chambre Syndicale for the prêt-à-porter designers, take place at Carousel du Louvre. At the other, sponsored by the Fédération, the mass-market prêt-à-porter collections are exhibited at the Porte de Versailles Exhibition Center. This trade show, known as Prêt-à-Porter Paris, brings together more than a thousand exhibitors from all over the world. With each succeeding show, the press pays more attention and provides more coverage of this end of the French fashion business.

A semiannual men's ready-to-wear show, Prêt-à-Porter Mode Masculin, traditionally held in January and July, is as important to the men's fashion industry as the women's ready-to-wear shows are to the women's fashion industry.[13]

Italy

Italy is France's most serious rival in the fashion industry. It has long been recognized as a leader in men's apparel, knitwear, leather accessories, and textiles.

A centuries-old tradition of quality craftsmanship and a close relationship between designers and manufacturers are common features of Italy's otherwise disparate fashion houses. Ermenegildo Zegna, a firm that markets three lines of menswear, also produces men's textiles. Rather than economize on labor costs through offshore manufacturing to the extent that designers in other developed countries do, Italian designers rely more on domestic factories. Consequently, much of their output is in the luxury price ranges. Italian manufacturers are also the sources for materials and production for many foreign designers.

FIGURE 16.7 Valentino's Spring 2013 couture design.

Italian Couture

Italy has long had couture houses named for the famous designers who head them, such as Valentino (Figure 16.7) and Mila Schön. Its designers are members of Italy's couture trade group (a counterpart to the Chambre Syndicale) known as the Camera Nazionale della Moda Italiana. The Camera Moda organizes the biannual ready-to-wear fashion-week runway shows that take place in Milan each year in March and September. You can look up schedule and general information at the association's website, www.cameramoda.com.

Unlike French couture houses, Italian couture designers are not all located in a single city. Although Milan is the biggest fashion center, couture designers may be found in Rome, Florence, and other Italian cities.

Both Italian and French couture depend heavily on Italian fabric and yarn innovation and design. Most of the excitement today in print and woven textile design is created and produced in the fabric mills of Italy. Italian knits are also known for their avant-garde styles.

Only a handful of Italian houses have an haute couture business today. There are no haute couture runway shows in Italy. Valentino and Versace show their haute couture collections in Paris. They are scheduled one week prior to the Paris shows so that foreign buyers can cover both important fashion markets in a single trip.

Like their Paris counterparts, many Italian couture houses have set up boutiques for the sale of exclusive accessories and limited lines of apparel. The designs are usually those of the couture house staff, and the apparel and accessories are sometimes made in the couture workrooms. All items offered in boutiques bear the couture house label.

Italian couture designers also have established licensing agreements with foreign producers. Some design and produce uniforms for employees of business firms, most notably airlines and car rental agencies. Some accept commissions to create fashion products ranging from perfume to menswear to home furnishings.

Italian Ready-to-Wear

Italy began to develop both its women's and men's ready-to-wear industries along with its couture fashions. As a result, it started exporting earlier than France, and today its economy relies heavily on its exporting program. The textile, apparel, footwear, and leather goods industries account for one-fifth of Italy's exports. Much of this exported merchandise is in the medium- to high-price range, especially in knitwear and accessories.

Designers. Innovative Italian ready-to-wear designers make their shows as exciting as the Paris ready-to-wear shows have become. Giorgio Armani and Versace are considered the standard bearers for two very different definitions of Italian design. Versace is noted for brightly colored prints, and Armani for classic elegance combined with comfortable styling. Other well-known Italian ready-to-wear designers are equally protective of their reputations for distinctive, recognizable signature styles. Among the leading designers are Dolce & Gabbana, Gianfranco Ferré, Krizia, Missoni, and Miuccia Prada. Ferragamo and Gucci are major names in shoes and accessories, and Fendi in fur.

Trade Shows and Market Centers. Until the late 1960s, the most important Italian ready-to-wear shows were staged at the elegant Pitti and Strossi palaces in Florence. Milan grew as a fashion center in the 1970s, and many designers began to show there, in addition to or instead of Florence.

Moreover, Italy hosts a number of shows featuring the categories of apparel, accessories, and textiles, for which Italian designers and manufacturers are internationally renowned. Leather shoes, handbags, gloves, and small leather goods are one major segment of Italy's fashion industry. Other accessories that are world famous are knitted hats, scarfs, and gloves; and silk scarfs and ties. Como, located in Northern Italy, is the hub of Italy's silk industry. The surrounding area is also one of the most recognized areas for trade and production of quality silk fabrics. It is important to note that trade shows are often held in the regions where the respective industries are centralized.

Great Britain

For many years, London's Savile Row was for menswear what Paris has been for women's apparel—the fountainhead of fashion inspiration. Savile Row is a wonderful place where each suit is handcrafted for its new owner, a process known as *bespoke tailoring*. (*Bespoke*, an archaic word meaning "to have reserved in advance," is applied in England to men's clothing that is made to measure, a process that takes six to ten weeks.)

In the 1980s, Italy became the main source of European-styled menswear, and Britain's fashion reputation focused on the craftsmanship of its tailoring and the quality of its tweeds and woolens rather than on trendsetting designs. Then, in the late 1990s, the British fashion industry, harking back to its daring hippie, mod, and punk styles of the late 1960s and 1970s, began to revive its image as a place for cool, new designs. Today, London continues to offer innovative designs (Figure 16.8).

FIGURE 16.8 Burberry Prorsum's menswear line for Spring 2013.

British Couture

Although Britain has never supported a couture industry the way that France and Italy have, it does offer famous design schools, such as the Royal College of Art, the London College of Fashion, and Central St. Martin's. St. Martin's alumni include internationally famous names Alexander McQueen, Hussein Chalayan, Julien MacDonald, Stella McCartney, and Clements Ribeiro. In addition to their own lines, these designers have or have had designer posts at leading French fashion houses. Other recent graduates of these schools, both British and foreign, are bringing design back to London. Philip Treacy is a five-time winner of the British Accessory Designer of the Year award for his striking hats.

British Ready-to-Wear

Ready-to-wear was a minor industry in Britain until after World War II. The fact that it entered a period of expansion after the war is largely due to the efforts of the government. According to one English fashion authority, the government became the "fairy godmother" responsible for "the survival of [British] couture and the rapid development of [Britain's] large and excellent ready-to-wear trade."[14]

Vivienne Westwood is a talent who has sparked and shocked the London fashion scene with her unorthodox clothes and lifestyle since the mid-1970s. Today, she continues to be an innovator and leader of the avant-garde pack.

Trade Shows

After a dormant period in the late 1980s and early 1990s, today the British runway shows and trade shows are a required stop on the European fashion circuit. British and foreign designers are showing, and British and foreign audiences are looking.

Other European Countries

For leadership in Europe, the fashion industry definitely focuses on France, Italy, and Britain. Other countries do attract international interest, however. In the 1990s and the 2000s, the Belgian town of Antwerp became a high-fashion mecca. Antwerp natives, such as Dries Van Noten, Ann Demeulemeester, Martin Margiela, Veronique Branquinho, A.F. Vandevorst, and Raf Simons, have achieved great success with their innovative and creative clothes. Although all these designers show and have their business headquarters in Paris, some of them still live in Antwerp. Other European countries that have a presence on the global fashion market are Ireland, with its traditional garments and fine linen, and Spain, with its swimwear, lingerie, and bridal fashion tradeshows. As the European Economic Community and other factors globalize the economy, however, national boundaries could assume less significance than they once had.

Germany and Scandinavia

Until the mid-1980s, most American fashion buyers skipped Germany on their European buying trips. The country was still divided into East and West, and few West German designers were well known outside Europe. But a new wave of high-fashion women's designers is changing this. Two apparel firms, Escada and Mondi, are noteworthy successes with their high-fashion lines. Designers Hugo Boss and Wolfgang Joop have developed international followings.

Although Germany's fashion industry is relatively small, its international trade fairs have become a major source of fashion inspiration for new fabric and designs. The Igedo Company produces the CPD women's wear and menswear fashion shows twice a year in Düsseldorf. Interestingly, this company has exported the fashion trade show through joint ventures with exhibition producers in Hong Kong, London, and Beijing. For textiles, the major international show is Interstoff in Frankfurt, and Cologne hosts shows of menswear, sportswear, children's wear, and apparel production machinery.

Each of the four Scandinavian countries—Norway, Sweden, Denmark, and Finland—has its own fashion industries and specialties. However, even though each country has its roster of designers, the styles tend to be alike, with emphasis on simple silhouettes and sturdy materials like wool, leather, and linen.

Leather apparel, primarily in menswear, is a popular Swedish product. Both Sweden and Norway are among the important suppliers of mink and other furs to countries around the world. Birger Christensen and Saga are leading furriers.

Scandinavia also offers some interesting textile designs. The best known, internationally, is the work of Finland's Marimekko.

Excellent jewelry in all price ranges is available in Scandinavia. The area has long been known for its clean-cut designs in gold and silver. Some well-known, Swedish-born contemporary designers include expatriates Lars Nilsson and Richard Bengtsson.

Canada

The development of a group of innovative designers has given the Canadian fashion industry a growing sense of confidence that has paid off in real growth. The industry also has a strong relationship with the United States and vice versa—about 75 percent of Canada's apparel exports go to the United States.[15] There has

Natalie Massenet

NET-A-PORTER: ONE-CLICK WONDER

NET-A-PORTER'S FOUNDER and executive chairperson Natalie Massenet knew what the luxury consumer would respond to when she brought her "shopable magazine" vision to life in 2000. In her previous role as a fashion editor, Massenet observed a disconnect between what magazines were telling customers to buy and the merchandise that stores actually carried. Readers complained that they were not able to find the items they were reading about. Her answer was to create a pure-play luxury shopping destination on the Internet—and Net-A-Porter.com was born.

This was nearly a decade before fashion's adoption of everything digital—elaborate editorial content, interactive e-commerce platforms, and high-end fashion houses' embrace of social media were still in their infancy. The secret to Net-A-Porter's success is that it combines all of these things in a single shopping destination. It possesses one of the most well-curated collections of designer apparel and accessories for purchase online, delivered alongside a relevant and compelling weekly digital magazine.

In the early years it was difficult to get top brands to work with Net-A-Porter, but now they are clamoring to be considered. Stella McCartney, Yves Saint Laurent, Alexander Wang, and RM by Roland Mauret are among the designers who have created capsule collections for the site. Net-A-Porter's second e-tail site, THE OUTNET.com, sells stock from previous collections at a discount and has been very successful. Its launch was followed up by the first global menswear retail site, mrporter.com.

In the years since the launch of Net-A-Porter, mobile shopping has become increasingly important. Sixty percent of customers actively use a smart phone, and between 20 and 30 percent of all retail transactions are conducted on either a smart phone or tablet. Net-A-Porter updated its "What's New" app and saw more than a doubling in downloads, from 300,000 to more than 750,000. The company also has a new automated warehouse where orders will be packed and shipped six times more efficiently than the old rate.

The U.S. is the fastest-growing and largest market for Net-A-Porter, producing more than 30 percent of its business. Buying for this market has grown six times since the company expanded its business in 2006 (or eight times if including THE OUTNET and MR PORTER). To maintain this growth in the U.S., Net-A-Porter opened its first headquarters in New York City in June 2012.

THEN & NOW

also recently been an influx of U.S. retailers in Canada, including Target and Sears.

As the business relationship between the two countries grows stronger, fashion industry leaders in both Canada and the United States are pushing to streamline the safety and regulation process across the border. Sometimes, problems can occur when a U.S. retailer opens a store in Canada. It can discover that the apparel sourcing laws and regulations are different than back home. "We've become a unified retail marketplace and our main challenge is not where we source from, but the need to ensure the free flow of goods between Canada and the U.S.," says Bob Kirke, executive director of Canadian Apparel Federation, which is based in Ottawa.[16]

The Canadian fashion industry has two important centers: the largest is Montreal, in Quebec; second is Toronto, in Ontario. Canadian trade shows continue to grow and prosper. The North American Fur and Fashion exhibition has been in existence for more than three decades. "We're still trying to be more creative to become part of the global fashion world," says Chantal Durivage, copresident of Sensation Mode, which operates Montreal Fashion Week.

Fashion week in Toronto is considered part of the international fashion weeks (Figure 16.9), with World MasterCard as a sponsor. Fashion week appears to have caught the attention of the international media and foreign buyers, according to Robin Kay, president of the show and organizer of the Fashion Design Council of Canada.[17]

Well-known Canadian designers from Montreal include Andrea Lenczner and Christie Smythe, Zoran Dobric, Marisa Minicucci, Marie Saint Pierre, and Simon Chang. Popular designers from Toronto include Philip Sparks, Jeremy Laing, Kimberley Newport-Mimran, Brenda Beddome, Pat McDonagh, and Alfred Sung.

Internationally successful Toronto-based manufacturers and retailers include Club Monaco, M.A.C., and Roots. Roots made the U.S. uniforms for the Winter Olympics in 2002 and 2006. It was the first time the Winter Olympics used a company outside sportswear giants like Nike and Adidas. The value-driven Canadian brand Joe Fresh, known for its bright colors and contemporary styles, has also made a splash in the United States, opening up stores in New York City in late 2011. In 2012, the company announced a partnership with J.C. Penney to open branded boutiques in 700 of the department store's locations.[18]

Most Canadian apparel manufacturing is located in Montreal, but every province has a stake in the industry, and shows in each province bring local goods to

FIGURE 16.9 A look from Toronto's Fashion Week in 2012.

the attention of other Canadians and to buyers from the United States and around the world. Montreal and Toronto each have their own fashion week twice a year, where local men's and women's wear designers showcase their new collections in runway shows. Other women's apparel and accessories shows include Western Apparel Market in Vancouver, the Alberta Fashion Market in Edmonton, the Prairie Apparel Markets in Winnipeg, the Saskatoon Apparel Market, and Toronto's Mode Accessories show. Children's wear markets take place in Vancouver and Alberta, and the North American Fur and Fashion Exposition is featured at the Place Bonaventure in Montreal. Alberta, Montreal, Vancouver, and Toronto all host gift shows.

The Americas and the Caribbean Basin

By the mid-1970s, the Central and South American market could be added to the growing list of international fashion markets. The fashion world began visiting market centers in Rio de Janeiro, Buenos Aires, São Paulo (Figure 16.10), and Bogotá.

For buyers and producers from the United States and Canada, the signing of the North American Free Trade Agreement (NAFTA) in 1994 brought new possibilities in the Mexican market. The rest of Central and South America and the Caribbean countries began to

FIGURE 16.10 Andre Lima's design on the runway at São Paulo's Fashion Week Spring/Summer 2013.

press for inclusion in this trading pact. (NAFTA is discussed more in detail in Chapter 17.)

Two factors contributed to this new presence in the fashion world. The first was the appeal to Americans and entrepreneurs from other developed countries of cheap sources of materials and labor. The second was the conveniently corresponding development of a fashion industry in Mexico and Central and South America.

From the perspective of Mexico and the Central and South American governments, the fashion industry became a means of increasing their gross national product and their status in the world marketplace.

The combination of Central America and the West Indies have suffered from the economic downturn, but the Dominican Republic and Honduras remain major suppliers in the apparel and textile industries.[19]

Fashion Products

The fashion industry in the Americas and the Caribbean Basin offers fashion on three levels. First, several countries have developed their own high-fashion industries, many of which are ripe for import to the United States and Europe. The second level revolves around the development of fashion products that reflect each country's national heritage of crafts. With a renewed interest in ethnicity throughout the world, such products are welcome. Third and finally, Central America, South America, Mexico, and the West Indies have become important offshore sources of products made to North American manufacturers' specifications.

Handbag buyers seek out the better-quality goods of Argentina and go to Brazil for moderate-quality goods. Uruguay is another important source of moderate- to high-quality handbags.

The most important shoe center is Brazil, where manufacturers concentrate on creating a stylish product made from lasts that fit North American feet. Belts and small leather goods are the specialty of Brazil, Argentina, and the Dominican Republic.

Costume jewelry is another important product from this region. Ecuador, Peru, and Mexico export silver and gold jewelry of native design.

Trade Shows in the Americas and the Caribbean Basin

The single most important market center in South America is São Paulo, Brazil. At the turn of the millennium, the emergence of designer talents like Alexandre Herchcovitch, Rosa Chá, and Icarius de Menezes coincided with a major Brazilian boom in fashion in general. The appearance of superstar models like Gisele Bündchen in these designers' shows attracted enough attention to put São Paolo fashion week on the map. Since then, São Paolo fashion week has been steadily growing in importance, and it may become one of the most attended and publicized fashion events in the world. Other important international fairs featuring textiles and textile products as well as fashion accessories are held in Bogotá, Colombia; Lima, Peru; San Salvador, El Salvador; and Santiago, Chile.

These shows offer not only an opportunity for buyers from North America and elsewhere but also a place for U.S. textile producers to be seen by potential customers in the region.

Asia and Oceania

The major portion of imports from the Far East to the United States has been low-priced, high-volume merchandise, and hardly any of the apparel has qualified as "designer merchandise." However, this is changing, as fashion buyers can now find exciting, innovative styles offered by new design-oriented Asian stylists.

Buyers have used certain countries in the Far East as a market in which to have fashions they saw in the European fashion centers copied and adapted. A fashion buyer needs to know which areas in the Far East are best equipped to handle specific types of manufacturing. Japan and Hong Kong were once the two major contract, or copyist, countries. But Japan has upgraded its fashion image so that today it is a producer of outstanding high-styled, high-priced fashion apparel (Figure 16.11). Hong Kong is working to develop the apparel industry of China and promoting Chinese goods in its international trade fairs.

Japan

Mercedes-Benz Fashion Week Tokyo grows in importance every year. The increasing attention being paid to fashion week in Japan, according to retailers and executives at Japanese fashion brands, is due to the uniqueness of design from this country. The Japan Fashion Week Organization hosts the Mercedes-Benz Fashion Week Tokyo twice a year. The organization also provides information about Japan's textile and fashion products and services overseas (Figure 16.12).[20]

Japanese Ready-to-Wear. In the 1950s and 1960s, the Japanese faithfully copied Western trends. Ironically, in the 1970s, as Western dress had finally won acceptance in Japan, a group of highly original Japanese designers—Hanae Mori, Kenzo Takada, Issey Miyake, and Kansai Yamamoto—emerged. They first worked in Paris, where their lines were design sensations that rivaled the French prêt-à-porter designers. For over a decade, in fact, these daring designers were thought of as French rather than Japanese. Some of them still show in Paris.

Japanese Designers. In the early 1980s, a mostly new wave of avant-garde designers—Rei Kawakubo of Comme des Garçons, Yohji Yamamoto, and Matsuhiro Matsuda—stormed the American fashion scene.

Although these Japanese designers continue to be a force in the American fashion world, and no one disputes their creative brilliance, their clothes never became commercially successful in America. U.S. retailers had trouble mass-merchandising the designs, which appeal mostly to customers who are looking for strikingly unusual shapes and fabrics. Today, although their work is highly revered and regarded as a source of great inspiration for the fashion industry, they remain niche players in the market.

In the 1990s, the latest generation of Japanese designers, catering to a domestic market, have, like their British contemporaries, focused on retro pop cultural influences such as hippie beads and T-shirts and 1970s punk. Popular Japanese designers today include Yasutoshi Ezumi, Shinichiro Arakawa, Hiroaki Ohya,

FIGURE 16.11 Shiho Shiroma's "Lightning Trip" collection for Spring/Summer 2013.

FIGURE 16.12 The Japan Creation show offers visitors trends in fabric, color, and fashion.

Kosuke Tsumura, and Masaki Matsushima, and these designers tend to create technically ingenious designs based on a theme or concept.

China

In 2000, the United States entered a trade agreement with China that gave China normal trader status. This paved the way for the country's entry into the World Trade Organization (WTO). Since then, China's growth in the apparel industry has been clear. Among the products that China exports, one of the most sought after is silk. As the Chinese have become more proficient in finishing processes for weaving, printing, and dyeing, they have increased their exports of finished silk fabrics and apparel products. China is also the world's largest cotton producer, with an estimated crop of thirty-four million bales from 2012 to 2013.[21] Inexpensive plastic shoes, leather, and fur are other important exports. Several trade shows in Beijing and Shanghai have been instituted by Western-owned exhibition producers to promote Chinese leather to the international market.

Hong Kong. In July 1997, Hong Kong rejoined mainland China after 156 years as a British Crown colony. The world held its collective breath, waiting to see what would become of this quintessentially market-driven world trading center when it came under communist rule. The agreement between Britain and China calls for the governing of Hong Kong as a Special Administrative Region for fifty years, and local businesses are reassuring their international customers that Hong Kong will continue to offer all the advantages they have enjoyed plus more. In addition to the political change, Hong Kong has experienced a move in its economy from manufacturing to trade and service industries, and its trade shows, once focused on promoting its own goods, now concentrate on serving as an international marketplace. Some of the advantages of participating in Hong Kong trade shows include the following:

- A duty-free port where exhibitors can bring in their samples and sell them from the exhibition.
- A newly expanded convention and exhibition center.
- A central location in Asia, easily reached by air.
- A thriving hospitality industry with a growing number of hotels and world-class restaurants.

As trade shows continue to grow to accommodate China's prominence in the global market, Hong Kong is still relevant as a safe window to the mainland.

Hong Kong Fashion Week has long focused on design. The Hong Kong Trade Development Council sponsors more than twenty exhibitions. Among the most well known are Hong Kong Fashion Week, World Boutique, Hong Kong International Jewelry Show, Hong Kong Toys & Games Fair, Hong Kong Houseware Fair, and the Inno Design Tech Expo. UBM Asia, a trade show producer based in Hong Kong, produces the All China Leather Exhibition in Shanghai and the APLF-Materials Manufacturing and Technology Fair in Hong Kong—the premier events of their kind—and the Cosmoprof Asia beauty fair.

Notable Hong Kong designers include Vivienne Tam, Flora Cheong-Leen, and Barney Cheng.

India

India's centuries-old textile industry continues to make it a major force in the Asian textile market. India also has its own rapidly expanding fashion industry with a variety of homegrown designers. Most set up their businesses at the end of the 1990s in response to India's growing upper class and its appetite for global styles. New Delhi has two different fashion weeks. Since 1999, the city has hosted Lakmé Fashion Week, which draws tremendous attention and is produced by IMG, the same event-marketing conglomerate that runs New York's Fashion Week.

The Fashion Design Council of India produces a calendar of fashion events that includes the biannual pret weeks for women's wear, Wills Lifestyle India Fashion Week; a dedicated week for men's fashion, Van Heusen India Men's Week; and the annual platform for couture, Synergy I Delhi Couture Week.[22] The India Trade Promotion Organization conducts promotions and fashion events with major retailers and assists U.S. and European designers in developing sourcing contacts in India (Figure 16.13).

India is also the home of the largest hand-loom industry in the world, and cotton and silk are the strongest growth areas of the Indian textile industry. India is the second largest producer of silk and also the largest consumer of silk in the world. It is known for its production of mulberry, oak and tropical tasar, muga, and eri silks. India's textile and sericulture (the rearing of silkworms for the production of raw silk) industries are expected to grow, which will also generate more jobs.[23]

Other Asian Countries

The other countries of Asia, being smaller and, in many cases, less industrialized than those discussed previously, have less influence on the American apparel industry, but their roles as trading partners and sites of offshore production grow increasingly important.

Singapore has many of the advantages of Hong Kong—an easily accessible location, a multinational

FIGURE 16.13 Tarum Tahiliani's design from India's Fashion Week.

population, and expertise in international trade. It is Hong Kong's chief rival as a center for trade shows.

Korea, with a design history similar to Japan's, has some exciting young designers creating for the Korean fashion-conscious market. Much of the production of ready-to-wear in Korea is still contract work. But because of the fashion design movement among young Koreans, this is slowly beginning to change.

Indonesia, Thailand, Malaysia, Vietnam, and the Philippines are regarded by many Americans in the apparel industry as sites of offshore production, but that is only part of the story. As these developing countries become more industrialized and the standard of living improves, their own industries and markets are taking their place in the global economy. Thailand, for example, has for many years been a producer of fine printed silk and cotton.

Oceania

Australia is not a large producer in the textile and apparel industries, but it is known for wool. In 2009 to 2010 there were seventy-three million sheep shorn in Australia, which produced 340 million kilograms of greasy wool. Production is expected to continue to

FIGURE 16.14 Easton Pearson's design from an Australian trade show.

increase marginally at a steady rate.[24] Australia is also credited with the origin of UGG boots, which became a major trend in the United States in the 2000s.

New Zealand is similar to Australia in that it imports more than it exports. Its retail market operates approximately a season behind Europe and the United States. Due to this, local operators are able to purchase end-of-season surplus goods and see them at the start of the season in New Zealand.[25]

Trends in Global Fashion Markets

The fashion industry survives through change. International fashion markets are working furiously to keep up with the five major changes that are necessary to remain viable in a highly competitive global market as discussed in the following sections. There are international fashion weeks in Australia (Figure 16.14), Brazil, New Zealand, Canada, Columbia, Mexico, Iceland, Hong Kong, Thailand, Japan, and South Africa. Most of these fashion weeks are geared toward promoting the local designer industry, with the eventual goal of competing with the dominant world fashion capitals—New York, Milan, and Paris. Many also receive government sponsorships because they help promote trade and taxes and boost the local economy with big business for hotels and airlines. But there are also other important industry changes.

First, mart managements and trade associations in the United States have responded to industry growth, shifts in population, and changes in buying habits. Marts have also of necessity become more competitive

FIGURE 16.15 The WWDMAGIC show in Las Vegas attracts buyers from all over the globe. Contacts made at WWDMAGIC can lead to sales contracts during and after the show.

with one another. Elaborate promotions designed to lure buyers now routinely include offers of reduced airfare and hotel rooms. Seminars and cocktail receptions are further enticements. The move toward year-round service is another response to competition. Many facilities have expanded their exhibition space and provided access to secretarial and clerical services.

Second, the expense of attending markets and trade shows has had an impact on buyers and exhibitors at home and abroad. For example, the haute couture showings in Paris have become promotional events; buyers

FIGURE 16.16 The NuOrder System provides an online marketplace for the fashion industry, creating a system that streamlines the ordering process between buyers and brands.

attend them vicariously by reading the fashion press. Economic globalization has made fashion capitals like Paris, Milan, and New York showplaces for designers from all over the world, not just from the home country. Retail buying trips to the national and international market centers have become the province of senior staff, who must make decisions for more departments or store units. Designers and other vendors carefully weigh the costs and benefits of several less elaborate exhibitions against fewer, more lavish ones (Figure 16.15).

Third is another aspect of globalization: developing countries are now becoming major players in the fashion industries, primarily as sources of materials and production, but also as importers and exporters of finished goods.

Fourth is the increased use of online promotion and distribution of information (Figure 16.16). Buyers, press, and consumers can now access information instantly. Some people argue that all this product information has made the consumer's attention span for trends shorter. Photos of collections are now shown so quickly that the clothes may look old by the time they hit the stores. However, this increased marketing and promotion can help to spur sales.

Fifth is the U.S. Commerce Department's International Buyer's Program, a joint government-industry effort designed to increase U.S. export sales by promoting international attendance at major U.S. industry exhibitions. It provides practical, hands-on assistance to U.S. exhibitors interested in exporting and making contacts with prospective overseas trade partners.[26]

Summary and Review

A market is a meeting place of buyers and sellers. Retail buyers of fashion goods go to market several times a year during market weeks, at the market centers of New York, Los Angeles, and Miami, and regional marts in other cities, including Atlanta, Chicago, Dallas, and Denver. With the exception of New York, where an entire district serves as a marketplace, markets are located in large convention centers with exhibition halls called marts. In addition to visiting the manufacturers' sales representatives in their showrooms or multiline sales reps in temporary exhibition spaces, the buyers may attend trade shows and seminars sponsored by trade organizations.

In Europe, market weeks are semiannual. Designers' haute couture (custom designs) and ready-to-wear collections are shown in the market centers of Paris, Milan, and London. Numerous trade shows for apparel, accessories, and textiles are presented in other cities.

Quebec is the Canadian province with the largest fashion industry, but all the provinces have apparel manufacturers, and market weeks and trade shows are held in major cities across the country.

The Americas and the Caribbean Basin continue to develop as centers for the production of wool and wool products, leather goods, and costume jewelry.

Japan's fashion designers and producers operate on an international scale with showings, boutiques, and manufacturing facilities at home and abroad. The biggest international market for fashion goods in Asia is Hong Kong. Apparel businesses there are using their manufacturing and marketing expertise to develop the silk, leather, and fur industries on the Chinese mainland. China is also the world's largest cotton producer.

Cotton and silk are the strongest growth areas of the Indian textile industry, and the country continues to build its production and manufacturing industry.

Singapore, Indonesia, Thailand, Malaysia, Vietnam, and the Philippines also continue to increase their presence in the textile industry and their production and manufacturing services.

Australia is steadily producing wool. New Zealand purchases surplus goods from Europe and the United States.

The fashion industry is truly operating in a global economy.

For Review

1. What criteria must be met for an area to be considered a market center?
2. What support services for buyers are offered by the marts during and between market weeks?
3. What distinguishes New York City as the major fashion market center in the United States?
4. Describe the distinctive characteristics of the three regional market centers.
5. What are the advantages and disadvantages of trade shows?
6. What business activities have the Paris couture houses undertaken to offset the decline in sales of haute couture clothing?
7. Name the fashion products for which Italy and Britain, respectively, are considered leaders.
8. Name the fashion products for which Canada is considered a leader.
9. Name the fashion products for which Japan is considered a leader.
10. What role does Hong Kong play in the international fashion market?
11. What role does India have in the fashion industry?

For Discussion

1. Discuss the role of the Far East to producers and retailers of fashion goods. What are some current emerging global markets?
2. The reputation of Paris as a prime source of fashion inspiration began to develop several centuries ago as the result of many interrelating factors. Identify those factors and discuss their importance in the development of any major fashion design center.

Trade Talk

Define or briefly explain the following terms:

boutique
buyer's directory
créateur
couture house
couturier/couturière
domestic market
foreign market
market
market center
market week
mart
prêt-à-porter
sales representative
trade association
trade show

Chapter Seventeen
GLOBAL SOURCING AND MERCHANDISING

KEY CONCEPTS

- Means of importing for retailers and manufacturers
- The role of offshore production in product development
- The international balance of trade and its effects on the fashion industry
- International trading laws and agreements between the United States and its trading partners

Because nations are no longer able or willing to produce all the goods and services they need and want, they rely on one another to supply them with what they cannot or choose not to produce themselves. In the process, the world's nations have become economically interdependent. The world is, in effect, one huge global market. We are less a universe made up of individual nations and more one world. This process—whereby the nations of the world become more interlinked with one another—is called *globalization*. The fashion industry is very much a part of the global economy, so much so that those who work in the business invented a term to describe the process of shopping for and purchasing imported goods: **global sourcing** (Figure 17.1). When a firm in a country, such as the United States, buys foreign goods, it **imports** them (Figure 17.2). The country that furnishes the goods, such as Italy, **exports** them. Most countries are both importers and exporters, although, as we shall see, they do not necessarily do each activity in equal amounts.

Fashion producers, retailers, and consumers in the United States have learned to expect the variety and sophistication that imports provide. The world of international trading is undeniably a fascinating one; this is its great appeal. Long gone are the days when foreign buying in the fashion industry consisted of buyers traveling to France a few times a year for the haute couture shows. Even then, very few U.S. retail store buyers actually bought haute couture. They bought ideas and patterns—and then came home to have them produced by American manufacturers. Eventually, as the world experienced a strong and growing post–World War II economy, other European countries—Italy at first, and then other Western European nations—developed their own fashion industries and began luring foreign—that is, American—buyers.

The rest of the world soon followed. Asia, long a source of import goods in home furnishings and a few other specialized areas, went after the U.S. fashion market. Mexico and the Central and South American countries have been the most recent to tap into the

339

FIGURE 17.1 Traveling the globe is an everyday experience for today's buyers. Tsim Sha Shui, in Kowloon, is a neon-lit shopping district for expensive jewelry and clothing from around the world.

FIGURE 17.2 The United States often imports foreign goods from other countries.

mother lode that many consider the American fashion consumer market to be. In sub-Saharan Africa, the manufacture of textiles presents a promising prospect for export; the establishment of this industry would help rebuild the economies of nations recovering from decades of political and military upheaval.

American buyers have expanded their sources to cover, quite literally, the globe. There is no place in the world that fashion buyers do not travel to in order to obtain goods. Where the Far Eastern circuit once meant shopping the markets in Hong Kong and Taiwan for raw materials, it now also means traveling to Japan for high fashion and places such as India, Vietnam, Sri Lanka, Indonesia, Malaysia, and the Philippines for their growing number of fashion specialties. American buyers have learned to use a global market to their advantage, molding it to current trends such as private-label manufacturing and specification ordering. They have learned to work their way through the labyrinth of federal and international restrictions that regulate international trade.

Adding to the complexity of global sourcing is the increasing reliance of textile and apparel producers on **offshore production**, the use of foreign workers in one or more countries to complete the steps of manufacturing the goods that bear the producer's label. U.S.-owned firms, as well as companies based in Canada, Western Europe, and other industrialized nations, use a variety of arrangements to take advantage of the resources available in countries with developing textile and apparel industries. Company-owned factories abroad, contracts with factories owned by citizens of the foreign country, and joint ownership are all options. A garment may be made of fibers grown in one country, woven into fabric in another, cut in a third, and assembled in a fourth. Decisions of where and how such multinational goods will be made have implications for quality and production costs.

Importing by Retailers

Retailers are the primary importers of foreign goods in the fashion industry, although manufacturers also seek global sourcing. Retailers like imports for several reasons: their uniqueness, quality, cost, and the variety they add to their stock. They constantly seek merchandise that makes their stores stand out in special and unique ways that set them apart from the competition. Foreign merchandise often fits that bill.

Global sourcing is a complex and often complicated business. What makes a foreign source attractive—its low cost and promise of higher profits—can be lost or diminished in a matter of minutes if something goes wrong.

Anyone who intends to buy goods from a foreign country needs a thorough knowledge of its local laws and regulations, particularly the laws that regulate exporting and importing, the efficiency of the transportation system, and the availability and skill of the labor force. The buyer must be well versed on the tax system and exchange rates. He or she must understand local and national customs and must be well informed about the current political and economic climate. Finally, the buyer must be up-to-date on U.S. import–export regulations, including any pending legislation, and must know all this for any country in which he or she intends to do business. This is why importing is best done by someone with access to good suppliers and extensive experience in dealing with foreign manufacturers and import regulations.

To gain entry to foreign fashion markets, as well as to cover them extensively, U.S. buyers rely on the help and experience of intermediaries. These specialists help U.S. buyers shop in the international markets successfully. Foreign-made goods can be purchased at and by the following:

- Foreign fashion markets
- Store-owned foreign buying offices
- Commissionaires or independent agents
- Import fairs held in the United States
- Importers

American Buyers and International Fashion Markets

Buyers like and need to travel to foreign fashion markets so they can observe new trends firsthand and buy goods suited to their customers. The international markets offer a variety of goods, but not all of them are suited to the American marketplace. By personally shopping in international markets, often during market weeks, American buyers can be sure that they are obtaining goods that will sell at home. They are also able to soak up the cultural and social climates of the countries to which they travel, which in turn helps them translate what is new and exciting to their customers.

Store-Owned Foreign Buying Offices

Some stores—those that are large enough to do so or whose image is very special—maintain company-owned foreign buying offices. Buyers who work in these offices support and advise store buyers by surveying the market for new trends, supervising purchases, and following up on delivery. Because they are an extension of the store, buyers in foreign buying offices are often authorized to make purchases just as store buyers are when they shop in foreign and domestic markets.

If the purchase is part of a new trend, stores need the goods when they are still new and customers are still eager to buy them. If it is part of a foreign theme promotion, goods must be delivered while the promotion is in progress. Delivery—especially timely delivery—has been a major problem with imported goods.

Stores generally locate their buying offices in major fashion capitals such as Paris, Rome, London, Hong Kong, and Tokyo, from which their buyers can travel to smaller markets around the world.

Saks Fifth Avenue and Neiman Marcus maintain store-owned foreign buying offices, as do the big general-merchandise chains such as Sears, J.C. Penney, and Walmart. Some stores that cannot afford their own foreign buying offices subscribe to the services of independently owned buying offices with foreign facilities, which shop exclusively for their member stores. An example is the Doneger Group.

Foreign Commissionaires or Agents

In contrast to store-owned foreign buying offices are **commissionaires**, or foreign-owned independent agents. Commissionaires, whose offices are also located in key buying cities, tend to be smaller than store-owned offices. Commissionaires also represent both retailers and manufacturers.

Apart from these differences, though, they provide many of the same services as store-owned foreign buying offices. They often have specialized buyers, or market representatives, who work closely with clients, keeping them abreast of what is generally available and helping them locate specific goods. As is the case with store-owned buying offices, a substantial part of the staff's time is spent following up on purchases to make sure they are delivered when they are needed.

Unlike store buyers, who are authorized to purchase on the store's behalf, commissionaires do not purchase unless they have been authorized to do so.

Commissionaires are paid on a fee basis. Usually, they take a percentage of the **first cost** in the country of origin.

Foreign Import Fairs in the United States

Another way to buy foreign goods is to attend one or more of the foreign import fairs that are now regularly

GLOBAL RETAILERS:
THEY CAME, THEY SAW, THEY CONQUERED! OR DID THEY?

RETAILING TODAY IS a giant global force in what has become a small, small world. American companies have long been the leaders in retail store openings across the U.S., but retailers from around the world have begun to catch up. From Sweden came H&M; from England, Topshop; and Spain has given us Zara, Mango, and Desigual. Japan's Uniqlo is the latest global retailer to expand to the American market.

Uniqlo, Zara, and H&M, in particular, are three global retailers that are making strides by bucking traditional retail models. Uniqlo's focus is on quality and longevity. Their strategy is to avoid trendy fashions and build a supply chain to deliver technology-based, differentiated products that appeal to the masses. In contrast, Zara has built its strategy around consumer trends, embracing the fast-changing tastes of its customers. To do this successfully, Zara has developed a highly responsive supply chain that enables delivery of new fashions as soon as a trend emerges. H&M's strategy is a hybrid of the Uniqlo and Zara models. It manages to merge a commitment to longevity while staying responsive to fashion trends. What enables H&M to react quickly is its network of twenty to thirty production offices, which are placed close to its suppliers.

Despite their different retail strategies, all three companies understand that retail success doesn't come from guessing what the next hot style will be. Each of these companies has a deep understanding of their customers' wants and needs. A fashion retailer may have a few great merchants who are able to put together a string of winners, but being dependent on the keen eye of a few people is a risky strategy. Instead, these three companies have built systems for identifying consumer preferences.

At Uniqlo, getting consumer preferences right is extremely important because of its lengthy development cycles and long-term commitments to materials and products. For Zara, reacting to consumer demands is a core component of its competitive advantage, and H&M is well known for its focus on researching and predicting emerging trends. These three companies have institutionalized their sales forecasting process, which has resulted in greatly reducing their markdowns. Across the industry, 30-40 percent of products are sold at markdown prices, as compared to only 15-20 percent for these companies.

What is remarkable about Uniqlo, Zara, and H&M is that each company has abandoned the traditional retail model in favor of its own approach. Should we watch and learn or should we go where others have feared to tread—and do it the American way? It's all up to you!

FIGURE 17.3 Intertextile Beijing showcases apparel fabrics and accessories from China and around the world.

held in the United States. Many foreign countries participate in such shows or stage their own fashion fairs in the United States (Figure 17.3).

These shows perform two important functions. First, they give foreign manufacturers and designers the same chance to observe American culture that Americans get when they buy in foreign fashion markets. The result is usually closer collaboration between buyers and manufacturers to adapt styles and quality to American tastes. Second, they increase the size and depth of the import market by giving buyers of small- and intermediate-size stores who would not ordinarily tap into the foreign market a chance to do so. To provide their customers with imported merchandise, these buyers need not maintain foreign representatives or shop in the foreign markets, neither of which would be cost-effective for their operations.

Importing by U.S. Businesses

Last but hardly least in a market that relies on foreign goods, American buyers purchase from American-owned importing firms. Import firms shop in the international markets to purchase their own lines, which they put together and display to retailers. Shopping these lines gives small retailers an opportunity to purchase foreign fashion merchandise that would not otherwise be available to them. The drawback to this method is that it does not allow for the customized ordering that buyers from big stores and chains have come to expect.

U.S. manufacturers, initially upset about the growth of direct importing done by retailers, have turned to offshore sources for the same reasons that retailers do:

price advantage, exclusivity, and workmanship. Like retailers, they often cite high domestic labor costs as a primary reason for resorting to imports. But labor costs must be viewed in light of other considerations if a manufacturer is to maintain control of its brands' images. For example, a sportswear manufacturer may combine fine-quality knitwear produced overseas with domestically produced skirts or pants to create a line of separates.

Today, the increasing labor costs in China, high import duties, fluctuating currency exchange rates, and uncertainty over fuel costs are making manufacturing in the United States more appealing. With increased domestic manufacturing, there is also the opportunity for U.S. job growth. These shifts are causing companies to buy more goods that are "Made in America."[1]

A classic example of this is American Apparel. The company, known for trendy, undecorated T-shirts, underwear, jeans, and other apparel sold in more than 250 American Apparel stores around the world, continues to apply current trends by manufacturing its primary apparel exclusively in its Los Angeles facility and paying the highest wages in the industry worldwide at $12 to $14 per hour.[2]

Product Development: Specification and Private-Label Buying

In addition to importing unique or distinctive goods, many retail operations use product development to set their assortment apart from those of their competitors. They may rely on domestic manufacturers or foreign sources for specification and private-label buying.

FIGURE 17.4 By selling Arizona Jeans, J.C. Penney adds increased product diversity for customers and can bring in more revenue.

As discussed in Chapter 8, these two terms may be used to describe the same items of merchandise, but the meanings are slightly different. If the retailer agrees, the manufacturer may design private-label merchandise for the retailer. On the other hand, **specification buying** is a type of purchasing that is done to the store's rather than the manufacturer's standards. Retailers provide the standards and guidelines for the manufacture of clothes they order.

Today, big retailers like Saks, J.C. Penney, Macy's, Walmart, and Target are selling more private labels alongside their own brands (Figure 17.4). The inclusion of these labels offers increased diversity to customers and can bring in additional revenue.

International Balance of Trade

Just as there are two sides to every coin, there are also two sides to the global market. Throughout the early 1980s, the expanding international market seemed to work to everyone's advantage. The global market came about largely because the early 1980s were a period of prosperity at home and abroad. There was nothing wrong with a fashion market that was truly international so long as a balance was maintained between exports—what Americans sold abroad—and imports—what they bought abroad. For several decades, foreign countries were eager to import American-made goods, which were much sought after for their high quality.

Unfortunately, by the mid-1980s, the downside of a global market—what happened when the trade balance shifted—revealed itself. The U.S. dollar grew weak, which meant that American goods became expensive, often too expensive to be of interest for export. The American reputation for producing quality goods suffered by comparison as other nations learned how to turn out quality products. The Japanese were soon beating Americans at their own game—cars and electronics. And the clothing industry proved itself woefully inept at competing at all. At first, Americans bought foreign clothes because they were so much cheaper than domestically produced goods. Eventually, though, they began to buy them because of their excellent workmanship and distinctive design.

When the dollar weakened, foreign countries only increased their exports to the United States. The resulting tidal wave of imports caused severe trauma to American industry generally and to the U.S. apparel manufacturing industry specifically. As foreign producers gained ground, domestic producers lost out.

These few cold facts seem to paint a discouraging picture for the U.S. fashion industry, but a closer examination of the situation from several perspectives shows that the outlook is far from uniformly bleak. To understand the present state of the import–export market, it is important to know something about the **balance of trade**. This is the difference between the value of exports and the value of imports. When the value of goods that a country imports exceeds the value of its exports, it experiences a **trade deficit**. When a country's exports exceed its imports, it has a **trade surplus**.

The United States has been the world's largest clothing importer, buying nearly one-third of all the imported clothing in the world. However, with the recent push for the United States to manufacture more products domestically, there may be yet another shift in the deficit. The conditions that traditionally encouraged consumers to purchase domestic goods—a devalued dollar and heightened tariffs—seem to have done little to turn the American public away from foreign merchandise. While the promotion "Crafted with Pride in the U.S.A.," which urges Americans to buy American, has created a sentimental support for domestic goods, at the point of purchase, consumers seem less interested in the origin of the goods than in getting the best value at a given price point. Furthermore, the distinction between domestic and foreign goods is clouded by the widespread practice of offshore production. The name of a U.S.-owned company on a label does not indicate anything at all about the nationality of the workers who made the product or the origin of the materials they used.

Some people believe that sterner measures, such as higher tariffs, are necessary to protect American industry from imports. Others oppose such measures. They argue that the real problem is the inefficiency of American industry. These two groups support two opposing ideologies regarding the conduct of American business.

For many of the world's developing countries, the manufacturing of clothing and textiles for export is the first step toward a sound national economy. Around the world, trade statistics show that the industrial countries are relying more and more on imports while the developing countries are becoming the exporters. Indications are that the growth in the U.S. trade deficit has slowed, but thus far, the United States remains the single largest contributor to the world trade imbalance.

Protectionism

Protectionism is the name given to an economic and political doctrine that seeks to exclude or limit foreign goods. The opposing doctrine, **free trade**, supports the free exchange of goods among nations. Since the balance of trade affects the nation's economic health, and the federal government is constantly passing and revising legislation about importing and exporting, advocates of both doctrines are well represented in Washington, D.C., by lobbyists who seek to promote legislation supporting their views.

The first import restrictions on goods brought into the country date back to 1789, when the United States, a newly founded republic that was still mostly rural, feared that it would not be able to compete with the world's industrial powers. To reduce its considerable reliance on imported goods, it slapped a 50 percent tariff, or import tax, on seventy different articles imported from France and England. Tariffs have come and gone, but the debate over whether protectionism is good—or necessary—has persisted for more than 200 years.

In the fashion industry, the leading supporters of protectionist legislation are manufacturers, who are most hurt when Americans buy imported rather than domestic goods. Industry trade associations and UNITE HERE, the apparel and textile workers' union, offer the most organized support for protectionism. Most consumers recognize their work through their campaigns, "Crafted with Pride in the U.S.A." and "Made in the

FIGURE 17.5 Americans are encouraged to buy and support domestic goods.

U.S.A.," which encourage people to buy American (Figure 17.5). But the manufacturers have also mounted a behind-the-scenes campaign designed to inform retailers about the advantages of buying domestically produced goods.

Free Trade

Free traders believe that restrictions on trade will threaten the nation's ability to grow and compete in the global marketplace. Retailers and most consumers are among those who support free trade. They believe the buying public should be free to buy imported as well as domestic goods.

Except for those times when protectionists are active, free traders do not do much to promote their cause. In many respects, they already have the support of the federal government. The history of the United States as the model of a capitalistic economy, the financial interests of powerful U.S. businesses in multinational conglomerates, and the interrelationship of the nation's role in international politics with its position as an economic power all favor a free trade stance.

The struggle over free trade versus protectionism is played out in several arenas, such as international trading laws, U.S. regulations, and preferential programs sponsored by various trading nations.

International Trading Laws

In the global economy, trade is truly international, not merely a set of bilateral agreements among pairs of nations. (A *bilateral agreement* is one in which two countries reach an agreement.) The trade relationship between any two nations affects the relationship of each party with its other trading partners as well. International trade laws have therefore developed out of need.

Counterfeit
Products

COUNTERFEIT WARS GO HIGH TECH

AS AUTHORITIES HAVE cracked down on counterfeit designer goods around the world, the counterfeiters have changed their game. Instead of shipping containers filled with fake designer clothing, shoes, and perfume sold directly to wholesalers and retailers, the counterfeiters have gone online. Now, many counterfeit seizures include mail and express courier shipments purchased online by commercial enterprises or directly by consumers.

In the past, many counterfeit goods were obvious either because of their incredibly low prices or because of misspelled names and shoddy workmanship. Today, however, many of the websites that sell counterfeit designer goods are so sophisticated that they are able to fool even the most discerning customers and charge prices comparable to the actual designers. The added insult is the fact that many of these websites never ship the goods that customers purchase.

Federal authorities seize counterfeit websites and post seizure banners on them to let the public know that these URLs—which often incorporate the designer name—are not legitimate sites. Some examples of seized sites are tiffanyandcojewelrysale.

net, chanel2outlet.com, and toryburchoutletclearance. com. According to John Morton, the Director of U.S. Immigration and Customs Enforcement, seized counterfeit sites "target criminals making a buck by trying to trick consumers into believing that they were buying name-brand products from legitimate websites when in fact they were buying counterfeits from illegal but sophisticated imposter sites located overseas."

Pursuing criminal organizations that sell counterfeit copies of designer goods is extremely difficult because as soon as they're caught they set up another website with a new URL. Legal action against these criminal organizations is so expensive that only the largest companies can pursue it. However, three promising cases settled in U.S. Federal courts awarded Hermes International and Burberry Ltd. each $100 million and Michael Kors LLC received $2.4 million. The twist in these cases is that the courts are requiring third-party payment processors like PayPal to hand over any frozen assets in order to fulfill the monetary judgments. Unfortunately, even as these judgments were handed down, counterfeiters were already moving to Twitter, Pinterest, and Facebook to sell their goods, even creating their own fashion blogs from which to sell their counterfeit goods directly.

Trade Agreements

In 1947, the United States and twenty-three other nations met in Geneva, Switzerland, to write an agreement known as the **General Agreement on Tariffs and Trade (GATT)**. This agreement played a major role in reducing trade barriers and unifying trading practices among member nations. Membership grew to ninety-two, and representatives met every few years to negotiate new trade arrangements among member nations. In 1995, GATT was succeeded by the World Trade Organization, which has continued to adjust member agreements to meet the changing needs of the global economy.

Currently, the United States has free trade agreements (FTAs) in effect with seventeen countries. Many FTAs are bilateral agreements between two governments. However, some, like the **North American Free Trade Agreement (NAFTA)** and the **Dominican Republic–Central America–United States (CAFTA-DR)** FTAs, are multilateral. The CAFTA-DR includes the United States, Costa Rica, Dominican Republic, El Salvador, Guatemala, Honduras, and Nicaragua. As the apparel and textile supply chain grapples with higher labor, raw material, and transportation costs, markets closer to home, such as Central America and the Dominican Republic, are expected to gain substantial business through imports and exports.[3]

The United States also has a series of Bilateral Investment Treaties (BITs) that help to protect private investment, develop market-oriented policies in partner countries, and promote U.S. exports.[4]

However, the FTAs have come under a lot of criticism. One of the arguments is that the interests of powerful nations and corporations are shaping the terms of world trade. This could mean that the interests of the people would be compromised, while a decreasing number of people would prosper. It could also threaten the domestic industries of industrialized countries, whose production costs can't compete with those of developing nations.

Multi-Fiber Arrangement

In 1973, the United States and fifty-three other nations signed the first multinational agreement specifically regulating the flow of textile products. A primary purpose of the **Multi-Fiber Arrangement (MFA)** was to establish ground rules for bilateral agreements and unilateral actions designed to restrict the free flow of these products. The United States, Canada, and some of the industrialized nations of Western Europe wanted to protect their textile industries from cheaper imports from less developed countries.

The MFA was renewed twice without any essential changes in its stated purpose or goals. It was also renewed in 1986, but this time not without controversy. The 1986 renewal attempted to deal with two changes in the status of textile trade:

1. Growing pressure in the United States to enact tighter quotas on textile imports
2. The United States' insistence that the Big Three textile-exporting nations—Hong Kong, Korea, and Taiwan—revise their bilateral agreements with the United States.

Despite the substantial revision, many American producers felt the arrangement did not give them the measure of relief they sought. They pointed out, for example, that the MFA limits the number of units that can be brought into the country rather than the cost value of merchandise. Faced with quantity limits, many foreign producers have merely shifted to higher-priced merchandise, a move that hurts the domestic market even more than limiting cheap imports does.

The textile exporters were dissatisfied for the opposite reason. They did not want their fledgling textile export industries to be singled out for quotas at all. Particularly galling to these less developed nations was the imposition of protectionist policies by an organization that was supposedly formed to promote free trade. Like David battling Goliath, the exporters won, and the MFA was phased out over the period between 1995 and 2005. By January 2005, the quotas came to an end, and importing countries could no longer discriminate between exporters.

U.S. Regulation of Imports

Some of the specific measures the United States—or any other country—is liable to undertake or has undertaken to promote its own trade interests are quotas; tariffs and duties; social responsibility; and prevention of counterfeiting, black market, and gray market goods.

Import Quotas

Import quotas are limits set to restrict the number of specific goods that may be brought into the country for a specific period of time. Quotas, which are established either by presidential proclamation or legislation, are either absolute or tariff-rate.

Absolute Quotas

Absolute quotas limit the quantity of goods that may enter the United States. When the limit is reached, no more goods of that kind may be imported until the quota period ends. Absolute quotas may be global or directed to specific countries. Imports in excess of a quota may be exported or detained for entry during the next quota period. To keep accurate and consistent records of apparel and other textile imports, these items are counted in terms of square meter equivalents.

Tariff-Rate Quotas

Tariff-rate quotas set a limit after which a higher duty is charged on goods entering the country. When a certain number of goods have entered at the lower rate, U.S. Customs and Border Protection (CBP) raises the duty on any additional goods, which in effect also raises their price in the market.[5]

Tariffs and Duties

A **duty** or **tariff** is a fee assessed by the government on certain goods that it wishes to restrict or limit. Tariffs and duties are imposed on imported goods that the government wishes to make more competitive in price with domestically produced goods. The tax varies depending on the category of merchandise, but it is usually a percentage of the first cost.

Tariff Schedules 807 (9802) and 807A

Tariff Schedules of the United States had a clause known as Item 807 (renumbered 9802 in 1989 but still referred to by its old number within the apparel industry). It allowed cut piece goods and trim items to be exported from the United States, assembled or sewn abroad, and then returned to the United States with duties owed only on the value that was added abroad. In other words, duty was paid only on the labor that was done abroad—not the materials.

There was a revision, 807A, that required that the piece goods taken out of the country to be of U.S. origin. Item 807A is also referred to as Super 807, because it provided special access for goods that were domestically cut and made of U.S. fabrics.

Social Responsibility

The downside of relying on offshore production for cheap labor (Figure 17.6) became apparent to American fashion producers when sweatshop conditions in third-world countries—and even in some domestic factories employing illegal aliens—came to light in the mid-1990s. Horror stories of workers held in virtual captivity, required to work long hours for less than subsistence wages, and subject to corporal punishment for the slightest infraction of inhumane work rules made front-page news. Realizing the threat to their

reputations as good corporate citizens, many apparel manufacturers were quick to recognize the need for self-regulation.

The American Apparel Manufacturers Association of Arlington, Virginia, formed a twelve-member labor task force to address the sweatshop problem, and in August 1996, representatives of eighteen organizations, including human rights advocacy groups and labor unions, as well as apparel manufacturers and retailers, joined together in the White House Apparel Industry Partnership. This advisory panel established voluntary standards to help improve the working conditions in factories where members of the U.S. apparel industry do business. These standards are called the WRAP (Worldwide Responsible Accredited Production) principles. Global support for WRAP continues to grow monthly.

In 2000, the American Apparel Manufacturers Association merged with the Footwear Industries of America and The Fashion Association to become the American Apparel and Footwear Association (AAFA). The AAFA continues to demonstrate its commitment to responsible business practices.

Corporate social responsibility (CSR) is when a company not only fully complies with the obligations of legislation, but also accounts for how it integrates social and environmental factors into its global decision-making policies and practices. This is more of a common practice today than in the past.[6] Ann Inc. is an example of a company that has implemented a

FIGURE 17.6 Sewing is a major cost for most garments, which has led to global sourcing for cutting costs.

successful CSR program for the past decade. The company, for instance, provided 18,000 store associates with training in smart energy practices as part of a green initiative.[7]

Counterfeit, Black Market, and Gray Market Goods

Both importers and exporters are plagued by the illegal importing of counterfeit, black market, and gray market goods. **Counterfeit goods**, like counterfeit currency, are inferior imitations passed off as the genuine article (Figures 17.7). Luxury goods and designer brands are the chief objects of counterfeiters.

Counterfeiting flourishes for two main reasons. First, it is considered a high-return, low-risk business: counterfeiters can earn millions of dollars and are rarely caught. Counterfeiters are among the world's most ruthless criminals. They are known to have smuggled workers from Asia into places such as New York and Los Angeles and kept them locked up to assemble fakes that are imported in pieces.

While the U.S. government and many European governments are focusing on ways to catch and punish counterfeiters, the real challenge is learning how to rehabilitate the child labor force that the industry helps create. The International Labor Organization reports that around the world, an estimated 211 million children between the ages of five and fourteen are part of the labor force.[8] According to UNICEF's Geoffrey Keele, "We need to look at why children become laborers to begin with. That comes down to issues of poverty. Access to education and to health care will help keep them from being vulnerable to exploitation in the labor field, sexual exploitation, and trafficking."[9]

The sale of counterfeit goods at "bargain" prices devalues the real brand and deprives legitimate businesses of their fairly earned profits. U.S. Customs officials are authorized to seize imported counterfeit goods.

Another problem for manufacturers is **bootleg goods**. Many of these goods are not cheap rip-offs; rather, they cannot be distinguished from the real ones. They are made by the same manufacturers who make the real ones but who sell some goods to the black market. The **black market** is where illicit goods or commodities that are in violation of official regulations are traded.

Gray market goods are those that were not intended for sale in the country in which they are being sold. Sometimes called parallel imports, gray goods are legitimate products that are distributed through channels not authorized by their original manufacturer. An authentic sneaker manufactured for distribution

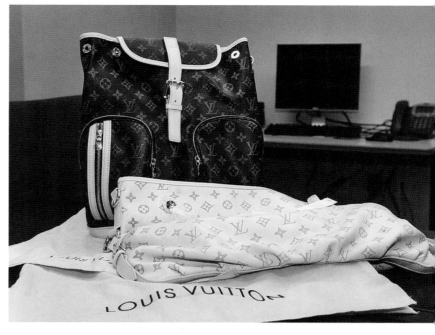

FIGURE 17.7 Counterfeit Louis Vuitton bags seized by U.S. Immigration and Customs.

in Europe, for example, is considered *gray* if it is sold in the United States instead. However, gray market goods can cause problems for vendors and consumers, especially in cases where legitimate gray market goods are mixed in with counterfeit products. The flood of gray market goods can also weaken sanctions against counterfeits.[10]

Penetration of the U.S. Market by Foreign Investors

Direct investment in U.S. properties and businesses is extremely attractive to foreigners. Because so many textiles and apparel items are imported into the United States, foreign investors have long been interested in buying into American textile and apparel manufacturing companies. Foreign investors, mostly from Europe and the Far East, have taken three routes to ownership: joint ventures, total ownership, and licensing. For example, L'Oréal of France purchased three important U.S. cosmetic labels: Maybelline, Redken, and Helena Rubinstein. Many retail operations have been foreign-owned for some time, and there is even more activity in this sector than in manufacturing. Other foreign retailing successes are H&M (Swedish owned), Zara (Spanish owned), Topshop (British owned) (Figure 17.8), and UNIQLO (Japanese owned).

New York's Madison Avenue, Chicago's Michigan Avenue, and Los Angeles's Rodeo Drive are lined with the boutiques of such Italian designers as Valentino, Armani, Ungaro, Dolce & Gabbana, Missoni, and Prada. Their presence in the United States is just a part of their global retailing strategy.

FIGURE 17.8 British-owned Topshop operates retail stores in the United States and globally.

Licensing

Investment by foreign manufacturers in the fashion industry is not entirely new. Licensing arrangements, which often involve ownership of domestic companies, were initiated over twenty-five years ago by companies such as Christian Dior, Pierre Cardin, and Hubert de Givenchy. Today, the European presence is widespread. For example, Donna Karan's and Marc Jacobs's collections are financed by the French LVMH (Louis Vuitton Moet Hennessy) family.

Penetration of Foreign Markets by U.S. Companies

To counterbalance foreign investment, American businesses have been interested in investing in foreign countries, where U.S. management is often welcomed because American know-how and standards for high quality are much-respected commodities. U.S. investment in foreign countries also helps the balance of trade. For example, J.Crew expanded its brand to China.

Licensing

Just as foreign manufacturers first penetrated the U.S. retail market with licensed products, so too have American companies been able to license products abroad. American character licenses such as Mickey Mouse, Kermit the Frog, Superman, and Miss Piggy have been great successes abroad, as have sports licenses and brand names, such as Nike, and designer names, such as Calvin Klein, Donna Karan, and Ralph Lauren.

Many companies today are switching from licensing to importing strategies in order to establish and strengthen brand identity. As international distribution continues to develop, U.S. manufacturers are finding that a mix of locally licensed product and U.S.-manufactured apparel is the most effective way to sell locally.

While the United States permits total ownership by foreign investors, most other countries only allow foreign investors to be partners or joint owners.

U.S. Exporting

Because the "Made in the U.S.A." label is desirable all over the world, the United States can export its fashion products around the globe. Increased U.S. exports, in fact, are seen by many industry experts as the solution to the U.S. trade deficit. The United States does not need to keep out foreign competitors as much as it needs to sell and promote its products abroad.

Although U.S. designer fashions are available in upscale department stores around the globe, a common strategy is to establish a presence in foreign markets with a freestanding "signature store," or boutique. The ability to monitor consumer reaction to the designer's merchandise allows for rapid adjustment to local tastes and preferences, just as is true at home. Bud Konheim, cofounder and CEO of Nicole Miller, predicted in 1996 that "by the end of the century, the term 'going global' will have lost its meaning. Foreign sales will just be another part of every firm's account list."[11] This certainly proved to be true, as today the term *global* is just one more part of the business.

Summary and Review

Through imports and exports and offshore and domestic production, the U.S. textile and apparel industry is a major player in the global economy. Importing is a major source of merchandise for retailers, who rely on visits to foreign markets, store-owned foreign buying offices, commissionaires, import fairs, and U.S. import firms. Apparel manufacturers are also purchasers of foreign products, especially fabrics and other materials and trimming. Retailers may develop products bearing their private label by having their designs produced by foreign manufacturers.

Over the years, U.S. apparel manufacturers have turned to offshore sources for all or part of the production of their goods, but increased production domestically is on the rise. Exports of U.S.-made fashion goods are a growing aspect of the country's role in global sourcing and merchandising. Some specific measures the United States is liable to undertake or has undertaken to promote its own trade interests are quotas; tariffs and duties; social responsibility; and prevention of counterfeiting, black market, and gray market goods. The United States participates in multi-national agreements such as those of the World Trade Organization and in separate trade agreements with individual countries or groups of countries.

U.S. and foreign businesses mutually penetrate each other's markets through licensing arrangements, investments in manufacturing, and establishment of retail outlets.

For Review

1. What advantages do imports give retailers?
2. Name the five ways foreign-made fashion merchandise can be purchased.
3. What are the two important functions of foreign import shows in the United States?
4. What concerns arise when retailers do specification buying of private-label merchandise?
5. Who are the advocates of protectionism in the fashion industry? Why?
6. Who are the advocates of free trade in the fashion industry? Why?
7. What is the purpose of the WTO? NAFTA? CAFTA-DR?
8. What are the provisions of Tariff Schedules 807 and 807A?
9. How do counterfeit goods affect the fashion industry?
10. What role does corporate social responsibility play in the fashion industry?

For Discussion

1. As a fashion consumer, do you advocate protectionism or free trade? What major items of your current wardrobe would you have been unable to purchase if broad protective legislation prohibiting imports had been in place?
2. What are the advantages of using a store-owned foreign buying office? A commissionaire?
3. What are the pros and cons for both domestic and offshore production?

Trade Talk

Define or briefly explain the following terms:

absolute quota
balance of trade
black market
bootleg goods
commissionaire
corporate social responsibility (CSR)
counterfeit goods
Dominican Republic–Central America–United States Free Trade Agreement (CAFTA-DR)
duty
export
first cost
free trade
General Agreement on Tariffs and Trade (GATT)
global sourcing
gray market goods
import
import quota
Multi-Fiber Agreement (MFA)
North American Free Trade Agreement (NAFTA)
offshore production
protectionism
specification buying
tariff
tariff-rate quota
trade deficit
trade surplus

Chapter Eighteen

FASHION RETAILING

KEY CONCEPTS

- History and development of fashion retailing in the United States
- Organization for buying and merchandising in department stores, specialty stores, and discount stores
- Organization for buying and merchandising in chains, leased departments, and franchises
- Operation of off-price retailers, factory outlet stores, category killers, boutiques, and showcase stores
- Operation of nonstore retailers, including direct sellers, catalog stores, TV home shopping, and Internet sites
- Trends in retail patterns

The business of everybody in the fashion business is store business, whether one designs, manufactures, buys, sells, promotes, displays, reports, or photographs clothes, shoes, accessories, or beauty products. Eventually, the goods must be where the people are, and the people must come to where the goods are, and what is in the stores must be desired and bought by people—people continuously "shopping"; seeing, desiring, paying, and possessing. That is store business, and, in one way or another, it is the business of everybody in the fashion business.

—Estelle Hamburger,
Fashion Business—It's All Yours,
Harper & Row, 1976[1]

Retailing is the business of buying and selling goods to those who will use them, the ultimate consumers. Retailing is a vital industry in the United States today. Contributing $2.5 trillion to the nation's annual gross domestic product (GDP), retail plays a big role in the economy.[2] **Fashion retailing** involves the business of buying and selling—or merchandising—apparel, accessories, and home fashions. It is the way fashion products are moved from the designer or manufacturer to the customer.

Retailing is in many ways the heart of the fashion industry. It is the most challenging end of the fashion business, existing as it does in a constant state of change. Retailers must, for example, be among the first to spot and act on new trends. They must be attuned to their customers' needs and desires to a degree that is

TABLE 18.1: *Top 10 Global Retail Leaders*

Company	Country of Origin	2010 Retail Sales ($U.S. Billion)
Walmart	U.S.	418,952
Carrefour	France	119,642
Tesco	U.K.	92,171*
Metro	Germany	88,931
Kroger	U.S.	82,189
Schwartz	Germany	79,119*
Costco	U.S.	76,255
The Home Depot	U.S.	67,997
Walgreen Co.	U.S.	67,420
Aldi	Germany	67,112*

*Sales-weighted, currency-adjusted composite growth rate
Source: "Global Powers of Retailing Top 250 Highlights,"
Stores magazine, January 2012, www.stores.org.

required in few other businesses. Retailers must react to a constantly changing economic climate. See Table 18.1 for a list of the top ten global retail leaders.

An extraordinary amount of planning and effort goes into the merchandising of fashion products. For people who are not in the fashion business, the process of merchandising fashion products can look very easy. Fashion moves from concept to customer; that is, it moves from designer to manufacturer to retailer to you—the customer! The most intricate part lies in the merchandising and retailing of the goods. As mentioned previously, an old adage among fashion retailers, called the five R's, stands for choosing:

- The right merchandise
- At the right price
- In the right place
- At the right time
- In the right quantities

If any one of these R's is incorrect, it will collapse all the R's. Think of it as smoothly juggling five balls at once. You must keep them all in the air at the same time; constantly moving, never touching. Your timing must be flawless. If you let one ball slip, they will all fall. And you must keep smiling and make it look effortless. That is like fashion merchandising—it looks easy but it is hard to do!

History and Development of Fashion Retailing

People have been swapping, trading, or selling one another's various goods for thousands of years. In Asia and the eastern Mediterranean, bazaars and marketplaces still operate on the sites they have occupied for centuries. Not until the mid-1800s and the opening of

the first department store—the Bon Marché in Paris—did modern merchandising as we know it begin to develop. Even then, it developed differently in the United States than in Europe. In this chapter, we explore the development of retailing in the United States.

Retailing in the United States grew directly out of the frontier. It was an attempt to meet the needs of countless numbers of settlers who were moving west to populate a huge country. The first settlements in the United States were situated along its eastern coast. There, settlers built cities and towns that resembled what they had left behind in Europe. Philadelphia, New York, and Boston were soon populous centers of commerce and culture. Their shops were patterned after those in London and Paris. No one is sure who should be credited with the founding of the first department store in the United States. Most authorities claim it was R. H. Macy in about 1860 (Figure 18.1). Others claim the first department store was The Fair in Chicago in 1874, or Wanamaker's in Philadelphia in 1876. On the frontier, however, such sophistication was not possible, nor would it have served the needs of western buyers. Instead, three elements—general stores, peddlers, and mail-order sellers—each uniquely geared to life on the frontier, combined to give birth to modern retailing in the United States.

General Stores

When the West was in the very early stages of settlement, there were no stores—and very few people to buy anything in them anyway. Apart from the settled

FIGURE 18.1 R.H. Macy's in New York City, 1908.

areas along the East Coast, most of North America was populated by Native Americans, fur traders, and explorers. Groups of Native Americans had long traded goods among themselves, and the Europeans who traveled west soon learned to follow suit. They began by trading with Native Americans, but soon European traders opened trading posts. There, fur traders swapped furs for basic supplies.

Gradually, as the West became more settled, and pioneer men and women moved across the country, trading posts evolved into **general stores**. Where trading posts had carried only such basics as guns, gun parts, and food supplies, general stores sought to expand their stock by adding such goods as saddles, salt pork, lamp oil, and even ladies' bonnets. Money was a scarce commodity on the frontier, so general stores were still willing to take goods as well as cash for payment. A farmer's wife might make bonnets or lace collars to exchange for the few supplies she needed from the general store. As people became more settled, they became interested in buying more than basic supplies, and general stores were soon stocking a greater variety of items such as dress fabric, sewing notions, and fancier bonnets.

Not surprisingly, in a place where life was spartan and store-bought goods were one of life's few pleasures, people liked to linger over their purchases. As a result, general stores also functioned as community social centers as well as gathering places for political debate. To this day, general stores still serve many small communities in rural areas of the United States.

Gradually, as settlers became more prosperous, the general stores stopped bartering and began to operate on a cash-only basis. The new influx of capital could be used for expansion. Over time, some general stores—such as Meier & Frank in Portland, Oregon, and Filene's in Boston—grew into full-fledged department stores.

Peddlers

Even with general stores located in communities and trading posts scattered along well-traveled trails, many homesteads were too isolated to make regular use of them. Itinerant peddlers began to service these remote customers. A peddler visited some areas only once a year, so he was accorded a warm welcome.

In many ways, peddlers were the first marketing experts. In addition to their wares, which typically consisted of pots and pans, shoes and boots, sewing notions, and a few luxury items such as lace, combs, and ribbons, they carried news of the latest fashions being worn in the cities back east. The reverse was also true, and they carried word back east about specific items that pleased or displeased customers in the Midwest or West.

Mail-Order Sellers

The final element in the development of modern retailing was the mail-order seller. Mail-order companies, which began in the late 1800s, serviced the rural areas of the United States. At that time, the United States was largely rural, so almost everyone was a mail-order customer. Montgomery Ward, which mailed its first catalog in 1872, was the first company to do the bulk of its business by mail. By 1894, it had a competitor, Sears, Roebuck and Co., and the mail-order business was in full swing (Figure 18.2). Such companies were able to operate only after the establishment of rural free delivery (RFD), a system of free mail delivery to rural areas, and later, parcel post, a system of low-cost mail delivery that replaced RFD.

The mail-order catalog brought a new and expansive world to the lives of rural Americans. Hundreds of fashion items, furnishings for the home, and tools for the farm were offered in the catalogs. The illustrations were clear, goods were described in detail, and best of all, from a farm person's point of view, prices were reasonable. The catalogs did not offer high fashion, but to rural women their variety and prices were still enough

FIGURE 18.2 In the latter part of the 19th century, the Sears, Roebuck and Co. catalogs opened a whole new world of fashion to rural Americans who lived far away from shops.

to delight. Those who had been limited to the scant provisions that a peddler was able to carry on his wagon or the barely filled shelves of general stores now felt as if the world was at their fingertips.

With the expansion of the Sears catalog in 1894, the fledgling company posted astonishing sales of $750,000 in 1895. By 1900, sales increased to more than $10,000,000.[3]

Traditional Types of Fashion Retailers

As the frontier turned into towns and cities, peddlers became sales representatives, and general stores and mail-order businesses evolved into something entirely different from their ancestors. Today, hundreds of thousands of retail stores exist to serve 311 million consumers in the United States.[4]

Retailers usually can be classified into one of two broad categories—general and specialized—depending on the kinds of merchandise they carry. In each of these categories are many different kinds of retail operations: department stores, specialty stores, chain operations, discount stores, and leased departments, to name a few. Almost all retail stores offer some form of mail-order or telephone buying service, and there are also retailers that deal exclusively in mail order. Most retailers also have Internet or e-commerce sites. Some stores have grown into giant operations, but many others are still small, independently owned and operated businesses.

The retail scene is dominated by **general merchandise retailers**, such as J.C. Penney, Sears, and Target. These retailers typically sell many kinds of merchandise in addition to clothing. They try to appeal to a broad range of customers. Most general merchandisers very broadly target their merchandise to several price ranges, and only a few limit themselves to narrow price ranges.

Specialty retailers, in contrast, offer limited lines of related merchandise targeted to a more specific customer. They define their customers by age, size, or shared tastes. Their customers are more homogeneous than those of general merchandisers. Examples are Crate and Barrel, Tiffany's, and Talbots.

Today, the differences between types of retailers are not as clearly defined as they used to be. It has, for example, become increasingly difficult to distinguish a department store from a chain operation, a discounter from an off-pricer, a franchiser from a chain. In this section, we look at three traditional types of fashion retailers: department stores, specialty stores, and discount stores.

Department Stores

The **department store** is the type of general retailer most familiar to the buying public. Many are even tourist landmarks. Few people, for example, visit New York without seeing Macy's or Bloomingdale's. In London, Harrods is a big tourist attraction, as is Le Printemps in Paris (Figure 18.3).

Department stores are in a state of flux that makes them difficult to define. The Census Bureau defines a department store as a retail store carrying a general line of apparel, home furnishings, and housewares, and employing more than fifty people. Despite this official definition, however, many department stores have eliminated their appliances and furniture departments.

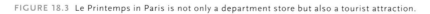

FIGURE 18.3 Le Printemps in Paris is not only a department store but also a tourist attraction.

356

TABLE 18.2 *Top 5 Department Stores in the United States*

Company	U.S. Retail Sales	No. of Stores
Sears Holdings	$35,362,000,000	3,484
Macy's	$24,864,000,000	852
Kohl's	$18,391,000,000	1,083
J.C. Penney	$17,659,000,000	1,099
Nordstrom	$9,624,000,000	204

Source: Adapted from "2011 Top 100 Retailers," *Stores* magazine, July 2011, www.stores.org.

Department stores reigned as the kings of retailers well into the 1960s, when there was only about four square feet of retail space per person in the United States. They had long dominated downtowns with main stores called *flagships*. In the 1960s and 1970s, department stores anchored malls. But in the turbulent 1980s, department stores failed all across the country, victims of overexpansion, mergers and acquisitions, and increased competition. By the mid-1990s, they came back strong, and in the twenty-first century, there was yet another shift. Chain specialty stores and category killers, which we will discuss later in this chapter, began to occupy a large percentage of retail space. Table 18.2 lists the five top department stores in the United States.

Before getting into the ways in which stores are changing, let us look at how various kinds of traditional retailers operate and merchandise themselves. As general merchandisers, department stores typically serve a larger portion of the community than other stores and often offer a variety of quality and price ranges. A department store usually offers a category of apparel at several price points, each in a different part of the store. Typical department stores offer dresses on many floors, in many departments, with varying rates of return.

Department stores have also traditionally enjoyed a certain prestige that often extends even beyond the communities they serve. They are usually actively involved in their communities. A department store, for example, will eagerly stage a fashion show for a local charity, knowing that such activities create goodwill and enhance the store's overall reputation.

Organization for Buying and Merchandising

Department stores are organized into special areas, or departments, such as sportswear, shoes, dresses, men's clothing, and furniture (Figure 18.4). Generally, buyers purchase for their departments, although in very

FIGURE 18.4 The traditional department store look features separate, departmentalized classifications, as in this shoe department at Macy's.

large department stores, even the departments may be departmentalized, with individual buyers purchasing only part of the stock for a department. In some sportswear departments, for example, one buyer may purchase tops, while another buys bottoms.

Entertainment Values

The weaving of entertainment into modern retailing is reshaping the shopping experience. Entertainment values in retailing are defined in a number of ways. The most traditional way is by having merchandise assortment. Many retailers think of their stores as theaters that provide entertainment. The walls are the stage, the fixtures are the sets, and the merchandise is the star. Other popular entertainment strategies include providing video walls and interactive Internet sites, arranging store visits by celebrities, presenting designer trunk shows, sponsoring charity fund-raisers, and on and on.

Contrary to the rumors that the department store is a dinosaur, many department stores are fighting back by adding entertainment value. One way that department stores have built relationships with their customers is through award and loyalty programs. These programs reward high-spending customers with bonuses and make members feel like they are part of a VIP club. The stores arrange events that range from meet-the-designer product launches to luncheons and cocktail parties. Macy's is one department store that has found ways to interact with customers of all age

FOREVER 21'S
FAST-FASHION EMPIRE

FOREVER 21'S SHOPPERS are young, grabby, and fast. They zoom through the store, ripping clothes from racks like birds swooping for fish. Few of them are aware that this American fashion chain started as a family business. Thanks to its "pile very high, sell very cheap" operation, it has been a phenomenal success.

How did the Changs, Korean immigrants who opened their first store in Los Angeles in 1984, become important players in "fast fashion"? Big dreams have ruined many retailers. Forever 21, however, has excelled at doing what most people didn't think was possible—selling clothes fast and cheap. Most retailers stay with dead inventory too long, but Forever 21 is all about movement into the store and out to the customer. The Changs figured out that if they order small enough batches of each style, shoppers will learn to buy what they like when they first see it—because the next week it might be gone! They also learned that new styles have to be displayed at the front of the store and these displays have to change daily.

For many shoppers, being able to find cheap copies of celebrity outfits and runway fashions wherever they can is a matter of pride. Forever 21 satisfies this longing and is known for reproducing famous designs and selling them very cheaply. In 2007, Diane Von Furstenberg filed a lawsuit against the retailer for duplicating her designs (as did Gwen Stefani, Ana Sui, and about forty other labels), though for the record, Forever 21 has never been found liable for copyright infringement.

From Forever 21 to H&M and Zara, trendy fast-fashion retailers are expanding across the U.S. to satisfy shoppers' demands for clothing that's cheap enough to purchase by the armload. Critics of fast fashion say it contributes to overconsumption, clogs landfills, and exploits workers in overseas sweatshops. Consumers argue that fashion is a form of self-expression and say stores like Forever 21 make style accessible to more people. According to Kirsten Osolind, president of Re:Invention, a marketing and innovation consulting firm, "The world is increasingly impulsive; fast fashion feeds on that impulsiveness and produces profits. [This] retail concept fits with a society that values instant gratification."

groups. For example, they have hosted events such as children's reading circles and registry planning parties for engaged couples.[5]

Specialty Stores

A **specialty store** carries a limited line of merchandise, whether it is clothing, accessories, or furniture (Figure 18.5). Examples of specialty stores include shoe stores, jewelry stores, maternity-wear stores, and boutiques. As noted, specialty merchandisers tend to target a more specific customer than do general merchandisers. They may offer a single line; just shoes, for example. Or they may offer related limited lines, for example, children's apparel, shoes, and other accessories. Or they may offer a subspecialty, like just athletic shoes, or just socks!

Another variation of the specialty store is the private-label retailer, which sells only what it manufacturers itself. Gap, Ann Taylor, and Brooks Brothers are leading examples.

Most of us are familiar with specialty stores but do not realize how varied they are. A specialty store can be one tiny hat shop, or it can be a chain of large, multidepartment stores such as Saks Fifth Avenue, which specializes in apparel. The latter is the type that *Stores* magazine reclassified as full-fledged department stores.

Most specialty stores in the United States are individually owned and have no branches. The composite sales of these single-unit specialty stores, however, represent only somewhat less than half of the total sales volume of all specialty stores. These stores are having an increasingly difficult time as harried consumers have less time to spend on shopping and want convenience and low prices.

Organization for Buying and Merchandising

In small specialty stores, the buying and merchandising are done by the owner or a store manager, sometimes with the assistance of a small staff. Large multidepartment specialty stores are organized along the lines of department stores, with buyers purchasing merchandise for their own departments. Multiunit specialty stores belonging to chain organizations are set up in a unique way that is described under chain organizations, later in this chapter.

Entertainment Values

Entertainment is a natural activity for specialty stores. In addition to exciting visual merchandising, many specialty stores offer related entertainment. Niketown began the trend with its video wall and then expanded to a Town Square with a staffed counter, banks of video monitors, and information about local and national

FIGURE 18.5 Brooks Brothers is a specialty store that is classically iconic but maintains a unique look.

sports teams. REI is a specialty store that offers more than just sporting equipment. Some of their locations offer bike and ski repair areas, seasonal gear rental areas, community rooms, and rock climbing walls. Another example is Williams-Sonoma, specialty retailer of home furnishings and gourmet cookware. It offers a variety of cooking classes at its stores in addition to a monthly cookbook club.

Discount Stores

The discount business got its start after World War II, when servicemen and servicewomen came home with a well-thought-out agenda for their lives: get married, establish a home, and start a family. Within a few years, with the help of the GI Bill, which funded both education and mortgages, many had managed to achieve at least one of their wishes. Millions of new houses had been built in new suburban towns. The next step was to furnish them.

Discounters saw a need and began to fill it. The first discounters sold household goods. They ran weekend operations, usually setting up shop in an empty warehouse, barn, or lot just outside the city limits. Their stock varied from week to week, but they managed to have what people needed. One weekend, toasters were featured; on another, bath and bed linens were on sale. The selection was not particularly good, but the prices were right, so people came to buy. Through word of mouth, discount businesses began to grow. Some even expanded into permanent stores.

FIGURE 18.6 Discounters, like Century 21, make a profit by keeping their overhead low.

The discounters sold name-brand merchandise at less than retail prices. They did it by keeping their overhead low and offering minimal services—two facets of discount selling that prevail to this day. Cash-and-carry was the rule.

Fair trade laws made the sale of goods at more than retail or "list" price illegal. Discounters discovered, however, that the fair trade laws did not apply to selling lower than list price. Soon they were doing exactly that. In a sense, the fair trade laws, designed to prevent gouging by retailers, made the discounter's low price more recognizable and reputable.

Today, a **discount store** is any retail operation that sells goods at less than full retail prices (Figure 18.6). Discounters are called *discount stores, mass merchandisers, promotional department stores,* and *off-pricers.*

TABLE 18.3 *Top 5 Discount Stores in the United States*

RANK	CHAIN (HEADQUARTERS)	U.S. RETAIL SALES
1	Walmart (Bentonville, AR)	307,736,000,000
2	Target (Minneapolis, MN)	65,815,000,000
3	Costco (Issaquah, WA)	78,394,000,000
4	Meijer (Grand Rapids, MI)	15,319,000,000
5	Dollar General (Nashville, TN)	13,035,000,000

Source: Adapted from "2011 Top 100 Retailers," *Stores* magazine, July 2011, www.stores.org.

Discounters, which may be either general or specialty merchandisers, may sell everything from cosmetics, accessories, and apparel to health and beauty aids to major appliances (Table 18.3).

Discount stores are operated in different formats, as follows:

Discount department stores are retailers that offer well-known branded apparel at 20 to 60 percent off regular department store prices. The store format resembles that of a department store.

Discount general merchandisers are retailers like Walmart and Carrefour that carry a broad range of products, from apparel to electronics, typically private label and basics. Their prices are lower than department stores or specialty stores.

Warehouse clubs stock a limited number of apparel stock-keeping units (SKUs)—generally whatever brands they can buy. Customers are usually required to pay a membership fee in order to shop at the store, but the benefits are bargain prices at large quantities—mostly for products outside of apparel. Examples of warehouse clubs include Costco Wholesale, Sam's Club, and BJ's Wholesale Club, Inc.

Discount/off-price specialty stores offer low-price apparel from private labels and typically lower-end brands, with the exception of H&M and similar stores that are partnered with designers and labels like Karl Lagerfeld and Stella McCartney to create exclusive lines that drive traffic and give the perception of higher quality and value at reasonable to inexpensive prices.

Hypermarkets typically offer discount grocery or superstore items and products commonly found in department stores. Apparel is not necessarily the focus in this category.

Organization for Buying and Merchandising

Early discounters searched the marketplace for close-out and special-price promotions. Their inventories consisted almost entirely of this type of goods. Today, discounters specialize in low-end open-market goods or special lines made exclusively for them. Most conventional retail operations do not want their buyers to purchase goods that will be sold to discounters, but this has not stopped manufacturers from making special lines for discounters. Some designers and manufacturers use discount outlets to sell their overstocks or slow-moving items.

Independently owned and nonchain discounters follow the same buying and merchandising practices as other retailers of similar volume and size. Chain discounters follow the usual practices of their business, with one exception. In chain discount buying, buyers are usually responsible for several departments rather than a single category of merchandise.

Figures show that 19.3 percent of all apparel sales in the country take place in discount stores.[6] Ninety million people—or approximately one-third of the U.S. population—walk into a Walmart every week. The large and widespread customer base is one reason analysts and economic observers look to the retail giants as an indicator of the economic condition. Discounters have a tremendous stake in the future of fashion retailing.

Entertainment Values

Discounters added "greeters" early on to welcome people to their vast stores and direct them to the correct spot within the store. Some early discounters also used "blue light specials" to stimulate customer interest. Discounters in malls usually rely on the mall to draw and entertain customers, while they focus on keeping prices low. As people tire of plain stores with rows of fluorescent lights, and hundreds of counters in rigid rows, some discounters are upgrading their visual merchandising and looking for related entertainment values.

Forms of Ownership

There are four types of ownership commonly found in U.S. retailing today: sole proprietors, chains, leased departments, and franchises. Partnerships, once a very popular form of retail ownership (Sears, Roebuck and Co., Abraham and Straus, etc.), are seldom found today because of liability issues and tax considerations.

Owners use many different formats, including the traditional department store, specialty store, or discount store, or the newer off-price, factory outlet, or category killer formats.

Sole Proprietors

Sole proprietors, or owners, are the entrepreneurs who shaped American retailing. Many of the retailing greats, James Cash Penney, John Wanamaker, Adam Gimbel, and Isaac and Mary Ann Magnin, began as sole proprietors with a great idea and went on from there to found great retailing empires.

More than 90 percent of all U.S. retailers own and operate a single store. Sole proprietors usually have small stores because of the huge amount of capital required to support an adequate inventory for a large business. These **mom-and-pop stores** are usually single stores, managed by the owner with a few assistants. They are most frequently specialty stores, because department stores require more space and more inventory. If the owner prospers and expands to more than four stores, he or she is said to have a *chain*.

Chain Organizations

A **chain organization** is a group of centrally owned stores, four or more according to the Census Bureau definition, each of which handles similar goods and merchandise. A chain organization may be local, regional, or national, although it is the national chains that have had the largest impact on retailing. They also may be general or specialty merchandisers, and depending on the kind of stores they are, they will target their customer broadly or narrowly. A chain organization can be a mass merchandiser known for its low prices; a department store known for high-quality, midprice goods; or a specialty merchandiser selling exclusive designs at high prices. Apparel chains may focus on a special size, age, or income group.

The oldest and best-known chain organizations are J.C. Penney and Sears, Roebuck and Co., which *Stores* magazine categorizes as department stores (Figure 18.7). Other chains include Kmart and Walmart, which are categorized as discount stores. Prestigious specialty chains are Talbots and Eddie Bauer. An example of a smaller specialty chain is Hot Topic.

FIGURE 18.7 Sears, Roebuck and Co. is one of the oldest chain organizations.

Organization for Buying and Merchandising

Most chain stores are departmentalized, but not in the same way as department stores. Chain-store buyers are typically assigned to buy a specific category or classification of apparel within a department instead of buying all categories for a department the way a department-store buyer does. This practice is called **category buying** or **classification buying**. Buyers in department stores, in contrast, are said to be responsible for **departmental buying**.

A departmental buyer in a sportswear department, for example, would buy swimwear, tops, jeans, sweaters, and slacks. A chain-store buyer who bought in the sportswear department might buy only swimsuits or only swimwear accessories. Category buying is necessary because huge quantities of goods are needed to stock the individual stores of a chain operation. Some chain operations have merchandise units numbering in the hundreds of thousands.

In addition to centralized buying and merchandising, most chains also have a system of central distribution. Merchandise is distributed to the units from a central warehouse or from regional distribution centers. Computer systems keep track of stock so that it can be reordered as needed; they also keep buyers informed of what is selling.

Leased Departments

Leased departments are sections of a retail store that are owned and operated by outside organizations. The outside organization usually owns the department's stock, merchandises and staffs the department, and pays for its own advertising. It is, in turn, required to abide by the host store's policies and regulations. In return for the leasing arrangement, the outside organization pays the store a percentage of its sales as rent.

Leased departments work best where some specialized knowledge is required. Jewelry, fur, and shoe departments are often leased, as are beauty salons. Glemby Company and Seligman and Latz, for example, lease many of the beauty salons in stores.

Department stores, chains, and discount organizations will lease both service and merchandise departments, while specialty stores usually restrict leased operations to services, such as jewelry or shoe repair or leather and suede cleaning.

Organization for Buying and Merchandising

Leased operations vary from the independent who operates in only one store to major chain organizations that operate in many stores. In chain organizations, centralized buying and merchandising prevail. Supervisors regularly visit each location to consult with local sales staff and department store managers. At such meetings, they assess current sales, deal with any problems, and plan for the future.

As the buying and selling functions have become increasingly separate from one another, operators of leased departments enjoy a unique—and at this point, rather old-fashioned—position within the fashion industry. Most operate in a variety of stores. They are furthermore buyers who maintain daily contact with their markets and their suppliers, which allows them to make excellent projections about future trends as well as to give outstanding fashion guidance to their customers.

Franchises

Franchises established themselves as a viable form of retailing when shops featuring fast food, bath linens, cookware, fabrics, unfinished furniture, electronics, and computers were successfully franchised. In a **franchise** agreement, the franchisee (owner-operator) pays a fee plus a royalty on all sales for the right to operate a store with an established name in an exclusive trading area. The franchiser (parent company) provides merchandise and assistance in organizing and merchandising, plus training. Customers often think that franchises are chains because they look alike.

With the exception of one or two bridal wear franchises and the maternity shop Lady Madonna, the fashion industry was not part of the initial franchise boom. It seems to have made up for lost time, however, in the second wave of franchising that proliferated during the 1980s. Firms as diverse as Benetton and Gymboree have adopted this form of ownership. Athletic footwear, tennis apparel, and men's sportswear have all produced lucrative and popular franchises. The Athlete's Foot (now known as TAF), for example, which sells athletic footwear and activewear, has 446 locations in forty countries.[7]

Designers are also getting in on the act. Examples of successful worldwide franchises by designers are Ralph Lauren's Polo Shops, Calvin Klein shops, and Yves Saint Laurent's Rive Gauche shops.

Industry experts see no signs that franchising will slow its pace, and many feel that this form of retailing will continue to grow.

Other Types of Fashion Retailers Today

In addition to the traditional retail formats discussed earlier, a group of businesses has evolved that adapt some of the attributes of the traditional retailers with some new ideas. Types of retail formats popular today include off-price retailers, factory outlet stores, convenience stores, category killers, catalog showrooms, flea markets, and boutiques or showcase stores, among others. Many overlap with existing traditional formats. Many are chains. We focus on those that are most important to apparel, accessories, and home furnishings.

Off-Price Retailers

Off-price retailing is the selling of brand-name and designer merchandise at lower-than-normal retail prices when the products are at the late rise or early peak in the fashion cycle. In contrast, regular discounters sell merchandise in the late peak and decline stages of the fashion cycle.

The first major off-price retailer in the United States was Loehmann's, which set up shop in Brooklyn in 1920 to sell "better" women's wear. Until then, high-quality women's garments had been available only through exclusive department stores. The regular-priced stores, for their part, did not fail to notice the arrival of Loehmann's on the retail scene. Department stores demanded that the discounter remove the labels so customers would not know what they were buying. That convention held for decades, but labels are rarely removed today.

Off-price retailers attribute part of their success to their providing an invaluable service to manufacturers and price-conscious customers. Because manufacturers must commit to fabric houses so far in advance (up to eighteen months before garments will be in the stores), they risk not having enough orders to use the fabric they have ordered. For many years, manufacturers took a loss when this happened. Then in the 1980s, when they had fewer orders than anticipated, they turned to off-pricers, who often pay full price for the fabric if the manufacturers will make it into garments at a lower cost. The manufacturers can more easily afford to cut their production costs than the cost of material they have already paid for. Off-pricers have in effect helped to smooth out the cyclical and often financially disastrous course of apparel manufacturing. Customers, in turn, benefit from being able to buy garments very similar to those that are being sold in exclusive stores for less than they would pay in those stores.

Off-pricers managed to capture an important share of the brand-name market. The success of brand names such as Donna Karan, Bill Blass, and Calvin Klein meant that designers no longer had to give department store exclusives, and they were soon selling their products to off-pricers. More recently, however, many designers have begun to prefer selling their overstocks

FIGURE 18.8 T.J.Maxx stores successfully fill the consumer's appetite for brand-name and designer clothes at discounted prices.

in their own stores. This has put severe pressure on off-pricers like Loehmann's to get enough inventory.

One other disadvantage seems to be built into off-price retailing: off-price retailers get the goods later than regular-priced retailers. While a department store puts designer spring and summer clothing on the selling floor during the winter, the off-pricer does not get the same merchandise until several months later. As a result, the off-pricer has a shorter selling season than the regular-price retailer.

Industry experts worry that off-pricers will overextend themselves, as retailers did during the mid- to late 1980s, in the rush to cash in on a strong market. While Filene's Basement and Syms closed in 2012, other off-price retailers, like T.J.Maxx (Figure 18.8) and Marshalls, have fared better. Burlington Coat Factory turned in $3.85 billion in sales in 2011, a remarkable demonstration of the consumer's appetite for brand-name and designer garments at reduced prices.[8]

Factory Outlet Stores

Factory outlet stores, discount operations run by a manufacturer, or increasingly these days by a designer, are another booming area of discount retailing. Factory outlet stores began in the 1920s in New England. For many years, they experienced little or no growth. A manufacturer would open a little store in one corner of a plant to sell company products—slightly defective goods and overstocks—at reduced rates to company employees. Kayser-Roth and William Carter Co. were among the first to sponsor factory outlet stores. Other manufacturers followed suit, usually opening their outlets on the premises, which also always meant in the Northeast where the apparel factories were located. Over time, manufacturers opened their stores to the

RetailMeNot®
Score the Savings You Want™

Submit a Coupon | Community | Blog | Sign up | Login

Search for savings from your favorite stores **Search!**

e.g. sephora expedia home depot tax wayfair estee lauder priceline macy's

Coupon Codes | Free Shipping | Printable Coupons | Grocery Coupons | Browse by Category

JCrew
30% Off Sale Items + Free Shipping
Use Code **GOODNEWS**
Save an Extra 30% On Final Sale Items + Free Shipping on $175+. Ends 3/15/13.
See more coupons from JCrew

J.CREW

Expedia | ULTA | The Real Deal by RetailMeNot | ★macy's | OLD NAVY | J.CREW | NINE WEST

COUPON WEBSITES GAIN STEAM

COUPONS ARE A hot topic between retailers and customers. Some retailers revile them and are trying to break consumers' addiction to coupons; however, Cotter Cunningham, founder and CEO of whatissharkmedia.com, is trying not to let that happen. Cunningham owns a variety of coupon websites that provide customers with all the coupons they desire. One of the largest, RetailMeNot.com, offers 500,000 coupons for 100,000 stores. Half of the coupons come directly from retailers; others are posted by users. Within a year of its launch in 2011, the site reached 400 million visitors and shows no signs of stopping.

"Consumers find no shame in using coupons—they're even accepted at Nordstrom," Cunningham said. Coupons from RetailMeNot.com are similar to the coupons that are printed in Sunday newspaper supplements in that they function to bring in new customers or clear merchandise. The main difference, however, is that RetailMeNot.com can get coupons to customers in a much shorter period of time than traditional newspapers. "Brick-and-mortar retailers are looking to replace the Sunday supplement ads with online coupons," he said. "The cycle to print Sunday supplements takes twenty weeks. Online, we can put an ad up in thirty minutes to one hour."

Ironically, Cunningham says that online coupons can help brick-and-mortar stores compete with online retailers, specifically because coupons from RetailMeNot.com are for in-store use only. "We see our app fighting showrooming," Cunningham said. "There's a big trend of people in stores looking at, say, Gap T-shirts to make sure online and offline pricing are the same. The number one reason people follow brands is because they are looking for deals."

RetailMeNot.com partners with retailers and shows them how to use coupons profitably and efficiently. The company has figured out a way to connect coupons to shoppers' credit cards so discounts automatically appear on their receipts. Its coupons also feature numerical codes to make scanning easier.

At only three and a half years old, Cunningham's company received $750 million in venture capital, which it used to grow its market share of the retail industry. The company is thinking about an IPO in the next two years—are you interested?

buying public—that is, those who drove by their often obscure locations.

The proliferation of factory outlet stores can be traced to a recession in the early 1980s, which created a market for stores that could meet the demand for bargain-hungry shoppers. Not only did the already-established factory outlets, such as Warnaco, Inc., Manhattan Industries, and Blue Bell, continue to operate, but big-name designers such as Calvin Klein, Anne Klein, and Bill Blass and brand-name organizations like Adidas, Bass Shoes, and Van Heusen menswear opened factory outlet stores.

Factory stores also left the factory, often to band together with one another in malls. The latest development is the emergence of entire communities, such as Freeport, Maine; Manchester, Vermont; and Secaucus, New Jersey, devoted almost exclusively to the selling of factory outlet goods. The draw in Freeport was the presence of L.L.Bean, an established force in mail-order retailing that expanded its factory store outlet throughout the 1980s from a small outpost to a huge multibuilding operation. See Chapter 19 for a discussion of retail locations.

Like off-price discounters, factory outlets offer certain advantages to manufacturers and customers. Most important is that they provide manufacturers and designers with a backup channel of distribution, which improves inventory control. Canceled orders and overstocks can be funneled into off-price retailers, which, if run correctly, also can be enormous image enhancers. Not to be underestimated is the possibility of strong profits. An outlet buys merchandise from the parent company for 30 percent off the regular wholesale prices and sells it for the same markup percentage as regular-priced retailers.

Designers and brand-name manufacturers use their outlets for overstocks and canceled orders. Some better sportswear manufacturers have 100 to 150 outlet stores, but to avoid offending the department stores, they do not publicize them. Large manufacturers, such as Kayser-Roth and Carter, are careful to use their outlets only for closeouts and seconds. The latter are unwilling to risk offending department stores and other major customers with more direct competition.

Originally, most outlet stores were pipe-rack operations in dingy surroundings. Many looked like the factories out of which they had originally operated. Factory outlets now resemble regular-priced retailers more and more, offering attractive merchandise displays and customer service that compares to that offered by full-priced retailers. Today, consumers are still frequenting outlet centers, but in addition to good prices on quality merchandise, they also want outlets to provide

them with a similar shopping experience to what they would get at a full-price store. In response, retailers are turning away from warehouse-style outposts and constructing high-end discounted stores, complete with attractive decor and services such as personal style consultations. Outlet stores provide a lucrative niche market to retailers, especially those on the high end of the spectrum. Saks Fifth Avenue's Off Fifth (Figure 18.9), Michael Kors, Swarovski, and Juicy Couture are a few that consistently rank among the top twenty outlets in the United States. Nordstrom and Neiman Marcus have expanded their outlets at a rate that is six times faster than their full-price stores.[9]

Yet, ironically, factory outlet customers are not people who must look for bargains. Instead, they are people with incomes far above average. Their motto is "NPR" or "Never Pay Retail." For most of these customers, bargain hunting is a leisure pastime, one that could easily be given up if factory outlet stores had to raise prices or cut services.

Category Killers

Superstores or category specialists carry one type of goods that they are able to offer in great depth at low prices because of volume buying. They so dominate a market that they drive out or kill smaller specialty stores and so are known as **category killers**. They offer a narrow but deep assortment of goods in stores 8,000

FIGURE 18.9 The popularity of outlets like Saks Fifth Avenue's Off Fifth continues to increase.

square feet or larger. Because of their buying power they can get not only rock-bottom prices but also excellent terms and an assured supply of scarce goods.

Examples of category killers include Bed, Bath and Beyond, Home Depot, Toys "R" Us, and Best Buy. Typically these are huge, freestanding stores, often called **big boxes**. They are rarely located in malls. They carry thousands of related products, at low prices, which they think offset no-frills service and decor.

Boutiques/Showcase Stores

Although boutiques originated as small shops with French couture houses, they really came to life as small, individually owned shops in the antiestablishment 1960s. The first freestanding boutiques opened in London and quickly spread to the United States. Their appeal lies in their potential for individuality. These stores are often owned and operated by highly creative persons who are eager to promote their own fashion enthusiasms. Their target customers are like-minded souls who share their unique attitudes about dressing.

Some boutique owners design their own merchandise; others buy and sell other people's designs. Boutiques are one of the few outlets for avant-garde merchandise that is too risky for department and specialty stores to carry (Figure 18.10).

Department stores have not, however, been above capitalizing on the success of boutiques. Bloomingdale's and Henri Bendel in New York City revolutionized merchandising display in the 1960s when they created special shops-within-shops on their selling floors. Frequently organized around the collections of a single designer, in-store boutiques offered customers a more complete fashion look. They were a fad that did not pass, and many department stores are now organized along boutique lines.

A trend seen in boutiques has been for designers to open their own shops. The French designers were the first to experiment with freestanding boutiques in the United States, but American designers soon followed suit. Among the French who have opened successful boutiques in the United States are Cardin, Valentino,

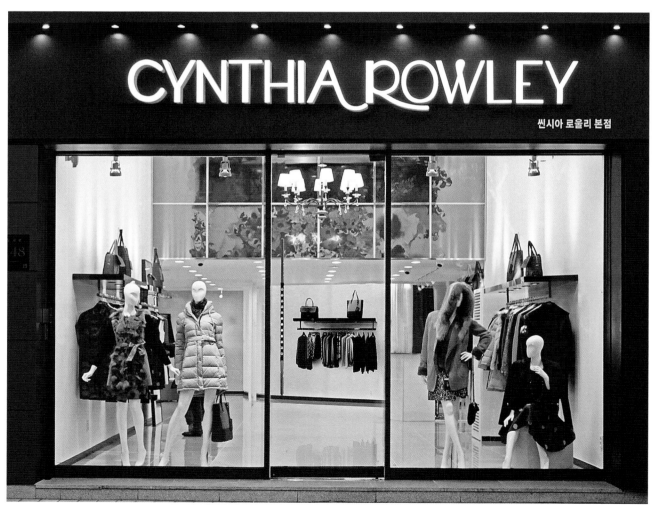

FIGURE 18.10 Cynthia Rowley's boutique in South Korea sells unique merchandise, with an inviting environment.

Yves Saint Laurent, and Givenchy. Italian designers and manufacturers such as Armani, Gucci, and Ferragamo were quick to follow. Successful British firms that pioneered in boutique selling on both sides of the Atlantic were Laura Ashley and Liberty of London.

Many American designers are expanding by opening showcase stores. A **showcase store** is a manufacturer's or designer's store that sells merchandise at the introductory and early-rise stages of the fashion cycle. In addition to generating income, showcase stores are testing grounds for new products. Ralph Lauren, Donna Karan, Calvin Klein, Tommy Hilfiger, Anna Sui, and Esprit operate showcase stores in addition to factory outlets. As lesser-known designers rush to open showcase stores, there is little doubt that this form of retailing will continue to grow.

Another trend in boutiques is the "vintage boutique" that features clothes and accessories from earlier decades. These small stores, long popular in major cities, have caught on in smaller communities across the country. The retro wave in fashion has also benefited many charities that sell used clothing, such as Goodwill Industries.

Nonstore Retailers

Nonstore retailing today is composed of four major formats: direct selling, catalog retailers, TV home shopping, and online shopping sites. The lines between these types are already starting to blur, as are those between nonstore retailers and traditional retailers. Store-based retailers are looking to expand their customer base through catalogs and electronic options. For example, not only have leading catalogers such as Lillian Vernon and Spiegel established major presences on the Internet, but retailers like J.C. Penney and Gap have giant online virtual storefronts.

Direct Selling

Direct selling, which used to be known as direct-to-the-home selling, is still a major force in the United States. In 2011, direct selling sales totaled $29.87 billion. Almost all the 15.6 million people who work in direct sales in the United States are independent part-time salespeople who buy merchandise from a large firm and distribute it by selling it to customers in their territories.[10]

Many fashion companies also sell in this way, mainly cosmetics, fragrances, and jewelry.

Catalog Retailers

Catalog retailing, or mail-order retailing, as it was traditionally called, has been popular in the United States since the 1880s. But by 1982, the explosive growth of

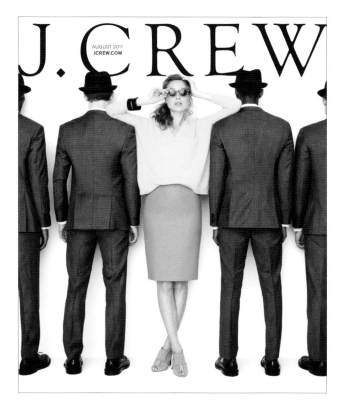

FIGURE 18.11 J.Crew has experienced remarkable sales from its catalogs, which also promote the company's online site.

mail-order retailers had reached such proportions that *Time* magazine ran a cover story on it. The evolution of air delivery and computerized distribution have played a vital role in increasing direct-mail and catalog sales. Companies are now able to target their customers in very specific ways, by age, income, geographic region, lifestyle, and interests. As a result, almost 90 percent of all catalog sales are now from specialized catalogs. Companies can use catalogs to link to their websites, in which the customer can find more promotions and products, and make purchases. Discount key codes on catalogs also provide sales for customers and can encourage purchases.

Not willing to rest on their laurels, catalogers have also sought new ways to develop their business. One way is to market around the world, where mail order has long been popular. U.S. catalogers like Lands' End, Eddie Bauer, Patagonia, J.Crew (Figure 18.11), Coldwater Creek, and Williams-Sonoma have experienced remarkable sales globally.

Retailers have established their own programs, and department store bills arrive stuffed with offers to purchase products. Some companies also send **magalogs**, which are catalogs that have editorial content, not just advertising.

However, there are a few big problems that plague catalog retailers: the steadily increasing cost of paper, growth in online shopping, the movement to be more green, and consistently higher return rates for products. Still, many customers respond enthusiastically to catalogs as providing entertainment, as well as another avenue to shop.

TV Home Shopping

One of the most talked-about developments in retailing has been the growth of home TV shopping, a form of retailing that takes the catalog sales techniques one step further. The potential of television as a direct-mail sales tool has long been recognized; witness the late-night gadget demonstrations and the ubiquitous storm window advertisements. Not until the advent of cable television, however, with its lower production standards and lower costs, was it feasible to produce infomercials and to set up home shopping services that sell an array of goods.

The cable TV infomercial, with its enthusiastic host and wildly appreciative audience, has been used to sell a large variety of goods, from Justin Bieber and Katy Perry for Proactiv to Susan Lucci's Malibu Pilates.

In 1977, the pioneer in the TV home shopping business was Home Shopping Network (HSN) of St. Petersburg, Florida. On the air twenty-four hours a day, seven days a week, HSN is the world's most widely distributed TV shopping network and offers customers an easy shopping experience with their remotes (Figure 18.12). It also has an e-commerce site and apps for the iPad and mobile phones. In 2011, HSN had grown into

a global multichannel retailer with a customer reach of 95.5 million U.S. households.[11]

HSN is a subsidiary of IAC and delivers its merchandise not only through television but also online, through hsn.com. With more than 40,000 products, www.hsn.com is transforming itself to complement HSN's successful broadcast network.[12]

The second largest television shopping service is QVC of West Chester, Pennsylvania, with ninety-eight million viewers, but a substantially higher revenue than HSN. In May 2009, QVC became the first multimedia retailer to offer native high-definition service to customers. QVC offers on-screen demonstrations of merchandise that range from simple cookware to sophisticated electronics. QVC sells enormous amounts of apparel and accessories, especially jewelry, and a wide array of home furnishings, tabletop goods, and gift items. QVC has separate weekly shows for gold jewelry, silver jewelry, simulated-diamond jewelry, men's jewelry, and watches. Los Angeles designer Bob Mackie has made many appearances on QVC, selling out their stock of his scarfs and tops. Similarly, comedian Joan Rivers promotes her line of costume jewelry, effectively combining selling and entertainment. Isaac Mizrahi and Rachel Zoe have also sold their apparel on the network. Besides its TV shopping network, QVC operates sales from its website, www.qvc.com; mobile phone applications; and a retail operation in Mall of America in Bloomington called QVC@themall. QVC, which is owned by Denver-based media giant Liberty Media, has long been the gold standard for some shopping networks. Revenue reached $8.3 billion in 2011, with $2.6 billion of that total coming from e-commerce.[13]

ShopNBC, which is owned and operated by Value Vision, is a multichannel electronic retailer. This shopping network reaches seventy-three million homes in the United States through cable and satellite television. It, too, offers an extensive array of products including apparel and accessories from Anne Klein, Suzanne Somers, Ed Hardy, and Harley-Davidson. With flat-screen TVs and advances in technology, customers get a better view of the products, enticing them to place even more orders. For instance, ShopNBC programming is streamed live at www.shopnbc.com, on Facebook, and via apps on mobile devices.[14]

Online Shopping

Worldwide e-commerce totaled $961 billion in 2011.[15] And in November 2011, Cyber Monday (the Monday after Thanksgiving) raked in more than $1.3 billion—up 22 percent from Cyber Monday sales in 2010—to become the biggest online spending day in history.[16]

FIGURE 18.12 HSN, the TV shopping network, has grown into a global multichannel retailer.

Key reasons for the growth of online sales are the ease and quickness of shopping at any hour and from any place. To compensate for the lack of hands-on shopping, many sites allow customers to zoom in on images, see multiple views of products, or look at merchandise in different colors. However, customers may have found another strategy for shopping. As discussed in Chapter 15, a more recent trend in retail is called *showrooming*. This is when a customer shops in a brick-and-mortar store first but then makes the purchase online. According to an AlixPartners survey, a sampling of 2,010 adults indicated that more consumers are purchasing online after having shopped at or visited a physical store. Those ages 25 to 34 were the largest demographic group that showroomed, specifically in apparel and footwear categories. The top three online purchase drivers were free shipping/home delivery, lower prices, and the desired item not being available in the store (Figure 18.13).[17]

Another form of e-tailing is member-only and flash-sale websites. Four major players in the flash-sales arena are Gilt Groupe, HauteLook, Ideeli, and Rue La La. These sites give customers exclusive discounts with sales that last for only a certain number of hours, creating a sense of urgency to buy.

Today, retailers are expanding their thinking about who they are selling their products to and how. Companies understand that they must reach out to the millennial generation through apps, blogs, social media, and mobile devices in addition to traditional methods.

Mergers and Acquisitions

Until the 1930s, most department stores in the United States were independently owned. Most, in fact, were owned by the families whose names they bore, names such as Marshall Field, John Wanamaker, Gimbel Brothers, and J. L. Hudson. By the 1980s, most of these long-established stores had changed hands, and with these changes in ownership came new images and sometimes even new names.

So much change has occurred in the retail business recently that you need a scorecard to track the remaining players. Consolidations, changes in distribution channels, bankruptcies, altered buying organizations, and foreign investments have all caused the retail scene as we knew it to change.

Although mergers have taken their toll on the department stores, causing some old, established stores

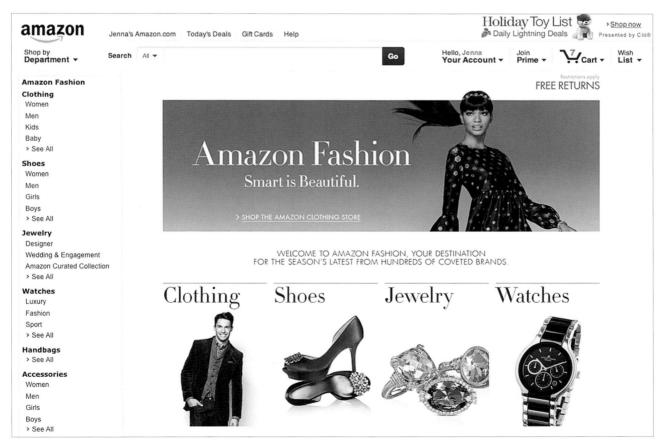

FIGURE 18.13 Amazon is an online-only site that offers competitive prices and deals on shipping costs for its customers globally.

to close their doors, some good has been served. Without mergers, many of the established department stores would not have survived the onslaught of competition from chains and discounters. In fact, mergers generally occur for one of two reasons: a need to reorganize for greater efficiency and a need to expand.

Merging for Efficiency and Expansion

Like everything in life, the only thing that has remained constant in the retail business over the last century is change. The trend toward mergers and consolidations started in 1896 when John Wanamaker acquired A. T. Stewart. But it was Fred Lazarus Jr. of the founding family of the original Lazarus Store in Columbus, Ohio, who consolidated the first retail giant with the purchase of the Shillito Store in Cincinnati and Filene's of Boston, with Abraham-Straus in New York joining them to form Federated Department Stores in 1930.

In the 1970s and 1980s, the big corporate merger trend picked up momentum with some of the most famous names in the business changing hands. Among the most memorable deals: Dayton Hudson bought Mervyns in 1978 and Marshall Field's at the beginning of 1990. Crown American Corp. bought Hess's Department Stores in 1979. Allied Stores Corp. picked up Garfinckel's, Raleighs, and Miller & Rhoads in 1981. Taubman bought Woodward & Lothrop in 1984 and John Wanamaker in 1986. P. A. Bergner acquired Boston Stores in 1985 and Carson Pirie Scott in 1989. May Department Stores acquired Associated Dry Goods in 1986 and Filene's and Foley's in 1986. L. J. Hooker, an Australian real-estate developer, bought Bonwit Teller, B. Altman, Sakowitz, and Parisian in 1987. Harcourt General bought Bergdorf and Neiman's in 1987. Dillard's acquired Joske's in 1987, half of Higbee's in 1988, D. H. Holmes in 1989, and Ivey's in 1990. Macy's added Bullock's, Bullock's Wilshire, and I. Magnin in 1988. Marks & Spencer bought Brooks Brothers in 1988, and Investcorp bought Saks in 1990.

The mergers and acquisitions of the 1970s and 1980s led to the restructuring and reorganization of the 1980s and 1990s, when many of these firms wound up in bankruptcy court or simply disappeared from the scene. Among the best known were the liquidation of B. Altman in 1989, Federated/Allied's Chapter 11 filing in January 1990, Carter Hawley Hale's bankruptcy in 1991, and Macy's bankruptcy in 1992.

In the twenty-first century, the mergers and acquisitions movement had a resurgence in the early 2000s, with one of the biggest happening in 2005. The two most notable deals included the acquisition of May Department Stores by Federated Department Stores in 2005, which changed its name to Macy's Inc. in 2007, and the purchase of Neiman Marcus Group by Texas Pacific Group/Warburg Pincus.

Other high-profile retail deals included Saks Incorporated selling its Parisian unit, and the acquisition of Lord & Taylor by Canada-based Hudson's Bay Company in 2012.[18] The merger and acquisition story is not over yet—stay tuned.

Trends: Changing Retail Patterns

Retail operations not only must constantly respond to change in their environments, but they themselves must also change if they are to survive. One theory, suggested by Malcolm P. McNair, retailing authority and professor emeritus at the Harvard Business School, describes the way in which retail organizations naturally change or evolve.

According to McNair's theory, called the "Wheel of Retailing," most retail organizations begin life as lower-priced distributors. They offer strictly functional facilities, limited assortments, and minimal customer services. As time elapses, the successful businesses need to grow in order to survive, so they begin to trade up in an effort to broaden their customer profile. Facilities are modernized. Store decor becomes more attractive. Assortments become more varied and of higher quality. Promotional efforts are initiated or increased, and some customer services are introduced.

The process of trading up, however, involves considerable capital investment in the physical plant, equipment, and stock. Operating expenses spiral. As a result, retailers are forced to charge higher prices to cover the increased cost of doing business. To justify the higher prices, they also begin to stock more expensive merchandise.

According to McNair's theory, as retailers move out of the low-priced end of the market into the moderate-to-high-priced field, they create a vacuum at the bottom of the retailing structure. The vacuum does not exist for long, though. Enterprising new retailers move quickly to fill the vacated and temporarily uncompetitive low-priced area to meet the demands of customers who either need or prefer to patronize low-priced retailers. This pattern keeps repeating itself as successful retailers trade up and new ones move into the vacuum. This theory also applies to catalog companies—Spiegel is one example of a firm that moved upscale.

Even those who move up must still constantly cope with the ever-changing nature of the fashion business.

In Chapter 19, the most important challenges and trends confronting today's retailers are discussed, along with strategies to overcome them.

Summary and Review

The history of fashion retailing in the United States is an interesting one. From general stores and peddlers to the earliest mail-order sellers, all early retailers sought customer satisfaction. Today's retailers seek the same goals through a variety of formats.

Three traditional retailing formats are the department store, the specialty store, and the discount store. Newer formats include off-price retailers, factory outlet stores, category killers, and boutiques and showcase stores. All of these formats can be owned in one of four ways: sole proprietors, chains, leased departments, or franchises.

Four types of nonstore retailing are popular today: direct selling, catalog or mail-order selling, TV home shopping, and online shopping. Mobile devices, social media, blogs, and apps are other ways in which retailers reach the millennial generation.

Mergers and acquisitions have changed the face of retailing as we knew it and will probably continue to do so. Malcolm McNair's theory of how retailers evolve and change proposes that most retailers begin as lower-priced distributors and then move upscale, creating an opportunity for new retailers to fill the lower-priced niche. McNair calls this the "Wheel of Retailing."

For Review

1. Name and briefly explain the characteristics and importance of three early forms of retail distribution in the United States.
2. How is the buying function handled by a department store?
3. What is a specialty store? How are buying and merchandising handled in a specialty store?
4. What is a chain organization? How are buying and merchandising handled in chain operations?
5. How do successful discounters make a profit?
6. What is a leased department, and how does it operate? Name the departments in a retail store that are frequently leased.
7. What is a category killer?
8. What stage or stages of the fashion cycle would most likely be emphasized by (a) a specialty store, (b) a department store, and (c) a discount store?
9. What is the difference between home TV shopping and online shopping?
10. According to Malcolm P. McNair, how do retail organizations typically evolve?

For Discussion

1. Compare and contrast the organization for buying and merchandising among (a) prestigious chain organizations, department stores, and large specialty stores; (b) discounters and off-price mass merchandisers; and (c) franchises and leased departments. Give examples of different types of retailers in your community.
2. What examples in your community can you cite that support McNair's theory of trading up by retailers?

Trade Talk

Define or briefly explain the following terms:

big box
category buying or classification
    buying
category killer
chain organization
departmental buying
department store
discount department store
discount general merchandiser
discount/off-price specialty store
discount store
factory outlet store
fashion retailing
franchise
general merchandise retailer
general store
hypermarket
leased department
magalog
mom-and-pop store
off-price retailing
showcase store
specialty retailer
specialty store
warehouse club

POLICIES AND STRATEGIES IN FASHION RETAILING

KEY CONCEPTS

- The six major merchandising policies that must be set by each retailer
- The five operational policies that must be set by each retail store
- The major strategies retailers are using to respond to customer concerns
- The major trends in merchandising and operational policies

Stores use their merchandising, operating, and location policies to differentiate themselves from the competition and to attract different kinds of customers. Successful retailers realize that "you cannot be all things to all people," as the old saying has it. So they carefully craft a unique mix of merchandise, policies, and store locations to attract a loyal customer following. At the same time, they must respond to changing trends—a challenging balancing act.

Merchandising Policies

Regardless of whether a retailer is a chain or a mom-and-pop operation, a general or specialty merchandiser, it seeks to maximize its profits by going after a target group of customers. To better target their customers, retailers establish **merchandising policies**. These are general and specific guidelines and goals established by store management and adjusted according to current trends and marketplace needs to keep the store on target.

Of the many elements that go into a store's merchandising policies, the six most important are the store's overall general goals regarding:

1. Stage of the fashion cycle that will be emphasized
2. Level of quality that will be maintained
3. Price range or ranges that will be offered
4. Depth and breadth of merchandise assortments
5. Brand policies
6. Exclusivity

Fashion Cycle Emphasis

As a means of establishing its image, every retailer decides to emphasize one phase of the fashion cycle over others. It then chooses its merchandise to fit that phase. Most stores want to ride the tide of new fashion. Few knowingly highlight styles once they have reached the decline stage, but stores still must choose whether to emphasize styles in their introductory, rise, culmination, or peak stages.

A retailer who chooses to buy styles in the introductory phase is opting to be a fashion leader, while a

FIGURE 19.1 Henri Bendel's target market has evolved over the years, starting with an emphasis on the niche, then expanding to a broader market, and finally back to a narrow focus.

store that waits for the styles to become slightly established, that is, to enter the rise stage, has decided to aim for being a close second to the fashion leader. Finally, a retailer may buy clothes in the culmination or peak stages, thus making itself a follower of fashion trends—as indeed most women and men are. The majority of stores across the country probably fall into this category.

Naturally, a store's choice about fashion emphasis must accord with its targeted customers' needs and wants. Henri Bendel in New York, which for many years had a reputation for extreme trendiness, knew that its target customers were a small, elite group of young and very stylish women who wanted to be the first to wear whatever was new (Figure 19.1). When The Limited bought Bendel, management changed Bendel's target customer and shifted the store's emphasis, moving from a position of fashion leadership to one of pursuing a broader market. In the late 1990s, it changed back to the narrower, less competitive niche of the fashion leader customer. Today, Bendel continues to nurture young, fashion-forward designers, with exclusive in-store boutiques and its Open See program. The Open See program, which seeks new talent, has launched the careers of designers like Todd Oldham, Anna Sui, James Purcell, Pamela Dennis, and Colette Malouf. It is held twice a year at Bendel's Fifth Avenue flagship store.[1]

Quality

Retailers can choose from three general levels of quality:

1. The top level, which involves the finest materials and workmanship
2. The intermediate level, which exhibits concern for quality and workmanship but always with an eye to maintaining certain price levels
3. The serviceable level, which involves materials and workmanship of a fairly low level, consistent with equally low prices

Just as retailers are known for their chosen emphasis within the fashion cycle, they are also known for their decisions regarding quality. Quality and high fashion, however, do not always go hand in hand. Although most introductory styles are high priced, this is not always the case. Some stores that assert themselves as fashion leaders do not bother with high quality, preferring merely to push what is new and exciting. In contrast, retailers that emphasize the rise or culmination stage also often stake their reputations on the high quality of their merchandise. They are thus able to emphasize their apparel's lasting qualities in ways that fashion leaders often cannot and do not want to do. One example is Sears's boy's wear, which stresses sturdy workmanship.

Once a store has set its quality policies, it must make more specific decisions, such as whether it will accept nothing less than perfect goods or whether it will permit irregulars and second-quality goods to be offered.

Price Ranges

What people earn affects what they can spend, especially for clothing, where a variety of choices regarding quality and price are available. As a result, pricing policies are an important merchandising decision. A store's pricing policies play a major role in determining the kinds of customers it will attract (Figure 19.2).

There is actually no direct correlation between price and quality. Items of relatively low quality may carry a high price tag if there is a reason for them to do so, such as the presence of a designer's name or the fact that they are in the introductory phase of the fashion cycle. Despite the lack of a correlation, however, most retailers do attempt to tie their price ranges to quality standards. A store policy of buying only top quality also permits high price ranges, whereas a store that features intermediate quality usually sets some bottom limits that it will not go below. Stores that emphasize serviceable quality usually tend to also emphasize their low prices. Ineffective pricing can drain a retailer's profits, muddle its image, and undermine customer trust.

Depth and Breadth of Assortments

An **assortment** refers to the range of stock a retailer features. A store can feature a **narrow and deep assortment** in which it stocks relatively few styles but has them in many sizes and colors. Or it can stock a **broad and shallow assortment** in which it offers many different styles in limited sizes and colors.

The two are mutually exclusive because space and cost are limiting factors in retail operations. A policy of stocking a broad assortment usually limits the depth to which those items can be stocked, and conversely, if depth is desired, variety must usually be limited. Prestige stores tend to stock broad and shallow assortments, offering small stocks of many styles in limited sizes and colors.

In stores that cater to midrange fashion and quality, assortments are broad and shallow early in a season when new styles are being tested. Once the demand for a style has become clear, the store begins concentrating on narrow and deep assortments of proven styles.

Mass merchandisers focus on narrow and deep assortments of styles in the culmination stage. Target, for example, has built an enviable reputation for fashionableness and fresh selection, yet its selections

FIGURE 19.2 Too many sales may undermine customers' trust (top), but flash-sale sites can entice customers to make purchases (bottom).

are not particularly deep. But its meticulous attention to housekeeping ensures that its counters and shelves give the impression of being well-stocked. Its apparel assortment is largely basics. But a handful of items in cutting-edge styles and colors give it an upscale look.

Brand Policies

Stores also must establish policies regarding the brands they will carry. A brand is a name, trademark, or logo that is used to identify the products of a specific manufacturer or seller. Brands help to differentiate products from their competition. Some brands, those associated with designers like Ralph Lauren, for example, acquire a special status that permits them to be sold at higher prices. Status and price, however, are not the only things that help a brand sell well. National brands and private labels have also become important.

A national brand, which identifies the manufacturer of a product, is widely distributed in many stores across the country. National brands, which hold out the promise of consistent quality, have become the backbone of many retailers' stocks. The names of some designers, such as Tommy Hilfiger and Eileen Fisher, to name but two, have become so well known to consumers that their labels are considered national brands. These name brands have acquired a value in the consumers' mind that is distinct from any intrinsic value in the products themselves. To minimize competition over national brands, some major retailers insist on buying exclusive

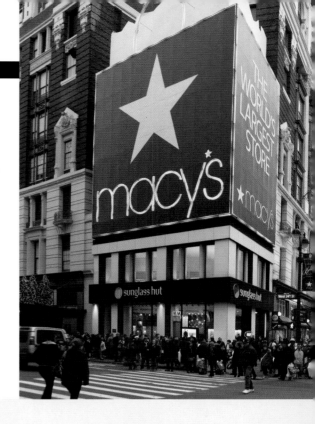

MACY'S INITIATIVE TO WOO MILLENNIALS

IN 2012 MACY'S revealed that over the next three years it hopes to capture more dollars from the Millennial customer, an age group with an estimated annual spending power of more than $65 billion. The initiative affects the retailer's organizational structure—this effort will move the company's focus beyond the seventy-six million baby boomers and toward their children and grandchildren. To do this, Macy's is adopting cutting-edge technologies to keep customers engaged, especially Millennial shoppers for whom cell phones, tablets, and social media are ingrained into daily life.

The Millennial customer is, in Macy's view, two distinct groups: the Mstylelab shopper, between the ages of thirteen and twenty-two, and the Impulse shopper, between the ages of nineteen and thirty. Macy's is aggressively building its Mstylelab and Impulse destination departments so that they are available in every store, some with an entire floor devoted to Millennials. Macy's is also developing brands just for the Millennial customer. Some of the highlights of their Millennial program include:

- Identifying customer lifestyle profiles for use by Macy's buying, planning, marketing, and visual merchandising teams.
- Developing new brands and fine-tuning its existing product assortment by location, based on geographic preferences.
- Training sales associates to better advise customers how to accessorize from head to toe.
- Redesigning Macy's internal organizational structure to speed up decision-making, product development, and alignment of resources across its buying staff, private brand developers, and merchandisers.

All of these initiatives are important because Macy's faces significant competition in the Millennial market from fast-fashion retailers like Zara and H&M. In Zara's case, the brand can develop and produce a collection within two weeks and get it into its stores. In order to stay relevant to the next generation of fashion consumers, Macy's must continue to reposition itself on the cutting edge of trends in product development and marketing.

styles, or **confined styles**, from national brand manufacturers.

Retailers are also riding the wave of popularity of brand names by promoting their own private labels or store brands. Store brands have proven to be an excellent way to meet price competition and achieve exclusivity, which is discussed in the following section.

Prestige specialty stores tend to feature their own store labels and designer names, a strategy Bergdorf Goodman pursued with a private-label collection of classic but luxurious sportswear. Many department stores have adopted private labels and brands with great success. Macy's with its INC, Charter Club, JM Collection, and Alfani collections is a prime example. When J.C. Penney started selling the Joe Fresh brand, it proved to be a top-selling brand online and has brought in new shoppers that wouldn't typically shop at J.C. Penney's.[2]

Mass merchandisers have always offered their own private labels, typically sold alongside unbranded merchandise, as a means of keeping prices low. Kmart, for example, sells "celebrity" lines, including apparel lines by Jaclyn Smith, Sofia by Sofia Vergara (Figure 19.3), and Dream Out Loud by Selena Gomez (for the juniors market). Target has established a slew of both clothing and beauty licenses through exclusive agreements and collaborations over the years with well-known designers such as Isaac Mizrahi, Missoni, Stephen Sprouse, Jason Wu, Mossimo, and Prabal Gurung.

Exclusivity

Exclusivity is something many stores strive for but few are able to achieve. Several store policies can help retailers establish a reputation for exclusivity.

1. They may prevail upon vendors to confine one or more styles to their store for a period of time and/or within their trading area.
2. They can buy from producers who will manufacture goods to their specifications.
3. They can become the sole agent within their trading area for new, young designers.
4. They can seek out and buy from domestic or foreign sources of supply that no one else has discovered.
5. They can create private labels.

However, the first two policies (confined lines and specification buying) are options only when a store

FIGURE 19.3 Kmart sells the private label Sofia by Sofia Vergara in its stores to attract new shoppers.

can place a large enough initial order to make production profitable for the manufacturer.

The last three policies do not necessarily demand high volume. They are thus invaluable to prestige stores that need exclusivity as part of their images but cannot hope to compete in volume with mass merchandisers or even big department stores.

Operational Store Policies

After a retailer has defined its target customers and set its merchandise policies in a manner designed to attract them, it must next establish **operational policies**. Often more specific in nature than merchandising policies, these are primarily designed to keep the customers once they are attracted enough to come into the store. What merchandising policies do to establish a retailer's image, operational policies do to build a store's reputation. Operational policies also serve to enhance merchandising policies. They establish such things as the store's ambiance, its customer services, its selling services, its promotional activities, and last but hardly least, its frequent shopper plans.

Ambiance

Ambiance, the atmosphere you encounter when you enter a store, does much to create the image of a store (Figure 19.4). Prestige department and specialty stores work hard to provide pleasant and even luxurious surroundings. Decor matters and usually consists of carpeted or wood floors, wood counters and display cases, and chandeliers and other expensive lighting. Dressing rooms are numerous, large, and private. The store is pleasing to the eye. Merchandise is attractively displayed on a variety of fixtures. Just think of the strong link between the store design of a Crate and Barrel and its displays and merchandise. Its use of textured woods, colorful textiles, and bright pottery has made its merchandise the stars of an exciting show.

Len Berry coined the term **sensory retailing**, which means in-store stimulation of all the customers' senses. Sensory retailing is becoming a more significant competitive weapon in retailing. Think of the sensuous aroma, mood music, and dramatic lighting of merchandise displays in a Victoria's Secret. In fact,

FIGURE 19.4 Alexander McQueen's store exhibits good visual merchandising, displays, and lighting, which sends a positive image to customers.

the music played in Victoria's Secret stores has become a successful business in itself. In the history of classical music, only eleven compact discs have sold more than a million copies. The label that released five of them is Victoria's Secret. This success has led to other retailers selling their own albums; among them are The Limited, Express, Lane Bryant, Polo, Gap, and Pottery Barn.

Retailers must create an experience and draw customers into it. Shoppers usually splurge on some items while attempting to save as much as possible on others. A retailer that maximizes customer involvement creates a unique experience for the shopper, drawing out the desire to splurge.

Retail environments that include education, allow sampling, and impart a feeling of pampering will entice the customer. Creating a welcoming atmosphere isn't simply about the lights and music—it must grow organically. By converging atmosphere, design, and merchandise, a retailer can create a unified story that sells its customer on the buying experience.[3]

In contrast, at low-range and discount stores, ambiance may count for little. The intention is to send the customer a clear message: shop here in less than luxurious surroundings, and we will give you the lowest possible price. Fixtures are usually plain, and garments are crowded on racks or "rounders," with supermarket-style signage. Fitting room space may be limited or may consist only of a large, shared dressing room, commonly referred to as a *snake pit* by customers.

Customer Services

Department stores pioneered in offering customer services. They were the first retailers to provide their customers with store charge privileges and generous return policies. Their willingness to accept merchandise returns, in fact, originated with John Wanamaker and his Philadelphia store of the same name. His first store, opened in 1876 in an old railroad freight station, was a men's clothing store. A year later, he added departments for ladies' goods, household linens, upholstery, and shoes, for a then-unheard-of total of sixteen departments. Wanamaker further shocked the retail world by advertising that if anything did not please "the folks at home" or was unsatisfactory for any other reason, it could be returned for a cash refund within ten days.

Today, it is commonplace for department and specialty stores to offer their customers an array of services designed to increase their edge over the competition. The more familiar customer services include several credit plans, liberal merchandise return policies, telephone ordering, free or inexpensive delivery, in-store restaurants, free parking, and a variety of services such as alterations and jewelry repair. As competition, particularly from chains and discounters, has increased, general merchandisers have met it by offering still more services, such as online ordering and extended shopping hours.

Discount stores, especially small ones, offer a more limited range of services than do department and specialty stores. Discounters took a lead in establishing extended hours. At small discount stores, transactions are usually on a cash-and-carry basis, although most accept major credit cards. Most large discounters offer their own credit plans, with greater emphasis on installment buying. Refund policies are less liberal than those of department stores; however, most discounters will accept unused goods (often for credit rather than cash) if they are returned in a specified period of time, usually seven to ten days. Delivery service, if available, is restricted to bulky items and usually costs extra.

Large discount chains like Target, proving Malcolm MacNair's theory discussed in Chapter 18, have raised their level of services. They have "guest amenity kiosks" with phones that shoppers can use to summon a salesperson or get a question answered. Target also has pint-size shopping carts to help keep shoppers' children amused. The Swedish discount chain IKEA offers play areas (Figure 19.5).

Selling Services

In all but the higher-priced specialty stores these days, self-service is the rule. In discount stores and low- to moderate-priced chain stores, clerks are present on the selling floor to direct customers to merchandise and ring up sales. In most department and specialty stores, salespersons are available on the sales floor to answer some questions and complete sales transactions.

The old service of catering exclusively to one client at a time, bringing clothes into the dressing room, and offering fit and style advice is gone in most department stores, probably forever. An exception to this rule is Nordstrom, which has maintained a high degree of selling services. In fact, it is the success of its sales help that has made Nordstrom one of the most successful specialty stores in America. Other very high-end specialty stores, such as Bergdorf Goodman and Lord & Taylor, also offer highly personalized selling techniques, which include recording what individual customers have purchased in the past and alerting them by phone or mail to new merchandise that may interest them. Very often, these high-level salespeople work on commission, so they have a real incentive to offer personalized service.

Despite the abundant lip service paid to customer service by more retail executives, a new study finds that poor in-store service is the biggest negative experience, generating negative word-of-mouth and resulting in lost sales.

The Retail Customer Dissatisfaction Study was conducted by the Verde Group and the Baker Retail Initiative at the University of Pennsylvania's Wharton School. Based on the study's findings, analysts at Verde and the Baker Retail Initiative have identified five core competencies that store associates must have to inspire customer loyalty:[4]

1. Engagement: Being polite, genuinely caring, and interested in helping, acknowledging, and listening
2. Executional Excellence: Patiently explaining and advising, checking stock, helping find products,

FIGURE 19.5 A child in a ball crawl at IKEA demonstrates this chain's strong customer service policies. They realize that if a child is content, Mom shops longer.

having product knowledge, and providing unexpected product quality
3. Brand Experience: Create exciting store atmosphere, consistently great product quality, and making customers feel like they're special and that they always get a deal
4. Expediting: Being sensitive to customers' time and long checkout lines; being proactive in helping speed up the process
5. Problem Recovery: Helping resolve and compensate for problems; upgrading quality and ensuring complete satisfaction

Promotional Activities

All retailers engage in some promotional activities, whether it is advertising or publicity. Advertising and publicity are a store's two chief means of communicating with its customers. How much a retail organization promotes itself, however, varies depending on the type of retail operation.

Discount stores are the heaviest promoters, and they rely heavily on advertising as opposed to publicity or public relations. All kinds of advertising—newspaper, television, radio, and direct mail—are employed to get their message across. Their advertising emphasizes low prices and in many instances invites customers to comparison shop. Discount operations tend to run frequent sales or special promotions. In a very popular promotion, IKEA, the Swedish home furnishings retailer, cooperated with public health officials in Houston to offer a day of free vaccinations and dental checkups for children of shoppers.

Compared with the discounters, department and chain stores and specialty stores engage in a more moderate amount of promotional activity, although, of course, large budgets are allotted for this purpose. Department stores rely most heavily on newspaper

DISCOUNTERS
ARE LEADING FIFTY YEARS OF RETAIL REVOLUTION

I T WAS A half century ago that discounters shook up the retail landscape, and the industry hasn't been the same since. In 1962, middle-class households were booming, as well as the first enclosed shopping malls that began popping up in the suburbs. Conditions were ripe for a new retail concept and over the course of that year, Walmart, Target, Kmart, and Kohl's opened their first stores.

Discounters expanded rapidly over the next decade, and by 1970, they had become part of the nation's lexicon. The 1990s saw two major retail shifts: the rise of megastores and e-commerce. Both Amazon and eBay launched in 1995. Walmart and Target moved online in 1996, but were slow to gain traction there. To diversify, Walmart, Kmart, and Target made big bets on the combined mass merchandise and supermarket concept, which was successful among consumers for whom time and convenience were at a premium. As discounters grew, they began to move away from the five-and-dime merchandising mentality and opted for better marketing. By 2000, a shift was under way—from merchants to marketers. It became just as important for discounters to develop, nurture, and promote a brand's personality as it was to move merchandise.

The 2000s were bookended by tough economies, with retailers scrambling to capture consumers' attention via big advertising budgets and escalating promotions. Today, discounters find themselves operating in a dramatically altered landscape. While they used to price products against department store prices, that is now an irrelevant argument. Consumers are educated and retailers have to come up with compelling offers that stand on their own.

On their golden anniversaries, what does the future look like for these discounting giants? Population growth is slowing, family units are evolving, and the minority is becoming the majority. Consumers are shifting from suburban to urban centers and they are shopping across a dizzying array of platforms. Media has become fragmented and e-commerce is shaping the industry. A revolution is happening, and discounters in particular must adapt to changing consumer preferences or risk becoming insignificant.

advertising, although some prestigious department and specialty stores also advertise in the major fashion magazines, local magazines, or cable television. Specialty chains like Gap, Esprit, and Pier 1 have begun to use general magazines as much as fashion magazines or shelter magazines to reach their target customers. Internet sites and social media are being used more frequently by both large and small retailers as ways to reach affluent customers interested in convenience.

The more prestigious stores use direct mail. Monthly bills, stuffed with advertising and special catalogs, are mailed regularly to charge customers. These retailers also do a moderate number of "special sale" and "special purchase" advertising campaigns. Sales are usually tied to special events, such as a holiday (the Columbus Day coat sales are one example), an anniversary, or an end-of-the-month clearance. Department stores were the leaders in pioneering traditional seasonal sales: white sales in January and August, back-to-school promotions in late summer and early fall.

The content of advertising varies with the type of retailer. Discount and mass merchandisers' ads are heavily product-oriented, displaying the product and its price in a direct manner. The prestige stores run some advertisements for individual items, but their advertisements are more likely to feature a designer or a new design collection. Advertisements may emphasize a new fashion look or trend at the expense of promoting the apparel in the ad.

Frequent Shopper Plans

A policy that the airlines have used to great advantage—the frequent flier plan—has been adopted by many other businesses. Also referred to as *loyalty marketing* or *customer retention programs*, this policy is also widely used by hotels, who reward frequent guests with special rates, their favorite newspaper, special easy checkout, and other perks. In today's "overstored" environment, retailers are searching for ways to stand out. Some retailers are adapting this policy by rewarding frequent shoppers with special sales, special discounts, newsletters, and clubs (Figure 19.6). This trend is spreading as retailers see the advantages of keeping existing customers and encouraging them to shop more often. The Foursquare app, which has a network of more than thirty million people worldwide, is another way for businesses to entice new customers and reward loyal ones. This app provides users with personalized recommendations and deals based on where they, or those with similar tastes, have been. It connects customers and retailers in a unique way and can be a rewarding tool for both of them.[5]

FIGURE 19.6 Loyalty and discount programs are a good way to advertise and encourage customers to shop, such as this one from CVS.

Shoe retailer DSW is another example of a company that offers a rewards program to its customers. DSW Rewards members earn points on every dollar they spend that add up to discounts on future purchases. The program also includes free shipping, personalized e-mail offers, a fashion newsletter, and a gift certificate on the member's birthday. Other companies with frequent shopper programs include Lands' End, the Children's Place, and Philips Electronics.

Location Policies

In addition to the ever-present neighborhood shopping center, retailers are exploring a wide range of locations, including larger malls, airports and train stations, and resort areas. They are using carts and kiosks, and even setting up traveling, pop-up shops. Experts classify shopping centers in many ways; for our purposes, we use the following simplified system.

Shopping Centers and Malls

A **shopping center** is a coordinated group of retail stores, plus a parking area. By 2010, there were 107,773 shopping centers in the United States.[6] Those shopping centers that are enclosed and climate-controlled are known as **malls** (Figure 19.7). While most malls have one floor, malls with two or three floors are becoming more common. In central business districts, more **vertical malls**, multistory buildings taller than they are wide, have been built to conserve valuable land. Water Tower Place in Chicago was the first vertical mall; it has seven levels of prestige stores and is next door to a Ritz-Carlton hotel.

Customers are increasingly seen as bored with cookie-cutter malls and stores. Too many malls look the same, contain the same stores, and lack any regional flavor. If dropped into the average mall, a customer would not know if he or she were in Alaska, Iowa, or Texas.

FIGURE 19.7 The Roosevelt Field shopping center offers a variety of retailers in one location.

The competition for customers is so great that existing malls feel they must continually renovate and expand, just to keep larger, newer centers from moving into their territory. Taubman Centers, Inc., a developer of malls, has incorporated interactive "entertainment-based" strategies. For example, it has turned the common areas in its malls into lounges that resemble plush hotel lobbies, built designated children's play areas, and created interactive demonstration areas that include mobile devices, game consoles, and other technological products.[7] (See Chapter 18 for other examples of entertainment values in retailing.)

Power centers or **power strips** are outdoor shopping centers that offer three or four category killers together, so that a range of merchandise is available at highly discounted prices. They may be built close to existing regional malls and contain off-price apparel retailers or category killers like the Cosmetic Center, Toys"R"Us, or Burlington Coat Factory. In the 1990s, these centers cannibalized market shares so fast that the traditional malls had to reinvent themselves to keep up with the competition. Some of the strategies that malls are using to attract shoppers are featuring new, innovative retailers for shoppers who are looking for something other than the usual national chains, and creating an interior mazelike layout that guides shoppers throughout different departments of a store and connects to other shops on the property.

Regional malls, for example, usually contain at least two "anchor" department stores, as well as many specialty stores and a food court or restaurants. Their trading area is at least a five-mile radius. Prestige regional malls may offer such services as weekend valet parking, free strollers, and free newspapers. Northbrook Court near Chicago offers lockers, a nursing lounge, and safety escorts.

Superregional malls are, as their name implies, even larger than regional malls, often containing up to one million square feet. They contain at least three department stores or major chain stores, with 100 to 300 specialty stores and services. Their trading area is up to an hour's driving time. An example is Oak Park Mall in Overland Park, Kansas, which has a concourse and an anchor, Nordstrom, as well as another Dillard's and an expanded J.C. Penney.

Another type of huge shopping center (four to five million square feet) has emerged in the last decade—the **megamall**. The first megamall was built in West Edmonton in Alberta, Canada, with over 800 stores. The largest megamall in the United States is the Mall of America, in Bloomington, Minnesota (Figure 19.8). With more than 500 specialty stores, it is ten times the size of an average regional mall. It combines shopping with entertainment in a major way: with fifty restaurants, seven nightclubs, fourteen movie theaters, and Camp Snoopy, an amusement park! To draw customers one weekend, the mall hired Ringo Starr and the Beach Boys to play at a Jam Against Hunger in its vast parking lot.

Outlet malls, like the various "Mills" developed by the Mills Corporation—Gurnee Mills, outside of Chicago;

FIGURE 19.8 The Mall of America in Bloomington, Minnesota.

FIGURE 19.9 London's Heathrow Airport mall.

Ontario Mills, in suburban Los Angeles; and Potomac Mills, outside of Washington, D.C.—are increasingly popular. Entertainment, like Gameworks and IMAX 3-D theaters, plays a key role in these developments.

Airport retailing as a whole is certainly nothing new. Food concessions have been in airports for decades. What is new is the number of well-known retailers, from the Disney Store to Gap to Victoria's Secret, that are opening in what are being called **air malls** (Figure 19.9). With plane traffic booming, and delays more frequent, airports have become some of the busiest street corners in America. The length of time that an average person stays in an airport is sixty-one minutes, just three minutes shorter than the time spent in a typical shopping mall. Furthermore, the typical air passenger is a high-end shopper, so average sales per square foot are more than $1,000 versus $225 for the typical suburban mall.

Lifestyle Retail Centers

Lifestyle centers are open-air shopping areas anchored by a multiplex cinema (or two) and a big bookstore, and they contain a collection of better restaurants that enjoy the terrific traffic that the movie crowd presents. They are upscale outdoor shopping areas designed to look like city streets, with an emphasis on spaces for people watching and shopping. The lifestyle center is designed in a zigzag pattern, so that from any given place, your eye catches a few more stores down the way. Placement

is everything. Marketers have discovered that today's time-pressed consumer will spend more if she can easily comparison shop among similar stores, so lifestyle centers will group, say, Ann Taylor, Coldwater Creek, and Talbots within fifty feet of one another. And it's around gathering spots—fountains, benches, and kids' play areas—that you will find impulse-purchase stores like Sunglass Hut or Build-a-Bear Workshop.

A mixture of uses, such as residences, office space, hotels, churches, and municipal facilities such as libraries, is typically included. In many ways, these centers attempt to re-create the traditional city center or downtown environment within the shopping center. As a result of the added amenities found in a lifestyle center, there are more reasons for consumers to visit and stay longer. The longer people stay, the more they spend.[8]

Resort Retailing

Progressive retailers are positioning themselves where their customers are when they are relaxed. For many, this has meant catalogs. For some others, however, it means putting stores in resort areas (Figure 19.10). In the ski resort town of Aspen, Colorado, for example, major retailers like Banana Republic and the Chanel Boutique have opened stores. Some resort towns have established themselves as unique shopping destinations. Seaside, a planned resort community in the Florida panhandle, is one such place. It has an open-air

FIGURE 19.10 Ralph Lauren's resort retailing store in Aspen.

bazaar called Perspicasity, which features the work of local craftspeople and retailers in intriguing displays of casual clothes and accessories.

Carts and Kiosks

Carts and kiosks are selling spaces in common mall areas and airports and train stations. Smaller and often on wheels, thus more flexible than even the smallest shop, **carts** are increasingly popular for selling accessories, T-shirts, and caps. Kiosks, on the other hand, are larger than carts and more stationary. Like a newsstand, a **kiosk** offers movable shelves or racks for merchandise. It is very popular for sunglasses, jewelry, and legwear.

Temporary and Pop-Up Shops

Temporary retailers, which typically set up shop in empty storefronts or kiosks or carts in malls, are a booming business. Temporary holiday shops became commonplace in the 1990s. Retailers trying to get consumers' attention attempt to create a sense of urgency to get people into stores to try out their clothes, their shoes, and any other new product. The store itself is the new limited edition—so limited, in fact, that it may last a mere ninety-six hours.

Retailers are adopting the concept of pop-up shop with gusto. A **pop-up shop** opens with great fanfare at an empty retail location for a few days in a major city or mall. And then, poof! It's gone. Retailers use pop-up stores to generate buzz and excitement around a new product launch. During the last several years, Target has opened pop-up stores that sell items from their designer collaborations. In 2011, the Missoni for Target pop-up shop in New York City was forced to close early because the inventory sold out in a matter of hours.[9] On the higher end of the fashion spectrum, in 2010 Dior opened up its first pop-up ever, in the design district of Miami. These temporary stores are a great way

for retailers to test out new products, as well as make a profit (Figure 19.11).

Retail Strategies

Customers are demanding more convenient shopping, more varied products, and lower prices at the same time that they are shifting their loyalty from retailer to retailer, shopping at Kmart one week and Macy's the next. Retailers have developed a number of strategies to respond to them. Let us examine retailer's responses in more detail.

Convenience

As life continues to grow faster-paced, customers continue to look for easier ways to shop. The consumer has less time, is smarter, and is more demanding. Surveys have found that a large number of shoppers will walk out of a store if the checkout lines are too long, the store is too crowded, or a salesperson is surly. More than 22 percent of shoppers report leaving a store for lack of sales help. Retailers are also contending with customers shopping online, which can deter shoppers from even entering a physical location. The four dimensions of customer convenience that retailers must consider are:

1. Locational—where customers have to go to make purchases
2. Time of day—when customers can make purchases
3. Process—ease and speed of shopping and returns
4. Assortment—what they can buy here and where else they will have to go

FIGURE 19.11 The Red Valentino pop-up greenhouse generates buzz and can attract new customers.

Customer Loyalty

Many types of retailers are experimenting with lifestyle and life-stage strategies to attract loyal customers. **Life-stage marketing** is a marketing strategy that targets a specific demographic. It has long been the specialty of catalog retailers in particular, and helps companies to make their products more relatable. In 2012, Ann Taylor signed on Kate Hudson to be the new face of the retailer (Figure 19.12). Hudson is a woman who "leads a full life and captures the spirit of the Ann Taylor woman," says Brian Lynch, brand president of the Ann Taylor division of Ann Inc.[10] The juniors apparel chains like Forever 21 and Urban Outfitters are well-known examples of life-stage retailers.

Differentiation

Differentiation can be achieved through proper positioning and image creation. With the glut of brands, it's imperative to create a distinctive image and niche in the consumer's mind. Retailers must stand out and build a presence everywhere that the customer shops, whether that is in the store's physical location, online, or via mobile devices—and today, most businesses consider all three.

Private-label merchandise is growing at an astronomical rate, as retailers try to differentiate themselves and their merchandise in response to customers' complaints about the sameness of merchandise everywhere. Private labels are discussed in Chapter 18.

Strategic Alliances

A **strategic alliance** is a form of business combination in which retailers and manufacturers join forces to operate more efficiently, thus improving both companies' profits while enabling them to give the customer a better product at a lower price. Although strategic alliances between retailers and manufacturers are difficult to form and to maintain, they are perceived as increasingly critical for success in today's highly competitive marketplace. One example of a profitable alliance is an agreement between Macy's Inc. and Tommy Hilfiger (owned by Phillips-Van Heusen Corp). Since 2008, Macy's has been the exclusive department store retailer in North America for the Tommy Hilfiger brand. The characteristics of strategic alliances as opposed to traditional retailer/manufacturer relationships are outlined in Table 19.1.

Trends in Retail Policies

Merchandising and operational policies continue to change at a dizzying rate. As the economy cycles through periods of boom and bust, retailers scramble

FIGURE 19.12 Ann Taylor features Kate Hudson in its advertisements to appeal to a specific customer.

to interpret and respond to changing customer needs and preferences. Of the many trends discussed in this chapter, two seem dominant: (1) technology and (2) creating new job opportunities. Let us look at each of these trends in more detail.

Technology

Retailers' use of new technology varies widely in sophistication and cost. It can be as simple as Gap providing sales associates with wireless headsets so that they can get inventory information for a customer immediately. Or the technology may be as complex as establishing a multibillion-dollar data warehouse of customer information.

Four ways that retailers are using technology are: faster delivery of products and information, data warehousing, communication, and e-tailing.

TABLE 19.1 *Characteristics of Traditional Relationships and Strategic Alliances*

TRADITIONAL APPROACH	ALLIANCE APPROACH
Individual goals	Shared common goals
Independent performance	Joint performance
Independently defined goals	Supply chain definitions
Sequential processes and activities	Simultaneous processes
Activities performed by individual companies	Partner with greatest competency performs the activity
Rewards competed for	Rewards shared
Penalties absorbed by supplier	Penalties or losses shared
Many suppliers	Few select suppliers
Sequential improvements	Continuous improvements
Information is kept secret	Information is shared

Adapted from Robin Lewis, "Partner or Perish," *WWD Infotracs: Strategic Alliances.*

Product and Information Delivery

To get the right product to the customer at the right time, manufacturers, shippers, and retailers are employing a variety of technological developments. As discussed in Chapter 8, there is the widespread use of bar codes, scanners, electronic data interchange, radio-frequency identification, product lifecycle management, and supply chain management among retailers.

Data Warehousing

To squeeze more profit out of each store, retailers have used a technique called data warehousing. A **data warehouse** is a repository that holds information about customers, transactions, and finances; it is also used for analysis and creating reports. Its role is to make this mass of data easily accessible by organizing it into categories like purchase history, vendors, sales promotions, and so forth. The data warehouse is typically separate from existing operational systems. Over the years, there have been many technological advancements to improve these systems and enhance efficiency.

Examples of retailers with large data warehouses include Walmart, Sears, and Target. Target was one of the first companies to set up a data warehouse. Lands' End uses its data warehouse to track out-of-stock items that customers order. Burlington Coat Factory uses its system to target big and tall customers for special promotions. At the North County Fair Mall in Escondido, California, mall managers can generate reports that show which stores mall patrons are shopping in, what they buy, and how much they spend. This information is then shared with the retailers in the mall.

Data warehousing can also be used as a powerful marketing tool. Customer profiling can help the retail staff target people who look like they fit the best-customer profile. Best-customer profiling also helps identify narrow targets within the highest revenue-generating customer base. According to a report from Oracle, the new breed of data warehouse must be able to capture and analyze social media, location information, sensor data, e-mail, audio, images, conversations, and many forms of machine-generated data.[11] Developments in data warehousing are currently being created to increase productivity in our businesses and the retail industry overall.

Communication

Companies use **videoconferencing** for a variety of purposes, including staff training, vendor conferences, and product development. Skype (owned by Microsoft), for example, allows for businesses and employees to communicate with one another from different locations. This is necessary today to maintain active

FIGURE 19.13 The eBay app offers shoppers easy online access for browsing and purchasing merchandise.

communication in our global businesses. It also cuts down on staff travel time and expenses, and can help to resolve problems more quickly and effectively. Additionally, many companies are using webinars for training, demonstrations, and promotion of products.

E-tailing

Online websites, mobile devices, blogs, and social media have changed the way retailers do business. **E-tailing** is defined as retail business that is conducted online, and it has become essential for businesses to keep up with their digital strategies, especially in the fashion industry. According to a report from NPD, apparel was the second most heavily shopped online category.[12]

Examples of successful retail websites are Amazon, eBay, and Macy's. Amazon reports show that the site is growing at five times the rate of overall retail and three times the rate of e-commerce in the United States. Another example is eBay (Figure 19.13), which reached a record $5 billion in mobile purchases (from smartphones and tablets) in 2011.[13] Promotion of merchandise and offering discounts through online sites, digital devices, and social media also help retailers expand their customer reach. (See also Chapter 17.)

Some retailers are exploring ways to apply digital strategies in their brick-and-mortar stores. For example, Piperlime, originally an online shop, opened a brick-and-mortar retail location in 2012. There are kiosks located throughout the store that link directly to Piperlime.com. They offer shoppers access to products online that may not be available in the store, and customers also receive free overnight shipping.[14] With this strategy, customers get to experience the retailer's online and physical store environment at the same time.

Creating New Job Opportunities

The human element remains a critical component of successful retailing. To develop a business that is truly customer-focused requires a greater investment in workers than most retailers were willing to make in the past.

The role of the buyer is also changing, especially in situations where retailers have strategic alliances with suppliers. Buyers can become trend analysts, trend-setters, and product developers. Additional employment opportunities exist for visual merchandisers and store designers, as chain stores try to customize each location. Even category killers are placing less emphasis on mass presentations of products. Experts predict that fashion retailers in particular will frequently change their total store environment to keep customers' interest. They are also creating positions to maintain their digital presence.

As discussed in earlier chapters, there is also a push for increased production and manufacturing domestically, which will create more jobs in the textile and apparel industry.

Summary and Review

There are six merchandising policies that every retailer must establish: (1) fashion cycle emphasis, (2) quality, (3) price ranges, (4) depth and breadth of assortments, (5) brand policies, and (6) exclusivity. Five major operational policies must also be determined: (1) ambiance, (2) customer services, (3) selling services, (4) promotional activities, and (5) frequent shopper plans.

Retail location policies include sites such as shopping centers, malls, downtown sites, resorts, carts and kiosks, and temporary and pop-up shops.

Emerging retail strategies include: (1) responding to customers' desire for convenience, (2) gaining customer loyalty, (3) differentiation, and (4) forging strategic alliances.

Trends in retail policies include improved technologies, such as (1) faster delivery of products and information, (2) data warehousing, (3) communication, and (4) e-tailing. Along with these developments come corresponding new job opportunities.

For Review

1. What are the six major merchandising policies that a retailer must establish?
2. What are the five types of operational policies that a retail store owner must establish?
3. What are the major kinds of shopping centers in the United States today?
4. What is the difference between a cart and a kiosk? Where can they usually be found?
5. What strategies are retailers using to respond to the customer's desire for more convenient shopping?
6. How are retailers responding to the decline of customer loyalty?
7. What are strategic alliances? What are their goals? Give some examples of these agreements.
8. Explain how technological developments in data warehousing and communication are being used in the fashion industries.
9. Name some new job opportunities that are being created in retailing today as a result of the trends mentioned in this chapter.

For Discussion

1. Compare and contrast the selling and fashion services of (a) department stores, (b) specialty stores, and (c) discount stores. Give examples of selling and fashion services offered by different types of retailers in your community.
2. Explain and discuss the following statement by Laurence Siegel, citing current examples to illustrate how it does or does not apply to your community:

> Traditional malls are all the same. They all have three or four anchors, a bunch of specialty stores in between, and maybe a multiscreen movie theater. There's little reason to drive past one to get to another.[15]

Trade Talk

Define or briefly explain the following terms:

air mall
ambiance
assortment
broad and shallow
    assortment
cart
confined style
data warehouse
e-tailing
kiosk
lifestyle centers
life-stage marketing
mall
megamall
merchandising policies
narrow and deep assortment
operational policies
outlet mall
pop-up shop
power center or strip
regional mall
sensory retailing
superregional mall
shopping center
strategic alliance
vertical mall
videoconferencing

Unit Six
THE AUXILIARY LEVEL: SUPPORTING SERVICES

The auxiliary services that support and enhance all the other levels of the fashion industries have an interconnecting role in the big fashion picture. Try to imagine a new fashion season without magazines, fashion stylists, trade shows, visual merchandisers, TV, blogs, advertising agencies, public relations agencies, and myriad other services that support and grow this phenomenon known as the fashion business. In this unit we explore the functions of magazines, newspapers, broadcast, TV, social media, fashion consultants, visual merchandisers, trade associations, and product development offices. You will develop a basic vocabulary and a working knowledge of the following:

- Chapter 20: The roles auxiliary services play in getting fashion information and products to the consumer.

Chapter Twenty
FASHION AUXILIARY SERVICES

KEY CONCEPTS

- Differences among advertising, publicity, and public relations
- Services provided to fashion merchandisers by such media as trade and consumer publications, broadcast media, and digital communication
- Role of store designers and visual merchandisers
- Information provided to fashion producers and retailers by fashion consultants and research agencies, trade associations and trade shows, and buying, merchandising, and product development offices

As consumers we expect to find what we want, when we want it, and where we want it every day of the year. In the fall, back-to-school merchandise had better be in stores, and the colors must be new and up-to-date. During the holiday months, gift merchandise and new items for holiday parties are expected. During spring and summer months, we expect new colors, silhouettes, and fabrics to brighten up our wardrobes and take us through spring days to the hot, muggy days of summer. How do the stores see into the future and anticipate our needs and wants? How do they keep stocks peaked when we want them and marked down when we are tired of them? They do not have crystal balls or fortune tellers leading the way; what they do have are the fashion auxiliary services.

As a professional in the fashion industry, you know that this marvelous spectacle did not occur by magic. In fact, it required elaborate planning and execution of plans for months in advance. As you enjoy the offerings for the upcoming season, you are well aware that preparations are already under way for the next season and for the seasons beyond.

Bringing you and your fellow consumers the styles you want to wear is so huge and all-encompassing a task that the fashion industry requires many support, or auxiliary, services. Some services—computer, book-keeping, legal—are typical of those needed by any business and may not be particularly tailored to the fashion business. Others, though, are specific to the fashion industry. Either they have been created specifically to serve it, as in the case of buying, merchandising, and product development organizations, or their function has been tailored to the fashion industry's specific needs, as in the case of advertising and public relations agencies, fashion magazines, and the variety of consultants and marketing groups. In this chapter, you will learn about the most important auxiliary services, such as trade and consumer fashion publications; the broadcast media; advertising and public relations agencies;

store design and visual merchandising services; consulting and market research groups; trade associations; and buying, merchandising, and product development organizations.

Fashion Auxiliary Services Offered by the Media

The media offer three broad categories of fashion auxiliary services: advertising, publicity, and public relations. **Advertising**, which appears in everything from magazines and newspapers to radio and television, is space and time that is paid for. **Publicity** is the free and voluntary mention of a firm, product, or person in the media. Its purpose is to inform or enhance public interest about something specific. **Public relations**, a broader term than publicity, is also a free and voluntary mention, but it is designed to enhance a long-term goal, such as the shaping of a company's public image. All three efforts are important elements of the remaining auxiliary services.

One difference between advertising and publicity/public relations is the amount of control a manufacturer or retailer can exercise over each. Since advertising is purchased, a great deal of control can be exercised over its execution. Public relations and publicity can be carefully developed and well presented to the media, but there is no guarantee that the material and information supplied will be used well—or used at all.

Many people think that broadcast media like cable TV and the Internet will completely replace more traditional media, like newspapers and magazines. However, others believe that this is debatable, or at least should be. Marc Brownstein, president of the Brownstein Group, presents the following question in an article for *Advertising Age*: "More and more ad dollars are moving from traditional media to digital, and that makes perfect sense. But there is an irrational shift to go all-digital. Just because it's the trendy thing to do, does it necessarily work?"[1] The answer to this remains to be seen, as companies continually try to figure out the right formula.

One way in which print media can connect with the digital world is through QR codes. **QR codes** are black-and-white boxes of pixels that encode links and information. These codes are often included in advertisements and link to a company's website or product information.

Fashion Magazines

Fashion magazines, which combine advertising, publicity, and public relations, came into existence about 150 years ago in the form of a single publication called *Godey's Lady's Book* (Figure 20.1). Prior to that, women discussed the newest fashions with one another but had no authoritative source from which they could learn what was new and exciting. The magazine's first editor, Sarah Josepha Hale, is now best remembered for

GODEY'S FASHIONS FOR DECEMBER 1861.

FIGURE 20.1 *Godey's Lady's Book* was the first fashion magazine.

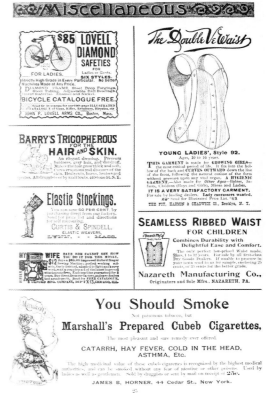

her early feminism, especially her struggle to help women win acceptance in professions, but her influence on fashion was equally important. *Godey's Lady's Book* reported on the latest styles and was the forerunner of today's fashion magazines, such as *Vogue* (Figure 20.2, left), *Harper's Bazaar, Glamour,* and *Seventeen* for young women.

For years, these magazines held sway, and while they competed with one another, they were not subject to new competition. The sheer volume of fashion magazines can be overwhelming, with new titles constantly launching. There are publications that cater to every style and demographic, from general consumers (*Elle* [Figure 20.2, right], *Glamour, Marie Claire,* and *Lucky*) to avante-garde fashion (*Nylon*) to celebrity-driven looks (*InStyle*). Magazines that appeal to specific ethnic markets include *Essence, Ebony,* and *Today's Black Woman,* for African Americans, and the bilingual *Latina,* for Hispanics. Even more specialized are such magazines as *Brides,* which report on wedding fashions. Fashion-driven websites also provide competition to the magazines; one is Style.com, which is owned by Condé Nast and gets an average of 2.7 million unique monthly visitors.[2]

Gentlemen's Quarterly (GQ) and *Men's Health* reported the biggest digital edition circulations in 2012 (based on combined print and digital figures) (Figure 20.3).[3] *Esquire,* which covers topics beyond fashion, is still widely regarded as an authority on the latest trends in menswear. Other men's magazines that cover fashion in addition to topics like health and sports include

FIGURE 20.2 Popular fashion magazines for women include *Vogue* (left) and *Elle* (right).

Details, Men's Fitness, Playboy, Men's Journal, Outside, FHM, and *Maxim.*

The **shelter magazines** are devoted to home fashions. Among the better known are *Elle Decor, Architectural Digest, House Beautiful, Martha Stewart Living, Wallpaper,* and *Surface.*

Fashion magazines' pages are filled with advertisements for apparel, cosmetics, and accessories. The business of reporting and interpreting the fashion news, however, is their primary function. Fashion editors visit manufacturers' showrooms to choose the latest fashions as subjects for articles and photographs in the editorial pages of their magazines. These visits provide opportunities for useful exchanges of information

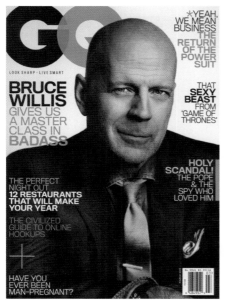

FIGURE 20.3 A popular fashion magazine for men includes *GQ,* which is available in both print (left) and digital (right) versions.

DIANA VREELAND: "YOU GOTTA HAVE STYLE"

D IANA VREELAND WAS the original American fashion editor and style arbiter, but she said that everything she learned about clothes she learned in Paris. A New York City socialite, her over-the-top personality and captivating sense of style set her on a path to fame and influence that no one could have predicted.

In 1936, while out dancing at the St. Regis Hotel, Vreeland was discovered by the editor in chief of *Harper's Bazaar*, who was so struck by Vreeland's personal style that she offered her a job. Vreeland protested that she'd never seen the interior of an office and never left the house before lunch, but she did need money to keep up her socialite's lifestyle. In the end, she accepted the job where she would stay for 26 years.

Vreeland started out at *Harper's* writing the "Why Don't You..." column that some have called the original blog. In it, she would ponder life and offer pithy advice such as, "Why don't you...wear velvet mittens with everything?" She was soon appointed fashion editor, and under her influence *Harper's*

began to reflect the style she encouraged in her readers: unconventional, revolutionary, shocking, and unexpected. She told her readers, "Fashion must be the most intoxicating release from the banality of the world." Always on the cutting edge, Vreeland was responsible for the magazine's first image of a bikini in 1947.

Fifteen years later, she left *Harper's* to become the editor in chief of *Vogue* magazine and later was hired as curator of the Metropolitan Museum of Art's Costume Institute. Over the course of her career she discovered stars (Lauren Bacall, Twiggy); helped launch designers (Manolo Blahnik, Diane von Furstenberg, Oscar de la Renta, the Missonis); and advised fashion icon Jackie Kennedy on matters of style. Most important, she encouraged women everywhere to embrace their lives as an adventure and to create their own personal style because "a new dress doesn't get you anywhere; it's the life you're living in the dress, and the sort of life you had lived before, and what you will do in it later."

Diana
Vreeland

about trends in markets that the manufacturers and publications share. In addition, most magazines prepare reports of their market research for the manufacturers and retailers that are both the subject of their editorial copy and their advertising accounts. These reports include reader surveys, such as those conducted by *Glamour*, and fashion forecasts of colors and styles for upcoming seasons. Like the fashion producers and retailers, the magazines must plan well in advance of offering their product to the public, so their reports can be relied upon for timely information.

Fashions that appear in magazine articles are accompanied by an **editorial credit**, a unique form of publicity that names the manufacturer and lists retail stores where the clothes may be purchased (Figure 20.4). Editorial credit benefits even stores that are not listed, for if they have seen a magazine in advance, they can often stock the fashions. For advertisers whose merchandise is featured and credited in the editorial pages of a magazine, this publicity reinforces the paid advertising message.

General Consumer Publications

General interest consumer publications also play a role in disseminating fashion news to the public. Practically every newspaper reports on fashion, and some, such as *The New York Times*, *Los Angeles Times*, *Chicago Tribune*, *The Wall Street Journal*, and *The Washington Post*, devote regular weekly sections to apparel and home fashion design. Their fashion editors cover fashion openings, press weeks, and trade shows around the world. *T* magazine (the *New York Times Style Magazine*) publishes special issues for men and women that include trends on fashion, accessories, beauty, and grooming. The magazine also has a design issue for home design. In *Paper*, *Time Out*, *City*, and other magazines that deal with pop culture, fashion gets extensive coverage. *Time*, *Newsweek*, and *People* provide occasional but important fashion coverage, as do the traditional women's magazines such as *Good Housekeeping* and *Ladies' Home Journal*. *Cosmopolitan*, whose primary market is young singles, has a circulation of 2.6 million. Other women's magazines that are geared toward women who are not full-time homemakers also carry fashion news for their market segments. Among the most influential are *Oprah* and *Working Mother*. *Seventeen* and *Teen Vogue* are designed for young teenagers. Women's sports magazines, such as *Self*, *Shape*, *Women's Health*, and *Fitness* include articles that cater to the fashion interests of female athletes and sports fans.

The New Yorker, *Vanity Fair*, *Harper's*, and *Atlantic Monthly* occasionally bring fashion news to their urbane, sophisticated audiences.

FIGURE 20.4 Editorial credits provide priceless promotion for designers and manufacturers.

Different language versions of *People*, *Playboy*, *Cosmopolitan*, *Harper's Bazaar*, *Elle*, and *Marie Claire* are also in the market. The Spanish version of *Reader's Digest*, called *Selecciones*, is widely circulated. The publicity departments of most stores across America usually have no difficulty getting their messages across in local newspapers because apparel stores are a major source of advertising revenue for newspapers.

Trade Publications

One of the most important aids to the merchandising of fashion is the **trade publication**. Unlike the fashion magazines, trade newspapers and magazines are published just for the industry. Many discourage subscriptions from people outside their field; few are available at newsstands, except in fashion markets and marts.

Just as general publications like city newspapers and national news magazines keep the public informed about what is going on in the world, trade publications keep their special readers informed about what is going

FIGURE 20.5 *Women's Wear Daily* is the leading trade publication in the fashion industry.

on in the fashion world—from the acquisition of raw materials to reports on retail sales. These publications announce new technical developments, analyze fashion trends, report on current business conditions, and generally help all who work in the fashion industry keep up-to-date on a staggering number of new products, techniques, and markets. Even government regulations are covered, as are personnel changes and classified ads for jobs.

The best-known fashion trade publication is *Women's Wear Daily* (Figure 20.5, left), often referred to as the bible of the industry. First published in 1910, it is one of the oldest publications of its kind. Beginning as a page in the *Daily Trade Record*, this newspaper quickly became a separate six-day-a-week publication. Since its inception, it has played a prominent role in the fashion business. *Women's Wear Daily*, called *WWD* by those who read it, is published daily and covers every aspect of the fashion industry, from fiber and fabric to apparel, from day-to-day developments to new directions and trends. In addition to its business reporting around the globe, *WWD* covers the social scene and trendsetters. In 2008, *WWD* started to incorporate men's coverage in its pages (Figure 20.5, right).

Footwear News covers its specialty as intensely as *WWD* covers the women's market. The youth market is covered in *Earnshaw's*. Department store and specialty store management and merchandising executives read *Stores* and *Chain Store Age*. The fiber and fabric professionals read *Apparel Magazine* and *Textile World*.

The Broadcast Media

Fashion merchandisers have a choice of standard broadcast mediums: television, cable television, and radio. Unlike the print media, the broadcast media are time, rather than space, oriented. Radio and television stations sell three levels of commercials, in descending order of cost: network, spot, and local.

Broadcast media focused on children have received a good deal of critical attention over the years. Many children's channels have been launched, and the kids' market seemed like a place of golden opportunity for advertisers. However, the climate slowed down at the turn of the millennium, and the children's channels that turned a profit were the already established and relatively inexpensive giants like Cartoon Network and Nickelodeon. There is also strong competition from the Disney Channel, with tween comedies such as *Phineas and Ferb* and *Wizards of Waverly Place* (Figure 20.6).

Television

One cannot turn on the television today without learning something about current apparel fashions. The fashion industry obtains invaluable publicity from the simple fact that everyone who acts in a show or hosts or appears on a newscast or talk show wants to—and usually does—wear the latest fashions.

In addition to this general across-the-board exposure, short segments on fashion are generally presented in many news and talk shows. News of the fashion world is reported, as are the latest styles. Occasionally,

FIGURE 20.6 Television shows, like *The Wizards of Waverly Place*, influence teen fashion and create trends.

manufacturers and designers get a chance to exhibit their work.

Network television advertising is expensive. Until the early 1980s, only huge companies such as Sears, Roebuck and Co. and J.C. Penney or fiber firms like DuPont and Monsanto could afford it. Increasingly, though, retailers and manufacturers have built television advertising into their budgets because they have seen that it is the best way to reach a generation reared on television. Manufacturers of sportswear—specifically, makers of jeans—were among the first to use television, but now designers such as Calvin Klein use television to transmit their fashion message. Sometimes designers or manufacturers offer retailers cooperative advertising with time for a voice-over for store advertising of their brand. The manufacturer can thus get a local advertising rate for the brand while the retailer gets the professionally produced commercial.

Because of the technical expertise and high level of quality required for network television, outside advertising agencies are usually hired to produce television advertising. Agencies develop an idea, present it in storyboard form to their client, photograph the advertisement, obtain or create the music, and provide files to individual stations for on-air viewing. Television commercials for national brands of apparel, such as Levi's jeans, are also sometimes seen in movie theaters as well.

Cable Television

Cable television has become an increasingly attractive option for fashion advertisers, largely because it costs so much less than network television. Many more outlets also exist for cable television, which reduces the competition to buy space. Cable television is also the home of the **infomercial**, the extended commercial in which a sponsor presents information about its product in a program format. Several celebrity-owned or celebrity-franchised cosmetics lines have relied on this advertising medium. The 1982 debut of the Home Shopping Network (HSN) marked the beginning of a new outlet for sales as well as advertising. QVC is another popular television shopping channel. (See Chapter 18 for more information on home shopping networks.)

Fashion-inspired cable television shows include *The Rachel Zoe Project* (Figure 20.7), on Bravo, and *Full*

FIGURE 20.7 *The Rachel Zoe Project* shows a glimpse of how stylists work in the fashion industry.

Frontal Fashion, on the Sundance Channel. E! Entertainment television offers *Fashion Police*, along with the Style network, a twenty-four-hour channel devoted to fashion and beauty.

One of the most successful and popular fashion shows on cable is *Project Runway*. Hosted by Tim Gunn and Heidi Klum, it has been a success since its beginning in 2004—so successful that Lord & Taylor has teamed up with *Project Runway* as the reality show's exclusive retail sponsor. Under the agreement with the Weinstein Company and Lifetime, as part of the grand prize, the winning designer currently gets the opportunity to sell an exclusive collection at Lord & Taylor and a fashion spread in *Marie Claire*.[4] Past retail sponsors for the show have included Bluefly.com, Piperlime.com, and Banana Republic. Neiman Marcus has provided accessories for the accessory wall in an all-star season of *Project Runway*.

Radio

While television is unsurpassed as a fashion advertising medium because of its visual qualities, radio is popular because it is inexpensive and can reach large but targeted audiences. Stations exist that serve only the youth market; others, such as classical radio stations, are geared toward an older market. Others broadcast news and can deliver to a captive audience during the morning and evening commutes, the so-called drive time.

The use of radio to sell fashion was tied to the rise of rock music in the 1950s and the youth-oriented market it created. The youth market has remained strong, but radio advertising, if chosen carefully, also reaches adults and families.

In terms of cost per customer reached, spot commercials on local radio stations are economical; most of the advertiser's customers live and work within the range of the station's signal. Commercials announcing sales and other storewide events can use radio effectively because they do not depend on visual appeals. To attract advertisers, stations provide assistance with the preparation of copy, which may be delivered by disc jockeys and other announcers.

Radio is also a source of publicity because products and fashion news are discussed on regular shows.

As with television, most retailers and manufacturers rely on outside agencies to write and produce radio commercials, although some use their in-house talent to prepare commercials and then hire time-buying groups to place them.

Digital Communication

Smart marketers acknowledge that they need to be everywhere the customer is. Websites, mobile devices,

FIGURE 20.8 YouTube broadcasts the latest designer runway videos on special fashion week channels.

apps, social media, and YouTube enable companies to reach customers through a variety of mediums, as well as respond to their specific needs at any given moment.

Apparel and accessories was one category that saw a great deal of growth in e-commerce during 2012. Other top categories included digital content and subscriptions, books, and magazines.[5] Digital forms of publications, along with advertising, can help to reach a wider audience and promote products and companies. Thus, this can create an increase in sales for categories such as apparel and accessories.

Social media has managed to make the global fashion industry seem small. As discussed in earlier chapters, social media are forms of electronic communication in which users create online communities and share information, including photos, videos, and messages. Companies have responded to the social media explosion by jumping onto social networking sites and accumulating fans on Facebook, while promoting new products, offering deals, and delivering real-time information. The bloggers, who have become just as famous as the designers themselves, send their reviews from the front row of fashion shows straight to the rest of the world. YouTube is another medium used to show off collections and related fashion videos as soon as a fashion event occurs (Figure 20.8).

Anyone can easily report, publish, and collaborate with others or give reviews. The phenomenon is changing the world from a one-to-many broadcast format to a many-to-many interactive conversation.

Advertising, Publicity, and Public Relations Agencies

Advertising, publicity, and public relations (PR) agencies do far more for the fashion industry than prepare and sell advertising. An agency in any of these three

FIGURE 20.9 Parker reaches the "city girl" customer not only with its clothing designs but also with the images used in its online advertising campaign.

FIGURE 20.10 This print advertisement for Alice and Olivia reflects the image and style of the company.

areas may be deeply involved in creating a multimedia campaign designed to shape the public's image of a client company. These campaigns are used for ongoing maintenance of a company's image as well as for an image change (Figures 20.9 and 20.10). PR firms can also perform damage control to protect brands.

Advertising Agencies

Advertising agencies provide many services, all of which are tied to the selling of commercial advertising space and/or time. Some agencies are specialized and deal only with one medium or one type of client,

while others are general, offering a full range of services for many different types of clients. Agencies vary from a one-person shop to a giant agency that employs hundreds of people around the world. Small agencies claim to offer personal attention, but even large agencies divide their staff into creative teams so that they, too, promise and often deliver a specialized service.

Small manufacturers and retailers and even fairly large department stores tend to rely on in-house advertising departments for all advertising except television and radio. Only the very large fiber and apparel companies regularly use advertising agencies, but those that can afford to do so find the investment worthwhile. In 2007, in an effort to boost sales and compete against Victoria's Secret, bra maker Playtex decided that it needed to try a new advertising strategy. It conducted focus groups across the country in order to better understand what customers thought about bras, how they chose them, and how they talked about them. These focus groups led to a winning ad campaign that helped boost the company's sales 3.4 percent in 2008, increase Web traffic on Playtexfits.com by 90 percent during the same time period, and get major coverage on television shows such as *The View* and *The Oprah Winfrey Show*. Playtex employed media agency Starcom to create a service-driven campaign called Girl Talk, which hinged on the fact that women talk about issues with their bras, such as fit and comfort, casually among friends. Girl Talk was honored with the AdweekMedia Plan of the Year for National TV and Cable.[6]

Public Relations Agencies

Public relations firms are involved in the creation of publicity as well as in public relations. Publicity and public relations require that the agency work closely with its client, keeping abreast of what is new and newsworthy and announcing it to the world, either through press releases (often with photographs), social media campaigns, or with story ideas presented to trade and consumer magazines and newspapers. As noted, public relations also involves, on a much deeper level, the shaping of a company's image. To this end, a public relations agency may suggest or help to plan and coordinate an event or activity, such as the rendering of a public service or gift to a charity or community, or the presentation of a scholarship or endowment to an institution or foundation. Examples include streetwear retailer Southpole sponsoring World of Dance, a traveling dance competition and exhibition, and creating an antibullying initiative, Speak Up, Step Up; Louis Vuitton teaming up with Italy's oldest film school, Centro Sperimentale di Cinematografia, to offer scholarships for low-income students; and fitness and lifestyle brand Athleta partnering with the nonprofit Girls on the Run.

The larger the company, the more likely it is to depend on an outside public relations firm. For example, KCD manages the public relations for the Victoria's Secret Fashion Show, a yearly event that is broadcast live online and on TV channels worldwide. Retailers, however, largely tend to have their own in-house publicity departments that work with top management to present the company's best face to the public. Among the well-known public relations agencies that specialize in the fashion industry are the huge Edelman, headquartered in Chicago; Cone Communications, in Boston; the Hart Agency, in Warwick, New York; and DeVries, in New York.

Other Advertising and Public Relations Services

Maintaining the corporate image of a fashion producer or retailer requires the services of a number of creative specialists, who may be company employees, agency employees, or freelancers. For example, **fashion stylists** may select and coordinate the apparel and accessories for store catalogs and print ads, for magazine articles, or for commercials. The job of the stylist involves juggling many tasks in one day, often including charming celebrities into posing in outfits they dislike. Many stylists work in either Los Angeles or New York, but more job opportunities are growing across the country. Hollywood's top stylists include Phillip Bloch, Jeannine Braden, Deborah Waknin, Lisa Michelle, Stacy Young, Rachel Zoe, and Patricia Field. Stylists must work cooperatively with the rest of the team: the photographers, the makeup artist, the hairdresser, the magazine editor, and the celebrity's agent or publicist.

Fashion illustrators' and photographers' work appears in advertising and in the editorial pages of consumer and trade publications. Skilled fashion photographers command creative control of a shoot as well as high pay.

Independent fashion show production companies offer their services to producers, retailers, and trade organizations.

Store Design and Visual Merchandising Services

Two important onsite promotional activities that support the selling of fashion merchandise are store design and visual merchandising. The layout and design of any retail business have an impact on sales. Even catalog retailers and others who do not come face-to-face with their customers have to consider how much room they have for inventory and how stock should be arranged to expedite finding items and filling orders. For the traditional retailer operating in a store, the selling floor serves the critical purpose of presenting the merchandise to the customer, a function that is essential in selling fashion goods, for which appearance is a primary feature. Manufacturers' and designers' showrooms are their selling floors and thus require the same attention to interior design and visual merchandising.

Store Design

Planning the layout for a store or department is even more daunting than designing the interior of one's own home. Some of the objectives are the same—visual appeal, ease of movement, and comfort, all within budget—but a space for the sale of merchandise must fulfill additional needs (Figure 20.11). The designer must be attuned to the tastes of the target customer, and the environment not only must be pleasant but also must encourage shopping and buying. Shoppers may regard their visit as a recreational activity, but for the store, it is a business trip, and everything possible must be done to gain the customers' business. Placement of fixtures must take into account security considerations and easy access to exits in case of fire. Local building codes for commercial buildings must be met, and to comply with the Americans with Disabilities Act, certain features, such as ramps to ensure wheelchair access and Braille on the elevator buttons, may be required. Meeting all of these demands calls for the services of a professional, not just any architect or interior designer but one who specializes in store design.

Fortunately, a retailer who moves into a mall or a manufacturer with a showroom at an apparel mart may be renting space that has already passed inspection.

FIGURE 20.11 The C. Wonder store layout is attuned to the tastes of its target customer.

Still, planning a selling area to maximize sales is not easy. Selecting fixtures that are suitable for the merchandise and the store image, choosing a color scheme, planning the lighting so that it will show off the merchandise in a flattering but accurate way—all these tasks and more must be considered. Major fashion designers, such as Ralph Lauren, have been known to supervise personally the furnishing and interior design of their boutiques within department stores as well as their freestanding outlets. As apparel designers have extended their business into home furnishings and even furniture lines, the connection between store design and fashion image has become even more pronounced. With the need for professional help as great as it is, the existence of trade shows and periodicals for store designers is not surprising.

Visual Merchandising

The term **visual merchandising** includes the arrangement and presentation of merchandise in store windows and on the selling floor. It covers the arrangement of items that are for sale as well as the display of sample items on mannequins and other props. The term is broader than the older term *display*, reflecting not only the *showing* of merchandise but the *reason* for showing it—namely, to sell it.

Like all other successful promotional activities, a store's visual merchandising supports and exemplifies the retailer's image. For example, a designer boutique,

though it may be small, is not cluttered (Figure 20.12). There is room for customers to step back and admire the exclusive merchandise. Coordinated and accessorized outfits are displayed to help customers assemble their own wardrobes. In the windows, no expense is spared to create an attention-getting environment for the featured merchandise. One or two outfits might be shown

FIGURE 20.12 Fixtures help to organize merchandise so customers can view all products easily.

in a setting in which they could be worn, or they may be set off in an empty space with dramatic lighting and a few well-chosen props. Perhaps the price is indicated on a small, discreetly placed sign.

In contrast, the mass-merchandiser's windows and selling floor send a message of availability and affordability. Windows are crowded with mannequins wearing a variety of outfits. Brightly colored banners announce bargain prices. Inside, closely packed racks house a full range of sizes and colors for each style. No exclusivity is offered here, and none is desired.

What these two examples have in common is that each reveals an image carefully planned to appeal to the target customer. For retailers from single-unit specialty shops to giant department store chains, visual merchandising is an essential promotional service. In larger stores, the work is typically carried out by a staff under the leadership of a visual merchandising director. At the corporate, regional, or store level, window and interior managers may help to coordinate the visual merchandising plan with the merchandising and advertising plans. The staff who execute the plan must include employees who are skilled in carpentry, lighting, sign making, collection of props, and dressing of mannequins—to name just some of their responsibilities. Small businesses, depending on their resources, may hire an independent visual merchandising firm or an individual freelancer. For help in deciding where to put merchandise on the selling floor, **planograms** are available. These computer-generated floor plans massage information about the sales of selected items or categories and factor those numbers in with other information about such items as the physical dimensions of the merchandise and the selling space. Feed that information to the computer, and it responds with a picture of the selling floor with merchandise in the best place.

Signs and Graphics

Signs and graphics enhance merchandise presentations both in windows and on the selling floor. Temporary signs to announce a sale or special event or inform shoppers of a price can be produced easily with computer software. More permanent signage, such as directional signs for elevators, escalators, and restrooms and signs identifying departments are more typically prepared by professionals. Like other aspects of visual merchandising, signs should be in keeping with the store's image.

Information Resources

The fashion business is so huge and complex that no one individual or company can keep abreast of everything that is happening in it. It is a business made up in large part of trends and news in addition to its products. As a result, the auxiliary service provided by fashion consultants and research agencies, whose role is to supply information, is vital to the industry.

Fashion Consultants and Information Services

Fashion consultants are individuals and groups who provide information and services to producers and retailers. Well-known consultants today are Kurt Barnard, Marvin Traub, and Walter F. Loeb. Firms working in the fashion and retailing consulting area today include Kurt Salmon Associates, in Atlanta; State Street Research, in Boston; Retail Management Consultants, in San Marcos, California; and WSL Strategic Retail, in New York City.

The Fashion Group International, Inc.

Another vital source of industry information is the Fashion Group, Inc., a nonprofit global association of professional women who work in the industry and the associated beauty and home fashions industries (Figure 20.13). It was founded in 1930 to create executive jobs for women. Over the ensuing decades, however, it has become an important consulting and research agency. Its services are offered to members and, in some instances, nonmembers. Originally a group of seventeen fashion leaders in New York, it now has more than 6,000 members in chapters in fashion centers across the world.

The Fashion Group is known for its exciting and prophetic fashion presentations. Through lavish fashion shows and fiber displays, it offers the fashion industry its expert and insightful analysis of upcoming trends. It covers the American, European, and Far Eastern fashion scenes. The Fashion Group maintains a valuable website (www.fgi.org), an online information service featuring directories of industry executives and professional services, calendars of events, trend reports and forecasts, a job bank, public announcements, and conferences.

Specialized Information Services

A number of services disseminate reports on various segments of the fashion industry. For example, Nigel French, a British company, issues reports on fabrics, knitwear, and color. The *International Colour Authority*, a British publication, and the Color Association of the United States specialize in reporting on color trends in women's and men's wear.

Market Research Agencies

Because knowing what is new and what is now is at the very heart of fashion, businesses in all segments

FIGURE 20.13 FGI publishes a bulletin that focuses on trends and events in the fashion industry.

of the industry avidly consume the raw data and trend analyses published by market research agencies. The services of these professional prophets are expensive, but many of their findings are made public in time to be useful to a larger following. Among the better-known agencies is Kurt Salmon Associates, known for its extensive work with textile and apparel manufacturers and softgoods retailers.

The major accounting firms also have special divisions devoted to the fashion industries. Ernst & Young, Deloitte & Touche, and PricewaterhouseCoopers all offer respected management consulting services on a global basis.

A breed of researchers and forecasters who rely on a variety of resources—including their own anecdotal observations and gut instincts as well as polls and surveys—is epitomized by Faith Popcorn. She has been called the Nostradamus of marketing. Popcorn started the Trend Bank in 1968. Through the Trend Bank, she has offered such hypotheses as Future Tense, EveVolution, 99 Lives, Cocooning, and AtmosFear, to name a few, which have proved to be right today. Popcorn started her career in advertising, and in 1974, she started BrainReserve. BrainReserve sprung from

the understanding that in order to properly position a brand, one needs to understand the future of the brand in the environment in which it exists. Today, BrainReserve has an expert panel of more than 10,000 visionaries worldwide, with experts from every industry and cultural area—media and medics to marketers and academics. These experts are constantly searching for clues and ideas that are the precursors to future trends.[7]

As consumers become more aware of trends, they become more aware that they are trendsetters, and the fashion industry, instead of attempting to dictate what will be worn next season, is actively seeking out the influential consumers and taking a cue from them.

Trade Associations and Trade Shows

Associations of manufacturers and retailers assist fashion buyers in many ways. The nature and frequency of assistance available, though, are not uniform throughout the industry, and buyers soon learn how much assistance will be forthcoming from their particular trade. (See Units Two, Three, and Four for the names and activities of trade associations and trade shows for the major segments of the fashion industry.)

Swarovski 2012 CFDA
Fashion Awards Party

CFDA:
AMERICAN FASHION'S
AMBASSADOR TO THE WORLD

THE COUNCIL OF Fashion Designers of America (CFDA) is on a mission to put the U.S. fashion industry back on the cutting edge with initiatives that support both emerging and established designers. In a few short years, its membership numbers have ballooned to over 400 members who reflect a wider spectrum of the industry, including creative directors from Kate Spade and J.Crew and four members from Calvin Klein, Inc.

Young design brands benefit from The Fashion Incubator, a CFDA program that provides low-cost studio space, business mentoring, educational seminars, and networking opportunities to winning designers for two years. Similarly, each year the CFDA/ Vogue Fashion Fund awards a substantial grant ($300,000 in 2012) and business mentoring from a team of fashion industry professionals. Past winners of the CFDA/Vogue Fashion Fund include American designers Alexander Wang, Joseph Altuzarra, and Proenza Schouler's Jack McCollough and Lazaro Hernandez. Other partnerships include the Diet Coke Young Designer Challenge, in which design students competed for the chance to have their Diet Coke T-shirt design featured in Target stores nationwide.

For more established designers, the CFDA is working to increase exposure to global business practices through programs like their China Exchange, which gives American designers a greater understanding of one of the fastest-growing consumer markets in the world. In its first trade, the China Exchange gave Jack McCollough and Lazaro Hernandez the opportunity to immerse themselves in the Shanghai fashion industry while China's Uma Wang received tips from Michael Kors in New York. Kors emphasized the importance of learning about global business when he said, "The world is tiny now. In 1981 when I was starting out, our idea of global was Canada."

At home, the CFDA helps established designers forge alliances with other industries from consumer goods to cars and coffee through the Business Services Network. Thanks in part to the CFDA, fashion is no longer considered a narrow interest of a small part of the population, but a part of our national art and culture enjoyed by everyone. This wider interest has propelled companies like Lexus, Gilt Groupe, and Printemps department store to seek affiliations with CFDA and its designers.

Retailers Group

The National Retail Federation (NRF) is the largest retail trade association in the United States, counting among its members all the major department and specialty stores. It disseminates information and advice through its monthly magazine, *Stores,* and other periodicals and through regional and national meetings. An annual general convention is sponsored by the NRF in New York City in January. Vendors of products and services as diverse as market research, management software, and shopping bags exhibit at this meeting. Members gather at seminars and workshops to learn from retailing authorities and from one another. A special feature at this convention is a session devoted to outstanding fashion promotions during the previous year.

Buyers Groups

Specialized associations or buying clubs provide an opportunity for an exchange of opinions and ideas among members. Retail buyers' groups also transmit the preferences of their members on matters as varied as the dates when lines should be opened and the appropriate sizes of stock boxes for specific products. Trade associations are often subsidized by outside sources, either the industry itself or a trade publication. Again, these associations are covered in Units Two, Three, and Four.

Trade Shows

Retail and manufacturing groups, as well as independent organizations, sometimes sponsor trade shows at which many exhibitors gather to show their products and lines in one place, usually a hotel or convention center. Trade shows save time that would otherwise be spent trudging from showroom to showroom and also provide buyers with a chance to meet and exchange ideas with one another. They are especially helpful in fashion areas made up of many small firms. Exhibitors also find them a place to meet their counterparts from other regions or countries.

The shoe, notions, piece-goods, and men's sportswear industries regularly sponsor trade shows. (See Chapter 16 for a discussion of trade shows and market weeks at U.S. and foreign markets and marts.)

Buying, Merchandising, and Product Development Organizations

Another type of auxiliary service—one developed especially for the fashion industry—is the **buying, merchandising, and product development organization**. This type of organization evolved from a service called a *resident buying office (RBO),* and to understand the function of a buying, merchandising, and product development organization, one must first know something about RBOs. The buying offices came into being to serve the ongoing needs of a store or group of stores for a steady supply of new merchandise. Because a store's buyers worked out of the store and made only occasional market trips, they came to rely on a service located at the market centers for ongoing, daily attention to the store's needs.

These offices continue to watch and report on fashion trends, help with strategic planning, make vendor recommendations, coordinate imports, and assist in product development. They help to organize fashion weeks and ensure that they go smoothly for their client stores' buyers. A good office continually adds to its list of services, and many have even expanded into areas such as sales promotion and advertising, personnel operations, and computer processing.

Location

Large firms, like the Doneger Group and Macy's Merchandising Group, are headquartered in New York City. However, a number of buying offices also have locations in Los Angeles or the West Coast. Marshall Kline Buying Service is an example of a Los Angeles–based buying office; it serves department stores and women's, men's, and children's apparel and home furnishings specialty stores. Some retail fashion chains, such as Ross Stores (a California off-price specialty chain), which maintain their own buying offices, have West Coast offices in Los Angeles.

The large buying, merchandising, and product development organizations also maintain branches abroad, and smaller companies have affiliates in the major foreign market centers.

Types of Ownership

Buying offices are either independent or store-owned. An independent office works for noncompeting clients that it seeks out, while a store-owned office is owned by a group of stores, or—less often—one store, for whom it works exclusively.

Independent Offices

Independent offices are more numerous than store-owned offices simply because relatively few retailing giants can afford to own and manage such a resource. The number of buying offices has declined in recent years because of mergers and acquisitions among their retailer clients and among buying offices themselves.

Independent offices typically represent noncompeting moderate-priced department and specialty stores in midsize and secondary markets. To avoid conflicts, most independents restrict themselves to one client in each trading area, although they may have clients who serve different market segments within a single area. For example, a resident office's clients within a trading area may include a department store; a bridal shop; a shoe store; stores specializing in activewear, men's sportswear, and children's wear; and stores catering to customers at different price points.

The staff familiarizes themselves with each client's needs and attempt to meet those needs with as wide a range of services as possible. One aspect of service that buying offices are promoting to attract new clients is personal attention. Small operations, which offer exclusivity to their customers, claim that in a business consumed by "mergermania," they are better able to service their clients, who may themselves be expanding, by continuing to provide personalized and individual service.

Larger firms have responded by forming divisions that cater to the needs of different groups of clients. The largest independent RBO—in fact, the largest RBO of any type—in the United States is the Doneger Group. Its ten divisions include specialized buying offices for retailers in such markets as apparel for large women, apparel for tall women, children's wear, menswear, home furnishings, and off-price retailing. Other divisions provide research and forecasting services and assistance in import and export.

Typically, an independent office charges each client store an annual, stipulated fee, which is based on the store's sales volume.

Store-Owned Offices

Store-owned offices are either associated or corporate owned. An **associated** or **cooperative office** is cooperatively owned and operated by a group of privately owned stores for their mutual use. It never takes outside private clients; membership is by invitation only. It is considerably more expensive than if the store were a client of an independent office because members buy shares in the cooperative when they join. The amount of shares that must be purchased is keyed to member stores' sales volume. One advantage of belonging to an associated office is that it provides members with an important exchange of information, often including financial information and merchandising experience.

The **corporate-owned** office, or **syndicated office**, as it is sometimes called, is maintained by a parent organization exclusively for the stores it owns. One advantage of this type of organization is that it can be given more authority than an independent office, although some corporate-owned offices still require authorization from store buyers for major purchases. For instance, Macy's, Inc. is an example of this type of office.

Functions of the Buying, Merchandising, and Product Development Organization

Even with instant forms of communication, the buying function benefits from the services of a representative and advisor who is actually at the market. Some of the functions that buying offices perform on behalf of their clients are purchasing, preparing for market weeks, importing, and developing products.

Purchasing

Buying offices offer store buyers' advice and support in various buying situations. For example, an office can place an order large enough to qualify for a manufacturer's quantity discount and then divide the goods among several small clients. The organization's staff can visit manufacturers' showrooms and make recommendations to their clients about specials, trends, and hot items. Size and location give the buying office clout with vendors when it comes to reordering in midseason or making sure that the right goods are delivered on schedule.

Preparing for Market Weeks

As noted in Chapter 16, market weeks are hectic times for fashion buyers, with many showroom visits and other information-gathering events. A buying office can provide services similar to those of a tour guide to make the buying trip smooth and efficient. Staff members visit the showrooms in advance and assess each manufacturer's lines on behalf of their various clients. When the store buyers arrive, the buying office may give presentations to let them know what to expect. Sometimes personnel from a buying office accompany visiting buyers to vendors' showrooms and offer on-the-spot advice about orders.

Importing

Many buying offices maintain divisions in key foreign cities or affiliate with a *commissionaires* overseas. (A commissionaire is an agent who represents stores in foreign markets. See Chapter 15 for further discussion.) Overseas divisions and commissionaires work closely with the merchandising division and with client stores. In addition to performing the buying functions of a domestic buying office, these services deal with the unique challenges of importing, such as quotas, tariffs, long lead times for delivery, and interpretation of the buyer's orders for vendors who speak a different language. Having an advisor and consultant overseas is especially beneficial for buyers who are attending a market week or trade show or having private-label goods produced in a foreign country.

Developing Products

Buying offices have played an important role in the development of private labels. Most corporate-owned buying offices have a private-label program for their member stores.

Corporate offices have also aggressively pursued private-label business and product development. Macy's, Inc. is an example of a company with a well-established product development and private-label program.

Summary and Review

Fashion producers and retailers depend on a variety of auxiliary services to support the merchandising function. Depending on the size and resources of a company, it may rely on its own staff for these services or hire outside firms to perform them.

The media regard fashion businesses as clients and offer assistance in preparing and placing advertising in newspapers, consumer and trade magazines, radio and television commercials, and online. To attract advertisers, the media offer fashion businesses color and style forecasts and other trend information. Advertising and public relations agencies also provide auxiliary services in placing paid advertisements and free publicity in the media. Store design and visual merchandising are other promotional services that may be performed by staff members or independent suppliers.

For information about industry trends and fashion forecasts, retailers and producers can take advantage of the services offered by fashion consulting firms, market research agencies, trade associations, and trade shows.

A source of information unique to the fashion industry is the buying, merchandising, and product development organization. This type of business began as resident buying offices, representing out-of-town retailers in the major markets. Some firms were independent, selling their services to noncompeting retailers. Others were corporate-owned, either as cooperatives owned by several retailers or as divisions of large retail chains. Resident buying offices have evolved into businesses that include wholesalers and producers among their clients and that provide a full range of services, including liaisons with vendors, advice and assistance in buying, merchandising, forecasting, and other information services.

For Review

1. What is the difference between advertising and publicity/public relations?
2. Describe the contents of *Women's Wear Daily*.
3. What are the advantages of television and radio for fashion exposure?
4. What tasks do public relations firms undertake for their clients?
5. What advantages do social media offer as a promotional medium?
6. How does a store design contribute to the store's image?
7. What resources are available to a small specialty store for effective visual merchandising?
8. Describe the research methods that trend forecasters use.
9. What is the major function of buying, merchandising, and product development organizations? What additional services do they perform?
10. What are the similarities and differences between independent and corporate buying, merchandising, and product development offices?

For Discussion

1. As a consumer, where do you get your information about fashion? How does each medium influence your buying decisions?
2. You own a small boutique that caters to upscale young women. What services of a buying, merchandising, and product development organization would be most useful to you? Why?

Trade Talk

Define or briefly explain the following terms:

advertising
associated or cooperative office
buying, merchandising, and product development organization
corporate-owned or syndicated office
editorial credit
fashion stylist
infomercial
planogram
public relations
publicity
QR codes
shelter magazines
trade publication
visual merchandising

GLOSSARY

Absolute quota A limit to the quantity of goods entering the United States. *Ch 17*

Activewear The sector of sportswear that includes casual attire worn for sports such as running, jogging, tennis, and racquetball. Sometimes called "active sportswear." *Ch 10*

Adaptations Designs that have all the dominant features of the style that inspired them but do not claim to be exact copies. *Ch 2*

Advertising The paid use of space or time in any medium. This includes newspapers, magazines, direct-mail pieces, shopping news bulletins, theater programs, catalogs, billboards, radio, TV, online, and mobile devices. *Ch 20*

Air malls Retail stores in airports. *Ch 19*

Ambiance The atmosphere encountered when entering a store. *Ch 19*

Anchor A design from a previous season reworked in a different color or fabric. *Ch 8*

Apparel contractor A firm whose sole function is to supply sewing services to the apparel industry. *Ch 8*

Apparel jobber (manufacturing) A firm that handles the designing, planning, and purchasing of materials, and usually the cutting, selling, and shipping of apparel, but does not handle the actual garment sewing. *Ch 8*

Apparel manufacturer A firm that performs all of the operations required to produce a garment. *Ch 8*

Aromatherapy Fragrant oils that are extracted from plants, herbs, and flowers, and that are used to stimulate or relax people. *Ch 14*

Assortment The range of stock a retailer features. See also *merchandise assortment*. *Ch 19*

Auxiliary level Composed of all the support services that are working with primary producers, secondary manufacturers, and retailers to keep consumers aware of the fashion merchandise produced for ultimate consumption. *Ch 5*

Baby-boom generation People born in the United States between 1946 and 1964; the largest generational group ever recorded. *Ch 3*

Balance of trade The difference between the value of exports and the value of imports. *Ch 17*

Bar code A pattern of dark bars and white spaces of varying length. *Ch 8*

Big boxes A concept for a store that presents a large selection of goods in a selling space oversized for its merchandise category. *Ch 18*

Bodywear Coordinated leotards, tights, and wrap skirts. *Ch 12*

Body wrap Herbs, seaweed, or mud applied directly to the body, which is then wrapped like a mummy to allow the substances to penetrate the pores. *Ch 14*

Bootleg goods Quality products made by the same manufacturer that produces the genuine branded products; these are sold to the black market. *Ch 17*

Boutique A shop associated with few-of-a-kind merchandise, generally of very new or extreme styling, with an imaginative presentation of goods. French word for "shop." *Ch 16*

Brand A name, trademark, or logo that is used to identify the products of a specific maker or seller and to differentiate the products from those of the competition. Also called "brand name." *Ch 6*

Brand-line representative (cosmetics) A trained cosmetician who advises customers in the selection and use of a specific brand of cosmetics, and handles the sales of that brand in a retail store. *Ch 14*

Bridal registry See *wedding registry. Ch 15*

Bridge (apparel—women's and menswear) A price zone that bridges the gap between designer and better prices. *Ch 10*

Bridge jewelry Merchandise ranging from costume to fine jewelry in price, materials, and newness of styling. *Ch 13*

Briolette An oval or pear-shaped gemstone cut in triangular facets. *Ch 13*

Broad and shallow assortment A store that offers many different styles in limited sizes and colors. *Ch 19*

Bundling Assembling the cut pieces of each pattern—sleeves, collars, fronts, and backs—into bundles according to their sizes. Usually done by hand. *Ch 8*

Buyer's directory A list (and often a map) of the manufacturers' showrooms in a particular market or mart; it is furnished to retail buyers to assist them in "working the market." *Ch 16*

Buying, merchandising, and product development office *Associated/Cooperative:* One that is jointly owned and operated by a group of independently owned stores. *Private:* One that is owned and operated by a single, out-of-town store organization and that performs market work exclusively for that store organization. *Salaried, Fee, or Paid:* One that is independently owned and operated and that charges the stores it represents for the work it does. *Syndicate/Corporate:* One that is maintained by a parent organization that owns a group of stores and performs market work exclusively for those stores. *Ch 20*

Carat A measure of weight of precious stones; equal to 200 milligrams or 1/142 of an ounce. See also *karat*. *Ch 13*

Career A profession for which one trains and which is undertaken as a permanent calling. *Career Project 1*

Career path or ladder The order of occupations in a person's life. *Career Project 2*

Category or classification buying A practice whereby a chain store buyer located in a central buying office is usually assigned to purchase only a specific category or classification of merchandise instead of buying all categories carried in a single department. See also *departmental buying*. *Ch 18*

Category killer Superstores or category specialists who so dominate a market that they drive out or "kill" smaller specialty stores. *Ch 18*

Chain organization A group of twelve or more centrally owned stores, each handling somewhat similar goods, which are merchandised and controlled from a central headquarters office (as defined by the Bureau of the Census). *Ch 18*

Chargebacks Financial penalties imposed on manufacturers by retailers. *Ch 8*

Classic A style or design that satisfies a basic need and remains in general fashion acceptance for an extended period of time. *Ch 2*

Chemise Sleep gowns with no waistlines. *Ch 12*

Collection A term used in the United States and Europe for an expensive line. *Ch 8*

Commissionaire (pronounced "ko-mee-see-oh-NAIR") An independent retailers' service organization usually located in the major city of a foreign market area. It is roughly the foreign equivalent of an American resident buying office. *Ch 17*

Computer-aided design (CAD) A computer program that allows designers to manipulate their designs easily. *Ch 8*

Computer-aided manufacturing (CAM) Stand-alone computerized manufacturing equipment, including computerized sewing, pattern-making, and cutting machines. *Ch 8*

Computer-integrated manufacturing (CIM) Many computers within a manufacturing company linked from the design through the production stages. *Ch 8*

Confined style(s) Styles that a vendor agrees to sell to only one store in a given trading area. See also *exclusivity*. *Ch 19*

Consignment selling When a manufacturer places merchandise in a retail store for resale but permits any unsold portion to be returned to the wholesale source by a specific date. *Ch 7*

Contemporary A type of styling and a price zone that is often also referred to as "updated," "better," or "young." Applies to all categories of apparel and furnishings. *Chs 9 and 10*

Contract buying See *specification buying*.

Contract tanneries Business firms that process hides and skins to the specifications of converters but are not involved in the sale of the finished product. *Ch 7*

Contractors See *apparel contractor*. *Ch 8*

Converter, leather Firms that buy hides and skins, farm out their processing to contract tanneries, and sell the finished product. *Ch 7*

Converter, textiles A producer who buys fabrics in the greige, contracts to have them finished (dyed, bleached, printed, or subjected to other treatments) in plants specializing in each operation, and sells the finished goods. *Ch 6*

Copycat scents Imitations of the aromas (and sometimes the packaging) of popular designer fragrances; sold at much lower prices. *Ch 14*

Corporate licensing The use of a company's name on (sometimes) related merchandise. *Ch 8*

Corporate-owned or syndicated office See *buying, merchandising, and product development office*. *Ch 20*

Corporate social responsibility (CSR) A company that not only fully complies with the obligations of legislation, but also accounts for how it integrates social and environmental factors into its global decision-making policies and practices. *Ch 17*

Cosmetics Articles other than soap that are intended to be rubbed, poured, sprinkled, or sprayed on the person for purposes of cleansing, beautifying, promoting attractiveness, or altering the appearance (as defined by the Federal Trade Commission). *Ch 14*

Costume jewelry Mass-produced jewelry made of brass or other base metals, plastic, wood, or glass, and set with simulated or nonprecious stones. Also called "fashion jewelry." *Ch 13*

Counterfeit goods Inferior imitations passed off as the genuine article. Luxury goods and designer brands are the chief objects of counterfeiters. *Ch 17*

Couture house (pronounced "koo-TOUR") An apparel firm for which the designer creates original styles. *Ch 16*

Couturier (male) or **couturière** (female) (pronounced "koo-tour-ee-AY" and "koo-tour-ee-AIR") The proprietor or designer of a French couture house. *Ch 16*

Créateurs (pronounced "kray-ah-TOURS") French ready-to-wear designers. *Ch 16*

Culmination (stage) See *fashion cycle*. *Ch 2*

Custom-made Clothing fitted specifically to the wearer. *Ch 9*

Cut-up trade Manufacturers of belts that are sold as part of a dress, skirt, or pants. *Ch 13*

Data warehouse A group of superpowerful computers hooked together and filled with easily accessible information about customers, transactions, and finances. *Ch 19*

Decline (stage) See *fashion cycle*. *Ch 2*

Demographics Population studies that divide broad groups of consumers into smaller, more homogeneous market segments; the variables include population distribution, age, sex, family life cycle, race, religion, nationality, education, occupation, and income. *Ch 3*

Departmental buying A practice whereby a department buyer is responsible for buying all the various categories of merchandise carried in that department. See also *category buying*. *Ch 18*

Department store As defined by the Bureau of the Census, a store that employs twenty-five or more people and sells general lines of merchandise in each of three categories: (1) home furnishings, (2) household linens and dry goods (an old trade term meaning piece goods and sewing notions), and (3) apparel and accessories for the entire family. *Ch 18*

Design A specific version or variation of a style. In everyday usage, however, fashion producers and retailers refer to a design as a "style," a "style number," or simply a "number." *Ch 2*

Details The individual elements that give a silhouette its form or shape. These include trimmings; skirt and pant length and width; and shoulder, waist, and sleeve treatment. *Ch 2*

Developed countries (DCs) Countries in the stage of economic development marked by a well-paid labor force and a high standard of living. *Ch 17*

Discount store A departmentalized retail store using many self-service techniques to sell its goods. It operates usually at low profit margins, has a minimum annual volume of $500,000, and is at least 10,000 sq. ft. in size. *Ch 18*

Discretionary income The money that an individual or family has to spend or save after buying such necessities as food, clothing, shelter, and basic transportation. *Ch 3*

Disposable personal income The amount of money a person has left to spend or save after paying taxes. It is roughly equivalent to what an employee calls "take-home pay," and provides an approximation of the purchasing power of each consumer during any given year. *Ch 3*

Diversification The addition of various lines, products, or services to serve different markets. *Ch 5*

Domestic market A fashion market center located in one's own country. *Ch 16*

Downward-flow theory The theory of fashion adoption which maintains that to be identified as a true fashion, a style must first be adopted by people at the top of the social pyramid. The style then gradually wins acceptance at progressively lower social levels. Also called the "trickle-down" theory. *Ch 4*

Drop (menswear) The difference in inches between the chest measurements of a suit jacket and the waist of the pants. The most common is the six-inch drop. *Ch 10*

Dual distribution A manufacturer's policy of selling goods at both wholesale and retail. *Ch 10*

Duty See *tariff*.

Editorial credit The mention, in a magazine or newspaper, of a store name as a retail source for merchandise that is being editorially featured by the publication. *Ch 20*

Electronic Data Interchange (EDI) The electronic exchange of machine-readable data in standard formats between one company's computers and another company's computers. *Ch 8*

Entrepreneurs People who start new business ventures. *Career Project 1*

Entry-level job One requiring little or no specific training and experience. *Career Project 1*

Environment The conditions under which we live that affect our lives and influence our actions. *Ch 3*

Erogenous Sexually stimulating. *Ch 4*

European styling (menswear) Features more fitted jackets that hug the body and have extremely square shoulders. *Ch 10*

Exclusivity Allowing sole use within a given trading area of a style or styles. An important competitive retail weapon. *Ch 19*

Export When a country provides goods to another country. *Ch 17*

Fabrics Materials formed from knitted, woven, or bonded yarns. *Ch 6*

Factor Financial institution that specializes in buying accounts receivable at a discount. *Ch 8*

Factory outlet store Manufacturer-owned store that sells company products at reduced prices in austere surroundings with minimum services. *Ch 18*

Fad A short-lived fashion. *Ch 2*

Fashion A style that is accepted and used by the majority of a group at any one time. *Ch 2*

Fashion business Any business concerned with goods or services in which fashion is an element—including fiber, fabric, and apparel manufacturing, distribution, advertising, publishing, and consulting. *Ch 2*

Fashion cycle The rise, widespread popularity, and then decline in acceptance of a style. *Rise:* The acceptance of either a newly introduced design or its adaptations by an increasing number of consumers. *Culmination:* That period when a fashion is at the height of its popularity and use. The fashion then is in such demand that it can be mass-produced, mass-distributed, and sold at prices within the reach of most consumers. *Decline:* The decrease in consumer demand because of boredom resulting from widespread use of a fashion. *Obsolescence:* When disinterest occurs and a style can no longer be sold at any price. *Ch 2*

Fashion industries Those engaged in producing the materials used in the production of apparel and accessories for men, women, and children. *Ch 2*

Fashion influential A person whose advice is sought by associates. A fashion influential's adoption of a new style gives it prestige among a group. *Ch 4*

Fashion innovator A person first to try out a new style. *Ch 4*

Fashion jewelry See *costume jewelry. Ch 13*

Fashion retailing The business of buying and selling—or merchandising—goods, apparel, accessories, and home fashions. *Ch 18*

Fashion trend See *trend.*

Fiber A threadlike unit of raw material from which yarn and, eventually, textile fabric is made. *Ch 6*

First cost The wholesale price of merchandise in the country of origin. *Ch 17*

Floor-ready Merchandise that has been ticketed with bar-coded price and packed in labeled cartons with all shipping documents attached. If the merchandise is a garment, it has been pressed and folded or hung on a hanger with a plastic bag over it. *Ch 8*

Foreign market Markets outside the domestic market; for example, to businesses in the United States, France is a foreign market. See also *market* and *domestic market. Ch 16*

Foundations The trade term for such women's undergarments as brassieres, girdles, panty girdles, garter belts, and shapers. *Ch 12*

Fragrance Includes cologne, toilet water, perfume, spray perfume, aftershave lotion, and environmental scents. *Ch 14*

Franchise A contractual agreement in which a firm or individual buys the exclusive right to conduct a retail business within a specified trading area under a franchiser's registered or trademarked name. *Chs 5 and 18*

Franchise distribution (cosmetics) The manufacturer or exclusive distributor sells directly to the ultimate retailer. *Ch 14*

Free trade The unrestricted exchange of goods between nations. *Ch 17*

Fur farming The breeding and raising of fur-bearing animals under controlled conditions. *Ch 7*

General Agreement on Tariffs and Trade (GATT) A 1947 agreement, between many countries, to reduce trade barriers and unify trading practices. It was replaced by the World Trade Organization (WTO) in 1995. *Ch 17*

Generation X The "baby bust" group, born from 1965 to 1976. *Ch 3*

Generation Y The second "baby boomlet" group, born from 1977 to 1987. *Ch 3*

General merchandise retailer Retail stores which sell a number of lines of merchandise—for example, apparel and accessories; furniture and home furnishings; household lines and dry goods; hardware, appliances, and smallwares—under one roof. Stores included in this group are commonly known as mass-merchandisers, department stores, variety stores, general merchandise stores, or general stores. *Ch 18*

General store An early form of retail store which carried a wide variety of mainly utilitarian consumer goods. *Ch 18*

Generic name Nontrademarked names assigned by the Federal Trade Commission to twenty-three manufactured fibers. *Ch 6*

Geographics Population studies that focus on where people live. *Ch 3*

Geotextiles Manufactured, permeable textiles currently used in reinforcing or stabilizing civil engineering projects. *Ch 6*

Global sourcing The process of shopping for and purchasing imported goods. *Ch 17*

Grading Adjustment of a style's sample pattern to meet the dimensional requirements of each size in which the style is to be made. Also referred to as "sloping." *Ch 8*

Gray market goods Goods not intended for sale in the country in which they are being sold, often with an invalid warranty. *Ch 17*

Greige goods (pronounced "grayzh goods") Fabric that has received no preparation, dyeing, or finishing treatment after having been produced by any textile process. *Ch 6*

Group A subdivision of a line, linked by a common theme such as color, fabric, or style. *Ch 8*

Haute couture (pronounced "oat-koo-TOUR") The French term literally meaning "fine sewing" but actually having much the same sense as our own term "high fashion." *Ch 16*

Hides Animals skins that weigh over 25 pounds when shipped to a tannery. *Ch 7*

High fashion Those styles or designs accepted by a limited group of fashion leaders—the elite among consumers—who are first to accept fashion change. *Ch 2*

High-fashion designer A person who creates designs, chooses the fabric, texture, and color for each design. Often, this person is involved with the development of the production model as well as with plans for the promotion of the line. A name designer may work for fashion houses, own his or her own firm, or work for a publicly owned firm. *Ch 8*

High-tech fabric A fabric that has been constructed, finished, or processed in a way that gives it certain innovative, unusual, or hard-to-achieve qualities not normally available. *Ch 6*

Home fragrances Fragrances used to scent a place rather than a person; also called environmental fragrances. *Ch 14*

Horizontal growth A company expands on the level on which it has been performing. See also *vertical growth*. *Ch 5*

Horizontal-flow theory The theory of fashion adoption that holds that fashions move horizontally between groups on similar social levels rather than vertically from one level to another. Also called the "mass-market theory." *Ch 4*

Import When a country buys goods from a foreign country. *Ch 17*

Import quota Limits set to restrict the number of specific goods entering a country. *Ch 17*

Inflation A substantial and continuing rise in the general price level. *Ch 3*

Innerwear The trade term for women's underwear; usually divided into foundations, lingerie, and loungewear. *Ch 12*

Inside shops Garment factories owned and operated by menswear manufacturers who perform all the operations required to produce finished garments. *Ch 10*

Intimate apparel The trade term for women's foundations, lingerie, and loungewear. Also called inner fashions, body fashions, and innerwear. *Ch 12*

Item house Contractors that specialize in the production of one product. *Ch 8*

Jobber A middleman who buys from manufacturers and sells to retailers. See also *apparel jobber*. *Ch 8*

Joint merchandising An arrangement in which a retail store pays part of the salary of the cosmetic/fragrance salespeople who represent one manufacturer's line. *Ch 14*

Karat A measure of the weight of the gold content of jewelry; abbreviated as "K." See also *carat*. *Ch 13*

Kiosk A stand that offers shelves or racks for merchandise. *Ch 19*

Kips Animal skins weighing from 15 to 25 pounds when shipped to a tannery. *Ch 7*

Knockoffs A trade term referring to the low-price copies of an item that has had good acceptance at higher prices. *Ch 2*

Leased department A department ostensibly operated by the store in which it is found but actually run by an outsider who pays a percentage of sales to the store as rent. *Chs 7 and 18*

Less developed countries (LDCs) Countries in the early stages of economic development; they have a low standard of living and lack a well-paid labor force. *Ch 17*

Let out (furs) A cutting and resewing operation to make short skins into longer-length skins adequate for garment purposes. *Ch 7*

Licensed trademark (fibers) A fiber's registered trademark used under a licensing agreement whereby use of the trademark is permitted only to those manufacturers whose end products pass established tests for their specific end use or application. *Ch 6*

Licensing An arrangement whereby firms are given permission to produce and market merchandise in the name of the licensor, who is paid a percentage of sales for permitting his or her name to be used. *Ch 5*

Life-stage marketing A marketing strategy that targets a specific demographic. It has long been the specialty of catalog retailers in particular, and helps companies to make their products more relatable. *Ch 19*

Lifestyle centers Open-air shopping areas anchored by a multiplex cinema (or two) and a big bookstore; they also contain a collection of restaurants. *Ch 19*

Line An assortment of new designs offered by manufacturers to their customers, usually on a seasonal basis. *Ch 5*

Line-for-line copies Exactly like the original designs except that they have been mass-produced in less expensive fabrics to standard size measurements. *Ch 8*

Lingerie A general undergarment category that includes slips, petticoats, camisoles, bras, panties, nightgowns, and pajamas. Underclothing is considered "daywear," while nightgowns and pajamas are classified as "sleepwear." *Ch 12*

Long-run fashion A fashion that takes more seasons to complete its cycle than what might be considered its average life expectancy. *Ch 2*

Loungewear The trade term for the intimate apparel category that includes robes, bed jackets, and housecoats. *Ch 12*

Mall An enclosed, climate-controlled shopping center. *Ch 19*

Manufactured fiber A fiber invented in a laboratory; also called "man-made" or "synthetic." *Ch 6*

Manufacturer See *apparel manufacturer*.

Marker (apparel manufacturing) A long piece of paper upon which the pieces of the pattern of a garment in all its sizes are outlined and which is placed on top of many layers of material for cutting purposes. *Ch 8*

Market (1) A group of potential customers. (2) The place or area in which buyers and sellers meet for the purpose of trading ownership of goods at wholesale prices. *Ch 16*

Market center A geographic center for the creation and production of fashion merchandise, as well as for exchanging ownership. *Ch 16*

Market segmentation The separating of the total consumer market into smaller groups known as "market segments." *Ch 3*

Market weeks Scheduled periods throughout the year during which producers and their sales representatives introduce new lines for the upcoming season to retail buyers. *Ch 16*

Marketing A total system of business activities designed to plan, price, promote, and place (distribute) products and services to present and potential customers. *Ch 2*

Mart A building or building complex housing both permanent and transient showrooms of producers and their sales representatives. *Ch 16*

Mass distribution (cosmetics) Third-party vendors, such as wholesalers, diverters, and jobbers, often interposed between the manufacturer and the retailer. *Ch 14*

Mass or volume fashion Those styles or designs that are widely accepted. *Ch 2*

Megamall Larger than a superregional mall, it contains four to five million square feet. *Ch 19*

Merchandise assortment A collection of varied types of related merchandise, essentially intended for the same general end-use and usually grouped together in one selling area of a retail store. *Broad:* A merchandise assortment that includes many styles. *Deep:* A merchandise assortment that includes a comprehensive range of colors and sizes in each style. *Narrow:* A merchandise assortment that includes relatively few styles. *Shallow:* A merchandise assortment that contains only a few sizes and colors in each style. *Ch 19*

Merchandising The planning required on the part of retailers to have, for a specific consumer target group, the right merchandise at the right time, in the right place, in the right quantities, at the right price, and with the right promotion. *Ch 2*

Merchandising policies Guidelines established by store management for merchandising executives to follow in order that the store organization may win the patronage of the specific target group(s) of customers it has chosen to serve. *Ch 19*

Merger The sale of one company to another with the result that only one company exists. *Ch 5*

Microfiber A fiber two or three times thinner than a human hair, and thinner than wool, cotton, flax, or silk fibers. It has a touch and texture similar to silk or cashmere, but is wrinkle-resistant. *Ch 6*

Millinery The women's hat industry. *Ch 13*

Minimum order The quantity, number of styles, and/or dollar amount required by the manufacturer in order to accept the retail store buyer's order. *Ch 8*

Mom-and-Pop store A small store run by the proprietor with few or no hired assistants. *Ch 18*

Multi-Fiber and Textile Arrangement (MFA) The first multinational agreement specifically regulating the flow of textile products; it is being phased out. *Ch 17*

Narrow and deep assortment One in which there are relatively few styles, but these styles are stocked in all available sizes and colors. *Ch 19*

Newly industrialized countries (NICs) Countries in the first stage of economic development; they have small-to-no export markets. *Ch 17*

North American Free Trade Agreement (NAFTA) An agreement that eliminated quotas and tariffs for goods shipped between Canada, the United States, and Mexico. *Ch 17*

Note (fragrances) Each scent that makes up a fragrance; notes vary in strength and duration. *Ch 14*

Obsolescence (stage) See *fashion cycle*.

Off-price retailing The selling of brand-name and designer merchandise at lower-than-normal retail prices when they are at the late rise or early peak in the fashion cycle. *Ch 18*

Offshore production The importation of goods by domestic apparel producers, either from their own plants operating in cheap, labor-rich foreign areas, or through their long-term supply arrangements with foreign producers. *Chs 8 and 17*

Operational policies Policies designed to keep customers once they are attracted to come into a store by establishing the store's ambiance, customer services, promotions, and frequent shopper plans. See also *merchandising policies*. *Ch 19*

Outlet mall A shopping center containing outlet stores and often entertainment facilities. *Ch 19*

Outpost Small accessory departments located next to apparel departments or near store entrances, sometimes with movable kiosks, carts, or racks. *Ch 13*

Outside shops See *apparel contractor*. *Ch 8*

Pelt The skin of a fur-bearing animal. *Ch 7*

Per capita personal income The wages, salaries, interest, dividends, and all other income received by the population as a whole, divided by the number of people in the population. *Ch 3*

Personal income The total or gross amount of income received from all sources by the population as a whole. It consists of wages, salaries, interest, dividends, and all other income for everyone in the country. See also *disposable personal income* and *discretionary income*. *Ch 3*

PETA People for the Ethical Treatment of Animals, a nonprofit organization devoted to animal rights. *Ch 7*

Piece-dyed The process of dyeing fabrics after they are knitted or woven; it gives the manufacturer maximum flexibility. See also *yarn-dyed*. *Ch 6*

Piecework A production method in which an operator sews only a section of the garment to speed the production process. See *section work*. *Ch 8*

Planogram A computer-generated floor plan that shows the selling floor with merchandise in the best position. *Ch 20*

Pop-up shop A promotion in which an empty retail location in a major city or mall opens for a few days to sell a specific product and then disappears. *Ch 19*

Power center or strip An outdoor shopping center that offers three or four category killers together. *Ch 19*

Premiums A gift-with-purchase offered by a manufacturer to promote a product. *Ch 14*

Prêt-à-porter (pronounced "preht-ah-por-TAY") A French term meaning ready-to-wear. *Ch 16*

Price zone A series of somewhat contiguous price lines that appeal to specific target groups of customers. *Ch 9*

Primary level Composed of the growers and producers of the raw materials of fashion—the fiber, fabric, leather, and fur producers who function in the raw materials market. *Ch 5*

Primary suppliers Producers of fibers, textile fabrics, finished leathers, and furs. *Ch 6*

Private label *or* **store brand** Merchandise that meets standards specified by a retail firm and that belongs to it exclusively. Primarily used to insure consistent quality of product as well as to meet price competition. *Ch 8*

Product development team A small group within a large apparel manufacturing firm that is responsible for one particular product line or brand. Usually consists of at least a merchandiser, designer, and product manager. *Ch 8*

Product manager See *specification manager.*

Profit The amount of money a business earns in excess of its expenses; net income. *Ch 5*

Prophetic styles Particularly interesting new styles that are still in the introductory phase of their fashion cycles. *Ch 4*

Protectionism An economic and political doctrine that seeks to exclude or limit foreign goods. *Ch 17*

Psychographics Studies that develop fuller, more personal portraits of potential customers, including personality, attitude, interest, personal opinions, and actual product benefits desired. *Ch 3*

Public relations Works to improve a client's public image and may develop long-range plans and directions for this purpose. *Ch 20*

Publicity The mention of a firm, brand, product, or person in some form of media. *Ch 20*

Purchasing power The value of the dollar as it relates to the amount of goods or services it will buy. A decline in purchasing power is caused by inflation. *Ch 3*

Quality Assurance (QA) Inspection of each component of a garment to ensure that it meets the standards established for it. *Ch 8*

Quick Response (QR) A strategy used by manufacturers to shorten the ordering cycle to compete with foreign imports. *Ch 8*

Quick Response (QR) codes Black-and-white boxes of pixels that encode links and information. These codes are often included in advertisements and link to a company's website or product information. *Ch 20*

Rack trade Refers to manufacturers of belts sold as separate fashion accessory items. *Ch 13*

Radio frequency identification (RFID) Electronic tags used for storing data; it includes a unique serial number that allows the tracking of products, cartons, containers, and individual items as they move through the supply chain. They hold more data than bar codes and can be read many times faster. *Ch 8*

Ramie A minor natural fiber from a woody-leafed Asian plant grown mostly in China. *Ch 6*

Readers Nonprescription reading glasses. *Ch 13*

Ready-to-wear (RTW) Apparel made in factories to standard size measurements. *Ch 9*

Recession A low point in a business cycle, when money and credit become scarce and unemployment is high. *Ch 3*

Regional mall An indoor shopping center with a trading area of at least a five-mile radius. It usually contains at least two anchor department stores, as well as many specialty stores and a food court or restaurants. *Ch 19*

Regular tanneries Those companies that purchase and process hides and skins to the specifications of converters but are not involved in the sales of the finished products. *Ch 7*

Resident buying office An old term used to describe a service organization located in a major market area that provides market information and representation to its noncompeting client stores. See *buying, merchandising, and product development office. Ch 20*

Retail level The ultimate distribution-level outlets for fashion goods directly to the consumer. *Ch 5*

Rise (stage) See *fashion cycle.*

Royalty fee Percentage of licensee sales paid to the licensor. See also *licensing. Ch 5*

Rubber-banding Cosmetic products that can be returned to the manufacturer and replaced with other products, if not sold within a specified period of time. *Ch 14*

Sales representatives Company representatives who exhibit merchandise to potential customers. *Ch 16*

Sample hand The designer's assistant who sews the sample garment. *Ch 8*

Secondary level Composed of industries—manufacturers and contractors—that produce the semifinished or finished fashion goods from the materials supplied by the primary level. *Ch 5*

Section work The division of labor in apparel manufacturing whereby each sewing-machine operator sews only a certain section of the garment, such as a sleeve or hem. *Ch 8*

Sensory retailing In-store stimulation of all the customer's senses, using pleasant aromas, mood music, dramatic lighting. *Ch 19*

Shelter magazines Home-decorating magazines. *Ch 20*

Shopping center A coordinated group of retail stores, plus a parking area. *Ch 19*

Short-run fashion A fashion that takes fewer seasons to complete its cycle than what might be considered its average life expectancy. *Ch 2*

Showcase store A manufacturer's or designer's store that sells merchandise at the introductory and early-rise stages of the fashion cycle. *Ch 18*

Showrooming A consumer who researches a product in the brick-and-mortar store first and then buys it online. *Chs 15 and 18*

Silhouette The overall outline or contour of a costume. Also frequently referred to as "shape" or "form." *Ch 2*

Skins Animal skins that weigh 15 pounds or less when shipped to a tannery. *Ch 7*

Sloping See *grading.*

Slop shops A name associated with the first shops offering men's ready-to-wear in this country. Garments lacked careful fit and detail work found in custom-tailored clothing of the period. *Ch 10*

Small leather goods A category that includes wallets, key cases and chains, jewelry cases, briefcases, and carrying cases for cell phones and laptop computers. *Ch 13*

Social media Forms of electronic communication in which users create online communities and share information, including photos, videos, and messages. *Chs 4, 9, and 10*

Spa Formerly "health spa," now a service business offering a wide variety of beauty treatments, including massages, manicures, pedicures, waxings, facials, aromatherapy, and thalassotherapy. *Ch 14*

Specialty retailers Stores that offer limited lines of related merchandise targeted to a more specific customer. *Ch 18*

Specialty store Stores that carry a limited line of merchandise, whether it is clothing, accessories, or furniture. *Ch 18*

Specification buying A type of purchasing that is done to the store's rather than to the manufacturer's standards. See also *private label. Chs 8 and 17*

Specification manager Manager who oversees the purchasing and manufacturing process for a private label. Also called "product manager." *Ch 8*

Spinnerette A mechanical device through which a thick liquid base is forced to produce fibers of varying lengths. *Ch 6*

Sportswear Casual wear that includes unconstructed jackets, knit and woven sports shirts, slacks, and leisure attire. *Chs 4, 9, and 10*

Spreader A laying-up machine that carries material along a guide on either side of a cutting table, spreading the material evenly, layer upon layer. *Ch 8*

Sterling silver A term used for jewelry and flatware with at least 92.5 parts of silver; the remaining 7.5 parts are usually copper. *Ch 13*

Strategic alliance A form of business combination in which a retailer and a manufacturer join forces to operate more efficiently, thus improving profits for both companies, while offering customers a better product at a lower price. *Ch 19*

Style A characteristic or distinctive mode of presentation or conceptualization in a particular field. In apparel, style is the characteristic or distinctive appearance of a garment, the combination of features that makes it different from other garments. *Ch 2*

Style number The number manufacturers and retailers assigned to a design. The number identifies the product for manufacturing, ordering, and selling. *Ch 2*

Stylist-designer A person who adapts or changes the successful designs of others. *Ch 8*

Suit separates (menswear) Sports jacket and trousers worn much as the tailored suit used to be. *Ch 10*

Sumptuary laws Laws regulating consumer purchases, for example, dress, on religious or moral grounds. *Ch 4*

Superregional mall Larger than a regional mall, often consisting of up to one million square feet, with at least three department or major chain stores, and one hundred to three hundred specialty stores. Their trading area is a distance up to one-hour's driving time away. *Ch 19*

Supply chain management (SCM) Allows companies to share forecasting, point-of-sale data, inventory information, and the supply and demand for materials or products. *Ch 8*

Sustainable use An environmental program that encourages land owners to preserve animal young and habitats in return for the right to use a percentage of the grown animals. *Ch 7*

Tabletop (goods) Categories of merchandise commonly found on tabletops, including dinnerware, glassware, flatware, hollowware, and giftware. *Ch 15*

Tailored-clothing firms Those menswear firms that produce structured or semistructured suits, overcoats, topcoats, sportcoats, and or separate trousers in which a specific number of hand-tailoring operations are required. *Ch 10*

Tanning The process of transforming animal skins into leather. *Ch 7*

Target market A specific group of potential customers that manufacturers and retailers are attempting to turn into regular customers. *Ch 3*

Tariff A fee assessed by a government on certain goods that it wishes to restrict or limit. *Ch 17*

Tariff-rate quota A set limit after which a higher duty is charged on goods entering the country. *Ch 17*

Taste The recognition of what is and is not attractive and appropriate. Good taste in fashion means sensitivity not only to what is artistic, but to these considerations as well. *Ch 2*

Textile fabric Cloth or material made from fibers by weaving, knitting, braiding, felting, crocheting, knotting, laminating, or bonding. *Ch 6*

Textile converter See *converter*.

Texture The look and feel of material, woven or unwoven. *Ch 2*

Thalassotherapy A skin treatment involving sea water, seaweed, or sea algae. *Ch 14*

Trade association Professional organizations for manufacturers or sales representatives. *Ch 16*

Trade deficit When the value of goods that a country imports exceeds the value of its exports. *Ch 17*

Trade publications Newspapers or magazines published specifically for professionals in a special field, such as fashion. *Ch 20*

Trade shows Periodic merchandise exhibits staged in various regional trading areas around the country by groups of producers and their sales representatives for the specific purpose of making sales of their products to retailers in that area. *Ch 16*

Trade surplus When a country's exports exceed its imports. *Ch 17*

Trend A general direction or movement. See also *fashion trend*. *Ch 2*

Trimmings All the materials—excluding the fabric—used in the construction of a garment; including braid, bows, buckles, buttons, elastic, interfacing, padding, self-belts, thread, zippers, etc. *Ch 6*

Trunk show A form of pretesting that involves a designer or manufacturer sending a representative to a store with samples of the current line, and exhibiting those samples to customers at scheduled, announced showings. *Ch 9*

Universal Product Code (UPC) The most widely accepted of a number of bar codes used for automatic identification of items scanned at retail cash registers. *Ch 8*

Upward-flow theory The theory of fashion adoption that holds that the young—particularly those of low-income families as well as those of higher income who adopt low-income lifestyles—are quicker than any other social group to create or adopt new and different fashions. *Ch 4*

Vermeil (pronounced "vur-MAY") A composite of gold over sterling silver. *Ch 13*

Vertical growth When a company expands on a different level than its original one. *Ch 5*

Vertical mall An indoor, multistory shopping center, taller than it is wide. *Ch 19*

Visual merchandising Everything visual that is done to, with, or for a product and its surroundings to encourage its sale. This includes display, store layout, and store decor. *Ch 20*

Wedding or bridal registry A store's list of a bridal couple's desired merchandise, upon which gift-givers' selections are recorded as they are purchased. Today it is often called merely a "gift registry" and is computerized. *Ch 15*

Wicking The ability of a fabric to carry the moisture of perspiration away from the skin. *Ch 12*

Yarn A continuous thread formed by spinning or twisting fibers together. *Ch 6*

Yarn-dyed Refers to dyeing yarns before they are woven or knitted; this process results in deep, rich colors. See also *piece-dyed*. *Ch 6*

REFERENCES

Chapter 1

Regina Lee Blaszczyk, ed., *Producing Fashion: Commerce, Culture, and Consumers* (Philadelphia: University of Pennsylvania Press, 2007).

Amy Fine Collins, "The Lady, the List, the Legacy," *Vanity Fair*, April 2004, pp. 260–274, 328–333.

Kathleen Craughwell-Varda, *Looking for Jackie: American Fashion Icons* (New York: Hearst, 1999).

Jane Farrell-Beck and Jean Parsons, *20th-Century Dress in the United States* (New York: Fairchild, 2007).

Jenna Weissman Joselit, *A Perfect Fit: Clothes, Character, and the Promise of America* (New York: Holt, 2002).

Eleanor Lambert, *Ultimate Style: The Best of the Best Dressed List* (New York: Assouline, 2004).

Valerie Bernham Oliver, *Fashion and Costume in American Popular Culture: A Reference Guide* (Westport, CT: Greenwood, 1996).

Caroline Rennolds Milbank, *New York Fashion: The Evolution of American Style* (New York: Abrams, 1996).

Thomas C. Reeves, *Twentieth-Century America: A Brief History* (New York: Oxford University Press, 2000).

Valerie Steele, *Fifty Years of Fashion: New Look to Now* (New Haven, CT: Yale University Press, 1997).

Valerie Steele, *Women of Fashion: Twentieth-Century Designers* (New York: Rizzoli, 1991).

FASHION FOCUS

John Heilpern, "Rucci's Rule," *Vanity Fair*, September 2011, p. 133.

Marc Karimzadeh, "Cutting His Own Way," *Women's Wear Daily*, December 19, 2011, p. 4.

The Fashion Center Business Improvement District, "Walk of Fame: Ralph Rucci," fashioncenter.com/fashion/fashion-attractions/the-walk-of-fame. Accessed March 2013.

THEN AND NOW

Amy Fine Collins, "Toujours Couture," *Vanity Fair*, September 2009, pp. 318, 321–322, 330.

Polly Guerin, "Couture Houses, Hoity Style Masters," PollyTalk.com, May 19, 2012, pp. 1–2.

Miles Socha, "Couture's Booming Markets," *Women's Wear Daily*, July 2, 2012, pp. 1, 7.

Chapter 2

1. George P. Fox, *Fashion: The Power That Influences the World. The Philosophy of Ancient and Modern Dress and Fashion* (London: Lange and Hellman, Printers & Stereotypers, 1850–1860–1872), Introduction, p. 20.
2. Brenda Polan and Roger Terdre, *The Great Fashion Designers* (London: Berg Publishers, 2009), p. 225.

3. Merriam-Webster, "Fashion," merriam-webster.com/dictionary/fashion. Accessed February 2013.
4. Miles Socha, "Museums Get Fashionable," *Women's Wear Daily*, December 30, 2011, pp. 10–11.
5. Ibid.
6. Peter F. Drucker, *Management Tasks, Responsibilities, Practices* (New York: Harper & Row, 1973), pp. 64–65.
7. Paul H. Nystrom, *Economics of Fashion* (New York: The Ronald Press, 1928), pp. 3–7; and *Fashion Merchandising* (New York: The Ronald Press, 1932), pp. 33–34.
8. Ibid., p. 7.
9. James Laver, *Taste and Fashion*, rev. ed. (London: George C. Harrop & Co., Ltd., 1946), p. 202.
10. Ruth La Ferla, "What They Design Real Women Wear," the *New York Times*, February 8, 2007, p. G1.
11. Irma Zandl, "How to Separate Trends from Fads," *Brandweek Online*, October 23, 2000.
12. Agnes Brooke Young, *Recurring Cycles of Fashion: 1760–1937* (New York: Harper & Brothers, 1937; reprint, New York: Cooper Square Publishers, Inc., 1966), p. 30.
13. "The Power of Clothing—Making the World a Better Place," uniqlo.com, August 16, 2011.
14. Maryam Banikarim, "Seeing Shades in Green Consumers," *Adweek*, April 19, 2010, p. 18. Full text copyright © 2010 Nielson Business Media, Inc.
15. Evan Clark, "Sustainable Apparel Coalition Created," *Women's Wear Daily*, March 1, 2011, p. 7b.
16. Sustainable Apparel Coalition, "About Us," apparelcoalition.org/higgoverview/. Accessed March 2013.

FASHION FOCUS

Elisa Lipsky-Karasz, "American Idol," *Harper's Bazaar*, June 2011, pp. 142–47.

Lisa Lockwood, "Designer's Shares Leap on Wall Street Debut," *Women's Wear Daily*, December 16, 2011, p. 4.

"Q & A: Michael Kors," *Women's Wear Daily*, March 9, 2011, p. 6.

THEN AND NOW

Thomas Lee, "Ralph Lauren: Très Geek," StarTribune.com, January 17, 2012, pp. 1–2.

Stephanie Schomer, "The Prince of Polo," FastCompany.com, September 2011, pp. 74–81.

Chapter 3

1. Michael Weiss, *The Clustered World* (New York: Little, Brown. 2000), c. 1.
2. SBI Business Insights, "U.S. Framework and VALS Types," strategicbusinessinsights.com/vals/ustypes.shtml. Accessed September 2012.

3. Ibid.

4. Ibid.

5. Quentin Bell, *On Human Finery* (London: Hogarth Press, 1947), p. 72.

6. Shobhana Chandra, "Consumer Spending in U.S. Rose in December as Incomes Surged," *Bloomberg*, January 31, 2013, bloomberg.com/news/2013-01-31/consumer-spending-in-u-s-climbed-in-december-as-incomes-surged.html. Accessed February 2013.

7. Experian, "The 2011 Discretionary Spend Report," experian.com/assets/.../2011-discretionary-spend-report.pdf. Accessed September 2012.

8. U.S. Census Bureau, "Income, Poverty and Health Insurance Coverage in the United States: 2011," September 12, 2012, census.gov/newsroom/releases/archives/income_wealth/cb12-172.html. Accessed February 2013.

9. *Webster's Tenth New Collegiate Dictionary* (Springfield, MA: Merriam-Webster, 1998).

10. Shobhana Chandra, "Consumer Spending in U.S. Rose in December as Incomes Surged," *Bloomberg*, January 31, 2013, bloomberg.com/news/2013-01-31/consumer-spending-in-u-s-climbed-in-december-as-incomes-surged.html. Accessed February 2013.

11. U.S. Census Bureau, "U.S. Census Bureau Projections Show a Slower Growing, Older, More Diverse Nation a Half Century from Now," December 12, 2012, census.gov/newsroom/releases/archives/population/cb12-243.html. Accessed March 2013.

12. Cecil Beaton, *The Glass of Fashion* (New York: Doubleday, 1954), pp. 335, 379–381.

13. U.S. Census Bureau, "The Two or More Races Population: 2010," September 2012, census.gov/prod/cen2010/briefs/c2010br-13.pdf. Accessed Feburary 2013.

14. Jennifer Steinhauer, "A Minority Market with Major Sales," *New York Times*, July 2, 1997, p. D1.

15. U.S. Census Bureau, "The Hispanic Population: 2010," May 2011, census.gov/prod/cen2010/briefs/c2010br-04.pdf. Accessed September 2012.

16. U.S. Census Bureau, "Overview of Race and Hispanic Origin: 2010," 2010 Census Briefs, March 2011, census.gov/prod/cen2010/briefs/c2010br-02.pdf. Accessed February 2013.

17. U.S. Census Bureau, "The Black Population: 2010," March 2012, census.gov/prod/cen2010/briefs/c2010br-06.pdf. Accessed February 2013.

18. Ibid.

19. U.S. Census Bureau, "The Asian Population: 2010," March 2012, census.gov/prod/cen2010/briefs/c2010br-06.pdf. Accessed February 2013.

20. Ibid.

21. U.S. Census Bureau, "Women's History Month: March 2011," January 26, 2011, census.gov/newsroom/releases/archives/facts_for_features_special_editions/cb11-ff04.html. Accessed September 2012.

22. Ibid.

23. Edward Sapir, "Fashion," *Encyclopedia of the Social Sciences*, vol. 6 (London: Macmillan, 1931), p. 140.

24. Bell, *On Human Finery*, p. 72.

25. Lisa Lockwood, "IMG Fashion, Rightster Team to Live-Stream Runway Shows," *WWD*, February 4, 2013, wwd.com/media-news/fashion-memopad/img-fashion-rightster-team-to-live-stream-runway-shows-6690040. Accessed February 2013.

26. Marisa Meltzer, "Thrill of the Haul," *Slate*, March 22, 2010, slate.com/id/2248295. Accessed February 2013.

27. Rachel Dardis, "The Power of Fashion," *Proceedings of the Twentieth Annual Conference, College Teachers of Textiles and Clothing, Eastern Region* (New York, 1966), pp. 16–17.

28. Paul H. Nystrom, *Economics of Fashion* (New York: Ronald Press, 1928), pp. 66–81.

FASHION FOCUS

Samantha Conti, "Hilfiger Road Trip Beginning at Oxford," *Women's Wear Daily*, p. 9.

Sharon Edelson, "Hilfiger's New House: Fifth Avenue Flagship A Big Move for Tommy," *Women's Wear Daily*, pp. 1, 20–21.

Bridget Foley, "Tommy at the Top," *Women's Wear Daily*, June 4, 2012, pp. 1, 4–5.

Lisa Lockwood, "Hilfiger's Silver Jubilee," *Women's Wear Daily*, July 28, 2010, p. 4.

THEN AND NOW

Samantha Conti, "Blow Archive Headed to Auction," *Women's Wear Daily*, May 18, 2010.

Samantha Conti, "Blow After Blow," *Women's Wear Daily*, November 11, 2010, p. 4.

Samantha Conti, "Blow's Wardrobe Sold," *Women's Wear Daily*, June 15, 2010, p. 3.

Amy Larocca, "The Sad Hatter," New York, July 23, 2007, pp. 39, 42.

J. J. Martin, "Why Fashion Needs Eccentrics," *Harper's Bazaar*, June 2007, pp. 47–51.

Chapter 4

1. James Laver, *Taste and Fashion*, rev. ed. (London: George G. Harrop, 1946), p. 52.

2. Thad Reuter, "E-Retail Spending to Increase 62% by 2016," *Internet Retailer*, internetretailer.com/2012/02/27/e-retail-spending-increase-45-2016. Accessed November 2012.

3. United States Department of Research, dol.gov/equalpay/#.UJLlULsv_M4. Accessed November 2012.

4. Pearl Binder, *Muffs and Morals* (London: George G. Harrop, 1953), pp. 162–164.

5. Elisabeth McClellan, *History of American Costume* (New York: Tudor Publishing, 1969), p. 82.

6. John Taylor, *It's a Small, Medium, and Outsize World* (London: Hugh Evelyn, 1966), p. 39.

7. *PR Newswire*, "Classroom School Uniforms Unveils 2011 School Uniform Survey" (July 25, 2011), prnewswire.com/news-releases/classroom-school-uniforms-unveils-2011-school-uniform-survey-126112303.html. Accessed March 2013.

8. Laver, *Taste and Fashion*, p. 201.

9. Agnes Brooke Young, *Recurring Cycles of Fashion: 1760–1937* (New York: Harper & Brothers, 1937; reprint New York: Cooper Square, 1966), p. 30.

10. A. L. Kroeber, "On the Principles of Order in Civilizations as Exemplified by Change in Fashion," *American Anthropologist*, vol. 21, July–September 1919, pp. 235–263.

11. Madge Garland, *The Changing Form of Fashion* (New York: Praeger, 1971), p. 11.

12. J. C. Flügel, *The Psychology of Clothes* (New York: International Universities Press, 1966), p. 163.

13. Laver, *Taste and Fashion*, p. 200.

14. Ibid., p. 201.

15. Cate T. Corcoran, "Reinventing Fashion via Crowdsourcing," *Women's Wear Daily*, July 26, 2010, p. 20, wwd.com/markets-news/ready-to-wear-sportswear/reinventing-fashion-via-crowdsourcing-3193600/print-preview/. Accessed March 2013.

16. Gabriel Tarde, *The Laws of Imitation* (New York: Henry Holt, 1903), p. 221.

17. Georg Simmel, "Fashion," *American Journal of Sociology*, vol. 62, May 1957, p. 545.

18. Charles W. King, "Fashion Adoption: A Rebuttal to the Trickle-Down Theory," *Proceedings of the Winter Conference* (New York: American Marketing Association, 1963), pp. 114–115.

19. Dwight E. Robinson, "The Economics of Fashion Demand," *The Quarterly Journal of Economics*, vol. 75, August 1961, p. 383.

20. King, "Fashion Adoption," pp. 114–115.

21. Quentin Bell, *On Human Finery* (London: Hogarth Press, 1947), p. 46.

22. Flügel, *Psychology of Clothes*, p. 140.

23. King, "Fashion Adoption," p. 124.

24. Flügel, *Psychology of Clothes*, p. 140.

25. Edward Sapir, "Fashion," *Encyclopedia of the Social Sciences*, vol. 6 (London: Macmillan, 1931), p. 140.

26. Simmel, "Fashion," pp. 543–544.

27. Flügel, *Psychology of Clothes*, p. 140.

28. Sapir, "Fashion," p. 140.

FASHION FOCUS

"Designer Inspirations," *Women's Wear Daily*, August 29, 2012, pp. 4–5.

THEN AND NOW

Bob Colacello, "Here's to the Ladies," *Vanity Fair*, February 2012, pp. 127, 130, 135, 140–141.

Christine Whitney, "Secrets of Today's 20 Most Stylish Women," *Harper's Bazaar*, pp. 86–87.

Chapter 5

1. U.S. Bureau of Labor Statistics, "Apparel Manufacturing: NAICS 315," bls.gov/iag/tgs/iag315.htm#about. Accessed February 2013.

2. Stephanie Rosenbloom, "Gap Acquires Athleta for $150 Million," *New York Times*, September 22, 2008, p. C13.

3. John Reynolds, "The Economic Impact of Franchising," *Franchising World*, June 2011, p. 44.

4. EPM Communications, "Fashion Licensing Shows Strongest Growth of Any Property Type," *The Licensing Letter*, June 2012, epmcom.com/public/Fashion_Licensing_Shows_Strongest_Growth_of_Any_PropertyType.cfm. Accessed February 2013.

5. EPM Communications, Inc., *International Licensing: A Status Report*, November 2012.

6. EPM Communications, Inc., "Disney Consumer Products Division Outperforms Company As a Whole," epmcom.com/public/TLLDA_Disney_Consumer_Products_Division_Outperforms_Company_As_A_Whole.cfm. Accessed February 2013.

7. Tony Lisanti, "Brand Licensing at Its Best: The Top 125 Global Licensors Report Reveals Continued Growth and Consumer Demand for Licensed Merchandise From Entertainment to Fashion to Corporate Brands," *License*, May 2011, p. 8. Gale Power Search. Web. 4 Sep. 2011.

8. Regina Molaro "Dressed for Success," *License! Global Supplement*, February 2007, vol. 10, p. 6.

9. Quentin Bell, *On Human Finery* (London: Hogarth Press, 1947), pp. 48–49.

10. Dwight E. Robinson, "Fashion Theory and Product Design," *Harvard Business Review*, vol. 36, November–December 1958, p. 129.

FASHION FOCUS

"Best British Fashion Designers of 2011," *BioSpectrum Asia*, December 29, 2011. Academic One File. Web. September 2, 2012.

Samantha Conti, "Burton Wins Top British Award," *Women's Wear Daily*, November 29, 2011, p. 2.

Samantha Conti, "McQueen Sets Retail Push," *Women's Wear Daily*, June 21, 2012, p. 1.

Miles Socha, "Meet Sarah Burton, McQueen's New Master," *Women's Wear Daily*, September 28, 2010, pp. 1, 7.

THEN AND NOW

Lisa Lockwood, "The New CEO: What It Takes In Today's World," *Women's Wear Daily*, July 23, 2012, pp. 1, 6–7.

Chapter 6

1. Jane Dorner, *Fashion in the Forties and Fifties* (New Rochelle, NY: Arlington House, 1975), p. 38.

2. "Overview: Cotton and Wool," United States Department of Agriculture Economic Research Service, ers.usda.gov/topics/crops/cotton-wool.aspx. Accessed November 2, 2012.

3. Ibid.

4. Faye Musselman, "Fabric Vendors are High on Hemp in Home Fashions," *Home Furnishing News*, May 7, 2001, p. 23.

5. "Fast Facts About American Wool," American Sheep Industry, Inc., April 2011.

6. American Fiber Manufacturers Association, fibersource.com/afma/afma.htm. Accessed November 2012.

7. Robert S. Reichard, "A First Look at 2013," *Textile World,* January/February 2013, textileworld.com/Articles/2013/ January/January_February_issue/Departments/ BusinessandFinancial.html. Accessed February 2013.

8. "Textiles," Environmental Protection Agency, July 26, 2011, epa.gov/osw/conserve/materials/textiles.htm. Accessed September 10, 2011.

9. Ibid.

10. Cotton Incorporated, "Cotton From Blue to Green," cottonfrombluetogreen.org. Accessed November 2012.

11. Ibid.

12. NatureWorks, natureworksllc.com/The-Ingeo-Journey/ Eco-Profile-and-LCA/Eco-Profile. Accessed February 2013.

13. Court Williams, "Second Nature," *Women's Wear Daily,* April 10, 2007.

14. Kristi Ellis, "U.S. Textile, Apparel Imports Down in June," *Women's Wear Daily,* August 12, 2011.

15. Kristi Ellis, "U.S. Mills Seeing CAFTA Benefits," *Women's Wear Daily,* August 15, 2011.

16. Kristi Ellis, "WWD Magic Preview: Textiles Key to National Export Initiative," *Women's Wear Daily,* August 9, 2011.

17. National Council of Textile Organizations (NCTO), U.S. Textile Industries, ncto.org/ustextiles/index.asp. Accessed February 2013.

18. Katya Foreman and Joelle Diderich, "Buyers Turn to Cotton Alternatives," *Women's Wear Daily,* February 22, 2011.

19. Bureau of Consumer Protection Business Center, "Clothes Captioning: Complying with the Care Labeling Rule," business.ftc.gov/documents/bus50-clothes-captioning- complying-care-labeling-rule. Accessed February 2013.

20. Fibre2Fashion, "ShanghaiTex 2013 to Have Digital Print- ing Machinery Zone," November 1, 2012, fibre2fashion .com/news/textilenews/newsdetails.aspx?news_ id=117614. Accessed February 2013.

21. Arthur Friedman, "New Focus on Next Gen Fabrics," *Women's Wear Daily,* August 1, 2011.

22. Ibid.

FASHION FOCUS

Columbia Sportswear Company, "Columbia Milestones," columbia.com/history/About_Us_History,default,pg. html. Accessed March 2013.

Jordan K. Speer, "Apparel's 2012 Top Innovators," *Apparel,* May 2012, pp. 14–15.

THEN AND NOW

"Denim Special," *Bazaar,* pp. 111–113, 115.

Christina Binkley, "How Can Jeans Cost $300?" *The Wall Street Journal,* July 7, 2011, pp. D1–D2.

Kim Friday, "Denim Through the Decades," *Women's Wear Daily,* September 7, 2012, p. 12.

Arnold J. Karr, "Jeans: From Workwear to Everywhere," *Women's Wear Daily,* September 7, 2012.

Chapter 7

1. Lynn M. Pearce, ed., "SIC 3111: Leather Tanning and Fin- ishing," *Encyclopedia of American Industries* (Gale, 2011), pp. 675–679.

2. IBISWorld, "Leather Tanning & Finishing in the U.S. Market Research Report, NAICS 31611," August 2012, ibisworld.com/industry/default.aspx?indid=367. Accessed February 2013.

3. ICTMN, "Reopened Ponca Tannery Revives 'Brain Tan- ning' Craft," April 4, 2011, indiancountrytodaymedia network.com/article/reopened-ponca-tannery-revives- brain-tanning-craft-26348. Accessed February 2013.

4. APLF, "About Us," aplf.com/AboutUs/tabid/1664/ language/en-US/Default.aspx. Accessed February 2013.

5. U.S. Hide, Skin and Leather Association, "Trade Issues," ushsla.org/ht/d/sp/i/26143/pid/26143. Accessed Febru- ary 2013.

6. Ibid.

7. The Fur Information Council of America, "FICA Facts," fur.org/fica-facts/. Accessed February 2013.

8. Fur Information Council of America, "New Vogue Fur Campaign Celebrates the Bright Future of Fur," October 23, 2012, fur.org/wp-content/uploads/New-Vogue-Fur- Campaign-Celebrates-the-Bright-Future-of-FurFINAL. pdf?995785. Accessed February 2013.

9. Julie Creswell, "Real Fur, Masquerading as Faux," *The New York Times,* March 19, 2013, nytimes. com/2013/03/20/business/faux-fur-case-settled-by- neiman-marcus-and-2-other-retailers.html. Accessed March 2013.

10. American Legend Cooperative, "About ALC," alcbusiness.com/corporate/. Accessed February 2013.

11. Fur Council of Canada, "Tips on Buying Fur," furfash- ions.com/buying_fur.aspx. Accessed February 2013.

12. Fur Information Council of America, fur.org. Accessed January 2013.

13. WeAreFur.com, "Markets," wearefur.com/about-fur/fur- facts. Accessed February 2013.

14. WeAreFur.com, "New European Textile Labelling Regula- tions," wearefur.com/our-trade/regulation. Accessed February 2013.

FASHION FOCUS

"Fur Now," *Women's Wear Daily,* January 12, 2012, pp. 1, 5.

"Furry Tale," *Women's Wear Daily,* March 11, 2011, pp. 1, 3, 5.

Brian Dunn, "Fur Price Hikes Trigger Caution," *Women's Wear Daily,* May 10, 2011, p. 5.

"The Runway Report," *Women's Wear Daily,* February 18, 2011, p. 3.

"The Runway Report," *Women's Wear Daily,* February 22, 2011, p. 3.

Hailey Branson-Potts, "West Hollywood Sheds Fur Sales," *Los Angeles Times,* September 21, 2011, articles.latimes. com/2011/sep/21/local/la-me-0921-fur-ban-20110921. Accessed March 2013.

Alyssa Giacobbe, "Fur is Flying Again," *New York,* January 16–23, 2012, pp. 57–64.

International Fur Trade Federation "Fashion, Fur, and the Next Generation," *Women's Wear Daily Collections,* pp. 1, 3.

Reuters, "West Hollywood Approves First Fur Ban in U.S.," baltimoresun.com, November 9, 2011.

THEN AND NOW

Loewe, "Heritage," loewe.com/us_en/heritage.html. Accessed March 2013.

Miles Socha (with contributions from Katya Foreman), "Loewe's Leather Focus," *Women's Wear Daily,* p. 1.

Chapter 8

1. Muditha M. Senanayake and Trevor J. Little, "'Measures' for New Product Development," *Journal of Textile and Apparel/Technology and Management,* vol. 1, no. 3, Spring 2001, p. 9.

2. Valerie Seckler, "NPD: National Brand Shoppers Outspend Private Label Fans," *WWD Infotracs* (Fashion Trends), February 28, 2006, p. 23.

3. Ibid.

4. Just-style.com, "Analysis: Private Labels Go Beyond the Stodgy Stage," May 9, 2007, just-style.com/comment/private-labels-go-beyond-the-stodgy-stage_id97261.aspx. Accessed February 2013.

5. "U.S. Retailers Rely on Exclusive Lines for Growth," *Apparel Online,* September 16, 2010, apparelresources. com/new/next.asp?cod=W&msg=11216. Accessed February 2012.

6. Marty Brochstein, "A Look at the Corporate Brand Sector," International Licensing Industry Merchandisers' Association Blog, October 14, 2011, licensing.org/news/blog/a-look-at-the-corporate-brand-sector/. Accessed September 2012.

7. Luisa Zargani, "Artistic License: The Valentino Name Has Graced Products Ranging from Furniture to Footwear," *Women's Wear Daily,* June 27, 2007, p. 22S.

8. Marty Brochstein, "A Look at the Corporate Brand Sector," International Licensing Industry Merchandisers' Association Blog, October 14, 2011, licensing.org/news/blog/a-look-at-the-corporate-brand-sector/. Accessed February 2012.

9. John Metzger, "Credit Insurance for Non-Factored Firms," *The Fashion Manuscript,* August 1997, p. 86.

10. Just-Style.com, "Coping with the High Cost of Raw Materials," May 2011, General OneFile. Web. Accessed September 2012.

11. Deena M. Amato-McCoy, "PLM: Streamlining for Bottom-Line Results: PLM Is Key to Successful, Streamlined, and Cost-Effective Production and Distribution for Firms Including Under Armour, Vesi Inc., Frazier Clothing Co., SA VA and More," *Apparel,* vol. 36, July 2011, General OneFile. Web. Accessed September 2012.

12. "RFID," *PC Magazine,* pcmag.com/encyclopedia_term/0,1237,t=RFID&i=50512,00.asp. Accessed February 2013.

FASHION FOCUS

"Juicy Taps New Chief," *Women's Wear Daily,* pp. 1, 10.

Evan Clark, "When Do Designers Reach the Next level?," *Women's Wear Daily,* February 13, 2012, pp. 1, 15, 16.

THEN AND NOW

Sara Bauknecht, "Clothing designers appeal to women's ego with vanity sizing," *Chicago Sun-Times,* April 1, 2012, suntimes.com/lifestyles/10515544-423/clothing-designers-appeal-to-womens-ego-with-vanity-sizing.html. Accessed March 2013.

Greg Lamm, "Will Those Pants Fit? New Technology at the Mall Aims to Help You Find Out," *Puget Sound Business Journal,* March 1, 2012, bizjournals.com/seattle/news/2012/03/01/will-those-pants-fit-new-technology.html. Accessed March 2013.

Ed Owen, "Tesco Launches Virtual 3D Fitting room," *BrandRepublic,* February 29, 2012, brandrepublic.com/news/1119577/. Accessed March 2013.

Marisa Peñaloza, "From Body Scan To Body Form: Sizing A Clothing Line," NPR, December 11, 2011, npr.org/2011/12/11/143004761/from-body-scan-to-body-form-sizing-a-clothing-line. Accessed March 2013.

Chapter 9

1. Emily Jane Fox, "Target Zeroes in on Exercise Fanatics," CNN Money.com, October 12, 2012, money.cnn.com/2012/10/12/news/companies/target-exercise-c9/index.html. Accessed February 2013.

2. Abram Brown, "Lululemon: Shapely Fit for a Growth Portfolio; Stock Trading at All-Time High," Forbes.com, March 23, 2012, forbes.com/sites/abrambrown/2012/03/23/lululemon-shapely-fit-for-a-growth-portfolio-stock-trading-at-all-time-high/. Accessed February 2013.

3. Christopher Murther, "Ski Fashion Trends for Winter 2013," *Boston Globe,* November 4, 2012, bostonglobe.com/lifestyle/travel/2012/11/03/ski-fashion-trends-for-winter/ofQV4pLvTEanv2jDWJUoCP/story.html. Accessed February 2013.

4. Kerry Medina, "The Knot.com and WeddingChannel.com Announce 2011 Wedding Statistics," TravelPulse, March 21, 2012, travelpulse.com/theknotcom-weddingchannelcom-announce-2011-wedding-statistics.html. Accessed February 2013.

5. Cecily Hall, "For Richer or Poorer," *Women's Wear Daily,* June 21, 2007, p. 12.

6. Destination Maternity Corporation, May 31, 2011.

7. Whitney Beckett, "Retail Sales of Licensed Merchandise Remain Stable at $71.25 Billion; DTR, 'Share-of-Mind' Key Issues," *The Licensing Letter,* January 1, 2007, p. 1.

FASHION FOCUS

"Brand New Bag," *Women's Wear Daily,* June 15, 2011, p. 1.

"Power of Two," *Women's Wear Daily,* June 5, 2012, p. 1.

"Sister Acts: Mister Blasberg's Best Dressed List: The Chicest Ladies of Summer 2011 Edition," *Harper's Bazaar,* harpersbazaar.com/fashion/fashion-articles/best-dressed-celebrities-090211#slide-9. Accessed March 2013.

Bridget Foley, "Scissor Sisters," *Women's Wear Daily,* May 31, 2011, pp. 8–10.

Marc Karimzadeh, "Keeping It Real," *Women's Wear Daily,* May 31, 2011, p. 12.

Vanessa Lau, "Kate and Laura Mulleavy's 'Swan' Song," *Women's Wear Daily,* December 2, 2010, p. 4.

Lisa Lockwood, "The Social Swirl," *Women's Wear Daily,* May 31, 2011, p. 14.

Evgenia Peretz, "The Rodarte Effect," *Vanity Fair,* pp. 341–346, 383–386.

THEN AND NOW

"Timeline: Highlights Through the Years, 1977–2012," *Women's Wear Daily,* May 1, 2012, pp. 10, 12, 14.

Rachel Brown, "Finding Riches in Retail," *Women's Wear Daily,* May 1, 2012, p. 16.

Arnold J. Karr, "American Dreamers," *Women's Wear Daily,* May 1, 2012, p. 8.

Chapter 10

1. Harry A. Cobrin, *The Men's Clothing Industry* (New York: Fairchild, 1970), p. 67.
2. Laura Putre, "How Hugo Boss Lost a Cleveland Union Battle," March 9, 2011, psmag.com/business-economics/how-hugo-boss-lost-a-cleveland-union-battle-27879/. Accessed February 2013.
3. Courtney Colavita, contributions by Amanda Kaiser, "Acting on Impulse: Men's Shopping Habits Have Become More Spontaneous, Opening Up New Opportunities for Retailers," *Daily News Record,* January 8, 2007, p. 38.
4. Jean E. Palmieri, "Part Two: Fairchild's Men's Wear CEO Summit, Retail Opportunities," *Women's Wear Daily,* April 7, 2011, p. 3B.
5. Nivedita Bhattacharjee, "U.S. Men's Clothing Sales Outpaces Women in 2011 Study," March 29, 2012, reuters.com/article/2012/03/29/retail-apparel-spending-idUSL3E8ET6FW20120329. Accessed February 2013.
6. Ibid.
7. Ibid.
8. Barbara Ettoie, "Business and Buttonholes," *New York Times,* October 28, 2007, p. F1.
9. Ray A. Smith, "A Real Savile Row," *Wall Street Journal,* April 14, 2007, p. P6.
10. "Investor Relations," menswearhouse.com. Accessed February 2013.
11. Ray A. Smith, "Men's Aisle Gets Crowded; More American Designers Target Guys with Luxury 'Classic' Lines, Trying to Tap Menswear Resurgence," *Wall Street Journal,* December 12, 2006, p. B1.
12. Lela London, "The Accessories Make the Man," Apparel Insiders, apparelinsiders.com/2012/07/the-accessories-make-the-man/. Accessed February 2013.
13. David Lipke, "Brooks Brothers Aims to Attract Young Shoppers," *Women's Wear Daily,* August 18, 2011, p. 1B.

14. Ray A. Smith, "Style & Substance: GQ Jr.: Menswear Brands Launch Lines for Younger Buyers," *Wall Street Journal,* February 5, 2007, p. B1.

FASHION FOCUS

David Lipke, "Reid Expands with Stores, E-commerce," *Women's Wear Daily,* pp. 1, 4.

THEN AND NOW

"Timeline: 1971-2011," *Women's Wear Daily,* June 2, 2011, pp. 4, 6.

Jean E. Palmieri, "A Hippie Makes Good," *Women's Wear Daily,* June 2, 2011, p. 2.

Jean E. Palmieri, "Creating a Culture of Fun and Fulfillment," *Women's Wear Daily,* June 2, 2011, p. 14.

Chapter 11

1. "Plaid City," *Women's Wear Daily,* February 14, 2001.
2. "Children's Wear—A Global Strategic Business Report," Global Industry Analysts, Inc., press release, January 13, 2011, strategy.com/pressMCP-5013.asp. Accessed January 2012.
3. Joyce Brothers, "How Clothes Form a Child's Self-Image," *Earnshaw's Infants', Girls' and Boys' Wear Review,* November 1979, p. 48.
4. WWD.com by Cotton Incorporated, "Tween Spirit: Post-Recession Tween Shoppers Remain Force at Retail," April 10, 2012, wwd.com/markets-news/textiles/the-power-of-youth-post-recession-tween-shoppers-remain-force-at-retail-5849340. Accessed February 2013.
5. Haya El Nassar, "Poor Economy Slows USA's Birthrate," *USA Today,* July 25, 2012, usatoday30.usatoday.com/news/nation/story/2012-07-25/low-US-birthrate-economy/56488980/1. Accessed February 2013.
6. T.L. Stanley, "Mother May I? Penny-Pinching Parents Might Not Be Spending on Themselves. But the Kids? That's a Different Story," *Adweek,* April 26, 2010, p. 12.
7. Allison Golub, "Size Matters," *Earnshaw's,* February 2007.
8. Urban, "EMP Report," p. 2.
9. WarnerBros.com, "Consumer Products," warnerbros.com/studio/divisions/consumer-products.html. Accessed February 2013.
10. Zak Stambor, "Children's Clothing Manufacturer Carter's Launches Two E-Commerce Sites," Internet Retailer, April 2, 2010, internetretailer.com/2010/04/02/childrens-clothing-manufacturer-carter-s-launches-two-e-com. Accessed February 2013.
11. "School Uniforms: Dressed for Success? The Effect of School Uniforms on Student Achievement and Behavior," *Education Week,* August 31, 2011, p. 4.
12. "JCPenney Launches 2006 Back-to-School Season; Company Leads Back-to-School Season with New Marketing Campaign, Styles and Brands; National Retailer Is Destination for Denim, Special Sizes, and School Uniforms." *Business Wire,* July 11, 2006.

13. "Manufacturers Expand Accessories I.Q. (French Toast Uniform L.L.C.)," *DSN Retailing Today,* May 22, 2006, p. 18.

FASHION FOCUS

Leonie Barrie, "US: Madonna to Launch Truth or Dare Lifestyle Brand," just-style.com, November 4, 2011. *General OneFile.* Web. September 8, 2012.

David Lipke, "Touring with Madonna," *Women's Wear Daily,* May 31, 2012, pp. 1, 8.

Julie Naughton, "9 Minutes with Madonna," *Women's Wear Daily,* April 16, 2012, pp. 1, 3.

Naomi Wolf, "Madonna: The Director's Cut," *Harper's Bazaar,* December 2011/January 2012, p. 274.

THEN AND NOW

Alix Browne, "Von Furstenberg's Next Generation," *The New York Times,* March 4, 2012, p. 3.

Rosemary Feitelberg, "Kids Get Trendy," *Women's Wear Daily,* January 9, 2012, p. 4.

Rosemary Feitelberg, "Mizrahi to Launch Babies Line," *Women's Wear Daily,* January 12, 2012, p. 8.

Karen Gram, "Designer Label Links with Gap," *The Vancouver Sun,* March 13, 2012, canada.com/nanaimodailynews/news/story.html?id=6293861. Accessed March 2013.

Daphne Merkin, "Les Enfants Terribles," *W Magazine,* March 2012, pp. 226, 228.

Chapter 12

1. Spanx, Inc. "About Us: Putting Her *Butt* on the Line Pays Off!", spanx.com/category/index.jsp?categoryId=4463905&clickId=topnav_aboutus_text. Accessed February 2013.

2. "Fashion Alert: Bad Bra Syndrome Is Sweeping the Nation. This August: Look for the Cure—Barely There Intimates Launches New Invisible Look," *PRNewswire,* August 17, 2006.

3. Olivia Bergin, "Miranda Kerr Reveals Her $2.5 Million Victoria's Secret 'Fantasy Bra,'" Telegraph.co.uk, October 20, 2011, fashion.telegraph.co.uk/article/TMG8838016/Miranda-Kerr-reveals-her-2.5million-Victorias-Secret-Fantasy-Bra.html. Accessed October 2012.

4. Natasha Montrose, "Yasmine Eslami Expands Lingerie Universe," *Women's Wear Daily,* August 1, 2011, p. 12.

5. Karyn Monget, "The Oprah Effect," *Women's Wear Daily,* January 24, 2011, p. 14B.

6. Karyn Monget, "First Lingerie Fashion Week to Debut," *Women's Wear Daily,* February 19, 2013, wwd.com/markets-news/intimates-activewear/first-lingerie-fashion-week-to-debut-6767306. Accessed February 2013.

7. Elizabeth Olson, "Finding the Right Fit, with Technology's Help," *New York Times,* August 16, 2012, nytimes.com/2012/08/17/business/media/finding-the-best-fitting-bra-with-technologys-help.html?_r=0. Accessed February 2013.

8. "Lululemon Athletica Inc. Announces Fourth Quarter and Full Year Fiscal 2011 Results," March 22, 2012, investor.lululemon.com/releasedetail.cfm?ReleaseID=658839. Accessed February 2013.

9. "Legwear, A Three Billion Dollar Baby," *Women's Wear Daily,* October 29, 2007.

10. Adrianne Pasquarelli, "LittleMissMatched Hits a Growth Spurt," Crain's New York, June 20, 2011, crainsnewyork.com/article/20110620/SMALLBIZ/110629986. Accessed February 2013.

11. Karyn Monget, "DKNY Legwear Links with Gossip Girl Designer," *Women's Wear Daily,* August 1, 2011, p. 12.

12. Wigwam Socks, wigwam.com/aboutus.aspx. Accessed February 2013.

FASHION FOCUS

Samantha Critchel, "Men's Underwear Getting a Little Extra Attention," *The Salt Lake Tribune,* February 6, 2012, p. 1.

Joelle Diderich, "Beckham's Underwear Revealed," *Women's Wear Daily,* January 5, 2012, p. MW2.

Joelle Diderich, "H&M Unveils David Beckham's Undies," *Women's Wear Daily,* January 4, 2012, wwd.com/fashion-news/intimates-activewear/hm-unveils-beckhams-undies-5452806. Accessed March 2013.

THEN AND NOW

Alexandra Jacobs, "Smooth Moves," *The New Yorker,* March 28, 2011, pp. 60, 63-64, 66-68.

Karyn Monget, "Celebrating Spanx at Bloomingdales" WWD.com, August 8, 2011, wwd.com/markets-news/intimates-activewear/celebrating-spanx-at-bloomingdales-5043080. Accessed March 2013.

Clare O'Connor, "Undercover Billionaire: Sara Blakely Joins the Rich List Thanks to Spanx," Forbes.com, March 26, 2012, forbes.com/sites/clareoconnor/2012/03/07/undercover-billionaire-sara-blakely-joins-the-rich-list-thanks-to-spanx/. Accessed March 2013.

Chapter 13

1. Office of the United States Trade Representative, "China," ustr.gov/countries-regions/china. Accessed February 2013.

2. Jennie Bell, "FN List: 10 Biggest Footwear Producers," *Footwear News,* October 8, 2012, wwd.com/footwear-news/business/fn-list-10-biggest-footwear-producers-6390753. Accessed February 2013.

3. American Apparel and Footwear Association, wewear.org/about/. Accessed February 2013.

4. Collective Brands, collectivebrands.com/about-collective/global-presence. Accessed February 2013.

5. American Apparel and Footwear Association, "AAFA Releases ShoeStats2011 Report," October 2011, wewear.org/aafa-releases-shoestats2011-report/. Accessed March 2013.

6. Accessories Magazine Staff, "NPD Group Reports on Footwear E-Commerce Shopping Behaviors," September 14, 2012, npd.com/wps/portal/npd/us/news/press-releases/pr_120912a/. Accessed February 2013.

7. Michelle Baran, "Shoe-Ins? Ready-to-Wear Tenderfeet like Zac Posen and Proenza Schouler Are Seeing the Benefits

of Adding Shoes to Their Mix, but Whether They Can Make Their Mark in the Footwear World Remains to Be Seen," *Footwear News,* January 22, 2007, p. 82.

8. Luxottica, luxottica.com. Accessed February 2013.

9. Marchon, "Corporate Overview," marchon.com/. Accessed February 2013.

10. "Revolutionary New Cuts Add Spice to Engagement Rings," Jewelry Information Center, jic.org. Accessed March 2008.

11. Kristina McKenna, "Briolettes Add Dimension to Design," *Jewelers Circular Keystone,* June 1, 2007, p. 178, jckonline .com/article/281613-Briolettes_Add_Dimension_to_ Design.php. Accessed February 2013.

12. William George Shuster, "Cartier Celebrates Santo's 100th: Honors Modern-Day Pioneers," *Jewelers Circular Keystone,* August 1, 2004.

13. Anthony DeMarco, "Swatch Group 2012 Gross Sales Up 14% to $8.88 Billion," January 10, 2013, forbes.com/sites/ anthonydemarco/2013/01/10/swatch-group-2012-gross-sales-up-14-to-8-88-billion/. Accessed February 2013.

14. Joelle Diderich, "Time as Luxury: Expensive Watches Boom as Investors Rush In," *Women's Wear Daily,* January 24, 2011, p. 1.

15. Ibid.

16. Swank, "Lifestyle Brands," swankinc.com/lifestyle-brands. Accessed February 2013.

FASHION FOCUS

Tory Burch LLC, "About the Company," toryburch.com/ about-us/about-us-main,default,pg.html. Accessed March 2013.

Marc Karimzadeh, "Uptown Girl: Tory heads to Madison," *Women's Wear Daily,* September 7, 2011, p. 9.

William Norwich, "What's Next, Tory?" *Town and Country,* September 2010, pp. 154–159.

Jessica Pressler, "Hers," *New York Magazine,* February 20–27, 2012, pp. 79–80, 82–86.

Michael Shnayerson, "An Empire of Her Own," *Vanity Fair,* February 2007, vanityfair.com/style/features/2007/02/ tory-burch-200702. Accessed March 2013.

Luisa Zargani "Tory Burch Makes Milan Statement," *Women's Wear Daily,* March 27, 2012, p. 3.

Luisa Zargani, "Tory Burch Opens Rome Unit," *Women's Wear Daily,* October 21, 2010, p. 3.

THEN AND NOW

"WWD Milestones: Coach at 70," *Women's Wear Daily,* September 26, 2011, pp. 1–3, 6–50.

Dianne M. Pogoda, "Leather Road," *Women's Wear Daily,* September 26, 2011, p. 4.

Chapter 14

1. Chris Tullett, "Global Goals," *Soap, Perfumery & Cosmetics,* October 1, 1995, p. 25.

2. Dorothy Carey, "Max Factor," *Economist,* June 15, 1966, p. 82.

3. Tony Case, "Dollars, Scents, and Eco-awareness," *Brandweek* (Cosmetics and Fragrances), June 18, 2007, p. 32.

4. Molly Prior, "Beauty Promises Strong M&A Outlook," *Women's Wear Daily,* January 6, 2012, p. 5.

5. Ibid.

6. Ibid.

7. Virginia Bonofiglio (Fashion Institute of Technology professor, cosmetics & fragrance department), author correspondence.

8. Ruth La Ferla, "No Nail Biting as Polishes Boom: Once Staid, Nail Polish Becomes Fashion Accessory," *New York Times,* April 4, 2012, nytimes.com/2012/04/05/fashion/ once-staid-nail-polish-becomes-fashion-accessory. html?pagewanted=all&_r=0. Accessed March 2013.

9. Ibid.

10. Stephen Fenichell, interview by Scott Simon, "Plastic— The Dominant Material of the Time," *Weekend Edition— Saturday,* National Public Radio, August 10, 1996.

11. Jennifer Wiel, "Choël: Innovation is Perpetual Driver," *Women's Wear Daily,* July 19, 2002, wwd.com/fashion-news/fashion-features/cho-235-l-innovation-is-perpetual-driver-760282?navSection=issues. Accessed March 2013.

12. Jess Halliday, "L'Oreal Ruling Sets Fragrance Precedent," *Cosmetics International,* August 13, 2004.

13. Federal Trade Commission, "Is it a Cosmetic, a Drug, or Both? (Or Is It Soap?)," July 8, 2002, updated April 30, 2012, fda.gov/Cosmetics/GuidanceCompliance RegulatoryInformation/ucm074201.htm. Accessed February 2013.

14. U.S. Food and Drug Administration, "Alpha Hydroxy Acids in Cosmetics," fda.gov/cosmetics/productand ingredientsafety/selectedcosmeticingredients/ ucm107940.htm. Accessed February 2013.

15. Jessica Best, "Animal Testing Legislation Passes New York Assembly," *Women's Wear Daily,* June 15, 2007, p. 12.

16. "Cosmetic Testing Without Animals," *Investor's Business Daily,* January 1, 2010, p. A02.

17. Cargo Cosmetics, "PlantLove," cargocosmetics.com/ products/plant-love. Accessed October 2012.

18. Andrea Nagel, "P&G Set to Begin New Sustainability Effort," *Women's Wear Daily,* December 12, 2010, p. 13

19. "Male Grooming: Market Grows at a Rapid Pace But Brands Need to Adapt," September 4, 2012, premiumbeautynews.com/en/male-grooming-market-grows-at,4457. Accessed October 2012.

20. Annamaria Andriotis, "10 Things the Beauty Industry Won't Tell You," *Smart Money,* April 20, 2011, smartmoney. com/spend/family-money/10-things-the-beauty-industry-wont-tell-you-1303249279432/. Accessed February 2013.

21. Racher Press, Inc, "Economic Clout of Asians, Hispanics Rising (Merchandising/Ethnic Hair & Skin Care)," *Chain Drug Review,* April 11, 2011, p. 24.

22. Elle Morris, "Ethnic Skin Care: An Opportunity for Personal Connection," *Global Cosmetic Industry,* December 2010, p. 38.

23. Christina Hilsenrath, "Ethnicity and Its Impact on the Beauty Business," NPD Group, press release, January 22,

2007, thefreelibrary.com/The+NPD+Group+reveals+ ethnicity's+impact+on+the+beauty+industry.- a0160927525. Accessed March 2013.

24. Faye Brookman, "Mass Shoppers Blur Ethnic Lines," *Women's Wear Daily,* March 16, 2007, p. 7.

25. Susan Dickenson, "Greener, Broader Marketplace Fuels Candle Sales," *Home Accents Today,* September 1, 2007, p. 9, homeaccentstoday.com/article/473608-Greener_ broader_marketplace_fuels_candle_sales.php. Accessed February 2013.

26. Export.gov, "Cosmetics and Toiletries (COS)," export.gov/ hongkong/eg_hk_027490.asp. Accessed February 2013.

27. "Trade Mission to India: New Delhi, Mumbai, and Bangalore," International Trade Administration, November 15–19, 2012, trade.gov/trade-missions/ mission-statements/beauty-and-cosmetics-trade-mission- to-india-november2010.asp. Accessed October 2012.

28. Sephora, "About Us," sephora.com/contentStore/ mediaContentTemplate.jsp?mediaId=10000020. Accessed February 2013.

29. Kline & Company, "Beauty Sales Through Alternate Channels Post a 21% Gain as U.S. Consumers Flock to the Internet and Television to Buy Cosmetics and Skin Care, According to a Newly Released Kline Report," press release, September 21, 2011, klinegroup.com/news/ beauty_sales092111.asp. Accessed April 2013.

30. Kline & Company, "Beauty Marketing Gone Social; However, not at the Expense of Traditional Marketing, Reports Kline," press release, January 16, 2012.

31. Business Wire, "Clinique Creates New Shopping Experience with Integrated Digital Technologies: Skin Care Diagnostic Tool on Apple iPAD® Leads the Way," February 25, 2011, businesswire.com/news/ home/20110225005538/en/Clinique-Creates-Shopping- Experience-Integrated-Digital-Technologies. Accessed February 2013.

32. Kline & Company, "Beauty Sales Through Alternate Channels Post a 21% Gain as U.S. Consumers Flock to the Internet and Television to Buy Cosmetics and Skin Care, According to a Newly Released Kline Report," press release, September 21, 2011, klinegroup.com/news/ beauty_sales092111.asp. Accessed April 2013.

33. The NPD Group, Inc., "NPD Reports Women Deem Anti-Aging Key Motivator When Purchasing Skincare Products," press release, January 20, 2010, npd.com/ wps/portal/npd/us/news/press-releases/pr_100120/. Accessed April 2013.

34. Alisa Marie Beyer, "The Age of Anti-Aging: A 360-Degree View," *GCI,* September 2010, p. 26.

35. Andrea Nagel, "Naturals to See Growth in 2008 with USDA Seals," *Women's Wear Daily,* July 6, 2007, p. 10.

FASHION FOCUS

"Shape Salutes Bobbi Brown: Her Easy-to-Wear Formulas Demystified Makeup, While Her Powerful Message of Self Acceptance Helped Us Feel More Confident in Our Own Skin," *Shape,* November 2011, p. 76. *General One- File.* Web. September 1, 2012.

Joan Juliet Buck, "The Mogul Next Door," *New York Times Magazine,* February 17, 2012, pp. 181–182.

Emily J. Minor, "More Than Skin Deep," *Success,* March 2012, pp. 68–70.

THEN AND NOW

Antoinette Alexander, "L'Oreal Fetes 100 Years in Beauty," *Drug Store News,* June 29, 2009, p. 64.

L'Oreal S.A. "SWOT Analysis," *Marketline,* June 15, 2012, pp. 4–8.

Chapter 15

1. "Will They Step up to the Plate? The Tabletop Industry Looks for Ways to Reverse Sales That Appear to Be on the Decline," *HFN,* September 8, 2008, p. 50, thefreelibrary. com/Will+they+step+up+to+the+plate%3F+The+tablet op+industry+looks+for+ways...-a0198545963. Accessed March 2013.

2. The Homer Laughlin China Company, "History of Fiesta," fiestafactorydirect.com/t-aboutfiesta.aspx. Accessed February 2013.

3. "The Truth About Thread Count," *New York,* February 16, 2009, p. 50.

4. Museum Store Association, msaweb.org, 2007.

5. XO Group Inc., xogroupinc.com/the-knot-inc-company. aspx. Accessed February 2013.

6. Susan Dickenson, "Home Decor Is Big Business At Online Retailer Hautelook.com," *Home Accents,* April 30, 2012, homeaccentstoday.com/article/550807-Home_de- cor_is_big_business_at_online_retailer_Hautelook_com. php. Accessed February 2013.

7. NPD Group, "The NPD Group Reports on the Trend of 'Showrooming' for the Home," February 29, 2012, npd.com/wps/portal/npd/us/news/press-releases/ pr_120229/. Accessed February 2013.

8. HGTV, hgtv.com/. Accessed February 2013.

FASHION FOCUS

"From Runway to Role Model: Celebrity Supermodels Are Introducing Brand Extensions: Marketing to Women: Addressing Women and Women's Sensibilities," *Business Insights: Essentials,* December 2011. Web. September 8, 2012.

Cindy Crawford, "Cindy Crawford Home," cindy.com/cindy- crawford-home. Accessed March 2013.

Diana Lyle, "Cindy Crawford," *Westlake Malibu Lifestyle Magazine,* November/December 2011 Holiday Issue, cindy.com/Westlake%20Malibu%20Lifestyle%20 Magazine%20November/December%202011%20 Holiday%20Issue. Accessed March 2013.

Moira Forbes, "Kathy Ireland: Swimsuit Cover Girl Turned $2 Billion Business Model," *Forbes,* February 13, 2012, forbes.com/sites/moiraforbes/2012/02/13/kathy- ireland-swimsuit-covergirl-turned-model-entrepreneur/. Accessed March 2013.

Kathy Ireland Worldwide, "About Kathy Ireland," http:// kathyireland.com/about-kathy/. Accessed March 2013.

THEN AND NOW

IKEA, "History of IKEA," http://www.ikea.com/ms/en_US/ about_ikea/the_ikea_way/history/. Accessed March 2013.

Justin Menza, "IKEA's Not Just for College Students," CNBC, October 1, 2012, cnbc.com/id/49241508. Accessed October 2012.

Chapter 16

1. NYC Fashion, "Resources for Emerging Designers," nycfashioninfo.com/design-support/other-resources. aspx. Accessed February 2013.

2. IMG, imgworld.com/about-us.aspx. Accessed February 2013.

3. Los Angeles County Economic Development Corporation, "2011 Otis Report on the Creative Economy of the Los Angeles Region," laedc.org/reports/2011OtisReport .pdf. Accessed February 2013.

4. California Market Center, "About the CMC," california marketcenter.com/faq/aboutus.php. Accessed February 2013.

5. Business & Industry, "Fashion & Apparel Manufacturers," October 2007, San Francisco Chamber of Commerce, sfchamber.com.

6. Renée Frojo, "S.F. Manufacturers Celebrate Job Growth in 2012," *San Francisco Business Times*, November 9–15, 2012, p. 5.

7. San Francisco Center for Economic Development, "Macy's West Sponsors Fashion Incubator San Francisco (FISF)," press release, sfced.org/about-sfced/press/2011/ macys-west-sponsors-fashion-incubator-san-francisco-fisf. Accessed February 2013.

8. Heidi Dillon, "Best Local Designers in Dallas," November 4, 2010, dfw.cbslocal.com/top-lists/best-local-designers- in-dallas/. Accessed February 2013.

9. Dallas Market Center, "About Dallas Market Center," dallasmarketcenter.com/about/?id=ql. Accessed February 2013.

10. Miami International Merchandise Mart, miamimerchan- disemart.com/index.html. Accessed February 2013.

11. The Fédération Française de la Couture, du Prêt-à-Porter des Couturiers et des Créateurs de Mode, "Federation," modeaparis.com. Accessed February 2013.

12. Contributor, "The French Contemporary Wave That's Reshaping Ready-to-Wear," *The Business of Fashion*, October 10, 2011, businessoffashion.com/2011/10/the- french-contemporary-wave-thats-reshaping-ready-to-wear. html. Accessed February 2013.

13. Mode à Paris, Fédération Française de la Couture, du Prêt-à-Porter des Couturiers et des Créateurs de Mode, modeaparis.com/en/fashion-shows/Schedules/Men-s- fashion. Accessed February 2013.

14. Madge Garland, *The Changing Form of Fashion* (New York: Praeger, 1971), p. 73.

15. Brian Dunn, "WWD Magic Preview: U.S., Canadian Spotlight," *Women's Wear Daily*, August 9, 2011, wwd.com/ business-news/government-trade/us-canada-strong-ties- but-problems-persist-5045720. Accessed February 2013.

16. Ibid.

17. Brian Dunn, "Growth Factor: The Canadian Fashion Industry Comes into Its Own," *Women's Wear Daily*, November 22, 2006, p. 14.

18. Lydia Dishman, "Joe Fresh Gives JCPenney a Smart Shot at Turnaround," July 25, 2012, forbes.com/sites/ lydiadishman/2012/07/25/joe-fresh-gives-jcpenney-a- smart-shot-at-turnaround/. Accessed February 2013.

19. Grace I. Kunz and Myrna B. Garner, *Going Global: The Textile and Apparel Industry*, 2nd ed. (New York: Fairchild, 2011), pp. 325–329.

20. Mercedes-Benz Fashion Week Tokyo, "About JFW Organization," tokyo-mbfashionweek.com/en/aboutus/. Accessed February 2013.

21. U.S. Department of Agriculture, "The World and United States Cotton Outlook," usda.gov/oce/forum/ presentations/CottonOutlook.pdf. Accessed February 2013.

22. Fashion Design Council of India, "About FDCI," willslifestyleindiafashionweek.com/fdci.php. Accessed February 2013.

23. Ministry of Textiles—Government of India, "Central Silk Board," csb.gov.in/silk-sericulture/silk/. Accessed February 2013.

24. Australian Wool Innovation Limited, "Australian Wool Production," wool.com/Media-Centre_Australian-Wool- Production.htm. Accessed February 2013.

25. Kunz and Garner, *Going Global*, pp. 384–385.

26. United States Department of Commerce, "Interna- tional Buyer Program Announces 2013 Roster Trade Shows," May 21, 2012, commerce.gov/blog/2012/05/21/ international-buyer-program-announces-2013-roster- trade-shows-0. Accessed February 2013.

FASHION FOCUS

Samantha Conti, "Stella McCartney Keeps It in the Family," *Women's Wear Daily*, December 9, 2011, p. 8.

Jessica Iredale, "Stella's Empire State," *Women's Wear Daily*, January 11, 2012, pp. 10–11.

Jessica Iredale, "Stella McCartney Moves to Soho," *Women's Wear Daily*, January 9, 2012, p. 7.

Karyn Monget, "Stella McCartney's Take on Lingerie," *Women's Wear Daily*, November 28, 2011, p. 8.

Justine Picardie, "Stella's Star Power," *Harper's Bazaar*, September 2012, pp. 538, 540–541, and 548.

Amy Spindler, "Stella McCartney: Ready for Chloe," *The New York Times*, April 22, 1997, nytimes.com/1997/04/22/ style/stella-mccartney-ready-for-chloe.html. Accessed March 2013.

THEN AND NOW

Rachel Strugatz, "Net-a-porter Land in NYC," *Women's Wear Daily*, June 26, 2012, p. 12.

Chapter 17

1. Andria Cheng, "'Made in America' Becomes More Fashionable with Luxury Brands," *Wall Street Journal*,

January 18, 2013, online.wsj.com/article/BT-CO-20130118-709995.html. Accessed February 2013.

2. David Lipke, "American Apparel Taps Pricy New Financing," *Women's Wear Daily*, March 14, 2012, p. 6.

3. Kristi Ellis and Arthur Friedman, "U.S. Mills Seeing CAFTA Benefits," *Women's Wear Daily*, August 15, 2011, wwd.com/business-news/government-trade/us-mills-seeing-cafta-benefits-5065580. Accessed February 2013.

4. Office of the United States Trade Representative, "Trade Agreements," ustr.gov/trade-agreements. Accessed February 2013.

5. U.S. Customs and Border Protection, "Quotas Administration," cbp.gov/xp/cgov/trade/trade_programs/textiles_and_quotas/guide_import_goods/quota_admin.xml. Accessed March 2013.

6. Andrew C. Wicks, "Can Social Responsibility Sustain a Global Business?" *Washington Post*, March 2, 2013, washingtonpost.com/business/defining-corporate-social-responsibility-for-use-across-the-globe/2013/03/01/75d0b320-8036-11e2-a350-49866afab584_story.html. Accessed March 2013.

7. Arnold J. Karr, "Expect Expanded Breadth for CSR," *Women's Wear Daily*, October 10, 2011, wwd.com/business-news/government-trade/expect-expanded-breadth-for-csr-5279630?navSection=package&navId=5286080. Accessed March 2013.

8. Kristi Ellis and Arthur Friedman, "Industry Strikes Back at Gingrich Over Comments on Child Labor," *Women's Wear Daily*, December 12, 2011, p. 12.

9. Dana Thomas, "The Fake Trade: Wanted for Stealing Childhoods: Each Year Hundreds of Children Have No Choice but to Sacrifice Their Lives to Produce Counterfeit Goods," *Harper's Bazaar*, January 2007, p. 69.

10. Lisa Casabona, "Gray Goods Pose Problems," *Footwear News*, November 27, 2006, p. 10.

11. "Exports Hit Their Stride," *Women's Wear Daily*, August 7, 1996, p. 28.

FASHION FOCUS

Erica M. Blumenthal, "Into the Madhouse," *The New York Times*, October 13, 2011, p. E6.

Matthew Carroll, "How Fashion Brands Set Prices," Forbes.com, February 22, 2012, forbes.com/search/?q=How+Fashion+Brands+Set+Prices. Accessed March 2013.

Samantha Conti, "Uniqlo Sets Expansion, Focuses on Innovation," *Women's Wear Daily*, September 29, 2011, pp. 1, 8.

Sharon Edelson, "CEO: Fast Retailing on Track for $54B by 2020," *Women's Wear Daily*, October 14, 2011, p. 5.

Sharon Edelson, "Uniqlo to Launch U.S. E-commerce Site," *Women's Wear Daily*, October 18, 2012, p. 1.

Kerry Folan, "Is Uniqlo Having a Fashion Identity Crisis?" Racked.com, August 23, 2012, racked.com/archives/2012/08/23/uniqlo-confirms-ecommerce-launch-for-fall.php. Accessed March 2013.

Dhani Mau, "Uniqlo Plots World Domination with More U.S. Stores and Ecommerce," Fashionista.com, September 24, 2012, fashionista.com/2012/08/uniqlo-plots-

world-domination-plans-to-launch-ecommerce-and-expand-stores-in-the-us/. Accessed March 2013.

Ashley Milne-Tyte, "Japan's Uniqlo Eyes Manhattan, And More," NPR.org, October 21, 2011, www.npr.org/2011/10/21/141560807/japans-uniqlo-eyes-manhattan-and-more. Accessed March 2013.

Greg Petro, "The Future of Fashion Retailing: The Zara Approach (Part 2 of 3)," Forbes.com, October 25, 2012, forbes.com/sites/gregpetro/2012/10/25/the-future-of-fashion-retailing-the-zara-approach-part-2-of-3/. Accessed March 2013.

Greg Petro, "The Future of Fashion Retailing: The Zara Approach (Part 3 of 3)," Forbes.com, November 5, 2012, forbes.com/sites/gregpetro/2012/11/05/the-future-of-fashion-retailing-the-hm-approach-part-3-of-3/. Accessed March 2013.

Barbara Thau, "Can Uniqlo's Clever Clothes Refashion the U.S. Retail Market?," DailyFinance.com, October 29, 2011, dailyfinance.com/2011/10/29/can-uniqlos-clever-clothes-refashion-the-u-s-retail-market/. Accessed March 2013.

Bryant Urstadt, "Uniqlones," *New York Magazine*, May 17, 2010, pp. 46, 48–49, 105.

THEN AND NOW

"eBay and Council of Fashion Designers of America Roll Out 'You Can't Fake Fashion,'" *Entertainment Close-up*, February 13, 2012. General OneFile. Web. September 8, 2012.

"Intellectual Property Rights," *U.S Customs and Border Protection. U.S. Immigration and Customs Enforcement*, 2011, pp. 10, 13, 15–20.

Kristi Ellis, "Bust Shuts Down 70 Counterfeit Sites," *Women's Wear Daily*, July 13, 2012, p. 2.

Maura Kutner, "Buying the Real Thing on the Internet," *Bazaar*, 2011, p. 66.

Petah Marian, "UK: Egyptian Olympic Team Given Counterfeit Nike Gear," Just-style.com, July 26, 2012, Web. General OneFile. Web. September 8, 2012.

Adrianne Pasquarelli, "Designers Scratch Back, Tell Copycats to Knock It Off; Police the Internet, Push for New Laws; Fighting Counterfeits Can Be Costly," *Crain's New York Business*, February 6, 2012, p. 2.

Susan Reda, "The Most Counterfeited Product," Stores.org, March 2012, stores.org/content/most-counterfeited-products. Accessed March 2013.

Kitty So, "US: Interpol Global Register to Fight Fake Clothing," Just-style.com, July 26, 2012, General OneFile. Web. September 8, 2012.

Chapter 18

1. Estelle Hamburger, *Fashion Business—It's All Yours* (New York: Harper & Row), 1976.

2. National Retail Federation, "NRF Forecasts 3.4% Increase in Retail Sales for 2013," January 28, 2013, nrf.com/modules.php?name=News&op=viewlive&sp_id=1513. Accessed March 2013.

3. Cynthia Crossen and Kortney Stringer, "A Merchant's Evolution," *Wall Street Journal,* November 18, 2004, online.wsj.com/article/SB110073967320277510.html. Accessed February 2013.

4. U.S. Census Bureau, "Resident Population by Sex and Age: 1980-2010 (Table 7)," *Statistical Abstract of the United States: 2012,* p. 11, census.gov/compendia/statab/2012/tables/12s0007.pdf.

5. Macy's, "What's Happening," macys.com/store/event/index.ognc?action=search&storeId=70. Accessed February 2013.

6. Arnold J. Karr, "Mass Players See Drop in Share of Apparel Sales," *Women's Wear Daily,* July 13, 2011, p. 1.

7. Entrepreneur, "The Athlete's Foot," entrepreneur.com/franchises/athletesfootthe/282103-0.html#. Accessed March 2013.

8. David Moin, "Burlington Coat Taps Paul Metcalf," *Women's Wear Daily,* March 22, 2012, p. 8.

9. Sharon Edelson, "Outlets Add Service to the Price Proposition," *Women's Wear Daily,* August 1, 2011, p. 2011.

10. Direct Selling Association, "Fact Sheet: U.S. Direct Selling in 2011," dsa.org/research/industry-statistics/11gofactsheet.pdf. Accessed February 2013.

11. Reuters, "Profile: HSN Inc.," reuters.com/finance/stocks/companyProfile?symbol=HSNI.O. Accessed February 2013.

12. HSN.com, "HSN at a Glance," hsn.com/hsn-at-a-glance_at-3666_xa.aspx. Accessed February 2013.

13. QVC.com, "About QVC," qvc.com/AboutUsAboutQVC.content.html. Accessed March 2013.

14. ShopNBC, "Overview: Corporate Profile," shopnbc.mwnewsroom.com/. Accessed March 2013.

15. Abdul Montaqim, "Global E-commerce Sales Will Top $1.25 Trillion by 2013," June 14, 2012, internetretailer.com/2012/06/14/global-e-commerce-sales-will-top-125-trillion-2013. Accessed September 12, 2012.

16. comScore.com, "Cyber Monday Spending Hits $1.25 Billion to Rank as Heaviest U.S. Online Spending Day in History," November 29, 2011, comscore.com/Press_Events/Press_Releases/2011/11/Cyber_Monday_Spending_Hits_1.25_Billion. Accessed September 2012.

17. Vicki M. Young, "Consumers Embrace Showrooming," *Women's Wear Daily,* September 26, 2012, wwd.com/retail-news/trends-analysis/perfect-storm-drives-showrooming-6341635. Accessed March 2013.

18. Petah Marian, "U.S.: Hudson's Bay Co. Completes Lord & Taylor Acquisition," just-style.com, January 24, 2012.

FASHION FOCUS

"From Forever 21 to H&M, Trendy "Fast Fashion" Retailers Are Expanding in San Diego County and Across the U.S. to Satisfy Shoppers' Demands for Clothing That's Cheap Enough to Purchase By the Armload," UTSanDiego.com, August 22, 2012, p. 3.

"Forever 21 Expands in China with Support from L.A. Mayor," *Los Angeles Times,* December 6, 2011, latimesblogs.latimes.com/money_co/2011/12/forever-21-expands-in-china-with-support-of-la-mayor.html. Accessed March 2013.

Susan Berfield, "Forever 21's Fast (and Loose) Fashion Empire," *Bloomsburg Businessweek,* January 20, 2011, businessweek.com/magazine/content/11_05/b4213090559511.htm. Accessed March 2013.

Jon Caramanica, "Forever 21: Four Floors, One Mission. Go.," *The New York Times,* July 28, 2010, nytimes.com/2010/07/29/fashion/29CRITIC.html?_r=0. Accessed March 2013.

Sharon Edelson, "Forever 21 Unveiled on Fifth Ave.," *Women's Wear Daily,* November 19, 2010, p. 3.

Joyce Man, "Forever 21 Set Sights on Beijing and Shanghai," *Women's Wear Daily,* January 19, 2012, p. 3.

Seth Stevenson, "Zara Gets Fresh Styles to Stores Insanely Fast. How Do They Do It?" Slate.com, June 21, 2012, slate.com/articles/arts/operations/2012/06/zara_s_fast_fashion_how_the_company_gets_new_styles_to_stores_so_quickly_.html. Accessed March 2013.

Eva Wiseman, "The Gospel According to Forever 21," Guardian.co.nk, *The Observer,* July 17, 2011, guardian.co.uk/lifeandstyle/2011/jul/17/forever-21-fast-fashion-america. Accessed March 2013.

THEN AND NOW

RetailMeNot, Inc. "About Us," retailmenot.com/corp/. Accessed March 2013.

Sharon Edelson, "Coupon Web Site Gains Steam," *Women's Wear Daily,* July 23, 2012, p. 3.

Sarah Perez, "20 Major Retailers Launch Passbook-Enabled Coupons Via Digital Offers Giant Coupons.com," TechCrunch.com, October 23, 2012, techcrunch.com/2012/10/23/twenty-major-retailers-launch-passbook-enabled-coupons-via-digital-offers-giant-coupons-com/. Accessed March 2013.

Chapter 19

1. Henri Bendel, "Calling All Designers!," henribendel.com/on/demandware.store/Sites-HB-Site/default/GirlsPlayground-Folder?fdid=open-see. Accessed March 2013.

2. Phil Wahba, "J.C. Penney Overhauls Pricing Strategy As Sales Plummet," Reuters, February 2, 2013, reuters.com/article/2013/02/28/us-jcpenney-results-idUSBRE91Q19C20130228. Accessed March 2013.

3. Tracey Sherwood, "Selling the Experience: Customers Want Retailers to Appeal to Their Ideas of Luxury with Interactive Experience and Electric Atmosphere," *Global Cosmetic Industry,* September 2007, p. 68.

4. Verde Group, "New Retail Study Finds Not All 'Great Shopping' Experience Drive Shopper Loyalty," July 7, 2009, thefreelibrary.com/New+Retail+Study+Finds+Not+All+%22Great+Shopping%22+Experiences+Drive...-a0203188149. Accessed February 2013.

5. Foursquare, "About Foursquare," foursquare.com/about/. Accessed February 2013.

6. U.S. Census Bureau, "Statistical Abstract of the United States, 2012: Table 1061," census.gov/compendia/statab/2012/tables/12s1061.pdf. Accessed March 2013.

7. Brad Thomas, "Taubman Centers Reporting Strong Black Friday Traffic," *Forbes,* November 23, 2012, forbes.com/sites/bradthomas/2012/11/23/taubman-centers-reporting-strong-black-friday-traffic/. Accessed March 2013.

8. Cybele Weisser, "A Whole New Mall Game," *Money,* November 2006, p. 156.

9. Janet Ozzard, "Missoni for Target Pop-up Store Forced to Close Early," September 9, 2011, nymag.com/thecut/2011/09/missoni_for_target_closed.html. Accessed March 2013.

10. David Lipke, "Kate Hudson Re-ups with Ann Taylor," *Women's Wear Daily,* July 25, 2012, wwd.com/media-news/fashion-memopad/kate-hudson-re-ups-with-ann-taylor-6111325. Accessed March 2013.

11. Bob Evans, "Data Warehouse 2.0: The 10 Top Trends Driving the Revolution," *Forbes,* January 14, 2013, forbes.com/sites/oracle/2013/01/14/data-warehouse-2-0-the-10-top-trends-driving-the-revolution/2/. Accessed March 2013.

12. Arnold J. Karr, "Apparel Strongest Fashion Category Online: NPD," *Women's Wear Daily,* January 24, 2012, wwd.com/retail-news/direct-internet-catalogue/apparel-strongest-fashion-category-online-npd-5561920?module=today. Accessed March 2013.

13. Rachel Strugatz, "The Year in E-Tail: Lessons Learned and Looking Ahead," *Women's Wear Daily,* January 25, 2012, wwd.com/retail-news/direct-internet-catalogue/the-year-in-e-tail-lessons-learned-and-looking-ahead-5564660. Accessed March 2013.

14. PR Newswire, "Piperlime Opens First Store in New York's Soho Neighborhood," September 6, 2012, prnewswire.com/news-releases/piperlime-opens-first-store-in-new-yorks-soho-neighborhood-168747556.html. Accessed March 2013.

15. Reda, "Mills Find Cure for Outlet Doldrums by Focusing on Entertainment Theme," *Stores,* April 1997, p. 106.

FASHION FOCUS

Rachel Brown, "Next Generation: Millennials Seen Driving Retailing," WWD.com, April 19, 2012, wwd.com/retail-news/trends-analysis/gen-y-and-the-omni-channel-world-5865846?full=true. Accessed March 2013.

Samantha Critchell, "Luxury Fashion World Tweaking Its Style for Gen Y," *Associated Press,* February 13, 2012, washingtontimes.com/news/2012/feb/13/luxury-fashion-world-tweaking-its-style-for-gen-y/?page=all. Accessed March 2013.

Sarah Mahoney, "Macy's Launches Its Own Little Sitcom," *MediaPost,* September 10, 2012, mediapost.com/publications/article/182627/macys-launches-its-own-little-sitcom.html#axzz2U8E8LAIH. Accessed March 2013.

Jean E. Palmieri, "Macy's Initiative Targets Millenials," WWD.com, October 18, 2012, wwd.com/retail-news/department-stores/macys-initiative-targets-millennials-6429065?full=true. Accessed March 2013.

David Moin, "Macy's Sets Tech Push to Propel Growth," *Women's Wear Daily,* May 21, 2012, pp. 1, 8.

Vicki M. Young, "Macy's Sets Strategy for Gen-Y Shoppers," *Women's Wear Daily,* March 22, 2012, pp. 1, 6.

THEN AND NOW

Andria Cheng, "Wal-Mart Outlines Strategy," Online.wsj.com, October 10, 2012, online.wsj.com/article/SB10000872396390443749204578048842451207454.html. Accessed March 2013.

Sharon Edelson, "Wal-Mart Plots New Approach to Super-Centers," WWD.com, October 10, 2012, wwd.com/retail-news/mass-off-price/wal-mart-plots-new-approach-to-supercenters-6398531. Accessed March 2013.

Sharon Edelson, "Big, Bigger, Wal-Mart," *Women's Wear Daily,* March 28, 2012, pp. 6, 8, 10.

Feifi Sun, "Target Turns 50: How the Discount Chain Stays Chic," Style.Time.com, October 17, 2012, style.time.com/2012/10/17/target-turns-50-how-the-discount-chain-stays-chic/. Accessed March 2013.

Stone, Kenneth E.,"Impact of the Wal-Mart Phenomenon on Rural Communities." (Published in *Proceedings: Increased Understanding of Public Problems and Policies–1997.* Chicago, Illinois: Farm Foundation). Iowa State University, 2.econ.iastate.edu/faculty/stone/10yrstudy.pdf. Accessed March 2013.

Natalie Zmuda, "Walmart, Target, Kmart, Kohls: Leading 50 Years of Retail Revolution," *Advertising Age,* March 19, 2012, adage.com/article/news/walmart-target-kmart-kohl-s-lead-retail-revolution/233379//. Accessed March 2013.

Chapter 20

1. Marc Brownstein, "In the Rush to Digital, Leave Room for the Millions Who Still Like TV and Print," *Advertising Age,* December 28, 2011, adage.com/article/small-agency-diary/digital-ad-strategy-lead-lower-brand-awareness/231800/. Accessed March 2013.

2. Media kit, Style.com, condenast.com/brands/style. Accessed March 2013.

3. Josh Halliday, "GQ and Men's Health Reported the Biggest Sales in PPA digital report," *Guardian,* February 14, 2013, guardian.co.uk/media/2013/feb/14/gq-mens-health-digital-sales-abc. Accessed March 2013.

4. "About *Project Runway* Season 10," mylifetime.com/shows/project-runway/about. Accessed September 27, 2012.

5. Arnold J. Karr, "U.S. E-commerce Grows 14.3% in Q4," *Women's Wear Daily,* February 10, 2013, wwd.com/retail-news/financial/us-e-commerce-grows-143-in-q4-6711305?navSection=package&navId=6648662. Accessed March 2013.

6. Steve McClellan, "Starcom USA," *Brandweek*, June 15, 2009, p. AM10.
7. Faith Popcorn's Brain Reserve, faithpopcorn.com/. Accessed March 2013.

FASHION FOCUS

Reinaldo Herrera, "Divine Diana," *Vanity Fair*, September 2012, p. 158.
Nandita Khanna, "The Lady in Black," *Town and Country*, September 2011, p. 54.
Lisa Lockwood, "Vreeland's Legacy Gets Screen Time," *Women's Wear Daily*, August 16, 2011, pp. 9–10.
Marcy Medina, "Diana Vreeland Tapped for Rodeo Drive Walk of Style," *Women's Wear Daily*, August 9, 2012, wwd.com/fashion-news/fashion-scoops/vreeland-on-rodeo-6151972. Accessed March 2013.

Lisa Immordino Vreeland, "Diana Vreeland," *Harper's Bazaar*, August 2011, pp. 438, 440, 442, and 443.

THEN AND NOW

CFDA, "About," cfda.com/about/mission-statement. Accessed March 2013.
Rosemary Feitelberg, "CFDA/Vogue Fashion Fund Unveils China Initiative," *Women's Wear Daily*, March 6, 2012, wwd.com/fashion-news/designer-luxury/cfdavogue-fashion-funds-exchange-program-5774427. Accessed March 2013.
Marc Karimzadeh, "CFDA's 50 Year Mark: As Milestone Nears, Group Plots Growth Era," *Women's Wear Daily*, May 19, 2011, pp. 1, 8.
Marc Karimzadeh, "CFDA Welcomes 26 New Members," *Women's Wear Daily*, June 11, 2012, p. 2.

CREDITS

Illustrations by Barbara Barg Medley
Features design: Carly Grafstein

Unit 1 WWD/Giovanni Giannoni
Unit 2 WWD/Giovanni Giannoni
Unit 3 WWD/Giovanni Giannoni
Unit 4 WWD/Thomas Iannaccone
Unit 5 WWD/Kyle Ericksen
Unit 6 WWD/Francois Goize

Chapter 1
1.0 WWD/Giovanni Giannoni
1.1a Allan Grant//Time Life Pictures/Getty Images
1.1b Fairchild Archive
1.2 Condé Nast Archive
1.3 Courtesy of Library of Congress © 1895 Keppler & Schwarzmann
1.4 Courtesy of Library of Congress/Photo by Bain News Service, N.Y.C.
1.5 Condé Nast Archive/Photo by Horst P. Horst
1.6 Condé Nast Archive
1.7 Courtesy of Library of Congress
1.8 Courtesy of Library of Congress
1.9a Condé Nast Archive/Photo by Henry Clarke
1.9b Everett Collection
1.10 Francesco Scavullo/Condé Nast
1.11 Everett Collection
1.12 Mattel Michele/Corbis Sygma
1.13 WWD/Robert Mitra
1.14 WWD/George Chinsee

FASHION FOCUS
Toujours Couture
(left to right)
Courtesy of Fairchild Archive
Courtesy of Fairchild Archive
Courtesy of Fairchild Archive

THEN AND NOW
Rucci's Rule: Cutting His Own Way
(clockwise)
Courtesy of WWD/Thomas Iannaccone
Courtesy of WWD/George Chinsee
Courtesy of WWD/Thomas Iannaccone
Courtesy of WWD/John Aquino

Chapter 2
2.0 WWD/Giovanni Giannoni
2.1 WWD/Kyle Ericksen
2.2 WWD/Guy Marineau
2.3 Jeffrey Mayer/WireImage
2.4a WWD/Robert Mitra
2.4b Fairchild Archive
2.5a Fairchild Archive
2.5b Fairchild Archive
2.6 WWD/Giovanni Giannoni and Onnie Koski
2.7 WWD/Kyle Ericksen and Dominique Maitre
2.9 WWD/Yukie Kasuga
2.10 Courtesy of Pantone
2.12 Stan Badz/PGA TOUR/Getty Images
2.13 WWD/Thomas Iannaccone
2.15 CN Digital Studio
2.16 WWD/Steve Eichner
2.17a Fairchild Archive
2.17b Fairchild Archive
2.18 Fairchild Archive

FASHION FOCUS
Michael Kors: American Idol
(left to right)
Courtesy of Fairchild Archive
Courtesy of WWD/Kyle Ericksen
Courtesy of Fairchild Archive

THEN AND NOW
David Lauren: The Prince of Polo
(clockwise)
Courtesy of Fairchild Archive
Courtesy of WWD/John Aquino

Chapter 3
3.0 WWD/Thomas Iannaccone
3.1 Courtesy of VALS
3.2a © Corbis
3.2b © Tim Graham/Corbis
3.4a Condé Nast Archive
3.4b Condé Nast Archive
3.4c Condé Nast Archive
3.4d Condé Nast Archive
3.4e Gerard JulienAFP/Getty Images
3.4f Condé Nast Archive
3.7 WWD/Dominique Maitre
3.8 Tim Mosenfelder/Getty Images

FASHION FOCUS
Tommy Hilfiger: It's All About the Team
(left to right)
Courtesy of WWD/George Chinsee
Courtesy of WWD/Steve Eichner
Courtesy of Fairchild Archive

THEN AND NOW
Why Fashion Needs Eccentrics
(left to right)
Courtesy of WWD
Courtesy of Fairchild Archive

Chapter 4
4.0 WWD/George Chinsee
4.1 Courtesy of Nicole Miller
4.3 Library of Congress
4.4 Fuse/Getty Images
4.5 Farichild Archive
4.6 Farichild Archive
4.7 © Hulton-Deutsch Collection/Corbis
4.8 © Matthias Balk/dpa/Corbis
4.9 Farichild Archive
4.10 David Crump/WPA Pool/Getty Images
4.11 Farichild Archive
4.12 Kevin Mazur/WireImage
4.13 Courtesy of Calvin Klein
4.14 WWD/Steve Eichner
4.15 WWD/Steve Eichner
T01a © Bettmann/CORBIS
T01b Courtesy of Library of Congress
T01c Courtesy of Library of Congress
T01d Associated Press

FASHION FOCUS
Birth of a Notion
(left to right)
Courtesy of WWD
Courtesy of WWD
Courtesy of WWD

THEN AND NOW
The Ladies Who Lunch
(left to right)
Photo by Dimitrios Kambouris/Getty Images for
    Bloomingdale's
Courtesy of WWD/Steve Eichner

Chapter 5
5.0 WWD/Thomas Iannaccone
5.2 Courtesy of Yoox
5.3a-c Courtesy of Gap, Inc.
5.4 Fairchild Archive
5.5 Courtesy of WWD
5.7 WWD/Kyle Ericksen
5.8a Fairchild Archive
5.8b WWD/Thomas Iannaccone
5.8c airchild Archive
5.10 Fairchild Archive

FASHION FOCUS
Sarah Burton: Savage Beauty Refashioned
(left to right)

Courtesy of Fairchild Archive
Courtesy of Fairchild Archive
Courtesy of Fairchild Archive

THEN AND NOW
The New CEO: It Can Be You
Illustration by Carly Grafstein

Chapter 6
6.0 WWD/George Chinsee
6.1 Condé Nast Archive
6.2 © Luca Tettoni/Corbis
6.3 Fairchild Archive
6.4 AP Photo/Heribert Proepper
6.5 Fairchild Archive
6.7 WWD/Kyle Ericksen
6.9 Getty Images/Science-Foto
6.11 Fairchild Archive
6.12 Courtesy of Cotton, Inc.
6.13 Dex Image
6.14 Library of Congress
6.15 Tay Jnr/Getty Images
6.16 Courtesy of Pantone
6.17 Fairchild Archive
6.19 CN Digital Studio
6.20 Toni Passig/WireImage
6.21 Getty Images/Glowimages
T02a Wanner/Getty Images

FASHION FOCUS
Columbia Sportswear: A Different Kind of Adventure in Fibers,
    Fabrics, and Fashion
(left to right)
Courtesy of Columbia Sportswear
Courtesy of Columbia Sportswear

THEN AND NOW
Denim Through the Decades: The American Way—Jeans
(left to right)
Courtesy of WWD/Steve Eichner
Courtesy of WWD
Courtesy of Fairchild Archive

Chapter 7
7.0 WWD/Robert Mitra
7.2a Guang Niu/Getty Images
7.2b Guang Niu/Getty Images
7.3 © Losevsky Pavel/Alamy
7.4a Fairchild Archive
7.4b Fairchild Archive
7.5 Fairchild Archive
7.6 Library of Congress
7.7 Library of Congress
7.8a Fairchild Archive
7.8b WWD/Giovanni Giannoni
7.9 Courtesy of WWD/Steve Eichner

7.10a Courtesy of Peta
7.10b Michel Dufour/WireImage
7.11a Fairchild Archive
7.11b Fairchild Archive
7.12 STR/AFP/Getty Images
7.13 Liasion
7.14 Courtesy of WWD/Gionvanni Giannoni
7.15 Fairchild Archive
To1a Fairchild Archive
To1b Fairchild Archive
To1c Fairchild Archive
To2a Fairchild Archive
To2b Fairchild Archive
To2c Fairchild Archive
To2d Fairchild Archive
To3a Fairchild Archive
To3b Fairchild Archive
To3c Fairchild Archive
To3d Fairchild Archive

FASHION FOCUS
Fur Is Flying Again: Fashion, Fur, and the Next Generation
(clockwise)
Courtesy of WWD/Giovanni Giannoni
Courtesy of Fairchild Archive
Courtesy of WWD/Giovanni Giannoni
Courtesy of Fairchild Archive

THEN AND NOW
Loewe: Hide & Chic
© Loewe

Chapter 8
8.0 WWD/Robert Mitra
8.1 Fairchild Archive
8.2 Fairchild Archive
8.4a-d Jean Pierre Amet/BelOmbra/Corbis
8.5 William Taufic/Corbis
8.7 Courtesy of WWD/Jahir Amed
8.8 WWD/Thomas Iannaccone
8.9 Fairchild Archive
8.10 Courtesy of WWD/Frank Oudeman
8.11 Courtesy of WWD
8.13 Ocean Photography/Veer
8.14a Getty Images
8.14b Getty Images
8.15 WWD/Kyle Ericksen

FASHION FOCUS
When Do Designers Reach the Next Level?:
  The Magic Number
(left to right)
Photo by Carly Grafstein
Courtesy of WWD/John Aquino
Courtesy of Fairchild Archive

THEN AND NOW
Vanity Sizing
(clockwise)
Courtesy of Alvanon
Courtesy of Alvanon
Courtesy of Alvanon

Chapter 9
9.0 WWD/Robert Mitra
9.1 Courtesy of the H.W. Gossard Co.
9.2 Library of Congress
9.3 Courtesy of WWD/Giovanni Giannoni
9.4 Courtesy of WWD/Robert Mitra
9.5 Fairchild Archive
9.6a Courtesy of WWD/John Aquino
9.6b Courtesy of WWD/George Chinsee
9.7 Courtesy of WWD/Marcos Cullen
9.8 Fairchild Archive
9.9 Courtesy of ellentracy.com
9.10a Courtesy of WWD/Giovanni Giannoni
9.10b Courtesy of WWD/John Aquino
9.11 Fairchild Archive
9.12 Courtesy of IMG
9.13 Fairchild Archive

FASHION FOCUS
The Sister Act
(left to right)
Courtesy of WWD/Steve Eichner
Courtesy of WWD/John Aquino
Courtesy of WWD/Steve Eichner
Courtesy of Fairchild Archive

THEN AND NOW
Guess at 30: American Dreamers Paul and Maurice Marciano
(clockwise)
Courtesy of WWD/Kyle Ericksen
Courtesy of WWD/Donato Sardella
Courtesy of WWD/George Chinsee

Chapter 10
10.0 WWD/Robert Mitra
10.1 Library of Congress
10.2a Hulton Archive/Getty Images
10.2b WWD/Kyle Ericksen
10.3 Bettman/Corbis
10.4a © RMN-Grand Palais/Art Resource, NY
10.4b Image copyright © The Metropolitan Museum of Art.
   Image source: Art Resource, NY
10.4c Courtesy of WWD/Rodolfo Martinez
10.5 WWD/George Chinsee
10.6 Fairchild Archive
10.7 Fairchild Archive
10.8 Fairchild Archive
10.9 Fairchild Archive

Chapter 14

14.0 WWD/Todd Matarazzo
14.1 The Art Archive/Egyptian Museum Cairo/Dagli Orti
14.2 The Art Archive/Culver Pictures
14.3 Courtesy of WWD/George Chinsee
14.4 na
14.5 Fairchild Archive
14.6 Courtesy of WWD/Thomas Iannaccone
14.7 Courtesy of WWD/George Chinsee
14.8 Courtesy of WWD/John Aquino
14.9 Courtesy of WWD/Robert Mitra
14.10 Courtesy of WWD/Thomas Iannaccone
14.11 Courtesy of Whole Foods Market
14.12 Fairchild Archive
14.13 Fairchild Archive
14.14 Courtesy of Cover Girl
14.15 Courtesy of WWD/Kyle Ericksen
14.16 Fairchild Archive
14.17 WWD/Thomas Iannaccone
14.18 Fairchild Archive
14.19 Fairchild Archive

FASHION FOCUS

Bobbi Brown: Redefining Beauty
(clockwise)
Courtesy of WWD/Kyle Ericksen
Courtesy of WWD/George Chinsee

THEN AND NOW

Beauty is a Science
Photo by Carly Grafstein

Chapter 15

15.0 iStockphoto/© stocknroll
15.1 Fairchild Archive
15.2 Courtesy of WWD/John Aquino
15.3 Courtesy of WWD/John Aquino
15.4 Cheltenham Art Gallery & Museums, Gloucestershire, UK/The Bridegman Art Library
15.6 Courtesy of Macy's
15.7 Amanda Holmes/Arcaid/Corbis
15.8 © Elliott Kaufman/Corbis
15.9 Abode/Beateworks/Corbis
15.10 Courtesy of Macy's
15.11 Courtesy of Macy's
15.12 Courtesy of Crate and Barrell
15.13 Courtesy of Maison Objet
15.15 Fairchild Archive
15.6 Fairchild Archive
15.7 Courtesy of organicstyle.com

FASHION FOCUS

From Supermodels to Entrepreneurs
(left to right)
Courtesy of raymourflanigan.com
© Erik S. Lesser/epa/Corbis

THEN AND NOW

IKEA Isn't Just for College Students
© virtualphoto/istock photo

Chapter 16

16.0 WWD/Giovanni Giannoni
16.1 Fairchild Archive
16.2 Courtesy of Moda Manhattan
16.3 Fairchild Archive
16.4 Fairchild Archive
16.5 WWD/Giovanni Giannoni
16.6 WWD/Dominique Maitre
16.7 WWD/Giovanni Giannoni
16.8 WWD/Giovanni Giannoni
16.9 Fairchild Archive
16.10 Gamma-Rapho via Getty Images
16.11 WWD/Giovanni Giannoni
16.12 Fairchild Archive
16.13 Manan Vatsyayana/Afp/Getty Images
16.14 Ian Waldie/Getty Images
16.15 Fairchild Archive
16.16 Fairchild Archive

FASHION FOCUS

Stella's Star Power
(left to right)
Courtesy of Fairchild Archive
Courtesy of Fairchild Archive
Courtesy of Fairchild Archive

THEN AND NOW

Net-A-Porter: One-Click Wonder
(left to right)
Courtesy of net-a-porter.com
Courtesy of WWD/John Aquino

Chapter 17

17.0 Fairchild Archive
17.1 Guy Vanderelst/Getty Images
17.2 Fairchild Archive
17.3 Fairchild Archive
17.4 Thomas Iannaccone
17.5 (c) John Van Hasselt/Sygma/Corbis
17.6 Photo by STR/AFP/Getty Images
17.7 WWD
17.8 Fairchild Archive

FASHION FOCUS

Global Retailers: They Came, They Saw, They Conquered! Or Did They?
(left to right)
Courtesy of WWD/Kyle Ericksen
Courtesy of WWD/Kyle Ericksen
Courtesy of WWD/Thomas Iannaccone

THEN AND NOW
Counterfeit Wars Go High-Tech
Courtesy of WWD/John Aquino

Chapter 18
18.0 WWD/Kyle Ericksen
18.1 Courtesy of Macy's
18.2 AP Photo/Sears, Roebuck and Co.
18.3 Fairchild Archive
18.4 Fairchild Archive
18.5 WWD/Robert Mitra
18.6 Fairchild Archive
18.7 Fairchild Archive
18.8 AP Photo/Elise Amendola
18.9 Fairchild Archive
18.10 Fairchild Archive
18.11 Courtesy of J.Crew
18.12 Courtesy of HSN

FASHION FOCUS
Forever 21's Fast-Fashion Empire
(left to right)
Courtesy of WWD/George Chinsee
Courtesy of WWD/George Chinsee

THEN AND NOW
Coupon Websites Gain Steam
Courtesy of RetailMeNot.com

Chapter 19
19.0 WWD/Marcus Dawes
19.1 Fairchild Archive
19.2a Fairchild Archive
19.2b Courtesy of Hautelook
19.3 WWD/John Aquino
19.4 WWD/Akeroyd By Tim Jenkins
19.5 © Najlah Feanny/Corbis
19.6 Courtesy of CVS
19.7 Fairchild Archive
19.8 Fairchild Archive
19.9 Fairchild Archive

19.10 Fairchild Archive
19.11 Fairchild Archive
19.12 Courtesy of Ann Taylor
19.13 Courtesy of Ebay

FASHION FOCUS
Macy's Initiative to Woo Millennials
(left to right)
Courtesy of macy's.com
Courtesy of Fairchild Archive

THEN AND NOW
Discounters are Leading 50 Years of Retail Revolution
(left to right)
Courtesy of John Calabrese
Courtesy of WWD

Chapter 20
20.0 WWD/Giovanni Giannoni
20.1 Courtesy of Library of Congress
20.2b Courtesy of Elle Magazine
20.5 Courtesy of W Magazine
20.6a Courtesy of WWD
20.6b Courtesy of Men's Week
20.7 Disney Channel via Getty Images
20.8 NBCU Photo Bank via Getty Images
20.10 Courtesy of Parker
20.11a Courtesy of Alice + Olivia
20.11b Courtesy of Diane von Furstenberg
20.12 WWD/Kyle Ericksen
20.13 Getty Images for Gucci
20.14 Courtesy of fgi.org

FASHION FOCUS
Diana Vreeland:"You Gotta Have Style"
Courtesy of WWD

THEN AND NOW
CFDA: American Fashion's Ambassador to the World
Courtesy of WWD/Steve Eichner

INDEX

economic importance of, 89
federal laws affecting, 92, 93
forms of ownership in, 92, 93, 95–96
franchise, 95–96
growth and expansion in, 92–93
licensing, 96–97
manufacturer's role in, 99–101
retailer's role in, 101–2
scope of, 90–91
Butterick, Ebenezer, 190
Buttons, placement of, 69
Buyers
global sourcing and, 340
haute couture and, 339
international fashion markets and, 341
production planning and, 157–58
specification buying, 165, 344
Buyer's directory, 320
Buyers' groups, 405
Buying, merchandising, and product development organization, 405–7
functions of, 406–7
Buying behaviors
adapting to changes in, 203
impulse buying, 264
Buying cycle, 102
See also Fashion cycle
Buying power, 68
purchasing power of the dollar, 54–55
reductions in, 71

C

Cable television, 397–98
CAFTA-DR (Central America-Dominican Republic Free trade Agreement), 347
Caftans, 228
California king (bed sheet), 300
California market, 193, 202
California Market Center, 214
CaliforniaMart (Los Angeles), 319
Camera Nazionale della Moda Italiana, 327
Campaign for Safe Cosmetics, 278
Canada, fashion industry in, 329, 331
Capezio (manufacturer), 235
Carat (gems), 258
Cardin, Pierre, 165
menswear and, 193, 197
Care labels, for textiles, 121, 125–26
Caribbean Basin, fashion industry in, 331–32
Carter's (manufacturer), 209, 213, 217
Cartier, Jacques, 137–38
Cartier (jeweler), 257, 259, 262
Carts and kiosks, 384
Cartwright, Edmund, 119
Cassini, Oleg, 140
Casual apparel, 11, 34, 57, 59

dress-down Fridays, 20, 194–95
See also Sportswear
Catalog retailers, 367
children's wear, 217
intimate apparel, 231–32
mail-order sellers, 355–56
menswear, 203
Category buying, 362
Celebrity brands, 176
Celebrity culture, 21
Census Bureau, U.S., 49, 55, 356, 361
Central America, free trade and, 347
CFDA (Council of Fashion Designers of America), 321, 404
Chain organizations, 361
buying and merchandising in, 362
Chambre Syndicale de la Haute Couture Parisienne, 10, 325, 327
Chanel, Coco, 11, 23, 79, 269
costume jewelry of, 260
Chanel handbag, 248
Chanel No. 5 (fragrance), 269
Chanel suit, 15, 32, 44
Change, 41–43
futility of forcing, 42
meeting demand for, 43
Chang family, 358
Character licensing, 215, 233
home furnishings, 296
Chargebacks, 166
Chemise, 9, 228
Chenille robes, 228
Chicago Merchandise Mart, 309, 318, 319
Chief executive officer, 100
Child labor, 349
Children's apparel, 207–19
demographics and, 208–9
designers and, 210, 212
hats and caps, 253, 254
history of, 209
industry organization and operation, 209–11
infants' and toddlers' wear, 211
licensing in, 214
market centers, 213–14
merchandising and marketing, 213–15
product specialization in, 211
psychological importance of, 207–8
resale shops for, 217–18
role of fashion in, 211–13
school uniforms, 70–71, 218–19, 246
shoes, 245–46
size categories for, 209, 211
underwear and sleepwear, 233
watches, 262
Children's Orchard (resalers), 218
China
cosmetics market in, 284

Nielsen PRIZM system, 50–51
Nightwear
    lingerie and loungewear, 227, 228
    pajamas and sleepwear, 233
Nike (wholesaler), 242, 359
North American Free Trade Agreement, 331, 347
Note (fragrance), 272, 273
NPD Group, 178, 247, 311
    Cohen and, 195, 234, 235
    on ethnic market, 282–83
Nursing bra, 227
Nylon, for intimate apparel, 225
Nylon hosiery, 11, 235

O

Oaten, Mark, 137
Obsolescence stage (fashion cycle), 38
Oceania, 335
Off-price retailers, 183, 363
Offshore production, 165–66, 340, 345
    in Asia, 335
    social responsibility and, 348–49
    See also Global sourcing and merchandising
Oil tanning, of leather, 133
Olsen twins (Mary Kate and Ashley), 176
Onassis, Jacqueline Kennedy, 16, 260
One-stop shopping, 265
On Human Finery (Bell), 53
Online (Internet) sales, 232, 281, 336, 368–69
    counterfeit goods, 346
    coupons for, 364
    See also E-tailing
Online videos, 63
Oriental rugs, 303
Outlet malls, 382–83
Outlet stores, 163
Outside shop, 154

P

Packaging
    fragrance and cosmetics, 275, 280
    recyclable, 280
    socks, 238
Pajamas, 233
Pantone, 120, 121
Pantyhose, 45, 235–36
Paris
    department stores in, 356
    haute couture in, 325–26
Parker, Samuel, 130
Partnership, 92, 93
Patou, Jean, 11, 23
Patternmaker, 157
Peacock look, for men (1960s), 193, 197
Pearls, 258–59
    simulated, 260

Peddlers, 355
Peignoir, 228
Pelt production, 141
    See also Fur industry
Penney's (retailer). See J.C. Penney
Perfumes, 267, 272–73
Perry, Katy, 30
Persian lamb, 139
Personal goods, 248–49
Personal income, 54
Personal signature, 41
PETA (People for the Ethical Treatment of Animals), 140
Petites, 181
Phillips-Van Heusen (PVH), 97, 196
Photographers, 6, 400
Physical mobility, 62–63
Piecework, 154
Place settings, 306
Plateau, of fashion cycle, 38
Platinum jewelry, 257
Playtex (bra maker), 399
Plus-size market, 181
    belts, 251
    bras for, 228, 230
    children's wear, 211
Poiret, Paul, 8, 10, 23, 46, 97, 325
Policies and strategies in retailing, 373–87
    brand policies, 375, 377
    convenience in, 384–85
    customer service, 378–79
    depth and breadth of assortments, 375
    fashion cycle emphasis, 373–74
    location policies, 381–84
    merchandising, 372–77
    new job opportunities, 386–87
    operational policies, 377–81
    price ranges, 375
    quality levels, 374–75
    selling services, 379
    trends in, 385–87
Polyester blends, 194
Polyester fleece, 253
Polymers, 111
Pompadour, Madame de, 83
Popcorn, Faith, 403
Population studies, 50
    age mix in, 55–56
    size of population, 55
    See also Market segmentation
Pop-up shops, 384
Power centers/strips, 382
"Power dressing," for women, 18
Power lunch, 78
Power suit, for men, 190, 194
Prada, Miuccia, 27, 125
Predicting fashion. See Forecasting

functions of, 406–7
  independent, 405–6
  store-owned, 406
Resort retailing, 383–84
Resources, consumer, 53
  See also Economic environment
Retail buyers, 157–58
Retailers, 101–2
  accessories, 264–65
  bridge apparel and, 201
  customer preferences and, 102
  designer licensing and, 97
  fur industry, 143–44, 146
  home furnishings, 310–11
  importing by, 340–43
  manufacturers acting as, 163
  markdown sales, 46
  menswear trends, 203
  product development and, 102
  temporary, 384
  top ten global, 354
  types of, 101–2
  See also Boutiques; Department stores; Catalog retailers;
    Fashion retailing
Retailers group, 405
Retail level, 90
RetailMeNot.com, 364
Retail store brands, 162
Rhodes, Zandra, 17, 52
Rise stage (fashion cycle), 37–38
Roberts, Flori, 282
Rock-and-roll fashions, 79
Roddick, Anita, 271
Rowley, Cynthia, 125
Royalty fee, 96
Rubber-banding (product returns), 272
Rucci, Ralph, 14
Rug manufacturing, 303

S
Sack dress, 33. *See also* Chemise
Saint Laurent, Yves, 17, 28, 280
Sales promotion, 69, 76
  See also Promotion
Sales representatives, 319
Sample hand, 157
San Francisco, 322
São Paulo fashion week, 332
Sapir, Edward, 61, 84–85
Sassi, Stefano, 165
Savile Row (London), 197, 328
Scandinavia, fashion specialties of, 329
Scanners, 168
Scarfs, 254–55
Scent strips, 286
Schiaparelli, Elsa, 11, 12

School uniforms, 70–71, 218–19
  shoes for, 246
Schueller, Eugene, 276
Sears, Roebuck and Co., 355, 361
Seasonal change, 69
Seasonal classifications, 183
Seasonal color, 35
Seasonal lines, 152
Secondary level, of fashion business, 90
Section work, 154
Self-assurance, 64
Self belt, 251
Self-expression, 51, 86
Self-image, 207
Selling services, 379
Sensory retailing, 377–78
Separates, in menswear, 203
Sephora (retailer), 285
Sewing stage (apparel production), 158–59
Sex and the City (television series), 21, 63, 243
Sexuality, fashion game and, 73–74
Shapewear, 227–28, 230
  girdles and corsets, 45, 224
  Spanx, 224, 225, 226
Shelter magazine, 309, 393
Shift dress, 16, 33
Shirt styles, for men, 204
Shirtwaist, 173
Shiseido Co., 274
Shoes. *See* Footwear
ShopNBC (shopping network), 368
Shopping centers and malls, 381–83
Short-run (fashion), 39
Short-run (production), 200–201
Showcase stores, 366–67
SIC/NAICS codes, 166, 167
Signs and graphics, 402
Silhouette, 34
  recurrence of, 71
Silk, 109
  Indian, 334
  intimate apparel and, 224–25, 228
Silver jewelry, 257, 261
Simmel, George, 77
Simpson, Wallace. *See* Duchess of Windsor
Singapore, 334–35
Single-hand operation, 159
Size ranges
  children's apparel, 209, 211
  footwear, 242
  menswear, 201
  plus-sizes, 181, 211, 228, 230
  vanity sizing, 160
  women's apparel, 180–81
Skin care products, 268, 269, 274
  antiaging products, 288